The Process of American History

VOLUME I

EARLY AMERICA

THE PROCESS OF

EDITED BY

PAUL GLAD, *University of Wisconsin*
ALLEN WEINSTEIN, *Smith College*
JOSEPH BRENT III, *Federal City University*
R. JACKSON WILSON, *Smith College*

AMERICAN HISTORY

FROM COLONIAL BEGINNINGS

TO THE PRESENT

Volume I

EARLY AMERICA

Prentice-Hall, Inc., Englewood Cliffs, New Jersey

Glad, Weinstein, Brent, and Wilson

THE PROCESS OF AMERICAN HISTORY:
FROM COLONIAL BEGINNINGS TO THE PRESENT

Volume I: *Early America*

13–723239–X

Library of Congress Catalog Card Number 72–76311
Printed in the United States of America

Current printing (last digit):
10 9 8 7 6 5 4 3 2 1

Prentice-Hall International, Inc., *London*
Prentice-Hall of Australia, Pty. Ltd., *Sydney*
Prentice-Hall of Canada, Ltd., *Toronto*
Prentice-Hall of India Private Ltd., *New Delhi*
Prentice-Hall of Japan, Inc., *Tokyo*

Acknowledgments

The editors are grateful to the following publishers and individuals for permission to reprint selections in this volume:

THE AMERICAN POLITICAL SCIENCE ASSOCIATION for Louis Hartz, "American Political Thought and the American Revolution," *American Political Science Review* (June 1952), pp. 323–324, 329–333, 339–342.

BERNARD BAILYN for his article, "Political Experience and Enlightenment Ideas in Eighteenth-Century America," *American Historical Review*, LXVIII (January 1962), 339–341, 344–351.

STANLEY ELKINS and ERIC MCKITRICK for their article, "The Founding Fathers: Young Men of the Revolution," *Political Science Quarterly*, LXXVI (1961), 183–185, 192–200, 212–216.

HARCOURT, BRACE & WORLD, INC., for Vernon Louis Parrington, *Main Currents in American Thought* (New York: Harcourt, Brace & World, Inc., 1927, 1930), I, 16–22, 43–44, 46–47, 49–50, II, vii–viii, III, 401–413: copyright 1927, 1930 by Harcourt, Brace & World, Inc., renewed 1955, 1958 by Vernon Louis Parrington, Jr., Louise P. Tucker, and Elizabeth P. Thomas.

HARPER & ROW, PUBLISHERS, for Carl N. Degler, *Out of Our Past: The Forces That Shaped Modern America* (New York: Harper & Row, Publishers, © 1959 by Carl N. Degler), pp. 8–14.

HARVARD UNIVERSITY PRESS for Bernard Bailyn, *The Ideological Origins of the American Revolution* (Cambridge, Mass.: The Belknap Press of Harvard University Press, copyright 1967 by the President and Fellows of Harvard College), pp. 144–159; and Perry Miller, *Errand into the Wilderness* (Cambridge, Mass.: Harvard University Press, copyright 1956 by the President and Fellows of Harvard College), pp. 2–15.

HILL & WANG, INC., for Clarence Ver Steeg, *The Formative Years, 1607–1763* (New York: Hill & Wang, Inc., copyright 1964 by Clarence Ver Steeg), pp. 173–187.

HOLT, RINEHART & WINSTON, INC., for Frederick Jackson Turner, *The Frontier in American History* (New York: Holt, Rinehart & Winston, Inc., 1962), pp. 1–4, 65–66.

HOUGHTON MIFFLIN COMPANY for Edmund S. Morgan, "The American Revolution Considered as an Intellectual Movement," in Arthur M. Schlesinger, Jr., and Morton White, eds., *Paths of American Thought* (Boston: Houghton Mifflin Company, 1963), pp. 11, 22–32.

THE JOURNAL OF SOUTHERN HISTORY for Winthrop D. Jordan, "Modern Tensions and the Origins of American Slavery," *Journal of Southern History*, XXVIII (February 1962), 18–30. A somewhat modified and much more complete description of the origin of American slavery is in Winthrop D. Jordan, *White over Black: The Development of American Attitudes Toward the Negro, 1550–1812* (Chapel Hill: University of North Carolina Press, 1968).

Preface

A Dutch scholar, Johan Huizinga, has argued that history is "the intellectual form in which a generation renders account to itself of its past." Inevitably, the way any historian approaches his subject is to some degree determined by the needs and problems of his own time. Not only do students of history differ in their perspective from one generation to another, but they differ within a given generation in comprehension and analysis. This book explores the interpretive and chronological variance within American historiography and examines some of the central issues under scholarly debate. It is based on a belief in the value of historical dialogue, dialogue arising from different perceptions of historical change. To view history as a process by which succeeding generations have assessed their past requires continuous and critical reworking of current interpretation.

To portray the process of American history, we have divided each chapter into five parts. The first is an introduction to a particular topic such as Reconstruction, Progressivism, or the New Deal. The second part offers interpretations from one or more historians of an earlier generation. The third section of each chapter contains documents from the period in question. The fourth presents a sampling of recent historians' interpretations. Finally, each chapter concludes with a short historiographical note.

At this point a caveat is in order. We do not intend to suggest that those who wrote first on any given subject were either naïve or less perceptive than those who followed. In every era, one of the historian's chief functions is to pose meaningful questions about the past. The earlier historians whose work is represented in this collection performed this function admirably. In many cases they established the terms of subsequent historical debate. Often, the nature of that debate helped to shape the present, for people tend to act according to how they perceive the past.

Men are never completely the prisoners of any interpretation, of course, and changing conditions invariably make younger historians aware of problems that older ones never recognized. New awareness may lead to investigation of unused material, to a re-examination of already known documents, and to adoption of new methods of analysis. Thus, we are not arguing that later scholars necessarily are better than their predecessors; we are saying only that recent historical writing is generally more relevant to today's problems, if only because it is written by men influenced by these problems.

In time many of the "recent" interpretations in this collection will seem dated. No matter how inadequate or inaccurate they may appear to future historians, however, they will always reveal important characteristics of the mid-twentieth-century American mind. Histories written by some of the students who use this book will one day replace those written by the historians whose work is included in these pages.

THE EDITORS

Contents

3. THE TRANSIT OF MIND: BELIEF AND ITS OBJECTS IN EIGHTEENTH-CENTURY AMERICA

5. THE CONTOURS OF A NATIONAL SOCIETY

6. ANTEBELLUM SOCIAL THOUGHT, 1815–1860

7. THE POLITICS OF JACKSONIAN AMERICA

The Process of American History

VOLUME I

EARLY AMERICA

1. "O Strange New World": Patterns of Colonial Settlement

INTRODUCTION

From the beginning, many colonial settlers were missionaries, seeking either to convert or to eliminate first the ungodly, later the unenlightened, and, with the Revolution, the un-American. Groups such as the New England Congregationalists and the Pennsylvania Quakers saw the new landscape as a fitting backdrop for profound spiritual dramas conceived in Europe. Bound by older missions, many of them came to reproduce their old way of life in a new land, and only reluctantly did they recognize that in the settlement process they had built societies that differed in many fundamental respects from their abandoned England.

Whatever their degree of spiritual devotion, few colonists felt inhibited in advertising the material promise of American life in order to attract new immigrants. The most ardent of these early seventeenth-century recruiters, the redoubtable Captain John Smith, bombarded London readers with broadsides proclaiming the economic and social delights available to freemen willing to invest their labor and to gamble their future on the undeveloped continent: "What pleasure can be more than (being tired with any occasion a-shore, in planting Vines, Fruits, or Hearbs, in contriving their owne Grounds, to the pleasure of their owne mindes, their Fields, Gardens, Orchards, Buildings, Ships and other works, etc.) to recreate themselves before their owne doores in their owne boates upon the Sea . . . to pull up two pence, six pence, and twelve pence, as fast as you can ha[u]le and veare a line?" The opportunity to construct a new and unique society—a civilization that offered economic security to the lowly as well as moral reformation to the ungodly—seemed a realizable ambition to many of Smith's American contemporaries. The striking abundance of the North American continent made it seem an appropriate Eden in which to perform the moral pageants of a chosen people. "What so truly su[i]ts with honour and honestie," Smith mused in a 1616 tract, "as the discovering things unknowne? erecting Townes, peopling Countries, informing the ignorant, reforming things unjust, teaching virtue . . . ?"

Three years later, the first cargo of African slaves entered Jamestown harbor, a human cornerstone for the future system of commercial agriculture. From this point on, black men could find little comfort in John Smith's inquiry: "Who can desire more content [than migrating to America], that hath small meanes?" Slavery took root in every colony, North and South—on plantations, on small farms, in towns, and in the few cities.

The Puritan founding of Boston had begun a still-unfinished process of urbanizing the American wilderness. By the mid-eighteenth century, most American cities, although smaller than London, had populations comparable to those of almost any other English city. Even in the earliest settlements, primitive iron foundries and other colonial industries began a steady process of growth that threatened British concepts of imperial balance and led to passage of parliamentary regulations restricting the scope of provincial entrepreneurship. Whatever the status of the colonial moral drama by the time of the Revolution, American society's economic performance was high by all contemporary measurements.

The readings and documents that follow analyze the structure and diverse elements of provincial society and examine the phenomenon of that society's prosperity. Almost all of the selections offer insight into the problem of an evolving socio-economic system that reshaped the values and habits of those immigrants (including thousands of African slaves) who came to the North American coastal area. "America began as a sobering experience," Daniel Boorstin wrote in *The Americans: The Colonial Experience*. "A new civilization was being born less out of plans and purposes than out of the unsettlement which the New World brought to the ways of the Old." The pattern of economic and social "unsettlement" described in the succeeding pages should help illuminate the character and assumptions of the New Society over which Croevecour rhapsodized while asking his still-relevant question: "What, then, is the American, this new man?"

I. EARLY INTERPRETATIONS

The single most influential figure in twentieth-century American historical writing has probably been Frederick Jackson Turner. Turner's emphasis on the frontier as the key to American development is contained in the following selections from several of his most important essays. Turner's views on the frontier and on the impact of sectional patterns can also be found in the selection from James Truslow Adams, which summarizes the state of historical research on colonial economic and social history a generation or two ago.

FREDERICK JACKSON TURNER

. . . Up to our own day American history has been in a large degree the history of the colonization of the Great West. The existence of an area of free land, its continuous recession, and the advance of American settlement westward, explain American development.

Behind institutions, behind constitutional forms and modifications, lie the vital forces that call these organs into life and shape them to meet changing conditions. The peculiarity of American institutions is, the fact that they have been compelled to adapt themselves to the changes of an expanding people—to the changes involved in crossing a continent, in winning a wilderness, and in developing at each area of this progress out of the primitive economic and political conditions of the frontier into the complexity of city life. Said Calhoun in 1817, "We are great, and rapidly—I was about to say fearfully—growing!" [1] So saying, he touched the distinguishing feature of American life. All peoples show development; the germ theory of politics has been sufficiently emphasized. In the case of most nations, however, the development has occurred in a limited area; and if the nation has expanded, it has met other growing peoples whom it has conquered. But in the case of the United States we have a different phenomenon. Limiting our attention to the Atlantic coast, we have the familiar phenomenon of the evolution of institutions in a limited area, such as the rise of repre-

sentative government; the differentiation of simple colonial governments into complex organs; the progress from primitive industrial society, without division of labor, up to manufacturing civilization. But we have in addition to this a recurrence of the process of evolution in each western area reached in the process of expansion. Thus American development has exhibited not merely advance along a single line, but a return to primitive conditions on a continually advancing frontier line, and a new development for that area. American social development has been continually beginning over again on the frontier. This perennial rebirth, this fluidity of American life, this expansion westward with its new opportunities, its continuous touch with the simplicity of primitive society, furnish the forces dominating American character. The true point of view in the history of this nation is not the Atlantic coast, it is the Great West. Even the slavery struggle, which is made so exclusive an object of attention by writers like Professor von Holst, occupies its important place in American history because of its relation to westward expansion.

In this advance, the frontier is the outer edge of the wave—the meeting point between savagery and civilization. Much has been written about the frontier from the point of view of border warfare and the chase, but as a field for the serious study of the economist and the historian it has been neglected.

The American frontier is sharply distinguished from the European frontier—a fortified boundary line running through dense populations. The most significant thing about the American frontier is, that it lies at the hither edge of free land. In the census reports it is treated as the margin of that settlement which has a density of two or more to the square mile. The term is an elastic

---

[1] "Abridgment of Debates of Congress," v, p. 706.

Reprinted from Frederick Jackson Turner, "The Significance of the Frontier in American History" and "The First Official Frontier of the Massachusetts Bay," from THE FRONTIER IN AMERICAN HISTORY *(New York: Holt, Rinehart & Winston, Inc., 1962), pp. 1–4, 65–66.*

4

one, and for our purposes does not need sharp definition. We shall consider the whole frontier belt, including the Indian country and the outer margin of the "settled area" of the census reports. This paper will make no attempt to treat the subject exhaustively; its aim is simply to call attention to the frontier as a fertile field for investigation, and to suggest some of the problems which arise in connection with it.

In the settlement of America we have to observe how European life entered the continent, and how America modified and developed that life and reacted on Europe. Our early history is the study of European germs developing in an American environment. Too exclusive attention has been paid by institutional students to the Germanic origins, too little to the American factors. The frontier is the line of most rapid and effective Americanization. The wilderness masters the colonist. It finds him a European in dress, industries, tools, modes of travel, and thought. It takes him from the railroad car and puts him in the birch canoe. It strips off the garments of civilization and arrays him in the hunting shirt and the moccasin. It puts him in the log cabin of the Cherokee and Iroquois and runs an Indian palisade around him. Before long he has gone to planting Indian corn and plowing with a sharp stick; he shouts the war cry and takes the scalp in orthodox Indian fashion. In short, at the frontier the environment is at first too strong for the man. He must accept the conditions which it furnishes, or perish, and so he fits himself into the Indian clearings and follows the Indian trails. Little by little he transforms the wilderness, but the outcome is not the old Europe, not simply the development of Germanic germs, any more than the first phenomenon was a case of reversion to the Germanic mark. The fact is, that here is a new product that is American. At first, the frontier was the Atlantic coast. It was the frontier of Europe in a very real sense. Moving westward, the frontier became more and more American. As successive terminal moraines result from successive glaciations, so each frontier leaves its traces behind it, and when it becomes a settled area the region still partakes of the frontier characteristics. Thus the advance of the frontier has meant a steady movement away from the influence of Europe, a steady growth of independence on American lines. And to study this advance, the men who grew up under these conditions, and the political, economic, and social results of it, is to study the really American part of our history. . . .

In summing up, we find many of the traits of later frontiers in this early prototype, the Massachusetts frontier. It lies at the edge of the Indian country and tends to advance. It calls out militant qualities and reveals the imprint of wilderness conditions upon the psychology and morals as well as upon the institutions of the people. It demands common defense and thus becomes a factor for consolidation. It is built on the basis of a preliminary fur trade, and is settled by the combined and sometimes antagonistic forces of eastern men of property (the absentee proprietors) and the democratic pioneers. The East attempted to regulate and control it. Individualistic and democratic tendencies were emphasized both by the wilderness conditions and, probably, by the prior contentions between the proprietors and non-proprietors of the towns from which settlers moved to the frontier. Removal away from the control of the customary usages of the older communities and from the conservative influence of the body of the clergy, increased the innovating tendency. Finally the towns were regarded by at least one prominent representative of the established order in the East, as an undesirable place for the re-location of the pillars of society. The temptation to look upon the frontier as a field for investment was viewed by the clergy as a danger to the "institutions of God." The frontier was "the Wrong side of the Hedge."

But to this "wrong side of the hedge" New England men continued to migrate. The frontier towns of 1695 were hardly more than suburbs of Boston. The frontier of a century later included New England's colonies in Vermont, Western New York, the Wyoming Valley, the Connecticut Reserve, and the Ohio Company's settlement in the Old Northwest Territory. By the time of the Civil War the frontier towns of New England had occupied the great prairie zone of the Middle West and were even planted in Mormon Utah and in parts of the Pacific Coast. New England's sons had become the organizers of a Great New England in the West, captains of industry, political leaders, founders of educational systems, and prophets of religion, in a section that was to influence the ideals and shape the destiny of the nation in ways to which the eyes of men like Cotton Mather were sealed.

JAMES TRUSLOW ADAMS

At the opening of our period, we thus have to deal with a widely scattered and mainly agricultural population leading a hard-working, narrow, parochial and sometimes dangerous exist-

Reprinted from James Truslow Adams in PROVINCIAL SOCIETY, 1690–1763 (New York: The Macmillan Company, 1927), pp. 23–24, 320–23, by permission of the publisher.

ence in solitary farms, tiny hamlets, or at most in what would now be considered small villages. Few of these last, except in eastern Massachusetts and around Williamsburg, Virginia, were connected by even the shortest roads fit for wheeled traffic. It was a society in which all the conditions tended greatly to emphasize the solidarity of family life and that of the smaller political units. The collection of provinces with varied governments and religious beliefs was peopled by groups of differing nationalities yet, speaking broadly, all alike subject to the similar influences exerted by life in a new country and by fundamental similarities in the relations of the individual to his government. The eighteenth century was to be marked by growing differentiation in social and economic conditions, yet by an increasing tendency toward intellectual and political unity.

The young American society, or rather the collection of societies, which we have sketched only in broadest outlines, was closely articulated with others overseas. Indeed, these connections with other communities across the water were in many cases closer than those which bound the several continental colonies to one another. Politically, of course, all the colonies, island and continental alike, centered in England, and as there were no intercolonial political bonds there were no reasons for the New Englander and the South Carolinian, for example, to consider themselves as bound to one another in any closer relationship than each was bound to the Jamaican or Barbadian. Each was but a resident in an English colony, and the closeness of the relationship between any two of them could be based only upon the closeness of their social or economic ties. In fact there was far more intercourse between Boston and the West Indies, and between the West Indies and Charleston, than there was between Charleston and Boston. The absence of political ties binding a group of any of the colonies served to bring out more clearly the relationship of each to the only political entity of which it formed a part, the British Empire. That term, indeed, as used to include the overseas possessions, makes its first appearance in the decade we are discussing.

With England herself the relations of the colonists were of the closest sort and embraced every field of political, economic and social life, although the closeness of these relations varied to some extent in the different colonies. She was not merely the source of protection, the seat of power, the center of empire, but was still "home" in the speech of all Americans of English descent. At the opening of the eighteenth century there was no fully differentiated American life, no American people. There was merely a loose group of English colonies in the West Indies and on the American continent. The latter possessed, it is true, certain fundamental institutions in common and were subject to certain common influences, but as yet they were without any common consciousness, common culture or even a vague premonition of a common destiny.

• • •

In the two generations which we have covered from 1691 to 1763, the growth of the colonies had been most extraordinary, the population increasing nearly sevenfold. Instead of the scattered settlements in the nearly unbroken forest, separated from one another by leagues of Indian trails, there was now almost continuous settlement from Maine to Georgia, connected by a network of roads over many of which wheeled traffic was constant and on not

a few of which stagecoaches plied regularly several times weekly. When our story began, there was not a single newspaper in America and no public means of conveying letters from one isolated settlement to another. At the end, there was a score of well established and able journals carrying the news of all the colonies, and a post which brought even the most remote settlements into fairly economical touch with one another. In most of the colonies, with the increase of communication and papers, there had developed not only a local public opinion but some glimpse of a larger common life and destiny. In all of them, the formation of opinion had largely passed from religious to lay leaders, and politics had freed itself from clerical control. The transplanted curture, which we found slowly dying of inanition at the beginning of our survey, had given place to a vigorous development of native growth, and the content of colonial life had become vastly enriched. In commerce, the imports of manufactured goods from England had risen from approximately £140,000 in 1697 to £1,630,000 in 1763. Even local manufacturers had begun to compete with agriculture as a leading factor in at least one section. The frontier, which had been merely at the backdoor of the tidewater sections at the beginning, had been pushed far across the back country, even over the mountains, and in the whole tidewater section there was now a stability and an immunity from danger almost as great as in the mother country itself.

On the other hand, these very facts had brought into existence new animosities and divisions, and a sectionalism of deeply disruptive tendency. Although the tidewater sections of all the colonies had been brought far closer to one another than had been the case at the opening of the century, almost every colony now had its own problem in the conflict—economic, political and cultural—between its older portion and its newer frontier. Moreover, with the increased wealth and the fullness of cultural life, had also come an alignment between the rich and poor which was far more marked than anything which can be observed in the simpler days of the beginnings. Wealth had concentrated, and whereas the capitalist of the older towns was far richer than his grandfather had ever dreamed of becoming, the poor settler was no better, if as well, off as *his* grandfather had been. His house was no better, nor his food, nor his educational facilities, and on the other hand he was apt to be much farther removed from the centers of culture, was more despised by the rich, and was exploited by them in a way which the earlier frontiersmen had not been when they planted their homes on free land and but a short distance from tidewater. In the South the great planter, by the use of slave labor, had enormously increased the productive capacity of his plantation, but his poorer neighbor had gone down in the struggle, or moved away beyond the mountains where the blight of the comparison of Negro slavery with his own free labor did not fall. In the towns, theaters, concerts and art exhibitions added steadily to the amenities of life for those who dwelt in the ever enlarging stately Georgian mansions, but in the small houses of the farmer or mechanic the art of the people had deteriorated. New blood, also, had come into colonial life, and with the influx of Germans and Scotch the old racial solidarity and sentimental allegiance of the colonists had to a marked degree been lost. Nevertheless, the disappearance of the French power from Canada and the West by the Treaty of 1763 seemed for the time to offer boundless opportunity for expansion and to open new lands where the discontented and the exploited might find a freer and less hampered life.

II. DOCUMENTS

1. Americans and Europeans—I

The French colonial immigrant to the American colonies, Hector St. John de Crevecoeur, composed one of the most influential portraits of provincial life and national character ever written. The selection that follows is taken from his famous celebration of New World virtues, contained in the chapter "What Is An American." Note especially Crevecoeur's contrast of American experience with European practices, always to the detriment of the Old World. Compare also Crevecoeur's view of the purposes of American society with those held by Franklin, Edwards, Jefferson, and other major figures in eighteenth-century America.

HECTOR ST. JOHN
DE CREVECOEUR

WHAT IS AN AMERICAN

. . . He is arrived on a new continent; a modern society offers itself to his contemplation, different from what he had hitherto seen. It is not composed, as in Europe, of great lords who possess everything, and of a herd of people who have nothing. Here are no aristocratical families, no courts, no kings, no bishops, no ecclesiastical dominion, no invisible power giving to a few a very visible one; no great manufacturers employing thousands, no great refinements of luxury. The rich and the poor are not so far removed from each other as they are in Europe. Some few towns excepted, we are all tillers of the earth, from Nova Scotia to West Florida. We are a people of cultivators, scattered over an immense territory, communicating with each other by means of good roads and navigable rivers, united by the silken bands of mild government, all respecting the laws, without dreading their power, because they are equitable. We are all animated with the spirit of an industry which is unfettered and unrestrained, because each person works for himself. If he travels through our rural districts he views not the hostile castle, and the haughty mansion, contrasted with the clay-built hut and miserable cabin, where cattle and men help to keep each other warm, and dwell in meanness, smoke, and indigence. A pleasing uniformity of decent competence appears throughout our habitations. The meanest of our log-houses is a dry and comfortable habitation. Lawyer or merchant are the fairest titles our towns

Reprinted from Hector St. John de Creve-coeur, LETTERS FROM AN AMERICAN FARMER *(New York, 1927), pp. 35–37, 39–40, 54–57.*

afford; that of a farmer is the only appellation of the rural inhabitants of our country. It must take some time ere he can reconcile himself to our dictionary, which is but short in words of dignity, and names of honour. There, on a Sunday, he sees a congregation of respectable farmers and their wives, all clad in neat homespun, well mounted, or riding in their own humble waggons. There is not among them an esquire, saving the unlettered magistrate. There he sees a parson as simple as his flock, a farmer who does not riot on the labour of others. We have no princes, for whom we toil, starve, and bleed: we are the most perfect society now existing in the world. Here man is free as he ought to be; nor is this pleasing equality so transitory as many others are. Many ages will not see the shores of our great lakes replenished with inland nations, nor the unknown bounds of North America entirely peopled. Who can tell how far it extends? Who can tell the millions of men whom it will feed and contain? for no European foot has as yet travelled half the extent of this mighty continent. . . .

What attachment can a poor European emigrant have for a country where he had nothing? The knowledge of the language, the love of a few kindred as poor as himself, were the only cords that tied him: his country is now that which gives him land, bread, protection, and consequence: *Ubi panis ibi patria,* is the motto of all emigrants. What then is the American, this new man? He is either an European, or the descendant of an European, hence that strange mixture of blood, which you will find in no other country. I could point out to you a family whose grandfather was an Englishman, whose wife was Dutch, whose son married a French woman, and whose present four sons have now four wives of different nations. *He* is an American, who, leaving behind him all his ancient prejudices and manners, receives new ones from the new mode of life he has embraced, the new government he obeys, and the new rank he holds. He becomes an American by being received in the broad lap of our great *Alma Mater*. Here individuals of all nations are melted into a new race of men, whose labours and posterity will one day cause great changes in the world. Americans are the western pilgrims, who are carrying along with them that great mass of arts, sciences, vigour, and industry which began long since in the east; they will finish the great circle. The Americans were once scattered all over Europe; here they are incorporated into one of the finest systems of population which has ever appeared, and which will hereafter become distinct by the power of the different climates they inhabit. The American ought therefore to love this country much better than that wherein either he or his forefathers were born. Here the rewards of his industry follow with equal steps the progress of his labour; his labour is founded on the basis of nature, *self-interest;* can it want a stronger allurement? Wives and children, who before in vain demanded of him a morsel of bread, now, fat and frolicsome, gladly help their father to clear those fields whence exuberant crops are to arise to feed and to clothe them all; without any part being claimed, either by a despotic prince, a rich abbot, or a mighty lord. Here religion demands but little of him; a small voluntary salary to the minister, and gratitude to God; can he refuse these? The American is a new man, who acts upon new principles; he must therefore entertain new ideas, and form new opinions. From involuntary idleness, servile dependence, penury, and useless labour, he has

passed to toils of a very different nature, rewarded by ample subsistence.—This is an American. . . .

An European, when he first arrives, seems limited in his intentions, as well as in his views; but he very suddenly alters his scale; two hundred miles formerly appeared a very great distance, it is now but a trifle; he no sooner breathes our air than he forms schemes, and embarks in designs he never would have thought of in his own country. There the plenitude of society confines many useful ideas, and often extinguishes the most laudable schemes which here ripen into maturity. Thus Europeans become Americans.

But how is this accomplished in that crowd of low, indigent people, who flock here every year from all parts of Europe? I will tell you; they no sooner arrive than they immediately feel the good effects of that plenty of provisions we possess: they fare on our best food, and they are kindly entertained; their talents, character, and peculiar industry are immediately inquired into; they find countrymen everywhere disseminated, let them come from whatever part of Europe. Let me select one as an epitome of the rest; he is hired, he goes to work, and works moderately; instead of being employed by a haughty person, he finds himself with his equal, placed at the substantial table of the farmer, or else at an inferior one as good; his wages are high, his bed is not like that bed of sorrow on which he used to lie: if he behaves with propriety, and is faithful, he is caressed, and becomes as it were a member of the family. He begins to feel the effects of a sort of resurrection; hitherto he had not lived, but simply vegetated; he now feels himself a man, because he is treated as such; the laws of his own country had overlooked him in his insignificancy; the laws of this cover

10

him with their mantle. Judge what an alteration there must arise in the mind and thought of this man; he begins to forget his former servitude and dependence, his heart involuntarily swells and glows; this first swell inspires him with those new thoughts which constitute an American. What love can he entertain for a country where his existence was a burthen to him; if he is a generous good man, the love of this new adoptive parent will sink deep into his heart. He looks around, and sees many a prosperous person, who but a few years before was as poor as himself. This encourages him much, he begins to form some little scheme, the first, alas, he ever formed in his life. If he is wise he thus spends two or three years, in which time he acquires knowledge, the use of tools, the modes of working the lands, felling trees, etc. This prepares the foundation of a good name, the most useful acquisition he can make. He is encouraged, he has gained friends; he is advised and directed, he feels bold, he purchases some land; he gives all the money he has brought over, as well as what he has earned, and trusts to the God of harvests for the discharge of the rest. His good name procures him credit. He is now possessed of the deed, conveying to him and his posterity the fee simple and absolute property of two hundred acres of land, situated on such a river. What an epoch in this man's life! He is become a freeholder, from perhaps a German boor—he is now an American, a Pennsylvanian, an English subject. He is naturalised, his name is enrolled with those of the other citizens of the province. Instead of being a vagrant, he has a place of residence; he is called the inhabitant of such a county, or of such a district, and for the first time in his life counts for something; for hitherto he has been a cypher. I only repeat what I have heard many say, and no wonder their hearts should glow, and be agitated with a multitude of feelings, not easy to describe. From nothing to start into being; from a servant to the rank of a master; from being the slave of some despotic prince, to become a free man, invested with lands, to which every municipal blessing is annexed! What a change indeed! It is in consequence of that change that he becomes an American. This great metamorphosis has a double effect, it extinguishes all his European prejudices, he forgets that mechanism of subordination, that servility of disposition which poverty had taught him; and sometimes he is apt to forget too much, often passing from one extreme to the other. If he is a good man, he forms schemes of future prosperity, he proposes to educate his children better than he has been educated himself; he thinks of future modes of conduct, feels an ardour to labour he never felt before. Pride steps in and leads him to everything that the laws do not forbid: he respects them; with a heart-felt gratitude he looks toward the east, toward that insular government from whose wisdom all his new felicity is derived, and under whose wings and protection he now lives. These reflections constitute him the good man and the good subject. Ye poor Europeans, ye, who sweat, and work for the great—ye, who are obliged to give so many sheaves to the church, so many to your lords, so many to your government, and have hardly any left for yourselves—ye, who are held in less estimation than favourite hunters or useless lap-dogs—ye, who only breathe the air of nature, because it cannot be withheld from you; it is here that ye can conceive the possibility of those feelings I have been describing; it is here the laws of naturalisation invite every one to partake of our great labours and felicity, to till unrented, untaxed lands! Many, corrupted beyond the power of amendment, have brought with them all their vices, and disregarding the advantages held to them, have gone on in their former career of iniquity, until they have been overtaken and punished by our laws. It is not every emigrant who succeeds; no, it is only the sober, the honest, and industrious: happy those to whom this transition has served as a powerful spur to labour, to prosperity, and to the good establishment of children, born in the days of their poverty; and who had no other portion to expect but the rags of their parents, had it not been for their happy emigration. . . .

2. Planter Capitalism

WILLIAM FITZHUGH

TO OLIVER LUKE (BEDFORDSHIRE, ENGLAND)

August 15th. 1690

Honoured Sir: Your Son which I had always an Esteem for as a Country man & friend, . . . being coming to pay his Duty to you, & to crave your blessing & your advice, direction & assistance now [how?] to launch him out into some happy subsistence in this world. I have told himself, that if you could furnish him with a handsom farm in your part of your Estate there, it would be a comfortable subsistence, & which I believe would better sort with his Desires, now he has seen the trouble of travelling & settling, but if your conveniencys & occasions or indeed inclinations do'nt agree to such a Settlement, & that you continue your resolutions of settling him here, . . . then Sr. I will presume . . . to give you the best method for such a Settlement, which is by lodging in some Merchants hand in London 150 or 200£ for the buying,

Reprinted from Richard Beale Davis, ed., WILLIAM FITZHUGH AND HIS CHESAPEAKE WORLD, 1676–1701: THE FITZHUGH LETTERS AND OTHER DOCUMENTS *(Chapel Hill, N.C.: The University of North Carolina Press, 1963), pp. 79–80, by permission of the Virginia Historical Society.*

a good convenient seat of land, which upon so much ready money some may in a short time be purchased, & then about such another sum lodged in the hands of some of the Royall African Company who for that will engage to deliver Negroes here at 16 or 18 or to be sure at £20 p head, which purchase so made of Land & Negroes, the dependences upon a Settlement, so made, as horses, Cattle, hogs &c. are easily purchased here to begin with, & continually raised for a future support. Sr. A Settlement thus made, will make a handsom gentile & sure subsistence, & if there be any thing of Care & Industry may be improved, but cannot well be mischiefed Whereas if he should have three times the sums above mention'd, its certain it will yield him a great deal of Tobo., but if either neglect carelessness or unskilfullness should happen its all brought to nought, & if the best husbandry & the greatest forecast & skill were used, yet ill luck at Sea, a fall of a Market, or twenty other accidents may ruin & overthrow the best Industry . . . .

TO GEORGE MASON (BRISTOL)

July 21st. 1698

Sir: I desire you by the first good conveniency to send me these things following viz Two large Silver Dishes containing about 80 or 90 ounces each dish. A Dozen of Silver plates. Two silver bread plates, A pair of Silver Candlesticks large & fair. A pair of Silver snuffers & Stand. I cannot tell whether these things are to be bought in Bristol but from London I have had of the same sort, from Mr. Richard Smith & Mr. Elias Spinkes very substantiall & very good Silver, but refer the same wholly to your self, both where & to buy of whom only this I must tell you, that I would have no letters engraved upon them nor Coat of Arms, having a Servant of my own singular good Engraved, & so can save that money. Also I would have you send me a Callico quilted morning gown for myself, & a black Crape gown & petticoat for my wife.

. . .

TO EDWARD HAYWARD (LONDON)

July 21st. 1698

Sir: You were pleased to promise me punctually & without fail, to send me in by the first conveniency what books I sent for by you if to be had in Bristol or London, therefore assuring my self & depending wholly upon your promise I have neglected all other conveniencys to send for these books following by you viz. All the Statutes made since the twenty second of King Charles the second to this year. The 2nd. Part of Rushworth's Collections in 2 Volumes The third part of Rushworth's Collections in 2 volume Doctr. Thos. Burnet's Theory of the earth in English All the works of the Author of the whole Duty of man in one Volume. The Lord Bacon's Remains. Cotton's exact Abridgement of the Records of the Tower Buchanan's de jure Regni apud Scotos if to be had in English. Mr. Boyle's letter to a friend concerning specifick Physick. A large fair printed bible in quarto. A large common prayer book in folio. The secret History of King Chas the 2nd. & King James the 2nd. A Continuation of the secret History of Whitehall to Abdicaon &c An Historicall account of the memorable actions of King William the third. These are the books I desire you without fail to send me, I am sure you may have all but one, & that is Buchanan I cannot say whether ever it has been Englished the rest are every day to be had in London to be sure, some part in Bristol, therefore do not send me word some of them are not to be had. . . .

LORD ADAM GORDON

I arrived at Charlestown, the Metropolis of South Carolina, *on the 8th Decemr. 1764,* having landed at Beaufort in Port Royal Island, some days before from Savannah river, which divides it from Georgia, as an imaginary Line does this Province from North Carolina.

It is of all the Southern Provinces the most considerable, on account of the Number of Inhabitants, the quantity and the variety of its productions and Exports, and the good condition of its Inhabitants. There seems in general to be but two Classes of people—the planters who are the proprietors, and the Merchants who purchase and Ship the produce.

Rice and Indigo are the two grand Stables of this Province, of which very great quantities are annually made and Exported to Europe and elsewhere.—It

Reprinted from "The Journal of Lord Adam Gordon," in Newton D. Mereness, ed., TRAVELS IN THE AMERICAN COLONIES *(New York: The Macmillan Company, 1916), pp. 397–400, 404–407.*

has been augmenting annually in Numbers, wealth and Industry, since the Crown purchas'd out the Lords proprietors, and as none of its Exports or productions, interfere with those of the Mother Country, it will be prudent in her to give this Province all possible encouragement.

Almost every family of Note have a Town residence, to which they repair on publick occasions, and generally for the three Sickly months in the fall, it being a certainty, that the Town of Charles Town, is at present the most healt[h]y spot in the Province; fevers and other disorders are both less frequent in it, and less virulent in their Symptoms; this is attributed to the Air being mended by the Number of Fires in Town, as much as to its cool Situation, on a point, at the junction of the two navigable Streams, called Ashley and Cowper [1] Rivers.

The Inhabitants are courteous, polite and affable, the most hospitable and attentive to Strangers, of any I have yet seen in America, very clever in business, and almost all of them, first or last, have made a trip to the Mother-Country. It is the fashion indeed to Send home all their Children for education, and if it was not owing to the nature of their Estates in this Province, which they keep all in their own hands, and require the immediate overlooking of the Proprietor, I am of opinion the most opulent planters, would prefer a home life. It is in general believed, that they are more attached to the Mother Country, than those Provinces which lie more to the Northward, and which having hardly any Staple Commodities of their own growth, except Lumber, Stock and Horses, depend mostly on Smuggling Molasses and other Contraband Commodities.

[1] Cooper.

The Town of Charlestown is very pleasantly Seated, at the conflux of two pretty rivers, from which all the Country product is brought down, and in return all imported goods are sent up the Country.—The Streets are Straight, broad and Airy, the Churches are handsome; The other places of Worship are commodious, and many of the houses belonging to Individuals, are large and handsome, having all the conveniencies one sees at home.—There is a Law against building houses of Wood, which like other Laws in other Countries no body observes, however, the most considerable buildings are of Brick, the others of Cypress and yellow Pine. The houses now are about fifteen hundred, but increase annually in a very surprizing manner.

Their Bar, which is very intricate, seems their only defence, for tho' they have a Fort below the Town, and a kind of earthen Rampart, with some Tabby works, round particular parts of Charlestown, yet it would not be tenible, against attacks of Shipping, or from the land, and therefore must fall a prey to any Enemy, the moment we lose our Superiority at Sea.—A Forty Gun Ship has been in, but small Frigates and Sloops are generally employed on that Station.

. . .

The back Country towards the Cherokee Mounts and Nation, is all healthy and fertile land, producing large Oak, and other deciduous timber, and is finely watered, without much Sand or Pine-barren, but is not yet fully peopled;—In general what part of South Carolina is planted, is counted unhealthy, owing to the Rice-dams and Swamps, which as they occasion a great quantity of Stagnated water in Summer, never fails to increase the Number of Insects, and to produce fall fevers and Agues, dry gripes and other disorders, which are often fatal to the lower set of people, as well White as Black.—

Within these two or three last years, a pretty considerable quantity of Flax and Hemp, has been raised by the Germans and other back Settlers, which, as well as the produce of a considerable part of North Carolina, comes down to Charlestown in Waggons, drawn with four Horses, two abreast—perhaps at the distance of three hundred Miles—this would appear extraordinary at home, but it must be remember'd that they live at no more expence when travelling than they would at home, since the[y] lie in the woods all night, make a good fire to dress their Bacon, and turn their Horses loose near them, 'till day light, after which they proceed on their Journey, and carry back in Return what goods they stand in need of themselves, or for their neighbours in the back Settlements.

It is pretty singular to remark, that the Number of White Inhabitants, fit to bear Arms in one of their back Counties, called Craven County,—does, —at present exceed what was the Number of fighting Men, in all the Province Seven years ago,—from this—I conclude that the farther you go back from the Sea Board in America, the more fertile the land is, and the more healthy the Climate, for there the people increase and breed, and rear up more Children than towards the Pine barren and Sandy Shores.

The Tide Swamp land in these Southern Provinces is by much the most valuable, since, when they are properly banked in, and your trunks and dams in perfect good order, by a judicious use of these advantages, it is alternately equally capable and fit to produce the two great Staple Commodities—Vizt Rice and Indigo, the first requiring an uncommon degree of moisture or Water, and the last, dry

and rich land, altho' the light land very near the Shore, will fetch very Surprizing Crops of Indigo, for two or three years, but it must then be thrown out, and left to time to recover its fertility.

Poultry and Pork, particularly Hams are excellent here.—Beef and Mutton middling, and Fish very rare and dear; the general drink of the better people is Punch and Madeira Wine, and many prefer Grog and Toddy.—All the poor, and many of the Rich, eat Rice for Bread, and give it even a preference; they use it in their Cakes, called Journey Cakes and boiled, or else boiled Indian corn, which they call Hominy, and of this they have two sorts, the great and small—the last I think the best.

Upon the whole, this is undoubtedly one of the most opulent, and most increasing Colonies in America, and bids fair to exceed all the others, if it advances in the like proportion as it has done for forty years past.

. . .

The Soil of the lower part of Virginia is light, tho' often a whitish clay at bottom, producing the best Tobacco in the World, and many other useful Crops.—From the high Duty on that Commodity, its value is fallen, and many people are going upon Hemp, which it is hoped may succeed, if the Bounty is continued.

This Province was the first Settled of any on the Continent, it has always been a Loyal one.—The first Settlers were many of them younger Brothers of good Families, in England, who for different motives chose to quit home in search of better fortune, their descendants, who possess the greatest land properties in the Province, have intermarried, and have had always a much greater connection with, and dependance on the Mother Country, than any other Province, the nature of their Situation being such from the commodiousness and Number of Navigable rivers and Creeks, that they may Export to, and import from, home everything they raise or want, from within a few miles of their own houses, and cheaper than any neighbouring province could supply them. They have almost always lived in good harmony with their Governours, and with one another; they each live at their own Seats, and are seldom at Williamsburgh, but when the publick business requires their attendance, or that their own private affairs call them there, scarce any of the topping people have [a] house there of their own, but in the Country they live on their Estates handsomely, and plentifully, raising all they require, and depending for nothing on the Market.

Money is at present a scarce Commodity, all goes to England, and I am much at a loss to find out how they will find Specie, to pay the Duties last imposed on them by the Parliament.[2] I have had an opportunity to see a good deal of the Country, and many of the first people in the Province and I must Say they far exceed in good sense, affability, and ease, any set of men I have yet fallen in with, either in the West Indies, or on the Continent, this in some degree may be owing to there being most of them educated at home, but cannot be altogether the cause, since there are amongst them many Gentlemen, and almost all the Ladies, who have never been out of their own Province, and yet are as sensible, conver[s]able and accomplished people, as one would wish to meet with.

Upon the whole, was [it] the case to live in America, this Province, in point of Company and Climate, would be my choice in preference to any, I have yet seen; the Country in general is more cleared of wood, the houses are larger, better and more commodious than those to the Southward, their Breed of Horses extremely good, and in particular those they run in their Carriages, which are mostly from thorough bred Horses and country Mares,—they all drive Six horses, and travel generally from 8 to 9 Miles an hour—going frequently Sixty Miles to dinner—you may conclude from this their Roads are extremely good—they live in such good agreement, that the Ferries, which would retard in another Country, rather accelerate their meeting here, for they assist one another, and all Strangers with their Equipages in so easy and kind a manner, as must deeply touch a person of any feeling and convince them that in this Country, Hospitality is every where practised.

Their provisions of every kind is good, their Rivers supply them with a variety of Fish, particularly Crabs and Oysters,—their pastures afford them excellent Beef and Mutton, and their Woods are Stocked with Venison, Game and Hogs. Poultry is as good as in South Carolina, and their Madeira Wine excellent, almost in every house; Punch and small Beer brewed from Molasses is also in use, but their Cyder far exceeds any Cyder I ever tasted at home —It is genuine and unadulterated, and will keep good to the age of twelve years and more.—

The Women make excellent Wives, and are in general great Breeders.—It is much the fashion to Marry young and what is remarkable in a Stay I have made of near a Month in the Province—I have not heard of one unhappy couple.

The Numbers of Inhabitants in Virginia, are supposed to be not fewer than 444,000—of near equal proportions

2 The Stamp Act is here referred to.

16

of Whites and Blacks, the Mulatoes are much less frequently met with here, than in the more Southern Latitudes, and their Slaves in general are more handsome, and better Clothed than any I [have] seen elsewhere;—the generality of those born in the Province, are brought young to Church and Christen'd, and most Parishes have one, two or three very decent Churches in them, built of Brick and Sashed, in which, established Clergymen of the Church of England, officiate alternately. Norfolk is the Port of most traffick in Virginia, it contains above four hundred houses, has depth of Water for a Forty Gun Ship, or more, and conveniencies of every kind for heaving down, and fitting out large Vessels, also a very fine Rope-Walk. . . .

. . .

The quantity of Tobacco, exported at an Average, of Ten Years past from Virginia, is supposed to be from Fifty to Sixty thousand Hogsheads annually, at about a thousand neat pounds per Hogshead.

. . .

3. Slavery

If capitalism came to the New World on the first ships, as Carl Degler observed, then slavery soon followed in its wake. Random and usually unsuccessful efforts to enslave captured Indians were followed by more systematic and lasting enslavement of the unfortunate Africans brought to the port cities and towns of the mainland English colonies. By the end of the seventeenth century, slavery in some form existed in each of these colonies, in most obvious contradiction to libertarian claims made by Crevecoeur and other colonial enthusiasts. The practice of slavery was, until late in the eighteenth century, a national, not just a southern, institution. Puritan ship owners profited handsomely from exchanging Africans for Southern or West Indian gold. By 1770, Negro slaves represented 40 per cent of the population of the five original Southern colonies. The qualities of colonial slavery are evoked in the following documents and, more importantly, in the essay by Winthrop D. Jordan included later in this chapter.

MASSACHUSETTS BAY STATUTES

ACTS RESPECTING BILLS ASSIGNED AND BOND SLAVERY

Sect. 1. It is ordered by the authority of this court, that any debt or debts due upon bill or other specialty as-

Reprinted from Massachusetts Bay Colony statutes on slavery, in THE CHARTERS AND GENERAL LAWS OF THE COLONY AND PROVINCE OF MASSACHUSETTS BAY (Boston, 1814), pp. 52–53, 745–51.

signed to another, shall be as good a debt and estate to the assignee, as it was to the assignor, at the time of its assignation; and that it shall be lawful for the said assignee, to sue for, and recover the said debt upon bill, and so assigned, as fully as the original creditor might have done; provided the said assignment be made upon the back side of the bill or specialty. [1647.]
Sect. 2. It is ordered by this court, and the authority thereof; that there shall never be any bond slavery, villan-

age or captivity amongst us, unless it be lawful captives taken in just wars, as willingly sell themselves or are sold to us, and such shall have the liberties and christian usage which the law of God established in Israel concerning such persons doth morally require; provided this exempts none from servitude, who shall be judged thereto by authority. [1641.]

Sect. 3. The general court conceiving themselves bound by the first opportunity to bear witness against the heinous, and crying sin of man stealing, as also to prescribe such timely redress for what is past, and such a law for the future, as may sufficiently deter all others belonging to us to have to do in such vile, and most odious courses, justly abhorred of all good and just men, do order, that the negro interpreter, with others unlawfully taken, be by the first opportunity, at the charge of the country for the present, sent to his native country (Guinea) and a letter with him of the indignation of the court thereabouts, and justice thereof desiring our honoured governor would please to put this order in execution. [1646.]

AN ACT RELATING TO MULATTO AND NEGRO SLAVES

Whereas great charge and inconveniences have arisen to divers towns and places by the releasing and setting at liberty mulatto and negro slaves, for prevention whereof for the future,

Be it declared and enacted by his excellency the governor, council and representatives, in general court assembled, and by the authority of the same, that no mulatto or negro slave shall hereafter be manumitted, discharged or set free, until sufficient security be given to the treasurer of the town or place where such person dwells, in a valuable

sum, not less than fifty pounds, to secure and indemnify the town or place from all charge for or about such mulatto or negro, to be manumitted and set at liberty, in case he or she by sickness, lameness or otherwise, be rendered uncapable to support him or herself.

And no mulatto or negro hereafter manumitted shall be deemed or accounted free, for whom security shall not be given as aforesaid, but shall be the proper charge of their respective masters or mistresses, in case they stand in need of relief and support, notwithstanding any manumission or instrument of freedom to them made or given; and shall also be liable at all times to be put forth to service by the selectmen of the town. [June, 1703.]

AN ACT TO PREVENT DISORDERS IN THE NIGHT

Whereas great disorders, insolences and burglaries are oft times raised and committed in the night time by Indians, negro and mulatto servants and slaves, to the disquiet and hurt of her majesty's good subjects, for prevention thereof,

Be it enacted by his excellency the governor, council and representatives, in general court assembled, and by the authority of the same, that no Indian, negro or mulatto servant or slave, may presume to be absent from the families whereto they respectively belong, or be found abroad in the night time after nine o'clock, unless it be upon some errand for their respective masters or owners.

And all justices of the peace, constables, tithingmen, watchmen, and other her majesty's good subjects, being householders within the same town, are hereby respectively empowered to take up and apprehend, or cause to be apprehended any Indian, negro or mulatto servant or slave that shall be found abroad after nine o'clock at night, and shall not give a good and satisfactory account of their business, make any disturbance, or otherwise misbehave themselves, and forthwith convey them before the next justice of the peace, if it be not over late in the night, or to restrain them in the common prison, watch house, or constable's house, until the morning; and then cause them to appear before a justice of the peace, who shall order them to the house of correction to receive the discipline of the house, and then be dismissed; unless they be charged with any other offence, than absence from the families whereto they respectively belong, without leave from their respective masters or owners; and in such towns where there is no house of correction, to be openly whipped by the constable, not exceeding ten stripes. [October, 1703.]

AN ACT FOR THE BETTER PREVENTING OF A SPURIOUS AND MIXED ISSUE, &c.

Sect. 1. Be it enacted by his excellency the governor, council and representatives, in general court assembled, and by the authority of the same, that if any negro or mulatto man shall commit fornication with an English woman, or a woman of any other christian nation within this province, both the offenders shall be severely whipped at the discretion of the justices of assize, or court of general sessions of the peace within the county where the offence shall be committed; and the man shall be ordered to be sold out of the province, and be accordingly sent away within the space of six months next after such order made, and be continued in prison at his master's charge, until he be sent away; and the woman shall be enjoined to maintain the child,

if any there be, at her own charge; and if she be unable so to do, she shall be disposed of in service to some of her majesty's subjects within the province, for such term as the justices of the said court shall order, for the maintenance of the child.

And if any Englishman, or man of other christian nation within this province, shall commit fornication with a negro or mulatto woman, the man so offending shall be severely whipped, at the discretion of the justices of the court of assize, or court of general sessions of the peace, before whom the conviction shall be, and shall also pay a fine of five pounds to her majesty for and towards the support of the government, and be enjoined to maintain the child, if any there be; and the woman shall be sold, and sent out of the province, as aforesaid.

And if any negro or mulatto shall presume to smite or strike any person of the English, or other christian nation, such negro or mulatto shall be severely whipped, at the discretion of the justices before whom the offender shall be convicted.

Sect. 2. And be it further declared and enacted by the authority aforesaid, that none of her majesty's English or Scottish subjects, nor of any other christian nation within this province, shall contract matrimony with any negro or mulatto; nor shall any person, duly authorised to solemnize marriages, presume to join any such in marriage, on pain of forfeiting the sum of fifty pounds; one moiety thereof to her majesty, for and towards the support of the government within this province, and the other moiety to him or them that shall inform and sue for the same, in any of her majesty's courts of record within the province, by bill, plaint or information.

And no master shall unreasonably

deny marriage to his negro with one of the same nation; any law, usage or custom to the contrary notwithstanding.

Sect. 3. And be it further enacted by the authority aforesaid, that from and after the first day of May, in the year one thousand seven hundred and six, every master of ship or vessel, merchant or other person, importing or bringing into this province any negro or negroes, male or female, of what age soever, shall enter their number, names and sex in the impost office; and the master shall insert the same in the manifest of his lading, and shall pay to the commissioner and receiver of the impost four pounds per head for every such negro, male or female; and as well the master, as the ship or vessel wherein they are brought, shall be security for payment of the said duty; and both or either of them shall stand charged in the law therefore to the commissioner, who may deny to grant a clearing for such ship or vessel, until payment be made, or may recover the same of the master, at the commissioner's election, by action of debt, bill, plaint or information in any of her majesty's courts of record within this province.

And if any master of ship or vessel, merchant or other shall refuse or neglect to make entry as aforesaid of all negroes imported in such ship or vessel, or be convicted of not entering the full number, such master, merchant or other persons, shall forfeit and pay the sum of eight pounds for every one that he shall refuse or neglect to make entry of, one moiety thereof to her majesty for and towards the support of the government of this province, and the other moiety to him or them that shall inform of the same, to be recovered by the commissioner in manner as aforesaid.

And if any negro imported as aforesaid, for whom the duty is paid, shall be again exported within the space of twelve months, and be bona fide sold in any other plantation, upon due certificate thereof produced, under the hand and seal of the collector or naval officer in such other plantation, the importer here shall be allowed to draw back the whole duty of four pounds by him paid, and order shall be given accordingly. And the like advantage of the drawback shall be allowed to the purchaser of any negro sold within this province, in case such negro happen to die within the space of six weeks next after importation, or bringing into this province.   [October, 1705.]

AN ACT PROHIBITING THE IMPORTATION OR BRINGING INTO THIS PROVINCE ANY INDIAN SERVANTS OR SLAVES

Whereas divers conspiracies, outrages, barbarities, murders, burglaries, thefts, and other notorious crimes and enormities at sundry times, and especially of late, have been perpetrated and committed by Indians and other slaves, within several of her majesty's plantations in America, being of a malicious, surly and revengeful spirit, rude and insolent in their behaviour, and very ungovernable, the over great number and increase whereof within this province is likely to prove of pernicious and fatal consequence to her majesty's subjects and interest here, unless speedily remedied, and is a discouragement to the importation of white Christian servants, this province being differently circumstanced from the plantations in the islands, and having great numbers of the Indian natives of the country within and about them, and at this time under the sorrowful effects of their rebellion and hostilities,

Be it therefore enacted by his excellency the governor, council and representatives, in general court assembled, and by the authority of the same, that from and after the publication of this act, all Indians, male or female, of what age soever, imported or brought into this province, by sea or land, from any part or place whatsoever, to be disposed of, sold, or left within the province, shall be forfeited to her majesty for and towards the support of the government, unless the person or persons importing or bringing in such Indian or Indians shall give security at the secretary's office of fifty pounds per head, to transport and carry out the same again within the space of one month next after their coming in, not to be returned back to this province.

And every master of ship or other vessel, merchant or person whatsoever, importing or bringing into this province, by sea or land, any Indian or Indians, male or female, within the space of twenty-four hours next after their arrival or coming in, shall report and enter their names, number and sex, and give security in the secretary's office as aforesaid, on pain of forfeiting to her majesty for the support of the government the sum of fifty pounds per head, to be sued for and recovered in any of her majesty's courts of record, by action, bill, complaint or information.

And the fee to be paid for such entry and bond as aforesaid shall be two shillings and six pence, and no more. [August, 1712.]

AN ACT FOR THE PREVENTING OF PERSONS UNDER AGE, APPRENTICES OR SERVANTS, BEING TRANSPORTED OUT OF THE PROVINCE WITHOUT THE CONSENT OF THEIR MASTERS, PARENTS OR GUARDIANS

Whereas it has been complained of that persons under age, apprentices and servants, within this province do oftentimes get on board the outward bound vessels, and are there entertained by the masters or mariners, and actually transported to some parts beyond the seas, not only to the great loss and injury of their respective masters, &c. but also to the damage of the province,

Be it therefore enacted by his excellency the governor, council and representatives, in general court assembled, and by the authority of the same, that every master of any outward bound ship or vessel that shall hereafter carry or transport out of this province any person under age, or bought or hired servant or apprentice, to any parts beyond the seas, without the consent of such master, parent or guardian signified in writing, shall forfeit the sum of fifty pounds, the one half to and for the use of the province, the other half to and for the use of him that shall inform or sue for the same, and be further liable to an action in the law, at the suit of the parent, master or owner of such transported person, for any damages sustained by him or them. [October, 1718.]

JOHN WOOLMAN

My employer, having a negro woman, sold her, and desired me to write a bill of sale, the man being waiting who bought her. The thing was sudden; and though I felt uneasy at the thoughts of writing an instrument of slavery for one of my fellow-creatures, yet I remembered that I was hired by the year, that it was my master who directed me to do it, and that it was an elderly man, a member of our Society, who bought her; so through weakness I gave way, and wrote it; but at the executing of it I was so afflicted in my mind, that I said before my master and

Reprinted from THE JOURNAL AND OTHER WRITINGS OF JOHN WOOLMAN (*London: J. M. Dent & Sons, 1910), pp. 26–27, 52–53, 55–56, 63–64, 67.*

the Friend that I believed slave-keeping to be a practice inconsistent with the Christian religion. This, in some degree, abated my uneasiness; yet as often as I reflected seriously upon it I thought I should have been clearer if I had desired to be excused from it, as a thing against my conscience; for such it was. Some time after this a young man of our Society spoke to me to write a conveyance of a slave to him, he having lately taken a negro into his house. I told him I was not easy to write it; for, though many of our meeting and in other places kept slaves, I still believed the practice was not right, and desired to be excused from the writing. I spoke to him in good-will; and he told me that keeping slaves was not altogether agreeable to his mind; but that the slave being a gift made to his wife he had accepted her.

· · ·

Feeling the exercise in relation to a visit to the Southern Provinces to increase upon me, I acquainted our Monthly Meeting therewith, and obtained their certificate. Expecting to go alone, one of my brothers who lived in Philadelphia, having some business in North Carolina, proposed going with me part of the way; but as he had a view of some outward affairs, to accept of him as a companion was some difficulty with me, whereupon I had conversation with him at sundry times. At length feeling easy in my mind, I had conversation with several elderly Friends of Philadelphia on the subject, and he obtaining a certificate suitable to the occasion, we set off in the fifth month, 1757. Coming to Nottingham week-day meeting, we lodged at John Churchman's, where I met with our friend, Benjamin Buffington, from New England, who was returning from a visit to the Southern Provinces. Thence we crossed the river Susquehanna, and lodged at William Cox's in Maryland.

Soon after I entered this province a deep and painful exercise came upon me, which I often had some feeling of, since my mind was drawn toward these parts, and with which I had acquainted my brother before we agreed to join as companions. As the people in this and the Southern Provinces live much on the labor of slaves, many of whom are used hardly, my concern was that I might attend with singleness of heart to the voice of the true Shepherd, and be so supported as to remain unmoved at the faces of men.

· · ·

Having travelled through Maryland, we came amongst Friends at Cedar Creek in Virginia, on the 12th; and the next day rode, in company with several of them, a day's journey to Camp Creek. As I was riding along in the morning, my mind was deeply affected in a sense I had of the need of Divine aid to support me in the various difficulties which attended me, and in uncommon distress of mind I cried in secret to the Most High, "O Lord be merciful, I beseech thee, to thy poor afflicted creature!" And some time, I felt inward relief, and, soon after, a Friend in company began to talk in support of the slave-trade, and said the negroes were understood to be the offspring of Cain, their blackness being the mark which God sent upon him after he murdered Abel his brother; that it was the design of Providence they should be slaves, as a condition proper to the race of so wicked a man as Cain was. Then another spake in support of what had been said. To all which I replied in substance as follows: that Noah and his family were all who survived the flood, according to Scripture; and as Noah was of Seth's race, the family of Cain was wholly destroyed. One of them said that after the flood Ham went to the land of Nod and took a wife; that Nod was a land far distant, inhabited by Cain's race, and that the flood did not reach it; and as Ham was sentenced to be a servant of servants to his brethren, these two families, being thus joined, were undoubtedly fit only for slaves. I replied, the flood was a judgment upon the world for their abominations, and it was granted that Cain's stock was the most wicked, and therefore unreasonable to suppose that they were spared. As to Ham's going to the land of Nod for a wife, no time being fixed, Nod might be inhabited by some of Noah's family before Ham married a second time; moreover the text saith "That all flesh died that moved upon the earth." (Gen. vii. 21.) I further reminded them how the prophets repeatedly declare "that the son shall not suffer for the iniquity of the father, but every one be answerable for his own sins." I was troubled to perceive the darkness of their imaginations, and in some pressure of spirit said, "The love of ease and gain are the motives in general of keeping slaves, and men are wont to take hold of weak arguments to support a cause which is unreasonable. I have no interest on either side, save only the interest which I desire to have in the truth. I believe liberty is their right, and as I see they are not only deprived of it, but treated in other respects with inhumanity in many places, I believe He who is a refuge for the oppressed will, in his own time, plead their cause, and happy will it be for such as walk in uprightness before him." And thus our conversation ended.

· · ·

The prospect of a way being open to the same degeneracy, in some parts of this newly settled land of America, in respect to our conduct towards the negroes, hath deeply bowed my mind in this journey, and though briefly to relate how these people are treated is

no agreeable work, yet, after often reading over the notes I made as I travelled, I find my mind engaged to preserve them. Many of the white people in those provinces take little or no care of negro marriages; and when negroes marry after their own way, some make so little account of those marriages that with views of outward interest they often part men from their wives by selling them far asunder, which is common when estates are sold by executors at vendue. Many whose labor is heavy being followed at their business in the field by a man with a whip, hired for that purpose, have in common little else allowed but one peck of Indian corn and some salt for one week, with a few potatoes; the potatoes they commonly raise by their labor on the first day of the week. The correction ensuing on their disobedience to overseers, or slothfulness in business, is often very severe, and sometimes desperate.

Men and women have many times scarcely clothes sufficient to hide their nakedness, and boys and girls ten and twelve years old are often quite naked amongst their master's children. Some of our Society, and some of the society called Newlights, use some endeavors to instruct those they have in reading; but in common this is not only neglected, but disapproved. These are the people by whose labor the other inhabitants are in a great measure supported, and many of them in the luxuries of life. These are the people who have made no agreement to serve us, and who have not forfeited their liberty that we know of. These are the souls for whom Christ died, and for our conduct towards them we must answer before Him who is no respecter of persons. They who know the only true God, and Jesus Christ whom he hath sent, and are thus acquainted with the merciful, benevolent, gospel spirit, will therein perceive that the indignation of God is kindled against oppression and cruelty, and in beholding the great distress of so numerous a people will find cause for mourning.

. . .

From the Yearly Meeting in Virginia I went to Carolina, and on the 1st of sixth month was at Wells Monthly Meeting, where the spring of the gospel ministry was opened, and the love of Jesus Christ experienced among us; to his name be the praise.

Here my brother joined with some Friends from New Garden who were going homeward; and I went next to Simons Creek Monthly Meeting, where I was silent during the meeting for worship. When business came on, my mind was exercised concerning the poor slaves, but I did not feel my way clear to speak. In this condition I was bowed in spirit before the Lord, and with tears and inward supplication besought him so to open my understanding that I might know his will concerning me; and, at length, my mind was settled in silence. Near the end of their business a member of their meeting expressed a concern that had some time lain upon him, on account of Friends so much neglecting their duty in the education of their slaves, and proposed having meetings sometimes appointed for them on a week day, to be attended only by some Friends to be named in their Monthly Meetings. Many present appeared to unite with the proposal. One said he had often wondered that they, being our fellow-creatures, and capable of religious understanding, had been so exceedingly neglected; another expressed the like concern, and appeared zealous that in future it might be more closely considered. At length a minute was made, and the further consideration of it referred to their next Monthly Meeting. The Friend who made this proposal hath negroes; he told me that

he was at New Garden, about two hundred and fifty miles from home, and came back alone; that in this solitary journey this exercise, in regard to the education of their negroes, was from time to time renewed in his mind. A Friend of some note in Virginia, who hath slaves, told me that he being far from home on a lonesome journey had many serious thoughts about them; and his mind was so impressed therewith that he believed he saw a time coming when Divine Providence would alter the circumstances of these people, respecting their condition as slaves.

. . .

At Monalen a Friend gave me some account of a religious society among the Dutch, called Mennonists, and amongst other things related a passage in substance as follows: One of the Mennonists having acquaintance with a man of another society at a considerable distance, and being with his wagon on business near the house of his said acquaintance, and night coming on, he had thoughts of putting up with him, but passing by his fields, and observing the distressed appearance of his slaves, he kindled a fire in the woods hard by, and lay there that night. His said acquaintance hearing where he lodged, and afterward meeting the Mennonist, told him of it, adding he should have been heartily welcome at his house, and from their acquaintance in former time wondered at his conduct in that case. The Mennonist replied, "Ever since I lodged by thy field I have wanted an opportunity to speak with thee. I had intended to come to thy house for entertainment, but seeing thy slaves at their work, and observing the manner of their dress, I had no liking to come to partake with thee." He then admonished him to use them with more humanity, and added, "As I lay by the fire that night, I thought that as I was a man of substance thou wouldst have received me freely; but if I had been as poor as one of thy slaves, and had no power to help myself, I should have received from thy hand no kinder usage than they."

In this journey I was out about two months, and travelled about eleven hundred and fifty miles. I returned home under an humbling sense of the gracious dealings of the Lord with me, in preserving me through many trials and afflictions.

THOMAS JEFFERSON

ADVERTISEMENT FOR A RUNAWAY SLAVE

[7 September 1769]

Run away from the subscriber in *Albemarle,* a Mulatto slave called *Sandy,*

Reprinted from Julian Boyd, ed., THE PAPERS OF THOMAS JEFFERSON *(Princeton, N.J.: Princeton University Press, 1950), I, 33.*

about 35 years of age, his stature is rather low, inclining to corpulence, and his complexion light; he is a shoemaker by trade, in which he uses his left hand principally, can do coarse carpenters work, and is something of a horse jockey; he is greatly addicted to drink, and when drunk is insolent and disorderly, in his conversation he swears much, and his behaviour is artful and knavish. He took with him a white horse, much scarred with traces, of which it is expected he will endeavour to dispose; he also carried his shoemakers tools, and will probably endeavour to get employment that way. Whoever conveys the said slave to me in *Albemarle,* shall have 40 s. reward, if taken up within the county, 4 l. if elsewhere within the colony, and 10 l. if in any other colony, from

Thomas Jefferson.

4. Merchants and Town Life

The great majority of provincial Americans lived either in towns, on small farms, or on plantations, but a flourishing urban culture still managed to evolve in the few cities which existed largely as trading seaports within the mainland English colonies. The special flavor of provincial city life—its rowdy, zestful welcoming of all forms of experience brought from the European world outside—is captured in the affable travel memoirs of Dr. Alexander Hamilton, namesake of but no relation to the later Revolutionary leader. Hamilton's tour of the Northern colonies in 1744, undertaken after serious illness, introduced the Maryland physician to some of the more fascinating byways and habits of urban culture in Philadelphia, New York, and Boston, as the following selection indicates.

DR. ALEXANDER HAMILTON

Philadelphia

The country round the city of Philadelphia is level and pleasant, having

Reprinted from Carl Bridenbaugh, ed., GENTLEMAN'S PROGRESS: THE INTINERARIUM OF DR. ALEXANDER HAMILTON *(Chapel Hill, N.C.: The University of North Carolina Press, 1948), pp. 18–23, 25, 28–30.*

a prospect of the large river of Delaware and the province of East Jersey upon the other side. You have an agreeable view of this river for most of the way betwixt Philadelphia and Newcastle. The plan or platform of the city lyes betwixt the two rivers of Delaware and Skuylkill, the streets being laid out in rectangular squares which makes a regular, uniform plan, but upon that account, altogether destitute of variety.

Att my entering the city, I observed the regularity of the streets, but att the same time the majority of the houses mean and low and much decayed, the streets in generall not paved, very dirty, and obstructed with rubbish and lumber, but their frequent building excuses that. The State House, Assembly House, the great church in Second Street, and Whitefield's church are good buildings.

I observed several comicall grotesque phizzes in the inn where I put up which would have afforded variety of hints for a painter of Hogarth's turn. They talked there upon all subjects—politicks, religion, and trade—some tollerably well, but most of them ignorantly. I discovered two or three chaps very inquisitive, asking my boy who I was, whence come, and whither bound.

I was shaved by a little, finicall, humpbacked old barber who kept dancing round me and talking all the time of the operation and yet did his job lightly and to a hair. He abounded in compliments and was a very civil fellow in his way. He told me he had been a journeyman to the business for 40 odd years, notwithstanding which, he understood how to trim gentlemen as well (thank God) as the best masters and despaired not of preferment before he dyed.

I delivered my letters, went to dine with Collector Alexander, and visited severall people in town. In the afternoon I went to the coffee house where I was introduced by Dr. Thomas Bond to severall gentlemen of the place, where the ceremony of shaking of hands, an old custom peculiar to the English, was performed with great gravity and the usuall compliments. I took private lodgings att Mrs. Cume's in Chestnut Street.

Thursday, June 7th. I remarked one instance of industry as soon as I got up and looked out att my chamber window, and that was the shops open att 5 in the morning. I breakfasted with Mrs. Cume and dined by invitation with Dr. Thomas Bond where, after some talk upon physicall matters, he showed me some pretty good anatomical preparations of the muscles and blood vessels injected with wax.

After dinner Mr. Venables, a Barbadian gentleman, came in who, when we casually had mentioned the free masons, began to rail bitterly against that society as an impudent, assuming and vain caball pretending to be wiser than all mankind besides, an *imperium in imperio,* and therefor justly to be discouraged and suppressed as they had lately been in some foreign countrys. Tho' I am no free mason myself, I could not agree with this gentleman, for I abhorr all tyrannicall and arbitrary notions. I believe the free masons to be an innocent and harmless society that have in their constitution nothing mysterious or beyond the verge of common human understanding, and their secret which has made such a noise, I imagine is just no secret att all.

• • •

Friday, June 8. I dined att a taveren with a very mixed company of different nations and religions. There were Scots, English, Dutch, Germans, and Irish; there were Roman Catholicks, Church men, Presbyterians, Quakers, Newlightmen, Methodists, Seventh-day men, Moravians, Anabaptists, and one Jew. The whole company consisted of 25 planted round an oblong table in a great hall well stoked with flys. The company divided into committees in conversation; the prevailing topick was politicks and conjectures of a French war. A knott of Quakers there talked only about selling of flour and the low price it bore. They touch a little upon religion, and high words arose among some of the sectaries, but their blood was not hot enough to quarrell, or, to speak in the canting phraze, their zeal wanted fervency. A gentleman that sat next me proposed a number of questions concerning Maryland, understanding I had come from thence. In my replys I was reserved, pretending to know little of the matter as being a person whose business did not lye in the way of history and politicks.

In the afternoon I went to see some ships that lay in the river. Among the rest were three vessels a fitting out for privateers—a ship, a sloop, and a schooner. The ship was a large vessel, very high and full rigged; one Capt. Mackey intended to command her upon the cruise. Att 6 o'clock I went to the coffee house and drank a dish of coffee with Mr. Hasell.

After staying there an hour or two, I was introduced by Dr. Phineas Bond into the Governour's Club, a society of gentlemen that met at a taveren every night and converse on various subjects. The Governour gives them his presence once a week, which is generally upon Wednesday, so that I did not see him there. Our conversation was entertaining; the subject was the English poets and some of the foreign writers, particularly Cervantes, author of Don Quixote, whom we loaded with elogiums due to his character. Att eleven o'clock I left this club and went to my lodging.

Saturday, June 9th. This morning there fell a light rain which proved very refreshing, the weather having been very hot and dry for severall days. The heat in this city is excessive, the sun's rays being reflected with such power from the brick houses and from the street pavement which is brick. The people commonly use awnings of painted cloth or duck over their shop doors and windows and, att sunset, throw buckets full of water upon the pavement which gives a sensible cool. They are stocked with plenty of excellent water in this city, there being a pump att almost every 50 paces distance. There are a great number of balconies to their houses where sometimes the men sit in a cool habit and smoke.

The market in this city is perhaps the largest in North America. It is kept twice a week upon Wednesdays and Saturdays. The street where it stands, called Market Street, is large and spacious, composed of the best houses in the city.

They have but one publick clock here which strikes the hour but has neither index nor dial plate. It is strange they should want such an ornament and conveniency in so large a place, but the chief part of the community consisting of Quakers, they would seem to shun ornament in their publick edifices as well as in their apparrell or dress.

The Quakers here have two large meetings, the Church of England one great church in Second Street, and another built for Whitefield in which one tennent, a fanatick, now preaches, the Romans one chapell, the Anabaptists one or two meetings, and the Presbyterians two.

The Quakers are the richest and the people of greatest interest in this government; of them their House of Assembly is chiefly composed. They have the character of an obstinate, stiffnecked generation and a perpetuall plague to their governours. The present governour, Mr. Thomas, has fallen upon a way to manage them better than any of his predecessors did and, att the same time, keep pretty much in their good graces and share some of their favours. However, the standing or falling of the Quakers in the House of Assembly depends upon their making sure the interest of the Palatines in this province, who of late have turned so numerous that they can sway the votes which way they please.

Here is no publick magazine of arms nor any method of defense, either for city or province, in case of the invasion of an enemy. This is owing to the obstinacy of the Quakers in maintaining their principle of non-resistance. It were a pity but they were put to a sharp triall to see whether they would act as they profess.

I never was in a place so populous where the *goût* for publick gay diversions prevailed so little. There is no such things as assemblys of the gentry among them, either for dancing or musick; these they have had an utter aversion to ever since Whitefield preached among them. Their chief employ, indeed, is traffick and mercantile business which turns their thoughts from these levitys. Some Virginia gentlemen that came here with the Commissioners of the Indian Treaty were desirous of having a ball but could find none of the female sex in a humour for it. Strange influence of religious enthusiasm upon human nature to excite an aversion at these innocent amusements, for the most part so agreeable and entertaining to the young and gay, and indeed, in the opinion of moderate people, so conducive to the improvement of politeness, good manners, and humanity.

. . .

Monday, June 11th. The morning proved clear, and the air cool and refreshing, which was a great relaxation and relief after the hot weather that had preceded. I read Montaigne's Essays in the morning and was visited by Dr. Lloyd Zachary, a physician in this place.

I dined with Collector Alexander and went in the afternoon in the company of some gentlemen to attend the Governour to the Court House stairs where war was publickly to be proclaimed against France. There were about 200 gentlemen attended Governour Thomas. Coll. Lee of Virginia walked att his right hand, and Secretary Peters upon his left; the procession was led by about 30 flags and ensigns taken from privateer vessels and others in the harbour, which were carried by a parcell of roaring sailors. They were followed by 8 or 10 drums that made a confounded martiall noise, but all the instrumental musick they had was a pitifull scraping negroe fiddle which followed the drums and could not be heard for the noise and clamour of the people and the rattle of the drums. There was a rabble of about 4,000 people in the street and great numbers of ladies and gentlemen in the windows and balconies. Three proclamations were read: 1st, the King of England's proclamation of war against the French king; 2nd, a proclamation for the encouragement of such as should fit out privateers against the enemy; 3rd, the Governour of Pennsylvania's proclamation for that province in particular, denouncing war and hostility against France.

. . .

Tuesday, June 12th. I must make a few remarks before I leave this place. The people in generall are inquisitive concerning strangers. If they find one comes there upon the account of trade or traffick, they are fond of dealing with him and cheating him if they can. If he comes for pleasure or curiosity, they take little or no notice of him unless he be a person of more than ordinary rank; then they know as well as others how to fawn and cringe. Some persons there were inquisitive about the state of religion in Maryland. My common reply to such questions was that I studied their constitutions more than their consciences so knew something of the first but nothing of the latter.

They have in generall a bad notion of their neighbouring province, Maryland, esteeming the people a sett of cunning sharpers; but my notion of the affair is that the Pennsylvanians are not a whit inferior to them in the science of chicane, only their method of tricking is different. A Pennsylvanian will tell a lye with a sanctified, solemn face; a Marylander, perhaps, will convey his fib in a volley of oaths; but the effect and point in view is the same tho' the manner of operating be different.

In this city one may live tollerably cheap as to the articles of eating and drinking, but European goods here are extravagantly dear. Even goods of their own manufacture such as linnen, woolen, and leather bear a high price. Their government is a kind of anarchy (or no government), there being perpetual jarrs betwixt the two parts of the legislature. But that is no strange thing, the ambition and avarice of a few men in both partys being the active springs in these dissentions and altercations, tho' a specious story about the good and interest of the country is trumpt up by both; yet I would not be so severe as to say so of all in generall.

Mr. Thomas, the present governour, I believe is an upright man and has the interest of the province really att heart, having done more for the good of that obstinate generation, the Quakers, than any of his predecessours have done. Neither are they so blind as not to see it, for he shares more of their respect than any of their former governours were wont to do.

There is polite conversation here among the better sort, among whom there is no scarcity of men of learning and good sense. The ladies, for the most part, keep att home and seldom appear in the streets, never in publick assemblies except att the churches or meetings; therefor I cannot with certainty enlarge upon their charms, having had little or no opportunity to see them either congregated or separate, but to be sure the Philadelphian dames are as handsome as their neighbours.

The staple of this province is bread, flower, and pork. They make no tobacco but a little for their own use. The country is generally plain and levell, fruitfull in grain and fruits, pretty well watered, and abounding in woods backward. It is upon the growing hand, more than any of the provinces of America. The Germans and high Dutch are of late become very numerous here.

. . .

New York

Saturday, June 16. The following observations occurred to me: I found this city less in extent but, by the stir and frequency upon the streets, more populous than Philadelphia; I saw more shipping in the harbour; the houses are more compact and regular and, in generall, higher built, most of them after the Dutch model with their gravell ends fronting the street. There are a few built of stone, more of wood, but the greatest number of brick, and a great many covered with pan tile and glazed tile with the year of God when built figured out with plates of iron upon the fronts of severall of them. The streets, in generall, are but narrow and not regularly disposed. The best of them run parallell to the river, for the city is built all along the water. In generall this city has more of an urban appearance than Philadelphia. Their wharfs are mostly built with logs of wood piled upon a stone foundation. In the city are severall large publick buildings. There is a spacious church belonging to the English congregation with a pretty high but heavy, clumsy steeple built of freestone fronting the street called Broadway. There are two Dutch churches, severall other meetings, and a pretty large Town House at the head of Broadstreet. The Exchange stands near the water and is a wooden structure, going to decay. From it a pier runs into the water, called the Long Bridge, about 50 paces long, covered with plank and supported with large wooden posts. The Jews have one synagogue in this city. The women of fashion here appear more in publick than in Philadelphia and dress much gayer. They come abroad generally in the cool of the evening and go to the Promenade.

. . .

Tuesday, June 19th. The staple of New York is bread flower and skins. It is a very rich place, but it is not so cheap living here as att Philadelphia. They have very bad water in the city, most of it being hard and brackish. Ever since the negroe conspiracy, certain people have been appointed to sell water in the streets, which they carry on a sledge in great casks and bring it from the best springs about the city, for it was when the negroes went for tea water that they held their caballs and consultations, and therefor they have a law now that no negroe shall be seen upon the streets without a lanthorn after dark.

In this city are a mayor, recorder, aldermen, and common council. The government is under the English law, but the chief places are possessed by Dutchmen, they composing the best part of the House of Assembly. The Dutch were the first settlers of this province, which is very large and extensive, the States of Holland having purchased the country of one Hudson, who pretended first to have discovered it, but they att last exchanged it with the English for Saranam, and ever since there have been a great number of Dutch here, tho' now their language and customs begin pretty much to wear out and would very soon die were it not for a parcell of Dutch domines here who, in the education of their children, endeavour to preserve the Dutch customs as much as possible. There is as much jarring here betwixt the powers of the legislature as in any of the other American provinces.

They have a diversion here, very common, which is the barbecuing of a turtle, to which sport the chief gentry in town commonly go once or twice a week.

There are a great many handsome women in this city. They appear much more in publick than att Philadelphia. It is customary here to ride thro' the street in light chairs. When the ladys walk the streets in the daytime, they commonly use umbrellas, prettily adorned with feathers and painted.

There are two coffee houses in this city, and the northern and southern posts go and come here once a week. I was tired of nothing here but their excessive drinking, for in this place you may have the best of company and conversation as well as att Philadelphia.

Boston

I need scarce take notice that Boston is the largest town in North America, being much above the same extent as the city of Glasgow in Scotland and having much the same number of inhabitants, which is between 20 and 30 thousand. It is considerably larger than either Philadelphia or New York, but the streets are irregularly disposed and, in generall, too narrow. The best street in the town is that which runs down towards the Long Wharf which goes. by the name of King's Street. This town is a considerable place for shipping and carrys on a great trade in time of peace. There were now above 100 ships in the harbour besides a great number of small craft tho' now, upon account of the war, the times are very dead. The people of this province chiefly follow farming and merchandise. Their staples are shipping, lumber, and fish. The government is so far democratic as that the election of the Governour's Council and the great officers is made by the members of the Lower House, or representatives of the people. Mr. Shirly, the present Governour, is a man of excellent sense and understanding and is very well respected there. He understands how to humour the people and att the same time, acts for the interest of the Government. Boston is better fortified against an enemy than any port in North America, not only upon account of the strength of the Castle but the narrow passage up into the harbour, which is not above 160 foot wide in the channell att high water.

There are many different religions and perswasions here, but the chief sect is that of the Presbyterians. There are above 25 churches, chapells and meetings in the town, but the Quakers here have but a small remnant, having been banished from the province att the first settlement upon account of some disturbances they raised. The people here have lately been, and indeed are now, in great confusion and much infested with enthusiasm from the preaching of some fanaticks and New Light teachers, but now this humour begins to lessen. The people are generally more captivated with speculative than with practicall religion. It is not by half such a flagrant sin to cheat and cozen one's neighbour as it is to ride about for pleasure on the sabbath day or to neg-lect going to church and singing of psalms.

The middling sort of people here are to a degree disingenuous and dissembling, which appears even in their common conversation in which their indirect and dubious answers to the plainest and fairest questions show their suspicions of one another. The better sort are polite, mannerly, and hospitable to strangers, such strangers, I mean, as come not to trade among them (for of them they are jealous). There is more hospitality and frankness showed here to strangers than either at York or at Philadelphia. And in the place there is abundance of men of learning and parts; so that one is att no loss for agreeable conversation nor for any sett of company he pleases. Assemblys of the gayer sort are frequent here; the gentlemen and ladys meeting almost every week att concerts of musick and balls. I was present att two or three such and saw as fine a ring of ladys, as good dancing, and heard musick as elegant as I had been witness to anywhere. I must take notice that this place abounds with pretty women who appear rather more abroad than they do att York and dress elegantly. They are, for the most part, free and affable as well as pretty. I saw not one prude while I was here.

The paper currency of these provinces is now very much depreciated, and the price or value of silver rises every day, their money being now 6 for one upon sterling. They have a variety of paper currencys in the provinces; viz., that of New Hampshire, the Massachusetts, Rhode Island, and Connecticut, all of different value, divided and subdivided into old and new tenors so that it is a science to know the nature and value of their moneys, and what will cost a stranger some study and application. Dr. Dowglass has writ a compleat treatise upon all the different kinds of paper currencys in America, which I was att the pains to read. It was the expense of the Canada expedition that first brought this province in debt and put them upon the project of issuing bills of credit. Their money is chiefly founded upon land security, but the reason of its falling so much in value is their issuing from time to time such large summs of it and their taking no care to make payments att the expiration of the stated terms. They are notoriously guilty of this in Rhode Island colony so that now it is dangerous to pass their new moneys in the other parts of New England, it being a high penalty to be found so doing. This fraud must light heavy upon posterity. This is the only part I ever knew where gold and silver coin is not uncommonly current.

5. Americans and Europeans—II

Europeans regarded the "United States of America," founded after the successful revolt against England, with keen interest and even fascination. The character of Americans, their folkways, their values and aspirations served as subject matter for a large new body of literature, in which Meredic Louis Elie Moreau de Saint-Mery's unflattering account remains an impressive "hatchet job" on the new nation. On the other hand, Benjamin Franklin's pamphlet providing "information" for Europeans who wished to immigrate to the United States contained an intriguing assessment of revolutionary society by the most "American" of "Americans."

BENJAMIN FRANKLIN

INFORMATION TO THOSE WHO WOULD REMOVE TO AMERICA (1782)

Many Persons in Europe, having directly or by Letters, express'd to the Writer of this, who is well acquainted with North America, their Desire of transporting and establishing themselves in that Country; but who appear to have formed, thro' Ignorance, mistaken Ideas and Expectations of what is to be obtained there; he thinks it may be useful, and prevent inconvenient, expensive, and fruitless Removals and Voyages of improper Persons, if he gives some clearer and truer Notions of that

Reprinted from Ralph Ketcham, ed., THE POLITICAL THOUGHT OF BENJAMIN FRANKLIN *(Indianapolis and New York: The Bobbs-Merrill Company, Inc., 1965), pp. 336–341.*

part of the World, than appear to have hitherto prevailed.

He finds it is imagined by Numbers, that the Inhabitants of North America are rich, capable of rewarding, and dispos'd to reward, all sorts of Ingenuity; that they are at the same time ignorant of all the Sciences, and, consequently, that Strangers, possessing Talents in the Belles-Lettres, fine Arts, &c., must be highly esteemed, and so well paid, as to become easily rich themselves; that there are also abundance of profitable Offices to be disposed of, which the Natives are not qualified to fill; and that, having few Persons of Family among them, Strangers of Birth must be greatly respected, and of course easily obtain the best of those Offices, which will make all their Fortunes; that the Governments too, to encourage Emigrations from Europe, not only pay the Expence of personal Transportation, but give Lands gratis to Strangers, with Negroes to work for them, Utensils of Husbandry, and Stocks of Cattle. These are all wild Imaginations; and those who go to America with Expectations founded upon them will surely find themselves disappointed.

The Truth is, that though there are in that Country few People so miserable as the Poor of Europe, there are also very few that in Europe would be called rich; it is rather a general happy Mediocrity that prevails. There are few great Proprietors of the Soil, and few Tenants; most People cultivate their own Lands, or follow some Handicraft or Merchandise; very few rich enough to live idly upon their Rents or Incomes, or to pay the high Prices given in Europe for Paintings, Statues, Architecture, and the other Works of Art, that are more curious than useful. Hence the natural Geniuses, that have arisen in America with such Talents, have uniformly quitted that Country for Europe, where they can be more suitably rewarded. It is true, that Letters and Mathematical Knowledge are in Esteem there, but they are at the same time more common than is apprehended; there being already existing nine Colleges or Universities, viz. four in New England, and one in each of the Provinces of New York, New Jersey, Pensilvania, Maryland, and Virginia, all furnish'd with learned Professors; besides a number of smaller Academies; these educate many of their Youth in the Languages, and those Sciences that qualify men for the Professions of Divinity, Law, or Physick. Strangers indeed are by no means excluded from exercising those Professions; and the quick Increase of Inhabitants everywhere gives them a Chance of Employ, which they have in common with the Natives. Of civil Offices, or Employ-

ments, there are few; no superfluous Ones, as in Europe; and it is a Rule establish'd in some of the States, that no Office should be so profitable as to make it desirable. . . .

These Ideas prevailing more or less in all the United States, it cannot be worth any Man's while, who has a means of Living at home, to expatriate himself, in hopes of obtaining a profitable civil Office in America; and, as to military Offices, they are at an End with the War, the Armies being disbanded. Much less is it adviseable for a Person to go thither, who has no other Quality to recommend him but his Birth. In Europe it has indeed its Value; but it is a Commodity that cannot be carried to a worse Market than that of America, where people do not inquire concerning a Stranger, *What is he?* but, *What can he do?* If he has any useful Art, he is welcome; and if he exercises it, and behaves well, he will be respected by all that know him; but a mere Man of Quality, who, on that Account, wants to live upon the Public, by some Office or Salary, will be despis'd and disregarded. The Husbandman is in honor there, and even the Mechanic, because their Employments are useful. The People have a saying, that God Almighty is himself a Mechanic, the greatest in the Univers; and he is respected and admired more for the Variety, Ingenuity, and Utility of his Handyworks, than for the Antiquity of his Family. They are pleas'd with the Observation of a Negro, and frequently mention it, that *Boccarorra* (meaning the White men) *make de black man workee, make de Horse workee, make de Ox workee, make ebery ting workee; only de Hog. He, de hog, no workee; he eat, he drink, he walk about, he go to sleep when he please, he libb like a Gentleman.* According to these Opinions of the Americans, one of them would think himself more oblig'd to a Genealogist, who could prove for him that his Ancestors and Relations for ten Generations had been Ploughmen, Smiths, Carpenters, Turners, Weavers, Tanners, or even Shoemakers, and consequently that they were useful Members of Society; than if he could only prove that they were Gentlemen, doing nothing of Value, but living idly on the Labour of others, mere *fruges consumere nati,*[1] and otherwise *good for nothing,* till by their Death their Estates, like the Carcass of the Negro's Gentleman-Hog, come to be *cut up.*

With regard to Encouragements for Strangers from Government, they are really only what are derived from good Laws and Liberty. Strangers are welcome, because there is room enough for them all, and therefore the old Inhabitants are not jealous of them; the Laws protect them sufficiently, so that they have no need of the Patronage of Great Men; and every one will enjoy securely the Profits of his Industry. But, if he does not bring a Fortune with him, he must work and be industrious to live. One or two Years' residence gives him all the Rights of a Citizen; but the government does not at present, whatever it may have done in former times, hire People to become Settlers, by Paying their Passages, giving Land, Negroes, Utensils, Stock, or any other kind of Emolument whatsoever. In short, America is the Land of Labour, and by no means what the English call *Lubberland,* and the French *Pays de Cocagne,* where the streets are said to be pav'd with half-peck Loaves, the Houses til'd with Pancakes, and where the Fowls fly about ready roasted, crying, *Come eat me!*

Who then are the kind of Persons to whom an Emigration to America may be advantageous? And what are the Advantages they may reasonably expect?

Land being cheap in that Country, from the vast Forests still void of Inhabitants, and not likely to be occupied in an Age to come, insomuch that the Propriety of an hundred Acres of fertile Soil full of Wood may be obtained near the Frontiers, in many Places, for Eight or Ten Guineas, hearty young Labouring Men, who understand the Husbandry of Corn and Cattle, which is nearly the same in that Country as in Europe, may easily establish themselves there. A little Money sav'd of the good Wages they receive there, while they work for others, enables them to buy the Land and begin their Plantation, in which they are assisted by the Good-Will of their Neighbours, and some Credit. Multitudes of poor People from England, Ireland, Scotland, and Germany, have by this means in a few years become wealthy Farmers, who, in their own Countries, where all the Lands are fully occupied, and the Wages of Labour low, could never have emerged from the poor Condition wherein they were born.

From the salubrity of the Air, the healthiness of the Climate, the plenty of good Provisions, and the Encouragement to early Marriages by the certainty of Subsistence in cultivating the Earth, the Increase of Inhabitants by natural Generation is very rapid in America, and becomes still more so by the Accession of Strangers; hence there is a continual Demand for more Artisans of all the necessary and useful kinds, to supply those Cultivators of the Earth with Houses, and with Furniture and Utensils of the grosser sorts, which cannot so well be brought from Europe. Tolerably good Workmen in any of those mechanic Arts are sure to find Employ, and to be well paid for their Work,

[1] " . . . . . . born
Merely to eat up the corn."—Watts.

there being no Restraints preventing Strangers from exercising any Art they understand, nor any Permission necessary. If they are poor, they begin first as Servants or Journeymen; and if they are sober, industrious, and frugal, they soon become Masters, establish themselves in Business, marry, raise Families, and become respectable Citizens.

Also, Persons of moderate Fortunes and Capitals, who, having a Number of Children to provide for, are desirous of bringing them up to Industry, and to secure Estates for their Posterity, have Opportunities of doing it in America, which Europe does not afford. There they may be taught and practise profitable mechanic Arts, without incurring Disgrace on that Account, but on the contrary acquiring Respect by such Abilities. There small Capitals laid out in Lands, which daily become more valuable by the Increase of People, afford a solid Prospect of ample Fortunes thereafter for those Children. The Writer of this has known several instances of large Tracts of Land, bought, on what was then the Frontier of Pensilvania, for Ten Pounds per hundred Acres, which after 20 years, when the Settlements had been extended far beyond them, sold readily, without any Improvement made upon them, for three Pounds per Acre. The Acre in America is the same with the English Acre, or the Acre of Normandy.

MEREDIC LOUIS ÉLIE MOREAU DE SAINT-MÉRY

The New York streets are narrow, as are the sidewalks where such exist. Fur-

4

Reprinted from "The Bitter Thoughts of President Moreau," in Oscar Handlin, ed., THIS WAS AMERICA (Cambridge: Harvard University Press, 1949), pp. 92–103.

thermore, the entrances to cellars which open onto the sidewalks cut off much of their width. The cellars are very bad and very damp and, in rainy spells and floods, fill with water. The custom of building kitchens in the cellar is, however, less widespread than in Philadelphia. The streets are not very even and one can see all sorts of animals wandering about, particularly cows and pigs. On Saturdays the sidewalks and windows are cleaned. But no one thinks of removing the dead dogs, cats, and rats from the streets. In front of almost every door are two white seats facing each other at right angles to the house. There, in the summer, people enjoy the fresh air.

People commonly drink excellent water, coming from a spring and called tea water because it makes fine tea. It is carried to all the houses by 24 horse-drawn carts and costs a little more than one cent a bucket. The owner of the spring rents his wells and his pump, operated by two horses and a boy, for $1,000. The carters in turn buy the water for 1/16 of a dollar a cask.

About 200 orphans are now lodged in the poorhouse and raised at the expense of the city. They wear no special uniform, since the magistrates wish to spare them the humiliation of clothing that would mark their condition. In that respect they differ from the children of both sexes whom one sees dressed in blue every Sunday in Trinity (Episcopal) Church. The latter belong to the less fortunate families of that communion and receive an education and clothing from the corporation. The municipal government, however, has no sympathy with this English practice and, on the contrary, seeks to avoid any symbol that would disrupt civic unity.

In the Bridewell, or house of correction, are lodged convicts and slaves, punished by various tasks for the profit of the city. There is also a hospital on the left side of Broadway. This institution does not belong to the city, but was built by private subscription, and the subscribers, among whom are many Quakers, select the directors. The two-story building generally holds 50 to 60 invalids. Each has a wooden bed, a mattress, and sheets. The two sexes are separated and the Negroes are in a different room. There are besides four cells for the insane, one of which is now occupied. There is a surgeon attached to the hospital which altogether has 24 employees, and 4 doctors who serve without pay. The annual expenses are $2,000 to $3,000, toward which invalids of means pay $2.00 a week.

There is no uniformity to the character of the Americans in the United States, a country that fills a whole continent. Nevertheless, there are some traits that may be considered general. Notwithstanding an ostensible hatred for them, they really love and fear the English. Despite their pride, the Americans have a vague feeling that they are somehow inferior to the Britons. Their tastes, customs, and, most of all, their habits, make true Englishmen of them. If the former mother country were to exploit this tendency by sending here as ambassador a famous man, titled and rich, his parties and flattery would assure a popular conquest. Instead, the London government has not ceased, since the peace of 1783, to show by its conduct a marked disdain for the United States. It gave evidence of that sentiment in the choice of its first representative, Temple, whose behavior in America before the Revolution, whose debts and immoderate conduct, had left a feeling of dislike. Mr. Hammond, new to diplomacy, was also a poor choice; his distaste for Americans and

his temper prevented him from keeping quiet about anything, and sometimes gave a critical character to incidents he should not have noticed at all. Mr. Bond, the consul general, was born in America but hates the country intensely. He has no striking qualities except a strong influence over Mr. Hammond, which however is no sign of talent.

Despite everything, one is astonished at the rapidity with which Americans have formed settlements in the interior. Their manner of life seems well-adapted to such undertakings, and when the mercantile and grasping spirit makes room for the virtues proper to a great nation, this country will probably enjoy perfect peace, although the inhabitants of the eastern states scorn the southerners, the Virginians, Carolinians, and Georgians.

It is said that the American is the perfect mean between the European and the Indian. But it is evident that he is departing steadily from the latter and approaching the former. Indifferent to almost everything, he sometimes takes an energetic stand, and then follows it with a nonchalance which indicates that he is not capable of feeling real enthusiasm. That indifference sometimes seems basic to American character, and the embellishments of friendship and philanthropy foreign to it. Doctor Ross, a Scot established in Philadelphia, told me in 1795, "I've lived in Philadelphia more than ten years and belong to several societies in which my position as a physician has brought me many contacts, but there are nevertheless not even two American homes to which I could go for dinner without being invited."

There was an attempt in Philadelphia to assemble a purse for the American prisoners in Algeria, but it hardly raised 1,200 francs. The comedians of the city gave a performance for the benefit of the prisoners which yielded almost 6,000 francs, but without much public enthusiasm. Thus it was the very needy English players who showed most sensitivity for the unfortunate seamen who had traveled far from home in the interests of their country and had left their women and children behind in misery.

In the winter of 1793, in skating on the Delaware River near Philadelphia, a young man disappeared beneath the breaking ice. There were loud cries of distress, but after a few moments he reappeared and was drawn out, after which people began skating again. Fifteen minutes later another disappeared and was drowned, but the skating continued without any display of emotion.

The frontiersman offers complete proof of the American indifference in love and in friendship and of failure to form attachments to anything. In the course of a lifetime he may begin as many as four clearings. He abandons, without reluctance, the place where he first drew breath, the church in which he first perceived the idea of a supreme being, the tombs of his ancestors, the friends of his infancy, the companions of his youth, and all the pleasures of his society. He emigrates, especially if he is a northerner, to go South or West, to the backwoods of the United States on the Ohio, disposing of his property, selling the house, the wagon, the horse, the dog, anything that will fetch a price.

The American has no dignity when it comes to money. A rich Philadelphia merchant met me at my door in 1795 and, as if by chance, said, "Don't refuse me, I need six hundred dollars until tomorrow morning." But I didn't have the sum he wished. The next day he met me on South Fourth Street near his house and said, "You have no money, well, in a little while I'll have a lot."

Note that this merchant had only spoken to me once before in buying on credit.

As far as generosity is concerned, there is much disparity in the American character, which includes some traits close to stinginess. A senator, asked to buy a very beautiful harp for one of his daughters, said, "I'd buy it all right, but the expense of the strings is too high." A widow in Philadelphia took in a Frenchman to teach the language to her daughter. This rich woman, realizing that her daughter could not take her lesson one Saturday, demanded a proportionate reduction from the monthly price. Another scholar, a very distinguished gentleman, having been absent a week, was paid for two months in Portuguese money hard to discount.

Love of gold often goes so far as to overwhelm delicacy. A well-known Democrat learned that a London trading house in January 1796 was using the services of a rival American firm in the attempt, in behalf of the English government, to forestall the market in flour. He said to Talleyrand, "That's too bad of them; I let that London company make more money than the one they picked." As a result, this Democrat was instrumental in having the people reject the Anglo-American commercial treaty of 1795.

There is no security in business. A borrower must be dunned a hundred times before a loan is repaid. One of my friends, a merchant in Guadaloupe, sent $15,000 with an order to buy bank stock. He received an answer which read, "I have received and executed the orders of your letter of —." Three years later the Guadaloupian arrives and asks for his shares, which have risen in value. They tell him that they have resold them, but will reimburse him with interest. He refuses. But the lawyers advise him to settle because a trial would take four years and cost 6,000 francs. In the end he gets back only his $15,000. In the South the clerks have a poor reputation for trustworthiness. If they are alone they regularly sell above the price and pocket the difference.

It is almost impossible to get an American to undertake a job he never did or never saw done. It took remarkable exertions on my part to get a man to make me boxes of different dimensions to hold seals.

One of the factors that makes American character hard to understand is the circumstance that they originated in different nations and have kept some of the marks of that original influence. Among the white residents of Philadelphia, for instance, are Englishmen, Scots, Irishmen, and Europeans of all nations, to say nothing of native Americans born in the various states of the United States who also have a diversified European ancestry. Thus the Americans descended from Dutchmen unite to a high degree the indolence of the first people and the avarice of the second, which augments the avidity for profit characteristic of both countries. It is impossible to push stinginess any further. They hardly feed themselves and treat their slaves badly.

In the United States the manner of living is always the same. They breakfast at nine on ham or salt fish such as shad, accompanied by coffee or tea and slices of toasted bread and butter. Dinner at two o'clock contains no real soup, but sometimes broth. The main dish is an English roast with potatoes. Then come peas boiled in water on which they put butter which melts in the heat, or else a spicy sauce. Then there are eggs, boiled or fried; fish, broiled or fried; a salad which sometimes contains cabbage cut into very thin slices which each one seasons to taste in his own dish; pastries; and

sweets of which they are very fond. For dessert, there is a little fruit, cheese, or pudding. The whole meal is accompanied by cider, by weak or strong beer, and by claret. During the dinner and while they eat they follow the English custom of exposing on a buffet in the dining room all the silver of the household.

At the entremets, they bring in Bordeaux or Madeira wine which lasts through dessert, at the end of which the ladies retire to their own devices, leaving the men free to drink as much as they please, for they continue to pass the bottle around the table, each one helping himself in his turn. They give toasts, smoke cigars, and run to the corner of the room seeking in the vessel on the bedside stand the means of making room for more liquor. Finally, bored, exhausted, or drunk they leave the dinner table, having thus worked themselves well into the night.

At about seven or eight o'clock of the evenings when there are no formal dinners they have tea as in the morning, but with no meat. At tea the whole family is reunited and friends, acquaintances, and even strangers are invited. These are the three meals of the day, for there is no supper. Tea in the evening is accompanied by a boring and dull etiquette. The mistress of the house serves, and passes the cups around. Until you turn over the cup and put the spoon on top they will keep bringing you fresh cups. There are a thousand stories, true or false, of Frenchmen, ignorant of this customary signal, who were drowned with that beverage.

A letter of recommendation to an American, if it is not concerned only with business, is ordinarily good for a dinner. When one enters an American home to dine, one leaves stick, hat, and coat in the entrance hall. Then, if the host already has one or more guests, he takes the newcomer, who now seems to live in the house, by the hand and presents him in order to each person, giving his name and the name of the individual to whom he is being introduced. This wise custom would be worth introducing in France, for among the French one occasionally makes insulting remarks about people who are present but whom one does not know.

All Americans are smokers. They also chew and sometimes they indulge in both activities in the manner dear to sailors. But the American of either sex who takes snuff is a rare phenomenon. The women do not deform their noses and do not soil themselves in this exercise which, despite all the excuses invented by those Europeans who have the habit, is more contrary to propriety than useful to health.

Americans have a great love for oysters, which they eat at all hours, even in the streets. They are sold in open baskets, by the dozen or the hundred, and are hawked through the streets with horrible noises until ten at night. There is also immoderate use of hot liquids. Tea is drunk boiling hot, but in the summer the water is cold or iced. They like liquors—rum, brandy, whisky—and they mix brandy with what they call grog.

Fresh fruit is in good demand. They eat seven or eight times as much meat as bread and they sleep too long in feather beds. Although the painting in their houses is renewed almost every year at the beginning of the autumn, the Americans continue to live in their homes without interruption.

For hard work and solid character, the natives do not compare with the German-born who form a large part of the population. The Pennsylvania Germans are less often drunkards, and their families are larger, contain as many as 12 and 14 children, while in 27 American families I found only one of 13 and one of 12. The Quakers grow weaker in numbers because many of their children leave the sect.

There are few centenarians in the United States, and the stones of the Philadelphia cemetery reveal only one nonagenarian. Ordinarily the group within which deaths are most common is that between the ages of 35 and 45.

American men are in general well-built, but seem to lack vigor. They are tall and thin, especially the Quakers. They are negligent in dress, those in the cities more so than the others. Both sexes lack color, are brave, but often irresolute.

As far as white women in general are concerned, we may begin with a remark very flattering and appropriate for them: no woman in the United States, whatever be the rank at which she was born (unless it be the result of some accident) has one of those figures, very common in Europe, even in France, among the lower classes, that repulse by their sheer ugliness; eyes, bloodshot or bleary; misformed in features. If one meets such a figure, one may be sure that she was recently imported from elsewhere and not the product of a soil well-favored in this respect.

American girls are pretty, and their eyes are alive with expression; but their complexions are wan, bad teeth spoil the appearance of their mouths, and there is also something disagreeable about the length of their legs. In general, however, they are of good height, are graceful, and, in enumerating their charms, one must not forget the shapeliness of their breasts.

Philadelphia has thousands of beauties between fourteen and eighteen. To offer but a single proof: on the north side of Market Street, between Third and Fifth Street, on a single winter's day I saw four hundred young maidens promenading, each one of whom would surely have been followed in Paris, a seductive tribute that could be offered by perhaps no other city in the world.

But these girls soon become pale, and an indisposition which is reckoned among the most unfavorable for the maintenance of the freshness of youth is very common among them. They have thin hair and bad teeth, and are given to nervous illnesses. The elements which embellish beauty, or rather which compose and order it, are not often bestowed by the graces. Finally, they are charming, adorable at fifteen, dried up at twenty-three, old at thirty-five, decrepit at forty or fifty. It is no accident that the usual age of marriage-ableness is fourteen.

The period at which the power of reproduction ceases is generally between forty and forty-five, and that revolution so dangerous in our climates is there passed without accident.

Girls do not appear in society until puberty. But one is constantly astonished to see young and pretty maidens in the streets going back and forth to school. Their hair hangs long and they wear petticoats closed by a seam. But at the marriageable age their hair is raised by a comb. From that time on they show themselves to society, they become their own mistresses, may walk alone, and take a lover.

The choice of a lover is unexceptional, it is public, and the parents hardly take notice because such are the customs of the country. The chosen man comes into the house whenever he pleases. He takes the object of his affections for a walk wherever he likes. He often comes for her on Sunday in a cabriolet and brings her back in the evening without being questioned as to their doings.

Girls generally hold on to their lovers, at least unless urgent causes force him to leave. In that case, they will choose a second. Similar causes can lead to several shifts in affection. But if the lover remains in the same place, he is always bound by the same chains, unless, having exhausted the expectations of pleasure, he escapes by a criminal inconstancy, and lets loose a flood of tears from the sweetheart he betrayed.

But universal indignation and the marks of infamy will catch up with one who is known as a villainous seducer, the betrayer of a married woman, for instance, no matter to what point he might flee, so long as that point is in the United States. Never, no never, in this vast country will he be able to obtain any kind of a post, even that of a watchman.

It is true that one must know how to be virtuous by system and by disposition. A maiden trusts herself to the restraint of her lover and charges him with the preservation of a respect that she herself cannot always command. Each day they are left alone. Since it is the daughter in many homes who awaits the return of the servants whom nothing can hold in after evening, and who often do not return until midnight, her lover is her only protection. The father, mother, and the whole family go to sleep. The lover and his girl remain alone, and sometimes on returning, the servants find them fallen asleep and the candle gone out—so cold is love in this country!!

When a girl notes some coolness in the man of her choice, she publicly overwhelms him with the most bitter reproaches, and will make known her prior rights in no uncertain terms if another woman, either through accident or design, attempts to supplant her. Nevertheless, these American young ladies are cold and passionless.

They give always the impression of calculation. Without emotion enough to alter the expression they will engage for hours in that which ought not be tolerated except in the grip of an irresistible ecstasy.

In view of the unlimited freedom of the unmarried woman, it is astonishing to discover the eagerness of all to be married, for marriage brings about an absolute change in the life of the girl. She ceases to be the young, scatterbrained irresponsible, knowing no laws but caprice and the good humor of a lover. She becomes a woman who exists only for her husband and for the care of her household. She is little more than a nursemaid; often, indeed, the first and only servant. But that very eagerness is a consequence of selfish calculation, because it is commonly believed that failure to find a husband is a reflection of some fault which repels lovers.

I am about to say something almost incredible. These women without the capacity for true love or passion give themselves over at an early age to a sensual enjoyment of themselves. Nor are they strangers to the taste for the pleasures of a misguided imagination in a person of the same sex. Among the common people, say in the home of an innkeeper or shopkeeper, the daughters and servant girls sleep together. In the space of eight or ten years a girl may share her bed with fifty or sixty different creatures, of whom no more may be known than their names, who may be dirty, unhealthy, infected with communicable diseases, and with habits fatal to a young person.

The Philadelphia women are luxuriously supplied with shoes, with ribbons, and with lingerie, although they still lack gauze, laces, and artificial flowers. They have a habit, which they think in good taste, of letting the men pay for what they buy in the shops and forgetting to reimburse them. They have a decided taste for finery and a great desire to show themselves off, which is at once the consequence of, and contributes to, the love of finery. They are not, however, as well turned out as Frenchwomen.

Although in general one notices a great deal of modesty in the Philadelphia girls, their manners are not altogether pure, and the carelessness of some parents as to the way in which their daughters may have acquired trinkets which they did not give them must favor some indiscretions. These, however, will not spring from love, for Americans are not very sentimental. But the women do have certain ridiculous scruples about being unwilling to hear certain words pronounced. And the extent to which that scruple is observed discloses rather an excess of knowledge than of ignorance.

American women also have a false modesty that makes them unwilling to discuss, even with their husbands, bodily ailments that may become serious. That is the source of so many bad teeth, of stomach troubles, and of poor skins. Americans divide the whole body into two parts: from the top to the waist is the stomach; from there to the bottom, the limbs. Imagine then the difficulties of a doctor who must guess from these rudimentary indications the nature and the seat of an illness. The slightest contact is forbidden and the ill woman will, even at the risk of death, not make the vagueness more specific.

Here is an example. A young woman, having borne her first child, found one of her breasts cracked. She suffered terribly but would only tell the doctor that her stomach hurt. The illness got worse. A feminine neighbor to whom she spoke of the condition, but who was unable to convince her to be frank with the doctor, revealed the matter to me. I resolved to speak to this woman, using all the arts that her stubborn prejudices demanded. I referred to the risks she ran, the possibility of death, and its effect on the little boy she loved so much. I charged her with failure in a duty toward nature and religion, and warned her that her obstinacy was a form of suicide.

I spoke with such eloquence, that I convinced the patient, who made her difficulties clear to the doctor. She regained her health after a long treatment. But the upshot was that this young mother thereafter refused to speak to me or even to greet me despite her awareness that I was responsible for saving her life.

In the eyes of the Yankee ladies, French women are not quite proper because there are points at which their chemise shows. I am sorry to say, that precisely because the American girls have so much shame when it comes to anything that concerns that garment that they own few of them and consequently change them infrequently, the result being that these are not quite clean and often become depositories for marks of a need to which nature has subjected all animals.

The character of children is strongly conditioned by their upbringing and the examples they see about them. They are raised at home and generally are free and mischievous. They often exercise their mischievousness by annoying the little Negroes. They throw snowballs at passers-by, and I myself have not been exempt from experiences which testify to their poor upbringing. The very youngest children whose mothers work are kept in cradles which are rocked mercilessly from morning to night by the mother's foot, with such force that the infant must be in a con-

stant state of dizziness. If there are other women or children in the household, that task is relegated to them.

When the children are a little older they are sent to schools where they learn reading, writing, and arithmetic. As far as writing is concerned, these schools have a great advantage in uniformity of system. They all teach English and a legible hand. Consequently, a child taught writing in any part of the continent is sure to find the same practice and the same characters wherever he may go.

In almost every city on the continent, especially in the North, there are officials who warn the parents that they must send their children to school when they are seven years old. If the parents do not heed the advice they are warned again with a time limit, at the expiration of which the officials take the children to school.

The result of this minute care is that a man who knows how to read and write doubles the value of his intelligence, in a manner of speaking, over people who lack those two skills. All Americans of both sexes have those abilities. I remember while working in the admiralty in Martinique where it was my duty to receive declarations, I could always extend the pen to American sailors, while most Frenchmen were ignorant, a fact very offensive to my national pride.

When the children are still older they are sent to boarding schools, if the parents can afford the expense. There they are taught languages, Latin and Greek, for in North America the latter language is taught like Latin. But lazy and insubordinate children behave badly in these institutions, for the masters and instructors are only concerned with keeping them and give way to their whims with a most unhappily complaisance.

Americans are quarrelsome, and many quarrels lead to pugilism, an indication of their English origin. Boxing has its own rules and regulations. The two athletes choose their field of combat. They strip to the waist, keeping on only their undershirts, which they roll up to the elbows. At a given signal they run toward each other, striking at the stomach and face with blows whose force can only be appreciated by those who have participated in such events.

After each charge they step back, then take up the attack again. If one falls his adversary must not touch him as long as he is on the ground. But at the slightest movement to get up he has the right to knock him down again. No one steps in to separate the two contestants. A ring forms around the struggling men, and partisans urge their champions on. Until one is willing to quit, the other continues to beat him with his fists. Once having conceded defeat, the loser picks himself up, dresses, is free and can retire until a new challenge leads him back to the field of battle.

At the end of a fight one or both of the contestants is thoroughly beaten up, disfigured, covered with blood which pours from mouth and nose. Teeth are broken, eyes blackened and sometimes closed entirely. Most fights take place at night by moonlight, except when drunkenness precipitates the issue in open daylight and before the eyes of curious onlookers.

The Americans also follow the English mode when they use boxing matches for exercising their passion for betting. But cockfights are the chief recourse of gamblers. These take place every day. Men spend all their time and energy preparing cocks for battle. They miss no opportunity to train their animals and excite them to fight, regulating their diet and using hard liquor to that end. The cocks are armed with iron spurs and their crests are shaven to give less grip to the enemy. They are urged on by cries and ringed in to prevent flight. In the midst of a crowd, which might be entirely composed of Englishmen, but really is so only by inheritance, the fight goes on and pitiful birds, torn and dying, settle wagers, the profits of which are consumed in nearby taverns by the atrocious winners. I will only say of dueling with pistols that this English custom daily gains favor in the United States.

III. RECENT INTERPRETATIONS

By the time of the American Revolution, colonial society had reached a remarkable peak of economic sophistication compared with its position a century earlier—and even compared with the economic structure of contemporary England and Europe. A flourishing world trade, scattered but expanding manufacturing establishments throughout the provinces, a complex and lively commercial agriculture, booming coastal cities—all these testified to the economic dynamism of the eighteenth-century colonies on the eve of independence. The following three selections synthesize the current degree of historical understanding of colonial economic and social life in a number of major areas. Clarence Ver Steeg's impressive work, *The Formative Years, 1607–1763,* contains the best recent discussion of colonial economic practices. Winthrop D. Jordan's article on the roots of American slavery summarizes earlier literature on the question and presents a perceptive analysis of the relationship between racial prejudice and economic factors in the process of enslavement. Carl Bridenbaugh's numerous books and articles on colonial urban life have made him the undisputed historical master of this field. His analysis of the century of American urbanization under English rule is summarized in another selection.

CLARENCE VER STEEG

THE STRUCTURE OF THE PROVINCIAL ECONOMY

An analysis of the structure of the provincial economy—the changing land systems, the modification in the production and marketing of agricultural staples, the expansion of trade and the increased complexity of trade relationships, and the changing labor base—clearly reveals the emergence of an indigenous American capitalism, characterized by such manifestations as production for market, specialization, and accelerated accumulation of capital. Without this economic structure political maturity might very well have been impossible to achieve. The evolution and strength of the provincial economy required an adjustment in the relationship between Great Britain and its colonies, an adaptation of the imperial system to these new economic realities, but such an adjustment never materialized.

The land system in provincial America became increasingly related to economic enterprise rather than to individual or group needs. Land rather than being primarily an instrument of settlement became an investment and,

Reprinted from Clarence L. Ver Steeg, THE FORMATIVE YEARS, *1607–1763 (New York: Hill & Wang, 1964), pp. 173–87, by permission of the publisher.*

in some instances, an instrument of speculation. In some cases, the acreage of obtainable land grants was so great that only speculators could afford to invest in them. One impecunious individual did not have the means to survey such amounts of land or to obtain a patent. At times, small grants of fifty acres, a manageable farm for an individual without equipment or capital, were not economically feasible. The practice of William Byrd II, who received a large land grant early in the eighteenth century and who then encouraged Frenchmen to come to America and settle on the land, purchasing smaller grants as they were able, benefitted both parties to the contract. But when, as in New York, huge grants, obtained by dubious or even false means, were controlled so as to prohibit outright purchase of smaller plots by rank-and-file migrants, the speculator became a curse.

In New England, the land system was modified in two ways, the first affecting the towns and the second affecting the expanding frontier. Property owners of a town in the eighteenth century seldom lived in the town, a distinct contrast to the seventeenth century, when the town proprietors were also residents. The interests of the seventeenth-century proprietors and those of the town generally coincided, whereas the interests of the absentee proprietors of the eighteenth century were at times in direct conflict with those of the town residents.

A number of developments explain this change. First, the second- and third-generation Puritans were frequently forced to migrate elsewhere to find new and better opportunities. Town property, originally distributed on the basis of need—according to the size of a family, for example—tended to be purchased eventually by people who had accumulated money. Second, the hold of the church, although it continued to be strong, was no longer exclusively allied with political authority so that the seventeenth-century objective of establishing towns to preserve a precisely defined social-religious community was replaced by a new objective, to establish towns which could serve the economic needs of a given area. Third, capital accumulation in New England enabled successful enterprisers to purchase land either around the settled communities or on the frontier, in either case a dramatic modification of the town system effectively used in the original settlements.

The distribution of frontier land in eighteenth-century New England also followed a different pattern than in earlier years. Large grants were awarded to individual entrepreneurs who divided the land into smaller parcels which were resold to individuals rather than to groups. The aim, of course, was to make a profit, not to create a particular type of community. As a result, the towns founded in the frontier territory frequently differed in general purpose and tone from the towns founded in the seventeenth century.

The land system in some of the middle and most of the southern colonies was substantially modified. In the middle colonies, the price of land near the urban communities increased rather markedly. The original settlers who held these grants profited from the price rise, and new arrivals or second-generation provincials attracted to the land were compelled to seek opportunities in the less settled areas where land values were better suited to their means.

In New York speculation in large land patents, some of which originated in the seventeenth century, got out of hand. A contemporary observer remarked:

an unaccountable thirst for large Tracts of Land without the design of cultivation, hath prevailed over the inhabitants of this and the neighboring Provinces with a singular rage. Patents have been lavishly granted (to give it no worse term) upon the pretence of fair Indian purchases, some of which the Indians have alleged were never made but forged. . . . They say that the Surveyors have frequently run Patents vastly beyond even the pretended conditions or limits of sale.

Robert Livingston, founder of the eighteenth-century Livingston dynasty of New York, was able to piece together a manor of several hundred thousand acres by marrying into the Van Rensselaer family, by artful cultivation of the King's officials in the colony, but, most significantly, by taking two separated patents, one of 2,000 acres and the second of 600 acres, and obtaining a title for all the intervening land, amounting to 160,000 acres. Captain Lewis Evans, whose political connections proved highly advantageous, accumulated an excess of 300,000 acres of land within a few years of his arrival in New York. These large patents reflected an almost unchecked entrepreneurial spirit applied to accumulating the most accessible source of wealth, land. The unscrupulous agrarian enterprisers of the eighteenth century were not unlike their industrial counterparts in the nineteenth century, the major difference being that a monopoly over land was more difficult to establish than a monopoly over an industry.

It should be noted that the land policy of the Pennsylvania proprietors was, on the whole, more just. James Logan, who was closely connected with the Penn family, was able to secure some especially desirable grants, but such cases were exceptional. Thirty thousand German Palatinates, for example, who originally attempted to find agreeable opportunities in New York, eventually abandoned that colony in favor of Pennsylvania. Not only was land in Pennsylvania cheaper but a clear title was easy to obtain. Moreover, the new arrivals frequently settled on the frontier land owned by the Penn family, on the presumption that possession was nine tenths of the law.

In the seventeenth century, the distribution of land in the southern colonies had not been free from abuses, but in the 1690s and particularly after 1710, those families with position and influence within the colonies gained extensive new grants, bolstering their favorable economic position. Whereas in the seventeenth century the Northern Neck had been granted to a family outside the colony (thus arousing the antagonism of the Virginia planters), eighteenth-century grants were given to residents within the colony. Planter capitalism, which organized land resources and labor to produce a commodity for market, emerged triumphant.

Several results can be directly attributed to the modified land system. In certain colonies the engrossers of extensive holdings—the Livingstons in New York and the Carters in Virginia, to cite examples—were able to establish a landed aristocracy. Moreover, with social prestige and political position dependent upon land, a relatively rigid social system resulted, not so much in

terms of who had the right to vote, but in terms of who had the power. In provincial America, perhaps more than in any other period of American history, those considered the social and economic elite were also those who exercised the most political power. Political contests were frequently a clash between giants, each seeking an advantage in the division of the land resources.

The friction between the large landed proprietor and the rank-and-file provincial, in the settled regions as well as on the frontier, was heightened during the eighteenth century as choice land became scarcer. If the territory beyond the Appalachians had not been opened by the American Revolution, the restrictive land system which favored the established few in certain colonies would undoubtedly have created more intense friction than it did. Although the issue became increasingly important, in no colony had it become decisive by 1763. Either sufficient land was still available or the hope of land beyond the Appalachian ridge allayed fears of the future.

Colonial agriculture also reflected a maturing provincial rather than a primitive colonial economy. The self-sufficient farm, characteristic of the seventeenth century, persisted, particularly in certain areas within New England and to an extent within the middle colonies, but farming turned increasingly to the production of a cash crop and to those techniques of farming which could increase production. Equally important, each group of colonies began to specialize, to produce commodities which best suited its soil, climate, labor force, and capital assets.

New England, for example, turned to grazing and the production of meat products for export. Wheat, which had generally been the staple for New

England during the latter half of the seventeenth century, was now imported, for New England could not profitably compete with the new regions, just as the new regions could not, at the outset, compete with New England in grazing. Specialization reached such a point that Boston established a public granary in 1728 to guard against the possible shortage of cereals.

The middle colonies specialized in producing grains. The transfer of wheat production from New England to the middle colonies foreshadowed the march of wheat westward, a half pace behind the frontier. The statistics on the expansion of wheat production are spectacular. To illustrate, Philadelphia exported a limited quantity of wheat in 1700, but by 1765 it exported more than 350,000 bushels of wheat and more than 18,000 tons of flour. The port of New York exported approximately one third the amount exported by Philadelphia. The eighteenth-century farmer of New England and the middle colonies was as interested in markets and trade as was the merchant. The interrelation between agricultural production and overseas markets, characteristic of a flourishing commercial capitalism, suggests, in addition, that any restrictive trade provision affected the agrarians fully as much as the merchants.

The southern colonies not only increased their production of the first staple, tobacco, but to it were added additional staples, notably rice, indigo, and naval stores. In each case, the accelerating rate of export, which reflected the increase in production, was phenomenal. In rice alone, exports increased more than fourteen times between 1715 and the 1760s. More than half a million pounds of indigo were exported in the 1760s, even though indigo was not marketed until the 1740s.

Naval stores had been profitably produced in South Carolina in the early decades of the eighteenth century, but North Carolina became the pre-eminent supplier among the southern colonies after the 1720s. New England, of course, shared in the production of naval stores.

In animal husbandry, the application of capital to farming was evident. Cattle breeding, the breeding of horses in the middle and southern colonies for export to New England, and the breeding of horses for domestic use in the South, not to mention some sheep farming, unknown and impractical in the seventeenth century, illustrate the change in animal husbandry. . . .

In summary, certain general trends influenced the development of agriculture during the eighteenth century, each reflecting a growing early American capitalism. First, capital was applied on a major scale to agricultural production. Although southern planter capitalism is the most obvious example, this generalization is also applicable to much of the agricultural production of the middle colonies and New England. Second, specialization became an identifying trait in American agriculture, with each region producing those staples for which it was best suited. Third, this specialization greatly encouraged intercolonial trade, for as each region concentrated increasingly on a marketable staple, important requirements as well as attention to markets increased. The southern colonies imported meat products from New England; New England and the middle colonies imported tobacco from the southern colonies. The middle colonies exported wheat to the West Indies; the West Indies dispatched molasses to New England; and the southern colonies frequently imported slaves from the West Indies. The velocity of trade between various parts of the Empire cannot be measured statistically because duties within the Empire were not uniformly applied, but the interaction produced by specialization in agriculture was intensified.

The point could validly be made that the application of capital to agricultural production was greater in the West Indies than in the continental colonies, which raises the question, Why did an indigenous commercial capitalism grow up in the North American provinces but not in the British West Indies? The most plausible explanation seems to be that in the West Indies the large number of absentee landholders not only drained the profits from the islands, but also prevented the establishment of an indigenous institutional-economic structure. Coupled with self-government, this could have created a sphere of authority apart from that of Britain. The West Indies, dependent on the protected British sugar market, always remained an economic and colonial appendage of the mother country.

Agricultural produce figured extensively in the Atlantic trade of American provinces. England could absorb part of the tobacco production, most of the naval stores, indigo, furs, and lumber, and some of the rice, but many prominent exports, meat products, fishery products, wheat, flour, and the like, had to seek markets outside the imperial framework. Because northern Europe produced its own meat products and because its animal husbandry was often in advance of that of the colonies, provincial meat products found markets in southern Europe and the West Indies. The sugar islands in the West Indies served as a principal market for colonial fishery products, wheat and flour, and other foodstuffs. Thus, the export trade of the middle colonies and New England was primarily connected with the West Indies and southern Europe, whereas that of the southern colonies was related primarily to Britain.

Colonial imports included manufactured goods—furniture, clothing, glass, and luxury items—most of it from England, and such necessities as salt from southern Europe and sugar and molasses from the West Indies. Because of the dearness of labor, it too became a "commodity" for import, the indentures as well as the slaves. These requirements created financial problems, for the colonials did not have sufficient cash to pay for these imports.

As with all rapidly expanding economies, the capital accumulation within the colonies was not equal to the investment requirements, and outside money, therefore, was needed. Because money did not flow in as rapidly as the maturing economy required, the provincials resorted to other means, principally the issuance of paper currency and the creation of land banks. Paper currency was first adopted extensively in the 1690s, just as the indigenous commercial capitalism was emerging, and it became a favorite method to meet the shortage of money. Land banks, in which land was used to back the issue of banknotes, were, unfortunately, ill suited to the needs of the economy because of their inflexibility in extending credit when it was most in demand. With land in such abundance as a resource, however, it was natural that the provincials should look to it to solve the problem of a limited supply of money. Both expedients, the issuance of money and the creation of land banks, were finally prohibited by imperial legislation.

According to the available statistics, during the decade 1700–10 approximately £265,000 sterling of goods were exported annually to Great Britain from the colonies, and approximately £267,000 sterling of goods were imported annually into the colonies from Great Britain. During the decade 1760–70 more than £1,000,000 sterling of goods were exported annually to Great Britain from the colonies, and approximately £1,760,000 sterling of goods were imported annually into the colonies from Great Britain. Estimates have been made that the colonial trade represented one third of the English trade in 1770, whereas it constituted only one sixth of the English trade in 1700.

These figures, first of all, dramatize the growth of trade between the colonies and the Empire during the first half of the eighteenth century. Second, the total trade of the American provinces, conventionally estimated as twice the amount of the trade with the mother country, as shown by these statistics, reveals a vigorous, growing commercial capitalism. Third, these statistics emphasize the pronounced change in the balance between imports and exports. Whereas in the decade 1700–10 the colonies, valued as suppliers of goods for the mother country, were equally valuable as markets, by 1770 the colonies were almost twice as valuable as markets for English goods as they were as suppliers. In fact, the statistics, convincing as they are, tend to underplay the role of the American provinces as a market for English goods because once again the figure given is that of the English customs. The export figure does not include the transportation and shipping charges incurred in carrying the goods to America. The import figure generally does include these costs. Therefore, the figure of £1,000,000 tends to be inflated; the figure of

£1,760,000 tends to be deflated. As a result, the value of the British exports to America, in relationship to the imports, is even greater than the statistics indicate. Finally, it is axiomatic that finished goods find a market in a relatively sophisticated economy as opposed to one that is primitive, which reemphasizes the maturity of the American provincial economy.

Although the trend which made the American provinces a flourishing English market became increasingly obvious by the middle of the eighteenth century, the British imperial policy failed to alter either its theory or practice to accommodate to the new economic realities. Consequently, the American provincials struggled to search for ways to pay for English goods: by accumulating a credit balance in the British West Indies which could be transferred to England; by using payment for services in the intercolonial and Atlantic trade to offset the obligations incurred in England; and by trading illegally outside the British colonial system, with the French West Indies and occasionally the Spanish, in order to obtain goods and specie that could be used for remittances. Certain historians have suggested that Britain eventually acknowledged the vitality of the market in the continental colonies, but contemporary letters, pamphlets, instructions, and legislation do not sustain this thesis.

The spectacular increase in trade, emerging during the eighteenth century as the mainstream of commercial capitalism itself, produced the provincial merchant-capitalist. Each colony possessed a mercantile group, although in some colonies the group was much more powerful than in others. A network of mercantile connections was centered in Boston and reached into the shipping centers of Beverley, Marblehead, Providence, Newport, and other New England ports. The Belchers, the Wentworths, the Bowdoins, the Browns, and the Hopkinses, to name only a representative sample, became identified with the mercantile elite. Merchant groups in New York City gained an economic advantage which eventually affected its politics, and the Philadelphia mercantile community, essentially nonexistent in 1700, was by the 1760s one of the most energetic entrepreneurial communities within the British nation, the equal of Boston and of most outports within England itself. Charleston, secure in its strategic location where the Ashley and Cooper Rivers converge, had ready access to the interior and, as a result, it became a thriving center for great merchants ranging from the Wraggs to the Manigaults to the Laurenses.

Virginia's mercantile development was rather distinct. The early eighteenth century was characterized by the planter-merchant. As a planter his main preoccupation was administering extensive plantation holdings, but his location on the principal rivers made him into a merchant as well, an intermediary between the London, Bristol, or Glasgow merchant and the planter whose holdings were located in the interior. Robert "King" Carter, a prototype, managed his plantations, but he also ran a store to supply other, and frequently lesser, planters, and he imported slaves for resale. As the eighteenth century advanced, a full time mercantile community developed in Norfolk, which, because of its location, could service an extensive hinterland. Merchants began to congregate at other centers, near the headwaters of navigable rivers, and after 1760 a lively trade in the upcountry was pursued by

individuals, most notably the Allasons, whose livelihood depended solely upon it. The evolution of the trading community, therefore, proceeded through three phases: the planter (to the late seventeenth century); the planter-merchant (to the 1740s); and, finally, the full-fledged merchant.

The trade statistics of provincial America suggest that the vitality of the provincial economy was intimately dependent upon the prosperity of the general Atlantic community. Moreover, the commercial, market-oriented economy of the American provinces made them less rather than more self-sufficient. In contrast to nineteenth-century industrial capitalism in the United States, when the major market for finished goods was almost exclusively internal, the eighteenth-century economy was dependent on external markets for finished goods. Economic fluctuations in Britain and Europe, therefore, were a potent factor in the economic welfare of the colonies. Indeed, an entire history is yet to be written on the significance and interrelation of this community of interests among the peoples bordering both sides of the Atlantic. The inability of the United States to remain isolated immediately after the American Revolution was merely a projection of the experience of the provincial period.

A reduction in trade, either because markets failed or because war severed conventional trade channels, affected prosperity. During periods of depression, the American provincial did not starve, because sufficient foodstuffs and similar necessities (except salt) were readily obtained, but economic growth and economic vitality suffered. This generalization applies not only to the merchant but to the producer, the wheat farmer in Pennsylvania, the cattle producer of New England, the tobacco planter in Virginia, the rice planter in Carolina. The rise of commercial capitalism resulted in an intimate interweaving of the interests of provincial America with those of the Atlantic community.

The maturing provincial economy was also reflected in the rise of manufacturing. Although other commodities could be cited (the annual output of shipbuilders increased from four thousand tons in 1700 to thirty-five thousand tons in 1770), a sophisticated index is the production of iron. More pig iron was produced in the colonies around the mid-eighteenth century than was produced in England, because of the easy access of the ore and, more important, because of an abundant supply of wood for converting the ore into pig iron. Even the restrictive Iron Act, passed by Parliament in 1750, encouraged the production of pig and bar iron by permitting these products to enter England duty-free. Slitting mills, used to convert pig or bar iron into finished products, were, under the terms of the same Act, prohibited, as were plating forges and steel furnaces. Equally significant, in the present context, was the development of glassworks, flour mills, sawmills, and the like.

A discussion of the provincial economic structure would be incomplete without an examination of the skill and productivity of the labor force. In a rapidly expanding economy, labor is scarce and thus expensive. In the formative years expensive labor was a constant factor, alleviated in part by the influx of immigrants and by the accelerated population levels in the provincial period.

Reliable statistics on the labor force, not to mention a breakdown of figures within the labor force, are almost impossible to secure, but the general trend is well known. In the seventeenth century, the labor force in the southern colonies was composed principally of indentured servants; New England attracted free labor, although many families employed servants. In the eighteenth century, the indentured servant was principally drawn to the middle colonies, while the southern colonies became increasingly dependent on Negro slaves. New England, although it retained some indentured servants and continued to maintain a tradition of hiring servants, was still characterized by the family as a laboring force and the artisan plying his particular skill.

The demand for labor in each group of colonies depended largely upon its economic base. In the southern colonies, for example, where capitalism was applied to agriculture on a major scale, a large number of relatively unskilled laborers was in heavy demand. In the middle colonies, where small farming predominated, the labor needs varied, but characteristically a small farm required semiskilled labor and the towns required skilled artisans. In New England, skilled artisans found a ready market for their labor, though the semiskilled worker also was in demand.

With the growth of urban communities in the middle colonies—New York City and Philadelphia—and with the rise of Charleston as a port, the skilled laborer in the eighteenth century had a wider choice than he had had in the seventeenth century. The craftsman became an important citizen in the community, the backbone of a relatively prosperous, important labor group. A silversmith like Paul Revere not only made history but created works of such quality that they have become artifacts reflecting the life of his generation.

WINTHROP D. JORDAN

Thanks to John Smith we know that Negroes first came to the British continental colonies in 1619. What we do not know is exactly when Negroes were first enslaved there. This question has been debated by historians for the past seventy years, the critical point being whether Negroes were enslaved almost from their first importation or whether they were at first simply servants and only later reduced to the status of slaves. The long duration and vigor of the controversy suggest that more than a simple question of dating has been involved. In fact certain current tensions in American society have complicated the historical problem and greatly heightened its significance. Dating the origins of slavery has taken on a striking modern relevance.

During the nineteenth century historians assumed almost universally that the first Negroes came to Virginia as slaves. So close was their acquaintance with the problem of racial slavery that it did not occur to them that Negroes could ever have been anything but slaves. . . .

There has since been agreement on dating the statutory establishment of slavery, and differences of opinion have centered on when enslavement began in actual practice. Fortunately there has also been general agreement on slavery's distinguishing characteristics: service for life and inheritance of like obligation by any offspring. . . .

All this was a very small academic gale, well insulated from the outside world. Yet despite disagreement on dating enslavement the earlier writers . . . shared a common assumption

Reprinted from Winthrop D. Jordan, "Modern Tensions and the Origins of American Slavery," JOURNAL OF SOUTHERN HISTORY, *XXVIII (February 1962), 18–30, by permission of the publisher.*

which, though at the time seemingly irrelevant to the main question, has since proved of considerable importance. They assumed that prejudice against the Negro was natural and almost innate in the white man. . . .

Only when tensions over race relations intensified once more did the older assumption of natural prejudice crop up again. After World War II American Negroes found themselves beneficiaries of New Deal politics and reforms, wartime need for manpower, world-wide repulsion at racist excesses in Nazi Germany, and growingly successful colored anticolonialism. With new militancy Negroes mounted an attack on the citadel of separate but equal, and soon it became clear that America was in for a period of self-conscious reappraisal of its racial arrangements. Writing in this period of heightened tension (1949) a practiced and careful scholar, Wesley F. Craven, raised the old question of the Negro's original status, suggesting that Negroes had been enslaved at an early date. Craven also cautiously resuscitated the idea that white men may have had natural distaste for the Negro, an idea which fitted neatly with the suggestion of early enslavement. Original antipathy would mean rapid debasement.

In the next year (1950) came a sophisticated counterstatement, which contradicted both Craven's dating and implicitly any suggestion of early prejudice. Oscar and Mary F. Handlin in "Origins of the Southern Labor System" offered a case for late enslavement, with servitude as the status of Negroes before about 1660. Originally the status of both Negroes and white servants was far short of freedom, the Handlins maintained, but Negroes failed to benefit from increased freedom for servants in mid-century and became less free rather than more. Embedded in this description of diverging status were broader implications: Late and gradual enslavement undercut the possibility of natural, deep-seated antipathy toward Negroes. On the contrary, if whites and Negroes could share the same status of half freedom for forty years in the seventeenth century, why could they not share full freedom in the twentieth?

The same implications were rendered more explicit by Kenneth M. Stampp in a major reassessment of Southern slavery published two years after the Supreme Court's 1954 school decision. Reading physiology with the eye of faith, Stampp frankly stated his assumption "that innately Negroes *are,* after all, only white men with black skins, nothing more, nothing less." Closely following the Handlins' article on the origins of slavery itself, he almost directly denied any pattern of early and inherent racial antipathy: ". . . Negro and white servants of the seventeenth century seemed to be remarkably unconcerned about their visible physical differences." As for "the trend toward special treatment" of the Negro, "physical and cultural differences provided handy excuses to justify it." Distaste for the Negro, then, was in the beginning scarcely more than an appurtenance of slavery.

These views squared nicely with the hopes of those even more directly concerned with the problem of contemporary race relations, sociologists and social psychologists. Liberal on the race question almost to a man, they tended to see slavery as the initial cause of the Negro's current degradation. The modern Negro was the unhappy victim of long association with base status. Sociologists, though uninterested in tired questions of historical evidence, could not easily assume a natural prejudice in the white man as the cause of slavery.

Natural or innate prejudice would not only violate their basic assumptions concerning the dominance of culture but would undermine the power of their new Baconian science. For if prejudice was natural there would be little one could do to wipe it out. Prejudice must have followed enslavement, not vice versa, else any liberal program of action would be badly compromised. One prominent social scientist suggested in a UNESCO pamphlet that racial prejudice in the United States commenced with the cotton gin!

Just how closely the question of dating had become tied to the practical matter of action against racial prejudice was made apparent by the suggestions of still another historian. Carl N. Degler grappled with the dating problem in an article frankly entitled "Slavery and the Genesis of American Race Prejudice." The article appeared in 1959, a time when Southern resistance to school desegregation seemed more adamant than ever and the North's hands none too clean, a period of discouragement for those hoping to end racial discrimination. Prejudice against the Negro now appeared firm and deep-seated, less easily eradicated than had been supposed in, say, 1954. It was Degler's view that enslavement began early, as a result of white settlers' prejudice or antipathy toward the first Negroes. Thus not only were the sociologists contradicted but the dating problem was now overtly and consciously tied to the broader question of whether slavery caused prejudice or prejudice caused slavery. A new self-consciousness over the American racial dilemma had snatched an arid historical controversy from the hands of an unsuspecting earlier generation and had tossed it into the arena of current debate.

Ironically there might have been no

historical controversy at all if every historian dealing with the subject had exercised greater care with facts and greater restraint in interpretation. Too often the debate entered the realm of inference and assumption. For the crucial early years after 1619 there is simply not enough evidence to indicate with any certainty whether Negroes were treated like white servants or not. No historian has found anything resembling proof one way or the other. The first Negroes were sold to the English settlers, yet so were other Englishmen. It can be said, however, that Negroes were set apart from white men by the word *Negroes,* and a distinct name is not attached to a group unless it is seen as different. The earliest Virginia census reports plainly distinguished Negroes from white men, sometimes giving Negroes no personal name; and in 1629 every commander of the several plantations was ordered to "take a generall muster of all the inhabitants men woemen and Children as well *Englishe* as Negroes." Difference, however, might or might not involve inferiority.

The first evidence as to the actual status of Negroes does not appear until about 1640. Then it becomes clear that *some* Negroes were serving for life and some children inheriting the same obligation. Here it is necessary to suggest with some candor that the Handlins' statement to the contrary rests on unsatisfactory documentation. That some Negroes were held as slaves after about 1640 is no indication, however, that American slavery popped into the world fully developed at that time. Many historians, most cogently the Handlins, have shown slavery to have been a gradual development, a process not completed until the eighteenth century. The complete deprivation of civil and personal rights, the legal conversion of the Negro into a chattel, in short slavery as Americans came to know it, was not accomplished overnight. Yet these developments practically and logically depended on the practice of hereditary lifetime service, and it is certainly possible to find in the 1640's and 1650's traces of slavery's most essential feature.

. . .

In addition to these clear indications that some Negroes were owned for life, there were cases of Negroes held for terms far longer than the normal five or seven years. On the other hand, some Negroes served only the term usual for white servants, and others were completely free. One Negro freeman, Anthony Johnson, himself owned a Negro. Obviously the enslavement of some Negroes did not mean the immediate enslavement of all.

Further evidence of Negroes serving for life lies in the prices paid for them. In many instances the valuations placed on Negroes (in estate inventories and bills of sale) were far higher than for white servants, even those servants with full terms yet to serve. Since there was ordinarily no preference for Negroes as such, higher prices must have meant that Negroes were more highly valued because of their greater length of service. Negro women may have been especially prized, moreover, because their progeny could also be held perpetually. . . .

. . . Yet this is not the only evidence that Negroes were subjected to degrading distinctions not directly related to slavery. In several ways Negroes were singled out for special treatment which suggested a generalized debasing of Negroes as a group. Significantly, the first indications of debasement appeared at about the same time as the first indications of actual enslavement.

. . .

Virginia law set Negroes apart . . . by denying them the important right and obligation to bear arms. Few restraints could indicate more clearly the denial to Negroes of membership in the white community. This action, in a sense the first foreshadowing of the slave codes, came in 1640, at just the time when other indications first appear that Negroes were subject to special treatment.

Finally, an even more compelling sense of the separateness of Negroes was revealed in early distress concerning sexual union between the races. In 1630 a Virginia court pronounced a now famous sentence: "Hugh Davis to be soundly whipped, before an assembly of Negroes and others for abusing himself to the dishonor of God and shame of Christians, by defiling his body in lying with a negro." While there were other instances of punishment for interracial union in the ensuing years, fornication rather than miscegenation may well have been the primary offense, though in 1651 a Maryland man sued someone who he claimed had said "that he had a black bastard in Virginia." . . .

· · ·

One is confronted, then, with the fact that the first evidences of enslavement and of other forms of debasement appeared at about the same time. Such coincidence comports poorly with both views on the causation of prejudice and slavery. If slavery caused prejudice, then invidious distinctions concerning working in the fields, bearing arms, and sexual union should have appeared only after slavery's firm establishment. If prejudice caused slavery, then one would expect to find such lesser discriminations preceding the greater discrimination of outright enslavement.

Perhaps a third explanation of the relationship between slavery and preju-

dice may be offered, one that might fit the pattern of events as revealed by existing evidence. Both current views share a common starting point: They predicate two factors, prejudice and slavery, and demand a distinct order of causality. No matter how qualified by recognition that the effect may in turn react upon the cause, each approach inevitably tends to deny the validity of its opposite. But what if one were to regard both slavery and prejudice as species of a general debasement of the Negro? Both may have been equally cause and effect, constantly reacting upon each other, dynamically joining hands to hustle the Negro down the road to complete degradation. Mutual causation is, of course, a highly useful concept for describing social situations in the modern world. Indeed it has been widely applied in only slightly altered fashion to the current racial situation: Racial prejudice and the Negro's lowly position are widely accepted as constantly reinforcing each other.

This way of looking at the facts might well fit better with what we know of slavery itself. Slavery was an organized pattern of human relationships. No matter what the law might say, it was of different character than cattle ownership. No matter how degrading, slavery involved human beings. No one seriously pretended otherwise. Slavery was not an isolated economic or institutional phenomenon; it was the practical facet of a general debasement without which slavery could have no rationality. (Prejudice, too, was a form of debasement, a kind of slavery in the mind.) Certainly the urgent need for labor in a virgin country guided the direction which debasement took, molded it, in fact, into an institutional framework. That economic practicalities shaped the external form of debasement should not tempt one to forget, however, that slavery was at bottom a social arrangement, a way of society's ordering its members in its own mind.

CARL BRIDENBAUGH

ONE HUNDRED YEARS OF URBAN GROWTH

The first hundred years of town history on the American continent witnessed the foundation and gradual development of a truly urban society. The story of American life is customarily regarded as a compound of sectional histories, and in the early colonial period two sections are commonly considered,—the tidewater and the frontier. Yet the tidewater was itself divided, and if we consider the sections as social and psychological rather than as purely geographical entities, it is possible to distinguish three of them,—the rural, agricultural society of the countryside; the restless, advancing society of the frontier; and the urban, commercial society of the larger seaports. Beginning as small specks in the wilderness, the five communities grew from tiny villages into towns, and finally attained the status of small cities. With other village communities of similar interests and outlook which multiplied and grew in the eighteenth century, they emerged as a social and economic "section" extending the length of the Atlantic seaboard, and exhibiting definite urban characteristics in striking contrast to rural farming districts and wilder regions of the frontier. Life in urban areas produced its own peculiar problems to be faced,

Reprinted from Carl Bridenbaugh, CITIES IN THE WILDERNESS: URBAN LIFE IN AMERICA, 1625–1742 (New York: G. P. Putnam's Son, 1964), pp. 467–70, 478–79, 481, by permission of the publisher.

and the urban viewpoint, based upon continuous close contacts with Europe, derived less from agriculture than from trade. Commercially minded town society looked to the East rather than the West, and was destined from the first to serve as the connecting link between colonial America and its Old World parents.

The future of the colonial towns became immediately evident from the conditions surrounding their birth. Designed as trading communities, they were established on sites most favorable for the pursuit of commerce. They were the western outposts of European commercial expansion in the seventeenth century. City-dwellers from the Old World formed the larger proportion of early town populations, and from the start commercial relations with England or Holland were maintained. Most significantly, the founding process occurred at a time when western Europe, under Dutch and English leadership, was gradually outgrowing and casting off the limitations of medieval feudal economy. Colonial towns grew to maturity in the era of world expansion attending the emergence of modern capitalism, and being new communities, with few irrevocably established customs or traditions, they frequently adapted themselves to the economic drift with more ease and readiness than did the older cities of England. Moreover, the colonizing movement was itself an expression of early capitalistic activity. It called forth organized rather than individual efforts and resources, created new and wider markets for economic development, and opened up seemingly unlimited territories for imperialistic exploitation. It thus produced a marked effect upon Old World economy, accelerating the breakdown of local units of business, and facilitating the formation of larger and more complex organizations of commerce and finance.

The problems which confronted town-dwellers in America were not only those of urban communities, but of a pioneer society as well. Urban development depends largely upon community wealth, and upon the willingness of the group to devote portions of it to projects for civic betterment, or to consent to taxation for this purpose. To a considerable extent the nature of town governments and the extent of authority vested in them conditioned the expenditure of town wealth for community enterprises. Here the colonists were hampered by the traditional nature of the charters of medieval English municipal corporations, whose limitations ill accorded with circumstances in seventeenth and eighteenth century America, especially with the imperious demands for expansion and immediate activity in the New World. In New England towns a new political organization, the town meeting, developed, which exhibited considerable efficiency in the handling of urban problems. This institution was more immediately susceptible to social wants and requirements than were the aristocratic, self-perpetuating corporations founded in America after the example of English municipal governments. Its greater powers of local taxation, and the fact that it placed the spending of public moneys and the enactment of civic ordinances in the hands of those directly affected by these operations, made it a far more effective form of government for dealing with community problems. These problems were the greater, because in the first century of their history the five colonial seaports enjoyed a much more rapid physical growth than did the cities of contemporary Europe. The individual enterprise of American town-dwellers, and the

commercial expansion and prosperity they achieved, aided in the solution of these problems of town living, but much of the efficiency and success which attended their efforts may be attributed to the emergence in the New World of a relatively high sense of civic responsibility in the early eighteenth century, at a time when public consciousness in Europe had receded to an extremely low ebb.

The towns were primarily commercial communities seeking treasure by foreign trade, and their economic vitality and commercial demands led to their early breaking the narrow bonds of medieval economic practice to forge ahead on uncharted but highly profitable commercial adventures. All five, during their first century, developed from simple manorial organizations, completely dependent upon European connections, into full-fledged commercial centers, only partially tied to England, and in many cases competing with British cities for a share of imperial traffic. Boston entered early into the West Indian provision trade, thereby setting an example for other American commercial communities. Soon Massachusetts mariners were seeking to monopolize the colonial carrying traffic in ships of their own building, and the profits of carrier and middleman became the basis of the Bay town's prosperity. Her priority in this field gave her an advantage which other seaports did not begin to overcome until the fourth decade of the eighteenth century. A further foundation for urban economic prosperity lay in the existence of an expanding frontier society with its great need for manufactured products. This made possible an earlier development of the towns as distributing centers for a wide hinterland than was the case with English cities like Bristol, Norwich and

Exeter, and became in this first century as important a factor in the economic growth of New York, Philadelphia and Charles Town as in that of the New England metropolis. As a producer of staple goods for exchange in trade, Boston, with its limited back country was at a disadvantage. More fortunate were New York with its flour and furs, Philadelphia, with its great staples of wheat, meat and lumber, and Charles Town, which after 1710 found prosperity in the important South Carolina crops of rice and indigo. Eventually the communities enjoying this sound economic backing rose to threaten the supremacy of Boston in colonial trade, while Newport and Philadelphia cut heavily into the Bay town's West India commerce. In the eighteenth century also Newport attained importance in shipbuilding and the slave trade. By 1742 Boston merchants were facing a period of relative decline, while their competitors in other colonial towns found the volume and profits of their traffic steadily mounting.

Continual increase in the volume of colonial trade and enlargement of the territory served by the towns led to greater complexity in commercial relations. In the early years merchants performed all types of business, but toward 1700 their functions began to be more specialized. Retail merchandising having definitely emerged by 1700, the great merchant now dealt chiefly with larger operations of exporting, importing and wholesaling, leaving much of the small trade to the shopkeeper. Demands of trade had by 1710 necessitated the issuance of paper currency in most of the colonies, and the establishment of the colonial post office to serve intercolonial communication. Growing business further led to the creation of insurance offices and some extension of credit facilities. Profits from trade,

originally completely absorbed in shipbuilding ventures and industries subsidiary to shipping, now began to create a surplus which sought investment in land, or, in some communities, in the development of certain forms of manufacturing.

Economic prosperity thus made possible the rise of colonial cities. It led to physical expansion of town boundaries, and facilitated dealing with urban problems by corporate effort. Wealth wrung from trade, more than any other single factor, determined the growth of a town society, in which urban amusements and a colonial culture might thrive. This is not, however, to force the history of urban America within the narrow bounds of an exclusively economic interpretation. Social and intellectual development are dependent upon and conditioned by economic progress, but they are not its necessary and inevitable result. They are altered, encouraged or stifled by the action and influence of material forces, but they are not necessarily caused or even initiated solely by economic factors.

. . .

Social stratification further differentiated urban society from the easy democracy of the back country, where any man might own land and all must work with their hands. Distinctions between the well-to-do and the not-so-rich were perhaps relatively unimportant in the beginning, when society was still so fluid that luck or diligence might elevate a man above his fellows in a short time, but with the accumulation of wealth and economic power in the hands of a few, and the coming in of numbers of artisans, indentured servants and immigrant laborers, class lines tightened and society crystallized into easily recognizable categories of better, middling, and poorer sorts. In all towns native aristocracies were commercial in origin, even at Charles Town where they later sought land as a basis for social distinction. They consolidated their position by means of wealth from successful trading ventures, collecting thereby social prestige and political influence. They lived grandly, dressed gaily, kept horses and coaches, and employed the labor of the less fortunate. The commercial, political and social leadership of the towns was in their hands. Later, as urban life became more sophisticated, they contributed to the development of secular amusements and to the relaxation of earlier strict moral codes. They gained further brilliance by alliance with representatives of British officialdom in America. Below them the middle class, professional people, tradesmen and artisans, lived comfortably but more plainly, enjoying in prosperous times many of the good things of life, but in hard times feeling the pinch far more than did their wealthy neighbors. Steady laborers might know periods of prosperity, but many of them could be squeezed out by the vicissitudes of the economic cycle. They performed the menial labor of the towns, enlisted as common seamen, and constituted a group from which much urban poverty and disorder were recruited. Negro and Indian slaves, mere underprivileged pieces of property, rounded out the caste system as it developed itself in metropolitan America.

Save Newport, each of the towns had originally been dedicated to a dominant Protestant religious organization, but after a century of growth diversity, indifference and actual unbelief came to characterize the religious scene. The complexities of town society were in large measure responsible for this development, for different national or social groups soon evolved their favored sects and denominations. When the ministry could no longer speak with one voice to all elements of town populations, it lost much of its influence, both social and clerical, and the appearance of agnosticism and irreverence was rapid. In general, at the end of the first century, Anglicanism was in all towns the religion of officials and aristocrats; Quakerism and Congregationalism, which had once in their own localities enjoyed this favored position, had joined the ranks of middle class religions, which further included Baptists and Presbyterians; while for the common man a religious refuge was just appearing in the enthusiastic, emotional revivalism of Whitefield. Absence of devotion penetrated all classes; the poorer sort were largely indifferent to the attractions of religion, freethinking characterized such middle class groups as Franklin's Junto, and aristocrats indulged a fashionable Deism. In contrast, a stern and uniform religious fundamentalism for a much longer time characterized the rural communities of the countryside.

. . .

In these various ways the developments of a hundred years of life under relatively urban conditions created a society at once distinct from that of rural regions, whether tidewater or back country, and even further removed from that of the westward reaching frontier. The communal attitude toward the solution of the physical and social problems of diversified populations dwelling together in close propinquity, and the constantly widening outlook which material progress, commercial expansion, and contact with the larger world of affairs made possible, were its distinguishing characteristics. In general, this society was more cooperative and social, less individualistic in its outlook toward problems of daily life, far more susceptible to outside influences and examples, less aggressively independent than the society of frontier America. At the same time it was more polished, urbane, and sophisticated, more aware of fashion and change, more sure of itself and proud of its achievements, more able to meet representatives from the outside world as equals without bluster or apology than the rural society of the colonial back country. Because its outlook was eastward rather than westward, it was more nearly a European society in an American setting. It had appropriated various points on the American continent and transformed them as nearly as possible into likenesses of what it had known at home. It was itself less transformed in the process than might have been expected, because the contact with the homeland never ceased, but rather increased with the passage of years. Its importance to American life as a whole was therefore great. Here were centers of the transit of civilization from Old World to New,—five points at the least through which currents of world thought and endeavor might enter, to be like all other commodities assimilated and redistributed throughout the countryside. It was well for the future of national America that its society should not remain completely rural and agricultural, isolated and self-sufficient, ignorant of outside developments and distrustful of new ideas from abroad, as it might well have done had there been no cities. Instead, the five towns provided the nucleus for a wider and more gracious living in the New World.

HISTORIOGRAPHICAL NOTE

The assumption that our natural landscape did not exercise an immediate transforming effect on the character of American settlers would be more readily accepted by a historian like Clarence Ver Steeg than by Frederick Jackson Turner and his followers. As David Potter observed in *People of Plenty*, the "primary purpose" of Turner's famous essay on the significance of the frontier was to explain how and why Americans differed from European contemporaries even from the earliest settlements "and to show why certain traits were dominant in the American strain." In other words, Turner's description of American social and economic patterns, which strongly influenced an entire generation of historical colleagues like James Truslow Adams, served two functions. Not only did the frontier thesis embody what these historians considered the dominant patterns of development in colonial American civilization but, at the same time, it described the character and values of the emerging "new man," that distinctive "American" whom writers since Crevecoeur believed had been reborn spiritually in the wilderness setting.

More recent historians have emphasized other factors in colonial social and economic life, most especially a degree of development in the eighteenth-century mainland colonies that was high even when compared with contemporary Europe and Great Britain. Thus Carl Bridenbaugh, rejecting

Turner's confident belief that the major forces responsible for shaping a uniquely American culture had emerged from the stark confrontation of colonist and wilderness, has stressed instead the less dramatic interplay between the settlers and more urban environments, whether in towns or cities. Turner's archetypal American held the rude and presumably democratic perspectives of a small-holding independent yeoman. In contrast, the provincial world described by Ver Steeg, Bridenbaugh, Jordan, Bernard Bailyn, and other recent historians features a more complex and diverse cast of national characters, distinct from Europe perhaps in the widespread ownership of small land holdings but retaining the assumptions and outlines of a recognizable and accepted class structure. Positions of economic and political leadership now appear to have been filled by classes other than Turner's yeoman farmers: New England merchants operating intricate networks of global trade; Southern agrarian capitalists with extensive investments in slave labor, selling their plantation-grown tobacco, rice, cotton, and indigo in a fluctuating European market system; ambitious small manufacturers competing, often illegally, with English firms. The degree of urbanization in the American colonies, Bridenbaugh has argued, appeared significantly high compared with contemporary Europe, and the unresolved presence of large numbers of African slaves added an additional contradiction to Turner's bright vision of an emerging small, freeholder social democracy.

Recent historians have not abandoned completely the environmental analysis of American character and development. Basically, they have broadened the terms of that analysis, placing much less emphasis on the dominant role of physical environment. Contemporary scholars have stressed instead the transforming impact of the settlers' own artifacts and ambitions in developing the American landscape. "Man creates a secondary environment—the environment of the city, the environment of modern technology," David Potter noted, "which is in its origin cultural but in its completed form as purely physical as the weather or the terrain and which has increasingly influenced the lives of men, at the expense of the primary or natural environment." Urban growth, the capitalist ethos, European commercial and agricultural demands—these factors, to name only a few, are now seen to have supplemented the special influence of the wilderness frontier in molding the culture of provincial America. Many recent historians have abandoned the efforts of environmentalists like Turner to divide American and European national character into two distinct realms, arguing that this artificial polarizing of the two cultures wrenches the study of American institutions out of its proper European context. Ver Steeg and Bridenbaugh, for example, would probably agree that despite differences, eighteenth-century Americans retained to a large degree basic European social patterns.

Yet the force of Turner's doctrines and approach continues to influence the writing and reassessment of the American past. At least three modern reinterpretations argue for some variant of Turner's fundamental belief in the unique development of American culture and accept some sense of the frontier's dominant role in this development. David Potter's *People of Plenty* emphasizes the fact of economic abundance in accounting for American distinctiveness, abundance caused by the generosity of both "primary" and "secondary" environments, while Daniel Boorstin's *The Americans: The Colonial Experience* places an even starker emphasis on the manner in which the *physical* environment itself transformed the previously held values and expectations of European colonists. Louis Hartz, in *The Liberal Tradition in America,* also adapts a Turnerian model to examine the major differences between European and American liberal ideologies. "Turner was not wrong," Hartz concludes at one point, "but, in a way he scarcely understood, half right, for how could American liberalism flourish as it did without a frontier terrain free of Old World feudal burdens?" The historical tradition represented by the Turner-Adams selections, therefore, remains a lively and influential one among American historians, although subsequent studies of colonial social and economic development, including those of Bridenbaugh and Ver Steeg, have produced important refinements in the frontier thesis. Up to now, these revisions have modified significantly but not undermined fully the foundations of Turner's argument. The revisionists still await their own Turner.

2. *The Puritan Experience:*
Fathers and Sons

INTRODUCTION

The selections in this chapter from Puritan sources and by several modern historians of New England Puritanism all bear on the nature of the Puritan experience in early American history. In the broadest application of the term, a "Puritan" was any member of the reform wing of sixteenth- and seventeenth-century English Protestantism. Following the Anglican Church's codification of doctrine and establishment of rituals under Elizabeth I in the late sixteenth century, thousands of English Protestants continued to agitate for a more complete "reformation" of church practices. This general demand for a further religious "purification" of England involved the Puritan rejection of the Anglican Church's hierarchical structure, which offended the Puritan belief in the subordination of *all* churches before the ultimate spiritual authority of the Bible itself. The English Puritans considered themselves "Congregationalists," resting their system of church organization on belief in the spiritual self-sufficiency of each pastor and the small body of believers under him, all searching for their own spiritual redemption through constant self-scrutiny and a thorough application of Biblical teachings. Furthermore, the Puritans insisted on "cleansing" from the body of Anglican rituals, practices that they considered archaic and intolerable survivals from England's period of Roman Catholicism. The use of holy water, relatively lax religious tests for church membership, the wearing of vestments by clerics, and the acceptance of a system of bishops were only a few of the many features of Anglican worship that most Puritans found offensive.

Unlike the "Separatist" Pilgrims of Plymouth, however, who completely rejected affiliation with the Church of England, the Puritan settlers of Massachusetts Bay never disassociated themselves completely from Anglicanism. They considered themselves *"Non*separating" Congregationalists, charged by God with the spiritual mission of reforming the whole Anglican Church. Those who remained in England during the early decades of the seventeenth century and suffered the persecutions of James I and Charles I helped to organize the political and religious opposition to the Stuart monarchy which ended with the execution of Charles I and the temporary establishment of a somewhat-Puritan commonwealth under Oliver Cromwell. Similarly, the Puritans who removed themselves to Massachusetts Bay did so not only to worship according to their doctrines and to escape the dangers of a hostile monarchy and restrictive established church. They came, also, in the hope of establishing a religious order and society in the New World that would serve as a model for the reform of Church and State in the mother country. First-generation leaders of the colony like John Winthrop and John Cotton believed that the Puritan commonwealth at Massachusetts Bay and the other New England Puritan settlements would not only provide refuge for persecuted English brethren but would constitute a necessary advance-guard for the eventual completion of the reformation of Old England. Thus, Winthrop called upon his fellow passengers in the *Arbella* to establish a "Citty upon a Hill," reminding them that "the eies of all people are upon us," although probably only their English co-religionists paid any particular attention to this attempt to found a Puritan commonwealth in a distant land which had never experienced either absolute monarchy *or* established church.

Few historians have questioned the sincere religious motives of those who led the original migration to Massachusetts Bay. Although the Puritans did not eschew economic success, but welcomed it as a further sign that God endorsed their holy experiment, the purpose of their "errand" into the New England wilderness was to create a purified religious and civil society that could serve as a model for decadent Europe. In the early days of settlement, only a few of the New England leaders probably expected to be buried in New World soil. Once their brethren in the mother country had triumphed over Anglican and Stuart repression, surely the principles and practices of Massachusetts Bay would be transported joyously to a Puritan England, or so Winthrop and his colleagues reasoned. In this process, of course, the New England Puritan leaders expected to play a major role, a role based on their experiences in governing the Puritan commonwealth of Massachusetts Bay.

If historians have agreed on the *purposes* of the experiment, however, they have differed profoundly in interpreting the major *practices* of Puritan New England. Examining the life and institutions of the Bay Colony, a number of influential historians early in the twentieth century expressed judgments that fixed certain stereotypes of Puritanism firmly in the American mind. Essentially, they viewed the Massachusetts Bay experiment as a rigidly-theocratic state controlled by a small group of political oligarchs and ministers who held the majority of the colony's citizens in strict, unwilling social bondage, repressed psychologically but most especially in their sexual conduct. In recent decades, however, several American historians have questioned all of these older assumptions about the nature of New

England Puritanism. The following documents and historical selections examine both earlier and newer approaches to the meaning of the Puritan experience in America.

I. EARLIER INTERPRETATION

One of the most influential of the earlier twentieth-century analysts and critics of New England Puritanism was Vernon L. Parrington, the distinguished literary historian who evaluated the Puritan experience in the first volume of his *Main Currents in American Thought*. Parrington believed the Massachusetts Bay experiment to be a conscious and tyrannical theocracy in which the majority of settlers fearfully submitted to the will of a few fanatic religious and secular leaders. Parrington not only reflected the liberal-Progressive historical consensus on Puritanism of his own generation, but through his writings he helped drive this perspective even deeper into the American consciousness. The following selection incorporates the major elements in Parrington's interpretation of Puritanism.

VERNON LOUIS PARRINGTON

THE TRANSPLANTING OF IDEAS

The Great Migration, it will be remembered, fell in the time of the Laudean reaction, when the Presbyterian Utopia seemed remote and the hopes of the Puritan dreamers were fallen low. The Boston leaders quitted England ten years before Charles summoned the Long Parliament, and twelve before the royal standard was unfurled at Nottingham. The armed struggle for supremacy was far below the horizon, and the outlandish philosophies that later sectaries were to propagate so diligently were as yet little known in the land. The generous grain of liberal thought was still in the milk,

Reprinted from Vernon Louis Parrington, MAIN CURRENTS IN AMERICAN THOUGHT *(New York: Harcourt, Brace & World, Inc., 1927), I, 16–22, 43–44, 46–47, 49–50, by permission of the publisher.*

its fruitful doctrines unripened. The immigrant gentlemen who came to Massachusetts Bay were Puritan Anglicans who professed a hearty love for the mother church and were no friends to the principle of Separatism. They were potential Presbyterians who rejected alike the Arminianism of Laud and the autocracy of the bishops. It is reasonable to suppose that as strict Calvinists, trained in the ordinances as well as in the doctrine of the French theologian, they came hither with the conscious purpose of setting up the complete Genevan discipline in the new world. If such was their plan—and certainly before their coming over they seem not to have entertained any thoughts of Separatism—it received a check from the Plymouth influence and the Puritan experiment was turned aside from the path of its natural development.

It was a somewhat curious misadventure that was to entail unforeseen consequences. Except in matters of doctrine Pilgrim and Puritan consorted ill together. Their social antecedents were as unlike as their views on political and religious institutions. The intellectual leaders of Plymouth—whatever may be said of the London adventurers who joined the Holland group—had been nurtured in Elizabethan radicalism. They were Brownist-Separatists of plebeian origins, who had arrived at their conception of the true church from a close study of Biblical texts, with perhaps some admixture of Anabaptist influence, nearly a generation before the Stuarts came with their divine-right theory. During their years on the continent they lived remote from the current of events in England, and under the guidance of the tolerant Robinson they had been disciplined in the theory and practice of primitive Congregationalism. On their removal to America they brought with them a consciously democratic church order, that met their simple needs and had taken shape from the experience of daily life. This democratic model of church government was spontaneously supplemented by the plantation covenant of civil government drawn up aboard ship, which was to serve as the organic law of the new commonwealth. Two cardinal principles—which at bottom were one—thus found their way to New England in the *Mayflower:* the principle of a democratic church and the principle of a democratic state. When ten years later the Boston leaders were faced with the problem of erecting a social order, they accepted the Plymouth model of Congregationalism, but rejected the plantation covenant. They saw no need for the latter as they were already provided with an organic law. The charter which Winthrop was insistent upon bringing with them out of England was asserted to be the constitution of the common-wealth and, meticulously interpreted, was to determine largely the form and scope of the new political state. It was construed to grant a legal sanction to government; but as the charter of a Carolinian trading company it quite naturally restricted authority to the managing heads, and granted powers to its directors that were useful in managing trade ventures but might easily become intolerable if interpreted as the organic law of a commonwealth. With such enlargement of powers the directors of the corporation would constitute a political oligarchy. There was a striking difference, certainly, between the covenant of Plymouth and the charter-constitution of Massachusetts Bay, and a political philosopher could readily enough have foreseen the course that events would take in the Puritan commonwealth, given the men and the ideals in control.

The Puritan Presbyterian

To make clear what was involved in the attempt to adapt the Plymouth model of church government to the charter commonwealth, it is necessary to consider somewhat particularly the body of prejudice and principle brought to the new world aboard the *Lady Arbella,* as the Puritan contribution to New England. The capable leaders who created the early institutions of Massachusetts Bay colony were Jacobean Englishmen of middle station, halfway between the aristocrat and the burgess, with certain salient characteristics of both. Fashioned by a caste society, they transported to the little commonwealth an abundant heritage of class prejudice. They aspired to be reckoned gentlemen and to live in the new world as they had lived in the old, in a half feudal state, surrounded by many servants and with numerous dependents. They honored rank, were sticklers for precedence, respected class distinctions, demanded the hereditary rights of the gentry. They had been bred up in a static order where gentlemen ruled and the people obeyed, and they could not think in terms of the Plymouth plantation covenant, subscribed by all heads of families. To the modern reader of his journal there is something almost childish in Winthrop's insistence on public deference to his official position and his grief when the halberd-bearers refused to provide the usual formality to his little progresses. But if they aspired to be rated as gentlemen, there was much also of the burgess nature in them. They were potential capitalists, eager to accumulate ample landholdings, keen to drive a bargain, given to trade and as sharp an eye to the main chance as any London merchant. The community of goods that marked the early days of Plymouth they disliked so greatly as to account it almost sinful. In the infancy of the settlement they entered upon an active mercantile life, building their ships for the West Indian trade, joining in the fisheries off the Newfoundland coast, venturing far in pursuit of gain. Active, capable men, excellent administrators rather than speculative thinkers, stewards of the public interests as well as their own, they would take it ill to have their matured plans interfered with by busybodies and incompetents. Their own counsel sufficed them and they wanted no help from outsiders.

Endow such men with religious zeal; let them regard themselves as particular repositories of righteousness, give them a free hand to work out their program unhampered by rival policies, provide them with a handbook elaborated in complete detail by a master system-maker; and the result was certain. Their Utopia must be a close-knit church-state, with authority reserved to the aristocracy of Christian talent. It is needless to inquire whether a definite conception of a theocracy was in their minds before their coming over; some such order was clearly implicit in their religious fervor, their Hebraic theology, their Genevan discipline, their aristocratic prejudices. They might nominally accept the Plymouth model of church-government, but they would meddle with democracy in church and state no more than necessity compelled. Circumstances, as well as their own promptings, would counsel quite an opposite course. They were engaged in a difficult and perilous undertaking, begirt by wilderness enemies, and fearful of hostile interference by the home authorities. If the venture were to survive, a drift towards centralization of power was as natural as it was inevitable. The common security would not suffer any dispersion of forces or domestic bickerings over authority. Dissatisfied members must be held in subjection and dangerous swarmings from the mother-hive must be prevented. The principle of Separatism was *too* disruptive to insure cohesive solidarity; the parts must be welded into a protective whole; and for such business what ideal was more efficient than a theocracy with Jehovah substituted for King Charles—not openly and seditiously, but quietly, in the hearts of the people. The historian need not wander far in search of the origin of the theocratic principle; it is to be found in the self-interest of the lay and clerical leaders. Ambitious men could not have devised a fitter means to weld together the two groups of magistrates and ministers, and endow their charter prerogatives with divine sanction. The Stuarts were bunglers at the business in comparison with Winthrop and Cotton. But if they worked the metal to such shape as they chose we must not forget that it had been well heated in the smithy of John Calvin. Overlook that fact and the theocracy becomes incredible.

There are perhaps sufficient grounds to assume that some plan of minority control was worked out before the migration took place. The preliminary discussions in England had been long and the terms of the charter were carefully seen to. By its provisions the right of franchise rested with the freemen of the corporation, in number about a hundred and ten. Of the total body of freemen it was known that only a small group would undertake the venture; probably fewer than a score came over with the emigrants, and through removals and death the number was speedily reduced to about a dozen. This handful of freemen constituted the court, and chose the governor, deputy governor, and the assistants or magistrates. These latter were to number eighteen according to the charter provision; but with more offices than eligible candidates, the number was necessarily reduced, and six assistants with the governor came to be reckoned a quorum of the court with sovereign powers. It was a patriarchal undertaking, and to Carolinian gentlemen there was nothing unusual or unjust in a handful of leaders exercising plenary powers over the lives and fortunes of two thousand members of the commonwealth. If the charter could not have been construed as granting such powers, it is reasonable to assume that they would not have entered upon the business. The lay leaders were practical men. They had ventured their estates in the hope of bettering their condition, both spiritual and material, and with their personal fortunes at stake they were in no mind to intrust the fate of the undertaking to other hands

than their own. They loved power quite as much as did the ungodly, and accounting themselves God's stewards they reckoned it sin not to use it in his name. As Puritans they would not keep a weather eye on the majority will. God did not speak in the Scriptures through majority votes; his chosen were a minority, the remnant in Israel.

A further sanction was at hand. If these Hebraized Englishmen created a close corporation and ruled magisterially, if the order in the new church-state was inquisitorial and stern, it was in strict conformity with the teachings and example of Calvin. Men deeply read in the *Institutes,* familiar with the Genevan Ordinances and the practices of the Consistory, were not likely to discover in them any lessons in democratic toleration. Righteousness may be fearfully relentless, and John Calvin had been a tyrant on principle. Iron-willed and masterful, he had risen to power in the turbulent city-state of Geneva in sixteenth-century fashion. A few splotches of blood on the white garments of the Church did not greatly trouble him. He was never squeamish about ways and means of furthering the Lord's work. He violated the right of refuge to bring to the state the pantheistic Unitarian Servetus, and he thanked God when the bungling of the executioner prolonged the sufferings of certain others of his victims. The Genevan discipline was rigorous, and the clerical inquisitors were more relentless than the lay. The tyrannies that have been freely charged upon the New England oligarchy are easily explained in the light of the Calvinistic Ordinances. There were no whippings or banishments or hangings in early Pennsylvania where Quaker and Lutheran dwelt together in peace if not in fellowship. But they were New Testament men and not out of the

Old, like the Saints in Massachusetts Bay. They worshiped a God of love rather than a God of wrath.

Granted the conception on which the theocratic experiment went forward, namely, that Jehovah was the sole lawgiver and the Bible the sufficient statute-book; granted also that these priests and magistrates were stewards of God's will; and the centralization of power in the commonwealth becomes invested with a higher sanction than the terms of the charter. It was an oligarchy of Christian grace. The minister was the trained and consecrated interpreter of the divine law, and the magistrate was its trained and consecrated administrator; and both were chosen by free election of the Saints. If unfortunately the Saints were few and the sinners many, was not that a special reason for safeguarding the Ark of the Covenant from the touch of profane hands? Hence all legislative experiments by annually elected deputies, no matter how exactly those experiments might fall in with the wishes of the majority, were sternly frowned upon or skillfully nullified. Not only were such popular enactments, it was held, too often prompted by the carnal desires of the natural man, but they were no better than an insult to God, as implying the insufficiency of the Scriptures to every temporal need. Unregenerate and sinful men must have no share in God's work. The Saints must not have their hands tied by majority votes. This explains, quite as much as mere love of power, the persistent hostility of the leaders to every democratic tendency. Such institutions as grew up spontaneously out of the necessities of the situation, were sharply hedged about by restrictions. The town meeting, which was extra-legal under the charter, was safeguarded by limiting the right of voting to freemen, except in a few trivial matters;

and the more popular deputies, who inclined to become self-willed, were forced to accept the principle of magisterial veto on their actions. When a law was passed, it was purposely left vague as to penalties, in order to give a free hand to the judges to punish as they wished, and it was not till 1641, after much insistence from the representatives of the people, that Ward's Body of Liberties was finally adopted.

Later critics of Puritanism discover in the theocratic experiment of Massachusetts Bay a preposterous attempt to turn back the pages of history, and refashion Englishmen after an ungainly Hebraic pattern. But to the leaders of that experiment it seemed rather a Utopian venture to create in the new world a nobler social order than elsewhere existed. Whether such a society was either possible or desirable, has long since become only an academic question; what is more suggestive is the fact that in spite of some bitterness on the part of a small minority, the stewardship of an oligarchy remained the accepted principle of government in Massachusetts Bay until the vacating of the charter in 1684. That it lingered out so long a life is a testimony to the skillful opportunism of the leaders. They early adopted a strategic policy which the British ministry foolishly refused to adopt a hundred years later; they cautiously undermined any potential disaffection by admitting the wealthiest and most influential to the rights of freemen, thus allying the ambitious and capable members of society with the ruling group, and laying the foundations of a provincial aristocracy, which in the course of time would secularize the government and substitute an economic for a theocratic basis of authority. The loss of the charter only hastened what in the nature of things must have come about eventually. . . .

John Winthrop, Magistrate

If John Cotton embodied the ideal and polity of the theocratic ministry, John Winthrop represented the ideal and polity of the theocratic magistracy. Rulership in the new church-state, while nominally the function of lay officers, in reality was quite as much ecclesiastical as political. The civil authorities were chosen by a narrow body of orthodox electors with a single view to theocratic ends. To the traditional conception of magistracy, in which the gentlemen of the Migration had been reared, was now added a special function, the care of the church, "the maintenance of whose peace," John Cotton asserted, "is the chief end which God aimed at in the institution of magistracy." The career of John Winthrop in Massachusetts must be judged, therefore, from this twofold point of view. He was not exclusively, or chiefly, a civil governor, but a magistrate-elder; and his political conduct was determined by this dual character of his office. Unless one keeps in mind the theocratic framework of the early Massachusetts commonwealth, one cannot understand the limitations of his authority, or judge his conduct intelligently.

John Winthrop was a skillful executive upon whose shoulders largely rested the success or failure of the undertaking during the difficult early years. But he was very much more than that; he was a Puritan steward of temporal affairs, who accepted his stewardship as a sacred duty lying upon his conscience. A cultivated gentleman, "browghte Up amonge boockes & learned men," with a tender and sympathetic nature—inclining overmuch to mildness, as he confessed apologetically—by every right he belongs with that notable group of Puritans, with Eliot and Vane and Hutchinson and Milton, in whom the moral earnestness of Hebraism was tempered to humaner issues by a generous culture. There was in him not a little fruitful sap of Elizabethan poetry to quicken his thought, lifting him out of the petty world of Jacobean lawyer and landed gentleman, and opening his eyes to a vision of the future significance of the great venture to which he dedicated his later years. Grave and dignified, he looks out at us from his portrait with a certain stoic calm not untouched with sadness, as if this life had proved a serious business, filled with responsibilities and weighty matters, and darkened by sorrow and disappointment. The pagan *joie de vivre* of Elizabethan times is gone, and in its stead is a serious intelligence that must grapple with realities and shape them to its will.

. . .

In theocratic philosophy, therefore, the magistrate became no other than God's vicegerent, with authority beyond popular limitation or control. No English squire presumed to exercise the magisterial powers which Winthrop and his associates quietly usurped. Among other innovations they early claimed the right of veto on the acts of the deputies, and in reply to the dissatisfaction voiced at such arbitrary encroachment, Winthrop argued that the magisterial veto was no infringement on the liberties of the people, but was a means to "preserve them, if by any occasion they should be in danger: I cannot liken it better to anythinge than the brake of a windmill: w'ch hathe no power, to move the runninge worke: but it is of speciall use, to stoppe any violent motion, w'ch in some extraordinary tempest might endanger the wholl fabricke." The convenient weapon of divine sanction Winthrop did not scruple to use at need. Thus when a petition was presented for the repeal of a law which arbitrarily decreased the number of deputies, he denied the lawfulness of the procedure:

When the people have chosen men to be their rulers, now to combine together . . . in a public petition to have an order repealed . . . savors of resisting an ordinance of God. For the people, having deputed others, have no right to make or alter laws themselves, but are to be subject.

The old English right of petition, in short, was not a right in theocratic Massachusetts, and any unauthorized joining together of citizens for political purposes was a conspiracy against the will of God. The practical result of this doctrine of magisterial vicegerency was that a small group of freemen set up an unlimited oligarchy over some four or five thousand of their fellow Englishmen, even going so far as to advance the novel doctrine of a freehold tenure of power.

The doctrine of aristocratic stewardship has never been more skillfully presented. It is John Cotton's reply to Roger Williams, translated into political terms; the philosophy of natural rights whittled down to a covenant between God and man. It rests on the assumption of an absolute law, superior to expediency. But may not honest men disagree as to what constitutes the good, just, and honest? and may not godly authority imperceptibly slide over into plain tyranny? Although the Saints may have professed themselves satisfied with Winthrop's doctrine, the pages of early Massachusetts history bear ample record of the dissatisfaction of the sinners. Most of the difficulties experienced by Winthrop in his administration of the commonwealth had their root in this assumption of arbitrary power, the immediate outcome of which was a spontaneous development of incipient democracy. How far such an assumption of divine custodianship may lead a generous man from the path of justice, appears in his summing up of the case against Mistress Anne Hutchinson, who because she insisted upon her own interpretation of the good, just, and honest, was adjudged "A woman not only difficult in her opinions, but also of an intemperate spirit." "The ground work of her revelations is the immediate revelation of the spirit, and not by the ministry of the Lord . . . and this hath been the ground of all these tumults and troubles; and I would that those were all cut off that trouble us." The kernel of the offense for which Mistress Hutchinson was banished, is then laid bare: "We see not that any should have authority to set up any other exercise beside what authority hath already set up."

In this arbitrary judgment of Winthrop's—the natural fruit of the tree of theocratic stewardship—the "little speech" discovers its suitable commentary. Urged on by his bigoted associates, the kind-hearted governor descended to their level, and began the unhappy business of playing the tyrant under the pretense of scourging God's enemies. The lords-brethren served notice upon all dissenters that henceforth there must be no dissent in New England. The admirable courage of Mistress Hutchinson availed no more against the magisterial interpretation of the good, just, and honest, than the boldness of Roger Williams before her; or later, the zeal of the Baptists who were sent away by Endicott; or later still, the piety of the Quakers, who were whipped at the cart-tail and hanged, men and women both. The policy of the political stewardship of the best and wisest never had fuller trial, with abler or more conscientious agents, than in Massachusetts Bay; and its failure was complete. Such progress as Massachusetts made towards freedom and tolerance was gained in the teeth of theocratic opposition; New England democracy owes no debt to her godly magistrates.

Bred up in a half-feudal world, the leaders of the Migration remained patriarchal in their social philosophy, unable to adapt old prejudices to new conditions. Human motives are curiously mixed, human actions rarely consistent; and if the shortcomings of John Winthrop show blacker by contrast with the excellence of the ideal which he professed, the fault must be charged against his time and associates and not

against his manly, generous nature. Most English gentlemen of his day were steeped in a sodden Toryism, yet he earnestly desired to be a faithful steward of church and state. If as a gentleman he held firmly to the privilege of rulership, as a Christian he endeavored to rule honorably and in the fear of the Lord. If he followed the beaten path and tried to shape the great experiment by the traditional principles of his class; if his zeal at times led him into indisputable tyrannies; it was because he was led away from the light, not because he sought selfish ends. Godliness has its own special temptations, and it would be ungenerous to bear ill-will against so lovable a man.

II. DOCUMENTS

1. Purposes

On the first voyage of the "Great Migration" to New England, John Winthrop lectured his fellow Puritans on the purposes of their "errand into the wilderness." Winthrop's lay-sermon dwelt on the meaning of Puritanism in an "unreformed" world and on the problems that would face the ship's band of Puritans in creating their new community. Winthrop was the most important secular leader of Massachusetts Bay Colony in its first generation of settlement, and "A Modell of Christian Charity" offers many insights into the beliefs and practices that characterized this fledgling "Citty Upon a Hill."

JOHN WINTHROP

God Almightie in his most holy and wise providence hath soe disposed of the Condicion of mankinde, as in all

Reprinted from John Winthrop, "A Modell of Christian Charity," in Edmund S. Morgan, ed., PURITAN POLITICAL IDEAS, 1558–1794 *(Indianapolis and New York: The Bobbs-Merrill Company, Inc., 1965), pp. 89–93.*

times some must be rich some poore, some highe and eminent in power and dignitie; others meane and in subjeccion.

. . .

It rests now to make some applicacion of this discourse by the present designe which gave the occasion of writing of it. Herein are 4 things to be propounded: first the persons, 2ly, the worke, 3ly, the end, 4ly the meanes.

1. For the persons, wee are a Company professing our selves fellow members of Christ, In which respect onely though wee were absent from eache other many miles, and had our imploymentes as farre distant, yet wee ought to account our selves knitt together by this bond of love, and live in the exercise of it, if wee would have comforte of our being in Christ, this was notorious in the practise of the Christians in former times, as is testified of the Waldenses from the mouth of one of the adversaries Aeneas Sylvius, mutuo [solent amare] penè antequam norint, they use to love any of theire owne religion even before they were acquainted with them.

2ly. for the worke wee have in hand, it is by a mutuall consent through a speciall overruleing providence, and a more then an ordinary approbation of the Churches of Christ to seeke out a place of Cohabitation and Consorteshipp under a due forme of Government both civill and ecclesiasticall. In such cases as this the care of the publique must oversway all private respects, by which not onely conscience, but meare Civill pollicy doth binde us; for it is a true rule that perticuler estates cannott subsist in the ruine of the publique.

3ly. The end is to improve our lives to doe more service to the Lord the comforte and encrease of the body of christe whereof wee are members that our selves and posterity may be the better preserved from the Common corrupcions of this evill world to serve the Lord and worke out our Salvacion under the power and purity of his holy Ordinances.

4ly for the meanes whereby this must bee effected, they are 2fold, a Conformity with the worke and end wee aime at, these wee see are extraor-dinary, therefore wee must not content our selves with usuall ordinary meanes whatsoever wee did or ought to have done when wee lived in England, the same must wee doe and more allsoe where wee goe: That which the most in theire Churches maineteine as a truthe in profession onely, wee must bring into familiar and constant practise, as in this duty of love wee must love brotherly without dissimulation, wee must love one another with a pure hearte fervently wee must beare one anothers burthens, wee must not looke onely on our owne things but allsoe on the things of our brethren, neither must wee think that the lord will beare with such faileings at our hands as hee dothe from those among whome we have lived, and that for 3 Reasons.

1. In regard of the more neare bond of mariage, betweene him and us, wherein he hath taken us to be his after a most strickt and peculiar manner which will make him the more Jealous of our love and obedience soe he tells the people of Israell, you onely have I knowne of all the families of the Earthe therefore will I punishe you for your Transgressions.

2ly, because the lord will be sanctified in them that come neare him. Wee know that there were many that corrupted the service of the Lord some setting upp Alters before his owne, others offering both strange fire and strange Sacrifices allsoe; yet there came noe fire from heaven, or other sudden Judgement upon them as did upon Nadab and Abihu whoe yet wee may thinke did not sinne presumptuously.

3ly When God gives a speciall Commission he lookes to have it stricktly observed in every Article, when hee gave Saule a Commission to destroy Amaleck hee indented with him upon certaine Articles and because hee failed in one of the least, and that upon a

faire pretence, it lost him the king-
dome, which should have beene his reward, if hee had observed his Commission: Thus stands the cause betweene
God and us, wee are entered into Covenant with him for this worke, wee have
taken out a Commission, the Lord
hath given us leave to drawe our owne
Articles wee have professed to enterprise these Accions upon these and
these ends, wee have hereupon besought him of favour and blessing:
Now if the Lord shall please to heare
us, and bring us in peace to the place
wee desire, then hath hee ratified this
Covenant and sealed our Commission,
[and] will expect a strickt performance
of the Articles contained in it, but if
wee shall neglect the observacion of
these Articles which are the ends wee
have propounded, and dissembling with
our God, shall fall to embrace this present world and prosecute our carnall
intencions, seekeing greate things for
our selves and our posterity, the Lord
will surely breake out in wrathe against
us be revenged of such a perjured people and make us knowe the price of
the breache of such a Covenant.

Now the onely way to avoyde this
shipwracke and to provide for our posterity is to followe the Counsell of
Micah, to doe Justly, to love mercy, to
walke humbly with our God, for this
end, wee must be knitt together in this
worke as one man, wee must entertaine
each other in brotherly Affeccion, wee
must be willing to abridge our selves
of our superfluities; for the supply of
others necessities, wee must uphold a
familiar Commerce together in all
meekenes, gentlenes, patience and lib-
erallity, wee must delight in eache other, make others Condicions our owne
rejoyce together, mourne together,
labour, and suffer together allwayes
haveing before our eyes our Commission and Community in the worke, our

Community as members of the same
body, soe shall wee keepe the unitie of
the spirit in the bond of peace, the
Lord will be our God and delight to
dwell among us, as his owne people
and will commaund a blessing upon us
in all our wayes, soe that wee shall see
much more of his wisdome power good-
nes and truthe then formerly wee have
beene acquainted with, wee shall finde
that the God of Israell is among us,
when tenn of us shall be able to resist
a thousand of our enemies, when hee
shall make us a prayse and glory, that
men shall say of succeeding planta-
cions: the lord make it like that of
New England: for wee must Consider
that wee shall be as a Citty upon a
Hill, the eies of all people are uppon
us; soe that if wee shall deale falsely
with our god in this worke, wee have
undertaken and soe cause him to with-
drawe his present help from us, wee
shall be made a story and a by-word
through the world, wee shall open the
mouthes of enemies to speake evill of
the wayes of god and all professours
for Gods sake; wee shall shame the
faces of many of gods worthy servants,
and cause theire prayers to be turned
into Cursses upon us till wee be consumed out of the good land whether
wee are goeing: And to shutt upp this
discourse with that exhortacion of
Moses that faithfull servant of the Lord
in his last farewell to Israell Deut. 30.
Beloved there is now sett before us life,
and good, deathe and evill in that wee
are Commaunded this day to love the
Lord our God, and to love one another
to walke in his wayes and to keepe his
Commaundements and his Ordinance,
and his lawes, and the Articles of our
Covenant with him that wee may live
and be multiplied, and that the Lord
our God may blesse us in the land
whether wee goe to possesse it: But if
our heartes shall turne away soe that

wee will not obey, but shall be seduced and worshipp [serve *cancelled*] other Gods our pleasures, and proffitts, and serve them; it is propounded unto us this day, wee shall surely perishe out of the good Land whether wee passe over this vast Sea to possesse it;

Therefore lett us choose life, that wee, and our Seede, may live; by obeyeing his voyce, and cleaveing to him, for hee is our life, and our prosperity.

2. Government

Historians like Parrington drew heavily for their interpretation of Puritan political theory and practices on John Winthrop's "Speech to the General Court," delivered to that Massachusetts Bay government body immediately following Winthrop's acquittal on a charge of exceeding his authority as a magistrate (or chief executive) of the colony. Winthrop believed that human liberty derived ultimately from man's covenant with God and from all subsequent "covenants and constitutions, amongst men themselves." In the light of Parrington's charge that Winthrop and his associates "quietly usurped . . . authority beyond popular limitation or control," the selection from Winthrop's Journal *concerning the early popular demands in Massachusetts Bay for a written* Body of Laws *takes on some importance. Was Winthrop insisting in his "Speech" that the magistrates possessed unlimited authority, as Parrington suggested, and did the ordinary settlers of Massachusetts Bay appear to have been particularly docile about asserting their political rights?*

JOHN WINTHROP

September 7, 1639
The people had long desired a body of laws,[1] and thought their condition very unsafe, while so much power rested in the discretion of magistrates. Divers attempts had been made at former courts, and the matter referred to some of the magistrates and some of the elders; but still it came to no effect; for, being committed to the care of many, whatsoever was done by some, was still disliked or neglected by others. At last it was referred to Mr. Cotton and Mr. Nathaniel Warde, etc., and each of them framed a model, which were presented to this general court,

[1] *The Body of Liberties,* which at length came into existence in response to the desire of the people here referred to, is a code of great interest, esteemed in its time comparable only to Magna Charta and the Common Law of England, and important in the history of constitutional development. It was mainly the work of Nathaniel Ward, of Ipswich, a man of bright mind, well versed in the law, though Cotton had a hand in it. A work of value here is Whitmore, *The Colonial Laws of Massachusetts* (Boston, 1889). See also *Old South Leaflets,* no. 164, *The Massachusetts Body of Liberties,* with scholarly annotation by Edwin D. Mead.

Reprinted from James K. Hosmer, ed., WINTHROP'S JOURNAL *(New York: Barnes & Noble, 1908), I, 323, 324, and from "Speech to the General Court," in Perry Miller and Thomas H. Johnson, eds.,* THE PURITANS *(New York: Harper & Row, 1963), I, 205–7.*

and by them committed to the governor and deputy and some others to consider of, and so prepare it for the court in the 3d month next. Two great reasons there were, which caused most of the magistrates and some of the elders not to be very forward in this matter. One was, want of sufficient experience of the nature and disposition of the people, considered with the condition of the country and other circumstances, which made them conceive, that such laws would be fittest for us, which should arise pro re nata upon occasions, etc., and so the laws of England and other states grew, and therefore the fundamental laws of England are called customs, consuetudines. 2. For that it would professedly transgress the limits of our charter, which provide, we shall make no laws repugnant to the laws of England, and that we were assured we must do. But to raise up laws by practice and custom had been no transgression; as in our church discipline, and in matters of marriage, to make a law, that marriages should not be solemnized by ministers, is repugnant to the laws of England; but to bring it to a custom by practice for the magistrates to perform it, is no law made repugnant, etc. At length (to satisfy the people) it proceeded, and the two models were digested with divers alterations and additions, and abbreviated and sent to every town, (12,) to be considered of first by the magistrates and elders, and then to be published by the constables to all the people, that if any man should think fit, that any thing therein ought to be altered, he might acquaint some of the deputies therewith against the next court.

July 3, 1645

I suppose something may be expected from me, upon this charge that is be-fallen me, which moves me to speak now to you; yet I intend not to intermeddle in the proceedings of the court, or with any of the persons concerned therein. Only I bless God, that I see an issue of this troublesome business. I also acknowledge the justice of the court, and, for mine own part, I am well satisfied, I was publicly charged, and I am publicly and legally acquitted, which is all I did expect or desire. And though this be sufficient for my justification before men, yet not so before God, who hath seen so much amiss in my dispensations (and even in this affair) as calls me to be humble. For to be publicly and criminally charged in this court, is matter of humiliation, (and I desire to make a right use of it,) notwithstanding I be thus acquitted. If her father had spit in her face, (saith the Lord concerning Miriam,) should she not have been ashamed seven days? Shame had lien upon her, whatever the occasion had been. I am unwilling to stay you from your urgent affairs, yet give me leave (upon this special occasion) to speak a little more to this assembly. It may be of some good use, to inform and rectify the judgments of some of the people, and may prevent such distempers as have arisen amongst us. The great questions that have troubled the country, are about the authority of the magistrates and the liberty of the people. It is yourselves who have called us to this office, and being called by you, we have our authority from God, in way of an ordinance, such as hath the image of God eminently stamped upon it, the contempt and violation whereof hath been vindicated with examples of divine vengeance. I entreat you to consider, that when you choose magistrates, you take them from among yourselves, men subject to like passions as you are. Therefore when you see infirmities in us, you should reflect upon your own, and that would make you bear the more with us, and not be severe censurers of the failings of your magistrates, when you have continual experience of the like infirmities in yourselves and others. We account him a good servant, who breaks not his covenant. The covenant between you and us is the oath you have taken of us, which is to this purpose, that we shall govern you and judge your causes by the rules of God's laws and our own, according to our best skill. When you agree with a workman to build you a ship or house, etc., he undertakes as well for his skill as for his faithfulness, for it is his profession, and you pay him for both. But when you call one to be a magistrate, he doth not profess nor undertake to have sufficient skill for that office, nor can you furnish him with gifts, etc., therefore you must run the hazard of his skill and ability. But if he fail in faithfulness, which by his oath he is bound unto, that he must answer for. If it fall out that the case be clear to common apprehension, and the rule clear also, if he transgress here, the error is not in the skill, but in the evil of the will: it must be required of him. But if the case be doubtful, or the rule doubtful, to men of such understanding and parts as your magistrates are, if your magistrates should err here, yourselves must bear it.

For the other point concerning liberty, I observe a great mistake in the country about that. There is a twofold liberty, natural (I mean as our nature is now corrupt) and civil or federal. The first is common to man with beasts and other creatures. By this, man, as he stands in relation to man simply, hath liberty to do what he lists; it is a liberty to evil as well as to good. This liberty is incompatible and inconsistent with authority, and cannot endure the least restraint of the most just authority. The exercise and maintaining of this liberty makes men grow more evil, and in time to be worse than brute beasts: omnes sumus licentia deteriores. This is that great enemy of truth and peace, that wild beast, which all the ordinances of God are bent against, to restrain and subdue it. The other kind of liberty I call civil or federal, it may also be termed moral, in reference to the covenant between God and man, in the moral law, and the politic covenants and constitutions, amongst men themselves. This liberty is the proper end and object of authority, and cannot subsist without it; and it is a liberty to that only which is good, just, and honest. This liberty you are to stand for, with the hazard (not only of your goods, but) of your lives, if need be. Whatsoever crosseth this, is not authority, but a distemper thereof. This liberty is maintained and exercised in a way of subjection to authority; it is of the same kind of liberty wherewith Christ hath made us free. The woman's own choice makes such a man her husband; yet being so chosen, he is her lord, and she is to be subject to him, yet in a way of liberty, not of bondage; and a true wife accounts her subjection her honor and freedom, and would not think her condition safe and free, but in her subjection to her husband's authority. Such is the liberty of the church under the authority of Christ, her king and husband; his yoke is so easy and sweet to her as a bride's ornaments; and if through frowardness or wantonness, etc., she shake it off, at any time, she is at no rest in her spirit, until she take it up again; and whether her lord smiles upon her, and embraceth her in his arms, or whether he frowns, or rebukes, or smites her, she apprehends the sweetness of his love in all, and is refreshed, supported, and instructed by every such dispensation of his authority over her. On the other side, ye know who they are that complain of this yoke and say, let us break their bands, etc., we will not have this man to rule over us. Even so, brethren, it will be between you and your magistrates. If you stand for your natural corrupt liberties, and will do what is good in your own eyes, you will not endure the least weight of authority, but will murmur, and oppose, and be always striving to shake off that yoke; but if you will be satisfied to enjoy such civil and lawful liberties, such as Christ allows you, then will you quietly and cheerfully submit unto that authority which is set over you, in all the administrations of it, for your good. Wherein, if we fail at any time, we hope we shall be willing (by God's assistance) to hearken to good advice from any of you, or in any other way of God; so shall your liberties be preserved, in upholding the honor and power of authority amongst you. . . .

3. Theology

Among the ministers of Puritan New England, none was more eminent or influential than John Cotton of Boston, whose sermons were printed and read widely in both Old and New England. Cotton's plain but vivid portrayal (in the following selections) of the individual soul wrestling with itself, searching for evidence of God's grace, embodied the essence of the New England Puritan's doctrine of salvation. The Puritan believed that God had freely chosen to "covenant" with man in order to draw the human soul to its salvation. Since God's grace was freely willed, therefore, God had presumably predestined a select or "elect" group for salvation. The first generation New England ministers, however, stressed the importance of constant self-examination despite this predestination, in order to detect signs of what the ministers believed was the Deity's handiwork. In Edmund Morgan's words, they believed that this spiritual preparation would "facilitate the operation of God's saving grace when and if it should come." The doctrine of the "covenant of grace" and some of its implications for Puritan spiritual practices are described in these selections from John Cotton's sermons.

JOHN COTTON

"HYPOCRITES AND SAINTS"

Truly it is hard to perceive when men differ, and therefore it is not an easie matter to make such use of Sanc-

Reprinted from John Cotton, "The New Covenant" and "The Way of Life," in Perry Miller and Thomas H. Johnson, eds., THE PURITANS (New York: Harper & Row, 1963), I, 316–18.

tification, as by it to beare witnesse unto Justification: and it will be a very hard case and much more difficult, when men cannot feele the presence of spirituall gifts, but want spirituall light: and when they doe finde faith in themselves, they doe finde it in hypocrites also, even in hypocrites also, even faith to seek the Lord, & faith to waite upon him, and faith to apply him, saying, *My*

God, and faith to stay upon the *God of Israel;* and yet these men doe vanish away in hyprocrisie; this hypocrites may doe; seeing therefore what easines of errour may befall Christians, whether this or that grace be of the right stampe or no, it will behove Christians to be wary, for even Eagle-eyed Christians will have much adoe so to discerne of sanctification in themselves, before they see their justification, as to cut off all hypocrites from having the like in them, for the sanctified frame of Gods children, and that which seemeth to be like it in hypocrites, both of them spring from the holy Ghost, and both from faith: but now the Spirit of God hath further worke in his own people, beyond what he worketh upon others, though he melteth both, yet hypocrites are melted as iron, which will returne againe to his former hardnes, but his owne people are melted into flesh, which will never returne to his hardnes more, neither can they rest in any measure of softnes unto which they have attained, but still are carried toward Jesus Christ: so that the one is a temporary faith, and the other persevereth; though both worke in the name of Christ, yet this difference will be found between them, not only when hypocrites come to be blasted; but even in the middest of their profession: As for the faith of the Gospell of Jesus Christ, it is never president of its own power, but his strength lyeth out of himselfe in Christ; whereas hypocrites and legall Christians are confident of their faith, that they can make use of it unto such and such ends, they think they need no more but look up to Christ, and their worke is at an end; and such strength they finde in themselves, as that they doe not feare, but that they shall carry an end all their worke to Gods glory and their own:

whereas the strongest faith even of the *Thessalonians* (whose faith was such, as none of all the Churches went before them) if it be not supplyed and strengthened, they know, & the Apostle *Paul* knoweth that it will warpe & shrinke. This may we see by comparing, 1 *Thes.* 1. 3. with *Chap.* 3. 2, 10. And the faithfull people of God, *Isa.* 26. 12. acknowledge Him to *worke all their works for them.* And therefore as there is a reall difference in the presence of the Spirit; so also in the worke of faith in hypocrites, and the children of God, for the one putteth confidence in himselfe in the gift received, and the other in *Jehovah.* This is the first difference of Sanctification.

2. There is Difference also in the Rule whereby they are guided, though both seeke to the word of God & take delight in that, insomuch as you shall not be able to difference them there, yet a great difference there is in the apprehension of the word: the one is so confident of the comfort that he hath in the word, and he will be ready to take it ill at Gods hand, if he finde not acceptance before him: Now the other see the need they have of the Lord to maintaine their comfort for them. This manner of affection we finde in *David,* when the Lord had brought him and his people into a sweet frame and temper of spirit to offer willingly towards the building of the Temple; what saith *David* now? Doth he thinke this to be enough? No, no, but he prayeth to the Lord, 1 *Chron.* 29. 18. *O Lord God of Abraham, Isaack, and Israel our fathers keepe this for ever in the imagination of the thoughts of the heart of thy people, and prepare their heart unto thee.* Thus is he sensible that these comforts would soone faile them, & they should againe waxe barren and uncomfortable. And here is the nature of true Consolation

in Christ, to looke up unto the Lord to preserve and maintaine it, and so he is still drawne neerer & neerer to Christ. But now though both attend unto the Word, as their Rule of Sanctification, if you take it in the way, in which the one and the other hold it forth, yet there is a great difference. *Psal.* 119. 6. *Then shall I not be ashamed,* &c. Here is a Rule; what, may not hypocrites walke according to this rule? Truly they professe no lesse, and they think it enough, if they have but a Rule in their eye, and therfore under a spirit of bondage they are confident and say, *What soever the Lord commandeth us, we will heare it and doe it,* Deut. 5. 27. And what saith *Balaam; Though* Balaack *would give me an house full of silver and gold, I cannot goe beyond the Commandement of the Lord, Numb.* 22. 18. and yet he loved the wages of iniquity; and indeed those that undertake so much in their owne strength, they come afterward to be weary of the Lord, and weary of his Commandements: as *Amos* 8. 5. and they say at last, *It is in vaine to serve God, and what profit is it that we have kept his ordinances?* Mal. 3. 14. These are but like washed swine, that will crop grasse for a while in a faire Pasture, but if you keepe them long there, they will not delight in such manner of feeding, but will rather choose to go into the mire; but as for goats they will delight in the Commandments of the Lord, *Isa.* 58. 2. It is not a very hard thing unto them, nor grievous for them to keep solemne fasting dayes together, they come willingly, they delight to come, therefore the difference will be hardly discovered, and unles you be a Christian of a very cleere discerning, you will not finde the difference.

4. Society

As do people in any society, the Puritans sought their pleasures not only among those allowed to them but from those available. Anyone who skims quickly the records of the Massachusetts General Court or local New England court records for the seventeenth century can document this statement in exuberant detail. Thus, if the term "puritan" has been used to describe anti-sensual, socially conforming, and sexually repressed elements in American culture, the blame should not fall on the settlers of Massachusetts Bay. They were neither secretive nor squeamish about all forms of love and love-making, lawful or unlawful, and Puritan writings reveal no embarrassment in dealing with both the pleasures and the problems of the flesh. William Bradford, chief magistrate of Plymouth (neighbor colony to Massachusetts Bay), demonstrated in his letters an eminently practical understanding of the reasons for social misbehavior in a religious commonwealth, and the selection from the Massachusetts General Court order of 1688 illustrates the practical nature of Puritan response to problems of social control. Anne Bradstreet's poem, while written in seventeenth-century New England, retains its freshness of sentiment and expression today.

WILLIAM BRADFORD

It was strange to see and consider how wickedness grew and broke forth here in a land where it was so witnessed against, and so resolutely hunted down, and so severely punished when found out; as in no place that I have known or heard of; and to such an extent that they have been somewhat censured for the severity of their punishments. And yet all of this did not suppress the breaking out of sundry notorious sins, of which in this and other years we were given sad examples. There was not only incontinence between unmarried persons, for which many men and women were sharply punished, but also among married persons also. But that which is even worse, sodomy and other sins fearful to name broke out more than once. I say it may be justly marveled at, and cause us to fear and tremble at the thought of our corrupt natures, which are with so much difficulty bridled, subdued, and mortified—nay, and cannot be by any other means save the powerful grace of Christ's spirit. But, besides this, one reason may be that the Devil has a greater spite against the churches of Christ here because of their very determination to preserve holiness and purity and to punish the contrary wherever it arises in church or commonwealth, so that he might cast a blemish or stain upon them in the eyes of the world, which is usually over ready to pass judgment. I would rather think this than, as some have believed, that Satan has more power in these heathen lands than in more Christian nations, especially over the servants of God.

Another reason may be that, as with streams when their waters are stopped or dammed up, when evils find a passage they break forth with more violence, and make more noise and disturbance than when they are suffered to run quietly in their own channels. Wickedness, being here stopped by strict laws and narrowly looked into, so it cannot run its course freely, searches everywhere and at last breaks out when it gets an opening.

A third reason may be, as I am verily persuaded, that there are not more evils of this kind in proportion to our numbers than in other places; but they are here more discovered and seen and made public by search, inquisition, and punishment; for the church examines its members closely, and the civil magistrates too look into these matters more than elsewhere. Besides, the people are few in comparison with other places, where the very numbers make it possible to conceal evil more easily; here it is brought to light and set out plainly to view as on a hill.

. . .

It may be demanded how so many wicked persons and profane people should so quickly come to this land and mix among the settlers, seeing it was religious men who began the work and they came for religion's sake. I confess this may be marveled at, especially in time to come, when the reasons cannot be fully known; and all the more since here there were so many hardships to be overcome. I shall endeavor to give some answer. And first, as it says in the Gospel, it is ever to be remembered that where the Lord begins to sow good seed, there the envious man endeavors to sow tares. Men who had come over into a wilderness where there was much hard work to be done building and planting had to take what help they could get when they could not get the kind they wanted; thus many undis-

Reprinted from William Bradford, HISTORY OF PLYMOUTH (New York: Van Nostrand, 1948), pp. 384–85, 388–89.

ciplined servants were brought over, both men and women; who, when their time of service had expired, became heads of families, giving increase to this class. Another reason was that men finding so many good people willing to come to these parts began to make a trade of it, to transport passengers and their goods, hiring ships for that end; and then to make up their freight and increase their profits, they filled up their ships with any who had money to pay. And thus the country became pestered with many unworthy persons. Again, since the Lord's blessing usually follows His people in outward as well as spiritual things (though afflictions are mixed in too), many people cling to God's people, as they followed Christ, for the sake of the loaves (John, VI, 26; Exod., XII, 38). Others were sent by their friends in the hope that they would improve themselves; others that they might be freed of such burdens, and freed of the shame of dissolute relatives. And thus, by one means or another, in twenty years' time, it is a question if the greater number have not grown worse.

MASSACHUSETTS GENERAL COURT

In 1668 the General Court of Massachusetts ordered: that where any man is legally convicted to be the Father of a Bastard childe, he shall be at the care and charge to maintain and bring up the same, by such assistance of the Mother as nature requireth, and as the Court from time to time (according to circumstances) shall see most meet to

Reprinted from William H. Whitmore, ed., THE COLONIAL LAWS OF MASSACHUSETTS *(Boston, 1889), p. 257.*

Order; and in case the Father of a Bastard, by confession or other manifest proof, upon trial of the case, do not appear to the Courts satisfaction, then the Man charged by the Woman to be the Father, shee holding constant in it, (especially being put upon the real discovery of the truth of it in the time of her Travail) shall be the reputed Father, and accordingly be liable to the charge of maintenance as aforesaid (though not to other punishment) notwithstanding his denial, unless the circumstances of the case and pleas be such, on the behalf of the man charged, as that the Court that have the cognizance thereon shall see reason to acquit him, and otherwise dispose of the Childe and education thereof.

ANNE BRADSTREET

A LETTER TO HER HUSBAND, ABSENT UPON
  PUBLICK EMPLOYMENT

My Head, my heart, mine Eyes, my life,
    nay more,
My joy, my Magazine of earthly store,
If two be one, as surely thou and I,
How stayest thou there, whilst I at *Ipswich*
    lye?
So many steps, head from the heart to sever
If but a neck, soon should we be together:
I like the earth this season, mourn in black,
My Sun is gone so far in's Zodiack,
Whom whilst I 'joy'd, nor storms, nor frosts
    I felt,
His warmth such frigid colds did cause to
    melt.
My chilled limbs now nummed lye forlorn;
Return, return sweet *Sol* from *Capricorn*;
In this dead time, alas, what can I more
Than view those fruits which through thy
    heat I bore?
Which sweet contentment yield me for a
    space,
True living Pictures of their Fathers face.

O strange effect! now thou art *Southward*
  gone,
I weary grow, the tedious day so long;
But when thou *Northward* to me shall re-
  turn,
I wish my Sun may never set, but burn
Within the Cancer of my glowing breast,

The welcome house of him my dearest
  guest,
Where ever, ever stay, and go not thence,
Till natures sad decree shall call thee
  hence;
Flesh of thy flesh, bone of thy bone,
I here, thou there, yet both but one.

5. Purposes

*After a half-century of settlement in New England, many children of the
Puritan founders began to take rigorous inventory of the failures and
accomplishments of their New World experiment. Had God abandoned
his children of the covenant, many asked, leaving them corrupt and spiritually decayed in the wilderness? Would they ever return to a "reformed"
England, or did God intend to keep them in the New World, seeking His
glory in an American setting? There were as many answers to these questions as ministers, but all devout Puritans had to face these fundamental
questions of identity late in the seventeenth century: Who am I? What
remains of my Puritan heritage? What is my purpose in this wilderness?
In responding to these questions, the sons and grandsons of the founders
were not only confronting the challenges of their Puritan experience, but
they were beginning to face the burdens and promise of American life itself.
Two contrasting contemporary evaluations of the Puritan achievement
(or failure) are found in the selections from Michael Wigglesworth's elaborate poem, "God's Controversy with New-England," and in John Higginson's introduction to Reverend Cotton Mather's* Magnalia Christi Americana; or the Ecclesiastical History of New-England.

MICHAEL WIGGLESWORTH

GOD'S CONTROVERSY WITH NEW-ENGLAND

Are these the men that erst at my command
  Forsook their ancient seats and native
  soile,
To follow me into a desart land,
  Contemning all the travell and the toile,
Whose love was such to purest ordinances
  As made them set at nought their fair
  inheritances?

Are these the men that prized libertee
  To walk with God according to their
  light,
To be as good as he would have them bee,
  To serve and worship him with all their
  might,

Before the pleasures which a fruitfull field,
  And country flowing-full of all good
  things, could yield,

Are these the fold whom from the brittish
  Iles,
  Through the stern billows of the watry
  main,
I safely led so many thousand miles,
  As if their journey had been through a
  plain?
Whom having from all enemies protected,
  And through so many deaths and dangers
  well directed,

I brought and planted on the western
  shore,
  Where nought but bruits and salvage
  wights did swarm

(Untaught, untrain'd, untam'd by vertue's
    lore)
    That sought their blood, yet could not
        do them harm?
My fury's flaile them thresht, my fatall
    broom
    Did sweep them hence, to make my peo-
        ple elbow-room.

· · ·

Are these the men, that now mine eyes
    behold,
    Concerning whom I thought, and whil-
        ome spake,
First Heaven shall pass away together
    scrold,
    Ere they my lawes and righteous wayes
        forsake,
Or that they slack to runn their heavenly
    race?
    Are these the same? or are some others
        come in place?

If these be they, how is it that I find
    In stead of holiness Carnality,
In stead of heavenly frames an Earthly
    mind,
    For burning zeal luke-warm Indifferency,
For flaming love, key-cold Dead-hearted-
    ness,
    For temperance (in meat, and drinke, and
        cloaths) excess?

Whence cometh it, that Pride, and Luxurie
    Debate, Deceit, Contention, and Strife,
False-dealing, Covetousness, Hypocrisie
    (With such like Crimes) amongst them
        are so rife,
That one of them doth over-reach another?
    And that an honest man can hardly trust
        his Brother?

How is it, that Security, and Sloth,
    Amongst the best are Common to be
        found?
That grosser sins, in stead of Graces growth,
    Amongst the many more and more
        abound?
I hate dissembling shews of Holiness.
    Or practise as you talk, or never more
        profess.

Judge not, vain world, that all are hypo-
    crites

That do profess more holiness then thou:
All foster not dissembling, guilefull sprites,
    Nor love their lusts, though very many
        do.
Some sin through want of care and constant
    watch,
    Some with the sick converse, till they the
        sickness catch.

Some, that maintain a reall root of grace,
    Are overgrown with many noysome
        weeds,
Whose heart, that those no longer may take
    place,
    The benefit of due correction needs.
And such as these however gone astray
    I shall by stripes reduce into a better way.

Moreover some there be that still retain
    Their ancient vigour and sincerity;
Whom both their own, and others sins,
    constrain
    To sigh, and mourn, and weep, and wail,
        & cry:
And for their sakes I have forborn to powre
    My wrath upon Revolters to this present
        houre.

· · ·

Beware, O sinful Land, beware;
    And do not think it strange
That sorer judgements are at hand,
    Unless thou quickly change.
Or God, or thou, must quickly change;
    Or else thou art undon:
Wrath cannot cease, if sin remain,
    Where judgement is begun.

Ah dear New England! dearest land to me;
    Which unto God hast hitherto been dear,
And mayst be still more dear than former-
    lie,
    If to his voice thou wilt incline thine ear.

Consider wel & wisely what the rod,
    Wherewith thou art from yeer to yeer
        chastized,
Instructeth thee. Repent & turn to God,
    Who wil not have his nurture be de-
        spized.

Thou still hast in thee many praying saints,
    Of great account, and precious with the
        Lord,

Who dayly powre out unto him their
    plaints,
And strive to please him both in deed &
    word.

Cheer on, sweet souls, my heart is with you
    all,
And shall be with you, maugre Sathan's
    might:
And whereso'ere this body be a Thrall,
    Still in New-England shall be my delight.

JOHN HIGGINSON

It hath been deservedly esteemed one of the great and wonderful works of God in this *last age,* that the Lord stirred up the spirits of so many thousands of his servants, to leave the *pleasant land* of England, the land of their *nativity,* and to transport themselves, and families, over the *ocean sea,* into a *desert land* in America, at the distance of a *thousand leagues* from their own country; and this, meerly on the account of *pure and undefiled Religion,* not knowing how they should have their *daily bread,* but trusting in God for *that,* in the way of *seeking first the kingdom of God, and the righteousness thereof:* And that the Lord was pleased to grant such a gracious *presence* of his with them, and such a *blessing* upon their undertakings, that within a few years a *wilderness* was subdued before them, and so many Colonies planted, Towns erected, and Churches settled, wherein the true and living God in Christ Jesus, is worshipped and served, in a place where, time out of mind, had been nothing before but *Heathenism, Idolatry, and Devil-worship;* and that the Lord has added so many of the blessings of Heaven and earth for the

Reprinted from John Higginson, "An Attestation to This Church-History of New-England," in Cotton Mather, MAGNALIA CHRISTI AMERICANA *(Hartford, Conn., 1853), pp. 13–15, 18.*

comfortable subsistence of his people at these *ends of the earth.* Surely of this *work,* and of this *time,* it shall be said, what *hath God wrought!* And, *this is the Lord's doings, it is marvelous in our eyes!* Even so (O Lord) *didst thou lead thy people, to make thyself a glorious name!* Now, *one generation passeth away, and another cometh.* The *first generation* of our fathers, that began this plantation of New-England, most of them in their *middle age,* and many of them in their *declining years,* who, *after they had served the will of God,* in laying the *foundation* (as we hope) of *many generations,* and given an *example* of true *reformed Religion* in the *faith* and *order* of the gospel, according to their best light from the *words* of God, they are now *gathered unto their fathers.* There hath been *another generation* succeeding the *first,* either of such as come over with their parents very young, or were born in the country, and these have had the managing of the publick affairs for many years, but are apparently *passing* away, as their *fathers* before them. There is also a *third generation,* who are grown up, and begin to stand thick upon the stage of *action,* at this day, and these were all born in the country, and may call New-England their *native land.* Now, in respect of what the Lord hath done for these generations, succeeding one another, we have aboundant cause of Thanksgiving to the Lord our God, who hath so increased and blessed this people, that from a *day of small things,* he has brought us to be, what we now are. We may set up an EBENEZER, and say, "Hitherto the Lord hath helped us." Yet in respect of our *present state,* we have need earnestly to *pray,* as we are directed, "Let thy work farther appear unto thy servants, and let thy beauty be upon us, and thy glory upon our children; establish thou the works of these our hands; yea, the works of our hands, establish thou them."

For, if we look on the *dark side, the humane side* of this work, there is much of *humane weakness,* and *imperfection* hath appeared in all that hath been done by *man,* as was acknowledged by our *fathers* before us. Neither was New-England ever without some *father chastisements* from God; shewing that He is not fond of the *formalities* of any people upon earth, but expects the *realities* of *practical Godliness,* according to our profession and engagement unto him. Much more may we, the *children* of such *fathers,* lament our *gradual degeneracy* from that *life* and *power of Godliness,* that was in them, and the many *provoking evils* that are amongst us; which have moved our God severely to witness against us, more than in our *first times,* by his *lesser judgments* going before, and his *greater judgments* following after; he shot off his *warning-pieces first,* but his *murthering-pieces* have come after them, in so much as in these calamitous times, the changes of wars of Europe have had such a malignant influence upon *us* in America, that we are at this day *greatly diminished and brought low, through oppression, affliction, and sorrow.*

And yet if we look on the *light side,* the *divine side* of this work, we may yet see, that the *glory of God* which was with our *fathers,* is not wholly departed from us their *children;* there are as yet many *signs* of his *gracious presence* with us, both in the way of his *providences,* and in the use of his *ordinances,* as also in and with the *hearts* and *souls* of a considerable number of his people in New-England, that we may yet say, as they did, "Thy name is upon us, and thou art in the midst of us; therefore, Lord, leave us not!" As Solomon prayed, so may we, "The Lord our God be with us, as he was with our fathers; let him

not leave nor forsake us; but incline our hearts to keep his commandments." And then "that he would maintain his own, and his people's cause, at all times, as the matter may require."

For the Lord our God hath in his infinite wisdom, grace, and holiness, contrived and established His *covenant,* so as he will be the God of his *people* and of their *seed* with them, and after them, *in their generations;* and in the ministerial dispensation of the *covenant of grace,* in, with, and to his visible Church. He hath promised *covenant-mercies* on the condition of *covenant-duties:* "If my people, who are called by my name, shall humble themselves, and pray, and seek my face, and turn from their wicked ways, then will I hear their prayers, forgive their sins, and heal their land; and mine eyes, and mine heart, shall be upon them perpetually for good!" that so the *faithfulness* of God may appear in all generations for ever, that if there be any *breach* between the Lord and his *people,* it shall appear plainly to lye on his *people's* part. And therefore he has taken care, that his own *dealings* with his people in the course of his *providence,* and their *dealings* with him in the ways of *obedience* or *disobedience,* should be recorded, and so transmitted for the use and benefit of aftertimes, from generation to generation; as, (Exodus xvii. 14,) "The Lord said unto Moses, *write this for a memorial in a book;*" and, (Deut. xxxi. 19,) "Write ye this song for you, that it may be a witness for me against the children of Israel;" and (Psa. cii. 18,) "This and that shall be written for the generation to come, and the people that shall be created shall praise the Lord." Upon this ground it was said, (in Psal. xliv. 1,) "We have heard with our ears, O God, and our fathers have told us, what work thou didst in their days in times of old, how thou castest out the Heathen, and plantedst them;" (so likewise in Psal. lxxviii. v. 3 to the 8th). Upon the same account it may be said, (Psal. xlv. last,) "I will make thy name to be remembered to all generations:" and this is one reason why the Lord commanded so great a part of the *Holy Scriptures* to be written in an *historical way,* that the wonderful works of God towards his church and people, and their acting towards him again, might be known *unto all generations:* and after the *scripture-time,* so far as the Lord in his *holy wisdom* hath seen meet, he hath stirred up some or other to write the *acts and monuments* of the church of God in all ages; especially since the *reformation of religion* from antchristian darkness, was *vigorously,* and in a great measure *successfully,* endeavoured in the foregoing century, by such learned and pious persons as the Lord inclined and inabled thereunto.

And therefore surely it hath been a duty incumbent upon the people of God, in this our New-England, that there should be extant, a true *history* of the wonderful works of God in the late plantation of this part of America: which was indeed planted, not on the account of any *worldly interest,* but on a design of enjoying and advancing the true *reformed religion,* in a *practical way;* and also of the good hand of God upon it from the beginning unto this day, in granting such a measure of *good success,* so far as we have attained: such a work as this hath been much *desired,* and long *expected,* both at home and abroad, and too long delayed by *us,* and sometimes it hath seemed a hopeless thing ever to be attained, till God raised up the spirit of this learned and pious person, one of the sons of the *colledge,* and one of the ministers of the *third generation,* to undertake this work. His learning and Godliness, and *ministerial abilities,* were so conspicu-

ous, that at the age of *seventeen years,* he was called to be a publick preacher in Boston, the *metropolis* of the whole English America; and within a while after that, he was ordained *pastor* of the same church, whereof his own *father* was the *teacher,* and this at the unanimous desire of the people, and with the approbation of the *magistrates, ministers,* and *churches,* in the vicinity of Boston. And after he had, for divers years, approved himself in an exemplary way, and obliged his *native country,* by publishing many useful *treatises,* suitable to the *present state* of Religion amongst us, he set himself to write the *church-history* of New-England, not at all omitting his ministerial employments; and in the midst of many difficulties, tears, and temptations, having made a diligent search, collecting of proper materials, and selecting the choicest *memorials,* he hath, in the issue, within a few months, contrived, composed, and methodized the same into this form and frame which we here see: so that it deserves the name of, THE CHURCH-HISTORY OF NEW-ENGLAND.

. . .

Now the Lord our God, the faithful God, that *keepeth covenant and mercy to a thousand generations,* with his people; let him incline the heart of his people of New-England, to keep covenant and duty towards their God, to walk in his ways, and keep his commandments, that he may bring upon them the blessing of Abraham, the mercy and truth unto Jacob, the sure mercies of David, the grace and peace that cometh from God the Father, and the Lord Jesus Christ; and that the grace of our Lord Jesus Christ may be in and with these churches, from one generation to another, until the second coming of our Lord the Saviour Jesus Christ! *Unto him be glory and dominion, for ever and ever.* AMEN.

III. RECENT INTERPRETATIONS

Included here are three selections from among the many recent contributions to the literature on New England Puritanism. Edmund S. Morgan's biography of John Winthrop provides a strikingly different interpretation of Puritan government from the one offered by Vernon L. Parrington. Morgan questions the usefulness of viewing the Massachusetts Bay experiment as an "oligarchy," when an examination of its actual organization and the conduct of government by Winthrop and his associates reveals a less authoritarian strain of administration. Carl Degler's essay on Puritan society raises questions concerning many traditional and still prevalent American cultural stereotypes of "Puritanism." In the final selection, Perry Miller analyzes the impact of a half-century of American experiences on the purposes and values of the New England Puritans.

EDMUND S. MORGAN

When Winthrop and eleven other members of the Massachusetts Bay Company met at Cambridge, England, on August 26, 1629, they agreed to go to New England if the charter and headquarters of the company could be transferred with them. Ten of the twelve kept their pledge, eight of them arriving with Winthrop or shortly after. Besides these, Winthrop could count only four or five other members of the company in New England at the end of 1630. This handful of men was now the Massachusetts Bay Company and endowed with all the powers described in the charter which Winthrop guarded among his papers.

In the charter the King had granted authority "to make, ordeine, and establishe all manner of wholesome and reasonable orders, lawes, statutes, and ordinances, directions, and instructions,

Reprinted from Edmund S. Morgan, THE PURITAN DILEMMA: THE STORY OF JOHN WINTHROP *(Boston: Little, Brown & Co., 1958), pp. 84–86, 89–96, by permission of the publisher.*

not contrarie to the lawes of this our realm of England, as well for setling of the forms and ceremonies of government and magistracy fitt and necessary for the said plantation, and the inhabitants there and for nameing and stiling of all sortes of officers, both superior and inferior which they shall finde needeful for that government and plantation, and the distinguishing and setting forth of the severall duties, powers, and lymytts of every such office and place."

It was intended, of course, that these extensive powers should be exercised by a corporation meeting in England; but the charter did not say so, and the only actual limitation which the King placed on the company's governmental authority over Massachusetts Bay was that it should make no laws repugnant to the laws of England. Settlers going to the colony from England and their children born there were to enjoy "all liberties and immunities" that they would have had if they had been born in England. But English birth did not in 1630 confer the right to participate in government, and the charter did not specify that the consent of the settlers should be obtained for the laws made to govern them. Instead the company had full powers to legislate for the colony and to organize a government to carry out their decrees in any way they saw fit.

With regard to the organization and government of the company itself the charter was much more specific. The members, known as "freemen," were to meet four times a year in a "Great and General Court," to make laws for both company and colony. Once a year, at one of these courts, they would elect a governor, a deputy governor, and eighteen "assistants" for the coming year, to manage affairs between meetings of the General Court. This executive council was to meet every month. The governor or deputy governor and at least six of the assistants must be present also at every meeting of the General Court, but the charter did not specify that any other members must be present to constitute a quorum, so that these seven officers, in the absence of any other members, could presumably exercise all the powers of the General Court.

In Massachusetts, therefore, Winthrop and the dozen or so members of the company who came with him had unlimited authority to exercise any kind of government they chose over the other settlers. In order to satisfy the terms of the charter they had only to meet once a month as assistants (all but one of the members who are known to have migrated the first year were assistants) and four times a year as a General Court, though the two types of meeting would now be virtually indistinguishable in membership. Provided they followed this procedure and passed no laws repugnant to the laws of England, they could govern Massachusetts in any way they saw fit. And for that matter, who was to say what law was repugnant to

those of England? Who was to decide, who to correct them if they erred? Here was no King, Parliament, bishop, or judge to stand in their way.

A group of men as sure of their cause as were Winthrop and his friends must have been strongly tempted to establish themselves as a permanent aristocracy or oligarchy, holding fast the power granted in the charter and using it to enforce the special commission which they believed God had given them. They were a determined, stiff-jawed set, quick to anger and slow to laughter, as likely a group of oligarchs as ever assembled. . . .

• • •

Winthrop and the other members of the Bay Company were authorized by their charter to exercise absolute powers of government; they were endowed by temperament with the inclination to exercise those powers; and they were assisted by a philosophy of government which clothed every civil ruler in the armor of divine authority. How natural, then, that they should become a ruling oligarchy. They might readily have succumbed to the lust for power, since power lay unchallenged in their hands.

But they did not succumb.

They did not even keep the powers to which the charter entitled them.

After Winthrop had explored the bay and moved the headquarters of the colony from Salem to Charlestown, he summoned the assistants for their first meeting on August 23, 1630. There were seven members present besides himself and Dudley, and they got down to the business of government at once. They provided for the maintenance of two ministers, set maximum wages for workmen in various trades, and appointed a beadle "to attend upon the Governor, and alwaies to be ready to execute his commands in publique businesses." They also ordered that there should be regular meetings, or "courts," of the assistants and of the General Court, though the difference between the two would be a formality, since their membership would be virtually identical (unless future emigration brought over other company members without the status of assistant). On September 7 and September 28 they met again as assistants and exercised their authority in a variety of actions. They forbade the sale of firearms to the Indians; they put an embargo on corn; they seized Richard Clough's strong water because he sold too much of it to other men's servants; and they fined Sir Richard Saltonstall, one of their own number, for being absent from court.

Then on October 19 Winthrop summoned at Charlestown the first meeting labeled in the records as a General Court. For this day he and the seven company members who met with him had prepared a revolution that was to affect the history of Massachusetts from that time forward. The records described the event with tantalizing brevity: "For the establishing of the government. It was propounded if it were not the best course that the Freemen should have the power of chuseing Assistants when there are to be chosen, and the Assistants from amongst themselves to chuse a Governor and Deputy Governor, whoe with the Assistants should have the power of makeing lawes and chuseing officers to execute the same."

This was surely a strange proposal to make to a group of men all of whom were both freemen and assistants. Why, when there were no freemen but themselves in the colony, should they make provision for freemen electing the assistants and the assistants electing the other officers? One begins to get an inkling of what was happenning in the next sentence of the records: "This was fully assented unto by the generall vote

of the people, and ereccion of hands."

The "people" here referred to were not simply the eight company members present. This we can conclude from events that followed. Winthrop had apparently thrown open the first meeting of the General Court to the whole body of settlers assembled at Charlestown. Together they had established the first constitution of Massachusetts. It used the terminology of the charter, and presumably allowed the provisions of the charter not expressly revised to remain in effect. But by general vote of the people of Massachusetts, the assistants were transformed from an executive council into a legislative assembly; and the term "freeman" was transformed from a designation for the members of a commercial company, exercising legislative and judicial control over that company and its property, into a designation for the citizens of a state, with the right to vote and hold office. The right of the citizen freemen to vote, however, was confined to electing assistants. These assistants, and not the freemen themselves, were to make laws and appoint from their own number a governor and deputy governor.

This transformation of the Bay Company's charter into a constitution for government of the colony would scarcely have been necessary or desirable if the members of the company had intended to keep control in their own hands. The reduction of the freemen's role in the government and the securing of popular consent to this change presaged the admission to freemanship of a large proportion of settlers, men who could contribute to the joint stock nothing but godliness and good citizenship. The transformation of trading company into commonwealth was completed at the next meeting of the General Court, when one hundred and sixteen persons were admitted as freemen.

(This was probably most, if not all, of the adult males, excluding servants, then in the colony.) The new freemen then voted that elections should be annual and, doubtless at the behest of Winthrop, that "for time to come noe man shalbe admitted to the freedome of this body polliticke, but such as are members of some of the churches within the lymitts of the same." Though stated in the form of a limitation, this declaration was in fact an open invitation to every future church member in Massachusetts to take up the privileges of freemanship.

Since the people had no political rights under the charter, Winthrop had given them a role to which they had had no legal claim at all. That he confined the gift to church members was not surprising: he would scarcely have wished to take into partnership all of the multitude of men who might come to his colony for the wrong reasons, and the qualified franchise might also help attract the right kind of settlers. By limiting freemanship to church members he extended political rights to a larger proportion of the people than enjoyed such rights in England—and to people who were better qualified to use them than the mere possessors of a forty-shilling freehold. The question that needs to be answered is not why he limited suffrage but why he extended it. What induced Winthrop and the other members of the Bay Company to resign voluntarily the exclusive powers which the charter conferred on them and which their political beliefs and native dispositions made congenial?

Possibly they gave way to popular demand, but there is no evidence that any such demand existed. Possibly they felt a need to keep their own ranks filled. With sickness and death whittling away at their number, they were already close to the minimum quota of seven assist-

ants required by the charter for the holding of the Assistants Court (only six were required in the General Court). But granting their need to perpetuate themselves, they could still have filled vacancies with a few hand-picked men as the need arose. The charter gave them express permission to admit new members to the company if they chose, but it put them under no obligation to do so. Even a popular demand, if it existed, could have been met by a less drastic measure than the one they took.

The real answer as to why they opened the door to freemanship so wide is to be found in the terms of the commission with which they believed the colony was entrusted. The idea of a "covenant," or contract, between God and man occupied a pre-eminent place in their thought: it was the basis of an individual's salvation; it was the origin of every true church and also of every state. "It is of the nature and essence of every society," Winthrop once wrote, "to be knitt together by some Covenant, either expressed or implyed." God's special commission to Massachusetts was an implied covenant.

But there was more than one covenant involved in the establishment of any society. After the people joined in covenant with God, agreeing to be bound by his laws, they must establish a government to see those laws enforced, for they did not have enough virtue to carry out their agreement without the compulsive force of government. They must decide among themselves what form of government they wanted and then create it by a voluntary joint compact—a second covenant.

Winthrop evidently thought that the mere act of coming to Massachusetts constituted a sufficient acceptance of the basic covenant, the special commission which God had given the colony. But the second covenant, establishing the government, required a more explicit agreement. Though the King's charter gave the Bay Company a clear and exclusive right to govern the territory, the King's authority was insufficient. The "due form of government" which Winthrop believed the special commission called for could originate only from a covenant between the settlers and the men who were to rule them. Hence the extraordinary action of October 19, with its sequel, the extension of freemanship.

Winthrop did not believe that in extending freemanship he had transformed Massachusetts into a democracy. The legislative power was lodged not in the people but in a select group where, according to his reading of the Bible, it belonged. Nor was Winthrop's action in securing the consent of the people to his government an affirmation of the principle that governments derive their just powers from the consent of the governed. He did not believe that the officers chosen under the new system would be simply the agents of the people who elected them. Rulers, however selected, received their authority from God, not from the people, and were accountable to God, not to the people. Their business was to enforce the nation's covenant with God, and during their term of office, so long as they devoted themselves to this business, they were free to act as they thought best, suiting their actions to the circumstances.

Winthrop did believe that the people, or a properly qualified portion of them, were entitled to determine the form of government to be established over them and to select the persons who should run that government. These two operations performed, their role was played out until, under the form of government they had chosen, it was time to elect new rulers. If a ruler failed in his duty to enforce the laws of God, the people would be obliged to turn him out without waiting for election time. But so long as he did his duty, his authority was absolute, and, regardless of any errors of judgment he might make, the people were obliged to submit. Indeed, anything less than submission would be rebellion against the authority of God.

In Winthrop's view, then, he had not in any way limited or reduced the authority of government by extending to church members a voice in the selection of the men who were to exercise the authority. Rather he had given to government a practical strength which it could not otherwise have possessed, for Winthrop was enough of a politician to know that, regardless of any divine authority a ruler might claim, people would submit to him more readily if they had a voice in choosing him, especially a Puritan people well educated by their ministers in the principle of government based on covenant.

There was a danger, of course, that the people would choose the wrong kind of men to rule them. Government was a difficult business, not something that one honest man could do as well as another. It required not only virtue but learning and wisdom as well: learning because the laws of God were not so obvious that he who runs might read them, wisdom because the ruler must be able to apply the laws every day to new situations and choose the right law for the case in hand. But the limitation of freemanship to church members furnished some insurance against the wiles of demagogues. Winthrop counted on the ministers to give the people sound advice and to instruct them about the kind of men who were best fitted to rule.

The ministers must not seek public office themselves, and there was little likelihood that they would or that they would succeed if they did. Though the ministers enjoyed a powerful influence over their congregations, the shadow of Rome still lay heavily on the Puritans. None of them wanted a "theocracy" in the sense of a government by the clergy. Indeed, of all the governments in the Western world at the time, that of early Massachusetts gave the clergy least authority. As long as Winthrop lived, ministers neither sought nor obtained government office. Their advice was frequently asked and frequently given; their influence over the people was invaluable; but authority rested firmly in the hands of laymen.

CARL DEGLER

WERE THE PURITANS "PURITANICAL"?

To most Americans—and to most Europeans, for that matter—the core of the Puritan social heritage has been summed up in Macaulay's well-known witticism that the Puritans prohibited bear-baiting not because of torture to the bear, but because of the pleasure it afforded the spectators. And as late as 1925, H. L. Mencken defined Puritanism as "the haunting fear that someone, somewhere, may be happy." Before this chapter is out, much will be said about the somber and even grim nature of the Puritan view of life, but quips like those of Macaulay and Mencken distort rather than illumine the essential character of the Puritans. Simply because the word "Puritan" has become encrusted with a good many barnacles, it is worth while to try to scrape them off if we wish to gain an

Reprinted from Carl Degler, OUT OF OUR PAST: THE FORCES THAT SHAPED MODERN AMERICA *(New York: Harper & Row, 1959), pp. 8–14, by permission of the publisher.*

understanding of the Puritan heritage. Though this process is essentially a negative one, sometimes it is clarifying to set forth what an influence is *not* as well as what it is.

Fundamental to any appreciation of the Puritan mind on matters of pleasure must be the recognition that the typical, godly Puritan was a worker in the world. Puritanism, like Protestantism in general, resolutely and definitely rejected the ascetic and monastic ideals of medieval Catholicism. Pleasures of the body were not to be eschewed by the Puritan, for, as Calvin reasoned, God "intended to provide not only for our necessity, but likewise for our pleasure and delight." It is obvious, he wrote in his famous *Institutes,* that "the Lord have endowed flowers with such beauty . . . with such sweetness of smell" in order to impress our senses; therefore, to enjoy them is not contrary to God's intentions. "In a word," he concluded, "hath He not made many things worthy of our estimation independent of any necessary use?"

It was against excess of enjoyment that the Puritans cautioned and legislated. "The wine is from God," Increase Mather warned, "but the Drunkard is from the Devil." The Cambridge Platform of the Church of 1680 prohibited games of cards or dice because of the amount of time they consumed and the encouragement they offered to idleness, but the ministers of Boston in 1699 found no difficulty in condoning public lotteries. They were like a public tax, the ministers said, since they took only what the "government might have demanded, with a more *general imposition . . .* and it employes for the welfare of the publick, all that is raised by the *lottery.*" Though Cotton Mather at the end of the century condemned mixed dancing, he did not object to dancing as such; and his grandfather,

John Cotton, at the beginning saw little to object to in dancing between the sexes so long as it did not become lascivious. It was this same John Cotton, incidentally, who successfully contended against Roger Williams' argument that women should wear veils in church.

In matters of dress, it is true that the Massachusetts colony endeavored to restrict the wearing of "some new and immodest fashions" that were coming in from England, but often these efforts were frustrated by the pillars of the church themselves. Winthrop reported in his *History,* for example, that though the General Court instructed the elders of the various churches to reduce the ostentation in dress by "urging it upon the consciences of their people," little change was effected, "for divers of the elders' wives, etc., were in some measure partners in this general disorder."

We also know now that Puritan dress —not that made "historical" by Saint-Gaudens' celebrated statue—was the opposite of severe, being rather in the English Renaissance style. Most restrictions on dress which were imposed were for purposes of class differentiation rather than for ascetic reasons. Thus long hair was acceptable on an upper-class Puritan like Cromwell or Winthrop, but it was a sign of vanity on the head of a person of lower social status. . . .

If the Puritans are to be saved from the canard of severity of dress, it is also worth while to soften the charge that they were opposed to music and art. It is perfectly true that the Puritans insisted that organs be removed from the churches and that in England some church organs were smashed by zealots. But it was not music or organs as such which they opposed, only music in the meetinghouse. Well-known American and English Puritans, like Samuel Sewell, John Milton, and Cromwell, were sincere lovers of music. Moreover, it should be remembered that it was under Puritan rule that opera was introduced in England—and without protest, either. . . .

*   *   *

Some modern writers have professed to find in Puritanism, particularly the New England brand, evidence of sexual repression and inhibition. Though it would certainly be false to suggest that the Puritans did not subscribe to the canon of simple chastity, it is equally erroneous to think that their sexual lives were crabbed or that sex was abhorrent to them. Marriage to the Puritan was something more than an alternative to "burning," as the Pauline doctrine of the Catholic Church would have it. Marriage was enjoined upon the righteous Christian; celibacy was not a sign of merit. With unconcealed disapprobation, John Cotton told a recently married couple the story of a pair "who immediately upon marriage, without ever approaching the *Nuptial* Bed," agreed to live apart from the rest of the world, "and afterwards from one another, too. . . ." But, Cotton advised, such behavior was "no other than an effort of blind zeal, for they are the dictates of a blind mind they follow therein and not of the Holy Spirit which saith, *It is not good that man should be alone.*" Cotton set himself against not only Catholic asceticism but also the view that women were the "unclean vessel," the tempters of men. Women, rather than being "a necessary Evil are a necessary Good," he wrote. "Without them there is no comfortable Living for Man. . . ."

Because, as another divine said, "the Use of the Marriage Bed" is "founded in man's Nature" the realistic Puritans required that married men unaccompanied by wives should leave the colony or bring their wives over forthwith.

The Puritan settlements encouraged marriages satisfactory to the participants by permitting divorces for those whose spouses were impotent, too long absent, or cruel. Indeed, the divorce laws of New England were the easiest in Christendom at a time when the eloquence of a Milton was unable to loosen the bonds of matrimony in England.

Samuel Eliot Morison in his history of Harvard has collected a number of examples of the healthy interest of Puritan boys in the opposite sex. Commonplace books, for example, indicate that Herrick's poem beginning "Gather ye rosebuds while ye may" and amorous lines from Shakespeare, as well as more erotic and even scatological verse, were esteemed by young Puritan men. For a gentleman to present his affianced with a pair of garters, one letter of a Harvard graduate tells us, was considered neither immoral nor improper.

It is also difficult to reconcile the usual view of the stuffiness of Puritans with the literally hundreds of confessions to premarital sexual relations in the extant church records. It should be understood, moreover, that these confessions were made by the saints or saints-to-be, not by the unregenerate. That the common practice of the congregation was to accept such sinners into church membership without further punishment is in itself revealing. The civil law, it is true, punished such transgressions when detected among the regenerate or among the nonchurch members, but this was also true of contemporary non-Puritan Virginia. "It will be seen," writes historian Philip A. Bruce regarding Virginia, "from the various instances given relating to the profanation of Sunday, drunkenness, swearing, defamation, and sexual immorality, that, not only were the grand juries and vestries extremely vigilant in reporting these offences, but the courts were equally prompt in inflicting punishment; and that the penalty ranged from a heavy fine to a shameful exposure in the stocks . . . and from such an exposure to a very severe flogging at the county whipping post." In short, strict moral surveillance by the public authorities was a seventeenth-century rather than a Puritan attitude.

Relations between the sexes in Puritan society were often much more loving and tender than the mythmakers would have us believe. Since it was the Puritan view that marriage was eminently desirable in the sight of God and man, it is not difficult to find evidence of deep and abiding love between a husband and wife. John Cotton, it is true, sometimes used the Biblical phrase "comfortable yoke mate" in addressing his wife, but other Puritan husbands come closer to our romantic conventions. Certainly John Winthrop's letters to his beloved Margaret indicate the depth of attachment of which the good Puritan was capable. "My good wife . . . My sweet wife," he called her. Anticipating his return home, he writes, "So . . . we shall now enjoy each other again, as we desire. . . . It is now bed time; but I must lie alone; therefore I make less haste. Yet I must kiss my sweet wife; and so, with my blessing to our children . . . I commend thee to the grace and blessing of the lord, and rest. . . ."

. . .

It would be a mistake, however, to try to make these serious, dedicated men and women into rakes of the Renaissance. They were sober if human folk, deeply concerned about their ultimate salvation and intent upon living up to God's commands as they understood them, despite their acknowledgment of complete depravity and unworthiness. "God sent you not into this world as a Play-House, but a Work-house," one minister told his congregation. To the Puritan this was a world drenched in evil, and, because it truly is, they were essentially realistic in their judgments. Because the Puritan expected nothing, Perry Miller has remarked, a disillusioned one was almost impossible to find. This is probably an exaggeration, for they were also human beings; when the Commonwealth fell, it was a Puritan, after all, who said, "God has spit in our faces." But Professor Miller's generalization has much truth in it. Only a man convinced of the inevitable and eternal character of evil could fight it so hard and so unceasingly.

The Puritan at his best, Ralph Barton Perry has said, was a "moral athlete." More than most men, the Puritan strove with himself and with his fellow man to attain a moral standard higher than was rightfully to be expected of so depraved a creature. Hence the diaries and autobiographies of Puritans are filled with the most torturous probing of the soul and inward seeking. Convinced of the utter desirability of salvation on the one hand, and equally cognizant of the total depravity of man's nature on the other, the Puritan was caught in an impossible dilemma which permited him no rest short of the grave. Yet with such a spring coiled within him, the Puritan drove himself and his society to tremendous heights of achievement both material and spiritual.

PERRY MILLER

It was a happy inspiration that led the staff of the John Carter Brown

Reprinted from Perry Miller, ERRAND INTO THE WILDERNESS (Cambridge, Mass.: Harvard University Press, 1956), pp. 2–15, by permission of the publisher.

Library to choose as the title of its New England exhibition of 1952 a phrase from Samuel Danforth's election sermon, delivered on May 11, 1670: *A Brief Recognition of New England's Errand into the Wilderness.* It was of course an inspiration, if not of genius at least of talent, for Danforth to invent his title in the first place. But all the election sermons of this period—that is to say, the major expressions of the second generation, which, delivered on these forensic occasions, were in the fullest sense community expression—have interesting titles; a mere listing tells the story of what was happening to the minds and emotions of the New England people: John Higginson's *The Cause of God and His People In New-England* in 1663, William Stoughton's *New England's True Interest, Not to Lie* in 1668, Thomas Shepard's *Eye-Salve* in 1672, Urian Oakes's *New England Pleaded With* in 1673, and, climactically and most explicitly, Increase Mather's *A Discourse Concerning the Danger of Apostasy* in 1677.

All of these show by their title pages alone—and, as those who have looked into them know, infinitely more by their contents—a deep disquietude. They are troubled utterances, worried, fearful. Something has gone wrong. As in 1662 Wigglesworth already was saying in verse, God has a controversy with New England; He has cause to be angry and to punish it because of its innumerable defections. They say, unanimously, that New England was sent on an errand, and that it has failed.

To our ears these lamentations of the second generation sound strange indeed. We think of the founders as heroic men—of the towering stature of Bradford, Winthrop, and Thomas Hooker—who braved the ocean and the wilderness, who conquered both, and left to their children a goodly heritage. Why then this whimpering?

Some historians suggest that the second and third generations suffered a failure of nerve; they weren't the men their fathers had been, and they knew it. Where the founders could range over the vast body of theology and ecclesiastical polity and produce profound works like the treatises of John Cotton or the subtle psychological analyses of Hooker, or even such a gusty though wrongheaded book as Nathaniel Ward's *Simple Cobler,* let alone such lofty and righteaded pleas as Roger Williams' *Bloudy Tenent,* all these children could do was tell each other that they were on probation and that their chances of making good did not seem very promising.

Since Puritan intellectuals were thoroughly grounded in grammar and rhetoric, we may be certain that Danforth was fully aware of the ambiguity concealed in his word "errand." It already had taken on the double meaning which it still carries with us. Originally, as the word first took form in English, it meant exclusively a short journey on which an inferior is sent to convey a message or to perform a service for his superior. In that sense we today speak of an "errand boy"; or the husband says that while in town on his lunch hour, he must run an errand for his wife. But by the end of the Middle Ages, errand developed another connotation: it came to mean the actual business on which the actor goes, the purpose itself, the conscious intention in his mind. In this signification, the runner of the errand is working for himself, is his own boss; the wife, while the husband is away at the office, runs her own errands. Now in the 1660's the problem was this: which had New England originally been—an errand boy or a doer of errands? In which

sense had it failed? Had it been despatched for a further purpose, or was it an end in itself? Or had it fallen short not only in one or the other, but in both of the meanings? If so, it was indeed a tragedy, in the primitive sense of a fall from a mighty designation.

If the children were in grave doubt about which had been the original errand—if, in fact, those of the founders who lived into the later period and who might have set their progeny to rights found themselves wondering and confused—there is little chance of our answering clearly. Of course, there is no problem about Plymouth Colony. That is the charm about Plymouth: its clarity. The Pilgrims, as we have learned to call them, were reluctant voyagers; they had never wanted to leave England, but had been obliged to depart because the authorities made life impossible for Separatists. They could, naturally, have stayed at home had they given up being Separatists, but that idea simply did not occur to them. Yet they did not go to Holland as though on an errand; neither can we extract the notion of a mission out of the reasons which, as Bradford tells us, persuaded them to leave Leyden for "Virginia." The war with Spain was about to be resumed, and the economic threat was ominous; their migration was not so much an errand as a shrewd forecast, a plan to get out while the getting was good, lest, should they stay, they would be "intrapped or surrounded by their enemies, so as they should neither be able to fight nor flie." True, once the decision was taken, they congratulated themselves that they might become a means for propagating the gospel in remote parts of the world, and thus of serving as steppingstones to others in the performance of this great work; nevertheless, the substance of their decision was that they "thought it better to dislodge betimes to some place of better advantage and less danger, if any such could be found." The great hymn that Bradford, looking back in his old age, chanted about the landfall is one of the greatest passages, if not the very greatest, in all New England's literature; yet it does not resound with the sense of a mission accomplished—instead, it vibrates with the sorrow and exultation of suffering, the sheer endurance, the pain and the anguish, with the somberness of death faced unflinchingly:

May not and ought not the children of these fathers rightly say: Our fathers were Englishmen which came over this great ocean, and were ready to perish in this wilderness; but they cried unto the Lord, and he heard their voyce, and looked on their adversitie . . . .

We are bound, I think, to see in Bradford's account [of the Pilgrims] the prototype of the vast majority of subsequent immigrants—of those Oscar Handlin calls "The Uprooted": they came for better advantage and for less danger, and to give their posterity the opportunity of success.

The Great Migration of 1630 is an entirely other story. True, among the reasons John Winthrop drew up in 1629 to persuade himself and his colleagues that they should commit themselves to the enterprise, the economic motive frankly figures. Wise men thought that England was over-populated and that the poor would have a better chance in the new land. But Massachusetts Bay was not just an organization of immigrants seeking advantage and opportunity. It had a positive sense of mission—either it was sent on an errand or it had its own intention, but in either case the deed was deliberate. It was an act of will, perhaps of willfulness. These Puritans

were not driven out of England (thousands of their fellows stayed and fought the Cavaliers)—they went of their own accord.

So, concerning them, we ask the question, why? If we are not altogether clear about precisely how we should phrase the answer, this is not because they themselves were reticent. They spoke as fully as they knew how, and none more magnificently or cogently than John Winthrop in the midst of the passage itself, when he delivered a lay sermon aboard the flagship *Arbella* and called it "A Modell of Christian Charity." It distinguishes the motives of this great enterprise from those of Bradford's forlorn retreat, and especially from those of the masses who later have come in quest of advancement. Hence, for the student of New England and of America, it is a fact demanding incessant brooding that John Winthrop elected as the "doctrine" of his discourse, and so as the basic proposition to which, it then seemed to him, the errand was committed, the thesis that God had disposed mankind in a hierarchy of social classes, so that "in all times some must be rich, some poor, some highe and eminent in power and dignitie; others mean and in subjeccion." It is as though, preternaturally sensing what the promise of America might come to signify for the rank and file, Winthrop took the precaution to drive out of their heads any notion that in the wilderness the poor and the mean were ever so to improve themselves as to mount above the rich or the eminent in dignity. Were there any who had signed up under the mistaken impression that such was the purpose of their errand, Winthrop told them that, although other peoples, lesser breeds, might come for wealth or pelf, this migration was specifically dedicated to an avowed end that had nothing to do with incomes. We have entered into an explicit covenant with God, "we haue professed to enterprise these accions vpon these and these ends"; we have drawn up indentures with the Almighty, wherefore if we succeed and do not let ourselves get diverted into making money, He will reward us. Whereas if we fail, if we "fall to embrace this present world and prosecute our carnall intencions, seekeing great things for our selves and our posterity, the Lord will surely breake out in wrathe against us be revenged of such a periured people and make us knowe the price of the breache of such a Covenant."

Well, what terms were agreed upon in this covenant? Winthrop could say precisely—"It is by a mutuall consent through a specially overruleing providence, and a more than ordinary approbation of the Churches of Christ to seeke out a place of Cohabitation and Consorteshipp under a due forme of Government both civill and ecclesiasticall." If it could be said thus concretely, why should there be any ambiguity? There was no doubt whatsover about what Winthrop meant by a due form of ecclesiastical government: he meant the pure Biblical polity set forth in full detail by the New Testament, that method which later generations, in the days of increasing confusion, would settle down to calling Congregational, but which for Winthrop was no denominational peculiarity but the very essence of organized Christianity. What a due form of civil government meant, therefore, became crystal clear: a political regime, possessing power, which would consider its main function to be the erecting, protecting, and preserving of this form of polity. This due form would have, at the very beginning of its list of responsibilities, the duty of suppressing heresy, of subduing or

somehow getting rid of dissenters—of being, in short, deliberately, vigorously, and consistently intolerant.

Regarded in this light, the Massachusetts Bay Company came on an errand in the second and later sense of the word: it was, so to speak, on its own business. What it set out to do was the sufficient reason for its setting out. About this Winthrop seems to be perfectly certain, as he declares specifically what the due forms will be attempting: the end is to improve our lives to do more service to the Lord, to increase the body of Christ, and to preserve our posterity from the corruptions of this evil world, so that they in turn shall work out their salvation under the purity and power of Biblical ordinances. Because the errand was so definable in advance, certain conclusions about the method of conducting it were equally evident: one, obviously, was that those sworn to the covenant should not be allowed to turn aside in a lust for mere physical rewards; but another was, in Winthrop's simple but splendid words, "we must be knit together in this worke as one man, wee must entertaine each other in brotherly affection." we must actually delight in each other, "always having before our eyes our Commission and community in the worke, our community as members of the same body." This was to say, were the great purpose kept steadily in mind, if all gazed only at it and strove only for it, then social solidarity (within a scheme of fixed and unalterable class distinctions) would be an automatic consequence. A society despatched upon an errand that is its own reward would want no other rewards: it could go forth to possess a land without ever becoming possessed by it; social gradations would remain eternally what God had originally appointed; there would be no internal contention among groups or interests, and though there would be hard work for everybody, prosperity would be bestowed not as a consequence of labor but as a sign of approval upon the mission itself. For once in the history of humanity (with all its sins), there would be a society so dedicated to a holy cause that success would prove innocent and triumph not raise up sinful pride or arrogant dissension.

Or, at least, this would come about if the people did not deal falsely with God, if they would live up to the articles of their bond. If we do not perform these terms, Winthrop warned, we may expect immediate manifestations of divine wrath; we shall perish out of the land we are crossing the sea to possess. And here in the 1660's and 1670's, all the jeremiads of which Danforth's is one of the most poignant) are castigations of the people for having defaulted on precisely these articles. They recite the long list of afflictions an angry God had rained upon them, surely enough to prove how abysmally they had deserted the covenant: crop failures, epidemics, grasshoppers, caterpillars, torrid summers, arctic winters, Indian wars, hurricanes, shipwrecks, accidents, and (most grievous of all) unsatisfactory children. The solemn work of the election day, said Stoughton in 1668, is "Foundation-work"— not, that is, to lay a new one, "but to continue, and strengthen, and beautifie, and build upon that which has been laid." It had been laid in the covenant before even a foot was set ashore, and thereon New England should rest. Hence the terms of survival, let alone of prosperity, remained what had first been propounded:

If we should so frustrate and deceive the Lords Expectations, that his Covenant-interest in us, and the Workings of his Salvation be made to cease, then All were lost indeed; Ruine upon Ruine, Destruction upon Destruction would come, until one stone were not left upon another.

Since so much of the literature after 1660—in fact, just about all of it—dwells on this theme of declension and apostasy, would not the story of New England seem to be simply that of the failure of a mission? Winthrop's dread was realized: posterity had not found their salvation amid pure ordinances but had, despite the ordinances, yielded to the seductions of the good land. Hence distresses were being piled upon them, the slaughter of King Philip's War and now the attack of a profligate king upon the sacred charter. By about 1680, it did in truth seem that shortly no stone would be left upon another, that history would record of New England that the founders had been great men, but that their children and grandchildren progressively deteriorated.

This would certainly seem to be the impression conveyed by the assembled clergy and lay elders who, in 1679, met at Boston in a formal synod, under the leadership of Increase Mather, and there prepared a report on why the land suffered. The result of their deliberation, published under the title *The Necessity of Reformation,* was the first in what has proved to be a distressingly long succession of investigations into the civic health of Americans, and it is probably the most pessimistic. The land was afflicted, it said, because corruption had proceeded apace; assuredly, if the people did not quickly reform, the last blow would fall and nothing but desolation be left. Into what a moral quagmire this dedicated community had sunk, the synod did not leave to imagination; it published a long and detailed inventory of sins, crimes, misdemeanors, and nasty habits, which makes, to say the least, interesting reading.

We hear much talk nowadays about corruption, most of it couched in generalized terms. If we ask our current Jeremiahs to descend to particulars, they tell us that the republic is going on the rocks, or to the dogs, because the wives of politicians aspire to wear mink coats and their husbands take a moderate five per cent cut on certain deals to pay for the garments. The Puritans were devotees of logic, and the verb "methodize" ruled their thinking. When the synod went to work, it had before it a succession of sermons, such as that of Danforth and the other election-day or fast-day orators, as well as such works as Increase Mather's *A Brief History of the Warr With the Indians,* wherein the decimating conflict with Philip was presented as a revenge upon the people for their transgressions. When the synod felt obliged to enumerate the enormities of the land so that the people could recognize just how far short of their errand they had fallen, it did not, in the modern manner, assume that regeneration would be accomplished at the next election by turning the rascals out, but it digested this body of literature; it reduced the contents to method. The result is a staggering compendium of iniquity, organized into twelve headings.

First, there was a great and visible decay of godliness. Second, there were several manifestations of pride—contention in the churches, insubordination of inferiors toward superiors, particularly of those inferiors who had, unaccountably, acquired more wealth than their betters, and, astonishingly, a shocking extravagance in attire, especially on the part of these of the meaner sort, who persisted in dressing beyond their means. Third, there were heretics, especially Quakers and Ana-

baptists. Fourth, a notable increase in swearing and a spreading disposition to sleep at sermons (these two phenomena seemed basically connected). Fifth, the Sabbath was wantonly violated. Sixth, family government had decayed, and fathers no longer kept their sons and daughters from prowling at night. Seventh, instead of people being knit together as one man in mutual love, they were full of contention, so that lawsuits were on the increase and lawyers were thriving. Under the eighth head, the synod described the sins of sex and alcohol, thus producing some of the juiciest prose of the period: militia days had become orgies, taverns were crowded; women threw temptation in the way of befuddled men by wearing false locks and displaying naked necks and arms "or, which is more abominable, naked Breasts"; there were "mixed Dancings," along with light behavior and "Company-keeping" with vain persons, wherefore the bastardy rate was rising. In 1672, there was actually an attempt to supply Boston with a brothel (it was suppressed, but the synod was bearish about the future). Ninth, New Englanders were betraying a marked disposition to tell lies, especially when selling anything. In the tenth place, the business morality of even the most righteous left everything to be desired: the wealthy speculated in land and raised prices excessively; "Day-Labourers and Mechanicks are unreasonable in their demands." In the eleventh place, the people showed no disposition to reform, and in the twelfth, they seemed utterly destitute of civic spirit.

"The things here insisted on," said the synod, "have been oftentimes mentioned and inculcated by those whom the Lord hath set as Watchmen to the house of Israel." Indeed they had been, and thereafter they continued to be even more inculcated. At the end of the century, the synod's report was serving as a kind of handbook for preachers: they would take some verse of Isaiah or Jeremiah, set up the doctrine that God avenges the iniquities of a chosen people, and then run down the twelve heads, merely bringing the list up to date by inserting the new and still more depraved practices an ingenious people kept on devising. I suppose that in the whole literature of the world, including the satirists of imperial Rome, there is hardly such another uninhibited and unrelenting documentation of a people's descent into corruption.

I have elsewhere endeavored to argue [1] that, while the social or economic historian may read this literature for its contents—and so construct from the expanding catalogue of denunciations a record of social progress—the cultural anthropologist will look slightly askance at these jeremiads; he will exercise a methodological caution about taking them at face value. If you read them all through, the total effect, curiously enough, is not at all depressing: you come to the paradoxical realization that they do not bespeak a despairing frame of mind. There is something of a ritualistic incantation about them; whatever they may signify in the realm of theology, in that of psychology they are purgations of soul; they do not discourage but actually encourage the community to persist in its heinous conduct. The exhortation to a reformation which never materializes serves as a token payment upon the obligation, and so liberates the debtors. Changes there had to be: adaptations to environment, expansion of the frontier, mansions constructed, commercial

[1] See *The New England Mind: From Colony to Province* (1952), Chapter II.

adventures undertaken. These activities were not specifically nominated in the bond Winthrop had framed. They were thrust upon the society by American experience; because they were not only works of necessity but of excitement, they proved irresistible—whether making money, haunting taverns, or committing fornication. Land speculation meant not only wealth but dispersion of the people, and what was to stop the march of settlement? The covenant doctrine preached on the *Arbella* had been formulated in England, where land was not to be had for the taking; its adherents had been utterly oblivious of what the fact of a frontier would do for an imported order, let alone for a European mentality. Hence I suggest that under the guise of this mounting wail of sinfulness, this incessant and never successful cry for repentance, the Puritans launched themselves upon the process of Americanization.

However, there are still more pertinent or more analytical things to be said of this body of expression. If you compare it with the great productions of the founders, you will be struck by the fact that the second and third generations had become oriented toward the social, and only the social, problem; herein they were deeply and profoundly different from their fathers. The finest creations of the founders— the disquisitions of Hooker, Shepard, and Cotton—were written in Europe, or else, if actually penned in the colonies, proceeded from a thoroughly European mentality, upon which the American scene made no impression whatsoever. The most striking example of this imperviousness is the poetry of Anne Bradstreet: she came to Massachusetts at the age of eighteen, already two years married to Simon Bradstreet; there, she says, "I found a new world and new manners, at which my heart rose" in rebellion, but soon convincing herself that it was the way of God, she submitted and joined the church. She bore Simon eight children, and loved him sincerely, as her most charming poem, addressed to him, reveals:

If ever two were one, then surely we;
If ever man were loved by wife, then thee.

After the house burned, she wrote a lament about how her pleasant things in ashes lay and how no more the merriment of guests would sound in the hall; but there is nothing in the poem to suggest that the house stood in North Andover or that the things so tragically consumed were doubly precious because they had been transported across the ocean and were utterly irreplaceable in the wilderness. In between rearing children and keeping house she wrote her poetry; her brother-in-law carried the manuscript to London, and there published it in 1650 under the ambitious title, *The Tenth Muse Lately Sprung Up in America.* But the title is the only thing about the volume which shows any sense of America, and that little merely in order to prove that the plantations had something in the way of European wit and learning, that they had not receded into barbarism. Anne's flowers are English flowers, the birds, English birds, and the landscape is Lincolnshire. So also with the productions of immigrant scholarship: such a learned and acute work as Hooker's *Survey of the Summe of Church Discipline,* which is specifically about the regime set up in America, is written entirely within the logical patterns, and out of the religious experience, of Europe; it makes no concession to new and peculiar circumstances.

The titles alone of productions in the next generation show how concentrated have become emotion and attention upon the interest of New England, and none is more revealing than Samuel Danforth's conception of an errand into the wilderness. Instead of being able to compose abstract treatises like those of Hooker upon the soul's preparation, humiliation, or exultation, or such a collection of wisdom and theology as John Cotton's *The Way of Life* or Shepard's *The Sound Believer,* these later saints must, over and over again, dwell upon the specific sins of New England, and the more they denounce, the more they must narrow their focus to the provincial problem. If they write upon anything else, it must be about the halfway covenant and its manifold consequences—a development enacted wholly in this country—or else upon their wars with the Indians. Their range is sadly constricted, but every effort, no matter how brief, is addressed to the persistent question: what is the meaning of this society in the wilderness? If it does not mean what Winthrop said it must mean, what under Heaven is it? Who, they are forever asking themselves, who are we?—and sometimes they are on the verge of saying, who the Devil are we, anyway?

This brings us back to the fundamental ambiguity concealed in the word "errand," that *double entente* of which I am certain Danforth was aware when he published the words that give point to the exhibition. While it was true that in 1630, the covenant philosophy of a special and peculiar bond lifted the migration out of the ordinary realm of nature, provided it with a definite mission which might in the secondary sense be called its errand, there was always present in Puritan thinking the suspicion that God's saints are at best inferiors, despatched by their Superior upon particular assignments. Anyone who has run errands for other people, particularly for people of great importance with many things on their minds, such as army commanders, knows how real is the peril that, by the time he returns with the report of a message delivered or a bridge blown up, the Superior may be interested in something else; the situation at headquarters may be entirely changed, and the gallant errand boy, or the husband who desperately remembered to buy the ribbon, may be told that he is too late. This tragic pattern appears again and again in modern warfare: an agent is dropped by parachute and, after immense hardships, comes back to find that, in the shifting tactical or strategic situations, his contribution is no longer of value. If he gets home in time and his service proves useful, he receives a medal; otherwise, no matter what prodigies he has performed, he may not even be thanked. He has been sent, as the devastating phrase has it, upon a fool's errand, than which there can be no more shattering blow to self-esteem.

The Great Migration of 1630 felt insured against such treatment from on high by the covenant; nevertheless, the God of the covenant always remained an unpredictable Jehovah, a *Deus Absconditus.* When God promises to abide by stated terms, His word, of course, is to be trusted; but then, what is man that he dare accuse Omnipotence of tergiversation? But if any such apprehension was in Winthrop's mind as he spoke on the *Arbella,* or in the minds of other apologists for the enterprise, they kept it far back and allowed it no utterance. They could stifle the thought, not only because Winthrop and his colleagues believed fully in the covenant, but because they could see

in the pattern of history that their errand was not a mere scouting expedition: it was an essential maneuver in the drama of Christendom. The Bay Company was not a battered remnant of suffering Separatists thrown up on a rocky shore; it was an organized task force of Christians, executing a flank attack on the corruptions of Christendom. These Puritans did not flee to America; they went in order to work out that complete reformation which was not yet accomplished in England and Europe, but which would quickly be accomplished if only the saints back there had a working model to guide them. It is impossible to say that any who sailed from Southampton really expected to lay his bones in the new world; were it to come about—as all in their heart of hearts anticipated—that the forces of righteousness should prevail against Laud and Wentworth, that England after all should turn toward reformation, where else would the distracted country look for leadership except to those who in New England had perfected the ideal polity and who would know how to administer it? This was the large unspoken assumption in the errand of 1630: if the conscious intention were realized, not only would a federated Jehovah bless the new land, but He would bring back these temporary colonials to govern England.

In this respect, therefore, we may say that the migration was running an errand in the earlier and more primitive sense of the word—performing a job not so much for Jehovah as for history, which was the wisdom of Jehovah expressed through time. Winthrop was aware of this aspect of the mission—fully conscious of it. "For wee must Consider that wee shall be as a Citty upon a Hill, the eies of all people are uppon us." More was at stake than just one little colony. If we deal falsely with God, not only will He descend upon us in wrath, but even more terribly, He will make us "a story and a by-word through the world, wee shall open the mouthes of enemies to speake evill of the wayes of god and all professours for Gods sake." No less than John Milton was New England to justify God's ways to man, though not, like him, in the agony and confusion of defeat but in the confidence of approaching triumph. This errand was being run for the sake of Reformed Christianity; and while the first aim was indeed to realize in America the due form of government, both civil and ecclesiastical, the aim behind that aim was to vindicate the most rigorous ideal of the Reformation, so that ultimately all Europe would imitate New England. If we succeed, Winthrop told his audience, men will say of later plantations, "the lord make it like that of New England." There was an elementary prudence to be observed: Winthrop said that the prayer would arise from subsequent plantations, yet what was England itself but one of God's plantations? In America, he promised, we shall see, or may see, more of God's wisdom, power, and truth "then formerly wee have beene acquainted with." The situation was such that, for the moment, the model had no chance to be exhibited in England; Puritans could talk about it, theorize upon it, but they could not display it, could not prove that it would actually work. But if they had it set up in America—in a bare land, devoid of already established (and corrupt) institutions, empty of bishops and courtiers, where they could start de novo, and the eyes of the world were upon it—and if then it performed just as the saints had predicted of it, the Calvinist internationale would know exactly how to go about completing the already begun but temporarily stalled revolution in Europe.[2]

When we look upon the enterprise from this point of view, the psychology of the second and third generations becomes more comprehensible. We realize that the migration was not sent upon its errand in order to found the United States of America, nor even the New England conscience. Actually, it would not perform its errand even when the colonists did erect a due form of government in church and state: what was further required in order for this mission to be a success was that the eyes of the world be kept fixed upon it in rapt attention. If the rest of the world, or at least of Protestantism, looked elsewhere, or turned to another model, or simply got distracted and forgot about New England, if the new land was left with a polity nobody in the great world of Europe wanted —then every success in fulfilling the terms of the covenant would become a diabolical measure of failure. If the due form of government were not everywhere to be saluted, what would New England have upon its hands? How give it a name, this victory nobody could utilize? How provide an identity for something conceived under misapprehensions? How could a universal which turned out to be nothing but a provincial particular be called anything but a blunder or an abortion?

If an actor, playing the leading role in the greatest dramatic spectacle of the century, were to attire himself and put on his make-up, rehearse his lines, take a deep breath, and stride onto

[2] See the perceptive analysis of Alan Heimert (The New England Quarterly, XXVI, September 1953) of the ingredients that ultimately went into the Puritans' metaphor of the "wilderness," all the more striking a concoction because they attached no significance a priori to their wilderness destination. To begin with, it was simply a void.

the stage, only to find the theater dark and empty, no spotlight working, and himself entirely alone, he would feel as did New England around 1650 or 1660. For in the 1640's, during the Civil War, the colonies, so to speak, lost their audience. First of all, there proved to be, deep in the Puritan movement, an irreconcilable split between the Presbyterian and Independent wings, wherefore no one system could be imposed upon England, and so the New England model was unserviceable. Secondly —most horrible to relate—the Independents, who in polity were carrying New England's banner and were supposed, in the schedule of history, to lead England into imitation of the colonial order, betrayed the sacred cause by yielding to the heresy of toleration. They actually welcomed Roger Williams, whom the leaders of the model had kicked out of Massachusetts so that his nonsense about liberty of conscience would not spoil the administrations of charity.

In other words, New England did not lie, did not falter; it made good everything Winthrop demanded—wonderfully good—and then found that its lesson was rejected by those choice spirits for whom the exertion had been made. By casting out Williams, Anne Hutchinson, and the Antinomians, along with an assortment of Gortonists and Anabaptists, into that cesspool then becoming known as Rhode Island, Winthrop, Dudley, and the clerical leaders showed Oliver Cromwell how he should go about governing England. Instead, he developed the utterly absurd theory that so long as a man made a good soldier in the New Model Army, it did not matter whether he was a Calvinist, an Antinomian, an Arminian, an Anabaptist or even—horror of horrors—a Socininan! Year after year, as the circus tours this country, crowds

howl with laughter, no matter how many times they have seen the stunt, at the bustle that walks by itself: the clown comes out dressed in a large skirt with a bustle behind; he turns sharply to the left, and the bustle continues blindly and obstinately straight ahead, on the original course. It is funny in a circus, but not in history. There is nothing but tragedy in the realization that one was in the main path of events, and now is sidetracked and disregarded. One is always able, of course, to stand firm on his first resolution, and to condemn the clown of history for taking the wrong turning: yet this is a desolating sort of stoicism, because it always carries with it the recognition that history will never come back to the predicted path, and that with one's own demise, righteousness must die out of the world.

The most humiliating element in the experience was the way the English brethren turned upon the colonials for precisely their greatest achievement. It must have seemed, for those who came with Winthrop in 1630 and who remembered the clarity and brilliance with which he set forth the conditions of their errand, that the world was turned upside down and inside out when, in June 1645, thirteen leading Independent divines—such men as Goodwin, Owen, Nye, Burroughs, formerly friends and allies of Hooker and Davenport, men who might easily have come to New England and helped extirpate heretics—wrote the General Court that the colony's law banishing Anabaptists was an embarrassment to the Independent cause in England. Opponents were declaring, said these worthies, "that persons of our way, principall and spirit cannot beare with Dissentors from them, but Doe correct, fine, imprison and banish them wherever they have power soe to Doe."

There were indeed people in England who admired the severities of Massachusetts, but we assure you, said the Independents, these "are utterly your enemyes and Doe seeke your extirpation from the face of the earth: those who now in power are your friends are quite otherwise minded, and doe professe they are much offended with your proceedings." Thus early commenced that chronic weakness in the foreign policy of Americans, an inability to recognize who in truth constitute their best friends abroad.

We have lately accustomed ourselves to the fact that there does exist a mentality which will take advantage of the liberties allowed by society in order to conspire for the ultimate suppression of those same privileges. The government of Charles I and Archbishop Laud had not, where that danger was concerned, been liberal, but it had been conspicuously inefficient; hence, it did not liquidate the Puritans (although it made halfhearted efforts), nor did it herd them into prison camps. Instead, it generously, even lavishly, gave a group of them a charter to Massachusetts Bay, and obligingly left out the standard clause requiring that the document remain in London, that the grantees keep their office within reach of Whitehall. Winthrop's revolutionaries availed themselves of this liberty to get the charter overseas, and thus to set up a regime dedicated to the worship of God in the manner they desired —which meant allowing nobody else to worship any other way, especially adherents of Laud and King Charles. All this was perfectly logical and consistent. But what happened to the thought processes of their fellows in England made no sense whatsoever. Out of the New Model Army came the fantastic notion that a party struggling for power should proclaim that, once it captured the state, it would recognize the right of dissenters to disagree and to have their own worship, to hold their own opinions. Oliver Cromwell was so far gone in this idiocy as to become a dictator, in order to impose toleration by force! Amid this shambles, the errand of New England collapsed. There was nobody left at headquarters to whom reports could be sent.

Many a man has done a brave deed, been hailed as a public hero, had honors and ticker tape heaped upon him—and then had to live, day after day, in the ordinary routine, eating breakfast and brushing his teeth, in what seems protracted anticlimax. A couple may win their way to each other across insuperable obstacles, elope in a blaze of passion and glory—and then have to learn that life is a matter of buying the groceries and getting the laundry done. This sense of the meaning having gone out of life, that all adventures are over, that no great days and no heroism lie ahead, is particularly galling when it falls upon a son whose father once was the public hero or the great lover. He has to put up with the daily routine without ever having known at first hand the thrill of danger or the ecstasy of passion. True, he has his own hardships—clearing rocky pastures, hauling in the cod during a storm, fighting Indians in a swamp—but what are these compared with the magnificence of leading an exodus of saints to found a city on a hill, for the eyes of all the world to behold? He might wage a stout fight against the Indians, and one out of ten of his fellows might perish in the struggle, but the world was no longer interested. He would be reduced to writing accounts of himself and scheming to get a publisher in London, in a desperate effort to tell a heedless world, "Look, I exist!"

His greatest difficulty would be not the stones, storms, and Indians, but the problem of his identity. In something of this sort, I should like to suggest, consists the anxiety and torment that inform productions of the late seventeenth and early eighteenth centuries— and should I say, some thereafter? It appears most clearly in *Magnalia Christi Americana,* the work of that soul most tortured by the problem, Cotton Mather: "I write the Wonders of the Christian Religion, flying from the Depravations of Europe, to the American Strand." Thus he proudly begins, and at once trips over the acknowledgment that the founders had not simply fled from depraved Europe but had intended to redeem it. And so the book is full of lamentations over the declension of the children, who appear, page after page, in contrast to their mighty progenitors, about as profligate a lot as ever squandered a great inheritance.

And yet, the *Magnalia* is not an abject book; neither are the election sermons abject, nor is the inventory of sins offered by the synod of 1679. There is bewilderment, confusion, chagrin, but there is no surrender. A task has been assigned upon which the populace are in fact intensely engaged. But they are not sure any more for just whom they are working; they know they are moving, but they do not know where they are going. They seem still to be on an errand, but if they are no longer inferiors sent by the superior forces of the Reformation, to whom they should report, then their errand must be wholly of the second sort, something with a purpose and an intention sufficient unto itself. If so, what is it? If it be not the due form of government, civil and ecclesiastical, that they brought into being, how otherwise can it be described?

The literature of self-condemnation must be read for meanings far below the surface, for meanings of which, we may be so rash as to surmise, the authors were not fully conscious, but by which they were troubled and goaded. They looked in vain to history for an explanation of themselves; more and more it appeared that the meaning was not to be found in theology, even with the help of the covenantal dialectic. Thereupon, these citizens found that they had no other place to search but within themselves—even though, at first sight, that repository appeared to be nothing but a sink of iniquity. Their errand having failed in the first sense of the term, they were left with the second, and required to fill it with meaning by themselves and out of themselves. Having failed to rivet the eyes of the world upon their city on the hill, they were left alone with America.

HISTORIOGRAPHICAL NOTE

What, then, were the major distinguishing characteristics of New England Puritanism, as twentieth-century American historians have interpreted them? Writing in the 1920's as a liberal and Progressive, Vernon L. Parrington synthesized many criticisms of Puritan thought and society into a full scale indictment of the Massachusetts Bay experiment. Parrington believed Puritanism to have been inherently antithetical to the more religiously tolerant and politically democratic society that had begun to emerge in the

English colonies by the end of the Colonial period. "Later critics of Puritanism," he wrote, "discover in the theocratic experiment of Massachusetts Bay a preposterous attempt to turn back the pages of history." Earlier historians writing in the decades preceding the publication of the monumental *Main Currents in American Thought* paved the way for Parrington's eloquent attack on Puritanism. Especially important were a trio of latter-day descendants of that great neo-Puritan, John Adams. Brooks Adams (*The Emancipation of Massachusetts*), Charles Francis Adams (*Three Episodes in Massachusetts History*), and James Truslow Adams (*The Founding of New England*) all anticipated, in varying degrees, Parrington's influential critique of the Puritans as bigoted, narrow-minded, conformist, tyrannical, humorless fanatics, intent on imposing an arbitrary scheme of theocratic and oligarchical control upon the helpless majority of Massachusetts Bay settlers. Charles Francis Adams, for example, called the early years of Puritan settlement "the theologico-glacial period of Massachusetts," a geological simile favored also by James Truslow Adams, who shared Charles Francis's antipathy to Puritanism but believed that Puritan social beliefs and theology operated like a set of ideological masks behind which were hidden the aspirations of the New England *bourgeoisie* for wealth and power. The attack on early New England Puritanism reached its apex during the 1920's, with the publication of Parrington's *Main Currents* and J. T. Adams's *Founding of New England*, the witty cannonades of H. L. Mencken and the polemics of a major literary critic, Van Wyck Brooks. In *The Wine of the Puritans,* Brooks accused the early New England Congregationalists of having been the original source of subsequent anti-aesthetic, sexually repressed, prohibitionist, and fundamentalist tendencies within American culture. These critics all shared the conviction that in the Massachusetts Bay Puritan experience could be found the roots not only of contemporary American religious intolerance, sexual prudery, and social priggishness but of *all* aspects of American culture that offended them.

Starting in the 1920's, however, other American scholars began to reevaluate the Puritan contribution to American life, questioning almost all the criticisms leveled by Mencken, Parrington, Brooks, and others against the early New England settlers. These "revisionists" of previously held conceptions concerning American Puritanism, unlike most critics of Puritanism, carefully analyzed the basic sources for study of the period—sermons, diaries, letters, court and town records among them—turning out in the process a number of valuable monographs on the Puritan experience. The most important of these "revisionists," Perry Miller, examined the entire body of Puritan thought in a series of notable works, most extensively in two volumes on *The New England Mind,* in which, after studying the basic outlines of New England Congregationalist theology, he traced the impact of their seventeenth-century experiences in the New World on original Puritan beliefs. Miller's conclusions concerning the changes in

purpose wrought by their "errand into the wilderness" are summarized in
the selection included in this chapter.

In the period between the two world wars, a second major "revisionist"
interpreter of Puritanism, Samuel Eliot Morison, penned several gracefully
drawn portraits of Puritan life and culture in New England which changed
many previously held assumptions concerning the social and cultural life
of the Massachusetts Bay colony. In a series of works—including his three-
volume *History of Harvard College* during the colonial period, his sketches
of the *Builders of the Bay Colony,* and his study of the *Puritan Pronaos
(The Intellectual Life of Colonial New England)*—Morison recreated in
stunning outline the vigorous society and culture of the early Puritan
settlers, reminding his readers that if the Puritans were primarily spiritual
reformers, they were also Englishmen of the Elizabethan age, thoroughly
familiar with contemporary English intellectual life and addicted to many
of its social practices. As Richard Schlatter observed in a penetrating recent review of Puritan historiography, "Morison's Puritans are not only
believable humans who loved good beer and gay clothing: they were admirable men and women who preserved in the midst of the wilderness a passion for learning and education unique in modern history." The influence
of Morison's scholarly labors, as well as more recent works by students of
Puritan culture, can be seen in the lively and cogent essay by Carl Degler,
drawn from that author's interpretive volume on American history, *Out of
Our Past.*

Perry Miller's studies of New England theology had challenged James
Truslow Adams's contention that Puritan religious beliefs could be understood primarily as the rationale of ambitious theocrats anxious to maintain
their social control, and Samuel Eliot Morison objected vehemently to the
personification of Puritan society and culture as either "narrow" or "prud-
ish." A third historian, Edmund S. Morgan, a Harvard student of Miller
and Morison, questioned the traditional *political* analysis made by Parrington and most earlier historians, which viewed Massachusetts Bay Puritanism
as a tyranically ruled commonwealth dominated by a small group of
oligarchs. Morgan tried to demonstrate that John Winthrop and his fellow
members of the Massachusetts Bay Company did not behave nearly as
arbitrarily as they could have in the founding of the colony, and that the
Massachusetts Bay government under Winthrop and his associates willingly
extended the privileges of freemanship to all settlers who could meet the
requirements for church membership and property holding. Indeed, he
argued that the leaders of the colony were far from a rigid oligarchy and
made numerous concessions, as practical statesmen, to the wishes of the
majority of settlers in order to govern (as far as possible) with their consent.

In recent decades, many American historians have written on aspects
of New England Puritanism from this "revisionist" perspective, although it
would be inaccurate to treat these writers as members of a single historical

"school." Primarily, they share a common set of attitudes toward New England Puritanism: sympathy for the high religious motives that brought the Puritans to American shores, awareness of the difficulties faced by the Puritans in constructing and maintaining a political order and a society which could best fulfill their original religious motives for immigrating, and recognition of the profound impact that the American environment had on the sons and grandsons of the Puritan founders. The "revisionists" do not consider the Puritans *alien* to the subsequent American development of political democracy and religious tolerance as did Parrington; they view them instead as the first major case of acculturation in American history, of an immigrant group *adapting* Old World ideals to the changed circumstances of the New World. For example Daniel J. Boorstin, in his recent work, *The Americans—The Colonial Experience,* called the Puritans "practical" forebears of all those aspects of national character and institutions that Parrington considered distinctively "American." Boorstin followed Perry Miller in asserting that the Puritans, as other settlers who came to terms with the New World, were forced to abandon many of their original ambitions and much of their ideology: "A new civilization was being born less out of plans and purposes than out of the unsettlement which the New World brought to the ways of the Old." Do the "revisionist" studies of Puritan society and culture, however, really invalidate the conclusions of earlier commentators like Parrington and Brooks? Have the "revisionists" relied solely in their works on objective examination of new evidence and on more perceptive interpretation of familiar sources, *or* does their commitment to portraying Puritanism in its most favorable light sometimes cloud their historical judgment? The student must evaluate this question for himself, after reading carefully the documentary and historical selections in the chapter. Few of the recent interpreters of the Puritan experience— Miller, Morison, Morgan, and Degler among them—have feigned indifference toward their subject. For the most part, these historians are in sympathy with the basic features of Puritan life as they view it, and their writings offer a skillful and well-argued *defense* of Puritanism based on thorough scholarship.

3. The Transit of Mind: Belief and Its Objects in Eighteenth-Century America

INTRODUCTION

The world has paid close attention to the distinctly American pattern of ideas that emerged from the new society founded by those Puritans on the *Arbella* who heard their Chief Magistrate John Winthrop proclaim their community "as a Citie upon a Hill." During the colonial era, the beliefs and concepts that evolved reflected the peculiar impact of New World conditions on those who settled here. Men as distinct as Cotton Mather, Thomas Jefferson, Jonathan Edwards, and Benjamin Franklin all accepted the premise that the American experience, an experience each defined in startlingly different terms, was unique in world history. Whether as devout protagonists in a divine morality play or as restrained seekers after a rational life, many colonials felt themselves possessed of a special calling whose nature they strained constantly to interpret correctly.

Values changed with each generation. The Non-Separatist founders of a Christian commonwealth bred sons and grandsons more obsessed with redeeming individual sinners than with halting the decline of Puritan communalism. By the middle of the eighteenth century, fathers who had been reared on a modified but still stringent Calvinist doctrine found their offspring more responsive to rationalist and secular teachings. Skepticism and faith, inquiry and belief came to coexist uneasily within the tolerant and highly mobile context of American society. The sons of ministers often found careers as tradesmen and artisans, while their sons in turn might be drawn into a growing class of colonial lawyers. Traditionalist churchmen saw clear evidence of spiritual decline in this movement from religious to secular objects of intellectual concern and personal vocation. Historians have viewed the process more dispassionately, attempting to understand the shifting objects of belief in a maturing society.

I. EARLY INTERPRETATIONS

The following excerpt from Charles A. Beard's and Mary Beard's *Rise of American Civilization* illustrates a dominant belief among American historians of the Beards' generation and of earlier ones: colonial American civilization at the time of the Revolution was a provincial, derivative society, largely English in its ideologies, habits, and class assumptions, with little of the "Americanness" detected by more recent historians.

But many other early historians found specifically American qualities in the colonial experience. Such historians viewed the Great Awakening as more than simply an incident in the progress of evangelical Protestantism within the English colonies. These commentators, who are represented here by the selection by Charles H. Maxson, saw the Awakening as the intellectual forerunner of revolutionary political ideals and emphasized the revival's general educational and cultural influence. In older American history textbooks Maxson's work served as a major source for general discussions of the Awakening.

Of the three giants among American historians in the first three decades of the twentieth century—Frederick Jackson Turner, Charles A. Beard, and Carl Lotus Becker—Becker has remained the most neglected, even though his intellectual range probably exceeded that of both his distinguished contemporaries. In the selection that follows, Becker analyzes the evolution of American political thought during the Revolutionary era from its Lockean antecedents.

CHARLES A. BEARD
AND
MARY BEARD

PROVINCIAL AMERICA

The culture of the colonial period— its social and religious life, its intellectual and æsthetic interests, its apparatus for the diffusion of knowledge and artistic appreciation—was subject to the conditions common to all provincial civilizations. In its origins it was derivative: the whole conventional heritage, from its noblest ideals to its grossest vulgarities, was European, in a strict sense, English. Like the culture of every other age, it was contingent upon the prevailing economic order, the modes of securing a livelihood, the

disposition of classes, the accumulation of riches, the development of patronage and leisure, the concentration of population, and the diversification of practical experience. Of necessity also it was bent to the laws of change, affected in every sphere by transformations in the character and weight of economic classes, the growth of secular concerns, and the impact of fresh currents of opinion from abroad.

. . .

The essential forms of colonial culture, as we have said, were English in their origins. Eminent advocates for the Scotch, Irish, Dutch, Swiss, Welsh, Swedes, and Jews have entered pleas against this ruling in many a portly volume and have placed upon the record facts and arguments worthy of calm review. Some have gone far in their racial claims. One stout partisan has traced the political institutions of America back to Holland through the

Reprinted from Charles A. Beard and Mary R. Beard, THE RISE OF AMERICAN CIVILIZATION *(New York: The Macmillan Company, 1927), I, 122, 124–26, by permission of the publisher.*

migrating Pilgrims. Another has given the American Revolution the appearance of a phase in the long contest between Scot and Englishman. An eager Irishman has compiled from crumbling papers and mossy tombstones a mighty roll of O'Rourkes, O'Donahues, and O'Briens that makes colonial history resemble a glorious page in the tale of Erin's sons.

Nevertheless, when the last word is said for all the diverse elements in provincial life, certain indubitable facts obtrude themselves upon the view like giant boulders on a plain. Beyond question, the overwhelming majority of the white people in the colonies were of English descent; the arrangement of classes was English; the law which held together the whole social order was English in essence, modified, of course, but primarily English; the dominant religious institutions and modes of theology were English adaptations of Christianity; the types of formal education, the amusements, furniture, fashions, art, and domestic codes were all fundamentally English too. The language of bench and bar, pulpit and press, was English. Pamphlets and books of the epoch written in Dutch and German no doubt fill a large space on the library shelf; but in truth they are remarkable, not so much for their bulk, as for their relative insignificance when measured against the huge mountain of declamations and arguments in English that have come down from that provincial age. The list of Scotch and Irish soldiers in the revolutionary army is imposing; still more so is the register of Englishmen. Presbyterians of Pennsylvania fought well under Washington; the shot that was heard round the world was fired at Concord by a Puritan. Whether for praise, blame, or merriment, colonial America was basically English; it was governed under the auspices of the English ruling classes; its chief channels of communication with Europe ran along English routes.

The prevailing˙ class structure by which the provincial culture of America was so largely conditioned was derived in the main from the mother country. Although it is sometimes imagined, on the basis of schoolbook fictions, that the colonies were local democracies formed on the pure principles of a New World philosophy and founded on substantial economic equality, the facts of the case lend little color to that view. In reality, by the colonizing process, the middle orders of England—landed gentry of the minor rank, merchants, and yeomen—with their psychology and social values were reproduced in a new environment.

At home these classes had carried society forward on the long road from feudalism to the modern age; in America, freed from the immediate pressure of a titled aristocracy and clerical hierarchy, they advanced rapidly ahead of their English contemporaries in the degree of their sovereignty over matters of law, religion, intellect, and æsthetic interest. Every colony had this class heritage developed into a well-articulated scheme of social subordination. It is true that the status of the ruling element was not as plainly marked by legal signs as in the mother country and that the gates of entry were slightly more ajar but its grip upon industry and local politics was no less secure.

CHARLES H. MAXSON

. . . The Great Awakening has sometimes been represented as a tempest of

Reprinted from Charles H. Maxson, THE GREAT AWAKENING IN THE MIDDLE COLONIES (*Chicago*, 1920), *pp. 139–41, 143–44, 148–50.*

ungoverned passions that swept over the colonies, leaving wreckage everywhere in the alienations and divisions in families, neighborhoods, and churches, the undermining of cherished institutions, and a relapse into indifference, debauchery, and irreligion. An impartial study of the period, however, free from partisan and denominational bias, leads to a very different conclusion. It is that thousands and thousands were given by the Great Awakening a new view of life's values, and from this view were derived new energies and new sympathies which gave direction not only to the subsequent career of these thousands but to the development of the whole American people. It was more than wave on wave of excitement; it was a transforming process in the nation's life.

The background of the international revival, of which the Great Awakening was a part, was the decadent civilization of the eighteenth century. The trend of the age was away from religion, away from the ideality, strenuousness, and rigor of a former time. A new period of moral laxity, religious indifference, and philosophic revolt had opened in Europe. These influences were quickly felt in the colonies, for every window was open toward the home lands, but there was little communication of ideas between the colonies. Though the colonies differed greatly from each other in their religious conditions, there were causes of religious decline in all peculiar to colonial life.

What was to be done to stem the tide of irreligion? The word "conservatism" sums up the answer of the majority of the sincerely religious. The conservatives of each denomination revered their own particular creed as the creation of a superior race of men, and therefore as a finality. Several of these denominations were na-tional churches in the Old World. Therefore every reforming movement or spirit of change had to make headway against racial prejudices and veneration of ancestral faith. The customs of the past were invested with sanctity. Leaders sought to quarantine their people from the contagion of change. But the enthusiasm of the fathers could not be reproduced. The religion of the sons was without vitality and power.

Then it was that primitive Christianity sprang up in different parts of the world almost spontaneously, though generally there was an influence traceable to German Pietism. In the new teaching emphasis was not placed upon an inherited and formal profession, or upon the magic efficacy of ceremony, but upon an inner experience with its new passion for the service of God through the service of man. The seat of religion passed back from the head to the heart, and religion became again a force.

The Great Awakening in the Middle Colonies had several distinct sources. One of them was German Pietism. The revival at Germantown in 1722 may be selected somewhat arbitrarily as the date of the beginning of the Great Awakening among the Germans. Most assuredly the ministry of Frelinghuysen was an important source. His first ingathering in 1726 may be selected as the beginning of the Great Awakening among the Dutch. The establishment of the Log College in 1726, followed by the revivals of its early graduates in 1729 and 1732, was the third source, ranking second to none in the history of the Great Awakening in the Middle Colonies. This was the beginning of the revival among the Presbyterians. The Edwards revival of 1734 in its influence on New England men in the Middle Colonies was another source, evidenced by the revival at Newark in

1739. This influence in the Middle Colonies was cumulative, following and strengthening the earlier evangelical influences. The establishment of the Holy Club at Oxford and the coming of the Methodist evangelist to the Middle Colonies in 1739 were the fifth source of the Great Awakening in this section. It was then that the various streams united into a mighty river, a flood of flame, which swept over the country.

The name "Great Awakening" was especially appropriate to the Whitefield revival, which became powerful in the Middle Colonies and the coast region of the far southern provinces, and then in 1740 burst into astonishing flame in New England. A characteristic feature of the evangelical revival in this and in all lands was religious excitement, more intense than at any previous time since the Puritan Revival, and more widely extended than in any other religious movement since the Reformation. Waves of feeling, comparable to that seen in war or financial panic or political crisis, swept from community to community. The same phenomenon had appeared in the earlier Edwards revival, which began at Northampton and spread through western Massachusetts and Connecticut. Accordingly the name "Great Awakening" was applied in New England to these two waves of religious excitement. The subsequent Presbyterian and Baptist revivals in the South, the one beginning at Hanover in 1742 and the other at Sandy Creek in 1755, were in close dependence upon these earlier revivals and were quite as remarkable. Therefore they must be included in the four great revivals of the Great Awakening.

But the name must not be limited to the four most widespread excitements. Other revivals mentioned in the list of distinct sources of the Great Awakening in the Middle Colonies were certainly parts of it. There were many revivals in the Middle Colonies and in other sections, later than the Whitefield revival, which must be included, for they were all parts of the new religious quickening. Some were as late as the surprising outburst at Easthampton, Long Island, in 1764, under the pastorate of Samuel Buell. Recognition must also be given to the early successes of the Methodists before the Revolutionary War. Some of the revivals of the various denominations were quite as phenomenal, though circumscribed in extent, and some were quite as important in their ultimate results as were the four great revivals. The Great Awakening is therefore best defined, not as successive waves of religious excitement, but as an intercolonial evangelical movement, part of the Methodist Revival in the empire and part of the world-wide Evangelical Revival.

• • •

It is sometimes represented that the unprecedented success of the Great Awakening, in the face of bitter opposition and in spite of serious defects in itself, was due to the Calvinistic doctrines preached throughout the colonies. No doubt individual experiences of thousands were molded by the Calvinistic teaching in which they were drilled and by the form of that teaching employed by Whitefield, Tennent, and other leading evangelists. But the successful propagators of the revival in the colonies were not all Calvinists. The Moravians, Lutherans, and Methodists shared in it. When regarded as a world movement the success of the revival is clearly shown not to have been dependent upon any particular form of religious philosophy.

A more insistent question than creed

was polity. Church government, as well as civil government, has its constitutional questions, and these were hotly debated in the period of the Great Awakening. The conservatives were in the majority in the various denominations. The evangelicals were compelled to insist on the right of the individual to a wider liberty than the conservatives were disposed to grant him. The battle cry of the conservatives was therefore "order and discipline." Of the evangelicals it was "the right of conscience." They made a distinction between essential and circumstantial rules. The position of the evangelicals was strikingly similar to that of the Americans in their debate with England after the French and Indian War, for they sought to establish constitutional limitations upon the authority of rulers.

. . .

Humanitarian enterprises of many kinds, besides missionary endeavor, owe their inception to the new social consciousness that came with the Great Awakening. Sympathies were profoundly stirred. The people were awakened to a new interest in the orphan, the negro, the Indian, and the unfortunate whether at their doors or in the most distant provinces. The first word against slavery was spoken by men straight from the home of Pietism in Germany. The antislavery movement in New England was originated by Hopkins, one of the great evangelical leaders. In the South the New Side Presbyterians and the Baptists at an early day opposed slavery. The Methodist discipline took strong ground against the system. Much has been said of Whitefield's owning slaves as an endowment for the orphan house, but not enough of his clarion call, heard the whole length of the colonies, de-

manding for the slave humane treatment and Christian training. The mission to the African in America grew out of the Great Awakening and measurably prepared the negro for the enjoyment of liberty.

The return to the emotional experience of Paul, the doctrine of Luther, and the rigor of John Cotton, with the attendant burst of song and the practical demonstration of the inherent kindliness of the movement, gradually won over nearly every important branch of the Protestant church in America, with one significant exception. The Anglican church in the colonies spurned the aid of Whitefield and impotently pronounced suspension upon him. Wesley's preachers were equally disowned. This church became the last refuge of the conservatives. The Great Awakening built up popular denominations, each with a numerous following of earnest, enthusiastic members. These denominations commanded the respect of the whole American people, even of the irreligious. But the ancient national church of the English people fell into contempt. The Presbyterians and the Congregationalists united in an annual convention to combat what were regarded as the encroachments of the Anglican church, and particularly to prevent the appointment of an American bishop. This was one of the earliest examples of an intercolonial combination to bring pressure to bear upon the English ministry. The Great Awakening was a democratic religious movement, but the Anglican church became more and more a small aristocratic body, centering in an official class. The clergy therefore sought the advancement of their interests by intrigue with the authorities in England. They were suspected by the people of being the emissaries of a foreign government. They shared its fortunes.

Thus the revival united with other influences to subvert the Church of England in the colonies.

There is an intimate connection between the American Revolution and the intercolonial religious ferment which preceded it. The policy of the conservatives was divisive and isolating, but the evangelicals almost always advocated union and friendly co-operation. The revival spirit was always the foe of denominational and racial prejudices. The Great Awakening widened the horizon of the people, for it was the first intellectual movement in which all the colonies participated. Denominations that were aggressively evangelistic ignored provincial boundaries and built up constituencies which were intercolonial in character. The revival led to a very considerable movement of population. This helped create a common American spirit. The Anglican church was one of the ties uniting the colonies with the mother country. The combination against that church and the winning of a large part of its nominal membership weakened that tie. The community of feeling which the revival cultivated in the several Calvinistic bodies, the actual combination of some of them against the English church, and the fear of invasion by the English government of their religious liberties were evidences of a spiritual union of the colonies which was prophetic of a national union. In just the same way a century later the disruption of the great popular denominations upon a sectional question was prophetic of the Civil War. The Great Awakening prepared the way for the Revolutionary War. The denominations, like the Presbyterian and the Baptist, which were built up by the revival took almost unanimously the patriot side. It was their meeting-houses that were burned as nests of rebellion and their pastors that were hunted as instigators of treason.

The separation of church and state was an application of the principles of the Great Awakening and the Revolution. The democratic principles of both were contrary to the special privileges of established churches. The growth of great bodies which did not possess these privileges, like the Presbyterian and Baptist denominations, raised up powerful organizations which did not rest until every vestige of an establishment was erased from the statute books. This was the course in Virginia and other southern provinces. It was so in New York, where a law, passed by dissenters in their own interest, had been interpreted as the establishment of the Church of England in parts of the province. The same fate befell the churches of the standing order in Massachusetts and Connecticut.

CARL LOTUS BECKER

HISTORICAL ANTECEDENTS OF THE
DECLARATION: THE NATURAL
RIGHTS PHILOSOPHY

Whether the political philosophy of the Declaration of Independence is "true" or "false" has been much discussed. In the late eighteenth century it was widely accepted as a commonplace. At a later time, in 1822, John Adams made this a ground for detracting from the significance of Jefferson's share in the authorship of the famous document. He was perhaps a little irritated by the laudation which Fourth of July orators were lavishing on his friend, and wished to remind his countrymen that others had had a hand in

Reprinted from Carl Lotus Becker, THE DEC-
LARATION OF INDEPENDENCE *(New York: Alfred
A. Knopf, Inc., 1942), pp. 24–28, 71–79, by permission of the publisher.*

the affair. "There is not an idea in it," he wrote to Pickering, "but what had been hackneyed in Congress for two years before." This is substantially true; but as a criticism, if it was intended as such, it is wholly irrelevant, since the strength of the Declaration was precisely that it said what everyone was thinking. Nothing could have been more futile than an attempt to justify a revolution on principles which no one had ever heard of before.

In replying to Adams' strictures, Jefferson had only to state this simple fact.

Pickering's observations, and Mr. Adams' in addition, that it contained no new ideas, that it is a commonplace compilation, its sentiments hacknied in Congress for two years before . . . may all be true. Of that I am not to be the judge. Richard H. Lee charged it as copied from Locke's treatise on Government. . . . I know only that I turned to neither book nor pamphlet while writing it. I did not consider it as any part of my charge to invent new ideas altogether and to offer no sentiment which had ever been expressed before.

In writing to Lee, in 1825, Jefferson said again that he only attempted to express the ideas of the Whigs, who all thought alike on the subject. The essential thing was

Not to find our new principles, or new arguments, never before thought of, not merely to say things which had never been said before; but to place before mankind the common sense of the subject, in terms so plain and firm as to command their assent. . . . Neither aiming at originality of principles or sentiments, nor yet copied from any particular and previous writing, it was intended to be an expression of the American mind. . . . All its authority rests then on the harmonizing sentiments of the day, whether expressed in conversation, in letters, printed essays, or the elementary books of public right, as Aristotle, Cicero, Locke, Sidney, etc.

Not all Americans, it is true, would have accepted the philosophy of the Declaration, just as Jefferson phrased it, without qualification, as the 'common sense of the subject'; but one may say that the premises of this philosophy, the underlying preconceptions from which it is derived, were commonly taken for granted. That there is a 'natural order' of things in the world, cleverly and expertly designed by God for the guidance of mankind; that the 'laws' of this natural order may be discovered by human reason; that these laws so discovered furnish a reliable and immutable standard for testing the ideas, the conduct, and the institutions of men—these were the accepted premises, the preconceptions, of most eighteenth century thinking, not only in America but also in England and France. They were, as Jefferson says, the 'sentiments of the day, whether expressed in conversation, in letters, printed essays, or the elementary books of public right.' Where Jefferson got his ideas is hardly so much a question as where he could have got away from them.

Since these sentiments of the day were common in France, and were most copiously, and perhaps most logically, expressed there, it has sometimes been thought that Jefferson and his American contemporaries must have borrowed their ideas from French writers, must have been 'influenced' by them, for example by Rousseau. But it does not appear that Jefferson, or any American, read many French books. So far as the 'Fathers' were, before 1776, directly influenced by particular writers, the writers were English, and notably Locke. Most Americans had absorbed Locke's works as a kind of political gospel; and the Declaration, in its form, in its phraseology, follows closely certain sentences in Locke's second treatise on government. This is interesting, but it does not tell us why Jefferson, having read Locke's treatise, was so taken with it that he read it again, and still again, so that afterwards its very phrases reappear in his own writing. Jefferson doubtless read Filmer as well as Locke; but the phrases of Filmer, happily, do not appear in the Declaration. Generally speaking, men are influenced by books which clarify their own thought, which express their own notions well, or which suggest to them ideas which their minds are already predisposed to accept. If Jefferson had read Rousseau's *Social Contract* we may be sure he would have been strongly impressed by it. What has to be explained is why the best minds of the eighteenth century were so ready to be impressed by Locke's treatise on civil government and by Rousseau's *Social Contract*. What we have to seek is the origin of those common underlying preconceptions that made the minds of many men, in different countries, run along the same track in their political thinking.

. . .

The sum and substance of Locke's elaborate enquiry into the origin and character of government is this: since reason is the only sure guide which God has given to men, reason is the only foundation of just government; and so I ask, not what authority any government has in fact, but what authority it ought in reason to have; and I answer that it ought to have the authority which reasonable men, living together in a community, considering the rational interests of each and all, might be disposed to submit to willingly; and I say further that unless it is to be assumed that any existing government has of right whatever authority it exercises in fact, then there is no way of determining whether the au-

thority which it exercises in fact is an authority which it exercises of right, except by determining what authority it ought in reason to have. Stripped of its decorative phrases, of its philosophy of 'Nature' and 'Nature's God' and the 'Universal Order,' the question which Locke asked was a simple one: 'I desire to know what kind of government that is . . . where one man . . . may do to all his subjects whatever he pleases, without the least liberty to any one to question or control those who execute his pleasure?' This, generally speaking, was what the eighteenth century desired to know. The answer which it gave to that question seemed self-evident: Such a government is a bad government; since governments exist for men, not men for governments, all governments derive their just powers from the consent of the governed.

If the philosophy of Locke seemed to Jefferson and his compatriots just 'the common sense of the matter,' it was not because Locke's argument was so lucid and cogent that it could be neither misunderstood nor refuted. Locke's argument is not particularly cogent unless you accept his assumptions as proved, nor lucid until you restate it to suit yourself; on the contrary, it is lumbering, involved, obscured by innumerable and conflicting qualifications—a dreary devil of an argument staggering from assumption posited as premise to conclusion implicit in the assumption. It was Locke's conclusion that seemed to the colonists sheer common sense, needing no argument at all. Locke did not need to convince the colonists because they were already convinced; and they were already convinced because they had long been living under governments which did, in a rough and ready way, conform to the kind of government for which Locke furnished a reasoned foundation. The colonists had never in fact lived under a government where 'one man . . . may do to all his subjects whatever he pleases.' They were accustomed to living under governments which proceeded, year by year, on a tacitly assumed compact between rulers and ruled, and which were in fact very largely dependent upon 'the consent of the governed.' How should the colonists not accept a philosophy, however clumsily argued, which assured them that their own governments, with which they were well content, were just the kind that God had designed men by nature to have!

The general philosophy which lifted this common sense conclusion to the level of a cosmic law, the colonists therefore accepted, during the course of the eighteenth century, without difficulty, almost unconsciously. That human conduct and institutions should conform to the will of God was an old story, scarcely to be questioned by people whose ancestors were celebrated, in so many instances, for having left Europe precisely in order to live by God's law. Living by God's law, as it turned out, was much the same as living according to "the strong bent of their spirits." The strong bent of their spirits, and therefore God's law, had varied a good deal according to the locality, in respect to religion more especially; but so far as one could judge at this late enlightened date, God had showered his blessings indifferently upon all alike—Anglicans and Puritans, Congregationalists and Presbyterians, Catholics, Baptists, Shakers and Mennonites, New Lights and Old Lights. Even Quakers, once thought necessary to be hanged as pestilent blasphemers and deniers of God's will, now possessed a rich province in peace and content. Many chosen peoples had so long followed God's law by relying upon their own wits, without thereby running into destruction, that experience seemed to confirm the assertion that nature was the most reliable revelation of God's will, and human reason the surest interpreter of nature.

The channels through which the philosophy of Nature and Natural Law made its way in the colonies in the eighteenth century were many. A good number of Americans were educated at British universities, where the doctrines of Newton and Locke were commonplaces; while those who were educated at Princeton, Yale, or Harvard could read, if they would, these authors in the original, or become familiar with their ideas through books of exposition. The complete works of both Locke and Newton were in the Harvard library at least as early as 1773. Locke's works were listed in the Princeton catalogue of 1760. As early as 1755 the Yale library contained Newton's *Principia* and Locke's *Essay;* and before 1776 it contained the works of Locke, Newton, and Descartes, besides two popular expositions of the Newtonian philosophy. The revolutionary leaders do not often refer to the scientific or philosophical writings of either Newton or Locke, although an occasional reference to Locke's *Essay* is to be found; but the political writings of Locke, Sidney, and Milton are frequently mentioned with respect and reverence. Many men might have echoed the sentiment expressed by Jonathan Mayhew in 1766:

Having been initiated, in youth, in the doctrines of civil liberty, as they were taught by such men as Plato, Demosthenes, Cicero and other renowned persons among the ancients; and such as Sidney and Milton, Locke and Hoadley, among the moderns, I liked them; they seemed rational.

And Josiah Quincy expressed the common idea of his compatriots when, in

1774, he wrote into his will these words:

I give to my son, when he shall arrive at the age of 15 years, Algernon Sidney's Works, John Locke's Works, Lord Bacon's Works, Gordon's Tacitus, and Cato's Letters. May the spirit of Liberty rest upon him.

For the general reader, the political philosophy of the eighteenth century was expounded from an early date in pamphlet and newspaper by many a Brutus, Cato, or Popliocola. An important, but less noticed, channel through which the fundamental ideas of that philosophy—God, Nature, Reason— were made familiar to the average man, was the church. Both in England and America preachers and theologians laid firm hold of the Newtonian conception of the universe as an effective weapon against infidelity. Dr. Richard Bentley studied Newton in order to preach a 'Confusion of Atheism,' deriving a proof of Divine Providence from the physical construction of the universe as demonstrated by that 'divine theorist,' Sir Isaac Newton. What a powerful support to Revelation (and to Revolution) was that famous argument from design! The sermons of the century are filled with it—proving the existence and the goodness of God from the intelligence which the delicately adjusted mechanism of nature everywhere exhibited.

In 1750 there was published at Boston a book of Twenty Sermons, delivered in the Parish Church at Charleston, South Carolina, by the Reverend Samuel Quincy. In these sermons we find the Nature philosophy fully elaborated.

For a right knowledge of God by the Light of Nature, displays his several amiable Perfections; acquaints us with the Relation he stands in to us, and the Obligations we owe to him. . . . It teaches us that our greatest Interest and Happiness consists in loving and fearing God, and in doing his Will; that to imitate his moral Perfections in our whole Behaviour, is acting up to the Dignity of our Natures, and that he has endowed us with Reason and Understanding (Faculties which the Brutes have not) on purpose to contemplate his Beauty and Glory, and to keep our inferior Appetites in due Subjection to his Laws, written in our hearts.

In his famous election sermon of 1754, Jonathan Mayhew uses this philosophy, without the formulae, for deriving the authority of government. Government, he says,

is both the ordinance of God, and the ordinance of man: of God, in respect to his original plan, and universal Providence; of man, as it is more immediately the result of human prudence, wisdom and concert.

In later Massachusetts election sermons, from 1768 to 1773, we find both the philosophy and the formulae; the three concepts of God, Nature, and Reason, which Samuel Quincy made the foundation of religion, are there made the foundation of politics and government as well. And so there crept into the mind of the average man this conception of Natural Law to confirm his faith in the majesty of God while destroying his faith in the majesty of Kings.

English writers in the nineteenth century, perhaps somewhat blinded by British prejudice against the French Revolution and all its works, complacently took it for granted that the political philosophy of Nature and natural rights upon which the Revolution was founded, being particularly vicious must be peculiarly French; from which it followed, doubtless as the night the day, that the Americans, having also embraced this philosophy, must have been corrupted by French influence. The truth is that the philosophy of Nature, in its broader aspects and in its particular applications, was thoroughly English. English literature of the seventeenth and eighteenth centuries is steeped in this philosophy. The Americans did not borrow it, they inherited it. The lineage is direct: Jefferson copied Locke and Locke quoted Hooker. In political theory and in political practice the American Revolution drew its inspiration from the parliamentary struggle of the seventeenth

century. The philosophy of the Declaration was not taken from the French. It was not even new; but good old English doctrine newly formulated to meet a present emergency. In 1776 it was commonplace doctrine, everywhere to be met with, as Jefferson said, "whether expressed in conversation, in letters, printed essays, or the elementary books of public right." And in sermons also, he might have added. But it may be that Jefferson was not very familiar with sermons.

II. DOCUMENTS

1. Varieties of Religious Experience

After long and bitter dispute with his congregation, Jonathan Edwards, the leading figure in the Great Awakening in New England, was forced to leave his Northampton, Massachusetts parish. Before departing, Edwards preached one of the most powerful sermons ever delivered in America, a sermon that enunciated succinctly the principles of the religious revival. A selection from this sermon follows, along with a letter from Edwards to a fellow minister detailing his side of the dispute with his congregation. A careful reading of this document will reveal certain changes then taking place that bear not only on the religious issues in dispute but on the entire question of political authority. According to Edwards, the parishioners seemed reluctant to submit to dictation from above in almost any form. Finally, the selection from Jonathan Mayhew's famous "Discourse Concerning Unlimited Submission . . ." presents a defense of resistance to tyranny based on scriptural justifications. In writings and sermons such as the famous Mayhew address can be found the pivotal link between the seventeenth-century Puritan approach to unwanted religious authority and the eighteenth-century Lockean rationale that treated in secular terms the problem of political authority in the English experience.

JONATHAN EDWARDS

The improvement I would make of the things which have been observed,

Reprinted from Jonathan Edwards, "Farewell Sermon," in Clarence H. Faust and Thomas H. Johnson, eds., JONATHAN EDWARDS: REPRESENTATIVE SELECTIONS (New York, 1935), pp. 186–203.

is to lead the people here present, who have been under my pastoral care, to some reflections, and to give them some advice, suitable to our present circumstances; relating to what has been lately done, in order to our being separated, as to the relation we have heretofore stood in one to another; but expecting to meet each other before the great tribunal at the day of judgment.

The deep and serious consideration of that our future most solemn meeting, is certainly most suitable at such a time as this; there having so lately been that done, which, in all probability, will (as to the relation we have heretofore stood in) be followed with an everlasting separation.

How often have we met together in the house of God, in this relation? How often have I spoken to you, instructed, counselled, warned, directed and fed you, and administered ordinances among you, as the people which were committed to my care, and whose precious souls I had the charge of? But in all probability, this never will be again.

The prophet Jeremiah, (chap. xxv. 3.) puts the people in mind how long he had laboured among them in the work of the ministry; *From the thirteenth year of Josiah, the son of Amon, king of Judah, even unto this day, (that is, the three and twentieth year), the word of the Lord came unto me, and I have spoken unto you, rising early and speaking.* I am not about to compare myself with the prophet Jeremiah; but in this respect I can say as he did, that *I have spoken the word of God to you, unto the three and twentieth year, rising early and speaking.* It was three and twenty years, the 15th day of last February, since I have laboured in the work of the ministry, in the relation of a pastor to this church and congregation. And though my strength has been weakness, having always laboured under great infirmity of body, beside my insufficiency for so great a charge, in other respects, yet I have not spared my feeble strength, but have exerted it for the good of your souls. I can appeal to you, as the apostle does to his hearers, Gal. iv. 13. *Ye know*

how through infirmity of the flesh, I preached the Gospel unto you. I have spent the prime of my life and strength, in labours for your eternal welfare. You are my witnesses, that what strength I have had I have not neglected in idleness, nor laid out in prosecuting worldly schemes, and managing temporal affairs, for the advancement of my outward estate, and aggrandizing myself and family; but have given myself to the work of the ministry, labouring in it night and day, rising early and applying myself to this great business to which Christ appointed me. I have found the work of the ministry among you to be a great work indeed, a work of exceeding care, labour and difficulty: many have been the heavy burdens that I have borne in it, which my strength has been very unequal to. GOD called me to bear these burdens, and I bless his name, that he has so supported me as to keep me from sinking under them, and that his power herein has been manifested in my weakness; so that although I have often been troubled on every side, yet I have not been distressed; perplexed, but not in despair; cast down, but not destroyed.

But now I have reason to think, my work is finished which I had to do as your minister: you have publicly rejected me, and my opportunities cease.

How highly therefore does it now become us, to consider of that time when we must meet one another before the chief Shepherd? When I must give an account of my stewardship, of the service I have done *for,* and the reception and treatment I have had *among,* the people he sent me to: and you must give an account of your own conduct towards me, and the improvement you have made of these *three and twenty years* of my ministry. For then both you and I must appear together, and we both must give an account, in order to an infallible, righteous and eternal, sentence to be passed upon us, by him who will judge us, with respect to all that we have said or done in our meetings here, all our conduct one towards another, in the house of God and elsewhere, on sabbath-days and on other days; who will try our hearts, and manifest our thoughts, and the principles and frames of our minds, will judge us with respect to all the controversies which have subsisted between us, with the strictest impartiality, and will examine our treatment of each other in those controversies: there is nothing covered, that shall not be revealed, nor hid, which shall not be known; all will be examined in the searching, penetrating light of God's omniscience and glory, and by him whose eyes are as a flame of fire; and truth and right shall be made plainly to appear, being stripped of every veil; and all error, falsehood, unrighteousness and injury, shall be laid open, stripped of every disguise; every specious pretence, every cavil, and all false reasoning, shall vanish in a moment, as not being able to bear the light of that day. And then our hearts will be turned inside out, and the secrets of them will be made more plainly to appear than our outward actions do now. Then it shall appear what the ends are, which we have aimed at, what have been the governing principles which we have acted from, and what have been the dispositions, we have exercised in our ecclesiastical disputes and contests. Then it will appear, whether I acted uprightly, and from a truly conscientious, careful regard to my duty to my great Lord and master, in some former ecclesiastical controversies, which have been attended with exceeding unhappy circumstances, and consequences: it will appear, whether there was any just cause for the resentment which was manifested on those occasions. And then our late grand controversy, concerning the Qualifications necessary for admission to the privileges of members, in complete standing, in the Visible Church of Christ, will be examined and judged, in all its parts and circumstances, and the whole set forth in a clear, certain and perfect light. Then it will appear, whether the doctrine, which I have preached and published, concerning this matter, be Christ's own doctrine, whether he will not own it as one of the precious truths which have proceeded from his own mouth, and vindicate and honour, as such, before the whole universe. Then it will appear, what was meant by *the man that comes without the wedding garment;* for that is the day spoken of, Matt. xxii. 13. wherein such an one *shall be bound hand and foot, and cast into outer darkness, where shall be weeping and gnashing of teeth.* And then it will appear, whether, in declaring this doctrine, and acting agreeably to it, and in my general conduct in this affair, I have been influenced from any regard to my own temporal interest, or honour, or any desire to appear wiser than others; or have acted from any sinister, secular views whatsoever; and whether what I have done has not been from a careful, strict and tender regard to the will of my Lord and Master, and because I dare not offend him, being satisfied what his will was, after a long, diligent, impartial and prayerful, enquiry; having this constantly in view and prospect, to engage me to great solicitude, not rashly to determine truth to be on this side of the question, where I am now persuaded it is, that such a determination would not be for my temporal interest, but every way against it, bringing a long series of extreme difficulties, and plunging me into an abyss of trouble and sorrow. And then it will appear, whether my people have done their duty to their pastor, with respect to this matter; whether they have shown a right temper and spirit on this occasion; whether they have done me justice in hearing, attending to, and considering, what I had to say in evidence of what I believed and taught, as part of the counsel of God; whether I have been treated with that impartiality, candour and regard, which the just Judge esteemed due; and whether, in the many steps which have been taken, and the many things that have been said and done, in the course of this controversy, righteousness and charity and christian decorum have been maintained: or, if otherwise, to how great a degree these things have been violated. Then every step of the conduct of each of us, in this affair, from first to last, and the spirit we have exercised in all, shall be examined and manifested, and our own consciences will speak plain and loud, and each of us shall be convinced, and the world shall know; and never shall there be any more mistake, misrepresentation or misapprehension of the affair, to eternity.

This controversy is now probably brought to an issue, between you and me, as to this world; it has issued in the event of the week before last; but it must have another decision at that great day, which certainly will come, when you and I shall meet together before the great judgment seat: and therefore I leave it to that time, and shall say no more about it at present.

But I would now proceed to address myself particularly to several sorts of persons.

I. To those who are professors of godliness among us.

I would now call you to a serious consideration of that great day, wherein you must meet him, who has heretofore been your pastor, before the Judge, whose eyes are as a flame of fire.

I have endeavoured, according to my best ability, to search the word of God, with regard to the distinguishing notes of true piety, those by which persons might best discover their state, and most surely and clearly judge of themselves. And those rules and marks, I have from time to time, applied to you, in the preaching of the word, to the utmost of my skill, and in the most plain and searching manner, that I have been able; in order to the detecting the deceived hypocrite, and establishing the hopes and comforts of the sincere. And yet it is to be feared, that after all that I have done, I now leave some of you in a deceived deluded state; for it is not to be supposed, that among several hundred professors, none are deceived.

Henceforward, I am like to have no more opportunity to take the care and charge of your souls, to examine and search them. But still I intreat you to remember and consider the rules which I have often laid down to you, during my ministry, with a solemn regard to the future day, when you and I must meet together before our Judge; when the uses of examination you have heard from me, must be rehearsed again before you, and those rules of trial must be tried, and it will appear, whether they have been good or not, and it will also appear, whether you have impartially heard them, and tried yourselves by them; and the Judge himself, who is infallible, will try both you and me: and after this, none will be deceived concerning the state of their souls.

I have often put you in mind, that whatever your pretences to experiences, discoveries, comforts, and joys, have been; at that day, every one will be judged according to his works: and then you will find it so.

May you have a minister of greater knowledge of the word of God, and better acquaintance with soul cases, and of greater skill in applying himself to souls, whose discourses may be more searching and convincing; that such of you as have held fast deceit under my preaching, may have your eyes opened by his; that you may be undeceived before that great day.

What means and helps for instruction and self-examination, you may hereafter have, is uncertain; but one thing is certain, that the time is short; your opportunity for rectifying mistakes in so important a concern, will soon come to an end. We live in a world of great changes. There is now a great change come to pass; you have withdrawn yourselves from my ministry, under which you have continued for so many years: but the time is coming, and will soon come, when you will pass out of time into eternity; and so will pass from under all means of grace whatsoever.

The greater part of you who are professors of godliness, have, (to use the phrase of the apostle,) *acknowledged me in part.* You have heretofore acknowledged me to be your spiritual father, the instrument of the greatest good to you, that ever is, or can be, obtained, by any of the children of men. Consider of that day, when you and I shall meet before our Judge, when it shall be examined, whether you have had from me the treatment which is due to spiritual children, and whether you have treated me, as you ought to have treated a spiritual father. —As the relation of a natural parent brings great obligations on children, in the sight of God; so much more, in many respects, does the relation of a spiritual father, bring great obligations on such, whose conversion and eternal salvation they suppose God has made them the instruments of; 1 Cor. iv. 15. *For though you have ten thousand instructors in Christ, yet have ye not many fathers; for in Christ Jesus, I have begotten you through the gospel.*

II. Now I am taking my leave of this people, I would apply myself to such among them as I leave in a christless, graceless condition; and would call on such, seriously to consider of that solemn day, when they and I must meet before the Judge of the world.

My parting with you, is in some respects, in a peculiar manner, a melancholy parting; in as much as I leave you in the most melancholy circumstances, because I leave you in the gall of bitterness, and bond of iniquity, having the wrath of God abiding on you, and remaining under condemnation to everlasting misery and destruction. Seeing I must leave you, it would have been a comfortable and happy circumstance of our parting, if I had left you in Christ, safe and blessed in that sure refuge and glorious rest of the saints.—But it is otherwise, I leave you far off, aliens and strangers, wretched subjects and captives of sin and satan, and prisoners of vindictive justice; without Christ, and without God in the world.

Your consciences bear me witness, that while I had opportunity, I have not ceased to warn you, and set before you your danger. I have studied to represent the misery and necessity of your circumstances, in the clearest manner possible. I have tried all ways, that I could think of, tending to awaken your consciences, and make you sensible of the necessity of your improving your time, and being speedy in fleeing from the wrath to come, and thorough in the use of means for your escape and safety. I have diligently endeavoured to find out, and use, the most powerful motives, to persuade you to take care for your own welfare and salvation. I have not only endeavoured to awaken you, that you might be moved with fear, but I have used my utmost endeavours to win you: I have sought out acceptable words, that if possible, I might prevail upon you to forsake sin, and turn to God, and accept of Christ as your Saviour and Lord. I have spent my strength very much, in these things. But yet, with regard to you whom I am now speaking to, I have not been successful: but have this day reason to complain in those words, Jer. vi. 29. *The bellows are burnt, the lead is consumed of the fire, the founder melteth in vain, for the wicked are not plucked away.* It is to be feared, that all my labours, as to many of you, have served to no other purpose but to harden you; and the word which I have preached, instead of being a savour of life unto life, has been a savour of death unto death. Though I shall not have any account to give for the future, of such as have openly and resolutely renounced my ministry, as of a betrustment committed to me: yet remember you must give account for yourselves, of your care of your own souls, and your improvement of all means past and future, through your whole lives. God only knows what will become of your poor perishing souls, what means you may hereafter enjoy, or what disadvantages and temptations you may be under. May God in mercy grant, that however all past means have been unsuccessful, you may have future means, which may have a new effect; and that the word of God, as it shall be hereafter dispensed to you, may prove as the fire

and the hammer that breaketh the rock in pieces. However, let me now at parting, exhort and beseech you, not wholly to forget the warnings you have had while under my ministry. When you and I shall meet at the day of judgment, then you will remember them: the sight of me your former minister, on that occasion, will soon revive them in your memory; and that in a very affecting manner. O do not let that be the first time that they are so revived.

You and I are now parting one from another as to this world; let us labour that we may not be parted, after our meeting at the last day. If I have been your faithful pastor, (which will that day appear, whether I have or no), then I shall be acquitted, and shall ascend with Christ. O do your part, that in such a case, it may not be so, that you should be forced eternally to part from me, and all that have been faithful in Christ Jesus. This is a sorrowful parting, that now is between you and me; but that would be a more sorrowful parting to you than this. This you may perhaps bear without being much affected with it, if you are not glad of it; but such a parting, in that day, will most deeply, sensibly and dreadfully, affect you.

III. I would address myself to those who are under some awakenings.

Blessed be God, that there are some such, and that (although I have reason to fear I leave multitudes, in this large congregation, in a christless state), yet I do not leave them all in total stupidity and carelessness, about their souls. Some of you, that I have reason to hope are under some awakenings, have acquainted me with your circumstances; which has a tendency to cause me, now I am leaving you, to take my leave of you with peculiar concern for you. What will be the issue of your present exercise of mind, I know not: but it will be known at that day when you and I shall meet before the judgment seat of Christ. Therefore now be much in consideration of that day.

Now I am parting with this flock, I would once more press upon you the counsels I have heretofore given, to take heed of being slighty in so great a concern, to be thorough and in good earnest in the affair, and to beware of backsliding, to hold on and hold out to the end. And cry mightily to God, that these great changes, that pass over this church and congregation, do not prove your overthrow. There is great temptation in them; and the devil will undoubtedly seek to make his advantage of them, if possible, to cause your present convictions and endeavours to be abortive. You had need to double your diligence, and watch and pray, lest you be overcome by temptation.

Whoever may hereafter stand related to you, as your spiritual guide, my desire and prayer is, that the great Shepherd of the sheep would have a special respect to you, and be your guide, (for there is none teacheth like him,) and that he who is the infinite Fountain of light, would *open your eyes, and turn you from darkness unto light, and from the power of Satan unto God; that you may receive forgiveness of sins, and inheritance among them that are sanctified, through faith that is in Christ;* that so, in that great day, when I shall meet you again, before your Judge and mine, we may meet in joyful and glorious circumstances, never to be separated any more.

IV. I would apply myself to the young people of the congregation.

Since I have been settled in the work of the ministry, in this place, I have ever had a peculiar concern for the souls of the young people, and a desire that religion might flourish among them; and have especially exerted myself in order to it; because I knew the special opportunity they had beyond others, and that ordinarily those, whom God intended mercy for, were brought to fear and love him in their youth. And it has ever appeared to me a peculiarly amiable thing to see young people walking in the ways of virtue and christian piety, having their hearts purified and sweetened with a principle of divine love. And it has appeared a thing exceedingly beautiful, and what would be much to the adorning and happiness of the town, if the young people could be persuaded, when they meet together, to converse as christians, and as the children of God; avoiding impurity, levity, and extravagance; keeping strictly to the rules of virtue, and conversing together of the things of God, and Christ and heaven. This is what I have longed for: and it has been exceedingly grievous to me, when I have heard of vice, vanity and disorder, among our youth. And so far as I know my heart, it was from hence that I formerly led this church to some measures, for the suppressing of vice among our young people, which gave so great offence, and by which I became so obnoxious. I have sought the good and not the hurt of our young people. I have desired their truest honour and happiness, and not their reproach; knowing that true virtue and religion tended, not only to the glory and felicity of young people in another world, but their greatest peace and prosperity, and highest dignity and honour in this world, and above all things to sweeten and render pleasant and delightful even the days of youth.

But whether I have loved you and sought your good more or less, yet God in his providence, now calling me to part with you, committing your souls to him who once committed the pastoral care of them to me, nothing remains, but only (as I am now taking my leave of you) earnestly to beseech you, from love to yourselves, if you have none to me, not to despise and forget the warnings and counsels I have so often given you; remembering the day when you and I must meet again before the great Judge of quick and dead; when it will appear whether the things I have taught you were true, whether the counsels I have given you were good, and whether I truly sought your good, and whether you have well improved my endeavours.

I have, from time to time, earnestly warned you against frolicking (as it is called,) and some other liberties commonly taken by young people in the land. And whatever some may say, in justification of such liberties and customs, and may laugh at warnings against them, I now leave you my parting testimony against such things; not doubting but God will approve and confirm it, in that day when we shall meet before Him.

V. I would apply myself to the children of the congregation, the lambs of this flock, who have been so long under my care.

I have just now said, that I have had a peculiar concern for the young people: and in so saying, I did not intend to exclude you. You are in youth, and in the most early youth: and therefore I have been sensible, that if those that were young had a precious opportunity for their soul's good, you who are very young had, in many respects, a peculiarly precious opportunity. And accordingly I have not neglected you: I have endeavoured to do the part of a faithful shepherd, in feeding the lambs as well as the sheep. Christ did once commit the care of your souls to me as your minister; and you know, dear children, how I have instructed you, and warned you from time to time: you know how I have often called you together for that end: and some of you, sometimes, have seemed to be affected with what I have said to you. But I am afraid it has had no saving effect, as to many of you; but that you remain still in an unconverted condition, without any real saving work wrought in your souls, convincing you thoroughly of your sin and misery, causing you to see the great evil of sin, and to mourn for it, and hate it above all things; and giving you a sense of the excellency of the Lord Jesus Christ, bringing you, with all your hearts, to cleave to Him as your Saviour; weaning your hearts from the world; and causing you to love God above all, and to delight in holiness more than in all the pleasant things of this earth: and so that I now leave you in a miserable condition, having no interest in Christ, and so under the awful displeasure and anger of God, and in danger of going down to the pit of eternal misery.

But now I must bid you farewell: I must leave you in the hands of God. I can do no more for you than to pray for you. Only I desire you not to forget, but often think of the counsels and warnings I have given you, and the endeavours I have used, that your souls might be saved from everlasting destruction.

Dear children, I leave you in an evil world, that is full of snares and temptations. God only knows what will become of you. This the Scripture has told us, that there are but few saved: and we have abundant confirmation of it from what we see. This we see, that children die as well as others: multitudes die before they grow up; and of those that grow up, comparatively few ever give good evidence of saving conversion to God. I pray God to pity you, and take care of you, and provide for you the best means for the good of your souls; and that God himself would undertake for you, to be your heavenly Father, and the mighty Redeemer of your immortal souls. Do not neglect to pray for yourselves: take heed you be not of the number of those, who cast off fear, and restrain prayer before God. Constantly pray to God in secret; and often remember that great day, when you must appear before the judgment-seat of Christ, and meet your minister there, who has so often counselled and warned you.

I conclude with a few words of advice to all in general, in some particulars, which are of great importance in order to the future welfare and prosperity of this church and congregation.

1. One thing that greatly concerns you, as you would be an happy people, is the maintaining of *family order.*

We have had great disputes how the church ought to be regulated; and indeed the subject of these disputes was of great importance: but the due regulation of your families is of no less, and in some respects, of much greater importance. Every christian family ought to be, as it were, a little church, consecrated to Christ, and wholly influenced and governed by his rules. And family education and order are some of the chief of the means of grace. If these fail, all other means are like to prove ineffectual. If these are duly maintained, all the means of grace will be like to prosper and be successful.

Let me now, therefore, once more, before I finally cease to speak to this congregation, repeat and earnestly press the counsel, which I have often urged on heads of families here, while I was their pastor, to great painfulness, in teaching, warning and directing their children; bringing them up in the nurture and admonition of the Lord; beginning early, where there is yet opportunity; and maintaining a constant diligence in labours of this kind: remembering that, as you would not have all your instructions and counsels ineffectual, there must be government as well as instructions, which must be maintained with an even hand, and steady resolution; as a guard to the religion and morals of the family, and the support of its good order. Take heed that it be not with any of you, as it was with Eli of old, who reproved his children, but restrained them not; and that by this means you do not bring the like curse on your families, as he did on his.

And let children obey their parents, and yield to their instructions, and submit to their orders, as they would inherit a blessing, and not a curse. For we have reason to think, from many things in the word of God, that nothing has a greater tendency to bring a curse on persons, in this world, and on all their temporal concerns, than an undutiful, unsubmissive, disorderly behaviour in children towards their parents.

2. As you would seek the future prosperity of this society, it is of vast importance that you should avoid *contention.*

A contentious people will be a miserable people. The contentions, which have been among you, since I first became your pastor, have been one of the greatest burdens I have laboured under, in the course of my ministry: not only the contentions you have had with me, but those you have had one with another, about your lands, and other concerns: because I knew that contention, heat of spirit, evil speaking, and things of the like nature, were directly contrary to the spirit of christianity, and did, in a peculiar manner, tend to drive away God's spirit from a people, and to render all means of grace ineffectual, as well as to destroy a people's outward comfort and welfare.

Let me, therefore, earnestly exhort

you, as you would seek your own future good, hereafter to watch against a contentious spirit. *If you would see good days, seek peace and ensue it,* 1 Pet. iii. 10, 11. Let the contention, which has lately been about the terms of christian communion, as it has been the greatest of your contentions, so be the last of them. I would, now I am preaching my Farewell Sermon, say to you, as the apostle to the Corinthians, 2 Cor. xiii. 11, *Finally, brethren, farewell. Be perfect: be of one mind: live in peace: and the God of love and peace shall be with you.*

And here I would particularly advise those, that have adhered to me in the late controversy, to watch over their spirits, and avoid all bitterness towards others. Your temptations are, in some respects, the greatest: because what has been lately done is grievous to you. But, however wrong you may think others have done, maintain, with great diligence and watchfulness, a christian meekness and sedateness of spirit: and labour, in this respect, to excel others who are of the contrary part: and this will be the best victory: for *he that rules his spirit, is better than he that takes a city.* Therefore let nothing be done through strife or vainglory: indulge no revengeful spirit in any wise; but watch and pray against it: and by all means in your power, seek the prosperity of this town: and never think you behave yourselves as becomes christians, but when you sincerely, sensibly and fervently, love all men, of whatever party or opinion, and whether friendly or unkind, just or injurious, to you, or your friends, or to the cause and kingdom of Christ.

3. Another thing, that vastly concerns the future prosperity of the town, is, that you should watch against the encroachments of Error; and particularly *Arminianism,* and doctrines of like tendency.

You were many of you, as I well remember, much alarmed, with the apprehension of the danger of the prevailing of these corrupt principles, near sixteen years ago. But the danger then was small, in comparison of what appears now: these doctrines, at this day, are much more prevalent, than they were then: the progress they have made in the land, within this seven years, seems to have been vastly greater, than at any time in the like space before: and they are still prevailing, and creeping into almost all parts of the land, threatening the utter ruin of the credit of those doctrines, which are the peculiar glory of the gospel, and the interests of vital piety. And I have of late perceived some things among yourselves, that show that you are far from being out of danger, but on the contrary remarkably exposed. The elder people may perhaps think themselves sufficiently fortified against infection: but it is fit that all should beware of self-confidence and carnal security, and should remember those needful warnings of sacred writ, *Be not high minded but fear,* and *let him that stands, take heed lest he fall.* But let the case of the elder people be as it will, the rising generations are doubtless greatly exposed. These principles are exceedingly taking with corrupt nature, and are what young people, at least such as have not their hearts established with grace, are easily led away with.

And if these principles should greatly prevail in this town, as they very lately have done in another large town I could name, formerly greatly noted for religion, and so for a long time, it will threaten the spiritual and eternal ruin of this people, in the present and future generations. Therefore you have need of the greatest and most diligent care and watchfulness with respect to this matter.

4. Another thing which I would ad-

vise to, that you may hereafter be a prosperous people, is, that you would give yourselves much to prayer.

God is the fountain of all blessing and prosperity, and he will be sought to for his blessing. I would therefore advise you, not only to be constant in secret and family prayer, and in the public worship of God in his house, but also often to assemble yourselves in private praying societies. I would advise all such, as are grieved for the afflictions of Joseph, and sensibly affected with the calamities of this town, of whatever opinion they be, with relation to the subject of our late controversy, often to meet together for prayer, and cry to God for his mercy to themselves, and mercy to this town, and mercy to Zion, and to the people of God in general through the world.

5. The last article of advice, I would give, (which doubtless does greatly concern your prosperity,) is, that you would take great care with regard to the settlement of a minister, to see to it who or what manner of person he is, whom you settle: and particularly in these two respects.

(1.) That he be a man of thoroughly sound principles, in the scheme of doctrine which he maintains.

This you will stand in the greatest need of, especially at such a day of corruption as this is. And, in order to obtain such an one, you had need to exercise extraordinary care and prudence. I know the danger. I know the manner of many young gentlemen of corrupt principles, their ways of concealing themselves, the fair specious disguises they are wont to put on, by which they deceive others, to maintain their own credit, and get themselves into others' confidence and improvement, and secure and establish their own interest, until they see a convenient opportunity to begin, more openly, to broach and propagate their corrupt tenets.

(2.) Labour to obtain a man, who has an established character, as a person of serious religion and fervent piety.

It is of vast importance that those, who are settled in this work, should be men of true piety, at all times, and in all places; but more especially at some times and in some towns and churches. And this present time, which is a time wherein religion is in danger, by so many corruptions in doctrine and practice, is in a peculiar manner, a day wherein such ministers are necessary. Nothing else but sincere piety of heart is at all to be depended on, at such a time as this, as a security to a young man, just coming into the world, from the prevailing infection, to thoroughly engage him, in proper and successful endeavours, to withstand and oppose the torrent of error and prejudice, against the high, mysterious, evangelical doctrines of the religion of Jesus Christ, and their genuine effects in true experimental religion. And this place is a place, that does peculiarly need such a minister, for reasons obvious to all.

If you should happen to settle a minister, who knows nothing, truly, of Christ, and the way of salvation by him, nothing experimentally of the nature of vital religion; alas, how will you be exposed as sheep without a shepherd. Here is need of one in this place, who shall be eminently fit to stand in the gap, and make up the hedge, and who shall be as the chariots of Israel and the horsemen thereof. You need one, that shall stand as a champion, in the cause of truth and godliness.

Having briefly mentioned these important articles of advice, nothing remains, but that I take my leave of you, and bid you all farewell, wishing and praying for your prosperity. I would now commend your immortal souls to HIM, who formerly committed them to me; expecting the day, when I must meet you again before him, who is the Judge of quick and dead. I desire that I may never forget this people, who have been so long my special charge, and that I may never cease fervently to pray for your prosperity. May God bless you with a faithful pastor, one that is well acquainted with his mind and will, thoroughly warning sinners, wisely and skilfully searching professors, and conducting you in the way to eternal blessedness. May you have truly a burning and shining light set up in this candlestick; and may you not only for a season, but during his life, and that a long life, be willing to rejoice in his light.

And let me be remembered, in the prayers of all God's people, that are of a calm spirit, and are peaceable and faithful in Israel, of whatever opinion they may be, with respect to terms of Church Communion.

And let us all remember, and never forget, our future, solemn meeting, on that Great day of the Lord: the day of infallible and of the unalterable sentence. AMEN.

JONATHAN EDWARDS

TO THE REV. MR. JOSEPH BELLAMY

Northampton, Decem. 6, 1749
My Dear Friend:

As for the present state of things here with Regard to our Controversy, 'tis not very easy for me to give you an Idea of it, without writing a sheet or two of Paper. But in brief, things are in great Confusion: the Tumult is vastly greater than when you was here, and is rising higher & higher continually. The People have got their Resentments up to a

Reprinted from a letter of December 6, 1749, in Clarence H. Faust and Thomas H. Johnson, eds., JONATHAN EDWARDS: REPRESENTATIVE SELECTIONS *(New York, 1935), pp. 387–89.*

great Height towards you since you have been gone; and you are spoken of by 'em with great Indignation & Contempt. And I have been informed that Col. Williams of Weathersfield has written a Letter to one of the principal men of that Church, where in He speaks contemptibly & with Resentment of your & Mr. Searl's last visit here.—There have been abundance of meetings about our affairs since you was here, society meetings, & church meetings, & meetings—of Committees, of Committees of the Parish & Committees of the Church, Conferences, Debates, Reports, & Proposals drawn up, & Replies & Remonstrances. The People have a Resolution to get me out of Town speedily, that disdains all Controul or Check. To make the matter strong, there is a Precinct meeting kept alive by adjournment, They have already had three or four conventions and have a standing Committee of nineteen men (chiefly of such as are strongly engaged), to oversee and manage the affair affectually. And we have another committee of the church of 15 men (in the Choice of which they picked out those that are most violent) and these appointed for the same End. But not withstanding such great doings nothing is yet done or concluded, the true grand difficulties that the People stick at about calling a Council, are *first,* that they would have a Council all on their own side in the controversy; and are contriving & struggling to their utmost to cut me off from liberty of chusing any Part of the council of such as are of my opinion & *secondly,* they are utterly against a Council having Liberty to look into the whole state of our Case, and giving advice in General; but would tie them up to some Particulars, in Judging of which they think they can have no Power to look into & Condemn any thing in their conduct, or to thwart their designs. I have been openly reproached in Church meetings, as apparently regarding my own Temporal Interest more than the Honour of Christ & the good of the Church. As to the affair of a publick dispute, it was quickly at an End after you went from hence, The People at their next Parish meeting rejected it, as what would tend to make Parties among us. They seem to be determined that the arguments for my opinion shall never be publickly heard, if it be possible to prevent it the Church Committee have voted expressly that no Council shall have Power to give Advice in that matter i.e. whether I shall preach on the subject or no: & have drawn up a writing, containing 9 or 10 votes or conclusions of theirs, manifesting what They would have as to the measure that shall be taken relating to a Council to be called: and in the same writing have added at the End a Threatening, that If they & I don't agree, They will report it to the Church as their Opinion that the Church should vote that my opinion is so & so pernicious, & declare their desire of a speedy separation, & immediate Call a Council themselves to dismiss me.—

I might have observed before, that I have been informed that Rector Williams wrote 'em up advice, not to have a publick dispute; because it would tend to Parties.

You may easily be sensible dear sir, that 'tis a Time of great Trial with me, and that I stand in Continual need of the divine Presence & merciful Conduct in such a state of things as this. I need Gods Counsel in every step I take & every word I speak; so all that I do & say is watched by the multitude around me with the utmost strictness & with eyes of the greatest uncharitableness & severity and let me do or say what I will, my words & actions are represented in dark colours, and the state of Things

is come to that, that they seem to think it greatly concerns 'em to blacken me, & represent me in Odious Colours to the world, to justify their own Conduct —They seem to be sensible that now their Character can't stand unless it be on the Ruin of mine. They have publickly voted that they will have no more sacraments; & they have no way to justify themselves in that, but to represent me as very bad. I therefore desire dear sir, your fervent Prayers to God. If He be for me, who can be against me? If He be with me, I need not fear ten thousands of the People. But I know myself unworthy of his Presence & help, yet would humbly trust in his infinite Grace & all sufficience.

My Love to your spouse.
I am your Brother
& near Friend
Jonathan Edwards.

JONATHAN MAYHEW

The Apostle's doctrine, in the passage thus explained concerning the office of civil rulers and the duty of subjects, may be summed up in the following observations, viz.:

That the end of magistracy is the good of civil society, *as such.*

That civil rulers, *as such,* are the ordinance and ministers of God, it being by his permission and providence that any bear rule, and agreeable to his will that there should be *some persons* vested with authority in society, for the well-being of it.

That which is here said concerning civil rulers extends to all of them in

Reprinted from Jonathan Mayhew, "A Discourse Concerning Unlimited Submission and Nonresistance to the Higher Powers," in Bernard Bailyn, ed., PAMPHLETS OF THE AMERICAN REVOLUTION, I *(Cambridge, Mass., 1965), 220–22, 226, 231–42, 247.*

common: it relates indifferently to monarchical, republican, and aristocratical government, and to all other forms which truly answer the sole end of government, the happiness of society; and to all the different degrees of authority in any particular state, to inferior officers no less than to the supreme.

That disobedience to civil rulers in the due exercise of their authority is not merely a *political sin* but an heinous *offense against God and religion.*

That the true ground and reason of our obligation to be subject to the *higher powers* is the usefulness of magistracy (when properly exercised) to human society and its subserviency to the general welfare.

That obedience to civil rulers is here equally required under all forms of government which answer the sole end of all government, the good of society; and to every degree of authority in any state, whether supreme or subordinate.

(From whence it follows,

That if unlimited obedience and nonresistance be here required as a duty under any one form of government, it is also required as a duty under all other forms, and as a duty to subordinate rulers as well as to the supreme.)

And lastly, that those civil rulers to whom the Apostle enjoins subjection are the persons *in possession; the powers that be,* those who are *actually* vested with authortiy.

There is one very important and interesting point which remains to be inquired into; namely, the *extent* of that subjection *to the higher powers* which is here enjoined as a duty upon all Christians. Some have thought it warrantable and glorious to disobey the civil powers in certain circumstances, and, in cases of very great and general oppression when humble remontrances fail of having any effect, and when the public welfare cannot be

otherwise provided for and secured, to rise unanimously even against the sovereign himself in order to redress their grievances, to vindicate their natural and legal rights, to break the yoke of tyranny, and free themselves and posterity from inglorious servitude and ruin. It is upon this principle that many royal oppressors have been driven from their thrones into banishment, and many slain by the hands of their subjects. . . . But, in opposition to this principle, it has often been asserted that the Scripture in general (and the passage under consideration in particular) makes all resistance to princes a crime, in any case whatever.—If they turn tyrants and become the common oppressors of those whose welfare they ought to regard with a paternal affection, we must not pretend to right ourselves unless it be by prayers and tears and humble entreaties; and if these methods fail of procuring redress we must not have recourse to any other, but all suffer ourselves to be robbed and butchered at the pleasure of the *Lord's anointed,* lest we should incur the sin of rebellion and the punishment of damnation. For he has God's authority and commission to bear him out in the worst of crimes, so far that he may not be withstood or controlled. Now whether we are obliged to yield such an absolute submission to our prince, or whether disobedience and resistance may not be justifiable in some cases notwithstanding anything in the passage before us, is an inquiry in which we are all concerned; and this is the inquiry which is the main design of the present discourse.

• • •

And if we attend to the nature of the argument with which the Apostle here enforces the duty of submission to *the higher powers,* we shall find it to be such an one as concludes not in favor of submission to all who bear the *title* of rulers in common, but only to those who *actually* perform the duty of rulers by exercising a reasonable and just authority for the good of human society. This is a point which it will be proper to enlarge upon because the question before us turns very much upon the truth or falsehood of this position. It is obvious, then, in general that the civil rulers whom the Apostle here speaks of, and obedience to whom he presses upon Christians as a duty, are *good rulers,* such as are, in the exercise of their office and power, benefactors to society. . . .

. . .

Thus, upon a careful review of the Apostle's reasoning in this passage, it appears that his arguments to enforce submission are of such a nature as to conclude only in favor of submission *to such rulers as he himself describes;* i.e., such as rule for the good of society, which is the only end of their institution. Common tyrants and public oppressors are not entitled to obedience from their subjects by virtue of anything here laid down by the inspired Apostle.

I now add, farther, that the Apostle's argument is so far from proving it to be the duty of people to obey and submit to such rulers as act in contradiction to the public good and so to the design of their office, that it proves *the direct contrary.* For, please to observe, that if the end of all civil government be the good of society, if this be the thing that is aimed at in constituting civil rulers, and if the motive and argument for submission to government be taken from the apparent usefulness of civil authority, it follows that when no such good end can be answered by submission there remains no argument or motive to enforce it; and if instead of this good end's being brought about by submission, a *contrary end* is brought

about and the ruin and misery of society effected by it, here is a plain and positive reason against submission in all such cases, should they ever happen. And therefore, in such cases a regard to the public welfare ought to make us withhold from our rulers that obedience and subjection which it would, otherwise, be our duty to render to them. If it be our duty, for example, to obey our King merely for this reason, that he rules for the public welfare (which is the only argument the Apostle makes use of), it follows by a parity of reason that when he turns tyrant and makes his subjects his prey to devour and to destroy instead of his charge to defend and cherish, we are bound to throw off our allegiance to him and to resist, and that according to the tenor of the Apostle's argument in this passage. Not to discontinue our allegiance, in this case, would be to join with the sovereign in promoting the slavery and misery of that society the welfare of which we ourselves as well as our sovereign are indispensably obliged to secure and promote as far as in us lies. It is true the Apostle puts no case of such a tyrannical prince; but by his grounding his argument for submission wholly upon the good of civil society it is plain he implicitly authorizes and even requires us to make resistance whenever this shall be necessary to the public safety and happiness. Let me make use of this easy and familiar *similitude* to illustrate the point in hand. Suppose God requires a family of children to obey their father and not to resist him, and enforces his command with this argument: that the superintendence and care and authority of a just and kind parent will contribute to the happiness of the whole family so that they ought to obey him for their own sakes more than for his. Suppose this parent at length runs distracted, and attempts, in his mad fit, to cut all his children's throats. Now, in this case, is not the reason before assigned why these children should obey their parent while he continued of a sound mind, namely, *their common good,* a reason equally conclusive for disobeying and resisting him since he is become delirious and attempts their ruin? It makes no alteration in the argument, whether this parent properly speaking loses his reason, or does, while he retains his understanding, that which is as fatal in its consequences as anything he could do were he really deprived of it. This similitude needs no formal application.

But it ought to be remembered that if the duty of universal obedience and nonresistance to our king or prince can be argued from this passage, the same unlimited submission under a republican or any other form of government and even to all the subordinate powers in any particular state, can be proved by it as well: which is more than those who allege it for the mentioned purpose would be willing should be inferred from it. So that this passage does not answer their purpose, but really overthrows and confutes it. This matter deserves to be more particularly considered.—The advocates for unlimited submission and passive obedience do, if I mistake not, always speak with reference to kingly or monarchical government as distinguished from all other forms and with reference to submitting to the will of the king in distinction from all subordinate officers acting beyond their commission and the authority which they have received from the crown. It is not pretended that any persons besides kings have a divine right to do what they please so that no one may resist them without incurring the guilt of factiousness and rebellion. If any other supreme powers oppress the people it is generally allowed that the

people may get redress, by resistance if other methods prove ineffectual. And if any officers in a kingly government go beyond the limits of that power which they have derived from the crown (the supposed original source of all power and authority in the state), and attempt, illegally, to take away the properties and lives of their fellow subjects, they may be *forcibly* resisted, at least till application can be made to the crown. But as to the sovereign himself, he may not be resisted in any case, nor any of his officers while they confine themselves within the bounds which he has prescribed to them. This is, I think, a true sketch of the principles of those who defend the doctrine of passive obedience and nonresistance. Now there is nothing in Scripture which supports this scheme of political principles. As to the passage under consideration, the Apostle here speaks of civil rulers in *general,* of all persons in *common* vested with authority for the good of society, without any particular reference to one form of government more than to another or to the supreme power in any particular state more than to subordinate powers. The Apostle does not concern himself with the different forms of government. This he supposes left entirely to human prudence and discretion. Now the consequence of this is that unlimited and passive obedience is no more enjoined in this passage under monarchical government, or to the supreme power in any state, than under all other species of government which answer the end of government, or to all the subordinate degrees of civil authority, from the highest to the lowest. Those, therefore, who would from this passage infer the guilt of resisting kings in all cases whatever, though acting ever so contrary to the design of their office, must, if they will be consistent, go much farther, and infer from it the guilt of resistance under all other forms of government and of resisting *any petty officer* in the state, though acting beyond his commission, in the most arbitrary, illegal manner possible. The argument holds equally strong in both cases. All civil rulers, as such, are the *ordinance* and *ministers of God;* and they are all, by the nature of their office and in their respective spheres and stations, bound to consult the public welfare. With the same reason, therefore, that any deny unlimited and passive obedience to be here enjoined under a republic or aristocracy or any other established form of civil government or to subordinate powers acting in an illegal and oppressive manner, with the same reason others may deny that such obedience is enjoined to a king or monarch or any civil power whatever. For the Apostle says nothing that is *peculiar to kings;* what he says extends equally to *all* other persons whatever, vested with any civil office. They are all, in exactly the same sense, the *ordinance of God* and the *ministers of God;* and obedience is equally enjoined to be paid to them all. For, as the Apostle expresses it, *there is* NO POWER *but of God:* and we are required to *render to* ALL *their* DUES, and not MORE than their DUES. And what these *dues* are, and to *whom* they are to be *rendered,* the Apostle *saith not* but leaves to the reason and consciences of men to determine.

Thus it appears that the common argument, grounded upon this passage, in favor of universal and passive obedience really overthrows itself by proving too much, if it proves anything at all; namely, that no civil officer is, in any case whatever, to be resisted, though acting in express contradiction to the design of his office; which no man in his senses ever did or can assert.

If we calmly consider the nature of the thing itself, nothing can well be imagined more directly contrary to common sense than to suppose that *millions* of people should be subjected to the arbitrary, precarious pleasure of *one single man* (who has *naturally* no superiority over them in point of authority) so that their estates, and everything that is valuable in life, and even their lives also shall be absolutely at his disposal, if he happens to be wanton and capricious enough to demand them. What unprejudiced man can think that God made ALL to be thus subservient to the lawless pleasure and frenzy of ONE so that it shall always be a sin to resist him! Nothing but the most plain and express revelation from Heaven could make a sober impartial man believe such a monstrous, unaccountable doctrine; and, indeed, the thing itself appears so shocking—so out of all *proportion,* that it may be questioned whether all the *miracles* that ever were wrought could make it credible that this doctrine *really* came from God. At present, there is not the least syllable in Scripture which gives any countenance to it. The hereditary, indefeasible, divine right of kings, and the doctrine of nonresistance, which is built upon the supposition of such a right, are altogether as fabulous and chimerical as transubstantiation or any of the most absurd reveries of ancient or modern visionaries. These notions are fetched neither from divine revelation nor human reason; and if they are derived from neither of those sources, it is not much matter from *whence they come, or whither they go.* Only it is a pity that such doctrines should be propagated in society, to raise factions and rebellions, as we see they have in fact been, both in the *last* and in the *present* REIGN.

But then, if unlimited submission and passive obedience to the *higher powers* in all possible cases be not a duty, it will be asked, "How far are we obliged to submit? If we may innocently disobey and resist in some cases, why not in all? Where shall we stop? What is the measure of our duty? This doctrine tends to the total dissolution of civil government and to introduce such scenes of wild anarchy and confusion as are more fatal to society than the worst of tyranny."

After this manner, some men object; and, indeed, this is the most plausible thing that can be said in favor of such an absolute submission as they plead for. But the worst (or rather the best) of it is that there is very little strength or solidity in it. For similar difficulties may be raised with respect to almost every duty of natural and revealed religion.—To instance only in two, both of which are near akin, and indeed exactly parallel, to the case before us. It is unquestionably the duty of children to submit to their parents, and of servants to their masters. But no one asserts that it is their duty to obey and submit to them in all supposable cases, or universally a sin to resist them. Now does this tend to subvert the just authority of parents and masters? Or to introduce confusion and anarchy into private families? No. How then does the same principle tend to unhinge the government of that larger family, the body politic? We know, in general, that children and servants are obliged to obey their parents and masters respectively. We know, also, with equal certainty that they are not obliged to submit to them in all things without exception, but may, in some cases, reasonably and therefore innocently resist them. These principles are acknowledged upon all hands, whatever difficulty there may be in fixing the exact limits of submission. Now there is at least as much difficulty in stating the measure of duty in these two cases as in the cases of rulers and subjects. So that this is really no objection, at least no reasonable one, against resistance to the *higher powers:* or, if it is one, it will hold equally against resistance in the other cases mentioned. It is indeed true that turbulent, vicious-minded men may take occasion from this principle, that their rulers may, in some cases, be lawfully resisted, to raise factions and disturbances in the state and to make resistance where resistance is needless and therefore sinful. But is it not equally true that children and servants of turbulent, vicious minds may take occasion from this principle, that parents and masters may, in some cases, be lawfully resisted, to resist when resistance is unnecessary and therefore criminal? Is the principle in either case false in itself merely because it may be abused and applied to legitimate disobedience and resistance in those instances to which it ought not to be applied? According to this way of arguing there will be no true principles in the world, for there are none but what may be wrested and perverted to serve bad purposes, either through the weakness or wickedness of men.

A PEOPLE really oppressed to a great degree by their sovereign cannot well be insensible when they are so oppressed. And such a people (if I may allude to an ancient *fable*) have, like the Hesperian fruit, a DRAGON for their *protector* and *guardian;* nor would they have any reason to mourn if some HERCULES should appear to dispatch him. For a nation thus abused to arise unanimously and to resist their prince, even to the dethroning him, is not criminal, but a reasonable way of vindicating their liberties and just rights; it is making use of the means, and the only means, which God has put into their power for mutual and self-defense. And it would be highly criminal in them not to make use of this means. It would be stupid tameness and unaccountable folly for whole nations to suffer *one* unreasonable, ambitious, and cruel man to wanton and riot in their misery. And in such a case it would, of the two, be more rational to suppose that they did **NOT** *resist* than that they who did would *receive to themselves damnation.*

And

This naturally brings us to make some reflections upon the resistance which was made about a century since to that unhappy prince, KING CHARLES I, and upon the ANNIVERSARY of his death. This is a point which I should not have concerned myself about were it not that *some men* continue to speak of it, even to this day, with a great deal of warmth and zeal, and in such a manner as to undermine all the principles of LIBERTY, whether civil or religious, and to introduce the most abject slavery both in church and state: so that it is become a matter of universal concern. What I have to offer upon this subject will be comprised in a short answer to the following *queries,* viz.:

For what reason the resistance to King *Charles* the *First* was made?

By whom it was made?

Whether this resistance was REBELLION [1] or not?

How the *anniversary* of King *Charles's* death came *at first* to be

solemnized as a day of fasting and humiliation?

And lastly,

Why those of the episcopal clergy who are very high in the principles of *ecclesiastical authority* continue to speak of this unhappy man as a great SAINT and a MARTYR?

For what reason, then, was the resistance to King *Charles* made? The general answer to this inquiry is that it was on account of the *tyranny* and *oppression* of his reign. Not a great while after his accession to the throne he married a *French Catholic;* and with her seemed to have *wedded* the politics, if not the religion, of *France* also. For afterwards, during a reign, or rather a tyranny, of many years, he governed in a perfectly wild and arbitrary manner, paying no regard to the constitution and the laws of the kingdom by which the power of the crown was limited or to the solemn oath which he had taken at his coronation. It would be endless, as well as needless, to give a particular account of all the illegal and despotic measures which he took in his administration, partly from his own natural lust of power and partly from the influence of wicked counselors and ministers.—He committed many illustrious members of both houses of Parliament to the *tower* for opposing his arbitrary schemes.—He levied many taxes upon the people without consent of Parliament, and then imprisoned great numbers of the principal merchants and gentry for not paying them.—He erected, or at least revived, several arbitrary courts, in which the most unheard-of barbarities were committed with his knowledge and approbation.—He supported that more than fiend, Archbishop *Laud,* and the clergy of his stamp, in all their church tyranny and hellish cruelties.—He authorized a book

[1] N.B. I speak of rebellion, treason, saintship, martyrdom, etc., throughout this discourse only in the *scriptural* and *theological sense.* I know not how the *law* defines them; the study of *that* not being my employment.

in favor of *sports* upon the *Lord's day*, and several clergymen were persecuted by him and the mentioned *pious* bishop for not reading it to the people after *divine service.*—When the Parliament complained to him of the arbitrary proceedings of his corrupt ministers he told that *august body*, in a rough, domineering, unprincely manner, that he wondered anyone should be so foolish and insolent as to think that he would part with the meanest of his servants *upon their account.*—He refused to call any Parliament at all for the space of twelve years together, during all which time he governed in an absolute lawless and despotic manner.—He took all opportunities to encourage the *papists* and to promote them to the highest offices of honor and trust.—He (probably) abetted the horrid massacre in *Ireland,* in which two hundred thousand Protestants were butchered by the Roman Catholics.—He sent a large sum of money, which he had raised by his arbitrary taxes, into *Germany,* to raise foreign troops in order to force more arbitrary taxes upon his subjects.—He not only by a long series of *actions* but also in *plain terms* asserted an absolute uncontrollable power, saying even in one of his speeches to Parliament that as it was blasphemy to dispute what God might do, so it was sedition in subjects to dispute what the King might do.—Towards the end of his tyranny he came to the House of Commons with an armed force and demanded five of its principal members to be delivered up to him.—And this was a prelude to that unnatural war which he soon after levied against his own dutiful subjects, whom he was bound by all the laws of honor, humanity, piety, and, I might add, of *interest* also, to defend and cherish with a paternal affection. I have only time to hint at these facts in a

general way, all which, and many more of the same tenor, may be proved by good authorities: so that the *figurative* language which St. *John* uses concerning the just and beneficent deeds of our blessed Saviour may be applied to the unrighteous and execrable deeds of this prince, viz.: *And there are also many other things which* King Charles *did, the which, if they should be written every one I suppose that even the world itself could not contain the books that should be written.* Now it was on account of King *Charles's* thus assuming a power above the laws in direct contradiction to his coronation oath, and governing the greatest part of his time in the most arbitrary oppressive manner; it was upon this account that that resistance was made to him which at length issued in the loss of his crown and of *that head* which was unworthy to wear it.

But by whom was this resistance made? Not by a private *junto;* not by a small seditious *party;* not by a *few desperadoes* who, to mend their fortunes, would embroil the state; but by the LORDS and COMMONS of *England.* It was they that almost unanimously opposed the King's measures for overturning the constitution and changing that free and happy government into a wretched, absolute monarchy. It was they that, when the King was about levying forces against his subjects in order to make himself absolute, commissioned officers and raised an army to defend themselves and the public; and it was they that maintained the war against him all along, till he was made a prisoner. This is indisputable though it was not, properly speaking, the Parliament but the army which put him to death afterwards. And it ought to be freely acknowledged that most of their proceeding in order to get this matter effected, and particularly the court by which the King was at last tried and condemned, was little better than a mere mockery of justice.

The next question which naturally arises is whether this resistance which was made to the King *by the Parliament* was properly *rebellion* or not? The answer to which is plain, that it was not; but a most righteous and glorious stand made in defense of the natural and legal rights of the people against the unnatural and illegal encroachments of arbitrary power. Nor was this a rash and too sudden opposition. The nation had been patient under the oppressions of the crown even to *long suffering,* for a course of many years; and there was no rational hope of redress in any other way. Resistance was absolutely necessary in order to preserve the nation from slavery, misery, and ruin. And who so proper to make this resistance as the Lords and Commons—the whole representative body of the people—guardians of the public welfare; and each of which was, in point of legislation, vested with an equal, co-ordinate power with that of the crown? Here were *two* branches of the legislature against *one:* two which had law and equity and the constitution on their side, against one which was impiously attempting to overturn law and equity and the constitution, and to exercise a wanton licentious *sovereignty* over the properties, consciences, and lives of all the people: such a *sovereignty* as some inconsiderately ascribe to the supreme Governor of the world.—I say inconsiderately, because God himself does not govern in an absolutely arbitrary and despotic manner. The power of this Almighty King (I speak it not without caution and reverence); the power of this Almighty King is *limited by law,* not, indeed, by *acts of Parliament* but by the eternal *laws* of truth,

wisdom, and equity, and the everlasting *tables* of right reason—tables that cannot be *repeated,* or *thrown down* and *broken* like those of *Moses.* But King *Charles* sat himself up above all these as much as he did the written laws of the realm, and made mere humor and caprice, which are no rule at all, the only rule and measure of his administration. And now, is it not perfectly ridiculous to call resistance to such a tyrant by the name of *rebellion?—the grand rebellion?* Even that Parliament which brought King *Charles* II to the throne and which run *loyally mad* severely reproved one of their own members for condemning the proceedings of that Parliament which first took up arms against the former King. And upon the same principles that the proceedings of this Parliament may be censured as wicked and rebellious, the proceedings of those who, since opposed King *James* II and brought the Prince of *Orange* to the throne may be censured as wicked and rebellious also. The cases are parallel. But whatever *some* men may *think,* it is to be hoped that, for their own sakes, they will not dare to *speak* against the REVOLUTION, upon the justice and legality of which depends (in part) his present MAJESTY'S right to the throne.

. . .

To conclude: Let us all learn to be *free* and to be *loyal.* Let us not profess ourselves vassals to the lawless pleasure of any man on earth. But let us remember, at the same time, government is *sacred* and not to be *trifled* with. It is our happiness to live under the government of a PRINCE who is satisfied with ruling according to law, as every other *good prince* will. We enjoy under his administration all the liberty that is proper and expedient for us. It becomes us, therefore, to be contented and dutiful subjects. Let us prize our freedom but not *use our liberty for a cloak of maliciousness.* There are men who strike at *liberty* under the term *licentiousness.* There are others who aim at *popularity* under the disguise of *patriotism.* Be aware of both. *Extremes are dangerous.* There is at present amongst *us,* perhaps, more danger of the *latter* than of the *former.* For which reason I would exhort you to pay all due regard to the government over us, to the KING and all in authority, and to lead a *quiet and peaceable life.* And while I am speaking of loyalty to our *earthly prince,* suffer me just to put you in mind to be loyal also to the supreme RULER of the universe, *by whom kings reign and princes decree justice.* To which King eternal, immortal, invisible, even to the ONLY WISE GOD be all honor and praise, DOMINION and thanksgiving, through JESUS CHRIST our LORD. AMEN.

2. The Enlightened American

The spread of eighteenth-century European enlightenment ideas in America can be observed in the following documents. Franklin's "Rules for a Club Established for Mutual Improvement" and the injunctions of "Poor Richard" in "The Way to Wealth" offer a superb summary of the secular, middle-class ambitions of their author and the mercantile, urban culture in which he thrived. The entrepreneurial values characteristic of the American port cities, but spreading far into the interior, can be detected in the preachments and homilies for self-improvement that flowed from Franklin's pen. Philip Vickers Fithian's letter offers a revealing glimpse into the cultural aspirations of Virginia's plantation aristocracy, while Thomas Jefferson's advice to his young protégé, Peter Carr, remains perhaps the clearest statement of educational values made by a leader of the American Enlightenment.

Philip Freneau's poem and David Ramsay's comments on the Revolution's "influence on the minds and morals of the citizens" offer evidence of Americans' desire to secure the development of a national culture worthy of their recently-gained political independence.

BENJAMIN FRANKLIN

RULES FOR A CLUB ESTABLISHED FOR MUTUAL IMPROVEMENT

Previous Question, To Be Answered At Every Meeting

Reprinted from Benjamin Franklin, "Rules for a Club Established for Mutual Improvement" (1728) and from "The Way to Wealth" (1758), in Ralph Ketcham, ed., THE POLITICAL THOUGHT OF BENJAMIN FRANKLIN *(Indianapolis and New York: The Bobbs-Merrill Company, Inc., 1965), 128–30, 280–83, 288–89.*

Have you read over these queries this morning, in order to consider what you might have to offer the Junto touching any one of them? viz.

1. Have you met with any thing in the author you last read, remarkable, or suitable to be communicated to the Junto? particularly in history, morality, poetry, physic, travels, mechanic arts, or other parts of knowledge.

2. What new story have you lately heard agreeable for telling in conversation?

3. Hath any citizen in your knowledge failed in his business lately, and what have you heard of the cause?

4. Have you lately heard of any citizen's thriving well, and by what means?

5. Have you lately heard how any present rich man, here or elsewhere, got his estate?

6. Do you know of a fellow citizen, who has lately done a worthy action, deserving praise and imitation; or who has lately committed an error, proper for us to be warned against and avoid?

7. What unhappy effects of intemperance have you lately observed or heard; of imprudence, of passion, or of any other vice or folly?

8. What happy effects of temperance, of prudence, of moderation, or of any other virtue?

9. Have you or any of your acquaintance been lately sick or wounded? If so, what remedies were used, and what were their effects?

10. Whom do you know that are shortly going voyages or journeys, if one should have occasion to send by them?

11. Do you think of any thing at present, in which the Junto may be serviceable to *mankind,* to their country, to their friends, or to themselves?

12. Hath any deserving stranger arrived in town since last meeting, that you have heard of? And what have you heard or observed of his character or merits? And whether, think you, it lies in the power of the Junto to oblige him, or encourage him as he deserves?

13. Do you know of any deserving young beginner lately set up, whom it lies in the power of the Junto any way to encourage?

14. Have you lately observed any defect in the laws of your *country,* of which it would be proper to move the legislature for an amendment? Or do you know of any beneficial law that is wanting?

15. Have you lately observed any encroachment on the just liberties of the people?

16. Hath any body attack your reputation lately? And what can the Junto do towards securing it?

17. Is there any man whose friendship you want, and which the Junto, or any of them, can procure for you?

18. Have you lately heard any member's character attacked, and how have you defended it?

19. Hath any man injured you, from whom it is in the power of the Junto to procure redress?

20. In what manner can the Junto, or any of them, assist you in any of your honourable designs?

21. Have you any weighty affair on hand, in which you think the advice of the Junto may be of service?

22. What benefits have you lately received from any man not present?

23. Is there any difficulty in matters of opinion, of justice, and injustice, which you would gladly have discussed at this time?

24. Do you see any thing amiss in the present customs or proceedings of the Junto, which might be amended?

Any person to be qualified [as a member of the Junto], to stand up, and lay his hand upon his breast, and be asked these questions, viz.

1. Have you any particular disrespect to any present members? *Answer.* I have not.

2. Do you sincerely declare, that you love mankind in general, of what profession or religion soever? *Answer.* I do.

3. Do you think any person ought to be harmed in his body, name, or goods, for mere speculative opinions, or his external way of worship? *Answer.* No.

4. Do you love truth for truth's sake,

and will you endeavour impartially to find and receive it yourself, and communicate it to others? *Answer.* Yes.

THE WAY TO WEALTH

Courteous Reader, I have heard that nothing gives an Author so great Pleasure, as to find his Works respectfully quoted by other learned Authors. This Pleasure I have seldom enjoyed; for tho' I have been, if I may say it without Vanity, an *eminent Author* of Almanacks annually now a full Quarter of a Century, my Brother Authors in the same Way, for what Reason I know not, have ever been very sparing in their Applauses; and no other Author has taken the least Notice of me, so that did not my Writings produce me some solid *Pudding,* the great Deficiency of *Praise* would have quite discouraged me.

I concluded at length, that the People were the best Judges of my Merit; for they buy my Works; and besides, in my Rambles, where I am not personally known, I have frequently heard one or other of my Adages repeated, with, *as Poor Richard says,* at the End on't; this gave me some Satisfaction, as it showed not only that my Instructions were regarded, but discovered likewise some respect for my Authority; and I own, that to encourage the Practice of remembering and repeating those wise Sentences, I have sometimes *quoted myself* with great Gravity.

Judge then how much I must have been gratified by an Incident I am going to relate to you. I stopt my Horse lately where a great Number of People were collected at a Vendue of Merchant Goods. The Hour of Sale not being come, they were conversing on the Badness of the Times, and one of the Company call'd to a plain clean old Man, with white Locks, *Pray, Father Abraham, what think you of the Times? Won't these heavy Taxes quite ruin the Country? How shall we ever be able to pay them? What would you advise us to?*——Father *Abraham* stood up, and reply'd, If you'd have my Advice, I'll give it you in short, for a *Word to the Wise is enough,* and *many Words won't fill a Bushel,* as *Poor Richard says.* They join'd in desiring him to speak his Mind, and gathering round him, he proceeded as follows;

Friends, says he, and Neighbours, the Taxes are indeed very heavy, and if those laid on by the Government were the only Ones we had to pay, we might more easily discharge them; but we have many others, and much more grievous to some of us. We are taxed twice as much by our *Idleness,* three times as much by our *Pride,* and four times as much by our *Folly,* and from these Taxes the Commissioners cannot ease or deliver us by allowing an Abatement. However let us hearken to good Advice, and something may be done for us; *God helps them that help themselves,* as *Poor Richard* says, in his Almanack of 1733.

It would be thought a hard Government that should tax its People one tenth Part of their *Time,* to be employed in its Service. But *Idleness* taxes many of us much more, if we reckon all that is spent in absolute *Sloth,* or doing of nothing, with that which is spent in idle Employments or Amusements, that amount to nothing. *Sloth,* by bringing on Diseases, absolutely shortens Life. *Sloth, like Rust, consumes faster than Labour wears, while the used Key is always bright,* as *Poor Richard* says. But *dost thou love Life, then do not squander Time, for that's the Stuff Life is made of,* as *Poor Richard* says.—How much more than is necessary do we spend in Sleep! forgetting that *The* sleeping *Fox catches no Poultry,* and that *there will be sleeping enough in the Grave,* as *Poor Richard* says. If Time be of all Things the most precious, *wasting Time* must be, as *Poor Richard* says, *the greatest Prodigality,* since, as he elsewhere tells us, *Lost Time is never found again;* and what we call *Time-enough, always proves little enough:* Let us then up and be doing, and doing to the Purpose; so by Diligence shall we do more with less Perplexity. *Sloth makes all Things difficult, but Industry all easy,* as *Poor Richard* says; and *He that riseth late, must trot all Day, and shall scarce overtake his Business at Night.* While *Laziness travels so slowly, that Poverty soon overtakes him,* as we read in *Poor Richard,* who adds, *Drive thy Business, let not that drive thee;* and *Early to Bed, and early to rise, makes a Man healthy, wealthy and wise.*

So what signifies *wishing* and *hoping* for better Times. We may make these Times better if we bestir ourselves. *Industry need not wish,* as *Poor Richard* says, and *He that lives upon Hope will die fasting. There are no Gains, without Pains;* then *Help Hands, for I have no Lands,* or if I have, they are smartly taxed. And, as *Poor Richard* likewise observes, *He that hath a Trade hath an Estate,* and *He that hath a Calling, hath an Office of Profit and Honour;* but then the *Trade* must be worked at, and the *Calling* well followed, or neither the *Estate,* nor the *Office,* will enable us to pay our Taxes.—If we are industrious we shall never starve; for, as *Poor Richard* says, *At the working Man's House* Hunger *looks in, but dares not enter.* Nor will the Bailiff or the Constable enter, for *Industry pays Debts, while Despair encreaseth them,* says *Poor Richard.*—What though you have found no Treasure, nor has any

rich Relation left you a Legacy, *Diligence is the Mother of Good luck,* as *Poor Richard* says, *and God gives all Things to Industry.* Then *plough deep, while Sluggards sleep, and you shall have Corn to sell and to keep,* says *Poor Dick.* Work while it is called To-day, for you know not how much you may be hindered To-morrow, which makes *Poor Richard* say, *One To-day is worth two To-morrows;* and farther, *Have you somewhat to do To-morrow, do it To-day.* If you were a Servant, would you not be ashamed that a good Master should catch you idle? Are you then your own Master, *be ashamed to catch yourself idle,* as *Poor Dick* says. When there is so much to be done for yourself, your Family, your Country, and your gracious King, be up by Peep of Day; *Let not the Sun look down and say, Inglorious here he lies.* Handle your Tools without Mittens; remember that *the Cat in Gloves catches no Mice,* as *Poor Richard* says. 'Tis true there is much to be done, and perhaps you are weak handed, but stick to it steadily, and you will see great Effects, for *constant Dropping wears away Stones,* and by *Diligence and Patience the Mouse ate in two the Cable;* and *little Strokes fell great Oaks,* as *Poor Richard* says in his Almanack, the Year I cannot just now remember.

Methinks I hear some of you say, *Must a Man afford himself no Leisure?* —I will tell thee, my Friend, what *Poor Richard* says, *Employ thy Time well if thou meanest to gain Leisure;* and *since thou art not sure of a Minute, throw not away an Hour.* Leisure, is Time for doing something useful; this Leisure the diligent Man will obtain, but the lazy Man never; so that, as *Poor Richard* says, a *Life of Leisure* and a *Life of Laziness are two Things.* Do you imagine that Sloth will afford you more

Comfort than Labour? No, for as *Poor Richard* says, *Trouble springs from Idleness, and grievous Toil from needless Ease. Many without Labour, would live by their* WITS *only, but they break for want of Stock.* Whereas Industry gives Comfort, and Plenty, and Respect: *Fly Pleasures, and they'll follow you. The diligent Spinner has a large Shift;* and *now I have a Sheep and a Cow, every Body bids me Good morrow;* all which is well said by *Poor Richard.*

But with our Industry, we must likewise be *steady, settled* and *careful,* and oversee our own Affairs *with our own Eyes,* and not trust too much to others; for, as *Poor Richard* says,

I never saw an oft removed Tree,
Nor yet an oft removed Family,
That throve so well as those that settled be.

. . . Be *industrious* and *free;* be *frugal* and *free.* At present, perhaps, you may think yourself in thriving Circumstances, and that you can bear a little Extravangance [*sic*] without Injury; but

For Age and Want, save while you may;
No Morning Sun lasts a whole Day,

as *Poor Richard* says—Gain may be temporary and uncertain, but ever while you live, Expence is constant and certain; and *'tis easier to build two Chimnies than to keep one in Fuel,* as *Poor Richard* says. So *rather go to Bed supperless than rise in Debt.*

Get what you can, and what you get hold;
'Tis the Stone that will turn all your Lead
into Gold,

as *Poor Richard* says. And when you have got the Philosopher's Stone, sure you will no longer complain of bad Times, or the Difficulty of paying Taxes.

This Doctrine, my Friends, is *Reason* and *Wisdom;* but after all, do not depend too much upon your own *Industry,* and *Frugality,* and *Prudence,* though excellent Things, for they may all be blasted without the Blessing of Heaven; and therefore ask that Blessing humbly, and be not uncharitable to those that at present seem to want it, but comfort and help them. Remember *Job* suffered, and was afterwards prosperous.

And now to conclude, *Experience keeps a dear School, but Fools will learn in no other, and scarce in that;* for it is true, *we may give Advice, but we cannot give Conduct,* as *Poor Richard* says: However, remember this, *They that won't be counselled, can't be helped,* as *Poor Richard* says: And farther, That *if you will not hear Reason, she'll surely rap your Knuckles.*

Thus the old Gentleman ended his Harangue. The People heard it, and approved the Doctrine and immediately practised the contrary, just as if it had been a common Sermon; for the Vendue opened, and they began to buy extravagantly, notwithstanding all his Cautions, and their own Fear of Taxes. —I found the good Man had thoroughly studied my Almanacks, and digested all I had dropt on those Topicks during the Course of Five-and-twenty Years. The frequent Mention he made of me must have tired any one else, but my Vanity was wonderfully delighted with it, though I was conscious that not a tenth Part of the Wisdom was my own which he ascribed to me, but rather the *Gleanings* I had made of the Sense of all Ages and Nations. However, I resolved to be the better for the Echo of it; and though I had at first determined to buy Stuff for a new Coat, I went away resolved to wear my old One a little longer. *Reader,* if thou wilt do the same, thy Profit will be as great as mine.

PHILIP VICKERS FITHIAN

TO THE REVEREND ENOCH GREEN

Decemr 1st 1773

Revd Sir: As you desired I may not omit to inform you, so far as I can by a letter, of the business in which I am now engaged, it would indeed be vastly agreeable to me if it was in my power to give you particular intelligence concerning the state and plan of my employment here.

I set out from home the 20th of Octr and arrived at the Hon: Robert Carters, of Nominy, in Westmorland County, the 28th I began to teach his children the first of November. He has two sons, and one Nephew; the oldest Son is turned of seventeen, and is reading Salust and the greek grammar; the others are about fourteen, and in english grammar, and Arithmetic. He has besides five daughters which I am to teach english, the eldest is turned of fifteen, and is reading the spectator; she is employed two days in every week in learning to play the Forte-Piana, and Harpsicord— The others are smaller, and learning to read and spell. Mr Carter is one of the Councellors in the general court at Williamsburg, and possest of as great, perhaps the clearest fortune according to the estimation of people here, of any man in Virginia: He seems to be a good scholar, even in classical learning, and is remarkable one in english grammar; and notwithstanding his rank, which in general seems to countenance indulgence to children, both himself and Mrs. Carter have a manner of instructing and dealing with children far superior, I may say it with confidence, to any I have

Reprinted from H. D. Farish, ed., THE JOURNAL AND LETTERS OF PHILIP VICKERS FITHIAN *(Williamsburg, Va., 1943), pp. 34–35.*

ever seen, in any place, or in any family. They keep them in perfect subjection to themselves, and never pass over an occasion of reproof; and I blush for many of my acquaintances when I say that the children are more kind and complaisant to the servants who constantly attend them than we are to our superiors in age and condition. Mr Carter has an overgrown library of Books of which he allows me the free use. It consists of a general collection of law books, all the Latin and Greek Classicks, vast number of Books on Divinity chiefly by writers who are of the established Religion; he has the works of almost all the late famous writers, as Locke, Addison, Young, Pope, Swift, Dryden, &c. in Short, Sir, to speak moderately, he has more than eight times your number— His eldest Son, who seems to be a Boy of genius and application is to be sent to Cambridge University, but I believe will go through a course either in Philadelphia or Princeton College first. As to what is commonly said concerning Virginia that it is difficult to avoid being corrupted with the manners of the people, I believe it is founded wholly in a mistaken notion that persons must, when here frequent all promiscuous assemblies; but this is so far from the truth that any one who does practise it, tho' he is accused of no crime, loses at once his character; so that either the manners have been lately changed, or the report is false, for he seems now to be best esteemed and most applauded who attends to his business, whatever it be, with the greatest diligence. I believe the virginians have of late altered their manner very much, for they begin to find that their estates by even small extravagance, decline, and grow involved with debt, this seems to be the spring which induces the People of fortune who are the pattern of all behaviour here, to be frugal, and moderate.

THOMAS JEFFERSON

TO PETER CARR

Paris, August 10, 1787

Dear Peter:—I have received your two letters of December the 30th and April the 18th, and am very happy to find by them, as well as by letters from Mr. Wythe, that you have been so fortunate as to attract his notice and good will; I am sure you will find this to have been one of the most fortunate events of your life, as I have ever been sensible it was of mine. I enclose you a sketch of the sciences to which I would wish you to apply, in such order as Mr. Wythe shall advise; I mention, also, the books in them worth your reading, which submit to his correction. Many of these are among your father's books, which you should have brought to you. As I do not recollect those of them not in his library, you must write to me for them, making out a catalogue of such as you think you shall have occasion for, in eighteen months from the date of your letter, and consulting Mr. Wythe on the subject. To this sketch, I will add a few particular observations:

1. Italian. I fear the learning this language will confound your French and Spanish. Being all of them degenerated dialects of the Latin, they are apt to mix in conversation. I have never

seen a person speaking the three languages, who did not mix them. It is a delightful language, but late events having rendered the Spanish more useful, lay it aside to prosecute that.

2. Spanish. Bestow great attention on this, and endeavor to acquire an accurate knowledge of it. Our future connections with Spain and Spanish America, will render that language a valuable acquisition. The ancient history of that part of America, too, is written in that language. I send you a dictionary.

3. Moral Philosophy. I think it lost time to attend lectures on this branch. He who made us would have been a pitiful bungler, if he had made the rules of our moral conduct a matter of science. For one man of science, there are thousands who are not. What would have become of them? Man was destined for society. His morality, therefore, was to be formed to this object. He was endowed with a sense of right and wrong, merely relative to this. This sense is as much a part of his nature, as the sense of hearing, seeing, feeling; it is the true foundation of morality, and not the το καλον,[1] truth, &c., as fanciful writers have imagined. The moral sense, or conscience, is as much a part of man as his leg or arm. It is given to all human beings in a stronger or weaker degree, as force of members is given them in a greater or less degree. It may be strengthened by exercise, as may any particular limb of the body. This sense is submitted, indeed, in some degree, to the guidance of reason; but it is a small stock which is required for this: even a less one than what we call common sense. State a moral case to a ploughman and a professor. The former will decide it as

Reprinted from Thomas Jefferson, letter of August 10, 1787, in Adrienne Koch and William Peden, eds., THE LIFE AND SELECTED WORKS OF THOMAS JEFFERSON *(New York, 1944), pp. 429–34.*

1 The beautiful.

well, and often better than the latter, because he has not been led astray by artificial rules. In this branch, therefore, read good books, because they will encourage, as well as direct your feelings. The writings of Sterne, particularly, form the best course of morality that ever was written. Besides these, read the books mentioned in the enclosed paper; and, above all things, lose no occasion of exercising your dispositions to be grateful, to be generous, to be charitable, to be humane, to be true, just, firm, orderly, courageous, &c. Consider every act of this kind, as an exercise which will strengthen your moral faculties and increase your worth.

4. Religion. Your reason is now mature enough to examine this object. In the first place, divest yourself of all bias in favor of novelty and singularity of opinion. Indulge them in any other subject rather than that of religion. It is too important, and the consequences of error may be too serious. On the other hand, shake off all the fears and servile prejudices, under which weak minds are servilely crouched. Fix reason firmly in her seat, and call to her tribunal every fact, every opinion. Question with boldness even the existence of a God; because, if there be one, he must more approve of the homage of reason, than that of blindfolded fear. You will naturally examine first, the religion of your own country. Read the Bible, then, as you would read Livy or Tacitus. The facts which are within the ordinary course of nature, you will believe on the authority of the writer, as you do those of the same kind in Livy and Tacitus. The testimony of the writer weighs in their favor, in one scale, and their not being against the laws of nature, does not weigh against them. But those facts in the Bible which contradict the laws of nature, must be examined with more care, and under a variety of faces. Here you must recur to the pretensions of the writer to inspiration from God. Examine upon what evidence his pretensions are founded, and whether that evidence is so strong, as that its falsehood would be more improbable than a change in the laws of nature, in the case he relates. For example, in the book of Joshua, we are told, the sun stood still several hours. Were we to read that fact in Livy or Tacitus, we should class it with their showers of blood, speaking of statues, beasts, etc. But it is said, that the writer of that book was inspired. Examine, therefore, candidly, what evidence there is of his having been inspired. The pretension is entitled to your inquiry, because millions believe it. On the other hand, you are astronomer enough to know how contrary it is to the law of nature that a body revolving on its axis, as the earth does, should have stopped, should not, by that sudden stoppage, have prostrated animals, trees, buildings, and should after a certain time have resumed its revolution, and that without a second general prostration. Is this arrest of the earth's motion, or the evidence which affirms it, most within the law of probabilities? You will next read the New Testament. It is the history of a personage called Jesus. Keep in your eye the opposite pretensions: 1, of those who say he was begotten by God, born of a virgin, suspended and reversed the laws of nature at will, and ascended bodily into heaven; and 2, of those who say he was a man of illegitimate birth, of a benevolent heart, enthusiastic mind, who set out without pretensions to divinity, ended in believing them, and was punished capitally for sedition, by being

gibbeted, according to the Roman law, which punished the first commission of that offence by whipping, and the second by exile, or death *in furea.* . . .

Do not be frightened from this inquiry by any fear of its consequences. If it ends in a belief that there is no God, you will find incitements to virtue in the comfort and pleasantness you feel in its exercise, and the love of others which it will procure you. If you find reason to believe there is a God, a consciousness that you are acting under his eye, and that he approves you, will be a vast additional incitement; if that there be a future state, the hope of a happy existence in that increases the appetite to deserve it; if that Jesus was also a God, you will be comforted by a belief of his aid and love. In fine, I repeat, you must lay aside all prejudice on both sides, and neither believe nor reject anything, because any other persons, or description of persons, have rejected or believed it. Your own reason is the only oracle given you by heaven, and you are answerable, not for the rightness, but uprightness of the decision. I forgot to observe, when speaking of the New Testament, that you should read all the histories of Christ, as well of those whom a council of ecclesiastics have decided for us, to be Pseudo-evangelists, as those they named Evangelists. Because these Pseudo-evangelists pretended to inspiration, as much as the others, and you are to judge their pretensions by your own reason, and not by the reason of those ecclesiastics. Most of these are lost. There are some, however, still extant, collected by Fabricius, which I will endeavor to get and send you.

5. Travelling. This makes men wiser, but less happy. When men of sober age travel, they gather knowledge, which they may apply usefully for their country; but they are subject ever after to recollections mixed with regret; their affections are weakened by being extended over more objects; and they learn new habits which cannot be gratified when they return home. Young men, who travel, are exposed to all these inconveniences in a higher degree, to others still more serious, and do not acquire that wisdom for which a previous foundation is requisite, by repeated and just observations at home. The glare of pomp and pleasure is analogous to the motion of the blood; it absorbs all their affection and attention, they are torn from it as from the only good in this world, and return to their home as to a place of exile and condemnation. Their eyes are forever turned back to the object they have lost, and its recollection poisons the residue of their lives. Their first and most delicate passions are hackneyed on unworthy objects here, and they carry home the dregs, insufficient to make themselves or anybody else happy. Add to this, that a habit of idleness, an inability to apply themselves to business is acquired, and renders them useless to themselves and their country. These observations are founded in experience. There is no place where your pursuit of knowledge will be so little obstructed by foreign objects, as in your own country, nor any, wherein the virtues of the heart will be less exposed to be weakened. Be good, be learned, and be industrious, and you will not want the aid of travelling, to render you precious to your country, dear to your friends, happy within yourself. I repeat my advice, to take a great deal of exercise, and on foot. Health is the first requisite after morality. Write to me often, and be assured of the interest I take in your success, as well as the warmth of those sentiments of at-

tachment with which I am, dear Peter, your affectionate friend.

PHILIP FRENEAU

LITERARY IMPORTATION

HOWEVER we wrangled with Britain awhile
We think of her now in a different stile,
And many fine things we receive from her isle;
Among all the rest,
Some demon possessed
Our dealers in knowledge and sellers of sense
To have a good *bishop* imported from thence.

. . .

It seems we had spirit to humble a throne,
Have genius for science inferior to none,
But hardly encourage a plant of our own:
If a college be planned,
'Tis all at a stand
'Till in Europe we send at a shameful expense,
To send us a book-worm to teach us some sense.

Can we never be thought to have learning or grace
Unless it be brought from that horrible place
Where tyranny reigns with her impudent face;
And popes and pretenders,
And sly faith-defenders
Have ever been hostile to reason and wit,
Enslaving a world that shall conquer them yet.

Reprinted from Philip Freneau, "Literary Importation" (1788), in Harry Hayden Clark, ed., POEMS OF FRENEAU *(New York, 1929), pp. 94–95.*

DAVID RAMSAY

Previous to the American revolution, the inhabitants of the British colonies

Reprinted from David Ramsay, THE HISTORY OF THE AMERICAN REVOLUTION, *II (Trenton, N.J., 1811), 394–412.*

were universally loyal. That three millions of such subjects should break through all former attachments, and unanimously adopt new ones, could not reasonably be expected. The revolution had its enemies, as well as its friends, in every period of the war. Country religion, local policy, as well as private views, operated in disposing the inhabitants to take different sides. The New-England provinces being mostly settled by one sort of people, were nearly of one sentiment. The influence of placemen in Boston, together with the connexions which they had formed by marriages, had attached sundry influential characters in that capital to the British interest, but these were but as the dust in the balance, when compared with the numerous independent whig yeomanry of the country. The same and other causes produced a large number in New-York who were attached to royal government. That city had long been head quarters of the British army in America, and many intermarriages, and other connexions, had been made between British officers and some of their first families. The practice of entailing estates had prevailed in New-York to a much greater extent than in any of the other provinces. The governors thereof had long been in the habit of indulging their favorites with extravagant grants of land. This had introduced the distinction of landlord and tenant. There was therefore in New-York an aristocratic party, respectable for numbers, wealth and influence, which had much to fear from independence. The city was also divided into parties by the influence of two ancient and numerous families, the Livingstones and Delanceys. These having been long accustomed to oppose each other at elections, could rarely be brought to unite in any political measures. In this controversy, one almost universally took part with America, the other with Great-Britain.

The Irish in America, with a few exceptions were attached to independence. They had fled from oppression in their native country, and could not brook the idea that it should follow them. Their national prepossessions in favor of liberty, were strengthened by their religious opinions. They were presbyterians, and people of that denomination, for reasons hereafter to be explained, were mostly whigs. The Scotch, on the other hand, though they had formerly sacrificed much to liberty in their own country, were generally disposed to support the claims of Great-Britain. Their nation for some years past had experienced a large proportion of royal favor. . . .

Such of the Germans, in America, as possessed the means of information, were generally determined whigs, but many of them were too little informed, to be able to chuse their side on proper ground. . . .

The great body of tories in the southern states, was among the settlers on their western frontier. Many of these were disorderly persons, who had fled from the old settlements, to avoid the restraints of civil government. Their numbers were encreased by a set of men called regulators. The expense and difficulty of obtaining the decision of courts, against horse-thieves and other criminals, had induced sundry persons, about the year 1770, to take the execution of the laws into their own hands, in some of the remote settlements, both of North and South-Carolina. In punishing crimes, forms as well as substance, must be regarded. From not attending to the former, some of these regulators, though perhaps aiming at nothing but what they thought right, committed many offences both against

law and justice. By their violent proceedings regular government was prostrated. This drew on them the vengeance of royal governors. The regulators having suffered from their hands, were slow to oppose an established government, whose power to punish they had recently experienced. Apprehending that the measures of Congress were like their own regulating schemes, and fearing that they would terminate in the same disagreeable consequences, they and their adherents were generally opposed to the revolution.

Religion also divided the inhabitants of America. The presbyterians and independents, were almost universally attached to the measures of Congress. Their religious societies are governed on the republican plan.

From independence they had much to hope, but from Great-Britain if finally successful, they had reason to fear the establishment of a church hierarchy. Most of the episcopal ministers of the northern provinces, were pensioners on the bounty of the British government. The greatest part of their clergy, and many of their laity in these provinces, were therefore disposed to support a connexion with Great-Britain. The episcopal clergy in these southern provinces being under no such bias, were often among the warmest whigs. . . . Religious controversy was happily kept out of view: The well informed of all denominations were convinced, that the contest was for their civil rights, and therefore did not suffer any other considerations to interfere, or disturb their union.

The quakers with a few exceptions were averse to independence. In Pennsylvania they were numerous, and had power in their hands. Revolutions in government are rarely patronised by any body of men, who foresee that a diminution of their own importance, is likely to result from the change. Quakers from religious principles were averse to war, and therefore could not be friendly to a revolution, which could only be effected by the sword. Several individuals separated from them on account of their principles, and following the impulse of their inclinations, joined their countrymen in arms. The services America received from two of their society, generals Greene and Mifflin, made some amends for the embarrassment, which the disaffection of the great body of their people occasioned to the exertions of the active friends of independence.

The age and temperament of individuals had often an influence in fixing their political character. Old men were seldom warm whigs. They could not relish the great changes which were daily taking place. Attached to ancient forms and habits, they could not readily accommodate themselves to new systems. Few of the very rich were active in forwarding the revolution. This was remarkably the case in the eastern and middle states; but the reverse took place in the southern extreme of the confederacy. There were in no part of America, more determined whigs than the opulent slaveholders in Virginia, the Carolinas and Georgia. The active and spirited part of the community, who felt themselves possessed of talents, that would raise them to eminence in a free government, longed for the establishment of independent constitutions: But those who were in possession or expectation of royal favor, or of promotion from Great-Britain, wished that the connexion between the parent state and the colonies, might be preserved. The young, the ardent, the ambitious and the enterprising were mostly whigs, but the phlegmatic, the timid, the interested and those who wanted decision were, in general, favorers of Great-Britain, or at least only the lukewarm inactive friends of independence. . . . The convulsions of war afforded excellent shelter for desperate debtors. The spirit of the times revolted against dragging to jails for debt, men who were active and zealous in defending their country, and on the other hand, those who owed more than they were worth, by going within the British lines, and giving themselves the merit of suffering on the score of loyalty, not only put their creditors to defiance, but sometimes obtained promotion or other special marks of royal favor.

The American revolution, on the one hand, brought forth great vices; but on the other hand, it called forth many virtues, and gave occasion for the display of abilities, which, but for that event, would have been lost to the world. When the war began, the Americans were a mass of husbandmen, merchants, mechanics and fishermen; but the necessities of the country gave a spring to the active powers of the inhabitants, and set them on thinking, speaking and acting, in a line far beyond that to which they had been accustomed. The difference between nations is not so much owing to nature, as to education and circumstances. While the Americans were guided by the leading strings of the mother country, they had no scope nor encouragement for exertion. All the departments of government were established and executed for them, but not by them. In the years 1775 and 1776, the country being suddenly thrown into a situation that needed the abilities of all its sons, these generally took their places, each according to the bent of his inclination. As they severally pursued their objects with ardor, a vast expansion of the human mind speedily followed. This displayed itself in a variety of ways. It was found that the talents for great stations did not differ in kind, but only in degree, from those which were necessary for the proper discharge of the ordinary business of civil society. In the bustle that was occasioned by the war, few instances could be produced of any persons who made a figure, or who rendered essential services, but from among those who had given specimens of similar talents in their respective professions. Those who from indolence or dissipation, had been of little service to the community in time of peace, were found equally unserviceable in war. A few young men were exceptions to this general rule. Some of these, who had indulged in youthful follies, broke off from their vicious courses, and on the pressing call of their country became useful servants of the public; but the great bulk of those who were the active instruments of carrying on the revolution, were self-made, industrious men. These, who by their own exertions had established or laid a foundation for establishing personal independence, were most generally trusted, and most successfully employed in establishing that of their country. In these times of action, classical education was found of less service, than good natural parts, guided by common sense and sound judgment.

• • •

The Americans knew but little of one another, previous to the revolution. Trade and business had brought the inhabitants of their seaports acquainted with each other, but the bulk of the people in the interior country were unacquainted with their fellow citizens. A continental army, and Congress, composed of men from all the states, by freely mixing together, were assimilated into one mass. Individuals of both, mingling with the citizens, disseminated principles of union among them. Local prejudices abated. By frequent collision asperities were worn off, and a foundation was laid for the establishment of a nation, out of discordant materials. Intermarriages between men and women of different states were much more common than before the war, and became an additional cement to the union. Unreasonable jealousies had existed between the inhabitants of the eastern and of the southern states; but on becoming better acquainted with each other, these in a great measure subsided. A wiser policy prevailed. Men of liberal minds led the way in discouraging local distinctions, and the great body of the people, as soon as reason got the better of prejudice, found that their best interests would be most effectually promoted by such practices and sentiments as were favorable to union. . . .

• • •

The science of government, has been more generally diffused among the Americans by means of the revolution. The policy of Great-Britain, in throwing them out of her protection, induced a necessity of establishing independent constitutions. This led to reading and reasoning on the subject. The many errors that were at first committed by unexperienced statesmen, have been a practical comment on the folly of unbalanced constitutions, and injudicious laws. The discussions concerning the new constitution, gave birth to much reasoning on the subject of government, and particularly to a series of letters signed Publius, but really the work of Alexander Hamilton, in which much political knowledge and wisdom were displayed, and which will long remain a monument of the strength and acuteness of the human understanding in investigating truth.

• • •

As literature had in the first instance favored the revolution, so in its turn, the revolution promoted literature. The study of eloquence and of the belles lettres, was more successfully prosecuted in America, after the disputes between Great-Britain and her colonies began to be serious, than it ever had been before. The various orations, addresses, letters, dissertations and other literary performances which the war made necessary, called forth abilities where they were, and excited the rising generation to study arts, which brought with them their own reward. Many incidents afforded materials for the favorites of the muses, to display their talents. Even burlesquing royal proclamations, by parodies and doggerel poetry, had great effects on the minds of the people. . . .

. . .

From the latter periods of the revolution till the present time, schools, colleges, societies and institutions for promoting literature, arts, manufactures, agriculture, and for extending human happiness, have been increased far beyond any thing that ever took place before the declaration of independence. Every state in the union, has done more or less in this way, but Pennsylvania has done the most. The following institutions have been very lately founded in that state, and most of them in the time of the war or since the peace. An university in the city of Philadelphia; a college of physicians in the same place; Dickinson college at Carlisle; Franklin college at Lancaster; the protestant episcopal academy in Philadelphia; academies at Yorktown, at Germantown, at Pittsburgh and Washington; and an academy in Philadelphia for young ladies; societies for promoting political enquiries; for the medical relief of the poor, under the title of the Philadelphia dispensary; for

promoting the abolition of slavery, and the relief of free negroes unlawfully held in bondage; for propagating the gospel among the Indians, under the direction of the united brethren; for the encouragement of manufactures and the useful arts; for alleviating the miseries of prisons. Such have been some of the beneficial effects, which have resulted from that expansion of the human mind, which has been produced by the revolution, but these have not been without alloy.

To overset an established government unhinges many of those principles, which bind individuals to each other. A long time, and much prudence, will be necessary to reproduce a spirit of union and that reverence for government, without which society is a rope of sand. The right of the people to resist their rulers, when invading their liberties, forms the corner stone of the American republics. The principle, though just in itself, is not favorable to the tranquility of present establishments. The maxims and measures, which in the years 1774 and 1775 were successfully inculcated and adopted by American patriots, for oversetting the established government, will answer a similar purpose when recurrence is had to them by factious demagogues, for disturbing the freest governments that were ever devised.

War never fails to injure the morals of the people engaged in it. The American war, in particular, had an unhappy influence of this kind. Being begun without funds or regular establishments, it could not be carried on without violating private rights; and in its progress, it involved a necessity for breaking solemn promises, and plighted public faith. The failure of national justice, which was in some degree unavoidable, increased the difficulties of performing private engagements, and weakened that sensibility to the obligations of public and private honor, which is a security for the punctual performance of contracts.

In consequence of the war, the institutions of religion have been deranged, the public worship of the deity suspended, and a great number of the inhabitants deprived of the ordinary means of obtaining that religious knowledge, which tames the fierceness, and softens the rudeness of human passions and manners. Many of the temples dedicated to the service of the most high, were destroyed, and these, from a deficiency of ability and inclination, are not yet rebuilt. The clergy were left to suffer, without proper support. The depreciation of the paper currency was particularly injurious to them. It reduced their salaries to a pittance, so insufficient for their maintenance, that several of them were obliged to lay down their profession, and engage in other pursuits. Public preaching, of which many of the inhabitants were thus deprived, seldom fails of rendering essential service to society, by civilizing the multitude and forming them to union. No class of citizens have contributed more to the revolution than the clergy, and none have hitherto suffered more in consequence of it. From the diminution of their number, and the penury to which they have been subjected, civil government has lost many of the advantages it formerly derived from the public instructions of that useful order of men.

On the whole, the literary, political, and military talents of the citizens of the United States have been improved by the revolution, but their moral character is inferior to what it formerly was. So great is the change for the worse, that the friends of public order are loudly called upon to exert their utmost abilities, in extirpating the vicious principles and habits, which have taken deep root during the late convulsions.

III. RECENT INTERPRETATIONS

Louis Hartz confronts directly the insistence that American culture had been derived largely from English or European models before the Revolution. He argues for the existence from the beginning of a distinctly American cast of mind, shaped in large measure by the impact of the natural environment and the absence of certain social factors and restraints inherent in the European experience. Hartz presents an eloquent, if perhaps overdrawn, defense both of America's uniqueness and of its early "liberal tradition." The student may wish to examine carefully Hartz's addition to Tocqueville's famous sentence: "The great advantage of the American is that he has arrived at a state of democracy without having to endure a democratic revolution; *and that he is born free without having to become so*" (italics, Hartz's addition). In what manner and to what degree was the American really "born free without having to become so"?

Edmund Morgan's essay provides a perceptive analysis of the evolution of colonial intellectual modes in eighteenth-century America. Morgan carefully traces the movement, in intelligible fashion, from a primacy of religious concerns to a primacy of political concerns, bridging the gap between the rhetoric and concerns of the century's three great cultural experiences: the Great Awakening, the Enlightenment, and the Revolution. His summary of Revolutionary political ideals contains a shrewd discussion of these values.

Bernard Bailyn's analysis of the relationship between colonial political practices and Enlightenment thought in America before the Revolution modifies and calls into question Becker's analysis of the same theme. Bailyn, a leading scholar of provincial political development, suggests that the ideological patterns that emerged from the Revolution owed as much, if not more, to American colonial political experience as to any borrowed or inherited set of European perspectives on the relationship between freedom and authority.

LOUIS HARTZ

When the Americans celebrated the uniqueness of their own society, they were on the track of a personal insight of the profoundest importance. For the nonfeudal world in which they lived shaped every aspect of their social thought: it gave them a frame of mind that cannot be found anywhere else in the eighteenth century, or in the wider history of modern revolutions.

One of the first things it did was to breed a set of revolutionary thinkers in America who were human beings like Otis and Adams rather than secular prophets like Robespierre and Lenin. Despite the European flavor of a Jefferson or a Franklin, the Americans refused to join in the great Enlightenment enterprise of shattering the Christian concept of sin, replacing it with an unlimited humanism, and then emerging with an earthly paradise as

Reprinted from Louis Hartz, "American Political Thought and the American Revolution," AMERICAN POLITICAL SCIENCE REVIEW *(June 1952), pp. 323–24, 329–33, 339–42, by permission of the publisher.*

glittering as the heavenly one that had been destroyed. The fact that the Americans did not share the crusading spirit of the French and the Russians, as we have seen, is already some sort of confirmation of this, for that spirit was directly related to the "civil religion" of Europe and is quite unthinkable without it. Nor is it hard to see why the liberal good fortune of the Americans should have been at work in the position they held. Europe's brilliant dream of an impending millennium, like the mirage of a thirst-ridden man, was inspired in large part by the agonies it experienced. When men have already inherited the freest society in the world, and are grateful for it, their thinking is bound to be of a solider type. America has been a sober nation, but it has also been a comfortable one, and the two points are by no means unrelated.

• • •

The issue of history itself is deeply involved here. On this score, inevitably, the fact that the revolutionaries of 1776 had inherited the freest society in the world shaped their thinking in a most intricate way. It gave them, in the first place, an appearance of outright conservatism. We know, of course, that most liberals of the eighteenth century, from Bentham to Quesnay, were bitter opponents of history, posing a sharp antithesis between nature and tradition. And it is an equally familiar fact that their adversaries, including Burke and Blackstone, sought to break down this antithesis by identifying natural law with the slow evolution of the past. The militant Americans, confronted with these two positions, actually took the second. Until Jefferson raised the banner of independence, and even in many cases after that time, they based their claims on a philosophic synthesis of Anglo-American legal history and the reason of natural law. Blackstone, the very Blackstone whom Bentham so bitterly attacked in the very year 1776, was a rock on which they relied.

The explanation is not hard to find. The past had been good to the Americans, and they knew it. Instead of inspiring them to the fury of Bentham and Voltaire, it often produced a mystical sense of Providential guidance akin to that of Maistre—as when Rev. Samuel West, surveying the growth of America's population, anticipated victory in the revolution because "we have been prospered in a most wonderful manner." The troubles they had with England did not alter this outlook. Even these, as they pointed out again and again, were of recent origin, coming after more than a century of that "salutary neglect" which Burke defended so vigorously. And in a specific sense, of course, the record of English history in the seventeenth century and the record of colonial charters from the time of the Virginia settlement provided excellent ammunition for the battle they were waging in defense of colonial rights. A series of

circumstances had conspired to saturate even the revolutionary position of the Americans with the quality of traditionalism—to give them, indeed, the appearance of outraged reactionaries. "This I call an innovation," thundered John Dickinson, in his attack on the Stamp Act, "a most dangerous innovation."

Now here was a frame of mind that would surely have troubled many of the illuminated liberals in Europe, were it not for an ironic fact. America piled on top of this paradox another one of an opposite kind, and thus as it were, by misleading them twice, gave them a deceptive sense of understanding.

Actually, the form of America's traditionalism was one thing, its content quite another. Colonial history had not been the slow and glacial record of development that Bonald and Maistre loved to talk about. On the contrary, since the first sailing of the *Mayflower,* it had been a story of new beginnings, daring enterprises, and explicitly stated principles—it breathed, in other words, the spirit of Bentham himself. The result was that the traditionalism of the Americans, like a pure freak of logic, often bore amazing marks of anti-historical rationalism. The clearest case of this undoubtedly is to be found in the revolutionary constitutions of 1776, which evoked, as Franklin reported, the "rapture" of European liberals everywhere. In America, of course, the concept of a written constitution, including many of the mechanical devices it embodied, was the end-product of a chain of historical experience that went back to the Mayflower Compact and the Plantation Covenants of the New England towns: it was the essence of political traditionalism. But in Europe just the reverse was true. The concept was the darling of the rationalists

—a symbol of the emancipated mind at work.

Thus Condorcet was untroubled. Instead of bemoaning the fact that the Americans were Blackstonian historicists, he proudly welcomed them into the fraternity of the illuminated. American constitutionalism, he said, "had not grown, but was planned"; it "took no force from the weight of centuries but was put together mechanically in a few years." When John Adams read this comment, he spouted two words on the margin of the page: "Fool! Fool!" But surely the judgment was harsh. After all, when Burke clothes himself in the garments of Siéyès, who can blame the loyal rationalist who fraternally grasps his hand? The reactionaries of Europe, moreover, were often no keener in their judgment. They made the same mistake in reverse. Maistre gloomily predicted that the American Constitution would not last because it was created out of the whole cloth of reason.

But how then are we to describe these baffling Americans? Were they rationalists or were they traditionalists? The truth is, they were neither, which is perhaps another way of saying that they were both. For the war between Burke and Bentham on the score of tradition, which made a great deal of sense in a society where men had lived in the shadow of feudal institutions, made comparatively little sense in a society where for years they had been creating new states, planning new settlements, and, as Jefferson said, literally building new lives. In such a society a strange dialectic was fated to appear, which would somehow unite the antagonistic components of the European mind; the past became a continuous future, and the God of the traditionalists sanctioned the very arrogance of the men who defied Him.

This shattering of the time categories of Europe, this Hegelian-like revolution in historic perspective, goes far to explain one of the enduring secrets of the American character: a capacity to combine rock-ribbed traditionalism with high inventiveness, ancestor worship with ardent optimism. Most critics have seized upon one or the other of these aspects of the American mind, finding it impossible to conceive how both can go together. That is why the insight of Gunnar Myrdal is a very distinguished one when he writes: "America is . . . conservative. . . . But the principles conserved are liberal and some, indeed, are radical." Radicalism and conservatism have been twisted entirely out of shape by the liberal flow of American history.

What I have been doing here is fairly evident: I have been interpreting the social thought of the American revolution in terms of the social goals *it did not need to achieve*. Given the usual approach, this may seem like a perverse inversion of the reasonable course of things; but in a world where the "canon and feudal law" are missing, how else are we to understand the philosophy of a liberal revolution? The remarkable thing about the "spirit of 1776," as we have seen, is not that it sought emancipation but that it sought it in a sober temper; not that it opposed power but that it opposed it ruthlessly and continuously; not that it looked forward to the future but that it worshipped the past as well. Even these perspectives, however, are only part of the story, misleading in themselves. The "free air" of American life, as John Jay once happily put it, penetrated to deeper levels of the American mind, twisting it in strange ways, producing a set of results fundamental to everything else in American thought. The clue to these results lies in the following fact: the Americans, though models to all the world of the middle class way of life, lacked the passionate middle class consciousness which saturated the liberal thought of Europe.

There was nothing mysterious about this lack. It takes the contemptuous challenge of an aristocratic feudalism to elicit such a consciousness; and when Richard Price glorified the Americans because they were men of the "middle state," men who managed to escape being "savage" without becoming "refined," he explained implicitly why they themselves would never have it. Franklin, of course, was a great American bourgeois thinker; but it is a commonplace that he had a wider vogue on this score in Paris and London than he did in Philadelphia; and indeed there is some question as to whether the Europeans did not worship him more because he seemed to exemplify Poor Richard than because he had created the philosophy by which Poor Richard lived. The Americans, a kind of national embodiment of the concept of the bourgeoisie, have, as Mr. Brinkmann points out, rarely used that concept in their social thought, and this is an entirely natural state of affairs. Frustration produces the social passion, ease does not. A triumphant middle class, unassailed by the agonies that Beaumarchais described, can take itself for granted. This point, curiously enough, is practically never discussed, though the failure of the American working class to become class conscious has been a theme of endless interest. And yet the relationship between the two suggests itself at once. Marx himself used to say that the bourgeoisie was the great teacher of the proletariat.

There can, it is true, be quite an argument over whether the challenge of an American aristocracy did not in fact exist in the eighteenth century. One can point to the great estates of New York where the Patroons lived in something resembling feudal splendor. One can point to the society of the South where life was extraordinarily stratified, with slaves at the bottom and a set of genteel planters at the top. One can even point to the glittering social groups that gathered about the royal governors in the North. But after all of this has been said, the American "aristocracy" could not, as Tocqueville pointed out, inspire either the "love" or the "hatred" that surrounded the ancient titled aristocracies of Europe. Indeed, in America it was actually the "aristocrats" who were frustrated, not the members of the middle class, for they were forced almost everywhere, even in George Washington's Virginia, to rely for survival upon shrewd activity in the capitalist race. This compulsion produced a psychic split that has always tormented the American "aristocracy"; and even when wealth was taken for granted, there was still, especially in the North, the withering impact of a colonial "character" that Sombart himself once described as classically bourgeois. In Massachusetts Governor Hutchinson used to lament that a "gentleman" did not meet even with "common civility" from his inferiors. Of course, the radicals of America blasted their betters as "aristocrats," but that this was actually a subtle compliment is betrayed in the quality of the blast itself. Who could confuse the anger of Daniel Shays with the bitterness of Francis Place even in the England of the nineteenth century?

Thus it happened that fundamental aspects of Europe's bourgeois code of political thought met an ironic fate in the most bourgeois country in the world. They were not so much rejected as they were ignored, treated indifferently, because the need for their passionate affirmation did not exist. . . .

. . .

Here, then, is the master assumption of American political thought, the assumption from which all of the American attitudes discussed in this essay flow: the reality of atomistic social freedom. It is instinctive to the American mind, as in a sense the concept of the polis was instinctive to Platonic Athens or the concept of the church to the mind of the middle ages. Catastrophes have not been able to destroy it, proletariats have refused to give it up, and even our Progressive tradition, in its agonized clinging to a Jeffersonian world, has helped to keep it alive. There has been only one major group of American thinkers who have dared to challenge it frontally: the Fitzhughs and Holmeses of the pre-Civil War South who, identifying slavery with feudalism, tried to follow the path of the European reaction and of Comte. But American life rode roughshod over them—for the "prejudice" of Burke in America was liberal and the positive reality of Locke in America transformed them into the very metaphysicians they assailed. They were soon forgotten, massive victims of the absolute temper of the American mind, shoved off the scene by Horatio Alger, who gave to the Lockean premise a brilliance that lasted until the crash of 1929. And even the crash, though it led to a revision of the premise, did not really shatter it.

. . .

But, someone will ask, where did the liberal heritage of the Americans come from in the first place? Didn't they have to create it? And if they did, were they not at one time or another in much the same position as the Europeans? These questions drive us back to the ultimate nature of the American experience, and, doing so, confront us with a queer twist in the problem of revolution. No one can deny that conscious purpose went into the making of the colonial world, and that the men of the seventeenth century who fled to America from Europe were keenly aware of the oppressions of European life. But they were revolutionaries with a difference, and the fact of their fleeing is no minor fact: for it is one thing to stay at home and fight the "canon and feudal law," and it is another to leave it far behind. It is one thing to try to establish liberalism in the Old World, and it is another to establish it in the New. Revolution, to borrow the words of T. S. Eliot, means to murder and create, but the American experience has been projected strangely in the realm of creation alone. The destruction of forests and Indian tribes—heroic, bloody, legendary as it was—cannot be compared with the destruction of a social order to which one belongs oneself. The first experience is wholly external and, being external, can actually be completed; the second experience is an inner struggle as well as an outer struggle, like the slaying of a Freudian father, and goes on in a sense forever. Moreover, even the matter of creation is not in the American case a simple one. The New World, as Lord Baltimore's ill-fated experiment with feudalism in the seventeenth century illustrates, did not merely offer the Americans a virgin ground for the building of a liberal system: it conspired itself to help that system along. The abundance of land in America, as well as the need for a lure to settlers, entered so subtly into the shaping of America's liberal tradition, touched it so completely at every point, that Sumner was actually ready to say, "We have not made America, America has made us."

It is this business of destruction and creation which goes to the heart of the problem. For the point of departure of great revolutionary thought everywhere else in the world has been the effort to build a new society on the ruins of an old society, and this is an experience America has never had. Tocqueville saw the issue clearly, and it is time now to complete the sentence of his with which we began this essay: "The great advantage of the American is that he has arrived at a state of democracy without having to endure a democratic revolution; *and that he is born free without having to become so.*"

Born free without having to become so: this idea, especially in light of the strange relationship which the revolutionary Americans had with their admirers abroad, raises an obvious question. Can a people that is born free ever understand peoples elsewhere that have to become so? Can it ever lead them? Or to turn the issue around, can people struggling for a goal understand those who have inherited it? This is not a problem of antitheses such, for example, as we find in Locke and Filmer. It is a problem of different perspectives on the same ideal. But we must not for that reason assume that it is any less difficult of solution; it may in the end be more difficult, since antitheses define each other and hence can understand each other, but different perspectives on a single value may, ironically enough, lack this common ground of definition. Condorcet might make sense out of Burke's traditionalism, for it was the reverse of his own activism, but what could he say about Otis, who combined both concepts in a synthesis that neither had seen? America's experience of being born free has put it in a strange relationship to the rest of the world.

EDMUND S. MORGAN

In 1740 America's leading intellectuals were clergymen and thought about theology; in 1790 they were statesmen and thought about politics. A variety of forces, some of them reaching deep into the colonial past, helped to bring about the transformation, but it was so closely associated with the revolt from England that one may properly consider the American Revolution, as an intellectual movement, to mean the substitution of political for clerical leadership and of politics for religion as the most challenging area of human thought and endeavor.

．　．　．

Such indifference to religion, edged with hostility to the clergy, was the end product of the developments we have been tracing from the 1740's. But though the clergy could blame themselves for much of their loss of prestige and for much of the decline of popular interest in religion, it was Parliament's attempt to tax the colonists in the 1760's that caused Americans to transfer to politics the intellectual interest and energy that were once reserved for religion. This reorientation was directed partly by the clergy themselves. They had never stopped giving instruction in political thought; and (except for the Anglicans) throughout the 1760's and 1770's they publicly and passionately

Reprinted from Edmund S. Morgan, "The American Revolution Considered as an Intellectual Movement," in Arthur M. Schlesinger, Jr., and Morton White, eds., PATHS OF AMERICAN THOUGHT *(Boston: Houghton Mifflin Co., 1963), pp. 11, 22–32, by permission of the publisher.*

scored the actions of George III and his Parliament against the standards by which their English Puritan predecessors had judged and condemned Charles I.

Presbyterian and Congregational ministers also raised the alarm when a movement was set afoot for the establishment in the colonies of state-supported bishops. The American clergymen developed no new general ideas about government—there was no New Light in political thought, no New Politics to match the New Divinity—but the old ideas and those imported from English political theorists served well enough to impress upon their congregations the tyrannical nature of taxation without representation, and of bishops who might establish ecclesiastical courts with jurisdiction extending beyond their own denomination.

Although the clergy were a powerful influence in molding American political opinion during the Revolutionary period, they did not recover through politics the intellectual leadership they had already begun to lose. Their own principles barred them from an active role in politics. While they had always given political advice freely and exercised their influence in elections, most of them would have considered it wrong to sit in a representative assembly, on a governor's council, or on the bench. To them as to their Puritan ancestors the clerical exercise of temporal powers spelled Rome. A minister's business was, after all, the saving of souls. By the same token, however outraged he might be by the actions of the English government, however excited by the achievement of American independence, a minister could not devote his principal intellectual effort to the expounding of political ideas and political principles. As the quarrel with England developed and turned into a

struggle for independence and nationhood, though the ministers continued to speak up on the American side, other voices commanding greater attention were raised by men who were free to make a career of politics and prepared to act as well as talk.

There had always, of course, been political leaders in the colonies, but hitherto politics had been a local affair, requiring at most the kind of talents needed for collecting votes or pulling wires. A colonial legislative assembly might occasionally engage in debates about paper money, defense, or modes of taxation; but the issues did not reach beyond the borders of the colony involved and were seldom of a kind to challenge a superior mind. No American debated imperial policy in the British Parliament, the Privy Council, or the Board of Trade. The highest political post to which a man could aspire in the colonies was that of governor, and everywhere except in Connecticut and Rhode Island, this was obtained not through political success but through having friends in England. Few native Americans ever achieved it or even tried to.

But the advent of Parliamentary taxation inaugurated a quarter-century of political discussion in America that has never since been matched in intensity. With the passage of the Stamp Act in 1765, every colonial legislature took up the task of defining the structure of the British empire; and as colonial definitions met with resistance from England, as the colonies banded together for defense and declared their independence, politics posed continental, even global, problems that called forth the best efforts of the best American minds. In no other period of our history would it be possible to find in politics five men of such intellectual stature as Benjamin Franklin, John Adams, Alexander

Hamilton, James Madison, and Thomas Jefferson; and there were others only slightly less distinguished.

Whether they hailed from Pennsylvania or Virginia, New England or New York, the men who steered Americans through the Revolution, the establishment of a new nation, and the framing of the Constitution did not for the most part repudiate the political ideas inherited from the period of clerical dominance. Like the clergy, they started from a conviction of human depravity; like the clergy, they saw government originating in compact, and measured governmental performance against an absolute standard ordained by God. Like the clergy too, they found inspiration in the example of seventeenth-century Englishmen. Sometimes they signed their own attacks on George III or his ministers with the names of John Hampden, William Pym, or other Parliamentary heroes in the struggle against Charles I. They read the works of Harrington and of Harrington's later admirers; and after the Declaration of Independence, when they found themselves in a position similar to that of England in the 1650's, they drew heavily on the arsenal of political ideas furnished by these latter-day republicans.

Indeed, most of the ideas about government which American intellectuals employed first in their resistance to Parliament, and then in constructing their own governments, had been articulated earlier in England and were still in limited circulation there. The social compact, fundamental law, the separation of powers, human equality, religious freedom, and the superiority of republican government were continuing ideals for a small but ardent group of Englishmen who, like the Americans, believed that the British constitution was basically republican and drew in-

spiration from it while attacking the ministers and monarch who seemed to be betraying it. It is perhaps no accident that the work in which Americans first repudiated monarchy, *Common Sense,* was written by an Englishman, Thomas Paine, who had come to America only two years before.

But if Englishmen supplied the intellectual foundations both for the overthrow of English rule and for the construction of republican government, Americans put the ideas into practice and drew on American experience and tradition to devise refinements and applications of the greatest importance. That republican ideas, which existed in a state of obscurity in England, should be congenial in the colonies, was due in the first place to the strong continuing Calvinist tradition which had been nourished over the years by the American clergy. But fully as important was the fact that during a hundred and fifty years of living in the freedom of a relatively isolated and empty continent, the colonists had developed a way of life in which republican ideas played a visible part. When Parliamentary taxation set Americans to analyzing their relationship to the mother country, they could not escape seeing that the social, economic, and political configuration of America had diverged from that of England in ways that made Americans better off than Englishmen. And the things that made them better off could be labeled republican.

England's practical experience with republicanism had lasted only eleven years. With the return of Charles II in 1660, Englishmen repudiated their republic and the Puritans who had sponsored it. Though a small minority continued to write and talk about republicanism and responsible government, they wielded no authority. The

House of Commons grew more powerful but less common, and the main current of English national life flowed in the channels of monarchy, aristocracy, and special privilege. Americans, by contrast, though formally subjects of the king, had lived long under conditions that approximated the ideals of the English republican theorists. Harrington thought he had found in the England of his day the widespread ownership of property that seemed to him a necessary condition for republican government; but throughout the colonies ownership of property had always been more widespread than in England. Furthermore no member of the nobility had settled in America, so that people were accustomed to a greater degree of social as well as economic equality than existed anywhere in England.

During the 1640's and 1650's England had seen a rapid multiplication of religious sects, which produced a wide belief in religious freedom, but after the Anglican Church had reimposed its controls in the 1660's, the most that other denominations could hope for was toleration. In America, religious diversity had steadily increased, and with it came a religious freedom which, if still imperfect, surpassed anything England had ever known.

Though the English people had twice removed an unsatisfactory king, in 1649 and in 1688, the English government remained far less responsible and far less responsive to the people than any colonial government. While the members of Parliament disclaimed any obligation to their immediate constituents, the members of American representative assemblies knew that they were expected to look after the interests of the people who elected them. Nor were the voters in America only a small minority of the population as in England. In most colonies probably the great majority of adult males owned enough property to meet the qualification (which varied from colony to colony) for voting. In England, the government paid hundreds of office-holders whose offices, carrying no duties, existed solely for the enrichment of those who held them. In the colonies such sinecures were few. Americans thought that government existed to do a job, and they created no offices except for useful purposes.

Thus when the quarrel with Parliament began, the colonists already had what English reformers wanted. And the colonists were inclined to credit their good fortune not to the accident of geography but to their own superior virtue and political sophistication. The interpretation was not without foundation: since Calvinist traditions were still strong among them and since they had often learned of British republican ideas through the sermons of Calvinist clergymen, Americans retained what the Enlightenment had dimmed in England and Europe, a keen sense of human depravity and of the dangers it posed for government. Although their own governments had hitherto given little evidence of depravity, by comparison with those of Europe, they were expert at detecting it in any degree. They had always been horrified by the open corruption of British politics and feared it would lead to tyranny. When Parliament attempted to tax them and sent swarms of customs collectors, sailors, and soldiers to support the attempt, their fears were confirmed. In resisting the British and in forming their own governments, they saw the central problem as one of devising means to check the inevitable operation of depravity in men who wielded power. English statesmen had succumbed to it. How could Americans avoid their mistakes?

In the era of the American Revolution, from 1764 to 1789, this was the great intellectual challenge. Although human depravity continued to pose as difficult theological problems as ever, the best minds of the period addressed themselves to the rescue, not of souls, but of governments, from the perils of corruption. Of course the problem was not new, nor any more susceptible of final solution than it had been in an earlier time, but Americans in the Revolutionary period contributed three notable principles to men's efforts to deal with it.

The first principle, which evolved from the struggle with Parliament, was that the people of one region ought not to exercise dominion over those of another, even though the two may be joined together. It was an idea that overlapped and greatly facilitated the slower but parallel development of the more general belief in human equality. In objecting to British taxation in 1764 the colonists had begun by asserting their right to equal treatment with the king's subjects in Great Britain: Englishmen could not be taxed except by their representatives; neither therefore could Americans. Within a year or two the idea was extended to a denial that Parliament, representing the electors of Great Britain, could exercise any authority over the colonies. The empire, according to one American writer, was "a confederacy of states, independent of each other, yet united under one head," namely the king. "I cannot find," said another, "that the inhabitants of the colonies are dependent on the people of Britain, or the people of Britain on them, any more than Kent is on Sussex, or Sussex on Kent."

It took varying lengths of time for other Americans to reach the position thus anonymously expressed in the press in 1765 and 1766. Franklin stated it later in 1766; Jefferson, James Wil-

son, and John Adams had all expressed it by the beginning of 1775. It was frequently buttressed by the citation of precedents from English constitutional history, but it rested on a principle capable of universal application, the principle stated in the preamble of the Declaration of Independence, that every people is entitled, by the laws of nature and of nature's God, to a separate and equal station.

Before Independence this principle offered a means of reorganizing the British empire so as to defeat the tyranny which Americans thought English statesmen were developing in the extension of taxation. If a British legislature, in which the colonists were not represented, could govern them, then neither British nor colonial freedom could be safe. Americans without a voice in the government could not defend their rights against corrupt rulers. Englishmen, relieved of expenses by American taxation, might rejoice for the moment, but their rulers, no longer dependent on them financially, would be able to govern as they pleased and would eventually escape popular control altogether. The only solution was to give each legislature power only over the people who chose it.

In the 1770's England was unwilling to listen to the colonial arguments, but ultimately adopted the American principle in forming the Commonwealth of Nations. The independent United States applied the principle not only in the confederation of states but in the annexation of other areas. When Virginia in 1781 offered the United States Congress her superior claim to the old Northwest, it was with the stipulation that the region be divided into separate republican states, each of which was to be admitted to the Union on equal terms with the old ones. The stipulation, though not accepted by Congress at the time, was carried out in Jefferson's land ordinance of 1784 and in the Northwest Ordinance of 1787 which superseded it. The United States never wavered from the principle until after the Spanish-American War, when it temporarily accepted government of areas which it had no intention of admitting to the union on equal terms.

The second contribution of the American Revolutionists was an application of the assumption, implicit in the whole idea of a compact between rulers and people, that a people can exist as a people before they have a government and that they can act as a people independently of government. The Puritans had distinguished between the compact of a group of individuals with God, by which they became a people, and the subsequent compact between this people and their rulers, by which government was created. John Locke had similarly distinguished between the dissolution of society and of government, and so, at least tacitly, had the Revolutionists. They would have been more daring, not to say foolhardy, if they had undertaken to destroy the bonds of society as well as of government. But in their haste to form new governments after the royal government in each colony dissolved, the Revolutionists followed a procedure that did not clearly distinguish the people from the government. Provincial congresses, exercising a *de facto* power, drafted and adopted permanent constitutions, which in most cases then went into effect without submission to a popular vote.

When the Massachusetts provincial congress proposed to follow this procedure in 1776, the citizens of the town of Concord pointed out the dangerous opening which it offered to human depravity. A *de facto* government that legitimized itself could also alter itself. Whatever safeguards it adopted against corruption could easily be discarded by later legislators: "a Constitution alterable by the Supreme Legislative is no Security at all to the Subject against any Encroachment of the Governing part on any or on all of their Rights and priviliges." The town therefore suggested that a special popularly elected convention be called for the sole purpose of drafting a constitution, which should then be submitted to the people for approval.

It is impossible to determine who was responsible for Concord's action, but the protest displays a refinement in the application of republican ideas that does not appear to have been expressed before. Concord's suggestion was eventually followed in the drafting and adoption of the Massachusetts constitution of 1780 and of every subsequent constitution established in the United States. By it the subservience of government to the people was secured through a constitution clearly superior to the government it created, a constitution against which the people could measure governmental performance and against which each branch of government could measure the actions of the other branches. The separation of governmental powers into a bicameral legislature, an executive, and a judiciary, which was an older and more familiar way of checking depravity, was rendered far more effective by the existence of a written constitution resting directly on popular approval. The written constitution also proved its effectiveness in later years by perpetuating in America the operation of judicial review, of executive veto, and of a powerful upper house of the legislature, all of which had been or would be lost in England, where the constitution was unwritten and consisted of customary procedures that could be altered at will by Parliament.

Thus by the time the Revolution ended, Americans had devised a way to establish the superiority of the people to their government and so to control man's tyranny over man. For the same purpose Americans had formulated the principle that no people should exercise dominion over another people. But the way in which they first employed the latter principle in running the new nation did not prove satisfactory. As thirteen separate colonies the people of America had joined to combat Parliamentary taxation, and the result had been thirteen independent republics. It had been an exhilarating experience, and it had led them almost from the beginning to think of themselves in some degree as one people. But the thought was not completed: they did not coalesce into one republic with one government. Instead, as thirteen separate and equal peoples, they set up a "perpetual union" in which they were joined only through a Congress in which each state had one vote. They gave the Congress responsibility for their common concerns. But they did not give it the ordinary powers of a government to tax or legislate.

Because of the straightforward equality of the member states and because the Congress did not possess the means by which governments generally ran to tyranny, the confederation seemed a safe shape in which to cast the new nation. Actually danger lurked in the fact that the Congress had insufficient power to carry out the responsibilities which the states assigned to it. After the British troops were defeated and the need for united action became less obvious, state support of the Congress steadily declined. Without coercive powers, the Congress could not act effectively either at home or abroad, and the nation was increasingly exposed to the danger of foreign depredations. At the same time,

the state governments were proving vulnerable to manipulation by corrupt or ambitious politicians and were growing powerful at the expense not only of the Congress but of the people. Some undertook irresponsible inflationary measures that threatened property rights. Unless the state governments were brought under more effective control, local demagogues might destroy the union and replace the tyranny of Parliament with a new domestic brand.

Although a few men foresaw the drawbacks of a weak Congress from the beginning, most people needed time to show them. The Massachusetts legislature, perceiving that the experience of the state could be applied to the whole United States, in 1785 suggested a national constitutional convention to create a central authority capable of acting effectively in the interests of the whole American people. But in 1785, Americans were not yet convinced that what they had was inadequate. The Massachusetts delegates to the Congress replied to their state's suggestion with the same arguments that had in the first place prompted Americans to base their union on a weak coordinative Congress rather than a real national government: it would be impossible, they said, to prevent such a government from escaping popular control. With headquarters remote from most of its constituents, with only a select few from each state engaged in it, a national government would offer too many opportunities for corruption. The fear was supported by the views of respected European political thinkers. Montesquieu, who had been widely read in America, maintained that republican government was suited only to small areas. A confederation of republics might extend far, but a single republican government of large extent would either fall a prey to the ambitions of a few corrupt individuals, or else it would break up into a number of smaller states.

These sentiments were so widely held that they prevented any effort to establish a national government until 1787. And when a convention was finally called in that year it was charged, not to create a new government, but simply to revise the Articles of Confederation. The members of the convention, without authorization, assumed the larger task and turned themselves into a national Constitutional Convention. They did so because they became convinced that, contrary to popular belief, a large republic would not necessarily succumb to corruption. The man who persuaded the Convention, insofar as any one man did it, was James Madison, one of the delegates from Virginia.

In the month before the Convention assembled, Madison had drawn up some observations on the "Vices of the Political System of the United States." Following a hint thrown out by David Hume, he reached the conclusion that "the inconveniencies of popular States contrary to the prevailing Theory, are in proportion not to the extent, but to the narrowness of their limits." In the state governments that had operated since 1776, the great defect was a tendency of the majority to tyrannize over the minority. Madison took it as axiomatic that "in republican Government the majority however composed, ultimately give the law." Unless a way could be found to control them, the majority would inevitably oppress the minority, because the individuals who made up the majority were as susceptible as any king or lord to the operation of human depravity. The most effective curb, Madison suggested, was to make the territory of the republic so large that a majority would have difficulty forming. Men being hopelessly selfish would inevitably seek to capture the government

for selfish purposes, and in a small republic they might easily form combinations to secure the necessary majority. But in a large republic, "the Society becomes broken into a greater variety of interests, of pursuits of passions, which check each other, whilst those who may feel a common sentiment have less opportunity of communication and concert."

This insight, later given classic expression in the tenth *Federalist* paper, was the most fruitful intellectual achievement of the Revolutionary period, the third of the three principles mentioned earlier. It gave Madison and his colleagues at Philadelphia the courage to attempt a republican government for the whole nation. The constitution which they drew up would provide the American peoples with a government that would effectively make them one people. The government would incorporate all the protections to liberty that they still cherished from their British heritage; it would preserve both imported and home-grown republican traditions; and it would employ the political principles developed during the Revolution. It would be a government inferior to the people and one in which no people should have dominion over another, a government in which almost every detail was prompted by the framers' determination to control the operation of human depravity. Many Americans, doubting that the safeguards would work, opposed the adoption of the Constitution. But the character of American politics from 1789 to the present day has borne out Madison's observation: majorities in the United States have been composed of such a variety of interests that they have seldom proved oppressive, and the national government has been a stronger bulwark of freedom than the state governments.

The establishment of a national republic renewed the challenge which the contest with Great Britain had presented to the best minds of America. In the Constitutional Convention and in the conduct of the new national government, Americans found scope for talents that the Revolution had uncovered. Jefferson, Hamilton, Madison, and John Adams received from national politics the stimulus that made them great. The writings in which they embodied their best thoughts were state papers.

In the course of the nineteenth century the stimulus was somehow lost, in hard cider, log cabins, and civil war. Intellect moved away from politics; and intellectual leadership, having passed from clergy to statesmen, moved on to philosophers, scientists, and novelists. But during the brief period when America's intellectual leaders were her political leaders, they created for their country the most stable popular government ever invented and presented to the world three political principles which men have since used repeatedly and successfully to advance human freedom and responsible government.

BERNARD BAILYN

The political and social ideas of the European Enlightenment have had a peculiar importance in American history. More universally accepted in eighteenth-century America than in Europe, they were more completely and more permanently embodied in the formal arrangements of state and society; and, less controverted, less subject

Reprinted from Bernard Bailyn, "Political Experience and Enlightenment Ideas in Eighteenth-Century America," AMERICAN HISTORICAL REVIEW, *LXVII (January 1962), 339–41, 344–51, by permission of the publisher.*

to criticism and dispute, they have lived on more vigorously into later periods, more continuous and more intact. The peculiar force of these ideas in America resulted from many causes. But originally, and basically, it resulted from the circumstances of the prerevolutionary period and from the bearing of these ideas on the political experience of the American colonists.

What this bearing was—the nature of the relationship between Enlightenment ideas and early American political experience—is a matter of particular interest at the present time because it is centrally involved in what amounts to a fundamental revision of early American history now under way. By implication if not direct evidence and argument, a number of recent writings have undermined much of the structure of historical thought by which, for a generation or more, we have understood our eighteenth-century origins, and in particular have placed new and insupportable pressures on its central assumption concerning the political significance of Enlightenment thought. Yet the need for rather extensive rebuilding has not been felt, in part because the architecture has not commonly been seen as a whole—as a unit, that is, of mutually dependent parts related to a central premise—in part because the damage has been piecemeal and uncoordinated: here a beam destroyed, there a stone dislodged, the inner supports only slowly weakened and the balance only gradually thrown off. The edifice still stands, mainly, it seems, by habit and by the force of inertia. A brief consideration of the whole, consequently, a survey from a position far enough above the details to see the outlines of the over-all architecture, and an attempt, however tentative, to sketch a line—a principle—of reconstruction would seem to be in order.

A basic, organizing assumption of the group of ideas that dominated the earlier interpretation of eighteenth-century American history is the belief that previous to the Revolution the political experience of the colonial Americans had been roughly analogous to that of the English. Control of public authority had been firmly held by a native aristocracy—merchants and landlords in the North, planters in the South—allied, commonly, with British officialdom. By restricting representation in the provincial assemblies, limiting the franchise, and invoking the restrictive power of the English state, this aristocracy had dominated the governmental machinery of the mainland colonies. Their political control, together with legal devices such as primogeniture and entail, had allowed them to dominate the economy as well. Not only were they successful in engrossing landed estates and mercantile fortunes, but they were for the most part able also to fight off the clamor of yeoman debtors for cheap paper currency, and of depressed tenants for freehold property. But the control of this colonial counterpart of a traditional aristocracy, with its Old World ideas of privilege and hierarchy, orthodoxy in religious establishment, and economic inequality, was progressively threatened by the growing strength of a native, frontier-bred democracy that expressed itself most forcefully in the lower houses of the "rising" provincial assemblies. A conflict between the two groups and ways of life was building up, and it broke out in fury after 1765.

The outbreak of the Revolution, the argument runs, fundamentally altered the old regime. The Revolution destroyed the power of this traditional aristocracy, for the movement of opposition to parliamentary taxation, 1760–1776, originally controlled by conservative elements, had been taken over by extremists nourished on Enlightenment radicalism, and the once dominant conservative groups had gradually been alienated. The break with England over the question of home rule was part of a general struggle, as Carl Becker put it, over who shall rule at home. Independence gave control to the radicals, who, imposing their advanced doctrines on a traditional society, transformed a rebellious secession into a social revolution. They created a new regime, a reformed society, based on enlightened political and social theory.

But that is not the end of the story; the sequel is important. The success of the enlightened radicals during the early years of the Revolution was notable; but, the argument continues, it was not wholly unqualified. The remnants of the earlier aristocracy, though defeated, had not been eliminated: they were able to reassert themselves in the postwar years. In the 1780's they gradually regained power until, in what amounted to a counterrevolution, they impressed their views indelibly on history in the new federal Constitution, in the revocation of some of the more enthusiastic actions of the earlier revolutionary period, and in the Hamiltonian program for the new government. This was not, of course, merely the old regime resurrected. In a new age whose institutions and ideals had been born of revolutionary radicalism, the old conservative elements made adjustments and concessions by which to survive and periodically to flourish as a force in American life.

The importance of this formulation derived not merely from its usefulness in interpreting eighteenth-century history. It provided a key also for understanding the entire course of American politics. By its light, politics in America, from the very beginning, could be seen to have been a dialectical process in which an aristocracy of wealth and power struggled with the People, who, ordinarily ill-organized and inarticulate, rose upon provocation armed with powerful institutional and ideological weapons, to reform a periodically corrupt and oppressive polity.

In all of this the underlying assumption is the belief that Enlightenment thought—the reforming ideas of advanced thinkers in eighteenth-century England and on the Continent—had been the effective lever by which native American radicals had turned a dispute on imperial relations into a sweeping reformation of public institutions and thereby laid the basis for American democracy.

• • •

In every colony and in every legislature there were people who knew Locke and Beccaria, Montesquieu and Voltaire; but perhaps more important, there was in every village of every colony someone who knew such transmitters of English nonconformist thought as Watts, Neal, and Burgh; later Priestley and Price—lesser writers, no doubt, but staunch opponents of traditional authority, and they spoke in a familiar idiom. In the bitterly contentious pamphlet literature of mid-eighteenth-century American politics, the most frequently cited authority on matters of principle and theory was not Locke or Montesquieu but *Cato's Letters,* a series of radically libertarian essays written in London in 1720–1723 by two supporters of the dissenting interest, John Trenchard and Thomas Gordon. Through such writers, as well as through the major authors, leading colonists kept contact with a powerful tradition of enlightened thought.

This body of doctrine fell naturally into play in the controversy over the power of the imperial government. For the revolutionary leaders it supplied a common vocabulary and a common pattern of thought, and, when the time came, common principles of political reform. That reform was sought and seriously if unevenly undertaken, there can be no doubt. Institutions were remodeled, laws altered, practices questioned all in accordance with advanced doctrine on the nature of liberty and of the institutions needed to achieve it. The Americans were acutely aware of being innovators, of bringing mankind a long step forward. They believed that they had so far succeeded in their effort to reshape circumstances to conform to enlightened ideas and ideals that they had introduced a new era in human affairs. And they were supported in this by the opinion of informed thinkers in Europe. The contemporary image of the American Revolution at home and abroad was complex; but no one doubted that a revolution that threatened the existing order and portended new social and political arrangements had been made, and made in the name of reason.

Thus, throughout the eighteenth century there were prominent, politically active Americans who were well aware of the development of European thinking, took ideas seriously, and during the Revolution deliberately used them in an effort to reform the institutional basis of society. This much seems obvious. But, paradoxically, and less obviously, it is equally true that many, indeed most, of what these leaders considered to be their greatest achievements during the Revolution—reforms that made America seem to half the world like the veritable heavenly city of the eighteenth-century philosophers—had been matters of fact before they were matters of theory and revolutionary doctrine.

No reform in the entire Revolution appeared of greater importance to Jefferson than the Virginia acts abolishing primogeniture and entail. This action, he later wrote, was part of "a system by which every fibre would be eradicated of antient or future aristocracy; and a foundation laid for a government truly republican." But primogeniture and entail had never taken deep roots in America, not even in tidewater Virginia. Where land was cheap and easily available such legal restrictions proved to be encumbrances profiting few. Often they tended to threaten rather than secure the survival of the family, as Jefferson himself realized when in 1774 he petitioned the Assembly to break an entail on his wife's estate on the very practical, untheoretical, and common ground that to do so would be "greatly to their [the petitioners'] Interest and that of their Families." The legal abolition of primogeniture and entail during and after the Revolution was of little material consequence. Their demise had been effectively decreed years before by the circumstances of life in a wilderness environment.

Similarly, the disestablishment of religion—a major goal of revolutionary reform—was carried out, to the extent that it was, in circumstances so favorable to it that one wonders not how it was done but why it was not done more thoroughly. There is no more eloquent, moving testimony to revolutionary idealism than the Virginia Act for Establishing Religious Freedom: it is the essence of Enlightenment faith. But what did it, and the disestablishment legislation that had preceded it, reform? What had the establishment of religion meant in prerevolutionary Virginia? The Church of England was the state church, but dissent was tolerated well beyond the limits of the English Acts of Toleration. The law required nonconformist organizations to be licensed by the government, but dissenters were not barred from their own worship nor penalized for failure to attend the Anglican communion, and they were commonly exempted from parish taxes. Nonconformity excluded no one from voting and only the very few Catholics from enjoying public office. And when the itineracy of revivalist preachers led the establishment to contemplate more restrictive measures, the Baptists and Presbyterians advanced to the point of arguing publicly, and pragmatically, that the toleration they had so far enjoyed was an encumbrance, and that the only proper solution was total liberty: in effect, disestablishment.

Virginia was if anything more conservative than most colonies. The legal establishment of the Church of England was in fact no more rigorous in South Carolina and Georgia: it was considerably weaker in North Carolina. It hardly existed at all in the middle colonies (there was of course no vestige of it in Pennsylvania), and where it did, as in four counties of New York, it was either ignored or had become embattled by violent opposition well before the Revolution. And in Massachusetts and Connecticut, where the establishment, being nonconformist according to English law, was legally tenuous to begin with, tolerance in worship and relief from church taxation had been extended to the major dissenting groups early in the century, resulting well before the Revolution in what was, in effect if not in law, a multiple establishment. And this had been further weakened by the splintering effect of the Great Awakening. Almost everywhere the Church of England, the established church of the highest state authority, was embattled and defensive—driven to rely more and more on its missionary arm, the Society for the Propagation of the Gospel, to sustain it against the cohorts of dissent.

None of this had resulted from Enlightenment theory. It had been created by the mundane exigencies of the situation: by the distance that separated Americans from ecclesiastical centers in England and the Continent; by the never-ending need to encourage immigration to the colonies; by the variety, the mere numbers, of religious groups, each by itself a minority, forced to live together; and by the weakness of the coercive powers of the state, its inability to control the social forces within it.

Even more gradual and less contested had been the process by which government in the colonies had become government by the consent of the governed. What has been proved about the franchise in early Massachusetts—that it was open for practically the entire free adult male population—can be proved to a lesser or greater extent for all the colonies. But the extraordinary breadth of the franchise in the American colonies had not resulted from popular demands: there had been no cries for universal manhood suffrage, nor were there popular theories claiming, or even justifying, general participation in politics. Nowhere in eighteenth-century America was there "democracy"—middle-class or otherwise—as we use the term. The main reason for the wide franchise was that the traditional English laws limiting suffrage to freeholders of certain competences proved in the colonies, where freehold property was almost universal, to be not restrictive but widely permissive.

Representation would seem to be different, since before the Revolution complaints had been voiced against the inequity of its apportioning, especially in the Pennsylvania and North Carolina assemblies. But these complaints were based on an assumption that would have seemed natural and reasonable almost nowhere else in the Western world: the assumption that representation in governing assemblages was a proper and rightful attribute of people as such—of regular units of population, or of populated land—rather than the privilege of particular groups, institutions, or regions. Complaints there were, bitter ones. But they were complaints claiming injury and deprivation, not abstract ideals or unfamiliar desires. They assumed from common experience the normalcy of regular and systematic representation. And how should it have been otherwise? The colonial assemblies had not, like ancient parliaments, grown to satisfy a monarch's need for the support of particular groups or individuals or to protect the interests of a social order, and they had not developed insensibly from precedent to precedent. They had been created at a stroke, and they were in their composition necessarily regular and systematic. Nor did the process, the character, of representation as it was known in the colonies derive from theory. For colonial Americans, representation had none of the symbolic and little of the purely deliberative qualities which, as a result of the revolutionary debates and of Burke's speeches, would become celebrated as "virtual." To the colonists it was direct and actual: it was, most often, a kind of agency, a delegation of powers, to individuals commonly required to be residents of their constituencies and, often, bound by instructions from them—with the result that eighteenth-century American legislatures frequently resembled, in spirit if not otherwise, those "ancient assemblies" of New York, composed, the contemporary historian William Smith wrote, "of plain, illiterate husbandmen, whose views seldom extended farther than to the regulation of highways, the destruction of wolves, wild cats, and foxes, and the advancement of the other little interests of the particular counties which they were chosen to represent." There was no theoretical basis for such direct and actual representation. It had been created and was continuously reinforced by the pressure of local politics in the colonies and by the political circumstances in England, to which the colonists had found it necessary to send closely instructed, paid representatives—agents, so called—from the very beginning.

But franchise and representation are mere mechanisms of government by consent. At its heart lies freedom from executive power, from the independent action of state authority, and the concentration of power in representative bodies and elected officials. The greatest achievement of the Revolution was of course the repudiation of just such state authority and the transfer of power to popular legislatures. No one will deny that this action was taken in accordance with the highest principles of Enlightenment theory. But the way had been paved by fifty years of grinding factionalism in colonial politics. In the details of prerevolutionary American politics, in the complicated maneuverings of provincial politicians seeking the benefits of government, in the patterns of local patronage and the forms of factional groupings, there lies a history of progressive alienation from the state which resulted, at least by the 1750's, in what Professor Robert Palmer has lucidly described as a revolutionary situation: a condition

. . . in which confidence in the justice or reasonableness of existing authority is undermined; where old loyalties fade, obligations are felt as impositions, law seems arbitrary, and respect for superiors is felt as a form of humiliation; where existing sources of prestige seem undeserved . . . and government is sensed as distant, apart from the governed and not really "representing" them.

Such a condition had developed in mid-eighteenth-century America, not from theories of government or Enlightenment ideas but from the factional opposition that had grown up against a succession of legally powerful, but often cynically self-seeking, inept, and above all politically weak officers of state.

Surrounding all of these circumstances and in various ways controlling them is the fact that that great goal of the European revolutions of the late eighteenth century, equality of status before the law—the abolition of legal privilege—had been reached almost everywhere in the American colonies at least by the early years of the eighteenth century. Analogies between the upper strata of colonial society and the European aristocracies are misleading. Social stratification existed, of course; but the differences between aristocracies in eighteenth-century Europe and in America are more important than the similarities. So far was legal privilege, or even distinction, absent in the colonies that where it existed it was an open sore of festering discontent, leading not merely, as in the case of the Penn family's hereditary claims to tax exemption, to formal protests, but, as in the case of the powers enjoyed by the Hudson River land magnates, to violent opposition as well. More important, the colonial aristocracy, such as it was, had no formal, institutional role in government. No public office or function was legally a prerogative of birth. As there were no social orders in the eyes of the law, so there were no governmental bodies to represent them. The only claim that has been made to the contrary is that, in effect, the governors' Councils constituted political institutions in the service of the aristocracy. But this claim—of dubious value in any case because of the steadily declining political importance of the Councils in the eighteenth century—

cannot be substantiated. It is true that certain families tended to dominate the Councils, but they had less legal claim to places in those bodies than certain royal officials who, though hardly members of an American aristocracy, sat on the Councils by virtue of their office. Councilors could be and were removed by simple political maneuver. Council seats were filled either by appointment or election: when appointive, they were vulnerable to political pressure in England; when elective, to the vagaries of public opinion at home. Thus on the one hand it took William Byrd II three years of maneuvering in London to get himself appointed to the seat on the Virginia Council vacated by his father's death in 1704, and on the other, when in 1766 the Hutchinson faction's control of the Massachusetts Council proved unpopular, it was simply removed wholesale by being voted out of office at the next election. As there were no special privileges, no peculiar group possessions, manners, or attitudes to distinguish councilors from other affluent Americans, so there were no separate political interests expressed in the Councils as such. Councilors joined as directly as others in the factional disputes of the time, associating with groups of all sorts, from minute and transient American opposition parties to massive English-centered political syndicates. A century before the Revolution and not as the result of anti-aristocratic ideas, the colonial aristocracy had become a vaguely defined, fluid group whose power—in no way guaranteed, buttressed, or even recognized in law—was competitively maintained and dependent on continuous, popular support.

Other examples could be given. Were written constitutions felt to be particular guarantees of liberty in enlightened states? Americans had known them in the form of colonial charters and governors' instructions for a century before the Revolution; and after 1763, seeking a basis for their claims against the constitutionality of specific acts of Parliament, they had been driven, out of sheer logical necessity and not out of principle, to generalize that experience. But the point is perhaps clear enough. Major attributes of enlightened polities had developed naturally, spontaneously, early in the history of the American colonies, and they existed as simple matters of social and political fact on the eve of the Revolution.

But if all this is true, what did the Revolution accomplish? Of what real significance were the ideals and ideas? What was the bearing of Enlightenment thought on the political experience of eighteenth-century Americans?

Perhaps this much may be said. What had evolved spontaneously from the demands of place and time was not self-justifying, nor was it universally welcomed. New developments, however gradual, were suspect by some, resisted in part, and confined in their effects. If it was true that the establishment of religion was everywhere weak in the colonies and that in some places it was even difficult to know what was orthodoxy and what was not, it was nevertheless also true that faith in the idea of orthodoxy persisted and with it belief in the propriety of a privileged state religion. If, as a matter of fact, the spread of freehold tenure qualified large populations for voting, it did not create new reasons for using that power nor make the victims of its use content with what, in terms of the dominant ideal of balance in the state, seemed a disproportionate influence of "the democracy." If many colonists came naturally to assume that representation should be direct and actual, growing with the population and bearing some relation to its distribution, crown officials did not, and they had the weight of precedent and theory as well as of authority with them and hence justification for resistance. If state authority was seen increasingly as alien and hostile and was forced to fight for survival within an abrasive, kaleidoscopic factionalism, the traditional idea nevertheless persisted that the common good was somehow defined by the state and that political parties or factions—organized opposition to established government—were seditious. A traditional aristocracy did not in fact exist; but the assumption that superiority was indivisible, that social eminence and political influence had a natural affinity to each other, did. The colonists instinctively conceded to the claims of the well-born and rich to exercise public office, and in this sense politics remained aristocratic. Behavior had changed—had had to change—with the circumstances of everyday life; but habits of mind and the sense of rightness lagged behind. Many felt the changes to be *away from*, not *toward*, something: that they represented deviance; that they lacked, in a word, legitimacy.

This divergence between habits of mind and belief on the one hand and experience and behavior on the other was ended at the Revolution. A rebellion that destroyed the traditional sources of public authority called forth the full range of advanced ideas. Long-settled attitudes were jolted and loosened. The grounds of legitimacy suddenly shifted. What had happened was seen to have been good and proper, steps in the right direction. The glass was half full, not half empty; and to complete the work of fate and nature, further thought must be taken, theories tested, ideas applied. Precisely because so many social and institutional reforms had already taken place in Amer-

ica, the revolutionary movement there, more than elsewhere, was a matter of doctrine, ideas, and comprehension.

And so it remained. Social change and social conflict of course took place during the revolutionary years; but the essential developments of the period lay elsewhere, in the effort to think through and to apply under the most favorable, permissive, circumstances enlightened ideas of government and society. The problems were many, often unexpected and difficult; some were only gradually perceived. Social and personal privilege, for example, could easily be eliminated—it hardly existed; but what of the impersonal privileges of corporate bodies? Legal orders and ranks within society could be outlawed without creating the slightest tremor, and executive power with equal ease subordinated to the legislative: but how was balance within a polity to be achieved? What were the elements to be balanced and how were they to be separated? It was not even necessary formally to abolish the interest of state as a symbol and determinant of the common good; it was simply dissolved: but what was left to keep clashing factions from tearing a government apart? The problems were pressing, and the efforts to solve them mark the stages of revolutionary history.

In behalf of Enlightenment liberalism the revolutionary leaders undertook to complete, formalize, systematize, and symbolize what previously had been only partially realized, confused, and disputed matters of fact. Enlightenment ideas were not instruments of a particular social group, nor did they destroy a social order. They did not create new social and political forces in America. They released those that had long existed, and vastly increased their power. This completion, this rationalization, this symbolization, this lifting

into consciousness and endowing with   elements of social and political change
high moral purpose inchoate, confused   —this was the American Revolution.

HISTORIOGRAPHICAL NOTE

Earlier in the twentieth century, historians of colonial religious and intellectual life employed a fairly rigid set of categories with which to explain
the period's major cultural developments. Generally, they stressed on one
hand the European origins of and continuing European influence on provincial cultural life, viewing American thought as both inherited and derivative, a bastard cultural by-product of English and continental pene-
tration into virgin colonial minds. On the other hand, these scholars felt
that the English mainland settlers had contributed almost nothing original
or of value to the Old World in intellectual attainment before the Revolution. Charles and Mary Beard, Charles MacLean Andrews, and an entire
generation of colonial historians portrayed in abundant detail the British
philosophic influences which they believed had spawned American political
theory, the Lockean origins of New World rationalism, and the English
models behind eighteenth-century religious movements such as the Great
Awakening, Deism, and Unitarianism. Other historians such as Carl Becker
and Gilbert Chinard stressed the impact of the French Enlightenment on
American political ideology prior to the Revolution. Few scholars before
the last few decades attempted careful connections between the three most
significant cultural developments in late colonial America—the Great Awakening, the American Enlightenment, and Revolutionary political thought—
preferring to describe these different strands of provincial intellectual life
as patterns that drew their connections largely from the emerging sense of
American nationhood, if connected at all.

More recently, historians have found in the evolving patterns of colonial
experience much evidence of major transformations in eighteenth-century
American intellectual life. Edmund S. Morgan, Bernard Bailyn, Daniel
Boorstin, Louis Hartz, and other writers have discerned within the web of
colonial ideas and values the firm pre-Revolutionary foundations of a distinctively American culture. Indeed, Hartz and Boorstin have stimulated
an entire school of historical writing which has argued that a fully articulated and uniquely American frame of thought and belief existed almost
from the earliest settlements. Morgan and Bailyn make less sweeping and
perhaps more persuasive claims. Their works do not insist on the *inherent*
distinctiveness of American culture but on its *evolving* separateness from
European models, an evolution well under way by the early eighteenth
century. Both Morgan and Bailyn have taken the two major threads of
spiritual self-discovery in late colonial America—the Awakening and the
Enlightenment—and studied their reception by and transformation within

existing provincial social and intellectual worlds, paying particular attention to the way in which revivalist and rationalist ideologies meshed within the immediate pre-Revolutionary period. America may not have blossomed as a civilization, fully-dressed from birth in its own cultural garments as Boorstin, Hartz, and, earlier, Frederick Jackson Turner have all asserted. Still, recent students of colonial intellectual life have provided ample evidence of a flourishing, distinctive, and only partly-derivative life of the mind in America decades before the colonists cut their remaining *political* ties with the Old World.

4. Toward the New Nation: The Evolution of Political Loyalties in Eighteenth-Century America

INTRODUCTION

Writing on the study of eighteenth-century American political history, the historian Bernard Bailyn observed in a recent essay: "What is needed at this point is an effort not to unearth new information nor even to classify comprehensively the information we already have but to point to central themes, to establish essential characteristics, and to relate this early history to the later development of American politics." No one has contributed more to this search for synthesis than Bailyn himself who, along with other recent historians of colonial America, has abandoned the traditional attempt to simplify eighteenth-century political history by squeezing its contents into three conveniently-divided compartments: the "late colonial period," "Revolutionary era," and "Federalist decade." Recent historians such as Bailyn have recognized that the issues, rhetoric, and political structure of all three periods—roughly covered by the years 1700–1763, 1763–1789, and 1789–1800—reveal significant continuities and areas of overlap that earlier American political historians tended to minimize. One approach to these separate but related patterns of events involves a recognition of the importance to contemporaries of the problem presented by shifting political loyalties.

Few historians dispute the basic facts and the general background of America's colonial revolt against England, yet there are fundamental interpretive quarrels about the meaning and relative importance of the various "causes" of the Revolution. *Causa,* as the philosopher R. G. Collingwood pointed out, "originally meant 'guilt,' 'blame,' or 'accusation,' and when first it began to mean 'cause' . . . it was used [historically] for the cause of a war or the like." Whatever the cluster of circumstances, policies, and events pointed to in attempting to explain the causes of the American Revolution, historians have usually awarded a large measure of praise or blame for its occurrence to those aspects of eighteenth-century Anglo-American political relationships that they believed to be most significant. This process generally has involved the simultaneous application of two sets of historical judgments: the first on the potentialities and abuses of the English imperial system, whether before or after 1763; and the second on the depth of provincial political autonomy, again either before 1763 or under the impact of English colonial demands following the end of the Seven Years War. Using these judgments, American colonial historians have laid out certain inescapable moral and institutional guideposts in defining the boundaries of their analyses, guideposts through which the present student must navigate in order to comprehend the somber background of revolution and nation-building.[1] A great many modern historians have written intelligently on the "causes of the American Revolution" without arriving at any consensus, and because of the wealth of material on this theme available elsewhere, this subject is not confronted directly in this chapter. Still, in examining the problem of causation, the student might remember the useful cautionary words of William Dray. "All historians," Dray pointed out, use the concept of *cause* "in such a way that their value judgments are relevant to their causal conclusions—not just in the sense that they do in fact influence those conclusions, but in the sense that the conclusions are logically dependent on them."

Rather than summarize the dominant strands of opinion concerning the "causes of the Revolution," this chapter examines the three most important political "happenings" in eighteenth-century America: the development, in each mainland English province, of a local structure of power in the assemblies that claimed an increasing daily share of the colonists' loyalties long before 1763 when provincial grievances against England began to grow swiftly; the fusing of local patterns of allegiance into a national sense of "American" interests during the 1770's and 1780's, coming both as a cause and result of the transforming revolutionary experience; and, finally, the evolution of a distinctively American party system that reflected both the underlying political loyalties and the defined disagreements among leaders in the new republic.

In a functional analysis of politics, the historian's search for the location and operation of power relates closely to his examination of the patterns of loyalty or commitment that exist or emerge in the same political situation. "The sociological struggle of [political] parties," wrote Max Weber, "differs in a basic way according to the kind of communal action which they struggle to influence. . . . Above all else, [political groups] vary according to the structure of domination within the community." Through-

---

[1] Present historians remain indebted to George Bancroft's monumental nineteenth-century account of the Revolutionary experience and to Bancroft's eloquent twentieth-century legatees, Edmund S. Morgan and Forrest MacDonald. Similarly, students should keep in mind for future reading George Louis Beer's and Charles McLean Andrews' sympathetic older volumes on the British Empire before the Revolution along with Lawrence H. Gipson's more recent work on the same subject. The pioneering studies of class conflict during the Revolution by Carl Becker and Arthur M. Schlesinger, Sr., have been supplemented but not displaced in importance by Merrill Jensen's and Jackson Turner Main's more recent treatments.

out the eighteenth century, contending political groups sought obedience and loyalty from the colonists. Thus, fractious assemblies vied with imperial supporters, Patriots with Tories, framers of the new Constitution with its opponents, and finally, Federalists with Jeffersonians. Although the issues under dispute changed with each struggle, the unresolved dilemma remained that of determining the political future of the English settlements. The pattern of loyalties and beliefs that emerged from this century's series of political campaigns continues to define the basic conditions of American nationality today.

I. EARLY INTERPRETATIONS

The following three selections from Charles McLean Andrews and Charles A. Beard represent the most influential historical treatments of the major themes in eighteenth-century American political history available to scholars during the first four decades of this century. Only since World War II has Beard's economic analysis of the origins of the Constitution and of the first party system come under sustained revisionist attack. Similarly, Andrews' views on the background of colonial revolt, although not subjected to the same merciless scrutiny as Beardian doctrine, have also been revised and made more sophisticated by recent historians concerned with the political psychology which underlay the conflict over authority in the colonies. It is impossible for the student to go beyond a superficial understanding of the struggle for political loyalties in provincial and revolutionary America without first having paid careful attention to the works and conclusions of these two masters.

CHARLES McLEAN ANDREWS

THE BRITISH COLONIES IN AMERICA

More than three hundred years ago. a small group of able-bodied men landed on the soil of Virginia and founded the first permanent English settlement in the New World. This famous plantation, though numbering in its earlier years but a few hundred

Reprinted from Charles McLean Andrews, THE COLONIAL BACKGROUND OF THE AMERICAN REVOLUTION *(New Haven: Yale University Press, 1931), pp. 3, 5, 7–9, 12, 14–16, 24–28, 35–37, 41–42, 46–47, 50, 55, 61, 65, by permission of the publisher.*

souls and for a decade a victim of sickness, starvation, and a faulty system of government, was always more than a setting for the romantic adventures of John Smith, John Rolfe, and Pocahontas, more even than the birthplace in America of self-government and the cradle of a new republic. It was the beginning of a great experiment in the field of English colonization and overseas expansion, the starting point of a great world movement which to-day has spread to the farthermost parts of the earth. Our own country, which is a product of this movement, emerged from it as an independent national state, but only after one hundred and seventy-five years of membership in the British colonial family; and it is in the light of such association, therefore, that the colonial period of our history must be approached and, in the first instance, judged.

．．．

At the beginning of the seventeenth century no precedent existed for so novel an adventure in the field of maritime endeavor as that in Virginia promised to be. England, it is true, had a few palatinates along the Welsh and Scottish frontiers, a few plantations just begun in Ireland, a group of incorporated merchants residing in the Low Countries across the Channel, and here and there a trading factory in India; but her own history furnished her with no successful example of a permanent settlement three thousand miles away from her own shores, and the experiences of other nations gave no clue to the proper treatment of such a settlement or to the place it should occupy in any system of colonial administration. In other words, England began her career as the greatest and most prosperous colonizing power that the world has ever known without any fixed policy, in fact, without any clear idea of what she and her people were doing. When for one reason or another and for ends of their own devising, these Englishmen were leaving their country and going to lands far distant and little known, their government was giving scarcely more than legal sanction to a migration for which it was in no way responsible.

．．．

Even had the English government been able to conceive of a colonial organization at this period of its history, it would have been unable to develop a workable policy as long as it allowed these settlements in America

to remain under private control and to manage their own governments and own their own soil under the terms of the charters granted them by the king. Certainly the early Stuarts never tried to fashion a colonial policy, and their successors after the Restoration were hardly more aware than they had been that a colonial world was in the making. It is true that, more or less unconsciously, both the earlier and the later Stuarts were laying the foundations of a system that became very elaborate as the years passed; but at first their purposes, which were commercial rather than political or administrative, were based on the idea that the communities in America were agricultural plantations or tenancies rather than colonies; that they were valuable less as political organizations and centres of population than as farming areas, outposts of trade, and sources of wealth; and that they were to be monopolized on the productive side wholly by the mother country in accordance with the prevailing idea that the maritime kingdoms of Europe should keep their plantation trade to themselves. . . .

This policy of monopolizing the trade of dependent colonies was effectively applied before 1624 in the tobacco contracts with Virginia and Bermuda, but after 1628 it could not become operative on a large scale because England was distracted by dissensions at home, and without command of the sea was unable to carry on her colonial trade with any degree of success. . . . But after 1660 and the restoration of the Stuarts, a colonial idea emerges for the first time in English history; and the commission, which was sent to America in 1664 to capture New Netherland from the Dutch, received special instructions—namely, to investigate conditons in New England

—which have a true colonial ring. But this commission failed of its purpose; and as affairs at home improved very slowly, official supervision of the colonies remained in a very rudimentary state. Even the famous navigation acts of the years from 1651 to 1696 were at the bottom commercial not colonial, and England's interest in America during these years continued to be a matter of trade and not of organized control. Englishmen were feeling their way, as it were, passing laws and appointing councils for the oversight of trade and plantations, merely in the hope of making these distant agricultural settlements profitable to the mother state. At best, however, the efforts of this period were disordered and ill-directed, and the attempts that were made to put into efficient execution the regulations laid down in the various acts of trade and navigation make these years a time of almost hopeless confusion in methods of colonial management.

• • •

Thus it is not surprising that British statesmen in their concern for the security of trade and the necessity of adequate military defense, should have thought it wise to bring these loosely controlled and privately managed colonies into a closer unity under the crown; or that later, when the demands of trade and the pressure of the French peril in America actually made a solution of the problem imperative, they should decide to transform all the colonies into royal provinces and to administer them directly by means of royal officials and more or less after a common plan. . . .

Now with France as her greatest competitor, England became engaged in a titanic struggle for supremacy at sea, that is, in the world of commerce. Colonies meant trade, trade meant wealth, and wealth meant power, and power was the ultimate end to be gained in a conflict among maritime nations, where trade and conquest went together, and where, according to the doctrines of the time, competition, not coöperation, was the watchword. As the men of the eighteenth century saw it, this commercial rivalry was a mortal combat, to which the colonies were expected to contribute their part in furthering the victory of the mother country. Thus under William and Mary, Anne, and the first two Georges, the English government strove to make the colonies contribute to the advancement of England in the European world. It was inconceivable that they should be allowed a commercial freedom that would be all to the advantage of the enemy; while to suffer them to remain weak and disunited, with the French on their very borders, was to endanger the resources upon which England depended—fish, furs, and naval stores—and might easily result to England in the very loss of the colonies themselves.

. . . Whatever may be the colonial policy of Great Britain to-day, certainly *laissez faire* was not a doctrine that played any part in determining England's relations with her colonies during our colonial period. Nor was there anything in the conditions of that time, from the nationalistic point of view, to warrant England in adopting a "let alone" policy toward the colonists in America. On the contrary, everything in the situation confronting her demonstrated the utter folly of such a course. Under the pressure of this conviction, in the period from 1696 to 1754 —a period of American colonial history shamefully neglected by the historians —the statesmen and merchants of England formulated for the first time a clearly defined and widely accepted theory of colonial relationship, now familiar to us as the old British colonial system.

. . .

Thus it happened that by the middle of the eighteenth century every British colony, except Maryland, Pennsylvania, Connecticut, and Rhode Island, was in the king's hands; and even in the proprietary colonies of Maryland and Pennsylvania, which were returned to their owners in 1694 and 1715, traces of the royal connection remained. The deputy governors, who were appointed by the proprietors, had to be confirmed by the crown; the Penns lost the power of vetoing the laws passed in their colony; the governor of Maryland could not leave the province without the royal consent, and the laws enacted by its assembly, having been subject to the royal approval for twenty-five years, were expected to be sent to England for the king's inspection, a requirement rarely, if ever, complied with. . . .

Thus of some thirty or more colonies possessed by Great Britain during our colonial period, all but four eventually came directly under the control of the king and were governed according to a common plan. Largely because of the opposition of parliament, the executive authorities in England never succeeded in royalizing all the colonies and so laying the foundations for a uniform and centralized system of colonial administration; but they did succeed in royalizing most of them and in setting up a plan of control that was practically the same in all cases. After 1763 Great Britain, victor in the contest with France, was the head of a group of dependent communities stretching from the Gulf of St. Lawrence to the farthermost limits of the southern West Indies. Each was administered by a governor, a council, patent officials, and provincial officials, who by solemn oath swore allegiance to the king and looked to him as the legal source of all their authority. The very possession of such a colonial world transformed Great Britain from an island kingdom, such as she had been in Elizabeth's reign, into an oceanic dominion, and broadened the scope of her responsibilities from the four seas of the seventeenth century to the ocean-wide activities of the eighteenth. She became the centre of a far-flung line of settlements, which acknowledged the king as their sovereign, herself as their mother country, and her institutions as models of their own; and as far as the colonists thought about the matter at all, they accepted their connection with her as the normal condition of their lives and essential to their welfare and prosperity.

The only bond that held these British colonies together was their legal subordination to the authority of the British crown, for owing to various causes, such as isolation, local environment, religious differences, and admixture of racial stocks, they lacked the unity that might have been theirs had similar religious, economic, and social practices been common to them all. Yet, always, though more or less unconsciously, they tended toward uniformity of governmental procedure and used similar methods of increasing their self-governing powers. From 1690 to 1711 and again from 1744 to 1754, commissioners representing New England and New York and sometimes other colonies met at Albany or elsewhere for the purpose of taking the offensive against the French or of establishing more friendly relations with the Six Nations. Also, considerable coöperative intercolonial activity was stimulated by the various wars in which the colonists were engaged; but only when the British government took the initiative—and rarely even then—were system and efficiency, on any large scale, attained. They looked on each other as "foreigners," in the mediæval sense of the word, that is, as men of other communities, and frequently used the term to designate their neighbors. It is true that from time to time during the colonial period they evidenced some slight manifestations of mutual understanding, but except for Franklin's plan of union—the Albany plan of 1754—which met with little favor among themselves, they took no concerted action that can be interpreted as a self-conscious desire for union among themselves.

. . .

Thus the leading features of British history during our colonial period can be summed up in the words "expansion" and "centralization," processes which manifested themselves in ever widening spheres of commerce, colonies, and ocean supremacy. Britain's policy in regard to her plantations was to secure a more closely knit and efficient colonial administration in the interest of the trade of her merchants and the receipts of her own exchequer; whereas the colonials, though they accepted their obligations as loyal subjects of the crown, early began to strive for greater freedom of action than that which they had as colonies in the strictly legal sense of the term. As they found it increasingly irksome to meet the obligations imposed upon them by the customs system and the courts of vice-admiralty, they broke the law by which technically they were restrained, and trenched upon the prerogative to which legally they were subject.

. . .

. . . In 1691, when New York obtained the right to call a popular assembly, the last of the colonies which had been settled in the seventeenth century secured a government based on the Virginia model. Thus, by the beginning of the eighteenth century, every British colony in America had a representative assembly elected under a limited popular suffrage. As may be seen by studying the legislative history of Nova Scotia and the Floridas in the later period, the fact was accepted in England that a British colony, if it were to attract settlers and to attain the objects sought for in its promotion, had to be granted a certain measure of self-government. There was nothing either philanthropic or specially broadminded in the granting of self-government to a royal colony, for the principle underlying it partook of the nature of a business proposition.

In time, these representative assemblies increased the number and scope of their powers, and in the West Indies as well as on the American continent they opposed the feudal and royal powers wielded by the executive part of the government, and began to claim for themselves all the privileges and functions of the House of Commons in England. In Maryland, from 1660 to 1689, the struggle lay between the proprietor and the popular element. The former was attempting to run the government as a good deal of a family affair and was invoking a divine right of proprietors, which in some ways was even worse than a divine right of kings; whereas the latter was mutinous and given to faction and objected to those in office, on the ground that they were "proud and malicious" and sought "the utter ruin of the poor man." In the Carolinas, whose proprietors lived in England and in later years showed themselves incompetent and helpless, the struggle focused upon the famous Fundamental Constitutions of Locke, which at four several times were sent to South Carolina, and which, though accepted by individuals for the sake of their land titles, were rejected four times by the assembly there. In Pennsylvania trouble began soon after the English revolution of 1689 and was largely due to Penn's really extraordinary attempt to set up a liberal, Sydneyesque form of government under a charter that was mediæval in character. Penn met his match in David Lloyd, the champion of the assembly against the proprietary prerogatives, and lost the battle in 1701, when he was compelled to grant a "Charter of Privileges" that established the supremacy of a representative assembly in Pennsylvania.

With the close of this struggle—one of the most interesting in the constitutional history of the colonial period—feudal privilege, as a feature of government, may be said to have passed away in America; and thereafter the issue, both in the proprietary and in the royal colonies, took on the more modern form of executive authority versus popular control. Under this guise the outcome was far less certain, for the royal prerogative was an integral part of the British constitution and not an anachronism, as were the mediæval proprietary privileges. Though the assemblies did not deny the legality of the prerogative, as exercised in America through royal and proprietary appointees, yet they encroached upon it constantly in matters concerning their own organization, numbers, membership, duration of sitting, the appointment of judges, and, most important of all, the control of the finances, which, without a budget system of any kind, they managed as a rule very badly.

. . .

As time went on, the assemblies came to look on these rights and privileges as a part of their historical heritage, inherent in themselves as representative bodies of people; and they asserted, to quote from a Jamaican protest, that under the common law "no instruction from king or minister could abridge or annihilate their right to them." That these assemblies were going far beyond their functions as provincial councils appears not only in their claims of privilege and encroachments upon the powers of the governors, but also in their passing, as in the case of Maryland, an act of attainder—an exercise of legislative and judicial authority that belonged only to the highest court of the realm, the High Court of Parliament; or, as in the case of Massachusetts, an act of amnesty, which was something the House of Commons would not have presumed to do in the face of the king's control of the pardoning power.

One may not wonder, under the circumstances, that the Board of Trade, the Privy Council, British ministers, and legal advisers, refused to recognize the claims of the colonial assemblies to powers coequal with those of parliament or should have persisted in their refusal to do so down to the very eve of the Revolution. In 1772 the attorney-general of England, in a report which was approved by the Privy Council and its committee, having first declared that the assembly of St. Christopher had "corrupted its own constitution by affecting a power which they had not, analogous and coequal to that of the House of Commons in Great Britain," advised the king to instruct his governor "to keep his assembly within the legal bounds of a provincial council and to hinder them from usurping authorities inconsistent with the peace and good government of the island." That which was true of the West Indies was true of the continental colonies also. There could be no compromise between the view of the highest executive and legal authorities in England, on one hand, that the colonial assemblies, after one hundred and fifty years of growth and experience, were still merely provincial councils, possessed of limited and inferior powers, and the view of the colonists, on the other hand, that their assemblies had all the privileges of the House of Commons and, with some limitations, all the powers exercised by the parliament in Great Britain. These differences were irreconcilable, and the significance lies not in the fact of the conflict between the executive and legislative branches of the government—that is as old as assemblies themselves and is always with us—nor in the fact that a monarchical form of government was arrayed against one that was popular in character, though this was one of the fundamental points at issue; but in the existence in every colony of a miniature house of commons which was exercising full powers over legislation, membership, and finance, and claiming legislative equality with the highest legislative body of the realm. Such a claim affected the very constitution of the British empire itself, for it asserted that the empire was not a single state made up of a mother country and her dependencies, but rather a group of states equal in status, with coördinate legislatures and a common king.

This view of the constitution, based on actual conditions, was common enough in the colonies before the Revolution, and was apparently in the minds of those who were responsible for the form in which the Declaration of Independence was cast. . . .

. . . Colonial subordination to the authority of the mother country was no legal fiction, for the vast majority of the colonists accepted it as the normal condition of their lives. This was notably true after 1713, when colonial habits of business and opportunities for profit had become more settled, and people had adapted themselves to the requirements and advantages of the British system. Rigid though this system seemed to be in law, it was, in practice, flexible and sufficiently adjustable to the needs of the colonists to enable them to move easily and freely within its boundaries and, in the main, to prosper under the conditions it imposed. Complaints there were, as always there must be under any system of regulation and control; but these complaints have more to do with the way in which the system worked than with the principle of subordination which it involved. That constantly a half-conscious effort was being made by the colonists to loosen the bonds of dependence admits of no doubt, for independence, in many directions other than political, was achieved long before actual revolt began. But during the years before 1763 the colonists thought of themselves and called themselves the "fellow subjects" of the king's subjects at home, and, as a rule, were too much occupied in making a living to question the advantages of the British connection, or to doubt the legality of a system that offered so many opportunities for evasion. If we argue forward from the restlessness of the seventeenth century or backward from the discontent of the years after 1763, we can easily make ourselves believe that the colonists were in a chronic state of dissatisfaction with the restrictions imposed upon them by the British crown and parliament; but, in reality, in proportion to the total population, there were fewer among them who deliberately broke the laws that England enacted than there are among the citizens of the United States to-day who are deliberately breaking the Volstead Act; and fewer still openly raised their voices against England's interference in their affairs than opposed the adoption of the Federal Constitution in 1787 and 1788, or are to-day expressing their fears of a centralized Federal government. Those most affected by the navigation acts and other constraining measures were the merchants and men of business, and not the agricultural population; yet it was the "embattled farmer," and not the "embattled merchant," whose shot was heard round the world. Other causes, therefore, than the navigation acts and restrictive measures must be found for our Revolution.

He would be a poor historian indeed who believed that the colonists thought of themselves as living in independent communities, awaiting the time when as ripened fruit they should separate from the parent stem. . . .

But whereas the relations with the king were thus carefully defined and clearly understood by the colonists, those with parliament were very unsettled. The reason for this is clear, because parliament itself was growing and changing and demanding more and more power. Everyone agreed that the colonies were the king's, but the notion that parliament could legislate for all the king's dominions had hardly become, at the time of the settlement, a maxim of the English lawyer. . . .

There was always a certain amount of inconsistency in colonial points of view, and one must not look upon individual expressions of opinion as binding upon a whole people; but, generally speaking, it is safe to say that in the eighteenth century before 1763 the colonists did not seriously oppose the extension of English law to the colonies and made no denial of parliament's right to legislate for them. In the royal colonies the rule prevailed that "where the law of the colony was silent, that of England was to be pursued." . . .

The one thing to be kept in mind is that the right of parliament to legislate for the colonies was not expressly denied by the colonists themselves before 1765; for although they often succeeded in thwarting the royal will and evading the acts of parliament, they accepted their colonial status up to that time with a reasonable measure of equanimity and content, neither denying their dependence on the crown nor refusing to acknowledge the right of parliament to enact measures that were designed to bind them in matters of purely domestic concern. Nor did they raise the issue of parliamentary sovereignty until the events of the pre-Revolutionary period made it necessary for them to discover a constitutional argument that would serve as a pretext for revolt. John Adams's assertion, made in 1775, that the authority of parliament was never admitted as of right in the internal affairs of the colonies is, like other of Adams's statements, not in accord with the facts of the case. . . .

Thus, in the eighteenth century, Great Britain found herself in possession of a group of self-reliant, self-willed colonies, composed in the main of her own flesh and blood, and proud of the race from which they had sprung. These colonies were advancing rapidly out of their plantation state into that of self-governing communities, and were growing in self-consciousness, population, and the complexity of their economic and social needs. Almost unaware of their own strength, they accepted their position in the British colonial world as a natural and inevitable condition of the life in which they had been reared; and though constantly striving for a greater measure of freedom and self-government, as they attained to larger stature, they did not seriously contest the authority of king and parliament before the beginning of the pre-Revolutionary era. . . .

The major portion of the members of the Convention are on record as recognizing the claim of property to a special and defensive position in the Constitution.

In the ratification of the Constitution, about three-fourths of the adult males failed to vote on the question, having abstained from the elections at which delegates to the state conventions were chosen, either on account of their indifference or their disfranchisement by property qualifications.

The Constitution was ratified by a vote of probably not more than one-sixth of the adult males.

It is questionable whether a majority of the voters participating in the elections for the state conventions in New York, Massachusetts, New Hampshire, Virginia, and South Carolina, actually approved the ratification of the Constitution.

The leaders who supported the Constitution in the ratifying conventions represented the same economic groups as the members of the Philadelphia Convention; and in a large number of instances they were also directly and personally interested in the outcome of their efforts.

In the ratification, it became manifest that the line of cleavage for and against the Constitution was between substantial personalty interests on the one hand and the small farming and debtor interests on the other.

The Constitution was not created by "the whole people" as the jurists have said; neither was it created by "the states" as Southern nullifiers long contended; but it was the work of a consolidated group whose interests knew no state boundaries and were truly national in their scope.

CHARLES A. BEARD

FROM "ECONOMIC INTERPRETATION"

At the close of this long and arid survey—partaking of the nature of catalogue—it seems worth while to bring together the important conclusions for political science which the data presented appear to warrant.

The movement for the Constitution of the United States was originated and carried through principally by four groups of personalty interests which had been adversely affected under the Articles of Confederation: money, public securities, manufactures, and trade and shipping.

The first firm steps toward the formation of the Constitution were taken by a small and active group of men immediately interested through their personal possessions in the outcome of their labors.

No popular vote was taken directly or indirectly on the proposition to call the Convention which drafted the Constitution.

A large propertyless mass was, under the prevailing suffrage qualifications, excluded at the outset from participation (through representatives) in the work of framing the Constitution.

The members of the Philadelphia Convention which drafted the Constitution were, with a few exceptions, immediately, directly, and personally interested in, and derived economic advantages from, the establishment of the new system.

The Constitution was essentially an economic document based upon the

Reprinted from Charles A. Beard, AN ECONOMIC INTERPRETATION OF THE CONSTITUTION *(New York: The Macmillan Company, 1913), pp. 324–25, and from* ECONOMIC ORIGINS OF JEFFERSONIAN DEMOCRACY *(New York: The Macmillan Company, 1915), pp. 464–67, by permission of the publisher.*

concept that the fundamental private rights of property are anterior to government and morally beyond the reach of popular majorities.

FROM "ECONOMIC ORIGINS"

No one can spend the leisure of several years in the study of the period which saw the formation of the Constitution and the rise of Jeffersonian democracy without arriving at certain general reflections, which may or may not be worthy of the name conclusions, concerning the drift of events. Such conclusions as have been reached in the course of preparation of the essay on the Constitution and this volume are here set down for whatever value they may have. No pretence is made to infallibility, but there appears to be satisfactory historical evidence to support them.

It is established upon a statistical basis that the Constitution of the United States was the product of a conflict between capitalistic and agrarian interests. The support for the adoption of the Constitution came principally from the cities and regions where the commercial, financial, manufacturing, and speculative interests were concentrated and the bulk of the opposition came from the small farming and debtor classes, particularly those back from the sea board.

The capitalistic interests whose rights were especially safeguarded by the Constitution had been harried almost to death, during the few years preceding the adoption of the Constitution, by state legislation and by the weaknesses and futility of the government under the Articles of Confederation. They were, therefore, driven into a compact mass, cemented by a conscious solidarity of interest. In the contest for the Constitution, they formed

the aggressive party, and though a minority of the nation, they were able to wring from the reluctant voters a ratification of the new instrument of government, because the backwoods agrarians were uninformed and indifferent and from two-thirds to three-fourths of the electorate failed to vote one way or the other on the Constitution. In other words, though numerically in a minority, the party of the Constitution was able by virtue of its wealth, talents, solidarity, and political skill to carry through ratification in the face of a powerful opposition representing very probably the majority of the country.

The men who framed the Constitution and were instrumental in securing its ratification constituted the dominant group in the new government formed under it, and their material measures were all directed to the benefit of the capitalistic interests—i.e., were consciously designed to augment the fluid capital in the hands of security holders and bank stock owners and thus to increase manufacturing, commerce, building, and land values, the last incidentally, except for speculative purposes in the West. The bulk of the party which supported these measures was drawn from the former advocates of the Constitution.

The spokesmen of the Federalist and Republican parties, Hamilton and Jefferson, were respectively the spokesmen of capitalistic and agrarian interests. Their writings afford complete and abundant proof of this fact.

The party of opposition to the administration charged the Federalists with building up an aristocracy of wealth by the measures of the government and appealed to the mass of the people, that is, the farmers, to resist the exactions of "a moneyed aristocracy." The Republicans by thus declaring war on the rich and privileged drew to themselves the support not only of the farmers, but also of a considerable portion of the smaller tradesmen and mechanics of the towns, who had no very great liking for the "rich and well born." By the ten years' campaign against the ruling class, they were able to arouse the vast mass of the hitherto indifferent voters and in the end swamp the compact minority which had dominated the country.

Jefferson was peculiarly fitted to become the leader of the opposition party. He was a planter and thus regarded as the spokesman of the agrarian interest. As a slave-owner and member of the ruling aristocracy in Virginia he conciliated that portion of the South which might have been disturbed by some of the violent democratic theories associated with his name. He had taken no part in the making and ratification of the Constitution, and it was known that he gave aid and comfort to the opponents of ratification while avowing his approval of certain parts of that instrument of government. He was known to oppose slavery in theory, but his agents skilfully spread abroad his statement that the federal government could not interfere with that peculiar institution under the powers conferred upon it by the Constitution. In private correspondence, Jefferson had vigorously denounced the bank and funded debt as schemes for robbing the agrarian interests, and his views were widely circulated by his friends and enemies. But he did not commit himself to any radical schemes for repudiation or irregular reduction and upon his election he skilfully used and conciliated the very classes that he had denounced. His academic views assiduously circulated by his partisans pleased the temper of the agrarian masses, and his practical politics propitiated, rather than alienated, the capitalistic interests.

Jeffersonian Democracy did not imply any abandonment of the property, and particularly the landed, qualifications on the suffrage or office-holding; it did not involve any fundamental alterations in the national Constitution which the Federalists had designed as a foil to the levelling propensities of the masses; it did not propose any new devices for a more immediate and direct control of the voters over the instrumentalities of government. Jeffersonian Democracy simply meant the possession of the federal government by the agrarian masses led by an aristocracy of slave-owning planters, and the theoretical repudiation of the right to use the Government for the benefit of any capitalistic groups, fiscal, banking, or manufacturing.

II. DOCUMENTS

1. The Colonial Power Struggle

Earlier in the eighteenth century, decades before English efforts to tighten control had led to colonial resistance and eventually to revolution, the provincial assemblies had been slowly but steadily expanding their scope of authority at the expense of royal governors and other crown officials. In almost every colony, the struggle for local power between the assemblies and the governors led to charges of administrative despotism and counter-charges of the existence of revolutionary designs behind the assemblies' efforts to accumulate authority. Disputes over specific, tangible exercises of authority—perhaps over the salary of royal officials, the dispatch of provincial troops to Indian wars, the provisioning of royal military forces, or tax rates within the colony—led to intense suspiciousness between executive and legislature in each colony and to a general atmosphere of great political tension. These strains long preceded the grievances of 1763–1776 and set the context for colonial willingness to challenge all parliamentary or royal authority in the last years of English rule. The following selections from the writings and statements of the New York Assembly, the English Board of Trade, and the New York royal governor illustrate the undercurrent of hostility between crown and colonists that existed long before the actual revolutionary explosion. The selection from a 1720 number of "Cato's Letters" published in London by the radical pamphleteers, Trenchard and Gordon, reveals the continuing presence of anti-ministerial, covertly republican sentiment and ideas in eighteenth-century England itself.

NEW YORK ASSEMBLY

BOARD OF TRADE

Their Lordships are sorry to observe, that the Assembly have not only hitherto refused to comply in any sort with the Tenor of that Instruction, but they seem likewise in some of their Answers . . . to have forgot that Decency and Respect which is always due to their Governor, who has the honor to Represent His Majesty's Person. . . . The Consequence of which proceedings . . . must naturally be that His Majesty will find himself under a necessity of laying the Undutiful behaviour of the Province before the Legislature of Great Britain, not only in this single Instance, but in many others of the same Nature and Tendency, whereby it manifestly appears that this Assembly

Reprinted from JOURNAL, *New York Assembly, September 9, 1730, and April 10, 1733, in John F. Burns, "Controversies Between Royal Governors and Their Assemblies in the Northern American Colonies" (unpublished doctoral thesis, Villanova University, 1933).*

for some years past, have attempted by Unwarrantable Practices to weaken if not cast off the . . . Dependence which all Colonies ought to have on the Mother Country.

NEW YORK ASSEMBLY

After which came the Assembly's statement of its claims in the dispute:

All that this or former Assemblies have endeavored is, to preserve the Powers granted by Charter to the General Court, in making Laws as well for the Support of the Government, as any other Affair; that when their Constituents' Money is brought into the Treasury, good and wholesome Laws might be enacted, containing Restrictions, Limitations and Rules, in observance of which, the Money would be issued and disposed of by your Excellency with the advice and consent of His Majesty's Council, for the Ends and Purposes for which the People were taxed. This is a Liberty His Majesty's Colonies and Plantations are in the Use and Enjoyment of, notwithstanding the strong and repeated Efforts some of them have of late met with, to perswade and induce them to give it up.

WILLIAM SHIRLEY

TO GEORGE CLINTON [1]

New York, August 13th, 1748.
Sir: I am honoured with your Excellency's letter of the 5th instant in which you inform me, "That you are of opinion the present state of His Majesty's government within this Province requires the immediate attention of the Ministry" and are pleased to desire me "as His Majesty's service has brought me here, whereby I have an opportunity of fully informing myself of this matter from the Publick papers, and other information which your Excellency has directed Mr Colden to lay before me to consider the same and to represent it to the Duke of Bedford, as you believe I shall find things in such a state that I shall think it my duty to give my sentiments thereon." Upon which I am to acquaint your Excellency that according to your desire I have informed myself of the state of His Majesty's government within this Colony and find that several late innovations have been introduced by the Assembly into it, and incroachments made upon His Majesty's prerogative greatly tending to weaken his government, not only in the Colony of New York but in His Majesty's other Colo-

nies in North America, through the influence which so bad an example (in this Colony especially) may have among them; and I now send your Excellency a particular state of the innovations and incroachments which appear to me most materially to effect His Majesty's government, with my sentiments of what may be the most adviseable measures for putting an end to them, as may either serve for your Excellency's private consideration only, or be of use to you in making a representation of them, as you shall think fit to the Duke of Bedford; which I think will come more properly from your Excellency than from me.

And as I found it necessary in order to trace the beginning and growth of the several incroachments that have been made on the King's prerogative, as also to judge what might be the most proper steps for putting a stop to them, to look back into the state of the government under the Administrations of your Predecessors and compare it with the present state of it under your own, I have used the same method in drawing the following account of them, vizt.

It appears by the Acts of Assembly that at the entrance of Governours Hunter, Burnet, Montgomery, and Cosby, for about twenty eight years past, upon their respective Administrations the Establishments for the support of His Majesty's Government were made for the term of five years, and no application of any part of the money arising from the supplies granted to His Majesty for that purpose, except for the payment of the Treasurer and Members of the Assembly, was made in these Acts: but there was only one general appropriation in them, vizt *For the support of His Majesty's government;* and the money raised was thereby directed to be drawn out of the Treasury by warrants from the Gover-

[1] Docts. rel. to Col. Hist. of N. Y. 6, 432. This letter is printed in full to show the clearness with which Shirley warned against the growth of the power of the Assembly at the expense of the governor.

Reprinted from C. H. Lincoln, ed., THE CORRESPONDENCE OF WILLIAM SHIRLEY, *I (New York, 1912), pp. 441–49.*

nour with the advice and consent of His Majesty's Council, which it appears by the minutes of Council was done, and that £1560 p Annum, being at first and for several years afterwards equal in value to £1200 sterling (which sum the Govr is by His Majesty's 26th instruction directed to take out of his revenue within the Colony for his support) was constantly drawn out of the Treasury by him for that purpose, as also £400 p annum New York currency for fire wood and Candles for his Majesty's garrison there, and £200 p annum for the repairs of the fortifications; and no other grants or matters whatsoever were intermixed in the before mentioned Acts, except the Taxes and Supplies which constituted the Fund, out of which the salaries and allowances to the Governour, Judges and other Officers of the Government were to be paid.

It appears also by the minutes of Council that all other monies levied by Acts of Assembly were during that time drawn out of the Treasury by warrant from the Governour and Council.

And I find that during that time all publick warlike stores for the defence of the Colony were lodged in the King's Magazine with the Store Keeper and issued by order of the Governour in whose sole disposal they were.

And it does not appear that within this time the Assembly assumed to themselves the appointment of such officers, as it appertain'd to the Governour to appoint, or to nominate them to him, or turn them out of their posts or to create a dependency of them upon themselves by an extraordinary manner of making grants for their subsistence.

But I find that in the year 1743 upon your Excellency's first coming to the Administration the Assembly instead of making the before mentioned Establishment for the support of His Majesty's Government for the term of five years, pass'd an Act intituled "An Act for the payment of the Salaries, Services and Contingencies therein mentioned untill the 1st of September 1744 out of the funds appropriated for the support of the Government" and have continued this method of granting salaries for the support of the Governour and other officers from year to year only, ever since; and many other innovations tending to create an intire dependency of the Governour and other Officers upon the Assembly, and to weaken His Majesty's Government in this Colony, have been occasionally introduced from year to year by that Act.

As first, many other grants are tack'd in it to those made to the Governour, among which some have been made to persons under pretence of *Extraordinary Services* done by them, but in reality (as I am informed by Mr Colden) for composing and publishing libellous papers against your Excellency's Administration, others to an officer of their own appointment for keeping the gun powder provided for the defence of the Colony, others to their Agent in England whom they have in the same Act obtruded upon your Excellency with directions for him to take his instructions from a Committee of their own house, exclusive (as it appears) to the Governour and Council, others to Committees appointed by the Act for the Payment of Officers and Soldiers raised for the defence of the Colony, the allowance of whose Muster Rolls as well as their pay has been likewise committed wholly to them by the Act. Others to the Commissioners for Indian Affairs for payment of outscouts to be raised and employed by them solely at their discretion.

2dly. The Assembly have taken upon themselves contrary to the express directions of His Majesty's commission to his Governour by virtue of which their House sits, which orders "that all money raised by Acts of Assembly shall be issued out by warrants from the Governour with the Advice and Consent of the Council, and disposed of by the Governour for the support of the Government and not otherwise" to limit in the Act what sums of money thereby raised shall be drawn out of the Treasury by such warrants and all other sums of money rais'd by Act of Assembly ever since, except those specially directed by this Act, to be drawn out by warrant from the Governor in Council, have been issued out by virtue of the several Acts *without such Warrant.*

3dly. The grants to the Governor for his support and to the Chief Justice for his salary, provided in this Act, run thus (vizt) "To the Governour for administring the Government of this Colony from the 22nd of September 1743 to the first of September 1744 (and in like manner for other years) after the rate of £1560 *p* Annum" (which sum I observe is now according to the present exchange, sunk from its former value of £1200 sterling, to £900) "and to James DeLancey Esq. as Chief Justice of the Supreme Court &c for the same year after the rate of £300 *p* Annum"; and so to the other Justices of the Supreme Court and to several other officers of the Government by *name,* and in case of the death or removal of any of them within the year it is provided in the Act that no more of their salaries shall be paid than what was due at the time of their respective deaths or removals and that "the Remainder shall be kept in the Treasury 'till dispos'd of by Acts to be hereafter pass'd for that purpose." So that in case

the Governour or any of those officers dye or are superseded within the year, there is no provision for the support of the Lieut Governour or President of the Council in either of *their* Administrations during the remainder of the year, and untill the appointment of a new Governour, nor for the support of the successor of any other officer dying or removed within the year. And I would observe besides, that this new method of making personal grants to the Officers for the time being, seems plainly to imply that the Assembly, in case any of the officers should dye or be removed by the Governour, will not make provision for those whom he shall appoint to succeed them 'till they know who they are and how they approve of them.

4thly. It appears by the Minutes of the Assembly's proceedings that the Acts thus made for your Excellency's annual support are pass'd the last of the Sessions, and I am informed by Mr Colden that intimations have been given (as indeed the Assemblys delaying to compleat these Acts till the others of the same Session are consented to by your Excellency, is of its self) that unless you pass the others which are lay'd before you for your Consent, the Act for your support will not be passed.

It appears likewise that since the year 1743 considerable advances have been made by the Assembly towards usurping the nomination of Officers which it appertains to the Governour to appoint, and the power of turning such as are actually appointed by him, out of their posts, and that they have proceeded so far as even to appoint an Officer to keep part of the King's warlike Stores; one instance of which is, the Speaker's acquainting your Excellency in the name and by order of the Assembly and in their presence in the Council Chamber before the Council, that they had turned out one Mr Heath commission'd by you to be Land and Tyde Waiter for the Colony imposts, and chose Mr Brass into that post, whom they desired you would accordingly commissionate; which Mr Colden assures me was done when he was present at the Council Board. Another instance is, their message to your Excellency desiring you to appoint Mr Mills Sergeant at Arms, as appears by the minutes of their proceedings: another the committing the custody of the Gunpowder provided by them for the service of the King's garrison, to a person who had no authority from your Excellency to receive it, and for which he has a grant made him by Act of Assembly out of the money raised for the support of His Majesty's Government, and paid to him by the Treasurer, by virtue of the directions in that act, without any warrant from Your Excellency; all which appears by the Act itself.

The Assembly have likewise taken the custody and disposal of the gunpowder provided for the use of the King's garrison and defence of the Colony, out of your Excellency's hands into their own; which appears from their refusal to pass an Act pursuant to the recommendation in His Majesty's 77th instruction, for imposing a powder duty on every vessel that enters and clears, for furnishing the magazines with powder for the defence of the Colony (as is the method of most other Colonies, and was used not long since in this) that they might avoid having the powder lodged in the magazine with the Store Keeper and in the disposal of your Excellency. But instead thereof purchasing gunpowder out of the publick money granted to His Majesty for the support of his government, and which they call by a new distinction *the Colony's Powder* and order to

be lodged in the Colony's powder House in the custody of their own officer, and not to be issued by him without an Act of Assembly for that purpose, but to remain there subject to their own directions and disposal; and such quantities as are issued out by acts of Assembly for the service of His Majesty's forts at New York and Albany, are ordered to be delivered, not to the Store keeper there to be kept in the King's magazine, but to particular persons nominated from time to time in those Acts, by the Assembly.

And I find likewise they have taken from your Excellency the passing of the Muster Rolls of all the troops raised for the defence of the Colony (except the King's four Independent Companies) and issuing the pay for them and their officers, according to the Establishment made for that purpose, and committed it to persons specially appointed in their Acts; by which they likewise take upon them to draw money out of the Treasury for the pay, without warrant from the Governour.

And they have likewise taken upon them not only to give the like power to the Commissioners for Indian Affairs, with regard to the payment of outscouts, but even a power to raise and employ them at discretion.

I find also that since 1743, they have assumed the power of erecting, by Acts of Assembly, fortifications and ordering *in what manner* they should be raised, and committed the *execution* of this to the conduct and direction of persons specially appointed for that purpose, in their Act.

And they have still proceeded farther in your Excellency's absence at Albany and without your consent or privity, to take upon themselves in conjunction with the Council to fortify part of the City of New York with stockades and Blockhouses, as your self informed me.

Upon all which innovations and encroachments I shall only observe in general, that the Assembly seems to have left scarcely any part of His Majesty's prerogative untouched, and that they have gone great lengths towards getting the government, military as well as civil, into their hands.

I have omitted to take notice to your Excellency of the stile of the Colony Acts, which runs thus: "Be it enacted by His Excellency the Governour, the Council and the General Assembly *and it is hereby enacted by the Authority of the same"* as a designed incroachment; because I apprehend the latter part of it is not inserted in their acts with a view of claiming an independency on His Majesty in the passing of their laws or excluding His Majesty's royal authority to disallow them; but is a mere impropriety in them; However as the latter part of the enacting clause is not the proper stile of a subordinate government, and nothing should be permitted to be put into the Provincial Acts which may have a tendency to accustom the Assemblys to consider their power of passing laws, as compleat, without His Majesty's allowance of them, it should be omitted.

As to what may be the most adviseable measures for your Excellency to take in the present situation of affairs within your government, I think no time should be lost for letting the Assembly know you expect that for the future they should provide for the support of His Majesty's government in the same manner which former Assemblies used to do it in, except as to having the sums proposed to be drawn out of the Treasury for the Governours salary and other Allowances, and for the maintenance of the several officers, ascertained in the Act or Acts themselves (which I am of opinion the Assembly have a right to do) instead of intrust-ing it with the Governour and Council, as was the former method; also that your Excellency should insist in general to have His Majesty's government within the Province restored to its former state. And I think your Excellency will have an advantage for effecting this beyond any other person, as the innovations and incroachments have arisen under your administration (what was done in Mr Clark's time who was only an occasional Commander in Chief upon the death of Mr Cosby and till the appointment of a New Governour, I think can not be regarded in the case) and therefore that it must seem reasonable to the Assembly for you to insist upon putting a stop to them; whereas should a Lieut Governour or President of the Council attempt this in your Excellency's absence from your government, I can not think he would have the least weight with the Assembly for altering what the Chief Governour has yielded to; and should not this reformation of the government be made during your Excellency's administration, your successor will I fear find that the continuance of these innovations and incroachments during the whole time of *that,* will be a considerable barr to his getting the government restored to it's former state and make the Assembly more tenacious of these incroachments than they will probably be now.

I shall only add that as your Excellency must expect at first to meet with some reluctancy and opposition in the Assembly to giving up the points they have gained I would recommend it to your consideration whether if you could procure His Majesty's disallowance of one or more of the late Acts of Assembly, by which these innovations have been introduced, and an additional instruction for restraining you from giving your assent to the like for the future, to be transmitted you, it might not strengthen your Excellency's hands and facilitate your resettling the King's government upon it's former foot: I think it would go far towards it. Wishing your Excellency all possible success in this affair, I have the honour to be with the most perfect regard, Sir,

Your Excellency's most Obedient
and most humble Servt.

W. Shirley.

CATO'S LETTERS

Saturday, February 18, 1720.

WHAT MEASURES ARE ACTUALLY TAKEN BY WICKED AND DESPERATE MINISTERS TO RUIN AND ENSLAVE THEIR COUNTRY.

Sir: As under the best Princes, and the best Servants to Princes alone, it is safe to speak what is true of the worst; so, according to my former Promise to the Publick, I shall take the Advantage of our excellent King's most gentle Government, and the virtuous Administration of an uncorrupt Ministry, to warn Mankind against the Mischiefs which may hereafter be dreaded from corrupt ones. It is too true, that every Country in the World has sometimes groaned under that heavy Misfortune, and our own as much as any; though I cannot allow it to be true, what Monsieur *de Witt* has long since observed, that the *English* Court has always been the most thievish Court in *Europe.*

Few Men have been desperate enough to attack openly, and barefaced, the Liberties of a free People. Such avowed Conspirators can rarely succeed: The Attempt would destroy itself. Even

Reprinted from "Cato's Letters," No. 17, in David L. Jacobson, ed., THE ENGLISH LIBERTARIAN HERITAGE (Indianapolis and New York: The Bobbs-Merrill Company, Inc., 1965), pp. 51–56.

when the Enterprize is begun and visible, the End must be hid, or denied. It is the Business and Policy of Traytors, so to disguise their Treason with plausible Names, and so to recommend it with popular and bewitching Colours, that they themselves shall be adored, while their Work is detested, and yet carried on by those that detest it.

Thus one Nation has been surrendered to another under the fair Name of mutual Alliance: The Fortresses of a Nation have been given up, or attempted to be given up, under the frugal Notion of saving Charges to a Nation; and Commonwealths have been trepanned into Slavery, by Troops raised or increased to defend them from Slavery.

It may therefore be of Service to the World, to shew what Measures have been taken to corrupt Ministers, in some of our neighbouring Countries, to ruin and enslave the People over whom they presided; to shew by what Steps and Gradations of Mischief Nations have been undone, and consequently what Methods may be hereafter taken to undo others: And this Subject I rather choose, because my Countrymen may be the more sensible of, and know how to value the inestimable Blessing of living under the best Prince, and the best established Government in the Universe, where we have none of these Things to fear.

Such Traytors will probably endeavour first to get their Prince into their Possession, and, like *Sejanus,* shut him up in a little Island, or perhaps make him a Prisoner in his Court; whilst, with full Range, they devour his Dominions, and plunder his Subjects. When he is thus secluded from the Access of his Friends, and the Knowledge of his Affairs, he must be content with such Misrepresentations as they shall find expedient to give him. False Cases will be stated, to justify wicked Counsel; wicked Counsel will be given, to procure unjust Orders. He will be made to mistake his Foes for his Friends, his Friends for his Foes; and to believe that his Affairs are in the highest Prosperity, when they are in the greatest Distress; and that publick Matters go on in the greatest Harmony, when they are in the utmost Confusion.

They will be ever contriving and forming wicked and dangerous Projects, to make the People poor, and themselves rich; well knowing that Dominion follows Property; that where there are Wealth and Power, there will be always Crowds of servile Dependents; and that, on the contrary, Poverty dejects the Mind, fashions it to Slavery, and renders it unequal to any generous Undertaking, and incapable of opposing any bold Usurpation. They will squander away the publick Money in wanton Presents to Minions, and their Creatures of Pleasure or of Burthen, or in Pensions to mercenary and worthless Men and Women, for vile Ends and traiterous Purposes.

They will engage their Country in ridiculous, expensive, fantastical Wars, to keep the Minds of Men in continual Hurry and Agitation, and under constant Fears and Alarms; and, by such Means, deprive them both of Leisure and Inclination to look into publick Miscarriages. Men, on the contrary, will, instead of such Inspection, be disposed to fall into all Measures offered, seemingly, for their Defence, and will agree to every wild Demand made by those who are betraying them.

When they have served their Ends by such Wars, or have other Motives to make Peace, they will have no View to the publick Interest; but will often, to procure such Peace, deliver up the Strong-Holds of their Country, or its Colonies for Trade, to open Enemies,

suspected Friends, or dangerous Neighbours, that they may not be interrupted in their domestick Designs.

They will create Parties in the Commonwealth, or keep them up where they already are; and, by playing them by Turns upon each other, will rule both. By making the *Guelfs* afraid of the *Ghibelines,* and these afraid of the *Guelfs,* they will make themselves the Mediums and Balance between the two factions; and both Factions, in their Turns, the Props of their Authority, and the Instruments of their Designs.

They will not suffer any Men, who have once tasted of Authority, though personally their Enemies, and whose Posts they enjoy, to be called to an Account for past Crimes, though ever so enormous. They will make no such Precedents for their own Punishment; nor censure Treason, which they intend to commit. On the contrary, they will form new Conspiracies, and invent new Fences for their own Impunity and Protection; and endeavour to engage such Numbers in their Guilt, as to set themselves above all Fear of Punishment.

They will prefer worthless and wicked Men, and not suffer a Man of Knowledge or Honesty to come near them, or enjoy a Post under them. They will disgrace Men of Virtue, and ridicule Virtue itself, and laugh at Publick Spirit. They will put Men into Employments, without any Regard to the Qualifications for those Employments, or indeed to any Qualifications at all, but as they contribute to their Designs, and shew a stupid Alacrity to do what they are bid. They must be either Fools or Beggars; either void of Capacity to discover their Intrigues, or of Credit and Inclination to disappoint them.

They will promote Luxury, Idleness, and Expence, and a general Depravation of Manners, by their own Example, as well as by Connivance and publick

Encouragement. This will not only divert Mens Thoughts from examining their Behaviour and Politicks, but likewise let them loose from all the Restraints of private and publick Virtue. From Immorality and Excesses they will fall into Necessity; and from thence into a servile Dependence upon Power.

In order to this, they will bring into Fashion Gaming, Drunkenness, Gluttony, and profuse and costly Dress. They will debauch their Country with foreign Vices, and foreign Instruments of vicious Pleasures; and will contrive and encourage publick Revels, nightly Disguises, and debauched Mummeries.

They will, by all practicable Means of Oppression, provoke the People to Disaffection; and then make that Disaffection an Argument for new Oppression, for not trusting them any further, and for keeping up Troops; and, in fine, for depriving them of Liberties and Privileges, to which they are entitled by their Birth, and the Laws of their Country.

If such Measures should ever be taken in any free Country, where the People choose Deputies to represent them, then they will endeavour to bribe the Electors in the Choice of their Representatives, and so to get a Council of their own Creatures; and where they cannot succeed with the Electors, they will endeavour to corrupt the Deputies after they are chosen, with the Money given for the publick Defence; and to draw into the Perpetration of their Crimes those very Men, from whom the betrayed People expect the Redress of their Grievances, and the Punishment of those Crimes. And when they have thus made the Representatives of the People afraid of the People, and the People afraid of their Representatives; then they will endeavour to persuade those Deputies to seize the Government to themselves, and not to trust their Principals any longer with the Power of resenting their Treachery and Ill-Usage, and of sending honester and wiser Men in their room.

But if the Constitution should be so stubbornly framed, that it will still preserve itself and the People's Liberties, in spite of all villainous Contrivances to destroy both; then must the Constitution itself be attacked and broken, because it will not bend. There must be an Endeavour, under some Pretence of publick Good, to alter a Balance of the Government, and to get it into the sole Power of their Creatures, and of such who will have constantly an Interest distinct from that of the Body of the People.

But if all these Schemes for the Ruin of the Publick, and their own Impunity, should fail them; and the worthy Patriots of a free Country should prove obstinate in Defense of their Country, and resolve to call its Betrayers to a strict Account; there is then but one thing left for such Traytors to do; namely, to veer about, and, by joining with the Enemy of their Prince and Country, complete their Treason.

I have somewhere read of a Favourite and First Minister to a neighbouring Prince, long since dead, who played his Part so well, that, though he had, by his evil Counsels, raised a Rebellion, and a Contest for the Crown; yet he preserved himself a Resource, whoever got the better: If his old Master succeeded, then this *Achitophel,* by the Help of a baffled Rebellion, ever favourable to Princes, had the Glory of fixing his Master in absolute Power: But, as his brave Rival got the Day, *Achitophel* had the Merit of betraying his old Master to plead; and was accordingly taken into Favour.

Happy therefore, thrice happy, are we, who can be unconcerned Spectators of the Miseries which the greatest Part of *Europe* is reduced to suffer, having lost their Liberties by the Intrigues and Wickedness of those whom they trusted; whilst we continue in full Enjoyment of ours, and can be in no Danger of losing them, while we have so excellent a King, assisted and obeyed by so wise a Parliament.

2. The Revolutionary Moment

There are innumerable accounts of colonial grievances against England before the American Revolution, but none summarized the major lines of complaint as cleverly as did Benjamin Franklin's satiric 1773 tract, "An Edict by the King of Prussia." Franklin's pungent thrusts at the crown's arbitrary behavior toward the colonists retains its freshness and relevance even today. When the provincial leaders decided upon a Declaration of Independence in 1776, their agreement on the basic outlines of such a statement long preceded Jefferson's actual drafting of the document. As John Adams wrote in the following retrospective account of the episode, "There is not an idea in it but what had been hackneyed in Congress for two years before." For those Americans not convinced by the Declaration alone of the need for a complete break with England, there remained the powerful rhetoric of Tom Paine's slashing attack on monarchy contained in "The American Crisis: I," more familiarly known as part of his larger work, Common Sense. *No single piece of writing did more to undermine, for wavering colonists, the notion of royal legitimacy. No polemic did more to call into question any lingering provincial loyalty to the crown.*

BENJAMIN FRANKLIN

AN EDICT BY THE KING OF PRUSSIA

Dantzic, Sept. 5, [1773.]
We have long wondered here at the supineness of the English nation, under the Prussian impositions upon its trade entering our port. We did not, till lately, know the claims, ancient and modern, that hang over that nation; and therefore could not suspect that it might submit to those impositions from a sense of duty or from principles of equity.

Reprinted from Benjamin Franklin, "An Edict by the King of Prussia" (1773), in Ralph Ketcham, ed., THE POLITICAL THOUGHT OF BENJAMIN FRANKLIN *(Indianapolis and New York: The Bobbs-Merrill Company, Inc., 1965), pp. 264–69.*

The following Edict, just made publick, may, if serious, throw some light upon this matter.

"FREDERIC, by the grace of God, King of Prussia, &c. &c. &c., to all present and to come, (*à tous présens et à venir*,) Health. The peace now enjoyed throughout our dominions, having afforded us leisure to apply ourselves to the regulation of commerce, the improvement of our finances, and at the same time the easing our domestic subjects in their taxes: For these causes, and other good considerations us thereunto moving, we hereby make known, that, after having deliberated these affairs in our council, present our dear brothers, and other great officers of the state, members of the same, we, of our

204

certain knowledge, full power, and authority royal, have made and issued this present Edict, viz.

"Whereas it is well known to all the world, that the first German settlements made in the Island of Britain, were by colonies of people, subject to our renowned ducal ancestors, and drawn from their dominions, under the conduct of Hengist, Horsa, Hella, Uff, Cerdicus, Ida, and others; and that the said colonies have flourished under the protection of our august house for ages past have never been emancipated therefrom; and yet have hitherto yielded little profit to the same: And whereas we ourself have in the last war fought for and defended the said colonies, against the power of France, and thereby enabled them to make conquests from the said power in America, for which we have not yet received adequate compensation: And whereas it is just and expedient that a revenue should be raised from the said colonies in Britain, towards our indemnification; and that those who are descendants of our ancient subjects, and thence still owe us due obedience, should contribute to the replenishing of our royal coffers as they must have done, had their ancestors remained in the territories now to us appertaining: We do therefore hereby ordain and command, that, from and after the date of these presents there shall be levied and paid to our officers of the *customs,* on all goods, wares, and merchandizes, and on all grain and other produce of the earth, exported from the said Island of Britain, and on all goods of whatever kind imported into the same, a duty of four and a half per cent *ad valorem,* for the use of us and our successors. And that the said duty may more effectually be collected, we do hereby ordain, that all ships or vessels bound from Great Britain to any other part of the world, or from any other part of the world to Great Brit-

ain, shall in their respective voyages touch at our port of Koningsberg, there to be unladen, searched, and charged with the said duties.

"And whereas there hath been from time to time discovered in the said island of Great Britain, by our colonists there, many mines or beds of iron-stone; and sundry subjects, of our ancient dominion, skilful in converting the said stone into metal, have in time past transported themselves thither, carrying with them and communicating that art; and the inhabitants of the said island, presuming that they had a natural right to make the best use they could of the natural productions of their country for their own benefit, have not only built furnaces for smelting the said stone into iron, but have erected plating-forges, slitting-mills, and steel-furnaces, for the more convenient manufacturing of the same; thereby endangering a diminution of the said manufacture in our ancient dominion; —we do therefore hereby farther ordain, that, from and after the date hereof, no mill or other engine for slitting or rolling of iron, or any plating-forge to work with a tilt-hammer, or any furnace for making steel, shall be erected or continued in the said island of Great Britain: And the Lord Lieutenant of every county in the said island is hereby commanded, on information of any such erection within his county, to order and by force to cause the same to be abated and destroyed; as he shall answer the neglect thereof to us at his peril. But we are nevertheless graciously pleased to permit the inhabitants of the said island to transport their iron into Prussia, there to be manufactured, and to them returned; they paying our Prussian subjects for the workmanship, with all the costs of commission, freight, and risk, coming and returning; any thing herein contained to the contrary notwithstanding.

"We do not, however, think fit to extend this our indulgence to the article of wool; but, meaning to encourage, not only the manufacturing of woollen cloth, but also the raising of wool, in our ancient dominions, and to prevent both, as much as may be, in our said island, we do hereby absolutely forbid the transportation of wool from thence, even to the mother country, Prussia; and that those islanders may be farther and more effectually restrained in making any advantage of their own wool in the way of manufacture, we command that none shall be carried out of one county into another; nor shall any worsted, bay, or woollen yarn, cloth, says, bays, kerseys, serges, frizes, druggets, cloth-serges, shalloons, or any other drapery stuffs, or woollen manufactures whatsoever, made up or mixed with wool in any of the said counties, be carried into any other county, or be waterborne even across the smallest river or creek, on penalty of forfeiture of the same, together with the boats, carriages, horses, &c., that shall be employed in removing them. Nevertheless, our loving subjects there are hereby permitted (if they think proper) to use all their wool as manure for the improvement of their lands.

"And whereas the art and mystery of making hats hath arrived at great perfection in Prussia, and the making of hats by our remoter subjects ought to be as much as possible restrained: And forasmuch as the islanders before mentioned, being in possession of wool, beaver and other furs, have presumptuously conceived they had a right to make some advantage thereof, by manufacturing the same into hats, to the prejudice of our domestic manufacture: We do therefore hereby strictly command and ordain, that no hats or felts whatsoever, dyed or undyed, finished or unfinished, shall be loaded or put into or upon any vessel, cart, carriage, or horse, to be transported or conveyed out of one county in the said island into another county, or to any other place whatsoever, by any person or persons whatsoever; on pain of forfeiting the same, with a penalty of five hundred pounds sterling for every offence. Nor shall any hat-maker, in any of the said counties, employ more than two apprentices, on penalty of five pounds sterling per month; we intending hereby, that such hatmakers, being so restrained, both in the production and sale of their commodity, may find no advantage in continuing their business. But, lest the said islanders should suffer inconveniency by the want of hats, we are farther graciously pleased to permit them to send their beaver furs to Prussia; and we also permit hats made thereof to be exported from Prussia to Britain; the people thus favoured to pay all costs and charges of manufacturing, interest, commission to our merchants, insurance and freight going and returning, as in the case of iron.

"And, lastly, being willing farther to favour our said colonies in Britain, we do hereby also ordain and command, that all the *thieves,* highway and street robbers, house-breakers, forgerers, murderers, s[o]d[omi]tes and villains of every denomination, who have forfeited their lives to the law in Prussia; but whom we, in our great clemency, do not think fit here to hang, shall be emptied out of our gaols into the said island of Great Britain, for the better peopling of that country.

"We flatter ourselves, that these our royal regulations and commands will be thought just and reasonable by our much-favoured colonists in England; the said regulations being copied from their statutes of 10 and 11 William III. c. 10, 5 Geo. II. c. 22, 23, Geo. II. c. 29, 4 Geo. I. c. 11, and from other equitable laws made by their parliaments; or from instructions given by their Princes;

or from resolutions of both Houses, entered into for the good government of their *own colonies in Ireland and America.*

"And all persons in the said island are hereby cautioned not to oppose in any wise the execution of this our Edict, or any part thereof, such opposition being high treason; of which all who are suspected shall be transported in fetters from Britain to Prussia, there to be tried and executed according to the Prussian law.

"Such is our pleasure.
Given at Potsdam, this twenty-fifth day of the month of August, one thousand seven hundred and seventy-three, and in the thirty-third year of our reign.
"By the King, in his Council.
"RECHTMAESSIG, *Sec.*"

Some take this Edict to be merely one of the King's *Jeux d'Esprit:* others suppose it serious, and that he means a quarrel with England; but all here think the assertion it concludes with, "that these regulations are copied from acts of the English parliament respecting their colonies," a very injurious one; it being impossible to believe, that a people distinguished for their love of liberty, a nation so wise, so liberal in its sentiments, so just and equitable towards its neighbours, should, from mean and injudicious views of petty immediate profit, treat its own children in a manner so arbitrary and tyrannical!

JOHN ADAMS

The committee had several meetings, in which were proposed the articles of which the declaration was to consist,

Reprinted from a letter of August 6, 1822, in C. F. Adams, ed., THE WORKS OF JOHN ADAMS, *II (Boston, 1850), 512–15.*

and minutes made of them. The committee then appointed Mr. Jefferson and me to draw them up in form, and clothe them in a proper dress. The sub-committee met, and considered the minutes, making such observations on them as then occurred, when Mr. Jefferson desired me to take them to my lodgings, and make the draught. This I declined, and gave several reasons for declining. 1. That he was a Virginian, and I a Massachusettensian. 2. That he was a southern man, and I a northern one. 3. That I had been so obnoxious for my early and constant zeal in promoting the measure, that any draught of mine would undergo a more severe scrutiny and criticism in Congress, than one of his composition. 4. and lastly, and that would be reason enough if there were no other, I had a great opinion of the elegance of his pen, and none at all of my own. I therefore insisted that no hesitation should be made on his part. He accordingly took the minutes, and in a day or two produced to me his draught. Whether I made or suggested any correction, I remember not. The report was made to the committee of five, by them examined, but whether altered or corrected in any thing, I cannot recollect. But, in substance at least, it was reported to Congress, where, after a severe criticism, and striking out several of the most oratorical paragraphs, it was adopted on the fourth of July, 1776, and published to the world.

NOTES

It is due to Mr. Jefferson here to say that his recollection of the event here described, materially differs from this account. In the month of August, 1822, Colonel Timothy Pickering addressed to Mr. Adams a letter of inquiry, respecting the origin of the Declaration of Independence. His reply contains so many other interesting particulars, besides those which relate to the single purpose of the letter, that it appears peculiarly suitable for insertion in this place in full.

TO TIMOTHY PICKERING.

6 August, 1822.

Sir:—Your favor of the 2d instant has prescribed a dismal plan, which I was never very well calculated to execute; but I am now utterly incapable. I can write nothing which will not be suspected of personal vanity, local prejudice, or Provincial and State partiality. However, as I hold myself responsible at this age, to one only tribunal in the universe, I will give you a few hints at all hazards.

As Mr. Hancock was sick and confined, Mr. Bowdoin was chosen at the head of the Massachusetts delegation to Congress. His relations thought his great fortune ought not to be hazarded. Cushing, two Adamses, and Paine, all destitute of fortune, four poor pilgrims, proceeded in one coach, were escorted through Massachusetts, Connecticut, New York, and New Jersey, into Pennsylvania. We were met at Frankfort by Dr. Rush, Mr. Mifflin, Mr. Bayard, and several other of the most active sons of liberty in Philadelphia, who desired a conference with us. We invited them to take tea with us in a private apartment. They asked leave to give us some information and advice, which we thankfully granted. They represented to us that the friends of government in Boston and in the Eastern States, in their correspondence with their friends in Pennsylvania and all the Southern States, had represented us as four desperate adventurers. "Mr. Cushing was a harmless kind of man, but poor, and wholly dependent on his popularity for his subsistence. Mr. Samuel Adams was a very artful, designing man, but desperately poor, and wholly dependent on his popularity with the lowest vulgar for his living. John Adams and Mr. Paine were two young lawyers, of no great talents, reputation, or weight, who had no other means of raising themselves into consequence, than by courting popularity." * We were all suspected of having independence in view. Now, said they, you must not utter the word independence, nor give the least hint or insinuation of the idea, either in Congress or any private conversation; if you do, you are undone; for the idea of independence is as unpopular in Pennsylvania, and in all the Middle and Southern States, as the Stamp Act itself. No man dares to speak of it. Moreover, you are the representatives of the suffering State. Boston and Massachusetts are under a rod of iron. British fleets and armies are tyrannizing over you; you yourselves are personally obnoxious to them and all the friends of government; you have been long persecuted by them all; your feelings have been hurt, your passions excited; you are thought to be too warm, too zealous, too sanguine. You must be, therefore, very cautious; you must not come forward with any bold measures, you must not pretend to take the lead. You know Virginia is the most populous State in the Union. They are very proud of their ancient dominion, as they call it; they think they have a right to take the lead, and the Southern States, and Middle States too, are too much disposed to yield it to them."

This was plain dealing, Mr. Picker-

* Compare this with the language of the Rev. Jacob Duché, in his letter to General Washington: "Bankrupts, attorneys, and men of desperate fortunes, are the colleagues of Mr. Hancock." *Graydon's Memoirs of his own Time,* Littell's edition, Appendix, p. 432.

ing; and I must confess that there appeared so much wisdom and good sense in it, that it made a deep impression on my mind, and it had an equal effect on all my colleagues.

This conversation, and the principles, facts, and motives, suggested in it, have given a color, complexion, and character, to the whole policy of the United States, from that day to this. Without it, Mr. Washington would never have commanded our armies; nor Mr. Jefferson have been the author of the Declaration of Independence; nor Mr. Richard Henry Lee the mover of it; nor Mr. Chase the mover of foreign connections. If I have ever had cause to repent of any part of this policy, that repentance ever has been, and ever will be, unavailing. I had forgot to say, nor had Mr. Johnson ever been the nominator of Washington for General.

Although this advice dwelt on my mind, I had not, in my nature, prudence and caution enough always to observe it. When I found the members of Congress, Virginians and all, so perfectly convinced that they should be able to persuade or terrify Great Britain into a relinquishment of her policy, and a restoration of us to the state of 1763, I was astonished, and could not help muttering, in Congress, and sometimes out of doors, that they would find, the proud, domineering spirit of Britain, their vain conceit of their own omnipotence, their total contempt of us, and the incessant representation of their friends and instruments in America, would drive us to extremities, and finally conquer us, transport us to England for trial, there to be hanged, drawn and quartered for treason, or to the necessity of declaring independence, however hazardous and uncertain such a measure might be.

It soon became rumored about the city that John Adams was for independ-

ence. The Quakers and proprietary gentlemen took the alarm; represented me as the worst of men; the true-blue sons of liberty pitied me; all put me under a kind of coventry. I was avoided, like a man infected with the leprosy. I walked the streets of Philadelphia in solitude, borne down by the weight of care and unpopularity.* But every ship, for the ensuing year, brought us fresh proof of the truth of my prophecies, and one after another became convinced of the necessity of independence. I did not sink under my discouragements. I had before experienced enough of the wantonness of popularity, in the trial of Preston and the soldiers, in Boston.

You inquire why so young a man as Mr. Jefferson was placed at the head of the Committee for preparing a Declaration of Independence? I answer; It was the Frankfort advice, to place Virginia at the head of every thing. Mr. Richard Henry Lee might be gone to Virginia, to his sick family, for aught I know, but that was not the reason of Mr. Jefferson's appointment. There were three committees appointed at the same time. One for the Declaration of Independence, another for preparing articles of Confederation, and another for preparing a treaty to be proposed to France. Mr. Lee was chosen for the Committee of Confederation, and it was not thought convenient that the same person should be upon both. Mr. Jefferson came into Congress, in June, 1775, and brought with him a reputation for literature, science, and a happy talent of composition. Writings of his were handed about, remarkable for the peculiar felicity of expression. Though a

* Dr. Benjamin Rush says of the Author, in a manuscript in the Editor's hands,—"I saw this gentleman walk the streets of Philadelphia alone, after the publication of his intercepted letter in our newspapers, in 1775, an object of nearly universal scorn and detestation."

silent member in Congress, he was so prompt, frank, explicit, and decisive upon committees and in conversation, not even Samuel Adams was more so, that he soon seized upon my heart; and upon this occasion I gave him my vote, and did all in my power to procure the votes of others. I think he had one more vote than any other, and that placed him at the head of the committee. I had the next highest number, and that placed me the second. The committee met, discussed the subject, and then appointed Mr. Jefferson and me to make the draught, I suppose because we were the two first on the list.

The sub-committee met. Jefferson proposed to me to make the draught. I said, "I will not." "You should do it." "Oh! no!" "Why will you not? You ought to do it." "I will not." "Why?" "Reasons enough." "What can be your reasons?" "Reason first—You are a Virginian, and a Virginian ought to appear at the head of this business. Reason second—I am obnoxious, suspected, and unpopular. You are very much otherwise. Reason third—You can write ten times better than I can." "Well," said Jefferson, "if you are decided, I will do as well as I can." "Very well. When you have drawn it up, we will have a meeting."

A meeting we accordingly had, and conned the paper over. I was delighted with its high tone and the flights of oratory with which it abounded, especially that concerning negro slavery, which, though I knew his Southern brethren would never suffer to pass in Congress, I certainly never would oppose. There were other expressions which I would not have inserted, if I had drawn it up, particularly that which called the King tyrant. I thought this too personal; for I never believed George to be a tyrant in disposition and in nature; I always believed him to be

deceived by his courtiers on both sides of the Atlantic, and in his official capacity only, cruel. I thought the expression too passionate, and too much like scolding, for so grave and solemn a document; but as Franklin and Sherman were to inspect it afterwards, I thought it would not become me to strike it out. I consented to report it, and do not now remember that I made or suggested a single alteration.

We reported it to the committee of five. It was read, and I do not remember that Franklin or Sherman criticized any thing. We were all in haste. Congress was impatient, and the instrument was reported, as I believe, in Jefferson's handwriting, as he first drew it. Congress cut off about a quarter of it, as I expected they would; but they obliterated some of the best of it, and left all that was exceptionable, if any thing in it was. I have long wondered that the original draught has not been published. I suppose the reason is, the vehement philippic against negro slavery.

As you justly observe, there is not an idea in it but what had been hackneyed in Congress for two years before. The substance of it is contained in the declaration of rights and the violation of those rights, in the Journal of Congress, in 1774. Indeed, the essence of it is contained in a pamphlet, voted and printed by the town of Boston, before the first Congress met, composed by James Otis, as I suppose, in one of his lucid intervals, and pruned and polished by Samuel Adams.

Your friend and humble servant.

On the national anniversary succeeding the date of this letter, Colonel Pickering quoted the latter part of it, in the course of some remarks made by him at a celebration of the day in Salem. This drew forth a letter, from Mr. Jefferson to Mr. Madison, denying its accuracy, particularly in the matter of the sub-committee, and attributing the error to the failing memory of eighty-eight, the assumed age of Mr. Adams at the time.* Mr. Jefferson did not then know, what the present publication of the Autobiography shows, not to speak of Mr. Pickering's letter of inquiry, that almost the identical statement had been made, not only in conversation long before, but also in this record, by Mr. Adams, nearly twenty years earlier, so that, if it be an error, it cannot be attributed merely to age.

Perceiving also the awkward nature of the charge made by one—himself—having, at the moment, nearly attained fourscore, Mr. Jefferson disclaims all reliance upon his recollection, and appeals to the unequivocal authority of his notes, made at the time. This seemed conclusive testimony, sufficient to set the matter at rest forever. But if by those notes is to be understood no more than what has since been published under that name, in the first volume of his correspondence, it is clear, on examination, that they present no evidence, excepting that which may be implied by their affirming nothing in corroboration.

The question, in itself, does not rise beyond the character of a curiosity of literature, as the substantial facts in both accounts are the same. The case having been stated, the reader must be left to form his opinions from the materials before him.

Among the papers left by Mr. Adams, is a transcript, by his own hand, of the Declaration of Independence, very nearly as it appears in Mr. Jefferson's first draught. This must have been made by him before the paper had been subjected to any change in committee, as none of the alterations which appear

* Jefferson's *Memoir and Correspondence,* vol. iv. p. 375.

on the original, as made at the instance of Dr. Franklin, and but one of the two suggested by himself, are found there. Several variations occur, however, in the phraseology, and one or two passages are wholly omitted. The most natural inference is, that he had modified it to suit his own notions of excellence, without deeming the alterations worth pressing in committee. As Mr. Jefferson says that his draught was submitted separately, first to Mr. Adams, and afterwards to Dr. Franklin, the presence of this copy does not affect the question of the correctness of either version of the proceedings.

THOMAS PAINE

THE AMERICAN CRISIS: I

These are the times that try men's souls. The summer soldier and the sunshine patriot will, in this crisis, shrink from the service of their country, but he that stands it *now* deserves the love and thanks of man and woman. Tyranny, like hell, is not easily conquered; yet we have this consolation with us that, the harder the conflict, the more glorious the triumph. What we obtain too cheap, we esteem too lightly; it is dearness only that gives everything its value. Heaven knows how to put a proper price upon its goods, and it would be strange indeed if so celestial an article as freedom should not be highly rated. Britain, with an army to enforce her tyranny, has declared that she has a right (*not only to tax*) but *to bind us in all cases whatsoever;* and if being

Reprinted from Thomas Paine, "The American Crisis: I," in THE LIFE AND WORKS OF THOMAS PAINE *(New Rochelle, N.Y.: Thomas Paine National Historical Association, 1925),* II, 263–75.

bound in that manner is not slavery, then there is not such a thing as slavery upon earth. Even the expression is impious, for so unlimited a power can belong only to God.

Whether the independence of the continent was declared too soon or delayed too long I will not now enter into as an argument; my own simple opinion is that, had it been eight months earlier, it would have been much better. We did not make a proper use of last winter, neither could we while we were in a dependent state. However, the fault, if it were one, was all our own; [1] we have none to blame but ourselves. But no great deal is lost yet. All that Howe has been doing for this month past is rather a ravage than a conquest, which the spirit of the Jerseys, a year ago, would have quickly repulsed, and which time and a little resolution will soon recover.

I have as little superstition in me as any man living, but my secret opinion has ever been and still is that God Almighty will not give up a people to military destruction or leave them unsupportedly to perish who have so earnestly and so repeatedly sought to avoid the calamities of war by every decent method which wisdom could invent. Neither have I so much of the infidel in me as to suppose that He has relinquished the government of the world and given us up to the care of devils, and as I do not I cannot see on what grounds the King of Britain can look up to heaven for help against us; a common murderer, a highwayman, or a

---

[1] The present winter is worth an age if rightly employed, but if lost or neglected the whole continent will partake of the evil; and there is no punishment that man does not deserve, be he who or what or where he will, that may be the means of sacrificing a season so precious and useful. [From *Common Sense*, p. 25.]

house-breaker has as good a pretense as he.

. . .

As I was with the troops at Fort Lee, and marched with them to the edge of Pennsylvania, I am well acquainted with many circumstances which those who live at a distance know but little or nothing of. Our situation there was exceedingly cramped, the place being a narrow neck of land between the North River and the Hackensack. Our force was inconsiderable, being not one fourth so great as Howe could bring against us. We had no army at hand to have relieved the garrison, had we shut ourselves up and stood on our defense. Our ammunition, light artillery, and the best part of our stores had been removed, on the apprehension that Howe would endeavor to penetrate the Jerseys, in which case Fort Lee could be of no use to us; for it must occur to every thinking man, whether in the army or not, that these kind of field forts are only for temporary purposes and last in use no longer than the enemy directs his force against the particular object which such forts are raised to defend. Such was our situation and condition at Fort Lee on the morning of the twentieth of November, when an officer arrived with information that the enemy, with two hundred boats, had landed about seven miles above; Major General Greene, who commanded the garrison, immediately ordered them under arms and sent express to General Washington at the town of Hackensack, distant by the way of the ferry = six miles. Our first object was to secure the bridge over the Hackensack, which laid up the river between the enemy and us, about six miles from us and three from them. General Washington arrived in about three quarters of an hour and marched at the head of the troops toward the bridge, which place I expected we should have a brush for; however, they did not choose to dispute it with us, and the greatest part of our troops went over the bridge, the rest over the ferry, except some which passed at a mill on a small creek, between the bridge and the ferry, and made their way through some marshy grounds up to the town of Hackensack and there passed the river. We brought off as much baggage as the wagons could contain; the rest was lost. The simple object was to bring off the garrison and march them on till they could be strengthened by the Jersey or Pennsylvania militia, so as to be enabled to make a stand. We stayed four days at Newark, collected our outposts with some of the Jersey militia, and marched out twice to meet the enemy, on being informed that they were advancing, though our numbers were greatly inferior to theirs. Howe, in my little opinion, committed a great error in generalship in not throwing a body of forces off from Staten Island through Amboy, by which means he might have seized all our stores at Brunswick and intercepted our march into Pennsylvania; but if we believe the power of hell to be limited, we must likewise believe that their agents are under some providential control.

I shall not now attempt to give all the particulars of our retreat to the Delaware; suffice it for the present to say that both officers and men, though greatly harassed and fatigued, frequently without rest, covering, or provision— the inevitable consequences of a long retreat—bore it with a manly and martial spirit. All their wishes centered in one, which was that the country would turn out and help them to drive the enemy back. Voltaire has remarked that King William never appeared to full advantage but in difficulties and in action; the same remark may be made on

General Washington, for the character fits him. There is a natural firmness in some minds which cannot be unlocked by trifles, but which, when unlocked, discovers a cabinet of fortitude; and I reckon it among those kind of public blessings which we do not immediately see that God has blessed him with uninterrupted health and given him a mind that can even flourish upon care.

. . .

I once felt all that kind of anger which a man ought to feel against the mean principles that are held by the Tories: a noted one, who kept a tavern at Amboy, was standing at his door with as pretty a child in his hand, about eight or nine years old, as I ever saw, and after speaking his mind as freely as he thought was prudent, finished with this unfatherly expression, "Well! give me peace in my day." Not a man lives on the continent but fully believes that a separation must some time or other finally take place, and a generous parent should have said, "If there must be trouble, let it be in my day, that my child may have peace," and this single reflection, well applied, is sufficient to awaken every man to duty. Not a place upon earth might be so happy as America. Her situation is remote from all the wrangling world, and she has nothing to do but to trade with them. A man can distinguish himself between temper and principle, and I am as confident as I am that God governs the world that America will never be happy till she gets clear of foreign dominion. Wars without ceasing will break out till that period arrives, and the continent must in the end be conqueror; for though the flame of liberty may sometimes cease to shine, the coal can never expire.

America did not nor does not want force, but she wanted a proper application of that force. Wisdom is not the purchase of a day, and it is no wonder that we should err at the first setting off. From an excess of tenderness, we were unwilling to raise an army and trusted our cause to the temporary defense of a well-meaning militia. A summer's experience has now taught us better; yet with those troops, while they were collected, we were able to set bounds to the progress of the enemy, and, thank God! they are again assembling. I always considered militia as the best troops in the world for a sudden exertion, but they will not do for a long campaign. Howe, it is probable, will make an attempt on this city; should he fail on this side of the Delaware, he is ruined. If he succeeds, our cause is not ruined. He stakes all on his side against a part on ours; admitting he succeeds, the consequence will be that armies from both ends of the continent will march to assist their suffering friends in the middle states; for he cannot go everywhere, it is impossible. I consider Howe as the greatest enemy the Tories have; he is bringing a war into their country, which, had it not been for him and partly for themselves, they had been clear of. Should he now be expelled, I wish with all the devotion of a Christian that the names of Whig and Tory may never more be mentioned; but should the Tories give him encouragement to come or assistance if he come, I as sincerely wish that our next year's arms may expel them from the continent, and the Congress appropriate their possessions to the relief of those who have suffered in well-doing. A single successful battle next year will settle the whole. America could carry on a two years' war by the confiscation of the property of disaffected persons and be made happy by their expulsion. Say not that this is revenge; call it rather the soft resentment of a suffering people who, having no object in view but the *good* of *all,* have staked their *own all* upon a seemingly doubtful event. Yet it is folly to argue against determined hardness; eloquence may strike the ear and the language of sorrow draw forth the tear of compassion, but nothing can reach the heart that is steeled with prejudice.

Quitting this class of men, I turn with the warm ardor of a friend to those who have nobly stood and are yet determined to stand the matter out; I call not upon a few but upon all— not on *this* state or *that* state, but on *every* state—up and help us, lay your shoulders to the wheel, better have too much force than too little when so great an object is at stake. Let it be told to the future world that in the depth of winter, when nothing but hope and virtue could survive, that the city and the country, alarmed at one common danger, came forth to meet and to repulse it. Say not that thousands are gone, turn out your tens of thousands; throw not the burden of the day upon Providence, but "show your faith by your works," that God may bless you. It matters not where you live or what rank of life you hold, the evil or the blessing will reach you all. The far and the near, the home counties and the back, the rich and the poor will suffer or rejoice alike. The heart that feels not now is dead; the blood of his children will curse his cowardice who shrinks back at a time when a little might have saved the whole and made *them* happy. I love the man that can smile in trouble, that can gather strength from distress and grow brave by reflection. 'Tis the business of little minds to shrink, but he whose heart is firm and whose conscience approves his conduct will pursue his principles unto death. My own line of reasoning is to myself as straight and clear as a ray of light. Not all the treasures of the world, so far as I believe, could have induced me to support an offensive war, for I think it murder; but if a thief breaks into my house, burns and destroys my property, and kills or threatens to kill me or those that are in it and to "bind me in all cases whatsoever" to his absolute will, am I to suffer it? What signifies it to me whether he who does it is a king or a common man, my countryman or not my countryman; whether it be done by an individual villain or an army of them? If we reason to the root of things, we shall find no difference; neither can any just cause be assigned why we should punish in the one case and pardon in the other. Let them call me rebel and welcome, I feel no concern from it; but I should suffer the misery of devils were I to make a whore of my soul by swearing allegiance to one whose character is that of a sottish, stupid, stubborn, worthless, brutish man. I conceive likewise a horrid idea in receiving mercy from a being who, at the last day, shall be shrieking to the rocks and mountains to cover him and fleeing with terror from the orphan, the widow, and the slain of America.

3. The Drive Toward a New Frame of Government

Many revolutionary leaders were disturbed by the renewal of older patterns of colonial (now state) autonomy under the framework of the Articles of Confederation. The call for revision of the Articles—indeed, for an entirely new framework of government—came from many sources, and the following letters by Henry Knox and George Washington are but two of hundreds written by prominent patriots during the 1780's. Four of the six greatest figures of the Revolutionary era participated in the Philadelphia convention that drafted the Constitution. Washington, Madison, Hamilton, and Franklin attended, with Jefferson and John Adams absent on diplomatic assignments in Europe. Madison and Hamilton, of the four notables present, contributed most to the document that emerged from the convention. In their famous collaborative effort with John Jay, Hamilton and Madison used the Federalist Papers *as practical propaganda to help speed ratification of the new frame of government by the New York constitutional convention. Federalist Number 10 contains Madison's impressive analysis of the problems presented by political factions to the successful conduct of democratic government, while Federalist Number 26 includes a little-known discussion by Hamilton that anticipates the emergence of political parties (as yet unknown at the national level) under the new form of government. Franklin's closing speech to the Philadelphia convention crystallized Federalist sentiment on the need for the new Constitution, much as Tom Paine's* Common Sense *had epitomized patriot consensus (or the hope for such consensus) at the beginning of the Revolutionary experience.*

GEORGE WASHINGTON

TO JOHN JAY

Mount Vernon,
August 1, 1786

Your sentiments, that our affairs are drawing rapidly to a crisis, accord with my own. What the event will be, is also beyond the reach of my foresight. We have errors to correct. We have probably had too good an opinion of human nature in forming our Confederation. Experience has taught us, that men will not adopt and carry into execution measures the best calculated for their own good, without the intervention of a coercive power. I do not conceive we can exist long as a nation without having lodged somewhere a power, which will pervade the whole Union in as energetic a manner as the authority of the State governments extends over the several States.

To be fearful of investing Congress, constituted as that body is, with ample authorities for national purposes, appears to me the very climax of popular absurdity and madness. Could Congress exert them for the detriment of the public, without injuring themselves in an equal or greater proportion? Are not their interests inseparably connected with those of their constituents? By the rotation of appointment, must they not mingle frequently with the mass of citizens? Is it not rather to be apprehended, if they were possessed of the power before described, that their individual members would be induced to use them, on many occasions, very timidly and inefficaciously for fear of losing their popularity and future election? We must take human nature

Reprinted from John C. Fitzpatrick, ed., THE WRITINGS OF GEORGE WASHINGTON, *XXVIII (Washington, 1938), 216–17.*

as we find it. Perfection falls not to the share of mortals. Many are of opinion, that Congress have too frequently made use of the suppliant, humble tone of requisition in applications to the States, when they had a right to assert their imperial dignity and command obedience. Be that as it may, requisitions are a perfect nullity where thirteen sovereign, independent, disunited States are in the habit of discussing and refusing compliance with them at their option. Requisitions are actually little better than a jest and a by-word throughout the land. If you tell the legislatures they have violated the treaty of peace, and invaded the prerogatives of the confederacy, they will laugh in your face. What then is to be done? Things cannot go in the same train forever. It is much to be feared, as you observe, that the better kind of people, being disgusted with the circumstances, will have their minds prepared for any revolution whatever. We are apt to run from one extreme into another. To anticipate and prevent disastrous contingencies would be the part of wisdom and patriotism.

What astonishing changes a few years are capable of producing. I am told that even respectable characters speak of a monarchical form of government without horror. From thinking proceeds speaking; thence to acting is often but a single step. But how irrevocable and tremendous! What a triumph for our enemies to verify their predictions! What a triumph for the advocates of despotism to find that we are incapable of governing ourselves, and that systems founded on the basis of equal liberty are merely ideal and fallacious! Would to God that wise measures may be taken in time to avert the consequences we have but too much reason to apprehend.

Retired as I am from the world, I frankly acknowledge I cannot feel myself an unconcerned spectator. Yet, having happily assisted in bringing the ship into port, and having been fairly discharged, it is not my business to embark again on a sea of troubles. Nor could it be expected, that my sentiments and opinions would have much weight on the minds of my countrymen. They have been neglected, though given as a last legacy in the most solemn manner. I had then perhaps some claim to public attention. I consider myself as having none at present.

With sentiments of sincere esteem and friendship, I am, dear sir, etc.

HENRY KNOX

TO MERCY WARREN

New-York, 30th May, 1787
Madam:—Having but just returned from Philadelphia, it was only yesterday I had the honor to receive your favor of the 2d instant.

Respecting politicks, as you have given me the opportunity, I shall take the liberty of indulging confidentially a few reflections, relying on your goodness for an excuse if any sentiment should escape, which in appearance should seem to be contrary to our former opinions. . . .

That our system operates badly indeed, no person who knows the discontents, which pervade the United States will deny. Not only a ruined commerce, but such destruction of *moral principle* as must alarm every upright, and intelligent lover of his country. Anarchy with its horrid train of miseries seem ready to overwhelm this region marked by nature for happiness. Were we to

Reprinted from WARREN-ADAMS LETTERS, *II* (Boston: Historical Society, 1925), 294–96.

examine our political systems without prejudice, perhaps we shall there find the source of all the evils of which we complain, and of all those which we apprehend.

Our respectable and enlightened friend Mr. Adams's Book will be the surest basis of his reputation. It is true he has been a little unfortunate in his title. It is not a defence of the constitutions of the United States, it is rather a sarcasm on them. But it should have been entitled "The Soul of a free government." But still it will be the means of great good. It is a word spoken in season. He clearly points out one of the capital causes of our misery and prostrate character—the will, the caprice the headlong conduct, of a government without strong checks by different branches, or a division of power by a balance, A mad democracy sweeps away every moral and divine trait from the human character. Hence it is that reason Law, and patriotism is banished from almost every Legislature. Private convenience, paper money, and ex post facto Laws, are the main springs of the American governments.

In addition to these local evils all national character, and interests are lost by the monsterous system of State governments; which from their construction, compared with the general government, must necessarily produce the effects which we experience of overturning even almost the appearance of a general government. Granted says candor, but the remedy? pardon me, the convention is sitting—and shall one of the cincinnati presume to give his opinion?

I confess however, that my only hope of human assistance is founded on the convention. Should they possess the hardihood to be unpopular, and propose an efficient National government, free from the entanglements of the present defective state systems we may yet be a happy and great nation. But I have no expectations if their propositions should be truly wise, that they will be immediately accepted. I should rather suppose that they would be ridiculed in the same as was the ark of old, while building by Noah. But if human nature be influenced by invariable principles, we are on the eve of political storms.

If the convention should propose to erect a temple to liberty on the solid, and durable foundation of Law and Justice, all men of principle in the first instance will embrace the proposal. Demagogues and vicious characters will oppose for a while. But reason will at length triumph. But should the convention be desirous of acquiring present popularity; should they possess local and not general views; should they propose a patch work to the present wretchedly defective thing called the Confederation, look out ye patriots, supplicate Heaven! for you will have need of its protection!

. . .

. . . I wish at present to try the experiment of a strong *national republic*. The state governments should be deprived of the power of injuring themselves or the Nation. The people have parted with power enough to form an excellent constitution; But it is incorp[ora]ted and diffused among bodies which cannot use it to good purpose. It must be concentered in a national government, the power of which should be divided between a strong executive, a senate, and assembly. The powers which each should have, would be a subject of nice discussion and much detail. The time of the executive, and senate should be such as to give stability to the system. The Assembly to be for one two or at most three years. A Judicial to be

formed on the highest principles of Independency. This government should possess every power necessary for national purposes which would leave the state governments but very little. But every power should be defined with accuracy, and checked according to the highest human wisdom. An attempt to overleap the bounds of the constitution by those who are in the execution of it, should be certainly and severely punished.

JAMES MADISON

THE FEDERALIST NO. 10

November 22, 1787
To the People of the State of New York: Among the numerous advantages promised by a well constructed Union, none deserves to be more accurately developed than its tendency to break and control the violence of faction. The friend of popular governments, never finds himself so much alarmed for their character and fate, as when he contemplates their propensity to this dangerous vice. He will not fail therefore to set a due value on any plan which, without violating the principles to which he is attached, provides a proper cure for it. The instability, injustice and confusion introduced into the public councils, have in truth been the mortal diseases under which popular governments have every where perished; as they continue to be the favorite and fruitful topics from which the adversaries to liberty derive their most specious declamations. The valuable improvements made by the American Constitutions on the popular models, both ancient and modern, can-

Reprinted from THE FEDERALIST PAPERS, *Nos. 10 and 26, in Paul L. Ford, ed.,* THE FEDERALIST *(New York: Henry Holt & Co., 1898), pp. 54–59, 62, 165–67.*

not certainly be too much admired; but it would be an unwarrantable partiality, to contend that they have as effectually obviated the danger on this side as was wished and expected. Complaints are every where heard from our most considerate and virtuous citizens, equally the friends of public and private faith, and of public and personal liberty; that our governments are too unstable; that the public good is disregarded in the conflicts of rival parties; and that measures are too often decided, not according to the rules of justice, and the rights of the minor party; but by the superior force of an interested and over-bearing majority. However anxiously we may wish that these complaints had no foundation, the evidence of known facts will not permit us to deny that they are in some degree true. It will be found indeed, on a candid review of our situation, that some of the distresses under which we labor, have been erroneously charged on the operation of our governments; but it will be found, at the same time, that other causes will not alone account for many of our heaviest misfortunes; and particularly, for that prevailing and increasing distrust of public engagements, and alarm for private rights, which are echoed from one end of the continent to the other. These must be chiefly, if not wholly, effects of the unsteadiness and injustice, with which a factious spirit has tainted our public administrations.

By a faction I understand a number of citizens, whether amounting to a majority or minority of the whole, who are united and actuated by some common impulse of passion, or of interest, adverse to the rights of other citizens, or to the permanent and aggregate interests of the community.

There are two methods of curing the mischiefs of faction: the one, by removing its causes; the other, by controling its effects.

There are again two methods of removing the causes of faction: the one by destroying the liberty which is essential to its existence; the other, by giving to every citizen the same opinions, the same passions, and the same interests.

It could never be more truly said than of the first remedy, that it is worse than the disease. Liberty is to faction, what air is to fire, an aliment without which it instantly expires. But it could not be a less folly to abolish liberty, which is essential to political life, because it nourishes faction, than it would be to wish the annihilation of air, which is essential to animal life, because it imparts to fire its destructive agency.

The second expedient is as impracticable, as the first would be unwise. As long as the reason of man continues fallible, and he is at liberty to exercise it, different opinions will be formed. As long as the connection subsists between his reason and his self-love, his opinions and his passions will have a reciprocal influence on each other; and the former will be objects to which the latter will attach themselves. The diversity in the faculties of men from which the rights of property originate, is not less an insuperable obstacle to a uniformity of interests. The protection of these faculties is the first object of Government. From the protection of different and unequal faculties of acquiring property, the possession of different degrees and kinds of property immediately results: and from the influence of these on the sentiments and views of the respective proprietors, ensues a division of the society into different interests and parties.

The latent causes of faction are thus sown in the nature of man; and we see them every where brought into different degrees of activity, according to the different circumstances of civil society. A zeal for different opinions concerning religion, concerning Government and many other points, as well of speculation as of practice; an attachment to different leaders ambitiously contending for pre-eminence and power; or to persons of other descriptions whose fortunes have been interesting to the human passions, have in turn divided mankind into parties, inflamed them with mutual animosity, and rendered them much more disposed to vex and oppress each other, than to co-operate for their common good. So strong is this propensity of mankind to fall into mutual animosities, that where no substantial occasion presents itself, the most frivolous and fanciful distinctions have been sufficient to kindle their unfriendly passions, and excite their most violent conflicts. But the most common and durable source of factions, has been the various and unequal distribution of property. Those who hold, and those who are without property, have ever formed distinct interests in society. Those who are creditors, and those who are debtors, fall under a like discrimination. A landed interest, a manufacturing interest, a mercantile interest, a monied interest, with many lesser interests, grow up of necessity in civilized nations, and divide them into different classes, actuated by different sentiments and views. The regulation of these various and interfering interests forms the principal task of modern Legislation, and involves the spirit of party and faction in the necessary and ordinary operations of Government.

. . .

It is in vain to say, that enlightened statesmen will be able to adjust these clashing interests, and render them all subservient to the public good. Enlightened statesmen will not always be at the helm: Nor, in many cases, can such an adjustment be made at all, without taking into view indirect and remote considerations, which will rarely prevail over the immediate interest which one party may find in disregarding the rights of another, or the good of the whole.

The inference to which we are brought, is, that the *causes* of faction cannot be removed; and that relief is only to be sought in the means of controling its *effects*.

If a faction consists of less than a majority, relief is supplied by the republican principle, which enables the majority to defeat its sinister views by regular vote: It may clog the administration, it may convulse the society; but it will be unable to execute and mask its violence under the forms of the Constitution. When a majority is included in a faction, the form of popular government on the other hand enables it to sacrifice to its ruling passion or interest, both the public good and the rights of other citizens. To secure the public good, and private rights, against the danger of such a faction, and at the same time to preserve the spirit and the form of popular government, is then the great object to which our enquiries are directed. . . .

By what means is this object attainable? Evidently by one of two only. Either the existence of the same passion or interest in a majority at the same time, must be prevented; or the majority, having such co-existent passion or interest, must be rendered, by their number and local situation, unable to concert and carry into effect schemes of oppression. . . .

. . .

The other point of difference is, the greater number of citizens and extent of territory which may be brought within the compass of Republican, than of Democratic Government; and it is this circumstance principally which renders factious combinations less to be dreaded in the former, than in the latter. The smaller the society, the fewer probably will be the distinct parties and interests composing it; the fewer the distinct parties and interests, the more frequently will a majority be found of the same party; and the smaller the number of individuals composing a majority, and the smaller the compass within which they are placed, the more easily will they concert and execute their plans of oppression. Extend the sphere, and you take in a greater variety of parties and interests; you make it less probable that a majority of the whole will have a common motive to invade the rights of other citizens; or if such a common motive exists, it will be more difficult for all who feel it to discover their own strength, and to act in unison with each other. Besides other impediments, it may be remarked, that where there is a consciousness of unjust or dishonorable purposes, communication is always checked by distrust, in proportion to the number whose concurrence is necessary.

ALEXANDER HAMILTON

THE FEDERALIST NO. 26

. . . Even in some of the States . . . we find unnecessary declarations, that standing armies ought not to be kept up, in time of peace WITHOUT THE CONSENT OF THE LEGISLATURE—I call them unnecessary, because the reason, which had introduced a similar provision into the English bill of rights, is not applicable to any of the state constitutions.

The power of raising armies at all, under those constitutions, can by no construction be deemed to reside any where else, than in the legislatures themselves; and it was superfluous, if not absurd, to declare that a matter should not be done without the consent of a body, which alone had the power of doing it. Accordingly in some of those constitutions, and among others in that of this State of New-York; which has been justly celebrated both in Europe and in America as one of the best of the forms of government established in this country, there is a total silence upon the subject.

It is remarkable, that even in the two States,[1] which seem to have meditated an interdiction of military establishments in time of peace, the mode of expression made use of is rather cautionary than prohibitory. It is not said, that standing armies *shall not be* kept up, but that they *ought not* to be kept up in time of peace. This ambiguity of terms appears to have been the result of a conflict between jealousy and conviction, between the desire of excluding such establishments at all events, and the persuasion that an absolute exclusion would be unwise and unsafe.

. . .

Let us examine whether there be any comparison, in point of efficacy, between the provision alluded to and that which is contained in the New Constitution, for restraining the appropriations of money for military purposes to the period of two years. The former by aiming at too much is calculated to effect nothing; the latter, by steering clear of an imprudent extreme, and by being perfectly compatible with a proper provision for the exigencies

[1] Pennsylvania and North Carolina.

of the nation, will have a salutary and powerful operation.

The Legislature of the United States will be *obliged* by this provision, once at least in every two years, to deliberate upon the propriety of keeping a military force on foot; to come to a new resolution on the point; and to declare their sense of the matter, by a formal vote in the face of their constituents. They are not *at liberty* to vest in the executive department permanent funds for the support of an army; if they were even incautious enough to be willing to repose in it so improper a confidence. As the spirit of party, in different degrees, must be expected to infect all political bodies, there will be no doubt persons in the national Legislature willing enough to arraign the measures and criminate the views of the majority. The provision for the support of a military force will always be a favourable topic for declamation. As often as the question comes forward, the public attention will be roused and attracted to the subject, by the party in opposition: And if the majority should be really disposed to exceed the proper limits the community will be warned of the danger and will have an opportunity of taking measures to guard against it. Independent of parties in the national Legislature itself, as often as the period of discussion arrived, the state Legislature, who will always be not only vigilant but suspicious and jealous guardians of the rights of the citizens, against incroachments from the Fœderal government, will constantly have their attention awake to the conduct of the national rulers and will be ready enough, if any thing improper appears, to sound the alarm to the people and not only to be the VOICE but if necessary the ARM of their discontent.

BENJAMIN FRANKLIN

I confess that there are several parts of this constitution which I do not at present approve, but I am not sure I shall never approve them: For having lived long, I have experienced many instances of being obliged by better information or fuller consideration, to change opinions even on important subjects, which I once thought right, but found to be otherwise. It is therefore that the older I grow, the more apt I am to doubt my own judgment, and to pay more respect to the judgment of others. Most men indeed as well as most sects in Religion, think themselves in possession of all truth, and that whereever others differ from them it is so far error. Steele, a Protestant in a Dedication tells the Pope, that the only difference between our Churches in their opinions of the certainty of their doctrines is, the Church of Rome is infallible and the Church of England is never in the wrong. But though many private persons think almost as highly of their own infallibility as of that of their sect, few express it so naturally as a certain french lady, who in a dispute with her sister, said "I don't know how it happens, Sister but I meet with no body but myself, that's always in the right"—*Il n'y a que moi qui a toujours raison.*

In these sentiments, Sir, I agree to this Constitution with all its faults, if they are such; because I think a general Government necessary for us, and there is no form of Government but what may be a blessing to the people if well ad-

Reprinted from Benjamin Franklin, closing speech to the Constitutional Convention, September 17, 1786, in Ralph Ketcham, ed., THE POLITICAL THOUGHT OF BENJAMIN FRANKLIN *(Indianapolis and New York: The Bobbs-Merrill Company, Inc., 1965), pp. 400–402.*

ministered, and believe farther that this is likely to be well administered for a course of years, and can only end in Despotism, as other forms have done before it, when the people shall become so corrupted as to need despotic Government, being incapable of any other. I doubt too whether any other Convention we can obtain may be able to make a better Constitution. For when you assemble a number of men to have the advantage of their joint wisdom, you inevitably assemble with those men, all their prejudices, their passions, their errors of opinion, their local interests, and their selfish views. From such an Assembly can a perfect production be expected? It therefore astonishes me, Sir, to find this system approaching so near to perfection as it does; and I think it will astonish our enemies, who are waiting with confidence to hear that our councils are confounded like those of the Builders of Babel; and that our States are on the point of separation, only to meet hereafter for the purpose of cutting one another's throats. Thus I consent, Sir, to this Constitution because I expect no better, and because I am not sure, that it is not the best. The opinions I have had of its errors, I sacrifice to the public good—I have never whispered a syllable of them abroad—Within these walls they were born, and here they shall die—If every one of us in returning to our Constitutents were to report the objections he has had to it, and endeavor to gain partizans in support of them, we might prevent its being generally received, and thereby lose all the salutary effects & great advantages resulting naturally in our favor among foreign Nations as well as among ourselves, from our real or apparent unanimity. Much of the strength & efficiency of any Government in procuring and securing happiness to the people, depends on opinion, on the general opinion of the goodness of the Government, as well as of the wisdom and integrity of its Governors. I hope therefore that for our own sakes as a part of the people, and for the sake of posterity, we shall act heartily and unanimously in recommending this Constitution (if approved by Congress & confirmed by the Conventions) wherever our influence may extend, and turn our future thought & endeavors to the means of having it well administered.

On the whole, Sir, I cannot help expressing a wish that every member of the Convention who may still have objections to it, would with me, on this occasion doubt a little of his own infallibility—and to make manifest our unanimity, put his name to this instrument. . . .

4. The First Political Party System

The origins of the first American party system during the administrations of George Washington and John Adams involved complex and interlocking disputes over the basic constitutional, economic, and diplomatic policies to be pursued by the new federal government. The disputes centered around dramatic personality conflicts between Washington's chief cabinet ministers, Alexander Hamilton and Thomas Jefferson, each of whom took divergent positions on such central problems as the relative power of state and federal governments, the relation of American foreign policy to the

European quarrels between England and France, and the proper course of government in assisting national economic development. In reply to an inquiry by Washington in September 1792 concerning the reasons for their dispute and for the rise of factional spirit within his government, both Jefferson and Hamilton wrote long explanatory letters presenting their sides of the policy and personal quarrels that had emerged. Oddly, both letters were written on September 9, thus providing Washington with a serious political dialogue to accompany his morning meal the following day. Twenty years later, Jefferson engaged in a remarkably lively exchange with John Adams on the reasons behind the evolution of the party system, in which the Virginian tried to trace the ideological and historical context of American party development, while the dour Adams insisted on pointing waspishly to the practical quarrels—the "Loaves and Fishes"—behind the struggle for political power in the new republic. Both the Hamilton-Jefferson and Adams-Jefferson exchanges follow.

ALEXANDER HAMILTON

TO GEORGE WASHINGTON

Philadelphia, September 9, 1792.
Sir: I have the pleasure of your private letter of the 26th of August. The feelings and views which are manifested in that letter are such as I expected would exist. And I most sincerely regret the causes of the uneasy sensations you experience. It is my most anxious wish, as far as may depend upon me, to smooth the path of your administration, and to render it prosperous and happy. And if any prospect shall open of healing or terminating the differences which exist, I shall most cheerfully embrace it; though I consider myself as the deeply injured party. The recommendation of such a spirit is worthy of the moderation and wisdom which dictated it. And if your endeavors should prove unsuccessful, I do not hesitate to say, that in my opinion

Reprinted from Frederick C. Prescott, ed., ALEXANDER HAMILTON AND THOMAS JEFFERSON: REPRESENTATIVE SELECTIONS *(New York, 1934),* pp. 132–34.

the period is not remote, when the public good will require *substitutes* for the *differing members* of your administration. The continuance of a division there must destroy the energy of government, which will be little enough with the strictest union. On my part there will be a most cheerful acquiescence in such a result.

I trust, sir, that the greatest frankness has always marked, and will always mark, every step of my conduct towards you. In this disposition I cannot conceal from you, that I have had some instrumentality of late in the retaliations which have fallen upon certain public characters, and that I find myself placed in a situation not to be able to recede *for the present.*

I considered myself as compelled to this conduct by reasons public as well as personal, of the most cogent nature. I *know* that I have been an object of uniform opposition from Mr. Jefferson, from the moment of his coming to the city of New York to enter upon his present office. I *know* from the most authentic sources, that I have been the frequent subject of the most unkind whispers and insinuations from the same quarter. I have long seen a party formed in the Legislature under his auspices, bent upon my subversion. I cannot doubt from the evidence I possess, that the *National Gazette* was instituted by him for political purposes, and that one leading object of it has been to render me, and all the measures connected with my department, as odious as possible. Nevertheless, I can truly say, that, except explanations to confidential friends, I never directly or indirectly retaliated or countenanced retaliation till very lately. I can even assure you, that I was instrumental in preventing a very severe and systematic attack upon Mr. Jefferson by an association of two or three individuals, in consequence of the persecution which he brought upon the Vice-President, by his indiscreet and light letter to the printer, transmitting *Paine's* pamphlet.

As long as I saw no danger to the government from the machinations which were going on, I resolved to be a silent sufferer of the injuries which were done me. I determined to avoid giving occasion to any thing which could manifest to the world dissensions among the principal characters of the government; a thing which can never happen without weakening its hands, and in some degree throwing a stigma upon it.

But when I no longer doubted that there was a formed party deliberately bent upon the subversion of measures, which in its consequences would subvert the government; when I saw that the undoing of the funding system in particular (which, whatever may be the original merits of that system, would prostrate the credit and the honor of the nation, and bring the government into contempt with that description of men who are in every society the only

firm supporters of government) was an avowed object of the party, and that all possible pains were taken to produce that effect, by rendering it odious to the body of the people, I considered it as a duty to endeavor to resist the torrent, and, as an effectual means to this end, to draw aside the veil from the principal actors. To this strong impulse, to this decided conviction, I have yielded. And I think events will prove that I have judged rightly.

Nevertheless, I pledge my honor to you, sir, that if you shall hereafter form a plan to reunite the members of your administration upon some steady principle of coöperation, I will faithfully concur in executing it during my continuance in office; and I will not directly or indirectly say or do a thing that shall endanger a feud.

I have had it very much at heart to make an excursion to Mount Vernon, by way of the federal city, in the course of this month, and have more than once been on the point of asking your permission for it. But I now despair of being able to effect it. I am, nevertheless, equally obliged by your kind invitation.

With the most affectionate and faithful attachment, etc.

THOMAS JEFFERSON

TO THE PRESIDENT OF THE UNITED STATES

Monticello, September 9, 1792.
Dear Sir: I received on the 2d instant the letter of August 23d, which you did me the honor to write me; but the immediate return of our post, contrary to his custom, prevented my answer by that occasion. The proceedings of

Reprinted from Frederick C. Prescott, ed., ALEXANDER HAMILTON AND THOMAS JEFFERSON: REPRESENTATIVE SELECTIONS (*New York, 1934*), *pp. 312–22.*

Spain, mentioned in your letter, are really of a complexion to excite uneasiness, and a suspicion that their friendly overtures about the Mississippi, have been merely to lull us while they should be strengthening their holds on that river. Mr. Carmichael's silence has been long my astonishment; and however it might have justified something very different from a new appointment, yet the public interest certainly called for his junction with Mr. Short, as it is impossible but that his knowledge of the ground of negotiation, of persons and characters, must be useful and even necessary to the success of the mission. That Spain and Great Britain may understand one another on our frontiers is very possible; for however opposite their interests or disposition may be in the affairs of Europe, yet while these do not call them into opposite action, they may concur as against us. I consider their keeping an agent in the Indian country as a circumstance which requires serious interference on our part; and I submit to your decision whether it does not furnish a proper occasion to us to send an additional instruction to Messrs. Carmichael and Short to insist on a mutual and formal stipulation to forbear employing agents or pensioning any persons within each other's limits; and if this be refused, to propose the contrary stipulation, to wit, that each party may freely keep agents within the Indian territories of the other, in which case we might soon sicken them of the license.

I now take the liberty of proceeding to that part of your letter wherein you notice the internal dissensions which have taken place within our government, and their disagreeable effect on its movements. That such dissensions have taken place is certain, and even among those who are nearest to you in the administration. To no one have they given deeper concern than myself; to no one equal mortification at being myself a part of them. Though I take to myself no more than my share of the general observations of your letter, yet I am so desirous ever that you should know the whole truth, and believe no more than the truth, that I am glad to seize every occasion of developing to you whatever I do or think relative to the government; and shall, therefore, ask permission to be more lengthy now than the occasion, particularly calls for, or could otherwise perhaps justify.

When I embarked in the government, it was with a determination to intermeddle not at all with the Legislature, and as little as possible with my co-departments. The first and only instance of variance from the former part of my resolution, I was duped into by the Secretary of the Treasury, and made a tool for forwarding his schemes, not then sufficiently understood by me, and of all the errors of my political life, this has occasioned me the deepest regret. It has ever been my purpose to explain this to you, when, from being actors on the scene, we shall have become uninterested spectators only. The second part of my resolution has been religiously observed with the War Department; and as to that of the Treasury, has never been farther swerved from than by the mere enunciation of my sentiments in conversation, and chiefly among those who, expressing the same sentiments, drew mine from me. If it has been supposed that I have ever intrigued among the members of the Legislatures to defeat the plans of the Secretary of the Treasury, it is contrary to all truth. As I never had the desire to influence the members, so neither had I any other means than my friendships, which I valued too highly to risk by usurpations on their freedom of judgment, and the conscientious pursuit of their own sense of duty. That I have utterly, in my private conversations, disapproved of the system of the Secretary of the Treasury, I acknowledge and avow; and this was not merely a speculative difference. His system flowed from principles adverse to liberty, and was calculated to undermine and demolish the Republic, by creating an influence of his department over the members of the Legislature. I saw this influence actually produced, and its first fruits to be the establishment of the great outlines of his project by the votes of the very persons who, having swallowed his bait, were laying themselves out to profit by his plans; and that had these persons withdrawn, as those interested in a question ever should, the vote of the disinterested majority was clearly the reverse of what they made it. These were no longer the votes then of the representatives of the people, but of deserters from the rights and interests of the people; and it was impossible to consider their decisions, which had nothing in view to enrich themselves, as the measures of the fair majority, which ought always to be respected. If what was actually doing begat uneasiness in those who wished for virtuous government, what was further proposed was not less threatening to the friends of the Constitution. For, in a report on the subject of manufactures (still to be acted on), it was expressly assumed that the General Government has a right to exercise all powers which may be for the *general welfare,* that is to say, all the legitimate powers of government; since no government has a legitimate right to do what is not for the welfare of the governed. There was, indeed, a sham limitation of the universality of this power *to cases where money is to*

be employed. But about what is it that money cannot be employed? Thus the object of these plans, taken together, is to draw all the powers of government into the hands of the general Legislature, to establish means for corrupting a sufficient corps in that Legislature to divide the honest votes, and preponderate, by their own, the scale which suited, and to have that corps under the command of the Secretary of the Treasury, for the purpose of subverting, step by step, the principles of the Constitution, which he has so often declared to be a thing of nothing, which must be changed. Such views might have justified something more than mere expressions of dissent, beyond which, nevertheless, I never went. Has abstinence from the department, committed to me, been equally observed by him? To say nothing of other interferences equally known, in the case of the two nations, with which we have the most intimate connections, France and England, my system was to give some satisfactory distinctions to the former, of little cost to us, in return for the solid advantages yielded us by them; and to have met the English with some restrictions which might induce them to abate their severities against our commerce. I have always supposed this coincided with your sentiments. Yet the Secretary of the Treasury, by his cabals with members of the Legislature, and by high-toned declamations on other occasions, has forced down his own system, which was exactly the reverse. He undertook, of his own authority, the conferences with the ministers of those two nations, and was, on every consultation, provided with some report of a conversation with the one or the other of them, adapted to his views. These views, thus made to prevail, their execution fell, of course, to me; and I can safely appeal to you, who have seen all my letters and proceedings, whether I have not carried them into execution as sincerely as if they had been my own, though I ever considered them as inconsistent with the honor and interest of our country. That they have been inconsistent with our interest is but too fatally proved by the stab to our navigation given by the French. So that if the question be by whose fault is it that Colonel Hamilton and myself have not drawn together? the answer will depend on that to two other questions: whose principles of administration best justify, by their purity, conscientious adherence? and which of us has, notwithstanding, stepped farthest into the control of the department of the other?

To this justification of opinions, expressed in the way of conversation, against the views of Colonel Hamilton, I beg leave to add some notice of his late charges against me in Fenno's Gazette; for neither the style, matter, nor venom of the pieces alluded to, can leave a doubt of their author. Spelling my name and character at full length to the public, while he conceals his own under the signature of "An American," he charges me, 1st. With having written letters from Europe to my friends to oppose the present Constitution, while depending. 2d. With a desire of not paying the public debt. 3d. With setting up a paper to decry and slander the government. 1st. The first charge is most false. No man in the United States, I suppose, approved of every tittle in the Constitution; no one, I believe, approved more of it than I did, and more of it was certainly disapproved by my accuser than by me, and of its parts most vitally republican. Of this the few letters I wrote on the subject (not half a dozen I believe) will be a proof; and for my own satisfaction and justification, I must tax you with the reading

of them when I return to where they are. You will there see that my objection to the Constitution was that it wanted a bill of rights securing freedom of religion, freedom of the press, freedom from standing armies, trial by jury, and a constant habeas corpus act. Colonel Hamilton's was that it wanted a king and house of lords. The sense of America has approved my objection and added the bill of rights, not the king and lords. I also thought a longer term of service, insusceptible of renewal, would have made a President more independent. My country has thought otherwise, I have acquiesced implicitly. He wishes the General Government should have power to make laws binding the States in all cases whatsoever. Our country has thought otherwise: has he acquiesced? Notwithstanding my wish for a bill of rights, my letters strongly urged the adoption of the Constitution, by nine States at least, to secure the good it contained. I at first thought that the best method of securing the bill of rights would be for four States to hold off till such a bill should be agreed to. But the moment I saw Mr. Hancock's proposition to pass the Constitution as it stood, and give perpetual instructions to the representatives of every State to insist on a bill of rights, I acknowledged the superiority of his plan, and advocated universal adoption. 2d. The second charge is equally untrue. My whole correspondence while in France, and every word, letter, and act on the subject, since my return, prove that no man is more ardently intent to see the public debt soon and sacredly paid off than I am. This exactly marks the difference between Colonel Hamilton's views and mine, that I would wish the debt paid tomorrow; he wishes it never to be paid, but always to be a thing wherewith to corrupt and manage the Legislature:

3d. I have never enquired what number of sons, relatives, and friends of Senators, Representatives, printers or other useful partisans Colonel Hamilton has provided for among the hundred clerks of his department, the thousand excisemen, custom-house officers, loan-officers, etc., etc., etc., appointed by him, or at his nod, and spread over the Union; nor could ever have imagined that the man who has the shuffling of millions backwards and forwards from paper into money and money into paper, from Europe to America, and America to Europe, the dealing out of treasury secrets among his friends in what time and measure he pleases, and who never slips an occasion of making friends with his means, that such an one, I say, would have brought forward a charge against me for having appointed the poet Freneau, translating clerk to my office, with a salary of 250 dollars a year. That fact stands thus. While the government was at New York I was applied to on behalf of Freneau to know if there was any place within my department to which he could be appointed. I answered there were but four clerkships, all of which I found full, and continued without any change. When we removed to Philadelphia, Mr. Pintard, the translating clerk, did not choose to remove with us. His office then became vacant. I was again applied to there for Freneau, and had no hesitation to promise the clerkship for him. I cannot recollect whether it was at the same time, or afterwards, that I was told he had a thought of setting up a newspaper there. But whether then, or afterwards, I considered it as a circumstance of some value, as it might enable me to do, what I had long wished to have done, that is, to have the material parts of the Leyden Gazette brought under your eye, and that of the public, in order to possess yourself and them of a juster view of the affairs of Europe than could be obtained from any other public source. This I had ineffectually attempted through the press of Mr. Fenno, while in New York, selecting and translating passages myself at first, then having it done by Mr. Pintard, the translating clerk, but they found their way too slowly into Mr. Fenno's papers. Mr. Bache essayed it for me in Philadelphia, but his being a daily paper, did not circulate sufficiently in the other States. He even tried, at my request, the plan of a weekly paper of recapitulation from his daily paper, in hopes that that might go into the other States, but in this too we failed. Freneau, as translating clerk, and the printer of a periodical paper likely to circulate through the States (uniting in one person the parts of Pintard and Fenno), revived my hopes that the thing could at length be effected. On the establishment of his paper, therefore, I furnished him with the Leyden Gazettes, with an expression of my wish that he could always translate and publish the material intelligence they contained, and have continued to furnish them from time to time, as regularly as I received them. But as to any other direction or indication of my wish how his press should be conducted, what sort of intelligence he should give, what essays encourage, I can protest, in the presence of heaven, that I never did by myself, or any other, directly or indirectly, say a syllable, nor attempt any kind of influence. I can further protest, in the same awful presence, that I never did by myself, or any other, directly or indirectly, write, dictate, or procure any one sentence or sentiment to be inserted *in his, or any other gazette,* to which my name was not affixed or that of my office. I surely need not except here a thing so foreign to the present subject as a little paragraph about our Algerine captives, which I put once into Fenno's paper. Freneau's proposition to publish a paper, having been about the time that the writings of Publicola, and the discourses on Davila, had a good deal excited the public attention, I took for granted from Freneau's character, which had been marked as that of a good whig, that he would give free place to pieces written against the aristocratical and monarchical principles these papers had inculcated. This having been in my mind, it is likely enough I may have expressed it in conversation with others, though I do not recollect that I did. To Freneau I think I could not, because I had still seen him but once, and that was at a public table, at breakfast, at Mrs. Elsworth's, as I passed through New York the last year. And I can safely declare that my expectations looked only to the chastisement of the aristocratical and monarchical writers, and not to any criticisms on the proceedings of government. Colonel Hamilton can see no motive for any appointment, but that of making a convenient partisan. But you, Sir, who have received from me recommendations of a Rittenhouse, Barlow, Paine, will believe that talents and science are sufficient motives with me in appointments to which they are fitted; and that Freneau, as a man of genius, might find a preference in my eye to be a translating clerk, and make good title to the little aids I could give him as the editor of a gazette, by procuring subscriptions to his paper, as I did some before it appeared, and as I have with pleasure done for the labors of other men of genius. I hold it to be one of the distinguishing excellences of elective over hereditary successions, that the talents, which nature has provided in

sufficient proportion, should be selected by the society for the government of their affairs, rather than that this should be transmitted through the loins of knaves and fools, passing from the debauches of the table to those of the bed. Colonel Hamilton, alias "Plain Facts," says that Freneau's salary began before he resided in Philadelphia. I do not know what quibble he may have in reserve on the word "residence." He may mean to include under that idea the removal of his family; for I believe he removed himself, before his family did, to Philadelphia. But no act of mine gave commencement to his salary before he so far took up his abode in Philadelphia as to be sufficiently in readiness for the duties of the office. As to the merits or demerits of his paper, they certainly concern me not. He and Fenno are rivals for the public favor. The one courts them by flattery, the other by censure, and I believe it will be admitted that the one has been as servile, as the other severe. But is not the dignity, and even decency of government committed, when one of its principal ministers enlists himself as an anonymous writer or paragraphist for either the one or the other of them? No government ought to be without censors; and where the press is free, no one ever will. If virtuous, it need not fear the fair operation of attack and defence. Nature has given to man no other means of sifting out the truth, either in religion, law, or politics. I think it as honorable to the government neither to know, nor notice, its sycophants or censors, as it would be undignified and criminal to pamper the former and persecute the latter. So much for the past, a word now of the future.

When I came into this office, it was with a resolution to retire from it as soon as I could with decency. It pretty early appeared to me that the proper moment would be the first of those epochs at which the Constitution seems to have contemplated a periodical change or renewal of the public servants. In this I was confirmed by your resolution respecting the same period; from which, however, I am happy in hoping you have departed. I look to that period with the longing of a wave-worn mariner, who has at length the land in view, and shall count the days and hours which still lie between me and it. In the meanwhile, my main object will be to wind up the business of my office, avoiding as much as possible all new enterprise. With the affairs of the Legislature, as I never did intermeddle, so I certainly shall not now begin. I am more desirous to predispose everything for the repose to which I am withdrawing, than expose it to be disturbed by newspaper contests. If these, however, cannot be avoided altogether, yet a regard for your quiet will be a sufficient motive for my deferring it till I become merely a private citizen, when the propriety or impropriety of what I may say or do, may fall on myself alone. I may then, too, avoid the charge of misapplying that time which now, belonging to those who employ me, should be wholly devoted to their service. If my own justification, or the interests of the republic shall require it, I reserve to myself the right of then appealing to my country, subscribing my name to whatever I write, and using with freedom and truth the facts and names necessary to place the cause in its just form before that tribunal. To a thorough disregard of the honors and emoluments of office, I join as great a value for the esteem of my countrymen, and conscious of having merited it by an integrity which cannot be reproached, and by an enthusiastic devotion to their rights and liberty, I will not suffer my retirement to be clouded by the slanders of a man whose history, from the moment at which history can stoop to notice him, is a tissue of machinations against the liberty of the country which has not only received and given him bread, but heaped its honors on his head. Still, however, I repeat the hope that it will not be necessary to make such an appeal. Though little known to the people of America, I believe, that as far as I am known, it is not as an enemy to the Republic, nor an intriguer against it, nor a waster of its revenue, nor prostitutor of it to the purposes of corruption, as the "American" represents me; and I confide that yourself are satisfied that as to dissensions in the newspapers, not a syllable of them has ever proceeded from me, and that no cabals or intrigues of mine have produced those in the Legislature, and I hope I may promise both to you and myself, that none will receive aliment from me during the short space I have to remain in office, which will find ample employment in closing the present business of the department.

Observing that letters written at Mount Vernon on the Monday, and arriving at Richmond on the Wednesday, reach me on Saturday, I have now the honor to mention that the 22d instant will be the last of our post-days that I shall be here, and consequently that no letter from you after the 17th, will find me here. Soon after that I shall have the honor of receiving at Mount Vernon your orders for Philadelphia, and of there also delivering you the little matter which occurs to me as proper for the opening of Congress, exclusive of what has been recommended in former speeches, and not yet acted on. In the meantime and ever I am, with great and sincere affection and respect, dear Sir, your most obedient, and most humble servant.

THOMAS JEFFERSON

TO JOHN ADAMS

Monticello June 27, 1813.

And I too, my dear Sir, like the wood-cutter of Ida, should doubt where to begin, were I to enter the forest of opinions, discussions, and contentions which have occurred in our day. I should exclaim with Theocritus, Τί πρᾶτον καταλεξῶ; ἐπεὶ πάρα μυρία ειπῆν.[1] But I shall not do it. The summum bonum with me is now truly Epicurean, ease of body and tranquility of mind; and to these I wish to consign my remaining days. Men have differed in opinion, and been divided into parties by these opinions, from the first origin of societies; and in all governments where they have been permitted freely to think and to speak. The same political parties which now agitate the U.S. have existed thro' all time. Whether the power of the people, or that of the ἄριστοι ["aristocrats"] should prevail, were questions which kept the states of Greece and Rome in eternal convulsions; as they now schismatize every people whose minds and mouths are not shut up by the gag of a despot. And in fact the terms of whig and tory belong to natural, as well as to civil history. They denote the temper and constitution of mind of different individuals. To come to our own country, and to the times when you and I became first acquainted, we well remember the violent parties which agitated the old Congress, and their bitter contests. There you and I were together, and the Jays, and the Dickinsons, and other anti-independants were arrayed against us. They

[1] " 'What first shall I gather?' he said, gazing at the thousands of trees."

Reprinted from Lester J. Cappon, ed., THE ADAMS-JEFFERSON LETTERS *(Chapel Hill: University of North Carolina Press, 1959) II, 335–38.*

cherished the monarchy of England; and we the rights of our countrymen. When our present government was in the mew, passing from Confederation to Union, how bitter was the schism between the Feds and Antis. Here you and I were together again. For altho' for a moment, separated by the Atlantic from the scene of action, I favored the opinion that nine states should confirm the constitution, in order to secure it, and the others hold off, until certain amendments, deemed favorable to freedom, should be made, I rallied in the first instant to the wiser proposition of Massachusets, that all should confirm, and then all instruct their delegates to urge those amendments. The amendments were made, and all were reconciled to the government. But as soon as it was put into motion, the line of division was again drawn, we broke into two parties, each wishing to give a different direction to the government; the one to strengthen the most popular branch, the other the more permanent branches, and to extend their permanence. Here you and I separated for the first time: and as we had been longer than most others on the public theatre, and our names therefore were more familiar to our countrymen, the party which considered you as thinking with them, placed your name at their head; the other, for the same reason, selected mine. But neither decency nor inclination permitted us to become the advocates of ourselves, or to take part personally in the violent contests which followed. We suffered ourselves, as you so well expressed it, to be the passive subjects of public discussion. And these discussions, whether relating to men, measures, or opinions, were conducted by the parties with an animosity, a bitterness, and an indecency, which had never been exceeded. All the resources of reason, and of wrath, were exhausted by each party in support of it's own, and to prostrate the adversary opinions. One was upbraided with recieving the Antifederalists, the other the old tories and refugees into their bosom. Of this acrimony the public papers of the day exhibit ample testimony in the debates of Congress, of state legislatures, of stump-orators, in addresses, answers, and newspaper essays. And to these without question may be added the private correspondences of individuals; and the less guarded in these, because not meant for the public eye, nor restrained by the respect due to that; but poured forth from the overflowings of the heart into the bosom of a friend, as a momentary easement of our feelings. . . .

. . . To me then it appears that there have been differences of opinion, and party differences, from the first establishment of governments, to the present day; and on the same question which now divides our own country: that these will continue thro' all future time: that every one takes his side in favor of the many, or of the few, according to his constitution, and the circumstances in which he is placed: that opinions, which are equally honest on both sides, should not affect personal esteem, or social intercourse: that as *we* judge between the Claudii and the Grachi, the Wentworths and the Hampdens of past ages, so, of those among us whose names may happen to be remembered for awhile, the next generations will judge, favorably or unfavorably, according to the complexion of individual minds, and the side they shall themselves have taken: that nothing new can be added by you or me to what has been said by others, and will be said in every age, in support of the conflicting opinions on government: and that wisdom and duty dictate an humble resignation to the verdict of our future peers. In

doing this myself, I shall certainly not suffer moot questions to affect the sentiments of sincere friendship and respect, consecrated to you by so long a course of time, and of which I now repeat sincere assurances.

JOHN ADAMS

TO THOMAS JEFFERSON

Quincy June 30th. 1813
Dear Sir: . . . But to return, *for the present* to "The Sensations excited, in free yet firm Minds by the Terrorism of the day." You say, "none can conceive them who did not witness them, and they were felt by one party only".

Upon this Subject I despair of making myself understood by Posterity, by the present Age, and even by you. To collect and arrange the documents illustrative of it, would require as many Lives as those of a Cat. You never felt the Terrorism of Chaises Rebellion in Massachusetts. I believe You never felt the Terrorism of Gallatins Insurrection in Pensilvania: You certainly never reallized the Terrorism of Fries's, most outragious Riot and Rescue, as I call it, Treason, Rebellion as the World and great Judges and two Juries pronounced it. You certainly never felt the Terrorism, excited by Genet, in 1793, when ten thousand People in the Streets of Philadelphia, day after day, threatened to drag Washington out of his House, and effect a Revolution in the Government, or compell it to declare War in favour of the French Revolution, and against England. The coolest and the firmest Minds, even among the Quakers in Philadelphia, have given their Opinions to me, that nothing but the Yellow

Reprinted from Lester J. Cappon, ed., THE ADAMS-JEFFERSON LETTERS *(Chapel Hill: University of North Carolina Press, 1959) II, 346–48.*

Fever, which removed Dr. Hutchinson and Jonathan Dickenson Sargent from this World, could have saved the United States from a total Revolution of Government. I have no doubt You was fast asleep in philosophical Tranquility, when ten thousand People, and perhaps many more, were parading the Streets of Philadelphia, on the Evening of my Fast Day; When even Governor Mifflin himself, thought it his Duty to order a Patrol of Horse And Foot to preserve the peace; when Markett Street was as full as Men could stand by one another, and even before my Door; when some of my Domesticks in Phrenzy, determined to sacrifice their Lives in my defence; when all were ready to make a desperate Salley among the multitude, and others were with difficulty and danger dragged back by the others; when I myself judged it prudent and necessary to order Chests of Arms from the War Office to be brought through bye Lanes and back Doors: determined to defend my House at the Expence of my Life, and the Lives of the few, very few Domesticks and Friends within it. What think you of Terrorism, Mr. Jefferson? Shall I investigate the Causes, the Motives, the Incentives to these Terrorisms? Shall I remind you of Phillip Freneau, of Loyd? of Ned Church? of Peter Markoe[?] of Andrew Brown? of Duane? of Callender? of Tom Paine? of Greenleaf, of Cheetham, of Tennison at New York? of Benjamin Austin. at Boston? But above all; shall I request you, to collect the circular Letters from Members of Congress in the middle and southern States to their Constituents? I would give all I am worth for a compleat Collection of all those circular Letters. Please to recollect Edward Livingstones motions and Speeches and those of his Associates in the case of Jonathan Robbins.

The real terrors of both Parties have allways been, and now are, The fear that they shall loose the Elections and consequently the Loaves and Fishes; and that their Antagonists will obtain them. Both parties have excited artificial Terrors and if I were summoned as a Witness to say upon Oath, which Party had excited, Machiavillialy, the most terror, and which had really felt the most, I could not give a more sincere Answer, than in the vulgar Style "Put Them in a bagg and shake them, and then see which comes out first."

Where is the Terrorism now, my Friend? There is now more real Terrorism in New England than there ever was in Virginia. The Terror of a civil War, a La Vendee, a division of the States etc. etc. etc. How shall We conjure down this damnable Rivalry between Virginia, and Massachusetts? Virginia had recourse to Pensilvania and New York, Massachusetts has now recourse to New York. They have almost got New Jersey and Maryland, and they are aiming at Pennsilvania. And all this in the midst of a War with England, when all Europe is in flames.

I will give you a hint or two more, on the Subject of Terrorism. When John Randolph in the House and Stephens Thompson Mason in the Senate were treating me, with the Utmost Contempt, when Ned Livingston was threatening me with Impeachment for the murder of Jonathan Robbins *the native of Danvers in Connecticut.* When I had certain Information, that the daily Language in an Insurance Office in Boston, was, even from the Mouth of Charles Jarvis, "We must go to Philadelphia and dragg that John Adams from his Chair."

I tha[n]k God that Terror never Yet seized on my mind. But I have had more excitements to it, from 1761 to this day than any other Man. Name the other if you can. I have been disgraced and degraded and I have a right to complain. But as I always expected it, I have always submitted to it; perhaps often with too much tameness.

The amount of all the Speeches of John Randolph in the House for two or three Years is, that himself and myself, are the only two honest and consistent Men in the United States. Himself, eternally in Opposition to Government, and myself as constantly in favour of it. He is now in Correspondence with his Friend Quincy. What will come of it, let Virginia and Massachusetts Judge. In my next, you may find Something, upon "Correspondencies" Whigg and Tory; Federal and democratic; Virginian and Novanglian; English and French; Jacobinic and despotic, etc.

Mean time, I am as ever Your Friend,
JOHN ADAMS

III. RECENT INTERPRETATIONS

Historians in the past few decades have revised substantially their understanding of eighteenth-century American political processes. No major area
of colonial or revolutionary political life has escaped careful reassessment
using new evidence and, more significantly, new techniques of analysis
borrowed from psychology and other social sciences. Bernard Bailyn's study
of pre-revolutionary political psychology in colonial America and Han-
overian England, for example, offers a persuasive re-interpretation of the
entire eighteenth-century English political experience. Similarly, in reviewing the critics of Charles Beard's economic interpretation of the Constitution, Stanley Elkins and Eric McKitrick offer a perceptive analysis of the
forces that led to the Philadelphia convention based on a careful study of
revolutionary leadership. Finally, William Nisbet Chambers brings the
entire problem of party development into comparative focus in his examination of political behavior patterns in the new republic.

BERNARD BAILYN

A NOTE ON CONSPIRACY

As I have indicated at length in
Chapters III and IV, the conviction on
the part of the Revolutionary leaders
that they were faced with a deliberate
conspiracy to destroy the balance of the
constitution and eliminate their freedom had deep and widespread roots—
roots elaborately embedded in Anglo-
American political culture. How far
back in time one may trace these roots
it is difficult to say, but I have attempted
at least to illustrate in the pages above,
and to show in considerable detail else-

1 "The Origins of American Politics," in *Perspectives in American History*, I (1967).

Reprinted from Bernard Bailyn, THE IDEOLOG-
ICAL ORIGINS OF THE AMERICAN REVOLUTION
*(Cambridge, Mass.: Harvard University Press,
1967), pp. 144–159, by permission of the publisher and the author.*

where,[1] that the configuration of attitudes and ideas that would constitute
the Revolutionary ideology was present
a half-century before there was an actual Revolution, and that among the
dominant elements in this pattern were
the fear of corruption—of its anticonsti-
tutional destructiveness—and of the
menace of a ministerial conspiracy. At
the very first signs of conflict between
the colonies and the administration in
the early 1760's the question of motivation was openly broached and the imputation of secret purposes discussed. Early
in the controversy anti-administration
leaders like Oxenbridge Thacher could
only "suppose" for the sake of discussion "that no design is formed to enslave them," while pro-administration
partisans, like Martin Howard, Jr., were
forced to refute the charge of design.[2]

2 [Oxenbridge Thacher], *The Sentiments of a
British American* (Boston, 1764: JHL Pamphlet
8), p. 4; [Martin Howard, Jr.], *A Letter from a*

To be sure, the conviction that the colonies, and England itself, were faced with a deliberate, anti-libertarian design grew most quickly where the polarization of politics was most extreme and where radical leaders were least inhibited in expressing and reinforcing general apprehensions. But in some degree it was present everywhere; it was almost universally shared by sympathizers of the American cause. The views of John Dickinson are particularly interesting, not merely because, though the most cautious and reluctant of Revolutionary leaders, he so forcefully conveyed the idea of conspiracy, but because he understood so well the psychological and political effects of thinking in precisely these conspiratorial terms. Reviewing the crisis of Charles I's reign, he pointed out that

acts that might *by themselves* have been upon many considerations excused or extenuated derived a contagious malignancy and odium from other acts with which they were connected. They were not regarded according to the simple force of each but as parts of a system of oppression. Every one, therefore, however small in itself, became alarming as an additional evidence of tyrannical designs. It was in vain for prudent and moderate men to insist that there was no necessity to abolish royalty. Nothing less than the utter destruction of the monarchy could satisfy those who *had* suffered and thought they had reason to believe they always *should* suffer under it. The conse-

quences of these mutual distrusts are well known.[3]

The explosion of long-smoldering fears of ministerial conspiracy was by no means an exclusively American phenomenon. It was experienced in England too, in a variety of ways, by a wide range of the English political public. Under George III, George Rudé has pointed out, it was

widely believed . . . that the influence of the Crown was being used to staff the administration with new Favourites and "King's Friends," who formed a secret Closet party, beyond the control of Parliament and guided behind the scenes by the sinister combination of the Earl of Bute (who had resigned office in 1763) and the Princess Dowager of Wales. Opponents of the new system talked darkly of a repetition of "the end of Charles II's reign"—and such talk was not confined to the circles of the Duke of Newcastle and others, who might be inclined to identify the eclipse of their own public authority with that of the national interest.

Such expressions, Rudé concludes, "were common currency and abound throughout this period both in the press, in Burke's *Thoughts on the Present Discontents* (1770), in personal correspondence, pamphlet literature and speeches in Parliament."[4] Burke's *Thoughts* is particularly relevant to the American situation, for the apprehension that dominates that piece is in essence interchangeable with that of innumerable Revolutionary writers. Its argument that Parliament was on the brink of falling "under the control of an unscrupulous gang of would-be despots" who would destroy the constitution "was sufficiently widely believed," Ian Christie has written, "to give mo-

---

Gentleman at Halifax . . . (Newport, 1765: JHL Pamphlet 10), p. 6. Similarly, Daniel Dulany felt obliged to argue the point, writing in 1773, when he was neutral in his sympathies, that "I should hardly expect to find [substantial merchants] in a plot against liberty, since commerce is ever engrafted on the stock of liberty, and must feel every wound that is given to it." Elihu S. Riley, ed., *Correspondence of "First Citizen"—Charles Carroll of Carrollton, and "Antilon"—Daniel Dulany, Jr.* . . . (Baltimore, 1902), p. 35.

[3] Dickinson, *Farmer's Letters* (JHL 23), pp. 58–59 (cf. pp. 62–64).
[4] Rudé, *Wilkes and Liberty*, p. 186.

mentum in due course to a radical movement in the metropolis."[5] The specific identification in *Thoughts* of the conspiratorial cabal at work was distinctively Burke's, but those who most vehemently disagreed with him about the source and nature of the conspiracy were no less convinced that a conspiratorial cabal of some sort was in fact at work. Catharine Macaulay, speaking for the extreme radicals, found it in the "maneuvers of aristocratic faction and party" of which Burke and the Rockinghams were themselves the inheritors and which was based on "a system of corruption [that] began at the very period of the [Glorious] Revolution and . . . was the policy of every succeeding administration." Horace Walpole too felt that Burke had not gone back far enough: "The canker had begun in the administration of the Pelhams," in the effort of the clique around the Princess Dowager "to inspire arbitrary principles into her son [the future George III] and to instruct him how to . . . establish a despotism that may end in tyranny in his descendants."[6]

For Horace Walpole, therefore, the immediate villain was Bute, who had arrived on the scene, Walpole wrote, with the triple disability of being "unknown, ungracious, and a Scot"; his influence, it was believed, continued through the sixties unabated, and by the early 1770's "Lord North had flung himself into the hands of Lord Bute's junto." In believing this, Walpole was scarcely alone. The conviction that Bute's secret influence lay behind the troubles of the time was widespread in opposition circles in England as it was in America. Seven years after Bute left office, Chatham delivered a speech in the Lords against "the secret influence of an invisible power—of a favorite, whose pernicious counsels had occasioned all the present unhappiness and disturbances in the nation, and who, notwithstanding he was abroad, was at this moment as potent as ever." Rockingham, who was convinced that Bute's secret influence had destroyed his administration in 1765–66, wrote in 1767 that his party's "fundamental principle" was to resist and restrain "the power and influence of Lord Bute." More ordinary opinion was reflected by the printer and publicist William Strahan, who in fact thought well of Bute but who agreed that his secret influence remained paramount long after his resignation from office. Strahan's colleague in the press, John Almon, not only blamed the evils of the time on

5 Ian R. Christie, *Wilkes, Wyvill and Reform* (London, 1962), p. 32. Burke expressed his more general fears privately to his friend Charles O'Hara in the year the *Thoughts* was published: "Without some extraordinary change . . . the court [working with the mob] may assume as uncontrolled a power in this country as the King of Sweden has done in his, without running any risks or meeting any more opposition than is just convenient to give their measures the sort of countenance that things receive from the supposition of their having been fairly debated. I know that this has been said ever since the Crown has got its great influence in Parliament. But it was not truly said while the people preferred one man to another; it was not said truly while a new ministry supposed a new Parliament; it was not said truly whilst it required art, address, and influence to secure a majority. Whether or no things were prepared for this in the last reign I cannot justly say; but this sort of power was then either not fully discovered, or nobody chose to venture upon it." Burke to O'Hara, September 30, 1770, *The Correspondence of Edmund Burke* (Thomas W. Copeland, *et al.*, eds., Cambridge and Chicago, 1958–), II, 336–337.

6 Catharine Macaulay, *Observations on a Pamphlet, Entitled, Thoughts on the Cause of the Present Discontents* (3d ed., London, 1770), pp. 7, 13; Romney Sedgwick, ed., *Letters from George III to Lord Bute, 1756–1766* (London, 1939), p. xli.

Bute but believed that the Rocking-hams were secretly cooperating with him. Indeed, the image of Bute as a malevolent and well-nigh indestructible machinator was almost universal among the opposition. Propagated endlessly in pamphlets and newssheets of all sorts, caricatured in a torrent of lurid cartoons depicting " 'the thane' as the lover of the Princess Dowager of Wales . . . and thus the bestower of posts and pensions to hordes of hungry barbarous Scots to the exclusion of the English," the idea of Bute as the central plotter became one of the keystones in the structure of opposition ideology, and it contributed forcefully to the belief, in England as well as in America, that an active conspiracy against the constitution was underway.[7]

Not everyone, of course, even within opposition circles, agreed that there was a deliberate design to overthrow the balance of the constitution; fewer still agreed with the republican radicals that the Coercive Acts were intended to "enslave America; and the same minister who means to enslave them would, if he had an opportunity, enslave England." Yet Lord Dartmouth felt it necessary to refute that charge specifically, and while it is true, as Christie has explained, that "abundant evidence now available about the activities of court and gov-

ernment enables historians to dismiss this fear as a chimera," it is nevertheless also true that there was a "contemporary belief in such a threat," a belief that was associated with the American crisis and that proved to be "a powerful stimulus to demands for reform" in English domestic affairs. "The sophisticated members of political society rightly dismissed as rubbish the misconceived but genuine radical fear, that the triumph of British arms and authority in America would be followed by the extinction of British liberties at home," but the fear remained, widespread enough, powerful enough, to force disbelievers to acknowledge it and to confront it. Thus the cool, well-informed, and hard-headed Dr. John Fothergill, the secret negotiator between Franklin and Dartmouth in the winter of 1774–75, felt it necessary to explain that he did "not quite" credit the ministry with "endeavoring to enslave [the colonists] by system. I believe they are very happy if they can find expedients for the present moment." So too Strahan wrote rather desperately to his American correspondent that "I know the *good disposition* of the ministry towards you . . . *I know* there is no disposition, either in the King, the ministry, or the Parliament, to oppress America in any shape." [8]

That this was the issue, for thought-

---

[7] Horace Walpole, *Memoirs of the Reign of King George the Third* (Denis Le Marchant, ed., London, 1845), I, 10; III, 233; IV, 92; Hansard, *Parliamentary History*, XVI, 842 (cf. Walpole, *Memoirs*, IV, 94); Foord, *His Majesty's Opposition*, p. 314 and n. 2; J. A. Cochrane, *Dr. Johnson's Printer* (Cambridge, 1964), p. 173, n. 3; Harvey C. Mansfield, Jr., *Statesmanship and Party Government* (Chicago, 1965), p. 104; Christie, *Wilkes, Wyvill and Reform*, pp. 35, 11; M. Dorothy George. *English Political Caricature to 1792* (Oxford, 1959), I, 120–121. On the actuality of Bute's influence, see Richard Pares, *King George III and the Politicians* (Oxford, 1953), pp. 104–109.

[8] John Sawbridge, quoted in Gipson, *British Empire*, XII, 127, 136; Christie, *Wilkes, Wyvill and Reform*, pp. 127, 136, 223, 67; Fothergill to Lt. Col. Ironside, December 22, 1774, in *Bulletin of the Friends Historical Society*, 5 (1913), 5; Strahan to David Hall, August 24, 1770, November 10, 1768, *Pa. Mag.*, XI (1887–88), 351; X (1886), 464. Fothergill admitted, however, that there was a high degree of "national corruption," which he explained not as a result of "the riches of the east" but rather of the sensualism and libertinism generated by slavery that the West India planters brought back to England.

ful and informed people, on which decisions of loyalty to the government
turned is nowhere so clearly and sensi-
tively revealed as in the record Peter
Van Schaack left of his tormented
meditations of January, 1776. A well-
born, scholarly, and articulate New
Yorker of 29 who prepared himself for
deciding the question of his personal
loyalty by undertaking in seclusion a
critical examination of the works of
Locke, Vattel, Montesquieu, Grotius,
Beccaria, and Pufendorf, he noted first
his fear of the destructive consequences
of conceding Parliament's right to bind
the colonies in all cases whatsoever.
That danger, he wrote, was perfectly
clear. "But my difficulty arises from
this," he said:

that taking the whole of the acts complained of together, they do not, I think,
manifest a system of slavery, but may fairly
be imputed to human frailty and the difficulty of the subject. Most of them seem
to have sprung out of particular occasions,
and are unconnected with each other . . .
In short, I think those acts may have been
passed without a preconcerted plan of enslaving us, and it appears to me that the
more favorable construction ought ever to
be put on the conduct of our rulers. I cannot therefore think the government *dissolved;* and as long as the society lasts, the
power that every individual gave the society
when he entered into it, can never revert
to the individual again but will always remain in the community.* [*footnote:*] *
Locke.⁹

⁹ Henry C. Van Schaack, *The Life of Peter
Van Schaack* (New York, 1842), pp. 58, 56–57.
So too James Iredell, reconstructing in 1776 the
evolution of the policies of the Continental
Congress, explained that the starting point for
all policy decisions had been a careful estimation of the motivation of the ministry: had
Grenville, it was asked, "acted from *principle*
and not from any *bad motive*"? Iredell, "Causes
Leading up to the American Revolution," in
Griffith J. McRee, ed., *Life and Correspondence
of James Iredell . . .* (New York, 1857–58), I,
312 ff.

All of this, however, forms but one
side of the role of conspiratorial thinking in the advent of the Revolution.
There is an obverse to this that is of
great importance, though, since in the
end it was not in itself determinative
of events, it has of necessity been neglected in the chapter above.

The opponents of the Revolution—
the administration itself—were as convinced as were the leaders of the Revolutionary movement that they were
themselves the victims of conspiratorial
designs. Officials in the colonies, and
their superiors in England, were persuaded as the crisis deepened that they
were confronted by an active conspiracy
of intriguing men whose professions
masked their true intentions. As early
as 1760 Governor Bernard of Massachusetts had concluded that a "faction"
had organized a conspiracy against the
customs administration, and by the end
of the decade he and others in similar
positions (including that "arch-con-
spirator" Thomas Hutchinson) had
little doubt that at the root of all the
trouble in the colonies was the maneuvering of a secret, power-hungry cabal
that professed loyalty to England while
assiduously working to destroy the
bonds of authority and force a rupture
between England and her colonies.¹⁰

The charge was quickly echoed in
England. The Massachusetts Convention of 1768 elicited from the House of

¹⁰ Bernard's fear of a conspiratorial faction is
the main theme that runs through his extensive
correspondence of the 1760's (13 vols., Sparks
MSS, Houghton Library, Harvard University,
excerpted in *The Barrington-Bernard Correspondence . . .* , Edward Channing and A. C.
Coolidge, eds., Cambridge, 1912); see also Gipson, *British Empire*, X, 116; XI, 33–34, 155, 157,
159; Bernard to Earl of Halifax, December 2,
1763, in Josiah Quincy, Jr., *Reports of Cases
. . . in the Superior Court of Judicature . . .
Between 1761 and 1772 . . .* (Samuel M.
Quincy, ed., Boston, 1865), p. 394.

Lords resolutions based on the belief that "wicked and designing men" in the colonies were "evidently manifesting a design . . . to set up a new and unconstitutional authority independent of the crown of England." [11] Such dangerous charges, tantamount to treason but objectively indistinguishable from faction—which was itself, in eighteenth-century terms, merely the superlative form of party [12]—had been a source of concern in the colonies since the start of the controversy. Under Grenville, Arthur Lee wrote, "every expression of discontent . . . was imputed to a desire in those colonies to dissolve all connection with Britain; every tumult here was inflamed into rebellion." The fear that colonial leaders nursed secret ambitions that they masked, with greater or lesser success, by continuing professions of loyalty grew as the crisis deepened. If in 1771 Hutchinson, an equal with his arch-enemies the Adamses in detecting secret purposes behind open professions, could report with relief that "the faction in this province against the government is dying," he still felt it necessary to add "but it dies hard." After the Tea Party such cautious optimism faded, and officials confirmed once and for all their belief that malevolent factions were implacably at work seeking to satisfy hidden ambitions and to destroy the ties to England.[13]

Such charges were commonly heard: among crown officials, at every level; but also in other circles—among Tories, such as those in inland Worcester, Massachusetts, who defied the majority, and the leadership, of the Town Meeting, and published a denunciation of "the artful, crafty, and insidious practices of some evil-minded and ill-disposed persons who . . . intend to reduce all things to a state of tumult, discord, and confusion." The committees of correspondence, they declared, had been the illegal creations of "a junto to serve particular designs and purposes of their own . . . tending directly to sedition, civil war, and rebellion." [14]

Such denunciations of the work of seditious factions seeking private aims masked by professions of loyalty, which abound in the writings of officials and of die-hard Tories, reach the extreme of vilification in Chief Justice Peter Oliver's scurrilous *Origin & Progress of the American Rebellion* and attain the ultimate in respectability in George III's statement to Parliament of October 26, 1775—a statement that may be taken as the precise obverse of Jefferson's claim, in the Declaration of Independence, that there was a "design to reduce [the colonies] under absolute despotism."

The authors and promoters of this desperate conspiracy [George III informed Parliament] have in the conduct of it derived great advantage from the difference of our intentions and theirs. They meant only to amuse, by vague expressions of attachment to the parent state and the strongest protestations of loyalty to me, whilst they were preparing for a general revolt . . . The rebellious war now levied is . . . manifestly carried on for the purpose of establishing an independent empire.

11 Hansard, *Parliamentary History*, pp. 479, 478 (cf. Gipson, *British Empire*, XI, 234, 244).
12 "Faction is to party what the superlative is to the positive: party is a political evil, and faction is the worst of all parties." Bolingbroke, "The Idea of a Patriot King," in *Works* . . . (London, 1754), III, 83.
13 "Monitor IX," *Virginia Gazette* (R), April 21, 1768; Frothingham, *Warren*, p. 158.

14 William Lincoln, *History of Worcester, Massachusetts* . . . (Worcester, 1837), pp. 87, 88. (I owe this reference to Richard D. Brown.)

This charge, emanating from the highest source, could not be left unanswered, and there lies in the records of the Continental Congress an elaborate refutation of the King's accusation—an essay, remarkably verbose and rhetorical, crowded with exclamations and gesticulations—dashes, italics, and shouting capitals—yet full of subtle perceptions, that fills no less than thirteen pages in the printed *Journals* of the Congress. Cast in the form of an "Address to the Inhabitants of the Colonies," it was written by a committee headed by John Dickinson and James Wilson, and though it was tabled by the Congress because it seemed unduly apologetic and defensive at the time (February 1776) and, in Madison's phrase, was "evidently short of the subsisting maturity" of opinion then in favor of independence, it nevertheless remains a most revealing exposition of the intellectual, political, and psychological dilemmas created by an escalating mutuality of conspiratorial fears. The Crown's representation of the actions of the Congress as those of "a seditious and unwarrantable combination," Wilson and Dickinson wrote, is malicious and false.

We are, we presume, the first rebels and conspirators who commenced their conspiracy and rebellion with a system of conduct immediately and directly frustrating every aim which ambition or rapaciousness could propose. Those whose fortunes are desperate may upon slighted evidence be charged with desperate designs. But how improbable is it that the colonists who have been happy and have known their happiness in the quiet possession of their liberties; who see no situation more to be desired than that in which, till lately, they have been placed; and whose warmest wish is to be reinstalled in the enjoyment of that freedom which they claim and are entitled to as men and as British subjects—

how improbable is it that *such* would, without any motives that could tempt even the most *profligate* minds to crimes, plunge themselves headlong into all the guilt and danger and distress with which those that endeavor to overturn the constitution of their country are always surrounded and frequently overwhelmed? . . . Whoever gives impartial attention to the facts we have already stated and to the observations we have already made must be fully convinced that all the steps which have been taken by us in this unfortunate struggle can be accounted for as rationally and as satisfactorily by supposing that the defense and re-establishment of their rights were the objects which the colonists and their representatives had in view as by supposing that an independent empire was their aim. Nay, we may safely go farther and affirm, without the most distant apprehension of being refuted, that many of those steps can be accounted for rationally and satisfactorily only upon the former supposition and cannot be accounted for, in that manner, upon the latter . . . Cannot our whole conduct be reconciled to *principles and views of self-defense?* Whence then the uncandid imputation of *aiming at an independent empire?* Is no regard to be had to the professions and protestations made by us, on so many different occasions, of attachment to Great Britain, of allegiance to His Majesty, and of submission to his government upon the terms on which the constitution points it out as a duty and on which alone a *British sovereign* has a right to demand it? . . . But the nature of this connection, and the principles on which it was originally formed and on which alone it can be maintained seem unhappily to have been misunderstood or disregarded by those who laid and conducted the late destructive plan of colony-administration.

Their conclusion was resigned: "Let neither our enemies nor our friends make improper inferences from the solicitude which we have discovered to remove the imputation of aiming to establish an independent empire.

Though an independent empire is not our *wish*, it may—let your oppressors attend—it may be the fate of our countrymen and ourselves." [15]

By then, in February of 1776, the lines of political division had long since hardened; troops were engaged in hostilities. Yet the accusations of malign purpose continued, culminating on the American side in the enumeration of conspiratorial efforts that forms the substance of the Declaration of Independence, and on the English side in a group of publications refuting those charges. The most interesting, if not the ablest, of these replies is by the ubiquitous Thomas Hutchinson, an exile in England since 1774, and, though consulted by the ministry and honored by Oxford University, still desperately eager to convince the world that his original suspicions had been correct. His *Strictures upon the Declaration of the Congress at Philadelphia* was his penultimate effort (his *History* would be the last) to prove that "if no taxes or duties had been laid upon the colonies, other pretenses would have been found for exception to the authority of Parliament." For the colonies, he explained, had been "easy and quiet" before the famous controversies started; "but there were men in each of the principal colonies who had independence in view before any of those taxes were laid or proposed . . . Their design of independence began soon after the reduction of Canada." Failing to attain their goals by arguments from the natural rights of mankind, they

found "some grievances, real or imaginary, were therefore necessary." These they produced simply by seeing to it "that every fresh incident which could be made to serve the purpose . . . should be improved accordingly." Professions of loyalty and concessions were "only intended to amuse the authority in England." No indulgence short of independence could ever have satisfied them, "for this was the object from the beginning." The chiefs of the rebellion in each colony found grounds "to irritate and enflame the minds of the people and dispose them to revolt"; and so it was that "many thousands of people who were before good and loyal subjects have been deluded and by degrees induced to rebel." The design, Hutchinson concluded, after answering one by one every charge in the Declaration, "has too well succeeded." [16]

The accusations of conspiratorial designs did not cease with the pamphlet series touched off by the Declaration, nor even with the American successes in battle. They merely shifted their forms, and began a process of adaptation that has allowed them to survive into our own time. Just as radical pamphleteers in England, patriot historians in America, and such Whig leaders as the younger Pitt continued after the war to blame the Revolution on the deliberate malevolence of the administrations of the 1760's and 1770's, so loyalists like Galloway and Thomas Jones continued to "expose" the Americans' conspiracy; continued to argue

---

[15] Merrill Jensen, ed., *American Colonial Documents to 1776 (English Historical Documents*, IX, London, 1955), p. 851; *Journals of the Continental Congress, 1774–1789* (W. C. Ford, *et al.,* eds., Washington, D.C., 1904–1937), IV, 146n, 139, 141, 142, 144, 146. Cf. references in Burnett, *Letters*, I, 348, and *American Historical Review*, I (1895–96), 684 ff.

[16] John H. Hazelton, *The Declaration of Independence, Its History* (New York, 1906), pp. 232 ff.; [Thomas Hutchinson], *Strictures* . . . (Malcolm Freiberg, ed., Boston, 1958 [*Old South Leaflets*, no. 227]), pp. 5–7, 9. See also the English government's quasi-official 132-page *Answer to the Declaration of the American Congress* (London, 1776), written, on commission of the Treasury, by John Lind.

that no error had been committed by the government of George III in not conceding more to America since the colonists had been secretly determined from the start to cast off their dependence upon England; continued too to link the rebels with opposition factions in England; and began, in the nadir of military defeat, darkly to suggest that the strangely defeated commander in chief, Sir William Howe, was himself not above suspicion of secret collaboration with the faction that had carried out so successfully the long-planned design of independence.[17]

These wartime and postwar accusations were both an end and a beginning —an end of the main phase of the ideological Revolution and the beginning of its transmutation into historiography. Charges of conspiratorial design settled easily into a structure of historical interpretation, on the one hand by Hutchinson, in the manuscript third volume of his *History of . . . Massachusetts-Bay* (published 1828); by Peter Oliver, in his frenzied *Origin & Progress of the American Rebellion* (1781, published 1961); by Thomas Jones, in his *History of New York during the Revolutionary War* (1780–1790, published 1879); by Jonathan Boucher, in the book-length Introduction of his *View of the Causes and Consequences of the American Revolution* (1797);— and on the other hand by Mercy Otis Warren, in her three-volume *History of the . . . American Revolution* (1805); by David Ramsay, in his *History of the American Revolution* (1789);

17 On the supposed link-up among colonial conspirators, opposition factions in England, and the suspicious conduct of General Howe on the field of battle, see especially Joseph Galloway's *Historical and Political Reflections on the Rise and Progress of the American Rebellion* . . . (London, 1780), and his *A Reply to . . . Sir William Howe* . . . (London, 1780).

and by patriot historians of individual states: Belknap, Burk, Trumbull, Ramsay. These are the histories of participants, or near-participants: heroic histories, highly personified and highly moral, in which the conspiratorial arguments propounded during the Revolution are the essential stuff of explanation. These views, caricatured and mythologized in such immortal potboilers as Weems' *Washington,* survived almost unaltered through the next generation—survived, indeed, through the next two generations—to enter in a new guise into the assumptions of twentieth-century scholarship. The "progressive" historians of the early twentieth century and their successors of the post-World War I era adopted unknowingly the Tory interpretation in writing off the Revolutionary leaders' professed fears of "slavery" and of conspiratorial designs as what by then had come to be known as propaganda. They implied when they did not state explicitly that these extravagant, seemingly paranoiac fears were deliberately devised for the purpose of controlling the minds of a presumably passive populace in order to accomplish predetermined ends— Independence and in many cases personal advancement—that were not openly professed. No Tory or administration apologist during the Revolution itself ever assumed more casually than did such distinguished modern scholars as Philip Davidson and John C. Miller that the fears expressed by the Revolutionary leadership were factitious instruments deliberately devised to manipulate an otherwise inert public opinion. Conversely, nowhere in the patriot literature of the Revolution proper is there a more elaborate effort to prove that there was in actuality a ministerial conspiracy—a plot of King's friends aimed at victimizing the colonists—than that made by Oliver Dickerson in his *Navigation Acts and the American Revolution* (1951).[18]

But the eighteenth century was an age of ideology; the beliefs and fears expressed on one side of the Revolutionary controversy were as sincere as those expressed on the other. The result, anticipated by Burke as early as 1769, was an "escalation" of distrust toward a disastrous deadlock: "The Americans," Burke said, "have made a discovery, or think they have made one, that we mean to oppress them: we have made a discovery, or think we have made one, that they intend to rise in rebellion against us . . . we know not how to advance; they know not how to retreat . . . Some party must give way." [19]

STANLEY ELKINS AND ERIC McKITRICK

THE FOUNDING FATHERS: YOUNG MEN OF THE REVOLUTION

I

Charles A. Beard, who in 1913 published *An Economic Interpretation of*

Reprinted from Stanley Elkins and Eric Mc-Kitrick, "The Founding Fathers: Young Men of the Revolution," POLITICAL SCIENCE QUARTERLY, LXXVI (1961), 183–85, 192–200, 212–16, by permission of the publisher.

18 See especially Philip Davidson, *Propaganda and the American Revolution, 1763–1783* (Chapel Hill, 1941); John C. Miller, *Sam Adams, Pioneer in Propaganda* (Boston, 1936), and his *Origins of the American Revolution* (Boston, 1943). For an excellent account of the process by which the ideological arguments of participants in the Revolution became built into the structure of historical explanation, see Sydney G. Fisher, "The Legendary and Myth-making Process in Histories of the American Revolution," *Proceedings of the American Philosophical Society*, 51 (1912), 53–75.
19 *Sir Henry Cavendish's Debates of the House of Commons* . . . (John Wright, ed., London, 1841–1843), I, 398–399.

the Constitution of the United States, did more than any single figure to make of the Constitution something other than a topic for ceremonial praise. By calling it a product of economic forces, Beard established an alternative position and enabled the entire subject to become one for serious historical debate. He thus created the first real dialectic on the Constitution and Founding Fathers, and for that reason Beard's work must still be taken as the point of departure for any historical treatment of that subject.

For Beard, the reality behind the movement for a constitution in the 1780's was economic interest. The animating surge came from holders of depreciated Continental securities who were demanding that their bonds be paid at par, and from conservative elements throughout the Confederation who wanted a national bulwark against agrarian-debtor radicalism. Beard thus identified the Federalists as those who wanted protection for property, especially personal property. The Anti-Federalists, on the other hand, were the great mass of agrarian debtors agitating for schemes of confiscation and paper money inflation in the state legislatures. Their hard-earned taxes would go to support any new bonds that a stronger United States government might issue; conversely, further fiscal experimentation on their part would be checked by national power. The Anti-Federalists, those who opposed a new constitution, were therefore the radicals; the Federalists, who favored it, were the conservatives.

Beard's argument was immediately challenged and kept on being challenged, which helped it to retain the fresh attractiveness of an avant-garde position for many years. But the man's influence grew, and his work played a vital part in historical thinking until well after the Second World War. Historical thinking, however, has its own historical setting. Why should such a statement as Beard's not have been made until the twentieth century, more than 125 years after the event?

In the nineteenth century the American Constitution had operated as the central myth of an entire political culture. While that culture was still in the tentative stages of its growth, still subject to all manner of unforeseen menaces, and with very little that was nationally sacred, there reigned everywhere the tacit understanding that here was the one unifying abstraction, the one symbol that might command all loyalties and survive all strife. The Constitution thus served multiple functions for a society that lacked tradition, folk-memory, a sovereign, and a body of legend. The need to keep the symbol inviolate seems to have been felt more instinctively during its earlier history than later on. Public controversy of the bitterest kind might occur over the charter's true meaning; enemies might accuse each other of misconstruing the document; but one did not challenge the myth itself. Americans even fought a civil war with both sides claiming to be the true upholders of the Constitution. Thus it was natural that when the historians of the nineteenth century—Bancroft, Hildreth, Frothingham, Fiske, McMaster—came to describe the origins of the Constitution, they should reach for the non-controversial idiom and imagery of a Golden Age. The Supreme Law had been fashioned and given to the people by a race of classic heroes.[1]

America's veneration for its Constitution became steadily more intense in the years that followed the Civil War. Now it was the symbol not only of the Union, for which that generation had made such heavy sacrifices, but also of the unfettered capitalism which was turning the United States into one of the richest and most powerful nations in the world. The new material order—wasteful, disorderly, already acquainted with labor disturbances, yet immensely productive—was watched over by the benevolent and solicitous eye of the Constitution. . . .

. . .

II

In 1940 certain new and interesting corollaries were added to the mode of approach which, due so largely to Beard's example, had come to influence historical thinking on the formation of the Constitution. In that year Merrill Jensen published *The Articles of Confederation: An Interpretation of the Social-Constitutional History of the American Revolution, 1774–1781.* Jensen's own approach was consistent with most of the general principles which had been laid down by Beard. But whereas Beard's primary interest had been with the Federalists—the men who led and supported the campaign for a new constitution—Jensen turned his attention to the Anti-Federalists, those who had opposed the constitutional movement. What, he asked, was the nature of the political system which the Constitution displaced, and what were the aims and intentions of the men who had created that system?

---

[1] Richard B. Morris has pointed out that in Henry Dawson there was at least one exception to this universal veneration for the Constitution. Dawson in 1871 published an article wherein he deplored the ancestor-worship which already wreathed the Fathers and their work. See Morris, "The Confederation and the American Historian," *William and Mary Quarterly,* XIII, 3rd ser. (April 1956), pp. 139–56; Dawson, "The Motley Letter," *Historical Magazine,* IX, 2nd ser. (March 1871), pp. 157 *et seq.*

In the face of most prior opinion to the contrary, Jensen found in the Confederation just the sort of loose arrangement most favorable to democratic self-rule on the local and state level, inasmuch as the primary authority was located in the state legislatures. It was for achieving exactly this object, he thought, that the Confederation's strongest supporters—such leaders as Samuel Adams, Patrick Henry, Thomas Burke, and Richard Henry Lee—had pushed the Colonies into the Revolution in the first place. Conversely, those who opposed the Confederation were the men who had at first been reluctant to support the Revolution. They had feared the consequences of a break with England because that would remove the one central power strong enough to restrain the forces of local democracy. These men did, to be sure, join the Patriot forces after the break had become inevitable. Yet almost at once they began working for a continental government which might supply the stabilizing and conservative force previously maintained by the Crown. Their eventual triumph would come, of course, at Philadelphia in 1787.

In a second book, *The New Nation* (1950), Jensen considered the accomplishments of the Confederation, together with the social and economic conditions of the period from 1781 to 1789. He concluded that the "critical period" was really not so critical after all. American ships were not excluded from many foreign ports; tariff wars between states were the exception rather than the rule; the Confederation government had solved the problem of western lands and was well on the way to settling the outstanding boundary disputes. By 1786 the economic depression which had struck the country in 1784 was coming to an end. Even the problem of national credit was not so serious as the Federalists wanted people to believe, since a number of the states had assumed responsibility for portions of the Continental debt held by their own citizens. Had the states been brought to accept a national impost—a tariff duty on incoming foreign good levied solely and exclusively by Congress, the revenue of which would be reserved for the support of the government—the Confederation would have been fully capable of surviving and functioning as a true federal establishment.

The collapse of the Confederation, Jensen argued, was not the logical outcome of weakness or inefficiency. It was the result of a determined effort by a small but tightly-organized group of nationalists to impose a centralized government upon the entire country despite the contrary desires of great majorities everywhere:

Most of these men were by temperament or economic interest believers in executive and judicial rather than legislative control of state and central governments, in the rigorous collection of taxes, and, as creditors, in strict payment of public and private debts. . . . They deplored the fact that there was no check upon the actions of majorities in state legislatures; that there was no central government to which minorities could appeal from the decisions of such majorities, as they had done before the Revolution.

These were the men who conspired to overthrow the Confederation and who masterminded the triumph of the Constitution.

There were points at which Jensen had not seen eye to eye with Beard. He was more impressed, for instance, by the Fathers' general outlook and ideology than by their property holdings; unlike Beard, moreover, he denied that the Confederation era was a time of serious economic difficulty.

Yet he had actually strengthened the Beardian logic at more than one point, and the differences were minor in the light of the convictions which united the two in spirit and intention. The work of Merrill Jensen, like that of Beard and Parrington and J. Allen Smith before him, still balanced on the assumption that the energy behind the American Constitution was conspiratorial energy, and that the Constitution came into being by means of a coup d'état—through the plotting of a well-disciplined Toryish few against the interests of an unvigilant democratic majority.

Indeed, Merrill Jensen's *The New Nation*—published two years after the death of Charles Beard—was the last major piece of Constitution scholarship to be done in the Progressive tradition, and represented the end of an era. By that time, 1950, Beard's own notions had begun to arouse not the admiration, but the suspicion, of a new generation of postwar intellectuals.

III

A few modest little articles, case studies of ratifying conventions held in individual states in 1788, had begun appearing here and there in the regional quarterlies. In 1947 there was one by Philip Crowl on Maryland, another on North Carolina by William Pool in 1950, still another on Virginia by Robert Thomas in 1953. Such fragments, of course, could not be expected to cause much immediate stir. But these studies carried implications, similar in each case, that would prove in the long run profoundly damaging to the whole structure of Beardian scholarship and Beardian reasoning.

A major item in that reasoning had been Beard's assumption that the principle which differentiated Federalists from Anti-Federalists was the principle of class and property interests—that the Federalists as a group were upholding one kind of class interest and defending one form of property while the Anti-Federalists, presumably, represented something else, something basically opposed. For some reason, Beard had never taken the trouble to check the Anti-Federalist side of his equation. Thomas, in his study of the delegates to the Virginia ratifying convention (where the fight had been unusually bitter), discovered that the members of both sides held property of essentially the same kind, in approximately the same amounts, and represented the same social class—the planting gentry. The other studies showed a similar pattern. In short, the conflict over ratification was apparently fought out not between classes, but between cliques of the same ruling class within these states, and whatever the conflict's "real" basis, it was not a struggle over property rights as such. Beard's "class" and "property" formula was simply indeterminate; the story had to be found elsewhere.

By 1956, Beard's *Economic Interpretation* had been set up for the *coup de grâce*. The executioner was Robert E. Brown, a professor at Michigan State who had been at work for some time implacably compiling a catalogue of the Master's offenses. In his *Charles Beard and the Constitution,* published that year, Brown tracked Beard through every page of the latter's masterpiece and laid the ax to virtually every statement of importance that Beard had made in it. There was absolutely no correlation between the Philadelphia delegates' property holdings and the way they behaved on the question of a constitution. It was not true that large numbers of adult males were disfranchised; the suffrage was remarkably liberal everywhere. Farmers as a class were by no means chronically debtors; many were creditors and many others were both. The supporters of Shays' Rebellion (the debtors' uprising in western Massachusetts which occurred during the fall and winter of 1786–1787) were certainly not united against the Constitution; if they had been, it could never have been ratified, since the Shaysites had a clear majority at the time of the Massachusetts convention. Nor did the Philadelphia delegates know that the Continental debt would be funded at par. If they had, the banker Robert Morris, for one, would never have speculated in western lands with the thought of paying for them in depreciated Continental paper.

Not only was Beard's evidence inconclusive at all points, Brown insisted, but there were even occasions when the Master had not been above doctoring it. He edited Madison's Federalist No. 10 to eliminate all but its economic emphasis; he quoted only those passages of the Philadelphia debates that made the Fathers look least democratic; he arranged his treatment of the ratification process in an order that violated chronology, centered unjustified attention on states where hard struggles did occur, overlooked the ease with which ratification was achieved in other states, and thus created a wildly exaggerated picture of the opposition at large.

Brown's book was respectfully received; there was little inclination to dispute his arguments; no champions arose to do serious battle for the departed Beard. Some of the reviewers were a little dismayed at Brown's tone; they thought it need not have been quite so ferocious. And the book did seem to bear out the principle that any work of destruction in the realm of discourse, however necessary, must be executed within restrictions that make for a certain stultification. Richard

Hofstadter remarked in this connection that Brown was "locked in such intimate embrace with his adversary that his categories are entirely dictated by Beard's assertions." Even Brown, in his way, had toyed with the "reality" theme. He had exonerated the Fathers of conspiratorial intentions but convicted Charles Beard in their place: Beard had cooked the evidence, had conspired to hide the truth.

The first effort in recent years to view the Constitution all over again in a major way, shaking off the Beardian categories and starting as it were from scratch, has been undertaken by Forrest McDonald. *We The People,* published in 1958, was the first of a planned trilogy whose design was to survey anew the entire story of how the Constitution was brought into existence. Although McDonald, like Brown, felt it necessary to show the inadequacy of Beard's conclusions, his strategy was quite different from Brown's; it was undertaken less to discredit Beard than to clear the way for his own projected treatment of the great subject. In the *Economic Interpretation,* Beard had made a number of proposals for research which he himself had not performed—and never did perform—but which would, Beard felt, further corroborate his own "frankly fragmentary" work. McDonald began by undertaking the very research which Beard had suggested, and its results convinced him that Beard had simply asked all the wrong questions.

One of the things McDonald investigated in *We The People* was an assumption upon which Beard had put a great deal of stress, the notion of a fundamental antagonism between "personalty" and "realty" interests at the time of the Philadelphia Convention. ("Personalty" was wealth based on securities, money, commerce, or manufacturing; "realty" was landed property whose owners' outlook tended to be primarily agrarian.) He found that there was no such split in the Convention. The seven men who either walked out of the Convention or else refused to sign the completed document were among the heaviest security-holders there, and represented "an all-star team of personalty interests." In state after state, moreover, there was no appreciable difference between the property holdings of Federalists and Anti-Federalists. Finally, the three states that ratified the Constitution unanimously—Delaware, New Jersey, and Georgia—were overwhelmingly dominated by agrarian interests.

Unlike Brown, McDonald was quite unwilling to write off the possibility of an economic analysis (his book's subtitle was *The Economic Origins of the Constitution*); it was just that Beard's particular economic categories led nowhere. Beard's sweeping "personalty" and "realty" classifications were meaningless, and he had deceived himself profoundly in supposing that the Federalists' property interests "knew no state boundaries" but were "truly national in scope." On these two points of difference McDonald set up an entirely new and original research scheme, and in so doing effected a really impressive conceptual maneuver. He was quite ready, in the first place, to find "economic forces" behind the movement for a constitution, but these must be sought not in "classes" or in broad categories of property but rather in the specific business interests of specific groups in specific places. The other organizing category would be the individual states themselves. The political framework within which any group had to operate was still that imposed by the state; the states were, after all, still sovereign units, and the precise rela-

tionship between economic forces and political action depended almost entirely on the special conditions within those states, conditions which varied from one to the other.

By abandoning Beard's "national" framework and recasting the entire problem on a state-by-state basis, McDonald made it possible to see with a sudden clarity things which ought to have been obvious all along. The states where ratification was achieved most readily were those that were convinced, for one reason or another, that they could not survive and prosper as independent entities; those holding out the longest were the ones most convinced that they could go it alone. The reasons for supporting ratification might vary considerably from state to state. For Georgia, an impending Indian war and the need for military protection could transcend any possible economic issue; New York, at one time imagining for itself an independent political and economic future, would finally ratify for fear of being isolated from a system which already included ten states and which might soon be joined by a seceded New York City.

The single problem of the Continental debt took different forms in different states. New Jersey, Massachusetts, and New York had each assumed portions of the debt held by their own citizens, but New Jersey and Massachusetts found their obligations intolerably burdensome while New York did not. Massachusetts had put an excessively heavy load on its direct property and poll-tax system; thus any possibility of the debt's being funded by a new Federal government should have found both the Boston security-holder and the Shaysite debtor more than willing to support such a government—and this, it appears, is about what happened. In New York and New Jersey an additional key to the debt issue was the question of a national tariff. New York had a state tariff, which was part of a financial system worked out to service the debt, and for that reason the state had been reluctant to accept a national impost in 1786. New Jersey, on the other hand, with no ocean trade of any account and having to receive most of its imports through New York, had no such revenue, was hard pressed to maintain interest payments on its debt, and thus had everything to gain from both a national impost and a national funding system. New Jersey was one of the first to ratify, and did so unanimously.

Recognizing the importance of specific location made it also easier and more natural to appreciate the way in which particular interests in particular places might be affected by the question of a stronger national government. Boston shipping interests, for example, seem to have been less concerned in the 1780's over class ideology or general economic philosophy than over those conditions of the times which were especially bad for business. The British would not let them into the West Indies, the French were excluding their fish, and their large vessels were no longer profitable. A strong national government could create a navy whose very existence would reduce high insurance rates; it could guarantee an orderly tariff system that would remove all pressure for higher and higher state tariffs; and it could counter British and French discrimination by means of an effective navigation act. Manufacturing interests would also tend to favor the Constitution, though not necessarily on principle; the vigor of their support would depend on the size of their establishments and the extent to which they competed with England. Support from Pennsylvania iron and Connecticut textiles would be particularly energetic.

So also with the wheat and tobacco farmers of the Connecticut Valley, though not for the same reason. They had to pay import taxes to New York for the goods they bought (their crops were sold there); they were heavily taxed, at the same time, to support a state-funded debt which they would be only too glad to see removed by a central government. Farmers in the Kentucky area, on the other hand, could be very suspicious of a Constitution under which northeastern shipping interests might influence the government to surrender free navigation on the Mississippi in return for a favorable trade treaty with Spain.

Forrest McDonald's work, according to him, has only just begun; years of it still lie ahead. But already a remarkable precision of detail has been brought to the subject, together with a degree of sophistication which makes the older economic approach—"tough-minded" as it once imagined itself—seem now a little wan and misty. The special internal conditions of the several states now seem fully valid as clues to the ratification policies of those states, each in its separate turn. And there is a credibility about the immediate needs and aspirations of particular groups, and the way they varied from place to place, that Beard's "interests" never quite possessed—or if they did, they had long since lost their hold on the modern mind.

And yet there are overtones in McDonald's work—for all its precise excellence, perhaps partly because of it—that have already succeeded in creating a new kind of "reality" spell. McDonald is very open-minded about all the manifold and complex and contradictory forces that converged upon the movement for a constitution. But somehow the ones he takes most seriously—the "real" forces behind the movement—

were specific, particular, circumscribed, hard, and immediate. They were to be looked for mostly on the local level, because that is where one really finds things. A state—the largest permissible "reality" unit—was an agglomeration of specific, particular, immediate localities. There were interests to be served, political or economic, and they were *hard*. They were pursued rationally and without sentimentality; men came down where they did because their hard, immediate, specific interests brought them there. But are we prepared to say that the final result was just the sum—or extension—of these interests?

No doubt large enough numbers of people were convinced of the economic advantages they would gain under a new federal government that we may, thanks to Professor McDonald, account for a considerable measure of the support which the Constitution received. In places where there was a balance to tip, we have a much better idea of just how it happened. Still, Merrill Jensen pointed out some time ago that the economic situation was already somewhat on the mend by 1786. There were, moreover, certain powerful states such as Virginia and New York that might very well have thrived either as independent units or in coalitions with their immediate neighbors. And conditions in general could not have been so desperate that a national government was absolutely required for solving economic problems, let alone for staving off economic collapse. The steps actually taken were not the only ones possible; there were certainly alternatives, and it is hard to believe that they would all have led to disaster.

The new approach is extremely enlightening and useful. But has it yet taken on life? When will it fully engage the question of initiative and energy? How do we account for the dedication,

the force and éclat, of Federalist leadership? When all is said and done, we do not exactly refer to the "interests" of a James Madison. We wonder, instead, about the terms in which he conceives of personal fulfillment, which is not at all the same. What animates him? The nationalist movement *did* have a mystique that somehow transfigured a substantial number of its leaders. What was it like, what were its origins?

. . .

We have already seen that nineteenth century habits of thought created a ponderous array of stereotypes around the historic Philadelphia conclave of 1787. Twentieth century thought and scholarship, on the other hand, had the task of breaking free from them, and to have done so is a noteworthy achievement. And yet one must return to the point that stereotypes themselves require some form of explanation. The legend of a transcendent effort of statesmanship, issuing forth in a miraculously perfect instrument of government, emerges again and again despite all efforts either to conjure it out of existence or to give it some sort of rational linkage with mortal affairs. Why should the legend be so extraordinarily durable, and was there anything so special about the circumstances that set it on its way so unerringly and so soon?

The circumstances *were,* in fact, special; given a set of delegates of well over average ability, the Philadelphia meeting provides a really classic study in the sociology of intellect. Divine accident, though in some measure present in men's doings always, is not required as a part of this particular equation. The key conditions were all present in a pattern that virtually guaranteed for the meeting an optimum of effectiveness. A sufficient number of states were represented so that the delegates could, without   strain,   realistically   picture themselves as thinking, acting, and making decisions in the name of the entire nation. They themselves, moreover, represented interests throughout the country that were diverse enough, and they had enough personal prestige at home, that they could act in the assurance of having their decisions treated at least with respectful attention. There had also been at work a remarkably effective process of self-selection, as to both men and states. Rhode Island ignored the convention, and as a result its position was not even considered there. There were leading state particularists such as Patrick Henry and Richard Henry Lee who were elected as delegates but refused to serve. The Anti-Federalist position, indeed, was hardly represented at all, and the few men who did represent it had surprisingly little to say. Yates and Lansing simply left before the convention was over. Thus a group already predisposed in a national direction could proceed unhampered by the friction of basic opposition in its midst.

This made it possible for the delegates to "try on" various alternatives without having to remain accountable for everything they said. At the same time, being relieved from all outside pressures meant that the only way a man could expect to make a real difference in the convention's deliberations was to reach, through main persuasion, other men of considerable ability and experience. Participants and audience were therefore one, and this in itself imposed standards of debate which were quite exacting. In such a setting the best minds in the convention were accorded an authority which they would not have had in political debates aimed at an indiscriminate public.

Thus the elements of secrecy, the general inclination for a national government, and the process whereby the delegates came to terms with their colleagues—appreciating their requirements and adjusting to their interests—all combined to produce a growing esprit de corps. As initial agreements were worked out, it became exceedingly difficult for the Philadelphia delegates not to grow more and more committed to the product of their joint efforts. Indeed, this was in all likelihood the key mechanism, more important than any other in explaining not only the peculiar genius of the main compromises but also the general fitness of the document as a whole. That is, a group of two or more intelligent men who are subject to no cross-pressures and whose principal commitment is to the success of an idea, are perfectly capable—as in our scientific communities of today—of performing what appear to be prodigies of intellect. Moving, as it were, in the same direction with a specific purpose, they can function at maximum efficiency. It was this that the historians of the nineteenth century did in their way see, and celebrated with sweeping rhetorical flourishes, when they took for granted that if an occasion of this sort could not call forth the highest level of statesmanship available, then it was impossible to imagine another that could.

Once the Philadelphia Convention had been allowed to meet and the delegates had managed, after more than three months of work, to hammer out a document that the great majority of them could sign, the political position of the Federalists changed dramatically. Despite the major battles still impending, for practical purposes they now had the initiative. The principal weapon of the Anti-Federalists—inertia —had greatly declined in effectiveness, for with the new program in motion it was no longer enough simply to argue that a new federal government was unnecessary. They would have to take positive steps in blocking it; they would have to arouse the people and convince them that the Constitution represented a positive danger.

Moreover, the Federalists had set the terms of ratification in such a way as to give the maximum advantage to energy and purpose; the key choices, this time, had been so arranged that they would fall right. Only nine states had to ratify before the Constitution would go into effect. Not only would this rule out the possibility of one or two states holding up the entire effort, but it meant that the Confederation would be automatically destroyed as an alternative before the difficult battles in New York and Virginia had to be faced. (By then, Patrick Henry in Virginia would have nothing but a vague alliance with North Carolina to offer as a counter-choice.) Besides, there was good reason to believe that at least four or five states, and possibly as many as seven, could be counted as safe, which meant that serious fighting in the first phase would be limited to two or three states. And finally, conditions were so set that the "snowball" principle would at each successive point favor the Federalists.

As for the actual process of acceptance, ratification would be done through state conventions elected for the purpose. Not only would this circumvent the vested interests of the legislatures and the ruling coteries that frequented the state capitals, but it gave the Federalists two separate chances to make their case—once to the people and once to the conventions. If the elected delegates were not initially disposed to do the desired thing, there was still a chance, after the convention met, of persuading them. Due partly to the hampering factor of transportation and distance, delegates had to have considerable leeway of choice and what amounted to quasi-plenipotentiary pow-

ers. Thus there could be no such thing as a fully "instructed" delegation, and members might meanwhile remain susceptible to argument and conversion. The convention device, moreover, enabled the Federalists to run as delegates men who would not normally take part in state politics.

The revolutionary verve and ardor of the Federalists, their resources of will and energy, their willingness to scheme tirelessly, campaign everywhere, and sweat and agonize over every vote meant in effect that despite all the hair-breadth squeezes and rigors of the struggle, the Anti-Federalists would lose every crucial test. There was, to be sure, an Anti-Federalist effort. But with no program, no really viable commitments, and little purposeful organization, the Anti-Federalists somehow always managed to move too late and with too little. They would sit and watch their great stronghold, New York, being snatched away from them despite a two-to-one Anti-Federalist majority in a convention presided over by their own chief, George Clinton. To them, the New York Federalists must have seemed possessed of the devil. The Federalists' convention men included Alexander Hamilton, James Duane, John Jay, and Robert Livingston—who knew, as did everyone else, that the new government was doomed unless Virginia and New York joined it. They insisted on debating the Constitution section by section instead of as a whole, which meant that they could out-argue the Anti-Federalists on every substantive issue and meanwhile delay the vote until New Hampshire and Virginia had had a chance to ratify. (Madison and Hamilton had a horse relay system in readiness to rush the Virginia news northward as quickly as possible.) By the time the New York convention was ready to act, ten others had ratified, and at the final moment

Hamilton and his allies spread the chilling rumor that New York City was about to secede from the state. The Anti-Federalists, who had had enough, directed a chosen number of their delegates to cross over, and solemnly capitulated.

In the end, of course, everyone "crossed over." The speed with which this occurred once the continental revolutionists had made their point, and the ease with which the Constitution so soon became an object of universal veneration, still stands as one of the minor marvels of American history. But the document did contain certain implications, of a quasi-philosophical nature, that make the reasons for this ready consensus not so very difficult to find. It established a national government whose basic outlines were sufficiently congenial to the underlying commitments of the whole culture—republicanism and capitalism—that the likelihood of its being the subject of a true ideological clash was never very real. That the Constitution should mount guard over the rights of property—"realty," "personalty," or any other kind—was questioned by nobody. There had certainly been a struggle, a long and exhausting one, but we should not be deceived as to its nature. It was not fought on economic grounds; it was not a matter of ideology; it was not, in the fullest and most fundamental sense, even a struggle between nationalism and localism. The key struggle was between inertia and energy; with inertia overcome, everything changed.

There were, of course, lingering objections and misgivings; many of the problems involved had been genuinely puzzling and difficult; and there remained doubters who had to be converted. But then the perfect bridge whereby all could become Federalists within a year was the addition of a Bill of Rights. After the French Revolution, anti-constitutionalism in France would be a burning issue for generations; in America, an anti-constitutional party was undreamed of after 1789. With the Bill of Rights, the remaining opponents of the new system could say that, ever watchful of tyranny, they had now got what they wanted. Moreover, the Young Men of the Revolution might at last imagine, after a dozen years of anxiety, that *their* Revolution had been a success.

WILLIAM N. CHAMBERS

Political parties emerge out of certain sets of conditions, confront certain problems or loads in the political system, and perform interrelated functions which may include functions contributing to political integration. What the conditions are determines in part the shapes party structures will take, the functions they will perform, and how they will perform them. Yet the way in which political elites and party leaders handle political loads also determines the result in part and the impact parties may have on political development in general. In short there is a reciprocal relationship between political development and loads on the one hand and the effects of party action on the other. This relationship carries profound consequences for the political system, particularly in the era of national formation or nation-building.

Once political parties emerge, they may take on stable structures and establish stable patterns of interaction which constitute party systems. It is probably

Reprinted from William Nisbet Chambers, "Parties and Nation-Building in America," in Joseph LaPalombara and Myron Wiener, eds., POLITICAL PARTIES AND POLITICAL DEVELOPMENT *(Princeton: Princeton University Press, 1967), pp. 79–90, by permission of the publisher.*

more useful for analysis to think in terms of developing party systems rather than simply of parties. For the United States it is certainly true that the relationship between parties and national integration can be understood only in terms of the party system and the net balance of integrative and malintegrative consequences of that system as a whole. Approached in this way, early American experience provides a useful laboratory. The United States constituted the first modern "new nation" in the sense that the American people were the first to throw off colonial rule, establish an independent polity, and achieve a fresh national identity. It was also the United States that brought into being the first modern political parties and party system with the emergence of the Federalist and Republican formations within two decades of the assertion of independence. In short, American development presents a case study of nation-building and party-building of great potential use in general and comparative political analysis. The address to these phenomena here will be to discuss the context and conditions out of which early American parties arose, the shape parties took and the functions they performed, the character of the party system, and the net impact that system had on national integration. The effect of parties on integration was a kind of end-product of the totality of functions the parties performed and of their relationships with one another.

The discussion will focus on the Federalists and Republicans in the 1790's, the crucial party-building decade. Neither of these formations survived beyond the period around 1820, and the first American party system was followed by a second system in the Jacksonian era in the 1830's. Yet the parties of the 1790's marked the way for later Democrats, Whigs, and second Repub-

licans and for the party systems they evolved. These parties and systems showed important similarities to their predecessors as well as some differences.

I. BASIC CONDITIONS IN PARTY DEVELOPMENT

Political parties in America did not spring from growing resistance to colonial rule from 1763 to 1776 in a manner that is familiar in many new nations in Asia and Africa today. In the revolutionary struggle sharp divisions did develop between Patriots and Loyalists. The Patriots established committees of correspondence in the thirteen colonies or states, formed the Continental Congress as a coordinating agency for the revolutionary effort and as a quasi-government thereafter, and undertook other means of agitation, cooperation, and action. Yet the Patriots did not become a party in the full sense and did not persist as a distinct political formation past the period of the struggle for independence. Cleavage between so-called Federalists and anti-Federalists appeared in the controversy over the ratification of the new Constitution in 1788–1789. Yet once again these alignments did not take on party form, and the actual contest over ratification was waged among a pluralistic congeries of leaders and groups that varied significantly from place to place in the thirteen state arenas involved. In the internal politics of the several states, moreover, the contest for power was waged by a variety of factional formations rather than by parties. Only relatively advanced Pennsylvania developed something like a party system.

Thus the first American parties, or national parties, emerged out of new conflicts only in the 1790's. In terms of economic groups, what distinguished Federalists from Republicans were cleavages between mercantile, investing, and manufacturing interests and certain segments of agriculture on the one side and most planting and agrarian interests on the other. Differences also arose out of disagreements over the degree to which power should be consolidated in the new national government; over proposed policies to promote economic growth and capitalist development through government action; and over the extent to which foreign policy should be oriented toward traditionalist-monarchist England or revolutionary-republican France. Lastly, conflict grew out of contentions between leading personalities such as the Federalists Alexander Hamilton and John Adams on the one hand and the Republicans James Madison and Thomas Jefferson on the other, contentions that were sometimes as petty as they were colorful; and out of cleavages among a variety of other group, sectional, religous, local, and personal interests and persuasions. The whole story does not require retelling in its historical detail. The Federalists and Republicans also developed out of a set of basic conditions, which are more to the point here.

As a general theory or hypothesis, the most basic conditions associated with the development of political parties in the modern sense may be summarized under four major headings:

1) The emergence or prospect of a significant national or common political arena, within which influence or power may be sought with reference to the decision-making centers and the offices of a common political system.

2) The development of differentiation or complexity within the political system in terms of divergences in group structures and conflicts of interest and opinion and in terms of governmental structures and functions.

3) The emergence of social structures and of ideologies or utopias which permit or encourage some form of popular or mass politics and a substantial electorate.

4) A sense of felt need to develop political structures to establish relationships between leaders and popular followings if leaders are to win and hold power and governmental functions are to be performed.

This statement of conditions can readily be related to the American instance by mediating the general theory through statements of particular sets of conditions which, taken together, constitute an immediate-conditional or relative-historical explanation for the emergence of the first American parties. The recital of American conditions will be summarized as a set of middle-range generalizations about American political development.

1) *A national political arena was opened with the ratification of the new Constitution and the establishment of the national government in 1789.*

Even in the colonial years a considerable degree of intercolonial communication and what might be called continental consciousness, or proto-national identity, had begun to emerge on the American scene. This development at once helped to sustain and received new impetus from the Revolutionary War effort and the Continental Congress of 1775–1789. The limited powers of this Congress, however, together with the fact that it could not exercise direct power over citizens but was only a quasi-government which depended on the states, and the fact that the Congress consisted of delegates appointed by state legislatures rather than of representatives chosen by the voters, kept it from providing a truly national political arena. The new general government with its single indirectly elected executive and its representative two-house Congress did become the center of a rapidly developing national arena. It was in and around this government that groups, leaders, and parties struggled and the great issues of the day were fought out.

2) The indigenous pluralism within the American nation produced a high degree of differentiation among groups, social strata, and states or sections and a complex interplay of interests, loyalties, sentiments, and opinions; and most of these forces quickly found expression in politics and turned increasingly to the national scene.

The cross-currents which the pluralism of early American life threw up were complex indeed. There were small-freehold farmers and great planters owning thousands of slaves; merchants, shippers and shipbuilders, importers and exporters, investors, and struggling manufacturers; artisans or "mechanics"; varied ethnic stocks and different religious faiths; would-be "aristocrats" and nascent "democrats," and sanguine "Gallomen" and sober "Anglomen"; states competing with one another; and a host of subgroupings, such as near-subsistence farmers or farmers who looked to the market. There extended across the new nation a congeries of interests that had to be given expression and accommodated if the system was to sustain itself and perform its functions; and parties developed in considerable part as a response to such felt needs. Certain interstate comparisons are also revealing in connection with this condition for party formation. Indices are difficult to assign, but Pennsylvania exhibited a particularly high degree of differentiation in the interplay of interests, which helps to explain the fact that Pennsylvania alone developed a state party system in the 1780's and also moved rapidly toward shaping local units of

the national parties in the 1790's. A significant degree of complexity might also be attributed to New York, for example, where the pace of national party development was second only to that of Pennsylvania; but in New York old patterns of domination by great families and clique politics, characteristics which were much less in evidence in Pennsylvania, impeded party development. It may be suggested as a hypothesis that the higher the degree of differentiation of group and other relationships is in a political system, the greater is the probability for the development of political parties, though this probability may be reduced by the presence of other impending conditions. Such differentiation certainly existed in American national politics by the 1790's, as various group interests took on nation-wide form and sought national expression.

Substantial differentiation also characterized the national government. It was not only formally separated into executive, legislative, and judicial branches with distinct prescribed powers but the two houses of Congress had different electoral foundations and constituencies and somewhat different functions. The Constitution also provided among the various organs of government an intricate set of checks or reciprocal relationships that in effect constituted a further differentiation of functions. Again, parties arose in part in response to the problems leaders faced in trying to operate this complex governmental machinery effectively.

3) Social structures and basic perspectives in the American experience provided a strong impetus for popular involvement in politics, demands for representation and mechanisms of consent, and the emergence of a substantial electorate.

In comparison with contemporary

European societies American society was remarkably open, atomistic, affluent, and fluid. It was not bound to feudal traditions, graded structures of estates or classes, or old corporate configurations. Most men owned a piece of farm land or other property as a foundation for individual independence; a vast continent and its wealth of resources offered unprecedented opportunities; distances between rich and poor were not so great as they were in Old World societies; social distinctions and deference patterns were not so sharp or rigid, and there was no genuine aristocracy or fixed hierarchy; and social mobility was a frequent fact as well as a hope. Distinctions there were, particularly between great planters and lesser farmers and Negro slaves in the South; and where social gradations were particularly sharp and persistent, patterns of deference held on longer than they did elsewhere. Yet distinctions were generally on the wane, partly as a result of economic opportunity and partly because of the democratization that had accompanied the Revolution and swept many states in the 1780's. This development was furthered by the impact of the social outlook, *ethos*, or mood that Hartz has aptly called the American "liberal tradition." This fundamental perspective, with John Locke as its ideologue, was to develop steadily in American conditions from a utopia to an increasingly common general ideology and foundation for emerging consensus; and in drafting the Declaration of Independence, which became the basic statement of the American creed, Jefferson drew on Lockian ideas as "the common sense of the subject." The liberal tradition placed heavy stress on such important if sometimes conflicting values as free individualism, opportunity, individual achievement, equali-

tarianism, and liberal democracy. It is not surprising that movement toward democratic participation, representation, and consent was rapid, and it is also not surprising that these forces brought the emergence of an extensive electorate in state after state. In terms of interstate comparisons all of these forces and particularly the stress on equalitarianism and a mass base for politics were especially pronounced in Pennsylvania, where party action developed most rapidly. On the other hand equalitarianism and the extension of suffrage took hold more slowly in the Southern states, where full-scale party structures and action came comparatively late, although even there the impact of remaining tax or property qualifications on suffrage has been exaggerated by older historians.

It may be suggested as a further general hypothesis that the greater the degree to which equalitarian political ideologies and extended suffrage obtain, the greater is the probability that political parties will develop in the absence of other, impeding factors. Recent research findings for the American case indicate that after the Revolution the great majority of white adult males in an era of widely held agricultural property could vote. Not all of them did, but the democratic impulse and keen party competition brought voting participation in the period 1799–1802 and after to the substantial proportion of 39 per cent or more of white adult males in important elections, a level that was not to be exceeded until new party rivalry appeared in the Jacksonian era. Moreover access to other avenues to the political arena was comparatively open. Freedom of political belief, expression, and action was also generally accepted, despite important uncertainties and exceptions in the early years.

4) Within the context of these conditions, a sense of felt need gradually arose for efficient means to represent and combine interests, amass power, conduct elections, and manage government.

Innumerable obstacles stood in the way of party development, and no one set out to construct parties with a blueprint in mind. Men thought in terms of devices to meet immediate needs, or bickered about immediate interests; many important political figures including George Washington spoke out against the idea of parties. The process of party-building was one of groping expedients as well as brilliant innovations, and it was some time before leaders came to think consciously in party-building terms. Yet in the space of a few years after the ratification of the Constitution in 1789 stable structures were evolved, and the Federalist and Republican formations emerged as parties.

This analysis is hardly unique in its basic terms. It is consistent with suggestions contained in the classical work of Ostrogorski, with the emphasis Weber puts on the relationship between popular or mass politics and "parties of politicians," and with many of the ideas offered by Duverger. Yet the summary here is based primarily on investigation of the American instance. Circumstances will certainly reveal variations from context to context in the significance of any one condition in the development of political parties even though the general pattern of relevant conditions may remain constant. Indeed it may be argued that generic conditions as they affect the development of parties can be firmly established only in terms of comparative historical processes carefully analyzed through a theoretically oriented historiography or time-oriented science of

political development. As V. O. Key puts it: ". . . a conception of the party system must take into account its dimension of time. It may be useful to think of the party system as an historical process rather than as patterned and static institutional behavior. . . . if the party process is viewed through time, additional aspects of the working of party [systems] may be identified." This, presumably, is the task of developmental political science or analytical history.

A possible factor in party development as it has operated in many new nations today should be noted. This is the effect of external influences on the peoples of developing areas who are seeking to achieve the modernization that most Western societies have already accomplished. The adaptation of foreign ideas or models as part of the European legacy, including general models for political parties, has played a significant part in political development in Asia and Africa today, although of course local conditions continue to have profound effects. Such mimetic elements were virtually absent in the early American experience. The terms "Whig" and "Tory" had been in use in England for a century or more, but they denoted broad persuasions and shifting alliances of factions or personal clique-"connexions," in the old spelling and the old style, rather than parties as such; suffrage remained extremely narrow; and these early English political formations did not develop continuing and pervasive structures to provide stable links between leaders at the parliamentary center and substantial popular followings in the nation as a whole. It was not until the rise of the Liberal and Conservative formations after the limited first Reform Act of 1832 that England may be said to have arrived at genuine political parties. Nor were modern party models available in the 1790's in other European countries. In short the Federalist and Republican formations in the United States had to find their own way toward party structure and party action.

II. POLITICAL DEVELOPMENT, PARTY STRUCTURES, AND PARTY FUNCTIONS

The argument that American parties in the 1790's were the first modern parties is more than a mere historiographical contention. It involves conceptions of what a political party is and does and of how American parties were related to the whole question of political development, and a conceptual distinction between party politics and faction politics. Political development may be understood as a movement toward a political system which is capable of handling the loads it confronts, characterized by significant differentiation of structures and specificity of functions, increasingly centralized and able to maintain itself. It may not be as easy to measure political development as it would be to measure economic development, for example, yet one might argue that a highly developed political system is characterized by some measure of rationalized political efficiency, defined as a substantial degree of coherence in policy output and a capacity for innovation in the face of new problems. Parites and party systems may have an important impact on the course of such development.

In the American case the emergence of parties marked a significant elaboration of structures and a movement toward relative political efficiency. Before the advent of parties politics was a pluralistic, kaleidoscopic flux of personal cliques like those that gathered around the great magnate families in New York, caucuses of the sort that came and went in many New England towns, select and often half-invisible juntos in the capitals or courthouse villages in the Southern states, or other more or less popular but usually evanescent factions. All of these political formations in their pluralistic variety may be brought under the general heading of faction politics. With few exceptions such old-style "connexions" or multiple factions were characterized by lack of continuity from election to election, by tenuous or shifting relationships between leaders in government on one hand and the electorate on the other, by comparatively narrow ranges of support from interest groupings, and thus by a confusing degree of raw, unaggregated pluralism in politics. One result was that it was difficult for the voters to hold any one group of men responsible for the direction of public policy. Another was that policy-making was generally erratic or incoherent except where it was under the control of a dominant "connexion," clique, or junto.

The advent of the Federalists and Republicans as comprehensive parties, on the other hand, brought a new dualistic order into politics. The parties emerged as durable, differentiated, visible, rationalized formations which developed stable operating structures. Continuing relationships were evolved between leaders and cadre at the center of government and between lesser leaders and cadre in the states, counties, and towns; and in turn between this structure and broad popular followings in the electorate. It is appropriate in the American instance to consider the structure of leaders and cadre as "the party," or party proper, and its supporters or adherents in the public as its following. At the beginning American parties accomplished little toward organization strictly construed as a regularized differentiation of internal functions and corresponding division of labor. Indeed the Federalists never achieved significant organization, although the Republicans by the late 1790's and early 1800's devised party caucuses, conventions, and committees in several states which foreshadowed the full development of organization proper in the Jacksonian era. Yet both party structures in the 1790's did reach out to amass stable popular followings of considerable range and density that carried them well beyond the fluid and limited support pre-party factions had enjoyed. Lastly, both parties developed distinctive sets of in-group perspectives with emotional overtones, or ideologies, that helped to bind party structures together and popular followings to the parties. In short the first American parties can be described as developing historical patterns of stable structures linked to broad popular followings, with distinguishing ideologies, and as structures that were able and ready to perform crucial political functions. It is in terms of this general idea of what a party is that the Federalists and Republicans may be thought of as the first modern parties.

HISTORIOGRAPHICAL NOTE

There are a great many sources—some suited to comparative study, others significant in themselves—to which the student can apply for an understanding of eighteenth-century American political history. Lawrence Gipson's multi-volume study of *The British Empire in America,* for example, contains a great deal of information on the institutional structure of the imperial system—information that can be added to and extended by consulting Charles MacLean Andrews' *Colonial Background of the American Revolution.* Similarly, instead of examining Charles Beard's own pioneering work on the economic origins of the Constitution, the reader might consult either Merrill Jensen's or Jackson Turner Main's volumes on the Confederation period, which embody more recent and systematic presentations of neo-Beardian insights. Much of Bernard Bailyn's analysis of the psychological roots of Anglo-American conflict can also be derived from Jack P. Greene's invaluable monograph, *The Quest for Power: The Lower Houses of Assembly in the Southern Royal Colonies, 1689–1776.* The two major critical reassessments of Beard's interpretation of the Founding Fathers, both works absorbed and incorporated into the Elkins-McKitrick essay, are Robert E. Brown's *Charles A. Beard and the Constitution* and Forrest MacDonald's superbly researched *We The People: The Economic Origins of the Constitution.* Finally, those works that anticipated William Nisbet Chambers' functional analysis of the evolution of America's first party system include perceptive studies by the historians Joseph Charles, Noble Cunningham, and Stephen Kurtz along with *The First New Nation,* an essay by the sociologist Seymour Martin Lipset. This short list could be extended greatly without sacrificing quality because of the many fine recent monographs and articles that have deepened our understanding of colonial politics.

The essential distinction between earlier twentieth-century historians and more recent analysts, however, goes beyond disagreements over interpretive points, although these remain abundant. Certainly Beard's insistence on the recognizable socio-economic class interests involved in framing the Constitution and the first party system is challenged by both the Elkins-McKitrick career-line study of revolutionary leaders and the Chambers operational view of the Federalist-Jeffersonian party structure. But does it clarify historical understanding merely to designate Beard's views as "economic" and Chambers' as "political"—a common form of labeling? Similarly, is it sufficient to call Andrews' approach to colonial politics "institutional" and Bailyn's "psychological"? Would it not be more profitable instead, for example, to raise certain questions about the major concerns of each historian? Andrews is interested primarily in delineating the analogous patterns of conflict between assemblies and royal officials within each eighteenth-century mainland colony. Can his approach be contrasted with Bailyn's attempt to explain through comparative analysis why *parallel* political institutions in England and its American provinces led to fundamental conflicts of allegiance and authority? Similarly, can we still not learn more from carefully refining Beardian categories concerning economic response to the Constitution and to the new government than we can from discarding the categories entirely? Neither Chambers nor the co-authors of "Young Men of the Revolution" would dispute the continuing relevance of Beard's insights, properly qualified, to our understanding of the nation-building process. They would insist, however, on *enlarging* Beard's analysis of the factors that helped determine political response in the revolutionary nation. By directing attention to the personalities, vocational ambitions, sources of power, and ideological beliefs of the revolutionary generation—as well as to social class and economic interests—recent historians have continued sharpening the tools of social science employed by Beard himself.

To summarize, the two groups of historians represented in this chapter appear divided less by their interpretive quarrels, great as these are, than by the interest scholars have shown during the past few decades in establishing more precisely the dynamics behind changing patterns of political loyalties in the American experience. Armed with a variety of methodological tools from fields of social analysis—especially games theory technique, role- and career-line concepts, and other recent applications to the behavioral study of politics—historians have begun recasting our understanding of familiar stages in the evolution of American political growth.

5. The Contours of a National Society

INTRODUCTION

After 1815, distinct patterns of sectional and class differences emerged in American society. The sectional differences tended to produce discrete regional cultures, with values and folkways that separated them from other regions and from abstract, national experiences. Class differences took the form of economic, ethnic, and social groupings that tended to cut across regional boundaries. Differences and conflicts between sections and between social classes were promoted by two separate but related elements in American society: westward expansion and a revolution in industrial techniques. Taken alone, either the frontier or the development of industrial technology would have been enough to produce unusual kinds of social change and tension. Taken together, as they were in the American experience, the expansion to the west and the industrial revolution combined to create a new nation of extraordinary power and promise, but a nation distracted by uncertainty and divided by conflicts of interest and values.

The precise effects of westward expansion on American development are not always easy to trace. It is clear enough that, in one sense or another, the experience of the frontier tended to promote equalitarian "democracy." But in one context—a Kentucky revival setting, for example—equalitarianism might mean a radical moral individualism that denied the values of history and tradition. At another time and place—in an Illinois lawyer's experience, for instance—"democracy" could create a compelling rhetoric about the ways in which the fate of the common man was tied to the fate of the Union. In still another context of experience—that of a businessman in St. Louis or a cotton planter in Louisiana—equalitarianism might imply a struggle for individual economic success in a competitive society. These different meanings of the frontier experience were tied, in some measure, to the seaboard sources of the migration. When New England townsmen went over into upstate New York, Ohio, or northern Indiana, they established ways of thinking and acting that were quite different from the style created by the migration of planters from Georgia or Virginia into Alabama or Mississippi. The West might respond as a unified section to social and political issues that were connected to presumed oppression by the eastern "money power," but on other issues, most notably the issue of slavery, there was no recognizable, single "West," but at least two wests, perhaps three.

Sectional and regional differences complicated the impact of the industrial revolution. In the North and East, the Embargo and the War of 1812 helped speed the growth of manufacturing, the development of transportation, and the recruitment of an immigrant labor force. At first, the mill owners of New England tried to use native labor, but in the long run they had to turn to immigrants to run their machines and lay their rails. This labor force was never completely proletarianized, but it did become a distinct class element in the northern half of the United States. In the South, the new technology had a paradoxical effect. It did not promote, on the whole, the development of industry but, through the cotton gin, revitalized the agricultural economy of plantation slavery. The South was tied more and more tightly to external sources of capital and manufactured goods, especially to the financiers and manufacturers of New England. This odd bond between the "Lords of the Long Wharf, the Counting-House, and the Lash" led Ralph Waldo Emerson to remark that it was all very well to sing praise of the Union and to listen to orations on the Fourth of July, "but cotton thread is the Union." Meanwhile, the development of eastern city markets, combined with the steamboat, canals, and new railroads, molded the Northwest into a more or less distinct farming region. The pressures of geographic and economic expansion led to a pattern of "boom and bust," a pattern that left more western farmers in debt at the end of each cycle.

Whatever the region and whatever the particular effects of new technology, the most striking aspect of the nation at large was swift change. Problems were created faster than solutions were found. But to many, if not to most Americans, the problems did not seem insoluble or even critical. Social and economic change lent an air of almost boundless possibility and openness to American society. This powerful sense of the American future helped gloss over sectional and social conflicts, creating at least the illusion of a unified, homogeneous society. It was this America that met the eye of the most perceptive European visitor to the United States, Alexis de Tocqueville. To this French aristocrat, it seemed that "In America . . . there is only one society. It may be rich or poor, humble or brilliant, trading or agricultural; but it is composed everywhere of the same elements. The plane of a universal civilization has passed over it."

I. EARLY INTERPRETATION

The most sustained attempt to interpret American history along sectional lines has been the work of Frederick Jackson Turner. In 1893, Turner delivered a paper on "The Significance of the Frontier in American History," in which he argued that the frontier experience had done more than any other factor to mold American values and institutions. In the middle of the 1920's, Turner revised his concept and attempted to make it somewhat more subtle. Instead of treating the frontier as a passing experience, he described

267

the "West" as a permanent section, continuously asserting a distinct attitude against the East. American experience could be understood, Turner argued, only as a long attempt by the West to gain independence and pre-eminence, along with a parallel contest between North and South for control of the western empire. It was this three-cornered conflict, and not a simple North-South antagonism, that Turner thought explained the Civil War and much of the remainder of American history.

FREDERICK JACKSON TURNER

A generation ago I published . . . a paper which I had read at the summer meeting of the American Historical Association, on "The Significance of the Frontier in American History." The Superintendent of the Census had just announced that a frontier line could no longer be traced, and had declared: "In the discussion of its extent, its westward movement, etc., it cannot therefore any longer have a place in the census reports."

The significance in American history of the advance of the frontier and of its disappearance is now generally recognized. This evening I wish to consider with you another fundamental factor in American history—namely, the Section. Arising from the facts of physical geography and the regional settlement of different peoples and types of society on the Atlantic Coast, there was a sectionalism from the beginning. But soon this became involved and modified by the fact that these societies were expanding into the interior, following the frontier, and that their sectionalism took special forms in the presence of the growing West. Today we are substantially a settled nation without the overwhelming influence that accom-

Reprinted from Frederick Jackson Turner, "The Significance of the Section in American History," WISCONSIN MAGAZINE OF HISTORY (March 1925), pp. 255–65, by permission of the publisher.

panied the westward spread of population. Urban concentration, chiefly in the East, has reversed the movement to a considerable extent. We are more like Europe, and our sections are becoming more and more the American version of the European nation.

First let us consider the influence of the frontier and the West upon American sections. Until our own day, as I urged in that paper, the United States was always beginning over on its outer edge as it advanced into the wilderness. Therefore, the United States was both a developed and a primitive society. The West was a migrating region, a stage of society rather than a place. Each region reached in the process of expansion from the coast had its frontier experience, was for a time "the West," and when the frontier passed on to new regions, it left behind, in the older areas, memories, traditions, an inherited attitude toward life, that persisted long after the frontier had passed by. But while the influence of the frontier permeated East as well as West, by survival of the pioneer psychology and by the reaction of the Western ideals and life upon the East, it was in the newer regions, in the area called the West at any given time, that frontier traits and conceptions were most in evidence. This "West" was more than "the frontier" of popular speech. It included also the more populous transitional zone adjacent, which was still influenced by pioneer traditions and where economic society had more in common with the newer than with the older regions.

This "West," wherever found at different years, thought of itself and of the nation in different ways from those of the East. It needed capital; it was a debtor region, while the East had the capital and was a creditor section. The West was rural, agricultural, while the East was becoming more and more urban and industrial. Living under conditions where the family was the self-sufficing economic unit, where the complications of more densely settled society did not exist, without accumulated inherited wealth, the frontier regions stressed the rights of man, while the statesmen who voiced the interests of the East stressed the rights of property.

The West believed in the rule of the majority, in what John Randolph, the representative of the Virginia Tidewater aristocracy, called "King Numbers." The East feared an unchecked democracy, which might overturn minority rights, destroy established institutions, and attack vested interests. The buoyant, optimistic, and sometimes reckless and extravagant spirit of innovation was the very life of the West. In the East innovation was a term of reproach. It always "stalked" like an evil spirit. The East represented accumulated experience, the traditions of the family living generation after generation in a single location and under a similar environment. . . . But out in the newer West, through most of its history, men lived in at least two or three states in the course of their migrations. Of the hundred and twenty-four members of the first Wisconsin constitutional convention in 1846, the average was three states for each member. Four had moved eight times. Sixteen had lived in five or more different states, or foreign countries and states; six had lived in seven or more.

The West demanded cheap or free lands on which to base a democratic farming population. The ruling interests in the East feared that such a policy would decrease land values at home and diminish the value of lands which its capitalists had purchased for speculation in the interior. It feared that cheap lands in the West would draw Eastern farmers into the wilderness; would break down the bonds of regular society; would prevent effective control of the discontented; would drain the labor supply away from the growing industrial towns, and thus raise wages.

The West opened a refuge from the rule of established classes, from the subordination of youth to age, from the sway of established and revered institutions. Writing in 1694, when the frontier lay at the borders of Boston Bay, the Reverend Cotton Mather asked: "Do *Old* People any of them *Go Out* from the Institutions of God, swarming into New Settlements where they and their Untaught Families are like *to Perish for Lack of Vision?*" To their cost, he said, such men have "got unto the *Wrong side of the Hedge*" and "the angel of the Lord becomes their enemy."

No doubt all this makes too sharply contrasted a picture. But from the beginning East and West have shown a sectional attitude. The interior of the colonies on the Atlantic was disrespectful of the coast, and the coast looked down upon the upland folk. The "Men of the Western World" when they crossed the Alleghenies became self-conscious and even rebellious against the rule of the East. In the 1730's the Tidewater aristocracy was conquered by the Jacksonian democracy of the interior.

And so one could go on through the story of the antimonopolists, the Grangers, the Populists, the Insurgents, the Progressives, the Farmers' *Bloc,* and the La Follette movement, to illustrate the persistence of the sectionalism of the West, or of considerable parts of it, against the East.

Perhaps Eastern apprehension was never more clearly stated than by Gouverneur Morris, of Pennsylvania, in the Constitutional Convention of 1787. "The busy haunts of men, not the remote wilderness," said he, are "the proper school of political talents. If the Western people get the power into their hands they will ruin the Atlantic interests. The back members are always averse to the best measures." He would so fix the ratio of representation that the number of representatives from the Atlantic States should always be larger than the number from the Western States. This, he argued, would not be unjust "as the Western settlers would previously know the conditions on which they were to possess their lands." So influential was his argument that the convention struck out the provision in the draft which guaranteed equality with the old states to the states thereafter to be admitted to the Union. But on the motion that the representatives from new states should not exceed those from the Old Thirteen, the affirmative vote was cast by Massachusetts, Connecticut, Delaware, and Maryland; Pennsylvania was divided; and the motion was defeated by the votes of the Southern States plus New Jersey.

To the average American, to most American historians, and to most of the writers of our school textbooks (if one can trust the indexes to their books), the word *section* applies only to the struggle of South against North on the questions of slavery, state sovereignty, and, eventually, disunion.

But the Civil War was only the most drastic and most tragic of sectional manifestations, and in no small degree the form which it took depended upon the fact that rival societies, free and slave, were marching side by side into the unoccupied lands of the West, each attempting to dominate the back country, the hinterland, working out agreements from time to time, something like the diplomatic treaties of European nations, defining spheres of influence, and awarding mandates, such as in the Missouri Compromise, the Compromise of 1850, and the Kansas-Nebraska Act. Each Atlantic section was, in truth, engaged in a struggle for power; and power was to be gained by drawing upon the growing West. In the Virginia ratification convention of 1787 William Grayson, by no means the most radical of the members, said: "I look upon this as a contest for empire. . . . If the Mississippi be shut up emigrations will be stopped entirely. There will be no new states formed on the Western Waters. . . . This contest of the Mississippi involves the great national contest; that is whether one part of this continent shall govern the other. The Northern States have the majority and will endeavor to retain it." Similar conceptions abound in the utterances of North Atlantic statesmen. "It has been said," declared Morris in 1787, "that North Carolina, South Carolina and Georgia only, will in a little time have a majority of the people of America. They must in that case include the great interior country and everything is to be apprehended from their getting power into their hands."

If time permitted, it would be possible to illustrate by such utterances all through our history to very recent times how the Eastern sections regarded the West, with its advancing frontier, as the raw material for power.

To New England, until her own children began to occupy the prairies ("reserved by God," as her pioneers declared, "for a pious and industrious people"), this aspect of the West threatened to enable the South perpetually to rule the nation. The first great migration, the most extensive in the area covered, flowed into the interior from the Southern upland. Some of the extreme leaders of the New England Federalists did not so much desire to break away from the South as to deprive that section of the three-fifths representation for its slaves, and either to permit the Western States to leave the Union or to see them won by England. Then the Old Thirteen could be united under conditions which would check the expansion of the South and would leave New England in control.

Writing in 1786 Rufus King, of New York, later Senator and Minister to England, while admitting that it was impolitic at the time wholly to give up the Western settlers, declared that very few men who had examined the subject would refuse their assent "to the opinion that every Citizen of the Atlantic States, who emigrates to the westward of the Alleghany is a total loss to our confederacy."

Nature [he said] has severed the two countries by a vast and extensive chain of mountains, interest and convenience will keep them separate, and the feeble policy of our disjointed Government will not be able to unite them. For these reasons I have ever been opposed to encouragements of western emigrants. The States situated on the Atlantic are not sufficiently populous, and losing our men is losing our greatest source of wealth.

Of course the immediate complaint

in New England and New York was against the South itself, its Jeffersonian principles (so obnoxious to New England puritanism), its slavery, its pro-French sympathies. But all these gained much of their force by the conviction that the West was a reservoir from which the South would continue to draw its power. Among the proposals of the Hartford Convention was that no new state should be admitted into the Union without the concurrence of two thirds of both houses of Congress. Had this proposed amendment been made, the New England States with two other states in the Senate could have blocked the West from future statehood. The report warned the old states against "an overwhelming Western influence" and predicted that "finally the Western States, multiplied in numbers and augmented in population will control the interests of the whole." Nathan Dane, after whom Dane County in this state [Wisconsin] is named, furnished the argument for this proposed amendment by his elaborate tabulations and schedules. He pointed out that in the commercial states capital was invested in commerce, and in the slaveholding states in Western lands. When "Kentucky, Ohio and Tennessee were raised up by this interest & admitted into the Union, then the balance was, materially, affected. The non-commercial states pressed the admission of Louisiana and turned the balance against the Northeast." "It clearly follows," he reasoned, "that if a bare majority in Congress can admit new States into the union (all interior ones as they must be) at pleasure, in these immense Western regions, the balance of the union as once fairly contemplated, must soon be destroyed."

But Jackson defeated the British at New Orleans. The Mississippi Valley remained within the Union, Louisiana's interests became affiliated with the commercial states in many ways, and New England people poured so rapidly into the West that New England found in the northern half of the Valley the basis for a new alliance and new power as disturbing to the slaveholding South as the Southern and Western connection had been to New England.

By the middle of the century the South was alarmed at the Western power much in the way that New England had been. "I have very great fears," wrote Justice Campbell, later of the Federal Supreme Court, from Mobile to Calhoun in 1847, "that the existing territories of the United States will prove too much for our government. The wild and turbulent conduct of the members upon the Oregon question and their rapacity and greediness in all matters conected with the appropriation of the revenues induces great doubt of the propriety of introducing new States in the Union so fast as we do." Of the legislators from the Western States he said: "Their notions are freer, their impulses stronger, their wills less restrained. I do not wish to increase the number till the New States already admitted to the Union become civilized."

On the other hand, it must be clearly borne in mind that as the West grew in power of population and in numbers of new senators, it resented the conception that it was merely an emanation from a rival North and South; that it was the dependency of one or another of the Eastern sections; that it was to be so limited and controlled as to maintain an equilibrium in the Senate between North and South. It took the attitude of a section itself.

From the beginning the men who went West looked to the future when the people beyond the Alleghenies should rule the nation. Dr. Manasseh Cutler, the active promoter of the Ohio Company of Associates, which made the first considerable permanent settlement in the Old Northwest Territory, wrote in 1787 a *Description of Ohio*. Though himself the minister at Ipswich, in the heart of that stronghold of conservatism, the "Essex Junto," he declared that on the Ohio would be "the seat of empire" for the whole Union. Within twenty years, he predicted, there would be more people on the western side of the Allegheny watershed than in the East, and he congratulated these people that "in order to begin right there will be no wrong habits to combat and no inveterate systems to overturn—there will be no rubbish to remove before you lay the foundations." Evidently it did not take long to produce the Western point of view!

In the Senate in 1837 Benton, of Missouri, scorned the proposals of Calhoun regarding the disposition of the public domain, and boasted that after the census of 1840 had shown the weight of the West it would be so highly bid for that it would write its own bill. Perhaps the debate over the Compromise of 1850 brings out the self-assertive Western attitude in these years most clearly. Calhoun had argued that the equilibrium between North and South was being destroyed by the increase in free states made out of the Western territories. But Stephen A. Douglas, of Illinois, spoke for the West when he attacked the Southern statesman for the error of thinking of the West as property of the older sections. "What share had the South in the territories," he asked, "or the North, or any other geographical division unknown to the Constitution? I answer none— none at all." And Douglas calculated that if its right to self-determination were admitted, the West would form at least seventeen new free states, and that therefore the theory of equilibrium was a hopeless one.

It was not only the slavery struggle that revealed the Eastern conception of the West as merely the field of contest for power between the rival Atlantic sections, and the West's counter assertion of its own substantive rights. The same thing was shown in many different fields. For example, rival Eastern cities and states, the centers of power in their respective sections, engaged in contests for the commercial control of the Mississippi Valley by transportation lines. The contests between rival European powers for the control of the Bagdad railway, the thrust of Germany toward the rich hinterlands made up of the Balkans and India, and the project of "Central Europe" in the history of the World War, have a resemblance to these American sectional contests for the still more valuable hinterland of the Mississippi Valley. American sections did not go to war over their trade and transportation interests. Nevertheless, they recognized that there were such interests. A Southern writer in *DeBow's Review* in 1847 declared:

"A contest has been going on between the North and South not limited to slavery or no slavery—to abolition or no abolition, nor to the politics of either whigs or democrats as such, but a contest for the wealth and commerce of the great valley of the Mississippi— a contest tendered by our Northern brethren, whether the growing commerce of the great West shall be thrown upon New Orleans or given to the Atlantic cities."

Shortly after this, in 1851, the *Western Journal* of St. Louis published articles lamenting that "the Western

States are subjected to the relation of Provinces of the East" and that New Orleans was giving way to New York as their commercial city. Since (so the argument ran) exports can never build up a commercial city, the mouth of the Mississippi must be so improved that imports would enter the Valley by way of New Orleans. "Then," said the writer, "a line of cities will arise on the banks of the Mississippi that will far eclipse those on the Atlantic coast."

The middle of the century saw an extension of this sectional contest for economic power derived from the growing West; but it was the railroad trunk lines rather than the canals that occupied the foreground. The goal became the ports of the Pacific. The Memphis convention of 1845 and the Chicago convention of 1847 illustrate how interior cities were now repeating the rivalry for Western trade which had earlier been seen on the Atlantic Coast. The contests between New Orleans, Memphis, St. Louis, and Chicago influenced the Kansas-Nebraska Act, and the later strategy of the struggle for position between the Pacific railroads.

Throughout our history, then, there has been this sectionalism of West and East, and this Eastern conception of the West as recruiting ground merely for the rival Atlantic Coast sections. Nationwide parties have had their Eastern and Western wings, often differing radically, and yet able by party loyalty and by adjustments and sacrifices to hold together. Such a struggle as the slavery contest can only be understood by bearing in mind that it was not merely a contest of North against South, but that its form and its causes were fundamentally shaped by the dynamic factor of expanding Sections, of a West to be won.

II. DOCUMENTS

1. The West

Throughout his career as a historian, Frederick Jackson Turner insisted that it was the frontier that fostered the highest and most characteristic American virtues—democracy, individualism, patriotism, and the spirit of enterprise. But these virtues always had, as he knew, their opposite sides. Democracy could, and did, degenerate into conformity, individualism into lawlessness, patriotism into jingoism, and enterprise into ruthlessness. The experience of the West, in Turner's view, was a process of sloughing off inherited institutions and restraints. The frontier meant renewal, then, but renewal could pass over into barbarism, the perennial fear of eastern conservatives. In the 1843 record of a frontier fight included here, the kinds of violent barbarism associated with the West are very plain.

The exuberant boast of the young wharf fighter was "My finger-nails is related to a saw mill on my mother's side, and my daddy was a double-breasted catamount." In the West, this sort of unrestrained enthusiasm was the common property of folk rhetoric and of professional humorists. Turner's section, it seemed, produced not only a politics of free land and majority rule, but also a social life full of unrestrained enthusiasms. In the sphere of religion, enthusiasm was associated with revivalism as the characteristic frontier form of worship. The revival—to oversimplify the matter somewhat—replaced the theological rigor of the seventeenth century with the kinds of emotional ecstasies described in the second selection in this section. The revivals, which were almost continuous from 1800 to the Civil War, were important social cement in the West and Southwest. They promoted highly individualized raptures of religious emotion; but, at the same time, they were profoundly communal experiences that provided a ritualized setting in which scattered families could unite in a common experience.

Americans entertained ambivalent ideas about native Indians during the early centuries of the nation's history. To many Puritans, the Indian had represented an opportunity for spreading the light of the Gospel. Others, especially toward the end of the eighteenth century, began to paint the Indian in the colors of the "Noble Savage." But to most westerners, the Indian was simply a dangerous obstacle and nuisance. The selection from Hugh Henry Brackenridge develops the standard arguments of westerners on Indian removal. Brackenridge was a westerner and a democrat, but the abstractions of frontier equalitarianism did not, in Brackenridge's eyes, have any bearing on "the animals, vulgarly called Indians."

A FRONTIER BRAWL

Once upon a time we were coming down the Mississippi River, on our way to this city. Bunyan has written about a certain delectable spot, situated somewhere in Utopia; but had the pilgrim seen the Arkansas landing we are just now speaking of, he would have thrown down his scallop shell and staff, and cut dirt as if the gentleman in black, on a streak of double-milled electricity, was after him. Two flatboats constituted the wharf, and they were continually butting their heads together. Such was the energy and regularity of their movement against each other, that for a moment we fancied the doctrine of Pythagoras was true, and that the departed spirits of two antagonistic rams had entered the timbers of the flatboats, and thence the combative symptoms above spoken of. As soon as the steamboat was moored alongside this floating wharf, the rush to board her was tremendous. One man, dressed in a hunting shirt of coarse homespun, and a coonskin cap, with a knife, something like that which sailors wear, sticking in his girdle, was the first to get on the plank that led from the flatboat to the steamer, and in his hurry to get on board he was pushed into the water, by a gigantic fellow in a bearskin coat, a coarse wool hat, and a pair of green baize leggings. The immersion of the gentleman in the hunting shirt was altogether accidental, but it was sufficient foundation, in the estimation of the cavaliers of Arkansas, for the tournament ground to be marked off, and the trumpets to blow *"largesse"* to the knights of the coonskin cap and the green baize leggings.

As soon as the ducked man arose

Reprinted from THE SPIRIT OF THE TIMES, XII (February 18, 1843), 611.

from the top of the mulatto-colored river, he clenched one hand above his head, and hallowed, "Hold on there—you thin-milk-livered skunk! Hold on till I get on shore, and may I be cut up for shoe pegs if I don't make your skillet-faced phizcymahogany look like a cabbage made into sourkraut!"

"See here, stranger," replied the offender, "your duckin' was axesighdental; but if you want a tussel I am har—just like a fin on a cat-fish's back!"

"The plank was mine by seniority, as the doctors say, old cat skinner, and may I be ground up into gunpowder, if I don't light on to you like a bull bat on a gallinipper," remarked the dripping man, as he shook himself like a Newfoundland dog, and stepped on shore.

"Stranger," said the causer of the accident, while his eye gleamed like that of an enraged panther, and his fists clenched so forcibly that his nails were driven into the palms of his hands, "perhaps you don't know that I'm the man that fought with Wash. Coffee, and dirked wild Jule Lynch."

"May I run on a sawyer, and may my brains fall down into my boot heels as I am walking up a stony hill, if I care if you had a rough and tumble with the devil. You pushed me off the plank and you must fight," was the peaceable reply of the wet gentleman.

"See here, man," said the opponent of Wash. Coffee, as he bared his breast and pointed to a large scar that ran across three or four of his ribs, "Wild Jule done this, but I laid him up for a time—these big scratches on my face was got through my trying to hug a young bar—and this arm has been broken twice. I'm a cripple, but if you will fight, why strip and let's be at it."

In an instant a ring was made and the two combatants, when doffed of their clothing, looked like middle-aged

Titans, preparing for battle. The younger, who had fallen into the water was about twenty-eight years of age, and his opponent was thirty-four or five. With eyes made fiery by anger, and lips quavering with intense passion, the younger dealt his adversary a tremendous blow in the breast. Until this affront the elder man had maintained a strange coolness, and manifested a disposition rather in favor of an apology than anything else; but the instant he felt the blow his nostrils became white, and twitched like a steed's scenting the battle. Closing his teeth hard together, he planted himself for the attack, and as his adversary approached him, he dealt him a fierce lick on the side of the face with his iron-bound knuckles, that laid his cheek bone as bare as though the flesh had been chopped off by an ax. Smarting with rage the other returned the compliment, and as the blood gushed in a torrent from his mouth, he turned around and spit out one or two of his teeth that were hanging by the gums, and with a "rounder" as it is technically termed, he hit the younger man [sic] a blow on the temple that laid him on the beach with a dead, heavy sound, like that of a falling tree.

"Thar, I hope he is got enough," said the elder of the two, at almost every word stopping to spit out some fragment of his broken jaw. One of his companions handed him a flask of brandy, and with a long deep-drawn swallow, like that of a camel at a spring on an oasis, he gulped down enough of the fiery liquor to have made a common man mad.

"Enough," cried the other party, who had been in a like manner attended by his friends. "Yes, when I drink your heart's blood I'll cry enough, and not till then, come on, you white-wired—"

"See here, stranger, stop thar. Don't talk of my mother—She's *dead—God bless her! I'm a man from A to izzard —and you—you thin gutted wasp, I'll whip you now if I die for it!*"

With a shout from the bystanders, and passions made furious by hate and deep draughts of liquor, with a howl the combatants again went to work. Disengaging his right hand from the boa constrictor grip of his opponent, the younger brute buried his long talon-like nails directly under the eyelid of his victim, and the orb clotted with blood hung by a few tendons to his cheek! As soon as the elder man felt the torture, his face for an instant was as white as snow, and then a deep purple hue overspread his countenance. Lifting his adversary in the air as though he had been a child, he threw him to the earth, and clutching his throat with both hands, he squeezed it until his enemy's face became almost black. Suddenly he uttered a sharp quick cry, and put his hand to his side, and when he drew it away it was covered with blood! The younger villain, while on his back, had drawn his knife and stabbed him. As the elder of the combatants staggered up, he was caught by some of his friends, and holding him in their arms, with clenched fists they muttered curses toward his inhuman opponent, who being shielded by his own particular clique, made for the river and plunged in. When about half way across, he gained a small island, and rising to his full height, he flapped his hands against his sides and crow'd like a cock.

"Ruo-ru—oo-o! I can lick a steamboat! My finger-nails is related to a saw mill on my mother's side, and my daddy was a doublebreasted catamount! I wear a hoop snake for a neck-handkerchief, and the brass buttons on my coat have all been boiled in poison! Who'll Ru— oo—ru—ooo!"

JAMES ROSS

In the year 1799, several ministers of the Presbyterian Church, Elders Mc-Gready, Hodge, and Rankin, and one belonging to the Methodist Episcopal Church, Elder John McGee, held a sacramental meeting, at the old Red River Church, which stood on or near the same site as the church of that name now does. The meeting drew together a large congregation, considering the thinly settled country.

On Sunday Elder Hodge preached and, as he was often heard to say afterwards, addressed the assemblage with a freedom and power, never before felt. The hearers though riveted in their attention, remained silent and quiet. As he closed his discourse, Elder John McGee rose, singing,

> Come, Holy Spirit, Heavenly Dove,
>   With all thy quickening powers,
> Kindle a flame of sacred love,
>   In these cold hearts of ours.

He had not sung more than the verse quoted, when an aged lady, Mrs. Pacely, sitting quite across the congregation to the left, and Mrs. Clark, also advanced in years, seated to the right, began in rather suppressed but distinct tones, to hold a sort of dialogue with each other, and to reciprocate sentiments of praise and thanksgiving to the Most High, for his grace in redemption. Still the preacher sang on, and the venerable ladies praised God, in louder tones. The preacher, still singing came down from the pulpit, intending to take the hands of these two happy old sisters; shaking hands, however, as he passed along, with all those within his reach. Suddenly persons began to fall as he

Reprinted from James Ross, THE LIFE AND TIMES OF THE ELDER REUBEN ROSS *(Philadelphia, 1882), pp. 233–41.*

passed through the crowd—some as dead; some most piteously crying for mercy; and a few, here and there, lifting their voices high, in the praise of the Redeemer. Among these last was Elder William McGee, who fell to the floor, and, though shouting praises, was for some time so overpowered as to be unable to rise. The other ministers, Mc-Gready, Hodge, and Rankin, were so surprised and astonished at this apparent confusion in the house of the Lord, that they made their way out of the door, and stood asking each other in whispers, "what is to be done." Elder Hodge looking in at the door, and seeing all on the floor, praising or praying, said, "We can do nothing. If this be of Satan, it will soon come to an end; but if it is of God, our efforts and fears are in vain. I think it is of God, and will join in ascribing glory to his name."

He walked into the house where the others presently followed. Rapidly those who had fallen to the floor mourning and crying for mercy, arose, two or more at a time, shouting praise, for the evidences felt in their own souls, of sins forgiven—for "redeeming grace and dying love." So there remained no more place that day, for preaching or administering the Supper. From thirty to forty, that evening professed to be converted.

Thus began that wonderful religious movement, which not only pervaded Kentucky, Tennessee, and Ohio, but crossed the mountains, and spread over many of the states on the Atlantic seaboard. On account of the strange bodily agitations attending it, it was considered the most wonderful event of the times.

"The next appointment was for the Saturday and Sunday following, at what is to this day called the Beach Meeting House, situated a little south of the Cumberland Ridge, ten miles west of

Gallatin, Sumner County, Tennessee." Here a vast crowd assembled, and scenes similar to those at Red River Meeting house transpired. But the most wonderful meeting was at Muddy River Church, a few miles north of Russellville, Kentucky, the Sunday after. "The people came in from the two states twenty, thirty, fifty, and even a hundred miles. Some came in tented wagons, some in open wagons, some in carts, some on horse back, and many on foot."

The meeting house, hours before preaching commenced, could not seat the third part of those on the ground. And still they came by dozens, fifties, and hundreds. A temporary pulpit was quickly erected under the shady trees, and seats made of large trees felled and laid upon the ground. The preaching commenced, and soon the presence of the all-pervading Power was felt, throughout the vast assembly.

"As night came on it was apparent the crowd did not intend to disperse. What was to be done? Some took wagons, and hurried to bring in straw from barns and treading-yards. Some fell to sewing the wagon sheets together, and others to cutting forks and poles, on which to spread them. Counterpanes, coverlets, and sheets were also fastened together, to make tents or camps. Others were dispatched to town and to the nearest houses to collect bacon, meal, flour, with cooking utensils to prepare food for the multitude. In a few hours it was a sight to see how much was gathered together for the encampment."

"Fires were made, cooking begun; and by dark, candles lighted, and fixed to a hundred trees; and here was the first, and perhaps the most beautiful camp ground the world ever saw."

Burton W. Stone, at that time in the fellowship of the Presbyterian Church, and Pastor of the Cane Ridge and Concord congregation, in Bourbon County, Kentucky, heard of the mighty work going on in southern Kentucky, and determined to go down and see for himself. He seems to have been a man of fine talents, respectable learning, spotless character, and childlike simplicity; but easily attracted by what was strange and marvelous. Early in the spring of 1801, he set out for Logan County, to attend one of the great camp meetings.

"On arriving," he writes, "I found the multitude assembled on the edge of a prairie, where they continued encamped many successive days and nights, during all which time, worship was being conducted in some parts of the encampment. The scene to me was passing strange. It baffles description. Many, very many, fell down, as men slain in battle, and continued, for hours together, in a comparatively breathless and motionless state. Sometimes for a few moments reviving and exhibiting symptoms of life, by a deep groan, or piercing shriek, or by a prayer for mercy most fervently uttered. After lying thus for hours, they obtained deliverance. The gloomy cloud that had covered their faces, seemed gradually and visibly to disappear; and hope, in smiles, to brighten into joy. They would then arise, shouting deliverance, and address the surrounding multitude in language truly eloquent and impressive. With astonishment did I hear women and children declaring the wonderful works of God and the glorious mysteries of the gospel. Their appeals were solemn, heart-rending, bold, and free. Under such addresses, many others would fall down in the same state, from which the speakers had just been delivered.

"Two or three of my particular acquaintances from a distance, were struck down. I sat patiently by one of them, whom I knew to be a careless sinner, for hours, and observed with critical attention, every thing that passed, from the beginning to the end. I noticed the momentary revivings as from death, the humble confession, the fervent prayer and ultimate deliverance; then, the solemn thanks and praise to God, the affectionate exhortation to companions and to the people round to repent and come to

Jesus. I was astonished at the knowledge of gospel truth displayed in these exhortations. The effect was that several sank down into the same appearance of death. After attending to many such cases, my conviction was complete, that it was a good work, nor has my mind waverd since on the subject."

Elder Stone, in chapter sixth of his book, enumerates six kinds of bodily agitations during this great excitement. The falling exercise; the jerks; the dancing exercise; the barking exercise; the laughing exercise; and the singing exercise.

"The falling exercise," he says, "was very common among all classes both saints and sinners of every age, and every grade, from the philosopher to the clown. The subject of this exercise, would generally, with a piercing scream, fall, like a log, on the floor, earth, or mud, and appear as dead.

"The jerks cannot be so easily described. Sometimes, the subject of the jerks would be affected in the whole system. When the head alone was affected, it would be jerked backward and forward, or from side to side, so quickly that the features of the face could not be distinguished. When the whole system was affected, I have seen a person stand in one place, and jerk backwards and forward, in quick succession, their hands nearly touching the floor behind and before. All classes, saints as well as sinners, strong as well as weak, were thus affected. They could not account for it, but some have told me, these were among the happiest moments of their lives.

"The dancing exercise generally began with the jerks, and was peculiar to professors of religion. The subject, after jerking awhile, began to dance, and then the jerks would cease. Such dancing was indeed *heavenly* to the spectators. There was nothing in it like levity, or calculated to excite levity in beholders. The smile of heaven shone in the countenance of the subject, and assimilated to angels, appeared the whole person. [Rather highly colored!]

"The barking, as opposers contemptu-

ously called it, was nothing but the jerks. A person afflicted with the jerks, especially in the head, would often make a grunt or a bark, (if you please) from the suddenness of the jerk. This name "barking," seems to have had its origin from an old Presbyterian preacher of East Tennessee. He had gone into the fields for private devotion, and was seized with the jerks. Standing near a sapling, he caught hold of it, to prevent his falling, and as his head jerked back, he uttered a grunt or kind of noise similar to a bark, his face being turned upward. Some wag discovered him in this position, and reported that he found him barking up a tree.

"The laughing exercise was frequent, confined solely to the religious. It was a loud, hearty laughter, but one *sui generis*. It excited laughter in no one else. The subject appeared rapturously solemn, and his laughter excited solemnity in saint and sinner. It was truly indescribable.

"The running exercise, was nothing more than that persons, feeling something of these bodily agitations, through fear attempted to run away, and thus escape from them, but it commonly happened that they ran not far before they fell or became so greatly agitated, they could proceed no farther.

"The singing exercise is more unaccountable than anything I ever saw. The subject, in a very happy state of mind, would sing most melodiously, not from the mouth or nose, but from the breast entirely, the sound issuing thence. Such music silenced everything and attracted the attention of all. It was most heavenly. None could ever be tired of hearing it. Dr. J. P. Campbell and myself, were together at a meeting, and were attending to a pious lady thus exercised, and concluded it to be something beyond anything we had ever known in nature."

This is, in part, what Elder Stone saw and heard, when he visited Southern Kentucky, in 1801, at the commencement of these strange exercises, expressed in his *naive,* or artless way.

Lorenzo Dow, while on tour of preaching in 1804, says:

"I passed by a meeting house, where I observed the undergrowth had been cut down for a camp-meeting, and from fifty to one hundred saplings cut off about breast high, and on inquiring about it, learned that they had been left for the people to jerk by."

This excited his curiosity, and on going round, he "found where the people had laid hold of them and jerked so powerfully that, they had kicked up the earth, like horses in fly-time"! He believed the jerking was "entirely involuntary, and not to be accounted for, on any known principle."

Peter Cartwright, in his book, speaks of the strange bodily exercises of the times, and seems to have been rather amused at what he sometimes saw.

"Just in the midst of our controversies on the subject of the powerful exercises among the people under preaching, a new exercise broke out among us called the *jerks,* which was overwhelming in its effects upon the bodies and minds of the people. No matter whether they were saints or sinners, they would be taken under a warm song or sermon and seized with a convulsive jerking all over, which they could not by any possibility avoid. And the more they resisted, the more violently they jerked. If they would not strive against it and pray in good earnest, it would usually abate. I have seen more than five hundred persons jerking at once in my large congregations. Most usually, persons taken with the jerks, to obtain relief, as they said, would rise up and dance—some would run, but could not get away—some would resist,—on such the jerks were most severe.

"To see those proud young gentlemen and ladies, dressed in their silks, jewelry, and prunella from top to toe, take the jerks, would often excite my risibility. The first jerk or two you would see their fine bonnets, caps, and combs fly, and their long, loose hair crack almost as loud as a wagoner's whip."

He tells an amusing story of two young men who brought their sisters to meeting one day, each armed with a horsewhip, and told the crowd that if Cartwright gave their sisters the jerks, they intended to horse-whip him. The girls went in, took their seats, and the youngsters stood at the door. Being a little unwell that day, and having a vial of peppermint in his pocket, just as he rose to commence preaching he drank a little of it. The young fellows, keeping their eyes on him steadily, saw this. While in the midst of his sermon the girls fell to jerking violently. When he had finished, and came down from the pulpit, he was told by a friend to be on his guard, as there were some fellows at the door who intended to whip him. On hearing this, he went to them, and asked why they were going to whip him? They answered, because he had given their sisters the jerks. He told them he had not given them the jerks. They replied he had, for they saw him with the medicine he carried about with him for the purpose. He then said, if he had given the girls the jerks he reckoned he could give it to them too, and commenced taking his peppermint out. At this the young fellows wheeled, took to their heels, and he saw no more of them.

Elder Stone tells us he had never seen anyone injured by the jerks; but Elder Cartwright says:

"During a camp-meeting, at a place called the Ridge, in William McGee's congregation, there was a very large, drinking man, cursing the jerks and all religion together. Soon he commenced jerking himself and started to run, but could not get away. He then took out his bottle of whisky and swore he would drink the jerks to death, but jerked so violently he could not get the bottle to his mouth, though he tried very hard to do so. At length he fetched a very violent jerk, snapped his neck, fell, and soon expired, surrounded by a very large crowd."

After Elder Stone had spent some time in Southern Kentucky, he returned to Cane Ridge, and related the strange things he had seen and heard. The people seemed to be solemnly impressed, and much feeling was manifested. During the second sermon he preached, after his return, two little girls were struck down, and the most intense excitement ensued, which overspread the whole country. At some of the great camp-meetings that followed, it was thought that from twenty to twenty-five thousand people were present, and bodily exercises of the most wonderful character were there likewise.

HUGH HENRY BRACKENRIDGE

With the narrative enclosed, I subjoin some observations with regard to the animals, vulgarly called Indians. . . . Having an opportunity to know something of the character of this race of men, from the deeds they perpetrate daily round me, I think proper to say something on the subject. Indeed, several years ago, and before I left your city, I had thought different from some others with respect to the right of soil, and the propriety of forming treaties and making peace with them. . . .

• • •

On what is their claim founded?— Occupancy. A wild Indian with his skin painted red, and a feather through his nose, has set his foot on the broad continent of North and South America; a second wild Indian with his ears cut in ringlets, or his nose slit like a swine or

Reprinted from Hugh Henry Brackenridge, in Wilcombe E. Washburn, ed., THE INDIAN AND THE WHITE MAN *(New York, 1964), pp. 111–17.*

a malefactor, also sets his foot on the same extensive tract of soil. Let the first Indian make a talk to his brother, and bid him take his foot off the continent, for he being first upon it, had occupied the whole, to kill buffaloes, and tall elks with long horns. This claim in the reasoning of some men would be just, and the second savage ought to depart in his canoe, and seek a continent where no prior occupant claimed the soil. . . . Let a man in more modern times take a journey or voyage like Patrick Kennedy and others to the heads of the Mississippi or Missouri rivers, would he gain a right ever after to exclude all persons from drinking the waters of these streams? Might not a second Adam make a talk to them and say, is the whole of this water necessary to allay your thirst, and may I also drink of it?

The whole of this earth was given to man, and all descendants of Adam have a right to share it equally. There is no right of primogeniture in the laws of nature and of nations. There is reason that a tall man, such as the chaplain in the American army we call the High Priest, should have a large spot of ground to stretch himself upon; or that a man with a big belly, like a goodly alderman of London, should have a larger garden to produce beans and cabbage for his appetite, but that an agile, nimble runner, like an Indian called the Big Cat, at Fort Pitt, should have more than his neighbors, because he has traveled a great space, I can see no reason. . . .

• • •

It is a usual way of destroying an opinion by pursuing it to its consequence. In the present case we may say, that if the visiting one acre of ground could give a right to it, the visiting of a million would give a right on the same principle; and thus a few surly ill natured men, might in the earlier ages have excluded half the human race from a settlement, or should any have fixed themselves on a territory, visited before they had set a foot on it, they must be considered as invaders of the rights of others.

It is said that an individual, building a house or fabricating a machine has an exclusive right to it, and why not those who improve the earth? I would say, should man build houses on a greater part of the soil, than falls to his share, I would, in a state of nature, take away a proportion of the soil and the houses from him, but a machine or any work of art, does not lessen the means of subsistence to the human race, which an extensive occupation of the soil does.

Claims founded on the first discovery of soil are futile. When gold, jewels, manufactures, or any work of men's hands is lost, the finder is entitled to some reward, that is, he has some claims on the thing found, for a share of it.

When by industry or the exercise of genius, something unusual is invented in medicine or in other matters, the author doubtless has a claim to an exclusive profit by it, but who will say the soil is lost, or that any one can found a claim by discovering it. The earth with its woods and rivers still exist, and the only advantage I would allow to any individual for having cast his eye first on any particular part of it, is the privilege of making the first choice of situation. I would think the man a fool and unjust, who would exclude me from drinking the waters of the Mississippi river, because he had first seen it. He would be equally so who would exclude me from settling in the country west of the Ohio, because in chasing a buffalo he had been first over it.

The idea of an exclusive right to the soil in the natives had its origin in the policy of the first discoverers, the kings of Europe. Should they deny the right of the natives from their first treading on the continent, they would take away the right of discovery in themselves, by sailing on the coast. As the vestige of the moccasin in one case gave a right, so the cruise in the other was the foundation of a claim.

Those who under these kings, derived grants were led to countenance the idea, for otherwise why should kings grant or they hold extensive tracts of country. Men become enslaved to an opinion that has been long entertained. Hence it is that many wise and good men will talk of the rights of savages to immense tracts of soil.

What use do these ringed, streaked, spotted and speckled cattle make of the soil? Do they till it? Revelation said to man, "Thou shalt till the ground." This alone is human life. It is favorable to population, to science, to the information of a human mind in the worship of God. . . . To live by tilling is *more humano,* by hunting is *more bestiarum.* I would as soon admit a right in the buffalo to grant lands, as in Killbuck, the Big Cat, the Big Dog, or any of the ragged wretches that are called chiefs and sachems. What would you think of going to a big lick or place where the beasts collect to lick saline nitrous earth and water, and addressing yourself to a great buffalo to grant you land? It is true he could not make the mark of the stone or the mountain reindeer, but he could set his cloven foot to the instrument like the great Ottomon, the father of the Turks, when he put his signature to an instrument, he put his large hand and spreading fingers in the ink and set his mark to the parchment. To see how far the folly of some would go, I had once a thought of supplicating some of the great elks or buffaloes that run through the woods, to make me a grant of a hundred thousand acres of land and prove he had brushed the weeds with his tail, and run fifty miles.

I wonder if Congress or the different States would recognize the claim? I am so far from thinking the Indians have a right to the soil, that not having made a better use of it for many hundred years, I conceive they have forfeited all pretence to claim, and ought to be driven from it.

With regard to forming treaties or making peace with this race, there are many ideas:

They have the shapes of men and may be of the human species, but certainly in their present state they approach nearer the character of Devils; take an Indian, is there any faith in him? Can you bind him by favors? Can you trust his word or confide in his promise? When he makes war upon you, when he takes you prisoner and has you in his power will he spare you? In this he departs from the law of nature, by which, according to baron Montesquieu and every other man who thinks on the subject, it is unjustifiable to take away the life of him who submits; the conqueror in doing otherwise becomes a murderer, who ought to be put to death. On this principle are not the whole Indian nations murderers?

Many of them may have not had an opportunity of putting prisoners to death, but the sentiment which they entertain leads them invariably to this when they have it in their power or judge it expedient; these principles constitute them murderers, and they ought to be prevented from carrying them into execution, as we would prevent a common homicide, who should be mad enough to conceive himself justifiable in killing men.

The tortures which they exercise on the bodies of their prisoners, justify extermination. Gelo of Syria made war on the Carthaginians because they oftentimes burnt human victims, and made peace with them on conditions they would cease from this unnatural and cruel practice. If we could have any faith in the promises they make we could suffer them to live, provided they would only make war amongst themselves, and abandon their hiding or lurking on the pathways of our citizens, emigrating unarmed and defenceless inhabitants; and murdering men, women and children in a defenceless situation; and on their ceasing in the meantime to raise arms no more among the American Citizens.

2. The South

Brackenridge's defense of a policy that advocated the virtual extermination of the Indians was hard and brutal. The hardness and brutality were probably caused, in part, by the tension between his attitudes toward Indians and his "democratic" attitudes toward other social problems. This latent contradiction was much more easily overcome in the case of the Indian than in the case of the Negro. On one level of abstraction or another, white Americans—northerners, southerners, and westerners—were committed to the doctrine of the free and equal creation of all men. What, then, could they say about the millions of Negro slaves in their midst? After about 1830, growing numbers of radicals in the North and West began to insist that slavery was inconsistent with equalitarian principles and must be abolished, even at the cost of the Union itself. But before abolitionists became an important fact of life in America, Southern planters wrestled with rationales for racial inequality. One of the most succinct statements of white racism was written by the author of the Declaration of Independence, Thomas Jefferson. In a passage of his Notes on Virginia *on revisions of the state laws, Jefferson did defend a proposal to emancipate Virginia's slaves, but he then took up the question of whether the freed slaves should be sent out of the country or "integrated" into the community. He insisted that the blacks should be transported to Africa, giving reasons that were a model of attitudes toward the Negro which were shared by the great majority of white Americans, not just in the South but in the North and West as well.*

Jefferson's Notes *were an expression of a mental set fairly common among Virginia aristocrats at the end of the eighteenth century: opposition to slavery on principle, worry over the fact that the combination of tobacco and slavery was not profitable, foreboding about the future of Virginia, and a strong belief in the physical, mental, and moral superiority of the white over the black man. A half-century later, things had changed in the South. There was almost no opposition to slavery among the planters. The cotton gin had caused a tremendous expansion of the plantation economy and of the slave system with it. Aristocratic forebodings about the future were drowned out by a growing enthusiasm over "King Cotton" and even secession. And, in response to attacks from northern abolitionists and to occasional revolts and rumors of revolts at home, white southerners' attitudes toward blacks were harsher than Jefferson's had been. By 1850, however, there was a significant new element in the Southern social equation: the plantation wife. Women in all sections of the nation were much more self-conscious and insistent on their prerogatives in 1850 than in 1800, and the wives of the planters were no exception. In the following selections from her remarkable diary, Mary Boykin Chesnut, wife of a prominent South Carolina secessionist, revealed something of the anguish over slavery which ladies of her class shared with northern women like Harriet Beecher Stowe. The paradox of Jefferson was the combination of his theoretical equalitarianism and his commonplace racism. Mrs. Chesnut suffered through a different, though somewhat parallel paradox: an opposition to slavery based on the bitter experience of it, combined with an ardent support of the South's "War for Independence."*

THOMAS JEFFERSON

To emancipate all slaves born after the passing the act. The bill reported

Reprinted from Thomas Jefferson, NOTES ON VIRGINIA, *in Adrienne Koch and William Peden, eds.,* THE LIFE AND SELECTED WRITINGS OF JEFFERSON *(New York, 1944), pp. 255–62.*

by the revisers does not itself contain this proposition; but an amendment containing it was prepared, to be offered to the legislature whenever the bill should be taken up, and farther directing, that they should continue with their parents to a certain age, then to be brought up, at the public expense, to tillage, arts, or sciences, according to their geniuses, till the females should be eighteen, and the males twenty-one years of age, when they should be colonized to such place as the circumstances of the time should render most proper, sending them out with arms, implements of household and of the handicraft arts, seeds, pairs of the useful domestic animals, &c., to declare them a free and independent people, and extend to them our alliance and protection, till they have acquired strength; and to send vessels at the same time to other parts of the world for an equal number of white inhabitants; to induce them to migrate hither proper encouragements were to be proposed. It will probably be asked, Why not retain and incorporate the blacks into the State, and thus save the expense of supplying by importation of white settlers, the vacancies they will leave? Deep-rooted prejudices entertained by the whites; ten thousand recollections, by the blacks, of the injuries they have sustained; new provocations; the real distinctions which nature has made; and many other circumstances, will divide us into parties, and produce convulsions, which will probably never end but in the extermination of the one or the other race. To these objections, which are political, may be added others, which are physical and moral. The first difference which strikes us is that of color. Whether the black of the negro resides in the reticular membrane between the skin and scarf-skin, or in the scarf-skin itself; whether it proceeds from the color of the blood, the color of the bile, or from that of some other secretion, the difference is fixed in nature, and is as real as if its seat and cause were better known to us. And is this difference of no importance? Is it not the foundation of a greater or less share of beauty in the two races? Are not the fine mixtures of red and white, the expressions of every passion by greater or less suffusions of color in the one, preferable to that eternal monotony, which reigns in the countenances, that immovable veil of black which covers the emotions of the other race? Add to these, flowing hair, a more elegant symmetry of form, their own judgment in favor of the whites, declared by their preference of them, as uniformly as is the preference of the Oran-utan for the black woman over those of his own species. The circumstance of superior beauty, is thought worthy attention in the propagation of our horses, dogs, and other domestic animals; why not in that of man? Besides those of color, figure, and hair, there are other physical distinctions proving a difference of race. They have less hair on the face and body. They secrete less by the kidneys, and more by the glands of the skin, which gives them a very strong and disagreeable odor. This greater degree of transpiration, renders them more tolerant of heat, and less so of cold than the whites. . . . They seem to require less sleep. A black after hard labor through the day, will be induced by the slightest amusements to sit up till midnight, or later, though knowing he must be out with first dawn of the morning. They are at least as brave, and more adventuresome. But this may perhaps proceed from a want of forethought, which prevents their seeing a danger till it be present. When present, they do not go through it with more coolness or steadiness than the whites. They are more ardent after their female; but love seems with them to be more an eager desire, than a tender delicate mixture of sentiment and sensation. Their griefs are transient. Those numberless afflictions, which render it doubtful whether heaven has given life to us in mercy or in wrath, are less felt, and sooner forgotten with them. In general, their existence appears to participate more of sensation than reflection. To this must be ascribed their disposition to sleep when abstracted from their diversions, and unemployed in labor. An animal whose body is at rest, and who does not reflect must be disposed to sleep of course. Comparing them by their faculties of memory, reason, and imagination, it appears to me that in memory they are equal to the whites; in reason much inferior, as I think one could scarcely be found capable of tracing and comprehending the investigations of Euclid; and that in imagination they are dull, tasteless, and anomalous. It would be unfair to follow them to Africa for this investigation. We will consider them here, on the same stage with the whites, and where the facts are not apocryphal on which a judgment is to be formed. It will be right to make great allowances for the difference of condition, of education, of conversation, of the sphere in which they move. Many millions of them have been brought to, and born in America. Most of them, indeed, have been confined to tillage, to their own homes, and their own society; yet many have been so situated, that they might have availed themselves of the conversation of their masters; many have been brought up to the handicraft arts, and from that circumstance have always been associated with the whites. Some have been liberally educated, and all have lived in countries where the arts and sciences are cultivated to a considerable degree, and all have had before their eyes samples of the best works from abroad. The Indians, with no advantages of this kind, will often carve figures on their pages not destitute of design and merit. They will crayon out an animal, plant, or a country, so as to

prove the existence of a germ in their minds which only wants cultivation. They astonish you with strokes of the most sublime oratory; such as prove their reason and sentiment strong, their imagination glowing and elevated. But never yet could I find that a black had uttered a thought above the level of plain narration; never saw even an elementary trait of painting or sculpture. In music they are more generally gifted than the whites with accurate ears for tune and time, and they have been found capable of imagining a small catch. Whether they will be equal to the composition of a more extensive run of melody, or of complicated harmony, is yet to be proved. Misery is often the parent of the most affecting touches in poetry. Among the blacks is misery enough, God knows, but no poetry. Love is the peculiar oestrum of the poet. Their love is ardent, but it kindles the senses only, not the imagination. . . . The improvement of the blacks in body and mind, in the first instance of their mixture with the whites, has been observed by every one, and proves that their inferiority is not the effect merely of their condition of life. We know that among the Romans, about the Augustan age especially, the condition of their slaves was much more deplorable than that of the blacks on the continent of America. . . . Yet notwithstanding these . . . discouraging circumstances among the Romans, their slaves were often their rarest artists. They excelled too in science, insomuch as to be usually employed as tutors to their master's children. Epictetus, Terence, and Phaedrus, were slaves. But they were of the race of whites. It is not their condition then, but nature, which has produced the distinction. Whether further observation will or will not verify the conjecture, that nature has been less bountiful to them in the endowments of the head, I believe that in those of the heart she will be found to have done them justice. That disposition to theft with which they have been branded, must be ascribed to their situation, and not to any depravity of the moral sense. The man in whose favor no laws of property exist, probably feels himself less bound to respect those made in favor of others. When arguing for ourselves, we lay it down as a fundamental, that laws, to be just, must give a reciprocation of right; that, without this, they are mere arbitrary rules of conduct, founded in force, and not in conscience; and it is a problem which I give to the master to solve, whether the religious precepts against the violation of property were not framed for him as well as his slave? And whether the slave may not as justifiably take a little from one who has taken all from him, as he may slay one who would slay him? That a change in the relations in which a man is placed should change his ideas of moral right or wrong, is neither new, nor peculiar to the color of the blacks. Homer tells us it was so two thousand six hundred years ago.

Jove fix'd it certain, take whatever day
Makes man a slave, takes half his worth
away.

But the slaves of which Homer speaks were whites. Notwithstanding these considerations which must weaken their respect for the laws of property, we find among them numerous instances of the most rigid integrity, and as many as among their better instructed masters, of benevolence, gratitude, and unshaken fidelity. The opinion that they are inferior in the faculties of reason and imagination, must be hazarded with great diffidence. To justify a general conclusion, requires many observations, even where the subject may be submitted to the anatomical knife, to optical glasses, to analysis by fire or by solvents. How much more then where it is a faculty, not a substance, we are examining; where it eludes the research of all the senses; where the conditions of its existence are various and variously combined; where the effects of those which are present or absent bid defiance to calculation; let me add too, as a circumstance of great tenderness, where our conclusion would degrade a whole race of men from the rank in the scale of beings which their Creator may perhaps have given them. To our reproach it must be said, that though for a century and a half we have had under our eyes the races of black and of red men, they have never yet been viewed by us as subjects of natural history. I advance it, therefore, as a suspicion only, that the blacks, whether originally a distinct race, or made distinct by time and circumstances, are inferior to the whites in the endowments both of body and mind. It is not against experience to suppose that different species of the same genus, or varieties of the same species, may possess different qualifications. Will not a lover of natural history then, one who views the gradations in all the races of animals with the eye of philosophy, excuse an effort to keep those in the department of man as distinct as nature has formed them? This unfortunate difference of color, and perhaps of faculty, is a powerful obstacle to the emancipation of these people. Many of their advocates, while they wish to vindicate the liberty of human nature, are anxious also to preserve its dignity and beauty. Some of these, embarrassed by the question, "What further is to be done with them?" join themselves in opposition with those who are actuated by sordid avarice only. Among the Romans emancipation required but one effort. The slave, when made free, might mix with, without staining the blood of his master. But with us a second is necessary, unknown to history. When freed, he is to be removed beyond the reach of mixture. . . .

MARY BOYKIN CHESNUT

I have seen a Negro woman sold upon the block at auction. I was walking. The woman on the block overtopped the crowd. I felt faint, seasick. The creature looked so like my good little Nancy. She was a bright mulatto, with a pleasant face. She was magnificently gotten up in silks and satins. She seemed delighted with it all, sometimes ogling the bidders, sometimes looking quite coy and modest; but her mouth never relaxed from its expanded grin of excitement. I dare say the poor thing knew who would buy her. My very soul sickened. It was too dreadful. I tried to reason. "You know how women sell themselves and are sold in marriage, from queens downwards, eh? You know what the Bible says about slavery, and marriage. Poor women, poor slaves."

. . .

I wonder if it be a sin to think slavery a curse to any land. Men and women are punished when their masters and mistresses are brutes, not when they do wrong. Under slavery, we live surrounded by prostitutes, yet an abandoned woman is sent out of any decent house. Who thinks any worse of a Negro or mulatto woman for being a thing we can't name? God forgive us, but ours is a monstrous system, a wrong

Reprinted from Mary Boykin Chesnut, A DIARY FROM DIXIE, ed. Ben Ames Williams (Boston, 1949), pp. 10–11, 122–23, 226–28.

and an iniquity! Like the patriarchs of old, our men live all in one house with their wives and their concubines; and the mulattoes one sees in every family partly resemble the white children. Any lady is ready to tell you who is the father of all the mulatto children in every body's household but her own. Those, she seems to think, drop from the clouds. My disgust sometimes is boiling over. Thank God for my country women, but alas for the men! They are probably no worse than men everywhere, but the lower their mistresses, the more degraded they must be.

I think this journal will be disadvantageous for me, for I spend my time now like a spider spinning my own entrails, instead of reading as my habit was in all spare moments.

. . .

I hate slavery. You say there are no more fallen women on a plantation than in London, in proportion to numbers; but what do you say to this? A magnate who runs a hideous black harem with its consequences under the same roof with his lovely white wife, and his beautiful and accomplished daughters? He holds his head as high and poses as the model of all human virtues to these poor women whom God and the laws have given him. From the height of his awful majesty, he scolds and thunders at them, as if he never did wrong in his life. Fancy such a man finding his daughter reading "Don Juan." "You with that immoral book!" And he orders her out of his sight. You see, Mrs. Stowe did not hit the sorest spot. She makes Legree a bachelor.

Someone said: "Oh, I know half a Legree, a man said to be as cruel as Legree. But the other half of him did not correspond. He was a man of polished manners, and the best husband and father and church-member in the world." "Can that be so?" "Yes, I know it. And I knew the dissolute half of Legree. He was high and mighty, but the kindest creature to his slaves; and the unfortunate results of his bad ways were not sold. They had not to jump over ice blocks. They were kept in full view, and were provided for, handsomely, in his will. His wife and daughters, in their purity and innocence, are supposed never to dream of what is as plain before their eyes as the sunlight. And they play their parts of unsuspecting angels to the letter. They profess to adore their father as the model of all earthly goodness."

"Well, yes. If he is rich, he is the fountain from whence all blessings flow."

"The one I have in my eye, my half of Legree, the dissolute half, was so furious in his temper, and so thundered his wrath at the poor women that they were glad to let him do as he pleased if they could only escape his everlasting fault-finding and noisy bluster."

"Now, now, do you know any woman of this generation who would stand that sort of thing?"

"No, never, not for one moment. The make-believe angels were of the last century. We know, and we won't have it. These are Old World stories. Women were brought up not to judge their fathers or their husbands. They took them as the Lord provided, and were thankful."

"How about the wives of drunkards? I heard a woman say once, to a friend, of her husband, as a cruel matter of fact without bitterness and without comment: 'Oh, you have not seen him. He is changed. He has not gone to bed sober in thirty years.' She has had her purgatory, if not what Mrs. —— calls 'the other thing,' here in this world. We all know what a drunken man is. To think that for no crime a person may be condemned to live with one thirty years."

"You wander from the question I asked. Are Southern men worse because of the slave system, and the facile black women?"

"Not a bit! They see too much of them. The barroom people don't drink, the confectionery people loathe candy. Our men are sick of the black sight of them!"

"You think a nice man from the South is the nicest thing in the world?" "I know it. Put him by any other man and see!" "And you say there are no saints and martyrs now; those good women who stand by bad husbands? Eh?" "No use to mince matters. Every body knows the life of a woman whose husband drinks."

"Some men have a hard time, too. I know women who are—well, the very devil and all his imps." "Ah, but men are dreadful animals." "Seems to me those of you who are hardest on men here are soft enough with them when they are present. Now everybody knows I am 'the friend of man' and I defend them behind their backs as I take pleasure in their society, well, before their faces."

Our tongues went on. . . .

This Columbus [South Carolina] is the place for good living, pleasant people, pleasant dinners, pleasant drives. I feel that I have put the dinners in the wrong place. They are the climax of the good things here. This is the most hospitable place in the world, and the dinners are worthy of it. In Washington, there was an endless succession of state dinners. I was kindly used. I do not remember ever being condemned to two dull neighbors; one side or the other was a clever man. So I liked Washington dinners.

In Montgomery there were a few dinners, but the society was not smoothed down. It was—such as it was—given over to balls and suppers. In Charleston, Mr. Chesnut went to gentlemen dinners all the time. No ladies present. Flowers were sent to me, and I was taken to drive and asked to tea. There could not have been nicer suppers. In Richmond, there were balls which I did not attend —and very few to which I was asked; but Mr. Chesnut dined out nearly every day.

But then the breakfasts! The Virginia breakfast is a thing *comme il y en a peu* in the world. Always there were pleasant people. Indeed, I have had a good time everywhere; always clever people, and people I liked, and everybody so good to me.

Here in Columbia, the family dinners are the specialty. You call, or they pick you up and drive home with you. "Oh, stay to dinner," and you stay gladly. They send for your husband, and he comes willingly. Then comes apparently a perfect dinner—you do not see how it could be improved—yet they have not had time to alter things or add because of the additional guests. They have everything of the best. Silver, glass, china, table linen, damask, etc. The planters live "within themselves" as they call it; from the plantations come mutton, beef, poultry, cream, butter, eggs, fruits and vegetables. It is easy to live here, with a cook who has been sent to the best eating house in Charleston to be trained. Old Mrs. Chesnut's Romeo was apprenticed at Jones's, in town. I do not know where Mrs. Preston's got his degrees, but he deserves a medal.

And now for a document *à la* Stowe, about Mrs. Preston's butler, William, and his brother John, and his sister Maria. In Richmond, Mrs. Preston always engaged a room next or opposite hers for Maria, who was her maid. Maggie Howell and Mary Hammy were forced to hunt up a recalcitrant maid late at night. They found the maids sleeping under the roof, where it is almost impossible to stand. They were stretched out in that hot, suffocating place, like sardines in a box. "Maria, do you know how blest you are?" said Mary Hammy, after her return to cleaner and cooler regions. "But I must say that in that stifling low room, where our damsel was stowed away with her likes, packed as if in a box, we found them hilarious. The din was so great, we could hardly make ourselves heard."

Maria often smoothed a dress for me. She loved to talk of her marital relations. She was so sad and mysterious in her dark revelations, I cannot make them very clear. She was married, her husband ill-used her; he did something very bad, that is very wrong, and he left her and then he died. She had no children. Then she would go off to her family history, which I had heard from Mrs. Preston when we were at the Fauquier White Sulphur. This is not a pretty story, but Maria told it leaving out all ugly words. Her mother died when they were quite young. She belonged to a Scotchman, a doctor. Her master married a white lady who did not like Maria and her two brothers; but she was not bad to them while her husband lived. Then the Scotchman died, and the widow found these white-fathered children in her yard a blot on the Scotchman's escutcheon. She sent them to Columbia to be sold. They were delighted to be sold, for they hated her worse than she hated them. Mrs. Preston bought them.

Before I knew the history of the Walkers (William, Maria, John), I remember a scene which took place at a ball given by Mrs. Preston while Mr.

Preston was in Louisiana. Mrs. Preston was resplendent in diamonds, point lace, velvet train, etc. There is a gentle dignity about her which is very attractive, and her voice is low and sweet, and her will is iron. She is an exceedingly well-informed person, but quiet, retiring and reserved. Her apparent gentleness almost amounts to timidity. At that ball, Governor Manning said to me: "Look at sister Caroline! Does she look as if she had the pluck of a heroine?" "How?" "A little while ago, William came to tell her that his brother John was drunk in the cellar, mad with drink, and that he had a carving knife which he was brandishing in his drunken fury and keeping everybody from their business, threatening to kill anyone who dared to go in the basement. They were like a flock of frightened sheep down there. Caroline did not speak to one of us, but followed William down to the basement, holding up her skirts. She found the servants scurrying everywhere, screaming and shouting that John was crazy and going to kill them. John was bellowing like a bull of Basham, knife in hand, chasing them at his pleasure. Caroline walked up to him. 'Give me that knife.' He handed it to her; she laid it on a table. 'And now come with me,' she said, putting her hand on his collar. She led him away to the empty smoke house, and locked him in and put the key in her pocket; and she returned without a ripple on her placid face to show what she had done. She told me of it, smiling and serene as you see her now."

Before the war shut us in, Mr. Preston sent to the lakes for his salmon, to Mississippi for his venison, to England for his mutton and grouse. But the best dish at all of these houses is what the Spanish call "the hearty welcome." Thackeray says at every American table he was first served with "grilled hostess." At the head of the table sat a person fiery-faced, anxious, nervous, inwardly murmuring like Falstaff "would it were night, Hal, and all were well."

At Mulberry, the house is always filled to overflowing, and one day is curiously like another. People are coming and going, carriages driving up or driving off. It has the air of a watering place where one does not pay, and where there are no strangers. At Christmas, the china closet gives up its treasures. The glass, china, silver, fine linen reserved for grand occasions comes forth. But as for the dinner itself, it is only a matter of great quantity; more turkey, more mutton, more partridge, more fish—and more solemn stiffness. Usually, a half-dozen persons unexpectedly dropping in makes no difference; they let the housekeeper know, that is all.

3. The East

The dominant fact of life in Turner's West was the frontier farm. In the South it was plantation slavery, and in the Northeast, the rise of the factory. But these sectional differences were not simple and straightforward. The West was profoundly influenced by changes in transportation and agricultural technology, and even the cotton South was the product of technological change. Conversely, New England had once been a frontier, as had been the Virginia Tidewater. Thus in every part of the nation there

were contradictions and confusions, created in many instances by the graft-
ing of new techniques onto inherited patterns of belief and morality. In
New England, the introduction of the factory system was tied at first to
the traditional moral and social values of the Puritan townsmen. In the
first mills, native labor—usually "factory girls"—ran the machines. Owners
kept close touch with their plants and their employees, so that factories
bore some resemblance to old-fashioned town congregations. In his account
of the beginnings of the mills of Lowell, Massachusetts, Nathan Appleton
conveys a rich sense of these early associations between Puritanism and the
factory—including a passage reminiscent of worship, describing how the
investors "sat by the hour, watching the beautiful movement of this new
and wonderful machine." In the end, of course, the Northeast became the
home of an immigrant labor force and of capitalists who took no real in-
terest in the workings of their factories. But obsession with the Civil War,
among other things, postponed industrial crisis until the end of the century.

NATHAN APPLETON

My connection with the Cotton Manufacture takes date from the year 1811, when I met my friend Mr. Francis C. Lowell, at Edinburgh, where he had been passing some time with his family. We had frequent conversations on the subject of the Cotton Manufacture, and he informed me that he had determined, before his return to America, to visit Manchester, for the purpose of obtaining all possible information on the subject, with a view to the introduction of the improved manufacture in the United States. I urged him to do so, and promised him my co-operation. He returned in 1813. He and Mr. Patrick T. Jackson, came to me one day on the Boston exchange, and stated that they had determined to establish a Cotton manufactory, that they had purchased a water power in Waltham, (Bemis's paper mill,) and that they had obtained an act of incorporation, and Mr. Jackson had

*Reprinted from Nathan Appleton, *INTRODUC-
TION OF THE POWER LOOM AND THE ORIGIN OF
LOWELL *(Lowell, Mass., 1858), pp. 7–16, 32.*

agreed to give up all other business and take the management of the concern.

The capital authorized by the charter was four hundred thousand dollars, but it was only intended to raise one hundred thousand, until the experiment should be fairly tried. Of this sum, Mr. Lowell and Mr. Jackson, with his brothers, subscribed the greater part. They proposed to me that I should take ten thousand of this subscription. I told them that theoretically I thought the business ought to succeed, but all which I had seen of its practical operation was unfavorable; I, however, was willing to take five thousand dollars of the stock, in order to see the experiment fairly tried, as I knew it would be under the management of Mr. Jackson; and I should make no complaint under these circumstances, if it proved a total loss. My proposition was agreed to, and this was the commencement of my interest in the cotton manufacture.

On the organization of the Company I was chosen one of the Directors, and by constant communication with Messrs. Lowell and Jackson, was familiar with the progress of the concern.

The first measure was to secure the services of Paul Moody, of Amesbury, whose skill as a mechanic was well known, and whose success fully justified the choice.

The power loom was at this time being introduced in England, but its construction was kept very secret, and after many failures, public opinion was not favorable to its success. Mr. Lowell had obtained all the information which was practicable about it, and was determined to perfect it himself. He was for some months experimenting at a store in Broad street, employing a man to turn a crank. It was not until the new building at Waltham was completed, and other machinery was running, that the first loom was ready for trial. Many little matters were to be overcome or adjusted, before it would work perfectly. Mr. Lowell said to me that he did not wish me to see it until it was complete, of which he would give me notice. At length the time arrived. He invited me to go out with him and see the loom operate. I well recollect the state of admiration and satisfaction with which we sat by the hour, watching the beautiful movement of this new and wonderful machine, destined as it evidently was, to change the character of all textile industry. This was in the autumn of 1814.

Mr. Lowell's loom was different in several particulars from the English loom, which was afterwards made public. The principal movement was by a cam, revolving with an eccentric motion, which has since given place to the crank motion, now universally used; some other minor improvements have since been introduced, mostly tending to give it increased speed.

The introduction of the power loom made several other changes necessary in the process of weaving. The first was in the dressing, for which Mr. Horrocks of Stockport, had a patent, and of which Mr. Lowell obtained a drawing. On putting it in operation, an essential improvement was made, by which its efficiency was more than doubled. This Waltham dressing machine continues in use, with little change from that time. The stop motion, for winding on the beams for dressing, was original with this Company.

The greatest improvement was in the double speeder. The original fly-frame introduced in England, was without any fixed principle for regulating the changing movements necessary in the process of filling a spool. Mr. Lowell undertook to make the numerous mathematical calculations necessary to give accuracy to these complicated movements, which occupied him constantly for more than a week. Mr. Moody carried them into effect by constructing the machinery in conformity. Several trials at law were made under this patent, involving with other questions, one, whether a mathematical calculation could be the subject of a patent. The last great improvements consisted in a more slack spinning on throstle spindles, and the spinning of filling directly on the cops, without the process of winding. A pleasant anecdote is connected with this last invention. Mr. Shepherd, of Taunton, had a patent for a winding machine, which was considered the best extant. Mr. Lowell was chaffering with him about purchasing the right of using them on a large scale, at some reduction from the price named. Mr. Shepherd refused, saying "you must have them, you cannot do without them, as you know, Mr. Moody." Mr. Moody replied—"I am just thinking that I can spin the cops direct upon the bobbin." "You be hanged," said Mr. Shepherd.

292

"Well, I accept your offer." "No," said Mr. Lowell, "it is too late."

From the first starting of the first power loom, there was no hesitation or doubt about the success of this manufacture. The full capital of four hundred thousand dollars was soon filled up and expended. An addition of two hundred thousand was afterwards made, by the purchase of the place below in Watertown.

After the peace in 1815, I formed a new copartnership with Mr. Benjamin C. Ward. I put in the capital for the purpose of importing British goods, with the understanding that I was not to perform any part of the labor of carrying on the business. I was content with a moderate fortune, but not willing to disconnect myself entirely from business. An accidental circumstance occasioned the continuance of this copartnership until 1830.

At the time when the Waltham Company first began to produce cloth there was but one place in Boston at which domestic goods were sold. This was at a shop in Cornhill kept by Mr. Isaac Bowers, or rather by Mrs. Bowers. As there was at this time only one loom in operation, the quantity accumulating was not very great. However, Mr. Lowell said to me one day that there was one difficulty which he had not apprehended, the goods would not sell. We went together to see Mrs. Bowers. She said every body praised the goods, and no objection was made to the price, but still they made no sales. I told Mr. Lowell, the next time they sent a parcel of the goods to town, to send them to the store of B. C. Ward & Co., and I would see what could be done. The article first made at Waltham, was precisely the article of which a large portion of the manufacture of the country has continued to consist; a heavy sheeting of No. 14 yarn, 37

inches wide, 44 picks to the inch, and weighing something less than three yards to the pound.

That it was so well suited to the public demand, was matter of accident. At that time it was supposed no quantity of cottons could be sold without being bleached; and the idea was to imitate the yard wide goods of India, with which the country was then largely supplied. Mr. Lowell informed me that he would be satisfied with twenty-five cents the yard for the goods, although the nominal price was higher. I soon found a purchaser in Mr. Forsaith, an auctioneer, who sold them at auction at once, at something over thirty cents. We continued to sell them at auction with little variation of the price. This circumstance led to B. C. Ward & Co. becoming permanently the selling agents. In the first instance I found an interesting and agreeable occupation in paying attention to the sales, and made up the first account with a charge of one per cent commission, not as an adequate mercantile commission, but satisfactory under the circumstances. This rate of commission was continued, and finally became the established rate, under the great increase of the manufacture. Thus, what was at the commencement rather unreasonably low, became when the amount of annual sale concentrated in single houses amounted to millions of dollars, a desirable and profitable business.

Under the influence of the war of 1812, the manufacture of cotton had greatly increased, especially in Rhode Island, but in a very imperfect manner. The effect of the peace of 1815 was ruinous to these manufacturers.

In 1816 a new tariff was to be made. The Rhode Island manufacturers were clamorous for a very high specific duty. Mr. Lowell was at Washington, for a considerable time, during the session of Congress. His views on the tariff were much more moderate, and he finally brought Mr. Lowndes and Mr. Calhoun, to support the minimum of 6¼ cents the square yard, which was carried.

In June 1816, Mr. Lowell invited me to accompany him in making a visit to Rhode Island, with a view of seeing the actual state of the manufacture. I was very happy to accept his proposition. At this time the success of the power loom, at Waltham, was no longer matter of speculation or opinion: it was a settled fact. We proceeded to Pawtucket. We called on Mr. Wilkinson, the maker of machinery. He took us into his establishment—a large one; all was silent, not a wheel in motion, not a man to be seen. He informed us that there was not a spindle running in Pawtucket, except a few in Slater's old mill, making yarns. All was dead and still. In reply to questions from Mr. Lowell, he stated, that during the war the profits of manufacturing were so great, that the inquiry never was made whether any improvement could be made in machinery, but how soon it could be turned out. We saw several manufacturers; they were all sad and despairing. Mr. Lowell endeavored to assure them that the introduction of the power loom would put a new face upon the manufacture. They were incredulous;—it might be so, but they were not disposed to believe it. We proceeded to Providence, and returned by way of Taunton. We saw, at the factory of Mr. Shepherd, an attempt to establish a vertical power loom, which did not promise success.

By degrees the manufacturers woke up to the fact, that the power loom was an instrument which changed the whole character of the manufacture; and that by adopting the other improvements which had been made in machinery, the tariff of 1816 was sufficiently protective.

Mr. Lowell adopted an entirely new arrangement, in order to save labor, in passing from one process to another; and he is unquestionably entitled to the credit of being the first person who arranged all the processes for the conversion of cotton into cloth, within the walls of the same building. It is remarkable how few changes have since been made from the arrangements established by him, in the first mill built at Waltham. It is also remarkable, how accurate were his calculations, as to the expense at which goods could be made. He used to say, that the only circumstance which made him distrust his own calculations, was, that he could bring them to no other result but one which was too favorable to be credible. His calculations, however, did not lead him so far as to imagine that the same goods which were then selling at thirty cents a yard, would ever be sold at six cents, and without a loss to the manufacturer, as has since been done in 1843, when cotton was about five or six cents a pound. His care was especially devoted to arrangements for the moral character of the operatives employed. He died in 1817, at the early age of 42, beloved and respected by all who knew him. He is entitled to the credit of having introduced the new system in the cotton manufacture, under which it has grown up so rapidly. For, although Messrs. Jackson and Moody were men of unsurpassed talent and energy in their way, it was Mr. Lowell who was the informing soul, which gave direction and form to the whole proceeding.

The introduction of the cotton

manufacture in this country, on a large scale, was a new idea. What would be its effect on the character of our population was a matter of deep interest. The operatives in the manufacturing cities of Europe, were notoriously of the lowest character, for intelligence and morals. The question therefore arose, and was deeply considered, whether this degradation was the result of the peculiar occupation, or of other and distinct causes. We could not perceive why this peculiar description of labor should vary in its effects upon character from all other occupation.

There was little demand for female labor, as household manufacture was superseded by the improvements in machinery. Here was in New England a fund of labor, well educated and virtuous. It was not perceived how a profitable employment has any tendency to deteriorate the character. The most efficient guards were adopted in establishing boarding houses, at the cost of the Company, under the charge of respectable women with every provision for religious worship. Under these circumstances, the daughters of respectable farmers were readily induced to come into these mills for a temporary period.

The contrast in the character of our manufacturing population compared with that of Europe, has been the admiration of the most intelligent strangers who have visited us. The effect has been to more than double

the wages of that description of labor from what they were before the introduction of this manufacture. This has been, in some measure, counteracted, for the last few years, by the free trade policy of the government; a policy, which fully carried out, will reduce the value of labor with us, to an equality with that of Europe.

It was the Americans who first introduced the manufacture of heavy goods by the application of the least amount of labor to the greatest quantity of raw material, thus producing a description of goods cheaper to the consumer than any heretofore existing. This system the English have been obliged to follow, and have even adopted our name of domestics, whilst they have the advantage of using the cheaper cotton of India, which the Americans have not yet done, but which they will surely find themselves compelled to do.

In 1818, Mr. Calhoun visited the establishment at Waltham, with the apparent satisfaction of having himself contributed to its success. It is lamentable to think that in 1832, under the alluring vision of a separate Southern confederacy, he should have become the active enemy of the manufacture which was doing so much for the interest of the planters, and that the influence of his name has continued to keep them in that error.

III. RECENT INTERPRETATION

Some of the paradoxes and contradictions suggested by the preceding documents were explored with great subtlety by an English historian, Marcus Cunliffe, in his book, *The Nation Takes Shape*. Cunliffe recognized that Turner's sections were important and that they sometimes carried ideological associations: the association of "democracy" with the West, for example;

"Europe" with the East; or "aristocracy" with the seaboard South. But Cunliffe had the benefit of the work of two generations of post-Turner historians behind him, two generations that had been constantly debating and revising the Turnerian scheme of things. The outcome of the debates and the revisions, as Cunliffe saw it, was a very complex, subtle, and elusive picture of the young nation of the early nineteenth century. Turner's vision of young America was comparatively simple (though by no means simple-minded). Cunliffe, on the other hand, took complexity and contradiction as his starting points, and set out to explain how Americans had quickly developed into "a people at once erratic and straightforward, self-conscious and demonstrative, friendly and suspicious, tolerant and bigoted, radical and conservative, confident and nostalgic."

MARCUS CUNLIFFE

In summing up the quality of the period 1789–1837 two temptations should be avoided. One is that of investing it with a false aura of tranquillity. In some respects, especially up to 1815, it was a time of prolonged crisis, full of regret and foreboding, hostility and confusion. The other danger is of assuming that the period constitutes an "era" of its own, separate from what came before and after, instead of being merely a half-century removed from the continuum of American history.

There is nevertheless some point in regarding the period as an entity and in trying to identify its special features. After all, its terminal dates have a certain force. At least 1789 has, as the beginning of the United States under a new Constitution. The working-out of that Constitution, in its various governmental, judicial, political, economic, social, and patriotic implications, is in large part the story of the period. As for 1837, it or its near neighbors in the decade of the 1830's can be argued

Reprinted from Marcus Cunliffe, THE NATION TAKES SHAPE: 1789–1837 *(Chicago: University of Chicago Press, 1959), pp. 181–201, by permission of the publisher.*

to mark the inauguration of another era. . . .

Granted that there are some features of the time that disappear subsequently—its homogeneity of population and its pre-industrial economy are two of the chief examples—nevertheless, the American character seems to have been formed in essence within a generation of George Washington's accession to the presidency. How else are we to account for the remarkable freshness, even for the present day, of Alexis de Tocqueville's *Democracy in America,* which was based on a visit to the United States in 1831–32? "National character" is a hazy expression. But for our approximate purposes we may think of it as an assemblage of beliefs and patterns of behavior which are widely recognized, inside and outside the country in question, as being more common among its citizens than among those of other nations. If this clumsy description is acceptable, then we may go on to suggest that Tocqueville's diagnosis of American attitudes to commerce, to social class, to politics, to literature, and a dozen other matters could be applied with surprising relevance to the America of 1870 or even 1950.

One might object that Tocqueville

was not really writing about the United States but about the social and political phenomenon of democracy, and that his book is therefore not a guide to American character but a brilliant piece of intellectual prophecy relating to the whole Western world. The criticism cannot be altogether brushed aside. Now and then, in the interests of his thesis, he did overstress the "democratic" ethos of America and the correspondingly "aristocratic" nature of Europe, making the one stand schematically for tomorrow and the other for yesterday. However, the objection can be answered in large part by pointing out that Tocqueville's diary of his American travels—a day-to-day record—embodies the same observations. So, broadly speaking, do the travel narratives of other contemporary European visitors, and so do the commentaries by Americans of the period when they discuss their native qualities. Then, as now, the South was held to be an exception to the prevailing American mood of egalitarian bustle. Then, as now, the more recently settled western areas were praised by some witnesses for their additional informality or "democracy" and criticized by others for their excessive uncouthness. But on the whole, whether favorable or not, the picture drawn by Tocqueville and by lesser men was consistent and is still recognizable. . . .

To observers in the early nineteenth century, then, Americans seem restless, competitive, "go-ahead" (another revealing Americanism coined in Jackson's time), egalitarian, naïve, serious, coarse and importunate yet in some ways prim and moralistic, matter-of-fact and yet imbued with vague, soaring notions of American futurity. This last point was wittily made by Tocqueville, in the comment that the American mind is either concentrated upon

the practical and parochial or else diffused in vast and formless reverie, and that in between lies a vacuum. One could go on adding almost indefinitely to the list of American characteristics identified during the period, and nearly all would support the assertion that American "national character" has not altered fundamentally since its early definitions. Similarly, if we glance at the conflicting elements in the picture and at the actual controversies that have separated individual from individual and section from section in American history, there appear to be certain enduring features in the record.

However, . . . it is extremely difficult to analyze American experience in satisfactory terms. Some Europeans and a few disillusioned Americans during the period 1789–1837 gave up the effort or concluded that the effort was not worth making. The United States, they felt, was an unstable experiment, hopelessly divided within itself, lacking in all the necessary safeguards of true nationhood, like some badly designed Mississippi steamboat whirling downriver until the irrevocable collision or explosion shattered her. Even Tocqueville, immeasurably more judicious than most spectators, doubted whether the Union could long hold together—and of course it did not.

By contrast, a number of recent American historians have dwelt upon the essential soundness of their country's early disposition. Seizing like Tocqueville on the absence of feudalism as the basic clue to American national development—on the fact that she was "born in broad daylight," unhampered by the past, dating the origin of her own national epic no farther back than 1776 and therefore able to carry the national legend around with her, so to speak, as a portable heritage—seizing on this truth, these historians have interpreted America's past as an organic affair. American politics were to a considerable degree a matter of *ad hoc* local or sectional bargaining. American ideology was an affair of fine shades, qualifications, ambiguities, contradictions. Perhaps, in such a view, it could be held that Emerson came near to grasping a subtle truth. In his unsystematic, perceptive way he typified the American intellect. He may have touched the heart of American reality with his doctrine of "compensation," according to which dualities are friendly rather than inimical, since they cancel one another out and thus lead to a kind of equilibrium:

> Foolish hands may mix and mar;
> Wise and sure the issues are.
> Round they roll till dark is light.

Some of these newer interpretations are highly sophisticated, so much so that they come full circle and are able to make good use of the old cynical-contemptuous, European view of the United States as a mere shapeless agglomerate. Thus they might fasten upon and extract significance from a casual remark made by the British visitor Mrs. Trollope as she watched a Methodist camp meeting in Ohio. The passage as a whole, from her book *Domestic Manners of the Americans* (1832) is censorious. But she also admits, "I . . . experienced a strange vibration between tragic and comic feeling." In such an *eperçu* a modern commentator might find much food for thought, for it hints at the tantalizing oddity of some sides of American history that could mean little or could mean far more than appears at first glimpse. The revivalist frenzy Mrs. Trollope witnesses is cheap, banal, erotic. Yet it has a pathos, a novelty, a colloquial vigor, a directness of emotion that go deeper than the occasion—like that of a Negro spiritual (the word "spiritual" being both neologist noun and poignant adjective).

Between the sweeping disapproval of a Frances Trollope and the refined insights of a study like R. W. B. Lewis' *The American Adam: Innocence, Tragedy, and Tradition in the Nineteenth Century* (1955) come a quanitity of attempts to interpret American history in terms of some bold polarity. In the widest terms of all, the division is seen as that of America versus Europe, which can be taken to imply democracy versus rigidity, innocence versus experience, and so on. Or, in the influential thesis of Frederick Jackson Turner, as West versus East, which represents a not-too-different polarity. Some scholars, for instance, now expound American history within an "Atlantic community," within which in turn there is a boundary between West and East—a boundary that shifts steadily inland across America, so that during part of the nineteenth century the eastern seaboard of the United States is linked economically and culturally with Europe rather than with the trans-Appalachian West.

Or again, there is the familiar polarity of Jefferson versus Hamilton, which can be visualized as a contest between Republicanism and Federalism, or agrarianism and capitalism, or rural life and urbanism, or debtor and creditor, or free trade and the tariff, or Jacksonianism and the "Monster Bank," or state rights and centralization in government, or—by extension—North and South, which can be again stylized as a division between Massachusetts and Virginia or between freedom and slavery. Present in some interpretations is a theory of class conflict or of sectional controversy as being principally economic in origin.

There is much to be said for these

polarities. They have the merit of clarity. They satisfy our ingrained habit of thinking dualistically, in terms of body and soul, god and devil, and so on; we respond readily, for example, to Emerson's idea of an American schism between "the party of the Past and the party of the Future" or to George Bancroft's statement of an immemorial feud between "the capitalist and laborer, the house of Have and the house of Want." They escape the current tendency in historiography to explain away conflicts as mere smoke screens behind which men maneuver and chaffer for "real" benefits.

The arguments epitomized in the string of contests cited above *were* important to those involved in them. Apart from the slavery dispute, perhaps no American controversy was as implacable as some in Europe. They often seem almost pastorally mild after one has looked at the mortal enmities of the Old World during the period. But though in this sense they might be circumscribed quarrels, some of them implied profound differences of viewpoint on how to shape the future. Americans under their new Constitution were gravely conscious that their decisions would be imprinted upon and enlarged in the lives of successive generations. Theirs, they wished to believe, was *tabula rasa*—the clean slate.

But current historiography has nevertheless made some of these polarities seem blurred and dubious; Americans even more than the rest of mankind have been described as likelier to choose "and . . . and" than "either . . . or." . . . Republicanism versus Federalism and Jackson versus the B.U.S. are instances of contests that are by no means clear cut. It is not just that we are uncertain which side is hero and which villain, but that we are not always able to say with confidence which

side is which, so confusing and sudden are the shifts in allegiance. Moreover, though some of the polarities seem nearly synonymous and though all are to some extent linked with one another, it is not possible to arrange them meaningfully by parceling them into teams, like this:

America	Europe
West	East
Democracy	Aristocracy
Agrarianism	Capitalism
State Rights	Centralization
South	North

There is a rough correspondence, perhaps, in each of the two groups. But it is so rough as to be almost worthless. Worse than that, it is positively misleading. Overly simple groupings of this kind have led some American historians to attach a spurious dynamism to geography (for such men, one feels, if Bishop Berkeley had never written his celebrated line, "Westward the course of empire," it would have been necessary to invent it. How fitting that the line was stamped on the cover of the first volume of Bancroft's sonorously patriotic history, published in 1834). Others have exaggerated the difference between Europe and the United States, making Europe more tyrannical and obsolescent than it really was and the United States more freedom-loving and progressive than any nation could be under heaven. One can but maintain that Turner's frontier thesis, while "true" and "useful" within limits, suffers from being so simplistic in shape. In his day there were cogent reasons for attempting a synthesis of geography-*cum*-idealism. And in European history, partly because one is dealing with fixed geographical/ethnic areas, partly because of the severity of European controversies and their relation to a well-defined class and occupational structure, it *is* possible to make up quite coherent "teams" of the sort shown above.

For the United States, the thing cannot be done. As some recent neoconservative writings reveal, the teams will not line up properly. What is "South" doing in the left-hand table if "Aristocracy" is in the right-hand column? One cannot construct an American "conservative" or "liberal" genealogy by any straightforward method. The result is full of illegitimacies, adoptions, divorces, remarriages.

If two teams cannot be chosen, is there any other way of representing the issues of American history for the period (which, to reiterate, embodies or foreshadows most of the major problems in American domestic experience)? The word "polarity" suggests a slightly less obvious diagram, by reminding us of a compass. So let us construct a diagram of polarities set out as a kind of compass and using the same twelve labels as before. North, South, East, and West, though standing for states of mind as well as actual geographical areas of the United States, can be left in their conventional places, as if they were compass points.

This is a more plausible representation. If we regard each of the twelve "points" as a concept or a cluster of attitudes, then this diagram suggests better than the two-team listing the complexities of the American situation. In fact, the diagram could be thought of more fitly as a spectrum of continuous and continuously modified color, each "point" shading off into those adjacent. Neighboring attitudes are shown to bear a sympathetic relationship to one another—like that between "centralization" and "capitalism." In fact, so do any four attitudes within a quadrant—say "aristocracy," "South," "state rights," "agrarianism." The polar opposites can be seen as mutually antagonistic. Here is a pictorial representation that avoids some of the oversimplifications we have alluded to.

However, the diagram is still not really satisfactory, and no reshuffling of the points will altogether remedy its weaknesses. One trouble is that it perpetuates the notion that the West is more innately "American" than the East and that the West is almost diametrically opposed to "capitalism." Also, of course, the diagram is static. It does not take into account the fluctuations of American development: the process, for instance, by which North and West were drawn together, instead of West to South, or that by which "state rights" became a southern instead of a New England doctrine.

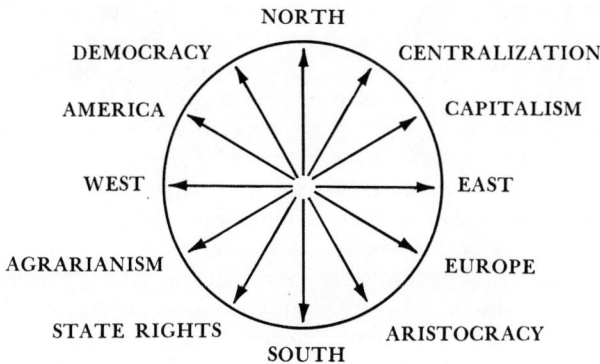

Like the effort to compile two rival teams, it overlooks a basic truth about America. This is the truth grasped by Tocqueville, though he missed some of the historical factors that underlay it and though he emphasized the Europe-America polarity a little too much: in comparison with at any rate the Europe of his father's day, the United States was an amazingly unformed and unfettered society. What was already formed, thanks to the British heritage and to the happy outcome of the Revolutionary War, was acquisitive, Protestant, libertarian, reasonably law-abiding. The rest was a matter for posterity to determine or, rather, for the Americans themselves to impose upon posterity, since they were free agents to a unique degree.

In this whole context rather than in preoccupation with the frontier, the United States was differentiated from Europe (though, in relation to the European continent, Britain itself was a more open and flexible society).

This is not to contend that America had no problems during the period or that she solved them. She was haunted by colonialism and wracked with dissension at the same time that she grew and thrived and exulted. But the point to stress, if we are searching for interpretations, is this: There are ideological polarities of real import. The nature and mission of the United States, the struggle to make it in a new likeness without reference to the Old World, constituted a vital quest, and the continuing influence of Europe posed a genuine dilemma. The wrangle over the balance between the federal government and the states, while it later lost much of its gravity, was during the period a weighty matter. The mutual hostilities of North and South embraced profound issues of government, political economy, and human nature.

These are all significant, and so are other issues. . . . Moreover, Americans alive between 1789 and 1837 took them seriously. But—and, here we reach the crux—though the polarities are more or less fixed, the personnel are not. The arguments stand fast, rooted in permanent considerations of law, order, and society, heavy and dignified (if not, as we have seen, speculative in the sense of academic philosophy). The men who employ the arguments, however, constantly change their own standpoints. They change their minds and their political parties, and the parties likewise reverse names and strategies. In 1815 New England and its "godlike" Daniel Webster adopt the extreme state-rights position, while the South and its spokesman John C. Calhoun breathe the spirit of nationalism. Fifteen years later, Calhoun and the South are sectionalist; Webster and his region stand for the federal Union. Similar examples can be found, not merely in politics, throughout the land and throughout the half-century.

Why? Not because politicians were all rogues or because Americans were all vulgar opportunists. But for two reasons. First, that since the United States was inchoate, there were no permanent sectional, political, economic, religious, or occupational groupings of the kind which are immediately recognizable in Europe and which impart a degree of coherence to European affairs even when these affairs include revolutions or other violent upheavals. American society was not entirely fluid; all sorts of rules and associations affected its operation. But they did not form inviolable taboos and imperatives. American society was tentative. Its rules could be modified; "joiners" could be and were "leavers," moving from one societal institution to another at will, and sometimes abruptly from one polar extreme to the other. Such looseness perhaps encouraged cynicism and corruptness of purpose, as permissive situations tend to. But expediency was not an inherent vice.

The second reason has already been suggested. It is that the range of possible choices was, by European standards, extraordinarily wide. Not merely was the American at liberty to change his occupation, his religious and political affiliations, his home and state; he saw before him all sorts of more solemn alternatives on which he was required by the nature of American democracy to have an opinion. His vote was endlessly solicited, his brain teased by conundrums about internal improvements, interstate commerce, the limits of suffrage, policy on land settlement, new states, tariffs. What he decided might make or mar his country. But how on such complex questions *could* he decide? No wonder that the average American changed his mind or did not bother to have an opinion or voted according to calculations of how his pocket would feel—and heavy financial stakes were frequently involved. Again, he was not being inherently irresponsible.

To recapitulate, the polarities are more or less fixed, the personnel are not. The people choose the position that matches their need or conviction of the moment and will shift to another if pressed. Some verities or some symbols of nationality—the Christian church, the Declaration of Independence, the Constitution, the memory of George Washington—are unchallenged in their broad generality; they are in the possession of virtually all Americans. The rest are a common heritage that may be repudiated or accepted as the situation dictates. The comedy of the situation is not lost upon Americans; one side of their nature, in the

eyes of European visitors, is a cliché-ridden pomposity that makes them talk all too often like Supreme Court justices or like Independence Day orators. But the other side is a glorious irreverence; they coin big, nonsensical words like "splendiferous," revel in mock solemnity, delight in puncturing the national self-image, for the disparity between the unchanging pieties of nationhood and the nimble uses to which they are put is rich material for the humorist.

A diagram that sought to convey something of this would be too complicated to depict here. In part, though, it could still be conceived of as a fixed compass card of concept polarities, except that we might remove the four geographical labels—North, South, East, West—from the card and perhaps substitute other polarities. On top of the fixed card we might visualize another, floating dial. The superimposed dial would represent various sectional, political, and occupational groups pivoted loosely above the permanent card, defining positions in relation to it: a dial fluctuating, swayed, so cynical-righteous that Tocqueville shuddered a little at the intellectual slovenliness of America, so unsteady that he foresaw the dismemberment of the Union, so buoyant that he rightly marveled at the fortuitous miracle of American democracy.

Such a device may serve to elucidate much that is characteristic and puzzling in American experience. From George Washington to Andrew Jackson (and since), it is the symbol of a people at once erratic and straightforward, self-conscious and demonstrative, friendly and suspicious, tolerant and bigoted, radical and conservative, confident and nostalgic. "Inconsistencies cannot both be right," says the philosopher Imlac in Samuel Johnson's *Rasselas;* "but, imputed to man, they may both be true."

His comment hints that one might enter similar claims on behalf of other peoples. Even so, as the events of the formative half-century from 1789 to 1837 may have made plain, it is no accident that while the American language abounds in such words and expressions as "footloose" and "every which way," many of America's national and state mottoes emphasize unity, sameness, perpetuity. Not all these expressions and mottoes were coined during the period but nearly all were anticipated then.

HISTORIOGRAPHICAL NOTE

The field of social history, while it is not exactly new to historians in the United States, is still underdeveloped in comparison with political history, and for the period between the American Revolution and the Civil War, social history is an especially sparse field. There are two basic reasons for this state of affairs. In the first place, the kinds of statistical data that must underlie sound modern social history are not easily available for the pre-Civil War period. More important, historians and sociologists have not yet developed the theories and hypotheses that will enable historians to work in social history with ease and fluency.

The slow progress of the social history of the period has interesting consequences. It is astonishing, for example, that a book written over 130 years ago is still one of the most valuable analyses of American society in the early nineteenth century. Alexis de Tocqueville's *Democracy in America* is still consulted by American historians, not as a document *from* the period but as an account *of* what American society was like in the years of Jackson and Emerson. Tocqueville worked entirely without the sophisticated techniques and hypotheses of modern scholarship. His insights were intuitive, his data thin, his biases powerful, but his work has not yet been replaced. Another consequence of the lack of work in social history is a virtual absence of material on the range of ordinary experiences typified by the documents in section two of this chapter. There are rare virtuoso technical performances on purely statistical data, such as Yasukichi Yasuba's *Birth Rates of the White Population in the United States, 1800–1860, an Economic Study* (Baltimore, 1961). And, at the other extreme, there are similarly polished books on writers, poets, and other intellectuals, the best of which is probably R. W. B. Lewis' *The American Adam: Innocence, Tragedy and Tradition in the Nineteenth Century* (Chicago, 1955). Yasuba's book is a highly technical study of the causes of a declining birth rate, with important implications concerning the influence of the frontier and industrial development, but its very technical subtlety puts it intellectually out of reach for many historians and most students. Lewis' *The American Adam* has implications as significant as those of Yasuba, but Lewis worked within a framework of literary criticism as technical in its way as Yasuba's statistics and has, similarly, failed to influence many historians working in the broader fields of social and political history.

Despite this general situation, there are a handful of recent books that brilliantly illuminate various features of the social landscape in America between the War of 1812 and the Civil War. Stanley Elkins' *Slavery: a Problem in American Institutional and Intellectual Life* (Second ed., Chicago, 1968) is a superb theoretical account of two separate social phenomena related to slavery and the Civil War. Elkins examines, in a highly innovative way, the effects of slavery on the social personality of the black man in America. And, as a parallel, he also probes the effect of the lack of institutional restraints and involvements on the abolitionists in the North. Elkins' hypotheses go to the quick of major questions about social experience in America, and they have both provoked controversy and stimulated new kinds of research.

Three distinct social groups were brought into existence as a direct result of the slave system: the slaves themselves, the abolitionists, and the planters. Elkins' *Slavery* is a fine introduction to the first two groups. By far the best work on the social psychology of the planters, however, is William R. Taylor's *Cavalier and Yankee: The Old South and the American National Character* (New York, 1969), which very skillfully traces the development of the mythic personalities of the cavalier and the yankee. *Cavalier and Yankee* can be read very profitably in conjunction with *The Mind of the South* (New York, 1941) by Wilbur J. Cash.

The best work on the West since Turner is Henry Nash Smith's *Virgin Land: The American West as Symbol and Myth* (New York, 1950). For Turner, the West was an actual social experience that remolded men's ways of thinking and acting. Smith, on the other hand, is concerned with the ways in which the West as an *idea* molded the social consciousness of Americans from Jefferson to Turner himself. Using folk-myth, popular magazines and novels, political documents, and literature about the West, Smith discusses the kinds of symbols that clustered around the frontier and formed what amounted to a national mythology about the meaning of American life.

A more recent and very compelling examination of the development of young America is an unfinished work of Perry Miller, *The Life of the Mind in America from the Revolution to the Civil War* (New York, 1965). Miller, who may have been America's finest modern historian, produced a superb analysis of the ways in which Americans interpreted and preserved their experience through the mechanism of evangelical revivals.

6. *Antebellum Social Thought,*
1815–1860

INTRODUCTION

If any one man could be said to represent the spirit of American society in the exuberant decades between 1815 and 1860, it would be Ralph Waldo Emerson. There was a dark side to Emerson, aspects of doubt and even tragedy, but in public, in the endless lectures and tours that made him famous as the "Sage of Concord," Emerson presented a buoyant, optimistic face. There were, he often said, only two "parties" in any society, a party of the past and a party of "movement," and he always associated himself with words and ideas like "movement," "growth," "freedom," "self-reliance," and "progress." In 1882, Emerson was asked to deliver a lecture about America as it had seemed in the years of his youth. He was by then an old man, and his memory for detail was cloudy, but he had no trouble recalling the spirit of the 1830's and 1840's. The "young men," he said, "were born with knives in their brain." His generation was committed to experiment, to criticism of old institutions and old ways of thought. It was, he went on, "the age of severance, of dissociation, of freedom, of analysis, of detachment. Every man for himself. . . . The social sentiments are weak; the sentiment of patriotism is weak; veneration is low; the natural affections feebler than they were. . . . There is an universal resistance to ties and ligaments once supposed essential to civil society. The new race is stiff, heady and rebellious; they are fanatic in freedom; they hate tolls, taxes, turnpikes, banks, hierarchies, governors, yea, almost laws."

Between the War of 1812 and the Civil War, Americans passed through an extraordinary experience. Everywhere, extremely rapid growth was the most obvious fact of life—in population, in territory, in transportation, and in agricultural and industrial production. This manifold experience of growth had a paradoxical effect on many Americans—Emerson's young men with "knives in their brain." It made them confident, even boastful, about such things as "progress" and "destiny," but rapid development also fed their attitude of relentless criticism of inherited ideas and institutions. Every received dogma and social arrangement was subjected to critical challenge. The churches—the most important social institution of the colonial period— were tested most severely. One by one states put an end to governmental support of religion. The power of the ministers over their congregations waned. The doctrines of colonial Puritanism, based on discipline and restraint, gave way to unrestrained and undisciplined revivalism. In politics, the party of restraint, the Federalist Party, withered away. One by one, restrictions on the political activities of the "common" man were cut away. Finally, the Union itself and the Constitution which was its cement, were challenged. Abolitionists in the North and "fire-eaters" in the South decided that the most general institution of all, the nation itself, ought to be dissolved.

But rebellion, criticism, and what Emerson called "severance" were only half the story. As Americans—especially the young ones—criticized and rejected received truths and organizations, they also set about making their own proposals for new ways of living. The outcome was a generation of radicalism with a harvest of unusual schemes for life. In the atmosphere of freedom generated by growth and criticism, young men and women seemed gripped by an extraordinary confidence that they could propose any scheme that came to mind—vegetarianism, communism, the abolition of slavery—found a community or movement on the idea, and wait for followers to swell the movement into a national crusade or revival.

As a result the intellectual history of the period is saturated with quixotic proposals for social reform. Most of these reform movements had as their primary goal some form of "liberation" for the individual, goals ranging from freeing men from the clutches of the rum habit to freeing slaves from their masters. But such generalized desires to liberate men from various forms of captivity, some real and some imagined, were balanced by a persistent fear of *too much* freedom, a longing for the restoration of restraint, discipline, and hierarchy. On the most obvious level, this fear of freedom was manifested in Southern defenses of slavery, but the same kind of fear led to the creation of religious "reform" movements like Mormonism or Shakerism, movements designed to restore order within new social arrangements.

From some angles, the history of the United States during the decades between 1815 and 1860 makes harmonious and digestible sense. The settlement of the frontier, the beginnings of industrialization, the emergence of political parties with sectional and economic components—all these broad tendencies fit together into a comprehensible pattern. But in the spaces left by such large tendencies, the intellectual life of Americans was varied, confused, and paradoxical. In the selections that follow, a few patches from a crazy-quilt are presented, not so much in order to summarize developments as to point to the perimeters of the subject.

I. EARLY INTERPRETATION

The first important attempt to write the intellectual history of the United States was made by Vernon Louis Parrington in *Main Currents of American*

Thought, published in 1927. The following selection is from the introduction to Parrington's second volume, which covered the period between 1800 and the Civil War, in which Parrington identified "romance" as the dominant theme of the period. His interpretation was fundamentally economic: The experience of expansion created an atmosphere of 'exuberance and experiment—the stuff of which "romance" is made. Into this setting came two powerful intellectual influences: French revolutionary ideology and the individualism of British political and economic thought. But Parrington was working under the influence of Frederick Jackson Turner, and he believed that economic development had had different results in different sections. The atmosphere of criticism and experimentation that Emerson described was therefore different in the North, the South, and the West, and the influence of French and British ideas was correspondingly sectionalized.

VERNON LOUIS PARRINGTON

. . . The half century that lay between these dramatic episodes [the War of 1812 and the Civil War] was a period of extravagant youth, given over to a cult of romanticism that wrought as many marvels as Aaron's rod. In the South, in New England, and on the western frontier, it laid hold of men's minds, consuming the stubble of eighteenth-century harvests, sweeping away the drab realisms of a cautious past, and offering in their stead more alluring ideals. Revolutions, greater and lesser, trod on each other's heels; the common adventure led into unexplored paths; and the final outcome for which it was all preparing was the emergence of a new middle class that in the succeeding half century was to subdue America to middle-class ends.

Such drastic overturnings of the customary and familiar, such swift ruptures with the past, quite evidently do not come from trivial causes. Men do

not put off the old before the new is ready; and if in those credulous years they turned romantic and refused to heed the counsels of experience, it was because the soil had been new-plowed for the growing of such crops as their fathers had not known. The grapes from which the wine of romance is vinted, it must not be forgotten, are rooted in the common earth. The loveliest romantic dreams spring from a parentage that is humbly prosaic. There is no more fruitful source of romantic hope than a fluid economics that overflows all narrow preëmptions and sweeps away the restrictions that hamper free endeavor. With fresh economic realms to conquer, the dullest plodder discovers a stimulus in anticipation that sets him upon creating a Utopia. The breaking up of the static, the bold adventuring upon new worlds, is the fertile soil in which romance springs most luxuriantly. It needs no uncommon eyes, surely, to discover in the swift changes that came to America in the wake of the second English war, the seedbed of those ebullient romanticisms which in politics and economics, in theology and literature, turned away so contemptuously from the homespun past. Of a sudden

Reprinted from Vernon Louis Parrington, MAIN CURRENTS IN AMERICAN THOUGHT *(New York: Harcourt, Brace & World, Inc., 1927-1930), II, vii–xiii, by permission of the publisher.*

America was becoming a new world with potentialities before undreamed of; and this new America was no longer content with the narrow ways of a more cautious generation. The older America of colonial days had been static, rationalistic, inclined to pessimism, fearful of innovation, tenacious of the customary. It conceived of human nature as evil, and accounting men incurably wicked, it opened no doors to Utopian dreams of a golden future. The round of daily life was confined within a narrow domestic economy, with few and rare changes in social status. Growth in population came mainly from natural increase. Exploitation was laborious, and such wealth as was laid by was gained in shop and field, in fisheries and shipping. With its expectations cramped by a drab agrarianism, it was content to remain primitively self-sufficient, not given to seeking riches by speculative short-cuts, clinging to the habitual, distrustful of change.

During the thirty-odd years between the Peace of Paris and the end of the War of 1812 that older America was dying. The America that succeeded was a shifting, restless world youthfully optimistic, eager to better itself, bent on finding easier roads to wealth than the plodding path of natural increase. It conceived of human nature as acquisitive, and accounting acquisitiveness a cardinal virtue, it set out to inquire what opportunities awaited it in the unexploited resources of the continent. The cautious ways of earlier generations were become as much out of date as last year's almanac. New commonwealths were arising in the wilderness; immigration from war-torn Europe was pouring in; wild lands were daily coming on the market. Money was to be made by the enterprising, and the multitude of the en-terprising was augmenting with the expansion of the settlements. The ideal of a static society having been put away, progress was assumed to be the first law of nature, and innovation was accepted as the sign and seal of progress. It was our first great period of exploitation, and from it emerged, as naturally as the cock from the mother egg, the spirit of romance, gross and tawdry in vulgar minds, dainty and refined in the more cultivated. But always romance. The days of realism were past, and it was quietly laid away with the wig and smallclothes of an outgrown generation.

Unfortunately economic romance is more imperious in its demands than literary romance. Its dreams follow objective desires, and in America of those days of new beginnings the desires of diverse economic groups conducted straight to antagonistic imperialisms. The major interests of the three great sections of the country differentiated more and more sharply. The East was discovering its Utopia in an industrial capitalistic order. With the flocking of immigrants to the factories began the extraordinary expansion of the cities and the movement of centralization that was eventually to transform America from a rural to an urban society, supplanting the farmer by the business man and disintegrating the traditional psychology. The new manufacturing and the new finance were subjecting an agrarian people to the dislocations and readjustments implied in the industrial revolution, the outcome of which no man could foresee. The reaction of this new industrialism upon the South was immediate. With the improvements in textile manufacturing came greater demands upon the new southern staple, and an agriculture that had long been static with its traditional crops of indigo, rice, and tobacco, began to look forward confidently to a Utopia founded on cotton, and conceived an imperialistic dream of expanding fields of white bolls and black slaves, reaching into Mexico and embracing the West Indies. The new South left off apologizing for slavery and hoping for its ultimate extinction. Slavery had become enormously profitable and it proposed to exploit the Negro as frankly as New England was exploiting the Irish immigrant, but more humanely if possible, in something of the patriarchal spirit.

Meanwhile in the Inland Empire was arising an economics that looked with little favor on the imperialisms of eastern capitalism or southern slavery; an economics equalitarian in temper, decentralizing in impulse; nourished on the idealism of the Declaration of Independence, but interpreting it to mean the natural right of every free citizen to satisfy his acquisitive instinct by exploiting the national resources in the measure of his shrewdness. Democratic in professions, it was middle-class in spirit and purpose. Discovering the inflowing tide of immigration to be favorable to speculation, it sought its Utopia in county-seat towns where land holdings mounted in value with every new wave. No narrow horizons bounded a realm that stretched to the Pacific and into the remote Northwest, and no stodgy ways of money-getting could satisfy men whose imaginations ranged through such spaces. This country was theirs to do with as they chose, and if eastern capitalism or southern slavery interfered with their inalienable rights, their Sharp's rifles were at hand for defense. In the vast territory drained by the Mississippi—the "Valley of Democracy," a recent writer has chosen to call it—was conceived what may be accounted the most romantic dream that ever visited the native mind of America. It impressed de Tocqueville, who discovered the poetry of America in this romance of a moving frontier, in the vision that led the pioneer on his conquering way westward, hewing at an interminable wilderness that was matched only by his ambitions.

Such swift expansions, such mounting romanticisms of temper, must inevitably provide themselves with correspondent philosophies to phrase the new aspirations. The nineteenth century was not content to think in the narrower terms of the eighteenth, but must refashion its thought to suit the romantic style. The modes which it came to accept were for the most part of European origin, adapted to new-world needs. From France and England, and later from Germany, came variant schools of romantic theory that at bottom were a common glorification of the ideal of individualism; and this very diversity of interpretation made possible in America an appeal to different classes and diverse interests, the sum total of which was a many-sided contribution to social theory, but a contribution which carried within it the seeds of later conflict.

The first stage in the romanticization of American thought resulted from the naturalization of French revolutionary theory. Its devious progress through the country can be traced fairly accurately. Landing first in Virginia in the early seventeen-seventies, it met with a hospitable reception from the generous planter society and spread widely there the fashion of Physiocratic agrarianism. Traveling thence westward into the Inland Empire it domesticated itself in frontier log cabins under the guise of an assertive individualism, to issue later as the coon-skin democracy of the Jacksonian revolution. Eventually reaching New England, the last haven and refuge of eighteenth-century realism, it disarmed Yankee antagonism by assuming the dress of Unitarianism and preached the doctrine of human perfectibility with such conviction as to arouse the conscience of New England to an extraordinary enthusiasm for reforming man and society. And coming finally to New York it inoculated the mind of the emerging proletariat with its doctrine of the rights of man, with Fourieristic and other Utopias, and turmoiled contemporary politics with equalitarian Locofoco programs. No other philosophy assumed so many and such attractive disguises, or wrought such changes in American ideals, as this French romanticism with its generous humanitarian impulses. The ground was ready for the seed it was to sow, and if in the judgment of a hostile philosophy the crop turned out to be tares, increasing thousands believed it to be excellent wheat, to the growing of which America was to be dedicated henceforth.

The rival philosophy, which came to view with increasing dislike the doctrines of French romanticism, was of English middle-class origin and sprang from the long struggle of that class to loose the hands of the landed gentry from control of the state. Phrased persuasively by Adam Smith, it embodied the principle of liberalism as that principle was understood by men of affairs. It conceived of a social Utopia that must result if economic forces were given free play; if governmental restrictions on trade were done away with and individual enterprise were free to buy and sell in the open market. Springing from the same root of individualism that brought forth French romanticism, it flowered in an economics that denied the aspirations of the French school. Assuming as its determining principle the common in-

stinct of acquisitiveness, it set up the economic man as the criterion of conduct and proposed to reorder society to the single end of trade. Thus sanctioned and given free rein, the principle of acquisitiveness set forth on its triumphant march through western civilization. Accepted by the English middle class as the ultimate social philosophy sufficient to all needs, it presented to willing eyes the ideal of exploitation as the goal of social progress.

But transported to America, the new philosophy soon discovered unforeseen obstacles in its path. The acquisitive instinct was here enormously strengthened by the vast unpreëmpted resources lying all about, but unfortunately those resources were too great or too speculative to be exploited by individual effort. Capital was wanting, and unless collective funds were available, exploitation must be slow and inadequate. There was need of the state to further the opening up of western lands and to throw its guardianship about an infant industrialism. Roads and canals could not wait on individual enterprise; tariffs and subsidies could flow only from the government. Hence arose a modification of *laissez faire,* from which resulted the theory that a democratic state stands in *loco parentis* to the economic interests of its citizens, and should guarantee the progressive well-being of strategic groups on whose prosperity depended the common well-being. It was this modification of the English philosophy that the Whig party came to embody in its platform, and which by pooling the interests of western speculators, eastern financiers and New England industrialists, sponsored the "American Plan," a curiously ingenious scheme to milk the cow and divide the milk among those who superintended the milking.

Meanwhile in the imperialistic South was arising a distinctive philosophy, native to the special conditions imposed by slavery, that was to set it apart from both eastern and western economics and draw it inevitably into a narrowing isolation. Frankly defensive in purpose, rejecting alike French equalitarianism and English individualism, it sought to justify the institution of slavery by an appeal to realism and square it to the theory of democracy by analogy with northern industrialism. The conception of a Greek democracy, which was the last citadel of the southern mind, was a skillful compromise between the antagonistic principles of aristocracy and democracy, the most romantic ideal brought forth by our golden age of romance. Assuming the middle-class principle of exploitation as the creative source of every civilization, it proposed to erect a free state on the basis of a slave proletariat after the model of ancient Athens. A democracy, it argued, is possible only among equals. In every society hitherto the inevitable inequality between economic classes has nullified every democratic program. Master and man, exploiter and exploited, are necessarily opposed in vital economic interests; and this potential clash, this fundamental antagonism of classes, has been intensified by the rise of industrialism. Exploitation has been brutalized by the impersonal wage-system,

and the proletariat has been reduced to sodden and embittered beasts. If now as honest realists we recognize frankly that equality cannot exist between inferior and superior races, if we accept the inevitable proletarian status of the Negro, if finally we concede the truism that the lifelong relations between master and slave are more humane than the temporary relations between wage-giver and wage-earner, we shall concern ourselves less with a romantic equalitarianism and more with a rational conception of a democracy of equals that may conceivably erect a civilization worthy of the name.

It was an ingenious theory, but unfortunately it left out of account the ambitions of the middle class, and it was this class that in the end destroyed it. Whether they will it or not, imperialisms have a way of clashing with rival imperialisms. Reality persists though romance may deny it, and in their several programs the three diverse sections of America were driving blindly to a collision. In that bitter collision the dream of the South was destroyed. With the overthrow of the aristocratic principle in its final refuge the ground was cleared of the last vestiges of the eighteenth century. Thenceforth America was to become wholly middle class, and such romance as it might bring forth was to be of another sort.

II. DOCUMENTS

1. The Assertion of Privacy

"Every man for himself" was Emerson's summary slogan. No cultural symbol in American history represented this spirit of romantic self-reliance better than the various frontiersmen—real and fictional—of the pre-Civil War decades. In real life, there were the exploits, factual and legendary, of a Daniel Boone or Davy Crockett. In fiction, there was the compellingly popu-

*lar figure of the hunter created by James Fenimore Cooper and known vari-
ously as Natty Bumppo, Leatherstocking, Deerslayer, and Hawkeye. The
hunter, either as a mythic Boone or as Leatherstocking, was the perfect
model of the self-sufficient individual. He rejected society, laws, customs,
manners, anything that threatened to hem in his liberated spirit. In the
selection from Cooper's* The Pioneers, *Leatherstocking has a bitter encounter with the forces of restraint and order. Accused of taking a buck out
of season, he defies a legal search party that comes to examine his hut; he is
then captured by a larger sheriff's party and taken to trial. The encounter
between him and the powers of social order, represented by the sheriff and
the court, is a classic example of the conflict between society and the free
hero of Parrington's "romance."*

*Leatherstocking's opposition to civil authority was fundamentally harm-
less. He asked only to be left alone in his forest, "where no man was ever
known to disturb another." But there were other men in real life who
pushed the assertion of private conscience to more subversive extremes.
William Lloyd Garrison, the great abolitionist leader, was (and is) one of the
most controversial Americans in our history. He was tenaciously active in
many reforms—temperance, abolition, peace, and others—and in every cause
he pressed the doctrine of the primacy of individual belief to its limits. In
the "Declaration of Sentiments" for a Peace Convention of 1838, which is
included here, Garrison spelled out the determination to "overthrow" every
civil institution and to replace governments and laws with the commands of
a Christian "conscience."*

*Translated into fiction, the assertion of private conscience yielded Leather-
stocking. Translated into reform, it yielded Garrison. An intellectual movement known as "Transcendentalism" developed in and around Concord,
Massachusetts, in the 1830's and 1840's, a movement that made individual
conscience or "spirit" the central doctrine of a philosophy. Transcendentalism was not a cohesive movement based on technical doctrines. It was, instead, a loose phenomenon committed to general claims that "spirit" was
fundamental, the material world in every way secondary, and the individual
"soul" the only thing of genuine value in experience. Economy, governments,
customs, and institutions were the general enemies against which the Transcendentalists set themselves. The third selection in this section is from a
brief history of the movement, written by Charles Mayo Ellis, one of the
minor but active Transcendentalists.*

*The most compelling American assertion of private conscience against
what Garrison called "the powers that be" was Henry David Thoreau's essay
on "Civil Disobedience." Thoreau was something of a composite of Leather-
stocking, abolitionist, and Transcendentalist. He was a woodsman, an active
opponent of slavery, and one of the principal spokesmen of the movement
which gathered around Emerson. He wrote "Civil Disobedience" in 1850 as
part of a protest against slavery and the Mexican War, but the essay easily*

*transcends the special circumstances under which it was written, and it has
served as something of a Bible for radicals, in America and abroad, down to
the present day.*

JAMES FENIMORE COOPER

When the sheriff thought time enough had elapsed for the different divisions of his force to arrive at their stations, he raised his voice in the silence of the forest, and shouted the watchword. The sounds played among the arched branches of the trees in hollow cadences; but when the last sinking tone was lost on the ear . . . no other noises were returned but the cracking of torn branches and dried sticks, as they yielded before the advancing steps of the officers. Even this soon ceased, as if by a common consent, when the curiosity and impatience of the sheriff getting the complete ascendency over discretion, he rushed up the bank, and in a moment stood on the little piece of cleared ground in front of the spot where Natty had so long lived. To his amazement, in place of the hut he saw only its smouldering ruins.

The party gradually drew together about the heap of ashes and the ends of smoking logs; while a dim flame in the centre of the ruin, which still found fuel to feed its lingering life, threw its pale light, flickering with the passing currents of the air, around the circle— now showing a face with eyes fixed in astonishment, and then glancing to another countenance, leaving the former shaded in the obscurity of night. Not a voice was raised in inquiry, nor

Reprinted from James Fenimore Cooper, THE PIONEERS; OR, THE SOURCES OF THE SUSQUEHANNA *(New York, 1823), pp. 346–348, 351–353, 360–363.*

an exclamation made in astonishment. . . .

The whole group were yet in the fulness of their surprise, when a tall form stalked from the gloom into the circle, treading down the hot ashes and dying embers with callous feet; and, standing over the light, lifted his cap, and exposed the bare head and weather-beaten features of the Leather-Stocking. For a moment he gazed at the dusky figures who surrounded him, more in sorrow than in anger before he spoke.

"What would ye with an old and helpless man?" he said. "You've driven God's creatur's from the wilderness, where His providence had put them for His own pleasure; and you've brought in the troubles and diviltries of the law, where no man was ever known to disturb another. You have driven me, that have lived forty long years of my appointed time in this very spot, from my home and the shelter of my head, lest you should put your wicked feet and wasty ways in my cabin. You've driven me to burn these logs, under which I've eaten and drunk —the first of Heaven's gifts, and the other of the pure springs—for the half of a hundred years; and to mourn the ashes under my feet, as a man would weep and mourn for the children of his body. You've rankled the heart of an old man, that has never harmed you or your'n, with bitter feelings toward his kind, at a time when his thoughts should be on a better world; and you've driven him to wish that the beasts of the forest, who never feast on the blood of their own families, was his kindred and race; and now, when he has come to see the last brand of his hut, before it is melted into ashes, you follow him up, at midnight, like hungry hounds on the track of a worn-out and dying deer. What more would ye have? for I am here—one too many. I come to mourn, not to fight; and, if it is God's pleasure, work your will on me."

When the old man ended he stood, with the light glimmering around his thinly covered head, looking earnestly at the group, which receded from the pile with an involuntary movement, without the reach of the quivering rays, leaving a free passage for his retreat into the bushes, where pursuit in the dark would have been fruitless. Natty seemed not to regard this advantage, but stood facing each individual in the circle in succession, as if to see who would be the first to arrest him. . . . The party now collected, and, preceded by the sheriff, with Natty in their centre, they took their way toward the village.

During the walk, divers questions were put to the prisoner concerning his reasons for burning the hut . . . , but to all of them he observed a profound silence, until, fatigued with their previous duties, and the lateness of the hour, the sheriff and his followers reached the village, and dispersed to their several places of rest, after turning the key of a jail on the aged and apparently friendless Leather-Stocking.

. . .

The long days and early sun of July allowed time for a gathering of the interested, before the little bell of the academy announced that the appointed hour had arrived for administering right to the wronged, and punishment to the guilty. . . .

When the judges were seated, the lawyers had taken possession of the table, and the noise of moving feet had ceased in the area, the proclamations were made in the usual form, the jurors were sworn, the charge was given, and the court proceeded to hear the business before them. . . .

. . . The usual forms were observed, when the foreman handed up to the bench two bills, on both of which the Judge observed, at the first glance of his eye, the name of Nathaniel Bumppo. It was a leisure moment with the court; some low whispering passed between the bench and the sheriff, who gave a signal to his officers, and in a very few minutes the silence that prevailed was interrupted by a general movement in the outer crowd, when presently the Leather-Stocking made his appearance, ushered into the criminal's bar under the custody of two constables. The hum ceased, the people closed into the open space again, and the silence soon became so deep that the hard breathing of the prisoner was audible.

Natty was dressed in his buckskin garments, without his coat, in place of which he wore only a shirt of coarse linen-check, fastened at his throat by the sinew of a deer, leaving his red neck and weather-beaten face exposed and bare. It was the first time that he had ever crossed the threshold of a court of justice, and curiosity seemed to be strongly blended with his personal feelings. He raised his eyes to the bench, thence to the jury-boxes, the bar, and the crowd without, meeting everywhere looks fastened on himself. After surveying his own person, as searching the cause of this unusual attraction, he once more turned his face around the assemblage, and opened his mouth in one of his silent and remarkable laughs.

"Prisoner, remove your cap," said Judge Temple.

The order was either unheard or unheeded.

"Nathaniel Bumppo, be uncovered," repeated the Judge.

Natty started at the sound of his name, and, raising his face earnestly toward the bench, he said:

"Anan!"

Mr. Lippet arose from his seat at the table, and whispered in the ear of the prisoner; when Natty gave him a nod of assent, and took the deer-skin covering from his head.

"Mr. District Attorney," said the Judge, "the prisoner is ready; we wait for the indictment."

The duties of public prosecutor were discharged by Dirck Van der School, who adjusted his spectacles, cast a cautious look around him at his brethren of the bar, which he ended by throwing his head aside so as to catch one glance over the glasses, when he proceeded to read the bill aloud. . . .

Natty listened to the charge with great attention, leaning forward toward the reader with an earnestness that denoted his interest; and, when it was ended, he raised his tall body to the utmost, and drew a long sigh. All eyes were turned to the prisoner, whose voice was vainly expected to break the stillness of the room.

. . .

"Do you plead guilty or not guilty?" said the Judge.

"I may say not guilty, with a clean conscious," returned Natty; "for there's no guilt in doing what's right; and I'd rather died on the spot, than had him put foot in the hut at that moment." [Leather-Stocking was charged with armed resistance to a search warrant. Evidence was presented, and the judge then charged the jury.]

It was now the duty of the Judge to deliver his charge. It consisted of a short, comprehensive summary of the testimony, laying bare the artifice of the prisoner's counsel, and placing the facts in so obvious a light that they could not well be misunderstood. "Living as we do, gentlemen," he concluded, "on the skirts of society, it becomes doubly necessary to protect the ministers of the law. If you believe the witnesses, in their construction of the acts of the prisoner, it is your duty to convict him; but if you believe that the old man, who this day appears before you, meant not to harm the constable, but was acting more under the influence of habit than by the instigations of malice, it will be your duty to judge him, but to do it with lenity."

As before, the jury did not leave their box; but, after a consultation of some little time, their foreman arose, and pronounced the prisoner:

"Guilty."

There was but little surprise manifested in the courtroom at this verdict, as the testimony, the greater part of which we have omitted, was too clear and direct to be passed over. The judges seemed to have anticipated this sentiment, for a consultation was passing among them also, during the deliberation of the jury, and the preparatory movements of the "bench" announced the coming sentence.

"Nathaniel Bumppo," commenced the Judge, making the customary pause.

The old hunter who had been musing again, with his head on the bar, raised himself, and cried, with a prompt, military tone:

"Here."

The Judge waved his hand for silence, and proceeded:

"In forming their sentence, the court have been governed as much by the consideration of your ignorance of the laws as by a strict sense of the importance of punishing such outrages as this of which you have been found guilty. They have therefore passed over the obvious punishment of whipping on the bare back, in mercy to your years; but, as the dignity of the law requires an open exhibition of the consequences of your crime, it is ordered that you be conveyed from this room to the public stocks, where you are to be confined for one hour; that you pay a fine to the State of one hundred dollars; and that you be imprisoned in the jail of this county for one calendar month, and, furthermore, that your imprisonment do not cease until the said fine shall be paid. I feel it my duty, Nathaniel Bumppo——"

"And where should I get the money?" interrupted the Leather-Stocking eagerly; "where should I get the money? you'll take away the bounty on the painters [panthers], because I cut the throat of a deer; and how is an old man to find so much gold or silver in the woods? No, no, Judge; think better of it, and don't talk of shutting me up in a jail for the little time I have to stay."

"If you have anything to urge against the passing of the sentence, the court will yet hear you," said the Judge mildly.

"I have enough to say agin' it," cried Natty, grasping the bar on which his fingers were working with a convulsed motion. "Where am I to get the money? Let me out into the woods and hills, where I've been used to breathe the clear air, and though I'm threescore and ten, if you've left game enough in the country, I'll travel night and day but I'll make you up the sum afore the season is over. Yes, yes—you see the reason of the thing, and the wickedness of shutting up an old man that has spent his days, as one may say, where he could always look into the windows of heaven."

"I must be governed by the law——"

"Talk not to me of law, Marmaduke Temple," interrupted the hunter. "Did the beast of the forest mind your laws, when it was thirsty and hungering for the blood of your own child? She was kneeling to her God for a greater favor than I ask, and he heard her; and if you now say no to my prayers, do you think he will be deaf?"

"My private feelings must not enter into——"

"Hear me, Marmaduke Temple," interrupted the old man, with melancholy earnestness, "and hear reason. I've travelled these mountains when you was no judge, but an infant in your mother's arms; and I feel as if I had a right and a privilege to travel them agin afore I die. Have you forgot the time that you come on to the lakeshore, when there wasn't even a jail to lodge in; and didn't I give you my own bear-skin to sleep on, and the fat of a noble buck to satisfy the cravings of your hunger? Yes, yes—you thought it no sin then to kill a deer! And this I did, though I had no reason to love you, for you had never done anything but harm to them that loved and sheltered me. And now, will you shut me up in your dungeons to pay me for my kindness? A hundred dollars! Where should I get the money? No, no —there's them that says hard things of you, Marmaduke Temple, but you ain't so bad as to wish to see an old man die in a prison, because he stood up for the right. Come, friend, let me pass; it's long sin' I've been used to such crowds, and I crave to be in the woods agin. Don't fear me, Judge—I bid you not to fear me; for if there's beaver enough left on the streams, or the buckskins will sell for a shilling apiece, you shall have the last penny of the fine. Where are ye, pups? come away, dogs, come away! we have a grievous toil to do for our years, but it shall be done—yes, yes, I've promised it, and it shall be done!"

It is unnecessary to say that the movement of the Leather-Stocking was again intercepted by the constable. . . .

"There must be an end to this," said the Judge, struggling to overcome his feelings. "Constable, lead the prisoner to the stocks. Mr. Clerk, what stands next on the calendar?"

Natty seemed to yield to his destiny, for he sank his head on his chest, and followed the officer from the courtroom in silence. The crowd moved back for the passage of the prisoner, and when his tall form was seen descending from the outer door, a rush of the people to the scene of his disgrace followed.

WILLIAM LLOYD GARRISON

Assembled in Convention, from various sections of the American Union, for the promotion of peace on earth and good-will among men, we, the undersigned, regard it as due to ourselves, to the cause which we love, to the country in which we live, and to the world, to publish a DECLARATION, expressive of the principles we cherish, the purposes we aim to accomplish, and the measures we shall adopt to carry forward the work of peaceful, universal reformation.

We cannot acknowledge allegiance to any human government; neither can we oppose any such government by a resort to physical force. We recognize but one KING and LAWGIVER, one JUDGE and RULER of mankind. We are bound by the laws of a kingdom which is not

Reprinted from William Lloyd Garrison, "Declaration of Sentiments Adopted by the Peace Convention," Boston, September 18–20, 1838, in WILLIAM LLOYD GARRISON, 1805–1879: THE STORY OF HIS LIFE AS TOLD BY HIS CHILDREN (Boston, 1894), IV, 230–234.

of this world; the subjects of which are forbidden to fight; in which MERCY and TRUTH are met together, and RIGHTEOUSNESS and PEACE have kissed each other; which has no state lines, no national partitions, no geographical boundaries; in which there is no distinction of rank, or division of caste, or inequality of sex; the officers of which are PEACE, its exactors RIGHTEOUSNESS, its walls SALVATION, and its gates PRAISE; and which is destined to break in pieces and consume all other kingdoms.

Our country is the world, our countrymen are all mankind. We love the land of our nativity only as we love all other lands. The interests, rights, liberties of American citizens are no more dear to us than are those of the whole human race. Hence, we can allow no appeal to patriotism, to revenge any national insult or injury. The PRINCE OF PEACE, under whose stainless banner we rally, came not to destroy, but to save, even the worst of enemies. He has left us an example, that we should follow his steps. . . .

. . .

The dogma, that all the governments of the world are approvingly ordained of God, and that THE POWERS THAT BE in the United States, in Russia, in Turkey, are in accordance with his will, is not less absurd than impious. It makes the impartial Author of human freedom and equality, unequal and tyrannical. It cannot be affirmed that THE POWERS THAT BE, in any nation, are actuated by the spirit or guided by the example of Christ, in the treatment of enemies; therefore, they cannot be agreeable to the will of God; and therefore, their overthrow, by a spiritual regeneration of their subjects, is inevitable.

We register our testimony, not only against all wars, whether offensive or defensive, but all preparations for war; against every naval ship, every arsenal, every fortification; against the militia system and a standing army; against all military chieftains and soldiers; against all monuments commemorative of victory over a fallen foe, all trophies won in battle, all celebrations in honor of military or naval exploits; against all appropriations for the defence of a nation by force and arms, on the part of any legislative body; against every edict of government requiring of its subjects military service. Hence, we deem it unlawful to bear arms, or to hold a military office.

As every human government is upheld by physical strength, and its laws are enforced virtually at the point of the bayonet, we cannot hold any office which imposes upon its incumbent the obligation to compel men to do right, on pain of imprisonment or death. We therefore voluntarily exclude ourselves from every legislative and judicial body, and repudiate all human politics, worldly honors, and stations of authority. If *we* cannot occupy a seat in the legislature or on the bench, neither can we elect *others* to act as our substitutes in any such capacity.

It follows, that we cannot sue any man at law, to compel him by force to restore anything which he may have wrongfully taken from us or others; but if he has seized our coat, we shall surrender up our cloak, rather than subject him to punishment.

• • •

The history of mankind is crowded with evidences proving that physical coercion is not adapted to moral regeneration; that the sinful dispositions of men can be subdued only by love; that evil can be exterminated from the earth only by goodness; that it is not safe to rely upon an arm of flesh, upon man whose breath is in his nostrils, to preserve us from harm; that there is great security in being gentle, harmless, long-suffering, and abundant in mercy; that it is only thê meek who shall inherit the earth, for the violent who resort to the sword are destined to perish with the sword. Hence, as a measure of sound policy—of safety to property, life, and liberty—of public quietude and private enjoyment—as well as on the ground of allegiance to HIM who is KING OF KINGS and LORD OF LORDS, we cordially adopt the non-resistance principle; being confident that it provides for all possible consequences, will ensure all things needful to us, is armed with omnipotent power, and must ultimately triumph over every assailing force.

• • •

But, while we shall adhere to the doctrine of non-resistance and passive submission to enemies, we purpose, in a moral and spiritual sense, to speak and act boldly in the cause of GOD; to assail iniquity, in high places and in low places; to apply our principles to all existing civil, political, legal and ecclesiastical institutions; and to hasten the time when the kingdoms of this world will have become the kingdoms of our LORD and of his CHRIST, and he shall reign for ever.

It appears to us a self-evident truth, that, whatever the gospel is designed to destroy at any period of the world, being contrary to it, ought now to be abandoned. If, then, the time is predicted when swords shall be beaten into ploughshares, and spears into pruning-hooks, and men shall not learn the art of war any more, it follows that all who manufacture, sell or wield those deadly weapons, do thus array themselves against the peaceful dominion of the SON OF GOD on earth.

Having thus briefly, but franky, stated our principles and purposes, we proceed to specify the measures we propose to adopt, in carrying our object into effect.

We expect to prevail through THE FOOLISHNESS OF PREACHING—striving to commend ourselves unto every man's conscience, in the sight of GOD. From the press, we shall promulgate our sentiments as widely as practicable. We shall endeavor to secure the co-operation of all persons, of whatever name or sect. The triumphant progress of the cause of TEMPERANCE and of ABOLITION in our land, through the instrumentality of benevolent and voluntary associations, encourages us to combine our own means and efforts for the promotion of a still greater cause. Hence, we shall employ lecturers, circulate tracts and publications, form societies, and petition our State and national governments, in relation to the subject of UNIVERSAL PEACE. It will be our leading object to devise ways and means for effecting a radical change in the views, feelings, and practices of society, respecting the sinfulness of war and the treatment of enemies.

In entering upon the great work before us, we are not unmindful that, in its prosecution, we may be called to test our sincerity, even as in a fiery ordeal. It may subject us to insult, outrage, suffering, yea, even death itself. We anticipate no small amount of misconception, misrepresentation, calumny. Tumults may arise against us. The ungodly and violent, the proud and pharisaical, the ambitious and tyrannical, principalities and powers, and spiritual wickedness in high places, may combine to crush us. So they treated the MESSIAH, whose example we are humbly striving to imitate. If we suffer with him, we know that we shall reign with him. We shall not be afraid of their terror, neither be troubled. Our confidence is in the LORD ALMIGHTY,

not in man. Having withdrawn from human protection, what can sustain us but that faith which overcomes the world? We shall not think it strange concerning the fiery trial which is to try us, as though some strange thing had happened unto us; but rejoice, inasmuch as we are partakers of CHRIST's sufferings. Wherefore, we commit the keeping of our souls to GOD, in well-doing, as unto a faithful Creator. FOR EVERY ONE THAT FORSAKES HOUSES, OR BRETHREN, OR SISTERS, OR FATHER, OR MOTHER, OR WIFE, OR CHILDREN, OR LANDS, FOR CHRIST'S SAKE, SHALL RECEIVE A HUNDRED FOLD, AND SHALL INHERIT EVERLASTING LIFE.

CHARLES MAYO ELLIS

The history of a man is not told by the account of the particles of matter of which his body is formed. He has an existence independent on the body —on the understanding—the material world or the spiritual. No logic is required to prove this. We cannot argue "I feel," or "I think, therefore I exist." The best argument to prove this is the simple statement—I am. We know that we exist. No proof of this can be adduced which is not based on the supposition of our existence.

Any theory which seeks to show that man is a mere "conformation of material particles," or "of those immaterial ideas the whole of which form the universe," leads to the conclusion that man does not exist. Matter may be in a form called human: there may be such an association of ideas as to form what might be named man, but the existence of the soul such a theory

Reprinted from Charles Mayo Ellis, AN ESSAY ON TRANSCENDENTALISM, *in Perry Miller, ed.,* THE AMERICAN TRANSCENDENTALISTS *(New York: Doubleday & Company, 1957), pp. 23–27.*

does not recognise. But besides matter and mind there is also man. If there is not there is no immortality, no life.

It cannot be that man is merely this, endowed with certain faculties—a sort of instrument; and that the soul is merely the sound of this instrument, which may make discord or harmony, as some philosophers have said. For how has this instrument conscious life? How can it hear the sounds if the sounds make up its existence? How does it feel the pulse of life beating in its bosom? Whence has it that other part which it uses as well as the body, and feels more called on to obey, which all the logic of perfect reason could not frame from all the matter in the universe? If man is but an instrument and his soul its music, why is not his soul dead when that is dumb? Why does he not cease to be when that is broken? Why does he feel within him longings, impulses, aspirations? How is it that he not only feels that he *is*—so that he may be associated with other matter, but that he himself possesses will and power —that he is not passive but active; not only is played upon, but plays, and finds within him what he has not gained from the world, what the world cannot get from him? Whence is he? If he is but body, how has he been produced by this mysterious association? What is he? If his body be himself, how can he use it? If he is matter, how can he know of the existence of God? How can he contemplate that which is not matter, the good, true, beautiful? He is not a book to be read, but he records and reads for himself.

Starting, then, with these, that man is and God is, which is involved in the first; the inquiry is, what has man? He has body, mind, *spirit;* affections, bodily, mental, *religious;* appetite, understanding, *religion.* And the latter he has and relies on as something distinct from the two former; not a combination of them. It is not because reason tells him that certain things are more for his animal comfort that he deems them right or beautiful, but because they answer the wants of the spiritual part of his nature.

Man knows of the existence of this spiritual element in his being as he knows of the existence of his mind or his body. He feels conscious of possessing it, feels it to be affected by outward objects, that some of these it loves, some it loathes. Its existence is known as that of the body, through the senses with which it is endowed.

What, then, is this part of man? Describe it. Whence, what, where? For what use? Now ask the same questions about the body. The body, you may call a structure of matter, endowed with senses by which it perceives the material world, with appetites which lead it to incorporate portions thereof with itself, and so to continue its existence. So of reason or the intellect; it is that, by whose senses, we perceive the intellectual world. This, too, has its appetites, and, making food of thought, adds to its strength and perpetuates its existence. It is the same with the religious, that which we call the highest part of our nature. This has the power of perceiving that which is independent of itself—true, good, and beautiful. For this it longs; this gives it strength and vigor. This is not doubted in every day life—all act upon it. We call him whom we find destitute of it an incomplete man, insane. Every one has the idea of God. This leads him to worship. No one can be deprived of it by education. Be where he may; do what he will, good or ill; he knows the right way. The impulses of his soul he may disregard, but he cannot deny them. To call for proof of their correctness is absurd. They are axiomatic. He knows that they are. He knows that it is by their aid alone that he perceives whatever else exists.

We have laws for the body. By exact conformity to them, by giving to each its proper food and exercise, we keep that harmony which is health. If we break these laws we incur pain, and disease ensues. The same is true of this other part of our nature. It may be strengthened by use, weakened by abuse. One part may be cultivated to an inordinate size at the expense of the rest—and the result will be deformity. But nothing can make that good which is wrong, nor that evil which is right. Nothing can deprive man of the sense of what is right. This is the law of nature—the same in all—the only foundation of practical religion, of government, laws, and the rule of right between man and man.

This, then, is the doctrine of Transcendentalism—the substantive, independent existence of the soul of man, the reality of conscience, the religious sense, the inner light, of man's religious affections, his knowledge of right and truth, his sense of duty, the *honestem* apart from the *utile*—his love for beauty and holiness, his religious aspirations—with this it starts as something not dependent on education, custom, command, or anything beyond man himself. These can only add new motives for obedience to that which he feels to be of imperative obligation; but they do not create and cannot contradict the law within him. This cannot be proved by evidence clearer than that which each man has of himself. Habit and education cannot eradicate it. Things may seem painful or inexpedient, but nothing can be just and true which this condemns. . . .

All the old systems start with the assumption of the reality of man's body and the material world, and that in the beginning man is nothing but this body. The inquiry then is, as to the ideas which are subsequently found in it, of truth, justice, beauty, God, infinity, the moral sense, his religious affections. What is their origin? How come they in the body. . . . If man does indeed find within him a page written out, his first thoughts should be whether it is in a language which he can read; what it says; whether it is the same in all other men; its relations; its use; last of all, its origin. But they are not. The first problem, nakedly stated, has always been this: Given the dead matter of the universe and the empty bodies made of it, to say how they are filled; and the answer is plain—with dead matter. Yet even this involves a new *assumption*. There must be a God, either force or Deity, to do even this. Thus this system ends in the denial of God and man.

Now this new system takes quite a different ground. In the first place, it says we have an independent existence, for we are conscious of it; we have reason, affections, religious sentiments, as well as bodies, whose existence is proved to us in the same manner as that of the bodies, through senses operated upon by that which is without them. Our sense of seeing is not created by the sun, though we are not made conscious of it till we open our eyes to the light. So with our sense of right or beauty, which we feel within us as soon as anything right or beautiful is presented to the organ which God has given us to perceive these. And as it recognises the existence of the soul as well as that of the body, and supposes the senses of the soul to be nothing introduced into the soul long after it begins to exist, but as original endowments, not effects, but conditions rather, of its existence, not thrown upon it by the world, it presents quite a different field from that of the old system. The existence of men's bodies and their senses, and the soul and its senses must both be referred to one source—God. Both are appealed to as facts in all reasonings. . . .

The results of the two systems may show their comparative merits. The old deriving all ideas from sensation, leads to atheism, to a religion which is but self-interest—an ethical code which makes right synonymous with indulgence of appetite, justice one with expediency, and reduces our love of what is good, beautiful, true and divine, to habit, association or interest. The new asserts the continual presence of God in all his works, spirit as well as matter; makes religion the natural impulse of every breast; the moral law, God's voice in every heart, independent on interest, expediency or appetite, which enables us to resist these; an universal, eternal, standard of truth, beauty, goodness, holiness, to which every man can turn and follow, if he will. . . .

HENRY DAVID THOREAU

I heartily accept the motto, "That government is best which governs least"; and I should like to see it acted up to more rapidly and systematically. Carried out, it finally amounts to this, which also I believe—"That government is best which governs not at all"; and when men are prepared for it, that will be the kind of government which they will have. Government is at best but an expedient; but most governments are usually, and all governments are sometimes, inexpedient. The objections which have been brought

Reprinted from Henry David Thoreau, "Civil Disobedience," in Carl Bode, ed., THE PORTABLE THOREAU (New York: The Viking Press, Inc., 1947), pp. 109–14, 122–23, 126–27, 133–37.

against a standing army, and they are many and weighty, and deserve to prevail, may also at last be brought against a standing government. The standing army is only an arm of the standing government. The government itself, which is only the mode which the people have chosen to execute their will, is equally liable to be abused and perverted before the people can act through it. Witness the present Mexican war, the work of comparatively a few individuals using the standing government as their tool; for, in the outset, the people would not have consented to this measure.

This American government—what is it but a tradition, though a recent one, endeavoring to transmit itself unimpaired to posterity, but each instant losing some of its integrity? It has not the vitality and force of a single living man; for a single man can bend it to his will. It is a sort of wooden gun to the people themselves. But it is not the less necessary for this; for the people must have some complicated machinery or other, and hear its din, to satisfy that idea of government which they have. Governments show thus how successfully men can be imposed on, even impose on themselves, for their own advantage. It is excellent, we must all allow. Yet this government never of itself furthered any enterprise, but by the alacrity with which it got out of its way. *It* does not keep the country free. *It* does not settle the West. *It* does not educate. The character inherent in the American people has done all that has been accomplished; and it would have done somewhat more, if the government had not sometimes got in its way. For government is an expedient by which men would fain succeed in letting one another alone; and, as has been said, when it is most expedient, the governed are most let alone by it. Trade and commerce, if they were not made of india-rubber, would never manage to bounce over the obstacles which legislators are continually putting in their way; and, if one were to judge these men wholly by the effects of their actions and not partly by their intentions, they would deserve to be classed and punished with those mischievous persons who put obstructions on the railroads.

But, to speak practically and as a citizen, unlike those who call themselves no-government men, I ask for, not at once no government, but *at once* a better government. Let every man make known what kind of government would command his respect, and that will be one step toward obtaining it.

After all, the practical reason why, when the power is once in the hands of the people, a majority are permitted, and for a long period continue, to rule is not because they are most likely to be in the right, nor because this seems fairest to the minority, but because they are physically the strongest. But a government in which the majority rule in all cases cannot be based on justice, even as far as men understand it. Can there not be a government in which majorities do not virtually decide right and wrong, but conscience?—in which majorities decide only those questions to which the rule of expediency is applicable? Must the citizen ever for a moment, or in the least degree, resign his conscience to the legislator? Why has every man a conscience, then? I think that we should be men first, and subjects afterward. It is not desirable to cultivate a respect for the law, so much as for the right. The only obligation which I have a right to assume is to do at any time what I think right. It is truly enough said that a corporation has no conscience; but a corporation of conscientious men is a corporation *with* a conscience. Law never made men a whit more just; and, by means of their respect for it, even the well-disposed are daily made the agents of injustice. A common and natural result of an undue respect for law is, that you may see a file of soldiers, colonel, captain, corporal, privates, powder-monkeys, and all, marching in admirable order over hill and dale to the wars, against their wills, ay, against their common sense and consciences, which makes it very steep marching indeed, and produces a palpitation of the heart. They have no doubt that it is a damnable business in which they are concerned; they are all peaceably inclined. Now, what are they? Men at all? or small movable forts and magazines, at the service of some unscrupulous man in power? . . .

The mass of men serve the state thus, not as men mainly, but as machines, with their bodies. They are the standing army, and the militia, jailers, constables, *posse comitatus*, etc. In most cases there is no free exercise whatever of the judgment or of the moral sense; but they put themselves on a level with wood and earth and stones; and wooden men can perhaps be manufactured that will serve the purpose as well. Such command no more respect than men of straw or a lump of dirt. They have the same sort of worth only as horses and dogs. Yet such as these even are commonly esteemed good citizens. Others—as most legislators, politicians, lawyers, ministers, and officeholders—serve the state chiefly with their heads; and, as they rarely make any moral distinctions, they are as likely to serve the devil, without *intending* it, as God. A very few—as heroes, patriots, martyrs, reformers in the great sense, and *men*—serve the state with their consciences also, and so necessarily resist it for the most part; and they are commonly treated as enemies by it. . . .

How does it become a man to behave toward this American government to-day? I answer, that he cannot without disgrace be associated with it. I cannot for an instant recognize that political organization as *my* government which is the *slave's* government also.

All men recognize the right of revolution; that is, the right to refuse allegiance to, and to resist, the government, when its tyranny or its inefficiency are great and unendurable. But almost all say that such is not the case now. But such was the case, they think, in the Revolution of '75. If one were to tell me that this was a bad government because it taxed certain foreign commodities brought to its ports, it is most probable that I should not make an ado about it, for I can do without them. All machines have their friction; and possibly this does enough good to counterbalance the evil. At any rate, it is a great evil to make a stir about it. But when the friction comes to have its machine, and oppression and robbery are organized, I say, let us not have such a machine any longer. In other words, when a sixth of the population of a nation which has undertaken to be the refuge of liberty are slaves, and a whole country is unjustly overrun and conquered by a foreign army, and subjected to military law, I think that it is not too soon for honest men to rebel and revolutionize. What makes this duty the more urgent is the fact that the country so overrun is not our own, but ours is the invading army.

. . .

Under a government which imprisons any unjustly, the true place for a just man is also a prison. The proper place today, the only place which

Massachusetts has provided for her freer and less desponding spirits, is in her prisons, to be put out and locked out of the State by her own act, as they have already put themselves out by their principles. It is there that the fugitive slave, and the Mexican prisoner on parole, and the Indian come to plead the wrongs of his race should find them; on that separate, but more free and honorable, ground, where the State places those who are not *with* her, but *against* her—the only house in a slave State in which a free man can abide with honor. If any think that their influence would be lost there, and their voices no longer afflict the ear of the State, that they would not be as an enemy within its walls, they do not know by how much truth is stronger than error, nor how much more eloquently and effectively he can combat injustice who has experienced a little in his own person. Cast your whole vote, not a strip of paper merely, but your whole influence. A minority is powerless while it conforms to the majority; it is not even a minority then; but it is irresistible when it clogs by its whole weight. If the alternative is to keep all just men in prison, or give up war and slavery, the State will not hesitate which to choose. If a thousand men were not to pay their tax-bills this year, that would not be a violent and bloody measure, as it would be to pay them, and enable the State to commit violence and shed innocent blood. This is, in fact, the definition of a peaceable revolution, if any such is possible. If the tax-gatherer, or any other public officer, asks me, as one has done, "But what shall I do?" my answer is, "If you really wish to do anything, resign your office." When the subject has refused allegiance, and the officer has resigned his office, then the revolution is accomplished.

But even suppose blood should flow. Is there not a sort of blood shed when the conscience is wounded? Through this wound a man's real manhood and immortality flow out, and he bleeds to an everlasting death. I see this blood flowing now.

. . .

I have paid no poll-tax for six years. I was put into a jail once on this account, for one night; and, as I stood considering the walls of solid stone, two or three feet thick, the door of wood and iron, a foot thick, and the iron grating which strained the light, I could not help being struck with the foolishness of that institution which treated me as if I were mere flesh and blood and bones, to be locked up. I wondered that it should have concluded at length that this was the best use it could put me to, and had never thought to avail itself of my services in some way. I saw that, if there was a wall of stone between me and my townsmen, there was a still more difficult one to climb or break through before they could get to be as free as I was. I did not for a moment feel confined, and the walls seemed a great waste of stone and mortar. I felt as if I alone of all my townsmen had paid my tax. They plainly did not know how to treat me, but behaved like persons who are underbred. In every threat and in every compliment there was a blunder; for they thought that my chief desire was to stand the other side of that stone wall. I could not but smile to see how industriously they locked the door on my meditations, which followed them out again without let or hindrance, and *they* were really all that was dangerous. As they could not reach me, they had resolved to punish my body; just as boys, if they cannot come at some person against whom they have a spite, will abuse his dog. I saw that the State was half-witted, that it was timid as a lone woman with her silver spoons, and that it did not know its friends from its foes, and I lost all my remaining respect for it, and pitied it.

Thus the State never intentionally confronts a man's sense, intellectual or moral, but only his body, his senses. It is not armed with superior wit or honesty, but with superior physical strength. I was not born to be forced. I will breathe after my own fashion. Let us see who is the strongest. What force has a multitude? They only can force me who obey a higher law than I. They force me to become like themselves. I do not hear of *men* being *forced* to live this way or that by masses of men. What sort of life were that to live? When I meet a government which says to me, "Your money or your life," why should I be in haste to give it my money? It may be in a great strait, and not know what to do: I cannot help that. It must help itself; do as I do. It is not worth the while to snivel about it. I am not responsible for the successful working of the machinery of society. I am not the son of the engineer. I perceive that, when an acorn and a chestnut fall side by side, the one does not remain inert to make way for the other, but both obey their own laws, and spring and grow and flourish as best they can, till one, perchance, overshadows and destroys the other. If a plant cannot live according to its nature, it dies; and so a man.

. . .

However, the government does not concern me much, and I shall bestow the fewest possible thoughts on it. It is not many moments that I live under a government, even in this world. If a man is thought-free, fancy-free, imagination-free, that which *is not* never for a long time appearing *to be* to him, unwise rulers or reformers cannot fatally interrupt him.

I know that most men think differently from myself; but those whose lives are by profession devoted to the study of these or kindred subjects content me as little as any. Statesmen and legislators, standing so completely within the institution, never distinctly and nakedly behold it. They speak of moving society, but have no resting-place without it. They may be men of a certain experience and discrimination, and have no doubt invented ingenious and even useful systems, for which we sincerely thank them; but all their wit and usefulness lie within certain not very wide limits. They are wont to forget that the world is not governed by policy and expediency. . . .

They who know of no purer sources of truth, who have traced up its stream no higher, stand, and wisely stand, by the Bible and the Constitution, and drink at it there with reverence and humility; but they who behold where it comes trickling into this lake or that pool, gird up their loins once more, and continue their pilgrimage toward its fountainhead.

No man with a genius for legislation has appeared in America. They are rare in the history of the world. There are orators, politicians, and eloquent men, by the thousand; but the speaker has not yet opened his mouth to speak who is capable of settling the much-vexed questions of the day. We love eloquence for its own sake, and not for any truth which it may utter, or any heroism it may inspire. Our legislators have not yet learned the comparative value of free trade and of freedom, of union, and of rectitude, to a nation. They have no genius or talent for comparatively humble questions of taxation and finance, commerce and manufactures and agriculture. If we

were left solely to the wordy wit of legislators in Congress for our guidance, uncorrected by the seasonable experience and the effectual complaints of the people, America would not long retain her rank among the nations. For eighteen hundred years, though perchance I have no right to say it, the New Testament has been written; yet where is the legislator who has wisdom and practical talent enough to avail himself of the light which it sheds on the science of legislation?

The authority of government, even such as I am willing to submit to—for I will cheerfully obey those who know and can do better than I, and in many things even those who neither know nor can do so well—is still an impure one: to be strictly just, it must have the sanction and consent of the governed. It can have no pure right over my person and property but what I concede to it. The progress from an absolute to a limited monarchy, from a limited monarchy to a democracy, is a progress toward a true respect for the individual. Even the Chinese philosopher was wise enough to regard the individual as the basis of the empire. Is a democracy, such as we know it, the last improvement possible in government? Is it not possible to take a step further towards recognizing and organizing the rights of man? There will never be a really free and enlightened State until the State comes to recognize the individual as a higher and independent power, from which all its own power and authority are derived, and treats him accordingly. I please myself with imagining a State at last which can afford to be just to all men, and to treat the individual with respect as a neighbor; which even would not think it inconsistent with its own repose if a few were to live aloof from it, not meddling with it, nor embraced by it, who fulfilled all the duties of neighbors and fellow men. A State which bore this kind of fruit, and suffered it to drop off as fast as it ripened, would prepare the way for a still more perfect and glorious State, which also I have imagined, but not yet anywhere seen.

2. The Fear of Freedom

Leatherstocking's forthright opposition to the law, Garrison's contempt for government, Thoreau's civil disobedience—all these emerged as part of what Parrington called "drastic overturnings of the customary and familiar." But "drastic overturnings" frighten men as often as they elate them. Parrington's "unexplored paths" did not always promote romance. They also prompted men and women to cast around for new clues to social order, for new organizations and restraints with which to discipline the individual citizen. In this section, we present three documents illustrating this kind of result of the fear of freedom.

The first document is a statement of belief written by a leader of the Shakers, or the "United Society of Believers in Christ's Second Appearing." The Shakers were one of a number of millennial and communal religious sects that appeared during the early decades of the nineteenth century. The sect was founded by a woman, "Mother" Ann Lee, at the end of the eighteenth century, but it did not blossom until the second quarter of the next century. The Shakers were committed to celibacy, to communism, and to discipline. Shakers found in their sect a release from individual competition and freedom. They also found a release from the fear of individual sin which had been exaggerated by the removal of traditional checks on private behavior. Finally, in their preoccupation with the second appearing of Christ, the Shakers found a way of analyzing their sense that history had gotten out of hand and was rushing headlong toward some unknown but violent ending.

A second kind of negative response to rapid and unsettling change was the political movement that came to be known as the "Know-Nothing" party. The party was the political arm of a secret society known as the "Order of the Star Spangled Banner." The Know-Nothings won control of Massachusetts in 1854, elected nine governors in 1855, and polled one-fourth of the presidential vote in the election of 1856. Their program was based on simple anti-Catholicism, and it fed on nativist fears that foreign immigrants were about to subvert the American way of life. But the party served a less obvious positive function for its members. It gave them a sense of belonging to a secret, powerful organization which might relieve them from a dread of individual isolation. This sense of belonging was reinforced by an elaborate organization and ritual that promised to restore the most important things which an excess of "liberty" had threatened: hierarchy, custom, and joint purpose. The second document in this section is a portion of the Know-Nothings' Constitution and ritual.

The fear of freedom was strongest, of course, in the slave-holding South, where "liberty" had a double and serious connotation. In the last selection in this section, George Fitzhugh, the most capable theoretical defender of slavery, argues that the libertarian assumptions of the Declaration of Independence were simply false. Governments, he insisted, were founded on force and sustained by inequalities among men. Fitzhugh appealed to "conservatives" in the North to recognize that they were as much in danger as the southern slaveholders, and to enter into an alliance with southern leaders. Laissez-faire individualism must be repudiated, he concluded, because "the masses require more protection, and the masses and philosophers equally require more of control."

THE SHAKER CREDO

It . . . is our faith . . . that there can be no Church in complete order according to the law of Christ, without a joint-interest and union, in which all the members have an equal right and privilege according to their calling and needs, in things spiritual and temporal. . . .

All the members who were received into the Church were to possess one joint-interest as a religious right; that is, all were to have just and equal rights and privileges according to their needs in the use of all things in the church —without any difference being made, on account of what any of us brought in, so long as we remained in obedience to the order and government of the Church, and were holden in relation as members. . . .

As it was not the duty nor purpose of the Church in uniting into Church-

Reprinted from A SUMMARY VIEW OF THE MIL-
LENNIAL CHURCH *(1848), in Marguerite Melcher,* THE SHAKER ADVENTURE *(Princeton, N.J.: Princeton University Press, 1941), pp. 89–91.*

order to gather and lay up an interest of this world's goods, but what we became possessed of by honest industry, more than for our own support, was to be devoted to charitable uses, for the relief of the poor and such other uses as the gospel might require. Therefore, it was and still is our faith never to bring debt or blame against the Church or each other for any interest or services which we have bestowed to the joint-interest of the Church, but freely to give our time and talents, as Brethren and Sisters, for the mutual good one of another and other charitable uses, according to the order of the Church.

God has begun to judge the nations of the earth, who have long been erring in judgment and straying from the paths of justice and truth; and this righteous judgment will never cease until the work of God shall be fully accomplished. . . .

. . . It will produce in the willing and obedient, the effectual destruction of all kinds of vice and immorality, and every principle of evil. It will enlighten mankind in the knowledge of the truth, and widely extend the benign principles of peace and good will to man. It will greatly increase the practical duties of humanity, benevolence and charity, and produce a universal diffusion of divine light, and the knowledge of salvation; and in the end it will effect the final decision and termination of the probationary state of all souls.

This Day of Judgment will be gradual and progressive, but certain and effectual; and will continue until a full and final separation shall be made between good and evil. Then shall the righteous no longer suffer under the oppressive hands of the wicked; nor shall the wicked any more shelter himself under the banners of the righteous; but each shall reap the reward of his own doings, whether they be good or evil: for God will search the heart and try the reins of every creature.

Then shall the covering be taken off from all people, and the veil be removed from all faces. Then shall Antichrist no longer beguile mankind with the mere name of religion in which there is no reality; nor his ministers any more deceive souls with the hope of salvation in their sins. Fraud and violence, theft and robbery, pride and ambition, malice and envy, falsehood and deception, and every species of wickedness will be completely uncovered, and appear in all their naked deformity; nor will it be in the power of man to conceal the smallest crime: for every secret sin will be fully brought to view. . . .

Let all lay aside the false doctrines of Antichrist, and consider and rightly appreciate this important truth; That man is a free agent, capable of thinking, believing and acting for himself; and therefore he is accountable to God

for the use and improvement he makes of his free agency, and must be judged and rewarded according to his works. The important period is fast approaching when the dividing line must be fully drawn, when the decisive sentence shall be pronounced: "He that is unjust, let him be unjust still; and he that is filthy, let him be filthy still; and he that is righteous let him be righteous still; and he that is holy let him be holy still. And behold I come quickly; and my reward is with me, to give every man according as his work shall be."

Tho' thousands in past ages, who conscientiously lived up to the best light they were able to obtain, were so far enlightened by the Spirit of God, as to see the natural tendency of indulging those inordinate desires which led to these baleful corruptions, and honestly took up their crosses, and, for a season, maintained a principle of continency; yet the fountain of iniquity was not discovered; the veil of the flesh, which is the covering that darkened the sight, was not yet removed. So great indeed has been the darkness which has covered the earth, and so benighted were the minds of the great mass of the professors of Christianity, that those souls who were thus partially enlightened, have generally been stigmatized as heretics, and have suffered great persecutions on account of their faith. And tho' such souls, like stars in the night, might shine in the midst of surrounding darkness; yet they could not dispel the darkness, nor enlighten the earth. This remained to be accomplished by the Spirit of Christ in the female. The dawning of the millennial day, and the rising of the Sun of Righteousness, having now commenced, will gradually disperse these clouds of darkness, and open the eyes of a benighted world.

THE KNOW-NOTHING RITUAL

"CONSTITUTION OF THE GRAND COUNCIL OF THE UNITED STATES OF NORTH AMERICA—ADOPTED UNANIMOUSLY, JUNE 17, 1854—THE ANIVERSARY OF THE BATTLE OF BUNKER HILL."

Article I.

This organization shall be known by the name and title of *The Grand Council of the United States of North America,* and its jurisdiction and power shall extend to all the states, districts, and territories of the United States of North America.

Article II.

A person to become a member of any subordinate council must be twenty-one years of age; he must believe in the existence of a Supreme Being as the Creator and Preserver of the Universe; he must be a native born citizen; a Protestant, born of Protestant parents, reared under Protestant influence, and not united in marriage with a Roman Catholic; Provided, nevertheless, that in this last respect, the state, district, or territorial council shall be authorized to so construct their respective constitutions as shall best promote the interest of the American cause in their several jurisdictions; And provided, moreover, that no member who may have a Roman Catholic wife shall be eligible to any office in this order.

Article III.

SEC. 1. The object of this organization shall be to resist the insidious policy of the Church of Rome, and other foreign influence against the institutions of our country by placing in all offices in the gift of the people, or by appointment, none but native born Protestant citizens. . . .

RITUAL.

First Degree Council.—Outside.

Marshal.—Gentlemen: Are you candidates for admission to this organization? [Each answers, "I am."]

Marshal.—Before proceeding further it is necessary that you take an obligation of secrecy.

Are you willing to take such an obligation? ["I am."]

Marshal.—You will now place yourselves in a position to receive it. [*Position.*—Place the right hand on the Holy Bible and Cross.]

Obligation.—You do solemnly swear upon this Holy Bible and Cross, before Almighty God and these witnesses, that you will not divulge any question now proposed to you, whether you become a member of this organization or not, and that you will never, under any circumstances, mention the name of any person or persons you see present, nor that you know such an organization to be in existence, and that you will true answers make to every question asked you to the best of your knowledge and belief: so help you God. ["I do."]

First Question.—Are you twenty-one years of age? ["I am."]

Second Question.—Do you believe in the existence of a Supreme Being, the Creator and Preserver of the Universe, and that an obligation at this time taken will be binding upon you through life? ["I do."]

Third Question.—Were you born within the limits or under the jurisdiction of the United States of America? ["I was."]

Fourth Question.—In religious belief are you a Roman Catholic? ["No."]

Reprinted from James P. Hambleton, A BIOGRAPHICAL SKETCH OF HENRY A. WISE *(Richmond, Va., 1856), pp. 47, 50–53.*

330

Fifth Question.—Have you or have you not been reared under Protestant influence? ["Yes," or "No."]

Sixth Question.—Are, or were, either of your parents Roman Catholic in religious belief? ["No."]

Seventh Question.—If married, is your wife a Roman Catholic? ["No," or "Yes,"—the answer to be valued as the Constitution of the State Council provide.]

Eighth Question.—Are you willing to use your influence and vote only for native born American citizens for all the offices of honor or trust in the gift of the people, to the exclusion of all foreigners and aliens, and of Roman Catholics in particular, and without regard to party predilections? ["I am."]

Inside.

Marshal.—Worthy President: I have examined these candidates, and finding them duly qualified, present them for obligation. [*If the examination in the ante-room gave evidence of even partial objection to any candidate the Marshal should state it to the President, before introducing the candidates.*]

President.—My friends: Previous to your uniting with and becoming members of this organization, it will be necessary for you to take upon yourselves a solemn obligation—one which we have all taken and intend sacredly to keep through life. It will not conflict with the duties you owe to yourselves, your families, your country, or your God. With this assurance are you still willing to proceed? [Each answers, "I am."]

Obligation.—You and each of you, of your own free will and accord, in the presence of Almighty God and these witnesses, your right hand resting on this Holy Bible and Cross, and your left hand raised towards Heaven, (or *if it be preferred,* your left hand rest-

ing on your breast and your right hand raised towards Heaven,) in token of your sincerity, do solemnly promise and swear that you will·not make known to any person or persons any of the signs, secrets, mysteries, or objects of this organization, unless it be to those whom, after due examination, or lawful information, you shall find to be members of this organization in good standing; that you will not cut, carve, print, paint, stamp, stain, or in any way, directly or indirectly, expose any of the secrets or objects of this order, nor suffer it to be done by others, if in your power to prevent it, unless it be for official instruction; that so long as you are connected with this organization, if not regularly dismissed from it, you will, in all things, political or social, so far as this order is concerned, comply with the will of the majority, when expressed in a lawful manner, though it may conflict with your personal preference, so long as it does not conflict with the Grand, State or Subordinate Constitutions, the Constitution of the United States of America, or that of the State in which you reside; and that you will not, under any circumstances whatever, knowingly, recommmend an unworthy person for initiation, nor suffer it to be done, if in your power to prevent it. You furthermore promise and declare that you will not vote, nor give your influence for any man for any office in the gift of the people, unless he be an American born citizen, in favor of Americans born ruling America, nor if he be a Roman Catholic, and that you will not, under any circumstances, expose the name of any member of this order, nor reveal the existence of such an organization. To all the foregoing you bind yourselves, under the no less penalty than that of being expelled from this order, and of having your name posted and circulated throughout all the different councils of the United States as a perjurer and as a traitor to God and your country, as a being unfit to be employed and trusted, countenanced or supported in any business transaction, as a person unworthy the confidence of all good men, and as one at whom the finger of scorn should ever be pointed. So help you God! [Each answers "I do."]

President.—Worthy Marshal: You will now present these brothers to the Secretary that he may record their names and residences; which being done, you will present them to the Instructor for final instruction.

Marshal.—Worthy Instructor: By direction of the Worthy President, I present to you these brothers for final instructions, they having signed the constitution.

Instructor.—Brothers: At the outer door you will make an ordinary alarm. When the wicket is opened, you will ask what is the pass? The outside sentinel will reply, give it—when you will give the term pass, and be admitted to the ante-room. You will then proceed to the inner door and give one rap. When the wicket is opened, give your name, the number of your council, the explanation of the term-pass, and the degree pass-word. If these be found correct, on being reported to the vice-president you will be admitted to the council. You will then proceed to the centre of the room, and address the president with the countersign, which is performed thus—[*Position*— the right hand placed on the heart and quickly withdrawn, the person remaining perfectly erect.] When this salutation is recognised, you will turn to the vice-president and address him in the same manner, who will also reply. You will then quietly take your seat. This sign is peculiar to this degree, and is never to be used outside of the council room. When retiring, you will address the officers in the same manner, and also give the degree pass-word to the inside sentinel.

The *term pass-word* is ————, [*the word to be established by each state council for its respective Subordinates.*] The *explanation of the term pass,* to be used at the inner door, is ————, [*to be established by each state, &c.*] The *degree pass-word* is twenty-one. The *traveling pass-word and explanation,* (which is changed annually by the grand president, and which is used only when the brother is traveling beyond the jurisdiction of his own state, district or territory,) is Yorktown—the place of final victory.

The sign of recognition is by placing the index finger of the right hand in the space between the buttons of the coat, vest or skirt, and elevating the thumb. The answer is given by placing the thumb of the right hand in the same place.

The grip is given in the form of a lady's slight shake of the hand, by bringing the three fingers of the right hand into such a position as to bring the thumb slightly upon the nail of the middle finger, dropping the hand immediately, when the following conversation ensues—the challenging party first saying what time? The answer, time for work. Then the response—are you, followed by the rejoinder, we are.

Public notice for mass meetings is given by means of a right angle triangular piece of paper, [a diagram is here given,] white in color. If information is wanted of the object of the gathering, or of the place, &c., the inquirer will ask of an undoubted brother only, have you seen SAM to-day? The reply will be go to ————, at ———— o'clock. A piece of paper of the same shape, red in color, will signify suspected danger.

If the color is red, with an equilateral triangular piece cut out, it will denote actual trouble, which requires that you come prepared to meet it.

Brothers, you are now initiated into and made acquainted with the work and organization of a council of this degree of the order; and here, upon the threshold of our institution, with the remembrance of your solemn obligation fresh upon us all, we extend to you the welcome and the sympathies of honest and patriotic hearts. In becoming members of this order, we do not compel you to act with us against your better judgment; and should you at any time wish to withdraw, from conscientious scruples, it will be our duty to grant you a dismission in good faith.

It has no doubt been long apparent to you, brothers, that foreign influence and Roman Catholicism have been making steady and alarming progress in our country. You cannot have failed to observe the significant transition of the foreign born and Romanist from a character quiet, retiring and even abject, to one bold, threatening, turbulent, and even despotic in its appearance and assumptions. You must have become alarmed at the systematic and rapidly augmenting power of these dangerous and unnatural elements of our national condition. So it is, brothers, with others besides yourselves, in every state of the Union. A sense of danger has struck the great heart of the nation. In every city, town and hamlet the danger has been seen and the alarm sounded. And hence true men have devised this order as a means of disseminating patriotic principles, of keeping alive the fire of national virtue, of fostering the national intelligence, and of advancing America and the American interest on the one side, and on the other of checking the stride of the foreigner or alien, of thwarting the machinations and subverting the deadly plans of the Jesuit and Papist.

GEORGE FITZHUGH

We do not agree with the authors of the Declaration of Independence, that governments "derive their just powers from the consent of the governed." . . . All governments must originate in force, and be continued by force. The very term, government, implies that it is carried on against the consent of the governed. Fathers do not derive their authority, as heads of families, from the consent of wife and children, nor do they govern their families by their consent. They never take the vote of the family as to the labors to be performed, the moneys to be expended, or as to anything else. Masters dare not take the vote of slaves as to their government. If they did, constant holiday, dissipation, and extravagance would be the result. Captains of ships are not appointed by the consent of the crew, and never take their vote, even in "doubling Cape Horn." If they did, the crew would generally vote to get drunk, and the ship would never weather the cape. Not even in the most democratic countries are soldiers governed by their consent, nor is their vote taken on the eve of battle. They have some how lost (or never had) the "inalienable rights of life, liberty, and the pursuit of happiness," and, whether Americans or Russians, are forced into battle without and often against their consent. The

Reprinted from George Fitzhugh, CANNIBALS ALL!, *ed. C. Vann Woodward (Cambridge, Mass.: Harvard University Press, 1960), pp. 243–249.*

ancient republics were governed by a small class of adult male citizens who assumed and exercised the government without the consent of the governed. The South is governed just as those ancient republics were. In the county in which we live, there are eighteen thousands souls, and only twelve hundred voters. But we twelve hundred, the governors, never asked and never intend to ask the consent of the sixteen thousand eight hundred whom we govern. Were we to do so, we should soon have an "organized anarchy." The governments of Europe could not exist a week without the positive force of standing armies.

They are all governments of force, not of consent. Even in our North, the women, children, and free negroes, constitute four-fifths of the population; and they are all governed without their consent. But they mean to correct this gross and glaring iniquity at the North. They hold that all men, women, and negroes, and smart children are equals, and entitled to equal rights. The widows and free negroes begin to vote in some of those States, and they will have to let all colors and sexes and ages vote soon, or give up the glorious principles of human equality and universal emancipation.

The experiment which they will make, we fear, is absurd in theory, and the symptoms of approaching anarchy and agrarianism among them leave no doubt that its practical operation will be no better than its theory. Antirentism, "vote-myself-a-farm-ism," and all the other Isms, are but the spattering drops that precede a social deluge.

Abolition ultimates in "Consent Government"; Consent Government in Anarchy, Free Love, Agrarianism, &c., &c., and "Self-elected Despotism" winds up the play.

If the interests of the governors, or governing class, be not conservative, they certainly will not conserve institutions injurious to their interests. There never was and never can be an old society, in which the immediate interests of a majority of human souls do not conflict with all established order, all right of property, and all existing institutions. Immediate interest is all the mass look to; and they would be sure to revolutionize government, as often as the situation of the majority was worse than that of the minority. Divide all property to-day, and a year hence the inequalities of property would provoke a re-division.

In the South, the interest of the governing class is eminently conservative, and the South is fast becoming the most conservative of nations.

Already, at the North, government vibrates and oscillates between Radicalism and Conservatism; at present, Radicalism or Black Republicanism is in the ascendant.

The number of paupers is rapidly increasing; radical and agrarian doctrines are spreading; the women and the children, and the negroes, will soon be let in to vote; and then they will try the experiment of "Consent Government and Constituted Anarchy."

It is falsely said, that revolutions never go backwards. They always go backwards, and generally farther back than where they started. The Social Revolution now going on at the North, must some day go backwards. Shall it do so now, ere it has perpetrated an infinitude of mischief, shed oceans of blood, and occasioned endless human misery; or will the Conservatives of the North let it run the length of its leather, inflict all these evils, and then rectify itself by issuing into military despotism? We think that by a kind of alliance, offensive and defensive, with the South, Northern Conservatism may now arrest and turn back the tide of Radicalism and Agrarianism. We will not presume to point out the whole means and *modus operandi.* They on the field of action will best see what is necessary to be done.

Whilst we hold that all government is a matter of force, we yet think the governing class should be numerous enough to understand, and so situated as to represent fairly, all interests. The Greek and Roman masters were thus situated; so were the old Barons of England, and so are the white citizens of the South. If not all masters, like Greek and Roman citizens, they all belong to the master race, have exclusive rights and privileges of citizenship, and an interest not to see this right of citizenship extended, disturbed, and rendered worthless and contemptible.

. . .

We think speculations as to constructing governments are little worth; for all government is the gradual accretion of Nature, time and circumstances. Yet these theories have occurred to us, and, as they are conservative, we will suggest them. In slaveholding countries all freemen should vote and govern, because their interests are conservative. In free states, the government should be in the hands of the land-owners, who are also conservative. A system of primogeniture, and entails of small parcels of land, might, in a great measure, identify the interests of all; or, at least, those who held no lands would generally be the children and kinsmen of those who did, and be taken care of by them. The frequent accumulation of large fortunes, and consequent pauperism of the masses, is the greatest evil of modern society. Would not small entails prevent this? All cannot own lands, but as many should own them as is consistent with good farming and advanced civilization.

The social institutions of the Jews, as established by Moses and Joshua, most nearly fulfill our ideas of perfect government.

A word, at parting, to Northern Conservatives. A like danger threatens North and South, proceeding from the same source. Abolitionism is maturing what Political Economy began. With inexorable sequence Let Alone is made to usher in No-Government. North and South our danger is the same, and our remedies, though differing in degree, must in character be the same. Let Alone must be repudiated, if we would have any Government. We must, in all sections, act upon the principle that the world is "too little governed." You of the North need not institute negro slavery, far less reduce white men to the state of negro slavery. But the masses require more of protection, and the masses and philosophers equally require more of control. Leave it to time and circumstances to suggest the necessary legislation; but rely upon it, "Anarchy, plus the street constable" won't answer any longer. . . .

. . .

There are three kinds of force that occur to us will sustain a government. First, "inside necessity," such as slavery, that occasions a few to usurp power, and to hold it forcibly, without consulting the many; secondly, the force of foreign pressure or aggression, which combines men and States together for common défence; and thirdly, the inherent force of a prescriptive or usurpative government, which sustains itself by standing armies. Such are all the governments of Western Europe. Not one of them could exist forty-eight hours, but for the standing armies. These standing armies became necessary and grew up as slavery disappeared. The old Barons kept the Canaille, the Proletariat, the Sans

Culottes, the Nomadic Beggars in order by lashing their backs and supplying their wants. They must be fed and kept at work. Modern society tries to effect this (but in vain) by moral suasion and standing armies. Riots, mobs, strikes, and revolutions are daily occurring. The mass of mankind cannot be governed by Law. More of despotic discretion, and less of Law, is what the world wants. We take our leave by saying "THERE IS TOO MUCH OF LAW AND TOO LITTLE OF GOVERNMENT IN THIS WORLD."

Physical force, not moral suasion, governs the world. The negro sees the driver's lash, becomes accustomed to obedient cheerful industry, and is not aware that the lash is the force that impels him. The free citizen fulfills *con amore,* his round of social, political, and domestic duties, and never dreams that the Law, with its fines and jails, penitentiaries and halters, or Public Opinion, with its ostracism, its mobs, and its tar and feathers, help to keep him revolving in his orbit. Yet, remove these physical forces, and how many good citizens would shoot, like fiery comets, from their spheres, and disturb society with their eccentricities and their crimes.

III. RECENT INTERPRETATION

All the documents in the preceding section have several characteristics in common: an impatience with existing institutions, a sense that the fate of American society was precarious, and an insistence that radical solutions of one kind or another were necessary. Fitzhugh and Garrison wanted very different things from life, and Thoreau and the Know-Nothings shared very few wishes or assumptions. But they, and many of their articulate contemporaries, agreed that they lived in a state of acute emergency of some sort, and that the emergency could *not* be met by existing institutions. Parrington's category of "romance" does not explain why so many men and women of the period were convinced that they and their country were in a crisis and that the churches, laws, and economic institutions which were already in existence simply could not deal with the situation. This question is brilliantly discussed in the following selection from Stanley Elkins' *Slavery.*

STANLEY ELKINS

By the 1830's the closest thing to an intellectual community in the United States consisted of men with no

Reprinted from Stanley Elkins, SLAVERY: A PROBLEM IN AMERICAN INSTITUTIONAL AND INTELLECTUAL LIFE *(Chicago: University of Chicago Press, 1959), pp. 141–164, by permission of the publisher.*

concrete commitment to the system at all. They were men who had no close commitment to any of society's institutions. They were truly men without responsibility.

The intellectual center of gravity had by this time somehow shifted. Its present location was not the Virginia Tidewater, not Philadelphia, not really New York, not even, in fact, quite

Boston. The nearest approach to such a center had withdrawn, rather symbolically, to a place *just outside* Boston, to the town of Concord. Living in Concord, or spending much time there, were persons all of whose names are now familiar: Ralph Waldo Emerson, Henry Thoreau, Bronson Alcott, George Ripley, Margaret Fuller, Theodore Parker, William Henry Channing, and others. These persons lived in a radically different age, and did their thinking in a radically changed setting, from that of such earlier intellectuals as Jefferson, Hamilton, Madison, and Adams.

The age had several characteristics which set it apart from that of forty years before and which left a decided mark upon its spiritual life. It . . . was an age featured by the breakdown of a number of key social institutions. During his own lifetime, the mature American of 1830 had seen stripped of their power all the establishments which a generation or so earlier had seemed to represent order—the church, the bar, the Federalist party, and the eastern merchant aristocracy. It was an age in which the individual had become an almost mystical symbol of promise. "In all my lectures," Emerson declared, "I have taught one doctrine, namely the infinitude of the private man." [1] It was also one in which nearly every form of public expression had taken on a prodigious quality of abstraction. Finally, it was an age which throbbed with the impulse to reform.

Some of this requires a certain amount of elaboration. Institutions, for example: what difference might the presence or absence of institutions, their thinness or thickness, make in the

texture of a man's thought? It was this very question that Henry James asked with regard to Hawthorne and what Hawthorne lacked. His famous answer was outrageously concrete:

The negative side of the spectacle on which Hawthorne looked out, in his contemplative saunterings and reveries, might, indeed, with a little ingenuity, be made almost ludicrous; one might enumerate the items of high civilization, as it exists in other countries, which are absent from the texture of American life, until it should become a wonder to know what was left. No State, in the European sense of the word, and indeed barely a specific national name. No sovereign, no court, no personal loyalty, no aristocracy, no church, no clergy, no army, no diplomatic service, no country gentlemen, no palaces, no castles, nor manors, nor old country houses, nor parsonages, nor thatched cottages, nor ivied ruins; no cathedrals, nor abbeys, nor little Norman churches; no great universities nor public schools—no Oxford, nor Eton, nor Harrow; no literature, no novels, no museums, no pictures, no political society, no sporting class—no Epsom nor Ascot! . . . The natural remark, in the almost lurid light of such an indictment, would be that if these things are left out, everything is left out.[2]

Sociologically, there seems to be much reason for taking James's statement seriously, however idiosyncratic its expression. What he might be saying is that artistic and intellectual activity at large must be nourished by a rich and complex profusion of "things," things which ought to have a certain sanction in antiquity—by no means a trivial point in itself. But there is an even larger principle involved, one to which "things" and "antiquity" are certainly related, but in rather a secondary way (Hawthorne's Salem was, after all, very old); the heart of the matter could be that these "facts" and

[1] *Journals of Ralph Waldo Emerson*, ed. Edward Waldo Emerson and Waldo Emerson Forbes (Boston: Houghton Mifflin, 1909–14), V, 380.

[2] Henry James, *Hawthorne* (New York: Harper, 1879), pp. 42–43.

"things" which James so valued were the signs, agents, and products of social institutions, of continuing institutions upon which one could count for mooring posts, for points of view, for centers of focus. It could be said that institutions define a society's culture, that they provide the stable channels, for better or worse, within which the intellectual must have his business—if, that is, his work is to have real consequences for society and if he himself is to have a positive function there. Institutions with power produce the "things" not only upon which one leans but also against which one pushes; they provide the standards whereby, for men of sensibility, one part of society may be judged and tested against another. The lack of them, moreover, removes the thinker not only from the places where power resides but also from the very *idea* of power and how it is used. "Power" is transformed into an abstraction. . . .

Society, institutions, power—all became abstractions, both in letters and in popular oratory. Where now was the setting in which the thinker might locate man, the object of his contemplation? The transcendent "individual" must be placed not in the society over which he had symbolically triumphed but in a transcendental universe—man himself became an abstraction. Success, energy, and power had for Americans made abstractions of everything; no one really needed to know or remember what had made them possible.

The very conception of their history itself which Americans could hold at this time was non-institutional, and this may shed some light on the abstract nature of both their thought and their morality. There were, for instance, at least two points of view (besides those of Lord North and George III) from which Americans

might have analyzed their Revolution. One was indicated by the language of the Declaration:

We hold these truths to be self-evident, that all men are created equal, that they are endowed by their Creator with certain inalienable Rights. . . . That whenever any Form of Government becomes destructive of these ends, it is the Right of the People to alter and abolish it, and to institute new Government. . . .

It was to some extent necessary that the revolutionary generation should conceive its great enterprise in such terms: mounting oppression and the right to smash all connections and begin anew. But there was another viewpoint, that of Edmund Burke. Burke's line of vision was fully English, and he had little use for the above sentiments; yet he was not unfriendly to the Revolution. He was always aware how relatively little was being smashed. He knew that the revolt of the Americans had sprung from a rude disruption of orderly expectations, that they were in fact struggling to conserve the institutions they already had, and that the very strength of those institutions pretty much guaranteed, in one form or another, that the Americans would succeed. Yet it was very difficult for any American to picture his Revolution on such grounds—grounds of "stability" rather than "change"—and for good reasons which Burke himself would have been the first to understand. The clearest social thought comes when basic institutional arrangements are threatened, and when revolutionists are truly forced to change these institutions, they become highly sensitive to them. But the American Revolution never really made this demand on its intellectuals. Its political and military leaders operated within institutional patterns long familiar to them, and, intellectually, all the Revolution required with the abstract ideals necessary to keep it going. Practically, it was an organizational genius for self-government acquired over generations that brought it to a successful conclusion. There were "changes," to be sure, but the major changes, which the Revolution did little more than legitimize, had already been accomplished over half a century before. It is an axiom in the theory of revolutions that an "orthodox" revolution, in the European sense, undergoes at least two phases. The first is that phase of militancy where ideals and slogans must be produced and proclaimed for the inspiration of the revolutionary movement. Necessary though they are, however, these ideals, being abstract and primarily moral in their nature, represent only one side of the movement's objectives; beyond a certain point there is danger that the abstractions may be taken too literally and may thus threaten the future stability of the revolutionary state. At this point—"Thermidor"—it may become necessary to eliminate the dedicated sloganeers, the Robespierres and Trotskys associated with the militant phase, and to formulate the objectives of the new state in more rational and pacific form. In our own Revolution this never occurred. Instead, the slogans themselves became enshrined in the minds and hearts of Americans, and to the generations that followed there seemed little reason why they should not be adequate to explain all the basic facts of the national experience.[3]

There had been one moment, indeed, when institutional arrangements had hung in the balance, and it was during this time that our best social thinking occurred. In the Philadelphia convention of 1787 and during the period of ratification that followed, men with specific stakes in society, men attached to institutions and with a vested interested in one another's presence, men aware of being engaged with concrete problems of power, wrote and debated a constitution and produced a treatise in political science—*The Federalist*—which remain as yet unmatched. They had, in short, all the prerequisites for intellectual efficiency. With much to push against and with both the opportunity and the necessity for testing their conceptions against those of one another, the common character of their work avoided much duplication of effort and eliminated the need for returning continually to first principles. But once again the very brilliant success of these men's efforts made it unnecessary to preserve the party they created, and made it possible for posterity to canonize their concrete achievement—the Constitution—into a shining moral abstraction. In short, a "withering-away of the state," at least in men's minds, never occurred more decisively than it did here; and we are brought back once more to the problem of "wisdom" and what, if anything,

[3] It might be added that the Declaration had been regarded all along not so much as a revolutionary manifesto, in the classic sense, but rather as a legal brief wherein the plaintiff epitomizes the reasons for a contemplated separation. Those elements in the revolutionary movement who might have been led to take the more sweeping assertions of universal equality too literally—the Tom Paines and Sam Adamses—had less, rather than more, influence as the movement developed into a drawn-out war. The Declaration's *obiter dicta* would thus never really be challenged one way or the other, and the Revolution never required a "Thermidor." As a result, the American people could accept the Declaration more or less *in toto* as a statement of the political theory on which the Republic rested, and if any test of its soundness were required, it was met by the success of the Revolution.

men in those days presumed to be wisdom's support. That support, as Emerson announced, was simply "character":

To educate the wise man, the State exists; and with the appearance of the wise man, the State expires. The appearance of character makes the State unnecessary. The wise man is the State. He needs no army, fort, or navy,—he loves men too well; no bribe, or feast, or palace, to draw friends to him: no vantage ground, no favorable circumstance. He needs no library, for he has not done thinking; no church, for he is a prophet; no statute book, for he is the lawgiver; no money, for he is value; no road, for he is at home where he is; no experience, for the life of the creator . . . looks from his eyes.[4]

The thinkers of Concord, who in the later thirties and forties would create an intellectual attitude at least coherent enough to be given a name— "Transcendentalism"—were men without connections. Almost without exception, they had no ties with the sources of wealth; there were no lawyers or jurists among them; none of them ever sat in a government post; none was a member of Congress; they took next to no part in politics at all; indeed, as Emerson remarked, "They do not even like to vote." [5] Not one of them wielded even the limited influence of a professor; they were scarcely on good terms with nearby Harvard itself, though all were well educated and several of them had studied there. They were all deeply concerned with religion and a number were ministers. Yet even here the bias was strongly anti-institutional, anti-formal, and individualistic.

Emerson had quit his Unitarian pastorate in 1832 in the conviction that he could administer the Lord's Supper only if the bread and wine were omitted from it; attacking the organized church as dead and worthless in his 1838 Divinity School address, he became *persona non grata* at Harvard and remained so for thirty years. George Ripley, declaring that "the truth of religion does not depend on tradition, nor historical facts, but has an unerring witness in the soul," [6] resigned from his pulpit in 1841 amid the protests of his admiring parishioners. Orestes Brownson had first joined the Presbyterian church but had remained in it for only two years, becoming a Universalist in 1824 and later a Universalist minister, though after a series of broils with other Universalists he drifted about as a freelance and eventually back to the church as a Unitarian. After four years of this he organized his own church, the "society for Christian Union and Progress"; then, having attacked both Protestantism and Catholicism in *New Views of Christianity, Society, and the Church* (1836), Brownson shocked New England liberals in 1844 by joining the Catholic church and violently attacking all its enemies. Theodore Parker was also a Unitarian minister but was never able to get along with other Unitarians. The Unitarians themselves had done what they could to get away from forms, traditions, and miracles, but Parker harassed them mercilessly for too much dependence on authority and for developing their own orthodoxies. Their organizational stability in Boston, loose and uncertain at best, was constantly being threatened by such episodes as Parker's attacks on the Divinity School, his denunciation of the Hollis Street

[4] "Politics," in *Emerson's Complete Works* (Cambridge: Riverside Press, 1883), III, *Essays, Second Series*, 206–7.

[5] "The Transcendentalist," in *Works*, I, *Nature, Addresses and Lectures*, 326.

[6] "Letter to the Church in Purchase Street," in O. B. Frothingham, *George Ripley* (Boston: Houghton Mifflin, 1882), pp. 84–85.

Council,[7] and his demand, in an ordination sermon in 1841, that "we worship as Jesus did, with no mediator, with nothing between us and the Father of all." [8] Parker never actually abandoned the pulpit, but a new church was founded for him which he ran on his own terms after having resigned his pastorate in West Roxbury. William Henry Channing, nephew of the founder of Unitarianism, William Ellery Channing, was constantly in and out of the church. He tried unsuccessfully in 1837 to organize a free church; he resigned a Unitarian pastorate after less than two years because he suspected Christianity of not being a divine institution and the Gospels of being unreliable; for two years Channing led an independent religious society in New York which fell apart when he went to Brook Farm in 1845, though he stayed there only a few months. After heading the "Religious Union of Associationists," whose object was the reign of love among mankind and which lasted about three years, Channing in middle life lapsed back into Unitarianism. The pathetic Jones Very, a poet of sorts as well as a man of religion, impressed the other Transcendentalists for a time with his intoxicated mysticism, but after his youthful inspiration had worn off he was unable to preach well because of shyness; aside from two temporary pastorates, Very lived the last forty years of his life in virtual retirement, a self-confessed "failure." At one time he had even been suspected of madness and had actually spent five weeks in an asylum, where he had successfully preached to the inmates his doctrine of "will-less existence." The only ministers connected with the Transcendentalist circle who retained at all times a stable relationship with the church were James Freeman Clarke and Frederic Henry Hedge, both of whom remained within the Unitarian fold and in later years took active roles in public life.

Certain features already mentioned as having become especially characteristic of the period at large—its abandonment of older institutional patterns, its exaltation of the individual and his limitless potentialities, the high-flown abstraction which national success permitted in public expression, the receptivity (charged with tension and guilt) toward the reform schemes which flourished in the middle thirties and early forties—all these features found their close counterparts in the attitudes and thought of the Transcendentalists. Their "revolt against the age" could be conceived and acted out only along lines which the age itself had laid down for them.

The anti-institutional impulse so strikingly evident even in the ministers' relationship with their own churches was also to be seen in the Transcendentalists' attitude toward institutions in general. "The difficulty," wrote Emerson, "is that we do not make a world of our own, but fall into institutions already made, and have to accommodate ourselves to them to be useful at all, and this accommodation is, I say, a loss of so much integrity and, of course, of so much power." [9] This echoed the earlier thoughts of William

[7] The Reverend John Pierpont in 1842 had denounced brewers and wine-bibbers from his pulpit and had actually called them by name. A council of clergymen rebuked Pierpont for using intemperate language, whereupon Parker denounced the council's decision as a "Jesuitical document in the interest of the liquor trade." See "The Hollis Street Council," *The Dial*, III (October, 1842), 201–21.

[8] Theodore Parker, *The Transient and Permanent in Christianity* (Boston: American Unitarian Association, 1908), p. 30.

[9] *Journals*, II, 448–49.

Ellery Channing, who had declared, "most of our civil institutions grow out of our corruptions." [10] The church as an institution was corrupt, and most of the Transcendentalists attacked it as such. "I hear a preacher announce for his text and topic the expediency of one of the institutions of his church. Do I not know beforehand that not possibly can he say a new and spontaneous word?" [11] Look not to the church for the meaning of Christianity, urged Theodore Parker, but to Jesus Himself: "He founds no institution as a monument of his words." [12] They turned their hostility not only upon the church but upon other establishments. Trade was denounced as an institutionalized web of corruption. Theodore Parker was not against businessmen as individuals ("Not all the merchants were bad," remarks his biographer) [13] but was very hard on them as a class. "All is the reflection of this most powerful class. The truths that are told are for them, and the lies." [14] Emerson said similar things about the "system," though he too made allowances for decent *individuals*.[15] The Transcendentalists at-

tacked all institutions and stood aloof from them—church, trade, even government itself. Especially noteworthy, as Perry Miller observes, was Henry Thoreau's "comprehensive resignation from all institutions he had never joined.[16] Everywhere a man goes, Thoreau complained, "men will pursue and paw him with their dirty institutions, and, if they can, constrain him to belong to their desperate oddfellow society." [17]

Here we get a sense of how dramatic was the contrast between these men and those of two generations earlier, and of how differently they looked at things. Thoreau's refusal to pay a poll tax, while sojourning at Walden, resulted in his being lodged overnight in the Concord jail, and the episode inspired him to declare, "I was never molested by any person but those who represented the State." [18] It was that very "State," of course, which had made it possible for Henry Thoreau to remain unmolested by any but itself— and that but once. The flourishing success of such a "State," there in the heart of New England, now enabled its

10 Quoted in John Reinhardt, "The Evolution of William Ellery Channing's Sociopolitical Ideas," *American Literature*, XXVI (May, 1954), 157.
11 "Self-Reliance," in *Works*, II, *Essays, First Series*, 55–56.
12 Parker, *The Transient and Permanent*, p. 2.
13 Henry S. Commager, *Theodore Parker* (Boston: Beacon Press, 1936), p. 183.
14 "A Sermon of Merchants," in Perry Miller (ed.), *The Transcendentalists: An Anthology* (Cambridge: Harvard University Press, 1950), p. 454.
15 "I content myself with the facts that the general system of our trade (apart from the blacker traits, which, I hope, are exceptions denounced and unshared by all reputable men), is a system of selfishness; is not dictated by the high sentiments of human nature; is not meas-

ured by the exact law of reciprocity, much less by the sentiments of love and heroism, but is a system of distrust, of concealment, of superior keenness, not of giving but of taking advantage." "Man the Reformer," in *Works*, I, 222.
16 *The Transcendentalists*, p. 258. Society's very instruments of communication were depraved: railroads ("We do not ride on the railroad; it rides upon us"), the post office ("There are very few important communications made through it"), or newspapers ("I never read any memorable news in a newspaper"). *Writings of Henry David Thoreau*, ed. B. Torrey and F. B. Sanborn (Boston: Houghton Mifflin, 1893–1900), II, *Walden, or Life in the Woods*, 102–3.
17 *Ibid.* "This, our respectable daily life, on which . . . our institutions are founded, is in fact the veriest illusion, and will vanish like the baseless fabric of a vision. . . ." *Writings*, VI, *Familiar Letters*, 162.
18 *Writings*, II, *Walden*, 190.

philosophers to contemplate the institutions it could do without and to hold up, as a serious philosophical alternative, the question of whether or not it needed any at all. Could he have foreseen it, this might well have confounded Theodore Parker's grandfather, who had commanded the militia on Lexington Green. And whereas few prose lyrics in praise of nature have so endeared themselves to us as Thoreau's *Walden* has, we might still ask whether *Walden*, as a paradigm of the good society, would have made much sense to James Madison.

It followed that the prime seat of virtue lay in the individual himself: "Transcendentalism says, the Man is all." [19] "What faculties slumber within," exclaimed William Ellery Channing, "weighed down by the chains of custom!" [20] To Frederic Henry Hedge, who inspired the first meetings of the "Transcendental Club," it was upon the individual that men must place the supreme hope of progress. "Let us ground it on universal Man, on the sight of the human will, and on the might of the human will, and on the boundless resources of the human mind." [21] A theory of infinite perfectibility flowed quite naturally from this, and the fellow seekers eagerly discussed its various possibilities. "I believe in Eternal Progression," wrote Margaret

Fuller to James Freeman Clarke; "I believe in a God, a Beauty and Perfection to which I am to strive all my life for assimilation." [22] George Ripley insisted that "man has the power of conceiving a perfection higher than he has ever reached. Not only so. He can make this perfection a distinct object of pursuit." [23] The same thought was announced by Bronson Alcott in even loftier terms: "Every soul feels at times the possibility of becoming a God; she cannot rest in the human, she aspires after the God-like. This instinctive tendency is an authentic augury of its own fulfillment. Men shall become Gods." [24] It was on the theme of individual perfectibility that the Transcendentalists' leading ideas on education were based. [25]

Did he [the Transcendentalist] take up the cause of education, it was as a believer in the latent capacity of every child, boy or girl; as an earnest wisher that such capacity might be stimulated by the best methods, and directed to the best ends. . . . Mr. Alcott's school . . . would have achieved

[22] *Memoirs of Margaret Fuller Ossoli*, ed. R. W. Emerson, W. H. Channing, and J. F. Clarke (London: R. Bentley, 1852), I, 177.

[23] George Ripley, *Discourse on the Philosophy of Religion* (Boston: J. Munroe, 1836), p. 39.

[24] *Dial*, I (July, 1840), 87.

[25] "It was the design of Providence," reasoned Sampson Reed, "that the infant mind should possess the germ of every science. If it were not so, they could hardly be learned." Elizabeth Peabody declared, "There is not a single thing that cannot be studied with comparative ease, by a child, who can be taught what faculties he must use, and how they are to be brought to bear on the subject, and what influence on those faculties the subject will have, after it is mastered." Sampson Reed, *Observations on the Growth of the Mind* (Boston: Crosby, Nichols, 1859), p. 45; Elizabeth Peabody, *Record of a School: Exemplifying the General Principles of Spiritual Culture* (Boston: Russell, Shattuck, 1836), p. xxi.

[19] *Journals*, VII, 268.

[20] Quoted in Van Wyck Brooks, *The Life of Emerson* (New York: Dutton, 1932), p. 37.

[21] "Progress of Society," in Miller, *Transcendentalists*, p. 74. "Character," according to the "Orphic Sayings" of Bronson Alcott, "is the only legitimate institution; the only legal influence." *The Dial*, I (July, 1840), 91. Emerson, in "Self-Reliance," exhorted the young man to throw aside the curtains of dead institutions and free his soul: ". . . under all these screens I have difficulty to detect the precise man you are. . . ." *Works*, II, 55.

such remarkable results had more faithful trial of its methods been possible.[26]

Even the agricultural communities (Brook Farm and Fruitlands) in which some of the Transcendentalists took part were conceived not as collective institutions but rather as "united individuals" gathered together to make self-perfection easier and to provide, as Elizabeth Peabody put it, "LEISURE TO LIVE IN ALL THE FACULTIES OF THE SOUL." [27] William Henry Channing put the aspirations of the whole group into a formula: "Trust, dare, and be; infinite good is ready for your asking; seek and find." [28]

That the age permitted its philosophers to abstract "man" so completely from his culture, with no sense of how much was thereby being taken for granted, should go far to explain the overwhelming abstractness of the Transcendentalists' thinking about everything—not only about "man" but about existence itself. Transcendentalists,

George Ripley declared, are so called "because they believe in an order of truths which transcends the sphere of the external sense. Their leading idea is the supremacy of mind over matter." [29] Frederic Henry Hedge managed to write whole passages on "society" in which there was not a single concrete word.[30] The lovable Bronson Alcott almost lived on abstractions. Emerson, with a certain mellow tolerance, noted of Alcott in his journal, "Particulars—particular thoughts, sentences, facts even—cannot interest him, except as for a moment they take their place as a ray from his orb. The Whole,—Nature proceeding from himself, is what he studies." Emerson would be astonished, "having left him in the morning with one set of opinions, to find him in the evening totally escaped from all recollection of them. . . ." [31] Although life at the Alcotts' had its genial side, the abstractions of the philosopher brought actual suffering to others. "At the very time," writes Harold Goddard, "when Alcott was entering in his Journal, 'All day discussing the endless infinite themes,' Mrs. Alcott was doing the endless

---

[26] Octavius Brooks Frothingham, *Trancendentalism in New England* (New York: Putnam, 1876), p. 156. Frothingham had personal recollections of many of the Transcendentalists.

[27] Elizabeth Peabody, "Plan of the West Roxbury Community," *The Dial*, II (January, 1842), 364. William Ellery Channing thought that the depressed condition of laborers after the 1837 panic was due to "the want of a strict economy"—they should have been realizing their true selves in cultural improvement. "Sure I am," he wrote, "that, were they to study plainness of dress and simplicity of living, for the purpose of their own true elevation, they would surpass in intellect, in taste, in honorable qualities, and in present enjoyment, that great proportion of the prosperous who are softened into indulgence or enslaved to empty show. By such self-denial, how might the burden of labor be lightened, and time and strength redeemed for improvement!" *The Works of William E. Channing, D.D.* (Boston, 1855), V, 211.

[28] *Memoirs of Margaret Fuller Ossoli*, II, 13.

[29] "Letter to the Church in Purchase Street," in Frothingham, *Ripley*, p. 84.

[30] "For, what is society, It is not a single people or generation, it is not a collection of individuals as such; but it is an intimate union of individuals, voluntarily coöperating for the common good, actuated by social feelings, governed by social principles, and urged onward by social improvements. Society, in this sense, has always been advancing, not uniformly, indeed, far from it,—sometimes the motion has not been perceptible, sometimes, it may be, there has been no motion at all,—but it has never lost ground;—whenever it has moved at all, it has moved forward." "Progress of Society," in Miller, *Transcendentalists*, p. 73.

[31] *Journals*, IV, 72; VI, 175, "Alcott drank water," commented Frederika Bremer, "and we drank fog."

finite chores."[32] At Fruitlands, Alcott and Charles Lane, in their heroic project of liberating the soul from its fetters of tradition and form, succeeded in shackling the household in an iron discipline which drove Mrs. Alcott close to distraction. "I am almost suffocated," she wrote furtively in her own journal, "in this atmosphere of restriction and form." The spartan diet was hard on her teeth, which were "very bad," and part of the routine involved everyone's keeping his hands "from each other's bodies."

All these causes have combined to make me somewhat irritable. . . . They all seem most stupidly obtuse on the causes of this occasional prostration of my judgment and faculties. I hope the solution of the problem will not be revealed to them too late for my recovery or their atonement for this invasion of my rights as a woman and a mother. Give me one day of practical philosophy. It is worth a century of speculation and discussion.[33]

But it was the restless Margaret Fuller, a woman of extaordinary intellectual capacities and strong sensibilities, who was the tragic figure of the Transcendentalists. The kindly reserve of Emerson, the dubious inspirations of the younger Channing, the vaporings of Alcott, the pale imitations in plaster at the Boston Athenaeum—to poor ardent Margaret there was nothing very *resistant* about all this. Almost too late, like a Henry James heroine, she

found what she needed in the thick life of Europe and in a love affair amid the passions of the Italian revolution of 1848. "Had I only come ten years earlier! Now my life must be a failure, so much strength has been wasted on abstractions, which only came because I grew not in the right soil."[34] The idyl was pathetically short, for very soon she had it all taken from her—husband, baby, her own life—in a storm at sea.[35]

The final element of interest to us in the thinking of the Transcendentalists—its overtone of guilt—was symptomatic of the reform impulses of the period. "I pray for the opportunity and will," wrote the anguished William Henry Channing to his mother in January, 1837, "to put forth all my powers rightly for the increase of good. . . . Self-satisfaction, or rather an easy conscience, I never yet enjoyed, and never deserved to, though perhaps I have by nature a self-tormenting disposition."[36] George Ripley's resignation from the pulpit was inspired by the conviction that his views did not have the reforming influence there that they should have had. "Blame me for it if you will," he wrote to his congregation in 1840, "but I cannot hold the degradation, the ignorance, the poverty, the vice, and the ruin of the soul, which is everywhere displayed in the very bosom of Christian society in our own city, while men look idly on, without a shudder."[37] Theodore Parker also worried over his relationship to the evils of the day. "It is a good thing, no doubt," he reflected,

Harold Clarke Goddard, *Studies in New England Transcendentalism* (New York: Columbia University Press, 1908), p. 158. Alcott's daughter Louisa May, when once asked to define a "philosopher," replied, "My definition is of a man up in a balloon, with his family and friends holding the ropes which confine him to earth and trying to haul him down." *Ibid.,* p. 158.

Odell Shepard, *Pedlar's Progress: The Life of Bronson Alcott* (Boston: Little, Brown, 1938), pp. 348, 351–53.

Memoirs, II, 225.

All three were drowned in a shipwreck off Fire Island, New York, in 1850.

Octavius B. Frothingham, *Memoir of William Henry Channing* (Boston: Houghton Mifflin, 1886), pp. 125–26.

Frothingham, *Ripley,* p. 74.

"that I should read the Greek Anthology and cultivate myself in my leisure, as a musk-melon ripens in the sun, but why should I be the only one of a thousand who has this chance?" [38] Even the serene Emerson was moved to exclaim, "Am I not too protected a person? Is there not a wide disparity between the lot of me and the lot of thee, my poor brother, my poor sister?" [39] Overwhelmed, for instance, by the evils of business life, Emerson was led to construct a web of guilt from which no one could be exempt.

We are all implicated of course in this charge; it is only necessary to ask a few questions as to the progress of the articles of commerce from the fields where they grew, to our houses, to become aware that we eat and drink and wear perjury and fraud in a hundred commodities. . . .

But by coming out of trade you have not cleared yourself. The trail of the serpent reaches into all the lucrative professions and practices of man. Each has its own wrongs. Each finds a tender and very intelligent conscience a disqualification for success. . . . Inextricable seem to be the twinings and tendrils of this evil, and we all involve ourselves in it the deeper by forming connections, by wives and children, by benefits and debts.[40]

"What is a man born for," he insisted, "but to be a Reformer, a Re-maker of what man has made; a renouncer of lies; a restorer of truth and good, imitating that great Nature which embosoms us all . . . ?" [41]

Such expressions were indicative of a phenomenon which was becoming noticeably widespread. It was apparent by the mid-1830's—with the appearance

[38] Quoted in Commager, *Theodore Parker*, p. 163.
[39] "New England Reformers," in *Works*, III, *Essays, Second Series*, 244.
[40] "Man the Reformer," in *Works*, I, 221, 223–24.
[41] *Ibid.*, p. 236.

of Transcendentalism, of abolitionism, of the reform-conscious Jacksonian "workingmen's parties"—that America was entering an extraordinary period of reform. The drive, momentarily halted with the panic and depression of the late thirties, burst forth once more in the forties in a veritable fury of reform projects of every imaginable sort—temperance, millenarianism, perfectionism, spiritualistic Shakerism, utopianism, pacifism. It could probably be said that much of the aggression which such activities surely generated found its satisfaction in the splurge of Manifest Destiny and war with Mexico in the middle and late forties, for by the 1850's a great number of the reform schemes so absorbing a few years earlier had lost their vitality. By then the field was vacated, so far as most people were concerned, to a single reform preoccupation—antislavery. That movement, present in some form since the early thirties and inflamed rather than alleviated by the exertions of the Mexican War, grew to formidable proportions in the 1850's.

• • •

It should . . . be recognized that in the history of American reform no direct correlation can be found between the extent of any given social evil and the intensity of the reform activity directed against it. It is frequently to be observed that some of the most notorious of abuses have been allowed to go unchallenged while others comparatively superficial may be attacked with inordinate energy, or that continuing ills may have been ignored at one time and ferociously denounced at another. Something more than the mere existence of such ills is therefore needed to explain the action which they may evoke.

The first element that a typical American reform situation appears to require is some sort of disruption of expectations, not necessarily connected with the actual objects of reform. This may be brought about in more than one way. One such way could be a depression bringing unemployment and sharp cutbacks in a variety of projects. But such a disruption might equally well be accomplished by a sharp upturn in prosperity, with its sweeping rearrangements of status and the dramatic appearance of a multitude of unsuspected possibilities. However, either way—and such a qualification might actually be called the second element needed for a reform situation—there must be *some* maneuvering space, an absence of *total* crisis conditions. A total involvement of energies in a crisis would leave none for a reform movement.[42]

A further element typifying reform activity in America has been the absence of clear institutional arrangements for channeling radical energy. We have never had a traditional orientation for such activity; no institutionalized radicalism has ever existed here. For those who, like Bismarck, have known how to read them, such arrangements in European society—for instance, the social-democratic and quasi-revolutionary parties—have tended to act as more or less dependable barometers of society's ills and discontents. The absence of anything of the sort in the America of the thirties and forties may in some measure account for the wild and unfocused quality of the various reform impulses of that period. This lack of channels seems to produce in the reformers a constant reconsideration of first principles, an urge to develop a great variety of new organizations,[43] and an overwhelming illusion of the individual's power to change society. While European radical movements have tended very often to *over*emphasize the institutional structure of their ac-

---

[42] This is a principle well known to labor leaders of the present day; it is one of their rules of thumb that the ideal setting for organizing activity is not in the trough of a depression, when poverty and hard times have become a reality (nor for that matter in a time of steady prosperity), but rather when things are either on the way up or on the way down. The classic statement of this idea was made by the French sociologist Émile Durkheim. Durkheim's problem was exactly parallel: tension produced by disrupted expectations. To measure this, he used the most extreme index he could find: the suicide rate in a given society. That rate increases, he discovered, not only with a sharp drop but also with a sharp upturn in prosperity. "If . . . industrial or financial crises increase suicides, this is not because they cause poverty, since crises of prosperity have the same result; it is because they are crises, that is, disturbances of the collective order. Every disturbance of equilibrium, even though it achieves greater comfort *and a heightening of general vitality*, is an impulse to voluntary death. Whenever serious readjustments take place in the social order, whether or not due to a sudden growth or to an unexpected catastrophe, men are more inclined to self-destruction." Émile Durkheim, *Suicide*, trans. John A. Spaulding and George Simpson (Glencoe, Ill.: Free Press, 1951), p. 246 (italics

added.) Thus the seemingly paradoxical connection between reform movements and suicide (each involving a form of aggression) lies in a condition from which either one or the other may be likely to result.

[43] Alexis de Tocqueville, traveling in the United States during a great reform epoch—the 1830's—was greatly struck by this. "The political associations that exist in the United States," he wrote, "are only a single feature in the midst of the immense assemblage of associations in that country. Americans of all ages, all conditions, and all dispositions constantly form associations. . . . If it is proposed to inculcate some truth or to foster some feeling by the encouragement of a great example, they form a society. Wherever at the head of some new undertaking you see the government in France, or a man of rank in England, in the United States you will be sure to find an association." *Democracy in America* (New York: Knopf, 1945), II, 106.

tivity,[44] the case in the United States has never been anything but the opposite. The initial burst of energy is typically dissipated for lack of a structure, and instead of leaving some residue of an organization, it leaves, more often than not, nothing at all.

Still another element of interest is the role of the intellectual in a reform situation. In Europe, the intellectual institutionally connected—with church, labor movement, or the like—is seen to act, in a crisis, along specified lines. He produces explanations for the followers of the institution, and his formulations, as a matter of course, give the institution a central place in the solution of the crisis. Certain things are thus expected of the intellectual; his role has specifications. The intellectual without connections, chronically the case in America, finds himself in a fundamentally different position. Society normally asks little or nothing of him; a reform situation, on the other hand, seems to present him with a role. Yet even here the only pressures exerted on him involve the maintenance of a steady stream of new and exciting ideas; his only measurement of effect must be that of audience appeal; his principal question must continue to be, How many are listening? The pressures he does not feel are the concrete demands of an institution as such; he feels no direct responsibility for a clientele; he has, in short, no vested interest. The result for the intellectual is a situation of no limits. His reform thinking will tend to be erratic, emotional, compulsive, and abstract.

It is in such a setting that guilt—always a necessary element in any reform movement anywhere—comes to assume a unique and disproportionate role in American reform activity. A gnawing sense of responsibility for the ills of society at large appears to be experienced most readily in this country by groups relatively sheltered, by groups without connections and without clear and legitimate functions (a prime example being furnished by the Transcendentalists), and by people who have seen older and honored standards transformed, modified, or thrown aside.

Reforming energy, or a sense of social responsibility, could be designated in terms other than "guilt." But the conditions of American society have made such energy peculiarly a personal, an individual, phenomenon. It is the absence of clear channels for the harnessing of these drives that has made it so. Contrasted with the civilizations of Europe, our Protestant culture with its strong secular inclinations has been conspicuous for its lack of institutions, religious or secular, among whose functions has been the absorption and transformation of guilt. Guilt must be borne as an individual burden to a degree not to be observed elsewhere. Guilt in a structured situation has formalized outlets, limits within which it may be expressed constructively and with effect. Otherwise, it has no such channels. It will thus accumulate, like static electricity; it becomes aggressive, unstable, hard to control, often destructive. Guilt may at this point be transformed into implacable moral aggression: hatred of both the sinner and the sin.

The morally implacable American has always been seen by the European as somehow unpredictable and dangerous. On the other hand, the European, to that same American, has immemorially evoked suspicions of

[44] Robert Michels, *Political Parties,* trans. Eden and Cedar Paul (Glencoe, Ill.: Free Press, 1949), describes and analyzes the inevitable bureaucratization of European Social Democratic movements.

cynicism, expediency, and corruption. This is because, between ourselves and the Europeans, the most basic conceptions of morality—of sin, of "the good" and "the bad"—have traditionally lain poles apart. All such conceptions have inevitably been formulated, in our culture, from the viewpoint of the individual looking outward; the individual in America has historically insisted upon his right to define sin for himself. The complex life of Europe, lived out century after century in the same place, has never been able to afford this. There, it has traditionally been regarded as much too dangerous to intrust the definition of iniquity to inspired itinerant preachers and young men on the make. Too much has been at stake: it is through the eyes of society that such matters have been seen; it is society's voice that has articulated them; it is within society's institutions that such formulations have been set down, conserved, and woven into the ancient fabric of custom. Between America and Europe a staggering range of cultural differences rests upon this single point: the meaning of "sin."

Let us picture, if possible, a stark "sin situation": the quasi-feudal community of pre-nineteenth-century Europe. Here we find a setting in which the perversion of power, always possible, could and did have immediate consequences—a setting in which the strong might at any time exploit the weak. Here the social arrangements, tightly knit, could afford little *physical* latitude; it was rarely possible for the oppressed to uproot themselves and move away. The setting, thus, was one in which "sin" meant something concrete—one in which terms had to be made with sin then and there. Sin was defined; arrangements in law and custom were worked out in the course of things for construing the responsi-

bilities of the strong and providing for the protection of the weak—the sacraments, *noblesse oblige,* "the right ordering of things." People who have thus lived with sin for centuries have become intimately acquainted with it; shock does not come to them so easily; their methods of dealing with sin do not appear as callous to themselves as to the innocent.

If, on the other hand, there were such a thing as a pure "innocence situation," it might look very much like nineteenth-century America. There, space and mobility prevented the development of a tight social structure in which one had to accept exploitation, aggression, lust, and avarice as a daily problem. There, in a symbolic if not quite a literal sense, the very space and mobility might offer something of a bargaining situation, functioning not only as a "safety valve" for the exploited but also as a warning to the exploiter. Such a setting is not the same as that in which the oppressed, having no such latitude as a possible alternative, must protect themselves by an intricate set of customs and standards which take into account the existence of sin—of man's tendency to exploit man. The result would be a different kind of conscience with dramatically different standards. The "innocence situation" in certain respects can make, and always has made, higher moral demands; for here the evidence seems to show, as it did to the Transcendentalists, that man's "nature" is indeed normally good. "Sin" thus becomes an abstraction, vague and sinister. One might still talk of greed and lust, but not concretely; social sins are indeed committed, but are somehow plotted in the dark by unseen forces. Such sins seem actually worse than if intimacy with them were more direct. Moreover, as social sin diminishes in concreteness and acquires an overwhelming emphasis on individual rather than social morality, sin is internalized and made "personal"; sins are invented which concern only oneself and the social consequences of which are relatively limited.[45]

It now remains only to ask what might happen when people to whom daily aggression is not a perennial problem, people who have no knowledge of the traditional mechanisms whereby such aggression is habitually controlled, are then brought face to face with concrete instances of violence, cruelty, lust, and injustice. The individual whose culture does not con-

tain formalized arrangements for the handling of such matters feels himself personally involved. He pictures direct retribution; this being impossible, he is oppressed by the accumulation of guilt without means of outlet. Having no experience with limited ways of coming to terms with exploitation, being pressed by cumulative and undischarged guilt, he makes an emotional demand for a total solution. Destroy the evil, he cries; root it up, wipe it out.

Such, then, are some of the considerations which make guilt a primary thing to watch in American reform movements. The easing of guilt is always a most important hidden function of such movements, and with this as a disproportionate element in their maintenance, we have a test for movements that seem to disintegrate without accomplishing anything; guilt may have been absorbed and discharged in ways which make unnecessary a literal attainment of the objective.[46] . . .

[45] I am here referring to the sins of consumption—the consumption, for example, of those narcotics (alcohol, nicotine, and so on) which may be socially tolerated but which appear at the same time to symbolize personal corruption. The same is true of certain amusements (dancing, cards, the theater) which, through society's eyes, function to divert the lusts of the flesh into harmless channels but which, from a "personal" viewpoint, seem to represent—if not actually to embody—those very lusts. Even fornication has traditionally been regarded among us more as a matter of personal defilement than as an act having possible social consequences. Actually all this should be said in the past tense. It was a wholesome morality, so long as relatively few strains were put on it, but its breakdown, having taken place over the first half of the present century, is now all but complete, except in areas of comparative isolation. Unavoidably, but unfortunately, the breakdown was accompanied by a kind of cynicism heavily laced with naïveté, and it left many wounds.

[46] Such an example may be found in the Progressive Era of the early twentieth century, during which Theodore Roosevelt served so admirable a function as the symbolic focus for reform. Among the most notable impulses of that period was the antitrust movement, prosecuted with such strenuosity by the President and with such minimal objective consequences. His successor, President Taft, who had none of Roosevelt's flair, was very unpopular among reformers, though his administration prosecuted twice as many antitrust suits and in half the time. For a discussion of the "guilt" theme, see Richard Hofstadter's *Age of Reform* (New York: Knopf, 1955), pp. 173–212.

HISTORIOGRAPHICAL NOTE

The books discussed in the Historiographical Note to Chapter Five (see pages 302–303) are equally relevant to the social thought of the period 1815–1860. Within the intellectual history of the period, however, the subject of reform has had its own more or less distinctive historiography. Each of the particular reform movements—temperance, women's rights, peace, Mormonism, and so forth—has received special treatment by historians. In addition, many historians have attempted to make sense out of reform as a general phenomenon.

The debate among twentieth-century historians has revolved around a simple but profound issue: what caused large numbers of white, prosperous, more or less secure Americans to involve themselves in movements that did not benefit them directly but instead tended to make them unpopular? Some historians have argued that men and women became reformers primarily because of the existence of objectively evil conditions which demanded correction. The primary cause of abolitionism, then, was the existence of slavery; the peace movement was a result of the horror and waste of war; the movement for women's rights was caused by the objective fact that women suffered from gross inequalities—and so on down the list of reforms. On the other side of the debate—which has never been entirely clear on either side—some historians have argued that reformers were really trying to solve their *own* problems, not those of slaves, drunkards, or oppressed women. According to this view, reform movements grew out of anxieties within the reformers, anxieties about social status, for example, or anxieties of a more sinister, psychological kind.

The first modern effort—after Parrington's—to bring all the reform movements of the antebellum years under one umbrella of interpretation was Alice Felt Tyler's *Freedom's Ferment: Phases of American Social History to 1860* (Minneapolis, 1944), a sympathetic catalogue of reform movements that took the causes of the agitation more or less for granted. Arthur Schlesinger, in an essay on *The American as Reformer* (Cambridge, 1950), argued that there was a continuous liberal tradition of reform in American history, a tradition with both religious and secular sources in the eighteenth century. In both the Tyler and Schlesinger interpretations, the reasons reformers seized on particular issues at particular times seem perfectly obvious and related to the objective conditions the reforms sought to cure. Similar sympathetic treatments of reform were included in two important books of the 1940's, Allan Nevins' *Ordeal of the Union* (New York, 1947), and Merle Curti's *The Growth of American Thought* (New York, 1943).

In the meantime, however, an alternative interpretation of reform had been developing. In 1906, Frank Tracy Carlton, in an essay on "Humanitarianism, Past and Present," *International Journal of Ethics* (1906), suggested that reform was the work of a former elite in a process of social decline. The internal sources of the antislavery movement were explored with a mixture of sympathy and criticism in Gilbert Barnes's *The Antislavery Impulse, 1830–1844* (New York, 1933). From the mid-thirties to the present, a number of historians, using Garrison as their symbolic type, have stressed the reformers' eccentricity and fanaticism. Hazel C. Wolf's *On Freedom's Altar: The Martyr Complex in the Abolition Movement* (Madison, Wisc., 1952), and Clyde S. Griffin's *Their Brothers' Keepers: Moral Steward-*

ship in the United States, 1800–1865 (New Brunswick, N.J., 1960) are two interesting and in some ways contrasting examinations of the psychological styles of reformers. The argument that the reformers were men and women beset by anxieties about their social status received its most influential recent statement in one of the essays in David Donald's *Lincoln Reconsidered* (New York, 1956). Stanley Elkins' *Slavery*, though it takes a less psychological and more intellectual approach to the abolitionists, contains the most serious modern indictment of the abolitionists' tactics, an indictment which Elkins implicitly extends to other reformers as well.

The abolitionists and other reformers have been defended in recent years against charges of fanaticism by scholars who have been deeply committed reformers themselves. Dwight L. Dumond's *Antislavery: The Crusade for Freedom in America* (Ann Arbor, Mich., 1961) was the climactic work of a scholar with a lifelong commitment to the ideals of the abolitionists. Louis Filler's *The Crusade Against Slavery, 1830–1860* (New York, 1960) is similarly sympathetic—and contains, incidentally, the best general bibliography on antebellum social reform. Most recently, Martin Duberman, himself very active in the movement for civil rights, has come ardently to the defense of the abolitionists, most pointedly in an essay on "The Abolitionists and Psychology," *The Journal of Negro History* (1962).

In the latter half of the 1960's, some historians have tried to redefine the debate over the reformers' personalities and motivations by putting the issue in a larger context. The most massive attempt at such a maneuver is David Brion Davis' *The Problem of Slavery in Western Culture* (Ithaca, N.Y., 1966). A brilliant essay on the intellectual and emotional implications of the reform ferment—which returns, in interesting ways, to some of Parrington's interpretive assumptions—is John L. Thomas' "Romantic Reform in America, 1815–1865," *American Quarterly* (1965). The quickest way for a student to familiarize himself with the current state of historical scholarship on the subject is through a small volume on *Antebellum Reform* (New York, 1967), edited by David Brion Davis.

7. The Politics of Jacksonian America

INTRODUCTION

Historians have generally characterized the period from the War of 1812 to the Mexican War as an era of development: the rise of the common man, the growth of political democracy and egalitarian ideology, the expansion of territorial nationalism. Only in recent years have scholars addressed themselves to the central paradox of American development during these decades, the vast and simultaneous increase in both individual freedom and national organization. Although there were occasional dissenters, most Jacksonians seemed comfortable with both trends, rarely inquiring into the possibility of contradictions. That political institutions had lost the uneasy balance between democratic principles and elitist practices characteristic of the founding generation seemed clear to most observers during the 1830's and 1840's.

Because of the controversial and popular presidency of Andrew Jackson, a second American party system evolved, more professional in its use of campaign techniques and in the degree of partisan organization than ever had been believed possible or desirable. Politics itself became an honorable, independent vocation for both Jacksonian and Whig stalwarts, and the remaining property qualifications that stood in the way of universal white male suffrage or office-holding were swept aside in state after state.

Although the new, popularly-based party coalitions fought bitterly over power at all levels of government, no issues appeared irreconcilable enough to disrupt the political system itself. Even the compelling symbolism of the Bank War, which pitted Democratic visions of a "Monster Bank" against Whig obsessions with "King Andrew" in the White House, failed to arouse popular passions to a pitch that professionals of both parties could not manipulate skillfully. Not until the slavery expansion question emerged— a consequence of the nation's easy victory over Mexico in 1848 and the resulting territorial acquisitions—did the parties face an issue that proved in the end too serious for compromise and too intractable to bury.

During the periods of alternating party control of the national government in the 1830's and 1840's, both Whigs and Democrats managed almost accidentally to change the presidency radically from the role originally envisioned by the founders. Under Presidents from Jackson to Taylor, the chief executive's office became the central organizing focus of the mass parties, sought and contested by political professionals or their military front-men rather than by true national notables as under the first party system. At the same time, presidential powers were strengthened through exercise—by use of the veto power, supervision of Western expansion, diplomatic successes, and military triumphs—until, by the 1850's, the presidency had become the crucial nationalizing institution in American political life.

Yet the office's weaknesses remained those of the party coalitions that selected its occupants. National parties, unmentioned in the Constitution and feared by the framers of that document, were the cement that bound together the transformed structure of Jacksonian politics. Their power derived from two sources: the patronage or spoils system that rewarded party regularity with political favors, and the convention and committee system that linked the professionals at every level—national, state, and local—with the electorate. In combination, these innovations strengthened the partisan base of presidential politics and linked the fate of domestic stability to the continued functioning of the party coalitions themselves, a lesson even many professionals learned belatedly during the 1850's, as they watched the older Jacksonian parties unravel under the pressures of the slavery question.

Democratic nationalism during the Jacksonian era fed directly upon the American population's relentless drive westward, which culminated in the huge territorial landgrab following the United States victory in the Mexican War. Most Americans found their belief in equality of opportunity compatible with the settlement and exploitation of the newly acquired land. Faith in an egalitarian political order and in the "manifest" virtues of continental expansionism seemed inseparable for Jacksonians, politicians, and public alike. Nor was this association of liberty and land new in American life. George Washington had taken time from his labors at Valley Forge to write his stepson: "Lands are permanent—rising fast in value—and will be very dear when our independency is established." Thomas Jefferson, although critical of the steady procession of frontier settlement beyond the Appalachians, still encouraged this movement with the Louisiana Purchase and spoke approvingly of an American "Empire for Liberty" in the uncharted West. Henry Clay, a second-generation Jeffersonian, based his case for war against England in 1810 on the popular Western belief in a "territorial imperative": "The conquest of Canada is in your power . . . The militia of Kentucky alone are competent to place Montreal and Upper Canada at your feet."

During the Jacksonian era, believers in a special American mission to those New World countries that lacked our own brand of political democracy, Anglo-Saxon freedom, and Protestant culture found encouragement in typical expansionist pronouncements such as Lewis Cass's 1847 declaration: "We must continue our occupation of Mexico, and push the invasion still further." What forced a halt, temporarily, to America's outward thrust during the 1850's was not an attack of conscience or moral uncertainty over such conquest but rather a critical bout of national indigestion. Territories conquered in the name of freedom could only be absorbed through organization, and beginning with the Congressional struggle over California in 1850, the slavery expansion issue ate at the structure of American politics for an entire decade. In the end, the consequences of expansion destroyed the prime agent of effective national cohesion, the political party system. The process of political disintegration is treated in another chapter. The pages that follow trace the evolution of democratization, party development, and territorial expansion during the Jacksonian era itself.

I. EARLY INTERPRETATION

In this sometimes sardonic account, Charles and Mary Beard attributed to long-range economic forces the democratic political changes in American life that capped the election of Andrew Jackson. These forces, which created new pools of mass political power in the working class and farming population, brought important structural reforms. Included among them were broadened suffrage, an end to most property requirements for office-holding, and increased popular influence on presidential politics through partisan institutions such as local committees, state conventions, and the spoils system. Just as important as these democratic changes, themselves, in the Beards' view, were the new political *styles* of Jacksonian America, which resulted from increased public interest, popular participation, and the professionalization of political life.

Political developments, in turn, accelerated the rise of a spirit of expansionist nationalism that was often rabid, aggressive, and intolerant. In this connection, the Beards considered America's drive westward a somewhat morally questionable extension of egalitarian tendencies, although they seemed to view the Mexican War itself as a pardonable example of democratic high spirits.

CHARLES A. BEARD AND MARY BEARD

JACKSONIAN DEMOCRACY—A TRIUMPHANT FARMER-LABOR PARTY

The creation of nine states beyond the mountains, accelerating the steady

Reprinted from Charles A. Beard and Mary Beard, THE RISE OF AMERICAN CIVILIZATION (New York: The Macmillan Company, 1930), pp. 542–52, 557, 581–83, by permission of the publisher.

movement of political power toward the West, was synchronous with profound social changes on the seaboard—changes equally disturbing to eastern gentlemen of the old school in wigs, ruffles, knee breeches, and silver buckles. While the widening agricultural area was sending an ever-increasing number of representatives to speak for farmers upon the floor of Congress, state after state on the Atlantic coast was putting ballots into the hands of laborers and mechanics whom the Fathers of the Republic had feared as Cicero feared the proletariat and desperate debtors of ancient Rome. Even Jefferson, fiery apostle of equality in the abstract, shrank at first from the grueling test of his own logic; not until long after the Declaration of Independence did he commit himself to the dangerous doctrine of manhood suffrage.

Expressing their anxieties in law, the framers of the first state constitutions, as we have noted, placed taxpaying or property qualifications on the right to vote. The more timid excluded from public office all except the possessors of substantial property; and those who stood aghast at the march of secularism applied religious tests that excluded from places of political trust Catholics, Jews, Unitarians, and scoffers who denied belief in hell. All people thus laid under the ban of the law they regarded as socially unsafe. "The tumultuous populace of large cities," ran the warning words of Washington, "are ever to be dreaded." In Jefferson's opinion also, "the mobs of the great cities" were "sores on the body politic."

Such was the prevailing view among the ruling classes of the time and it was founded on no mere theories of state. The conduct of the rioters in the days of the Stamp Act agitation, the fierce treatment meted out to Tories in the years of the Revolution, and the mass meetings of workingmen in New York and Philadelphia when the first state constitutions were being framed, all indicated that social forces of unknown power were stirring beneath the surface of society.

There was a brief period of peace and reaction while the Constitution was being launched but that was the calm before the storm. Washington had been safely installed only a few weeks when the alarm bell of the French Revolution gave the signal for an uprising of the sansculottes of the western world. Before long, in all the cities of the American seaboard, a movement for white manhood suffrage was in full swing. Indeed, the mechanics of Pennsylvania had already set an example in 1776 by forcing the adoption of a low taxpaying franchise which gave a broad popular base to the government and paved the way for a Jacobinical democracy. During Washington's first administration, in 1791, to be exact, Vermont came into the Union without property restrictions, and Delaware gave the ballot to all white men who paid taxes. Though reckoned among the conservative states, Maryland "shot Niagara" in 1809 by adopting manhood suffrage; and nine years later Connecticut, even less devoted to the quest for novelties, decided that all males who contributed a trivial sum to the support of the government could be trusted with the ballot.

The fire spread to Massachusetts. Into the state constitutional convention of 1820 strode radicals ready to strike down all the political privileges expressly accorded to property, raising anew the specter of Daniel Shays. Frightened at their demands, Daniel Webster, then in the prime of his manhood, and John Adams, at the close of his memorable career, joined in protesting against innovations. With his customary eloquence, Webster warned the convention that all the revolutions of history which had shaken society to its foundations had been revolts against property; that equal suffrage was incompatible with inequality in property; and that if adopted it would either end in assaults on wealth or new restraints upon democracy—a reaction of the notables. In spite of the fact that the argument was cogent, it did not rally the delegates as one man to the established bulwarks. The privileges of riches in the state senate were indeed retained but the straight property test for the suffrage was abandoned and a small taxpaying restriction adopted, merely to be swept away itself within a few years.

A similar contest took place in New York in 1821 when a band of Federalists in the constitutional convention argued, threatened, and raged to save the political rights of property, only to go down in defeat after gaining some petty concessions which were abolished within five years in favor of white manhood suffrage. From this struggle echoes were heard in Rhode Island where the mechanics of Providence, learning of Tammany's victory in New York, called for a similar unhorsing of the freeholders who ruled their own states. Unawed by their hue and cry, the conservatives stood firm while the tiny commonwealth founded by apostles of liberty was shaken by a long and stormy agitation over the rights of man. For nearly twenty years the tempest blew hard, provoking an armed uprising, known as Dorr's Rebellion, and culminating in the substitution of a taxpaying for the freehold qualification on the suffrage.

Equally obdurate were Virginia and North Carolina, notwithstanding the power of Jefferson's great name; the former would not let anybody but landowners vote until 1830; the latter did not surrender that restriction for twenty-six years. But the delay was not so significant, for the growth of the western counties in those two states gave them each a population of small farmers who had no more love for the planters on the coast than the Irish mechanics of New York City had for the stockholders in the United States

Bank. Thus it may be said that when the nineteenth century turned its first quarter, political power was slipping from the hands of seaboard freeholders, capitalists, and planters into the grip of frontier farmers—usually heavily in debt to the East for capital and credit—and into the hands of the working class of the industrial towns, already tinged with leveling doctrines from fermenting Europe.

As the cohorts of the new democracy marched in serried ranks upon the government, they inevitably modified the spirit and practice of American politics. First of all, they criticized the method of electing the President. Shrinking from the hubbub of popular agitations, the Fathers had sought to remove the choice of the chief magistrate as far as possible from the passions of the multitude; though impressed by the difficulties of the task they hoped to introduce a quiet, dignified procedure about as decorous as the selection of a college rector by a board of clerical trustees. To attain their end, they provided that the President of the United States and also the Vice-President should be carefully chosen by a small body of electors selected as the legislatures of the states might decide.

Given this choice, the legislatures, naturally greedy for power, proceeded to exercise the right themselves; but before long the new democracy was thundering at their doors, demanding the transfer of that sovereign prerogative to the voters at the polls. Slowly but surely the managers of politics yielded to the cry for the popular choice of the President; in 1824 only six states still allowed the legislatures to choose the presidential electors and eight years later but a single state, South Carolina, clung to the original mode. One of the great safeguards against the tyranny of majorities was now submerged in the tossing waves of democracy.

Yet the all-devouring populace was by no means satisfied with this gain, for the nomination of party candidates for President was still in the control of a small body of politicians known as the "congressional caucus." After the country divided into two parties, it became necessary for each of them to select its candidate in advance of the election; but of course the rank and file of its personnel could not assemble for that purpose in one forum, travel being tedious and expensive even for exalted officers. Accordingly the party members in Congress simply took upon themselves the high function. When the season for choosing the presidential candidate approached, the congressmen of each party met in caucus behind closed doors and agreed upon the dignitary to be put before the people. While the election of President and Vice-President was passing into popular control, the choice of candidates thus remained in the grip of a few managers in Washington.

To the new democracy this situation was intolerable and a roar of protest went up against it. In 1824, on the refusal of "old King Caucus" to nominate General Andrew Jackson, such a clatter was raised that never again did members of Congress dare officially to select the people's candidates for them. When the campaign of 1832 came around, there was substituted for the caucus an institution known as the nominating convention, an extra-legal party conference compsoed of faithful delegates chosen by local assemblies of loyal partisans. To be sure Senators and Representatives were always prominent in the convention but they were now faced by hundreds of party agents "fresh from the people," as Jackson was wont to say.

In fact, the grand convention was mainly ruled by office-holders and aspirants for office. While the election of the President was vested in the people legally, the choice of candidates, in fact, passed from the congressional monopoly to professional politicians at large. This transfer was noted by many eminent observers, especially by those who failed to win a nomination; and soon the convention was denounced in the vivid terms formerly applied to the caucus. Nevertheless, the new party institution took root and flourished; by 1840 it seemed as rigidly fixed as the Constitution itself. It also became at the same time the accepted organ of party operation in the lower ranges of state and county politics. Men who refused to abide by its decisions were anathematized and treated like social pariahs.

The profits as well as the powers of public office now became objects of interest to the new democracy. "To the victors belong the spoils," a slogan of New York politicians, was elevated to the dignity of a national principle in the age of Andrew Jackson. And yet it would be a mistake to assume that the doctrine was a product of the period. To the statesmen of ancient Rome the emoluments of office and the plunder of the provinces were matters of prime concern; the hands of the righteous Cicero were far from spotless. The government of England in the era of the Georges was an immense aggregation of sinecures and profitable positions, the impeccable Pitt having his Newcastle to distribute pelf among the beggars of the better sort that swarmed around Parliament.

In colonial America, contests over lucrative posts filled official circles with petty rackets; the thrifty Franklin made the most of his opportunity as royal postmaster-general of America. Once independence was established, there were problems of statecraft to be considered. Even the virtuous Washington, placed by a sense of honor and private fortune above jobbery in public offices, could not ignore its function in party management. In making his first appointments, he was careful to choose friends rather than enemies of the new Constitution, although he occasionally tried to clip the wings of especially dangerous critics by giving them places in the administration; and, taught by experience the perils of doubters in his own household, he finally vowed that he would henceforth select only well-disposed persons for office, on the highly defensible theory that no government can rely on its foes for success. Jefferson was equally careful, when removals, resignations, and deaths occurred, to make selections with reference to party loyalty.

This practice the labor and agrarian democracy which later swept into power merely amplified by ousting a larger proportion of office-holders and by avowing more frankly that the sweets of place were among the joys of victory. To this doctrine, they added another, namely, rotation in office, demanding that terms be short so that more party workers could share in the delights of conquest. The bucolic openly admitted the purpose; while the sophisticated argued that long tenure made officers lazy, bureaucratic, and tyrannical.

In either form the new gospel weighed heavily with farmers who seldom saw as much as a hundred dollars cash in the course of a whole year and with mechanics who labored at the bench or forge for seventy-five cents a day. To them a chance at the public "trough," as the phrase ran in gross colloquialism, was to be welcomed gratefully on any axiom of ethics. Indeed, it was often difficult to distinguish, except in mathematical terms, between those who suffered from the taint of vulgarity in office-seeking and those who united public emoluments and private retainers in the higher ranges of the public service. Whatever the niceties of the occasion required, it was clear to all that the advent of the farmer-labor democracy was bound to work changes in the more decorous proceedings handed down from the Fathers.

The flow of time in which occurred these modifications in American political life carried off the heroic figures of the Revolution and left the race to the fleet men of a new generation. Washington died in 1799, still "first in the hearts of his countrymen," as Light Horse Harry Lee said in the funeral oration. Patrick Henry had already gone to his long home; Samuel Adams was soon to follow. In 1804, Alexander Hamilton, in the prime of life, was shot in a duel by Aaron Burr. John Adams and Thomas Jefferson, old and bent under the weight of years, trudged on in the dusty way until 1826, when they died within a few hours of each other on July 4, reconciled and at peace. Charles Carroll, last surviving signer of the Declaration of Independence, lived to turn the first sod for the Baltimore and Ohio Railway on July 4, 1828, and to see with dimmed eyes the outlines of a progressive future; but in four years he too was no more. James Madison, philosopher of the Constitution, kept up the good fight long enough to write a ringing protest against nullification in South Carolina; then death carried him off at the ripe old age of eighty-five.

When the election of 1824 arrived, there was no Father of the republic, in the vigor of manhood and crowned with the halo of a romantic age, able to take up the office laid down by Colonel Monroe. Time as ever was ruthless. The Virginia succession had come to an end. Even the Federalist party, founded by Hamilton and Washington, was out of the field—or rather incorporated as a disturbing factor in the all-embracing Republican party of Jefferson. The "era of good feeling" was closing; buried or concealed hatreds were reviving. New men, looking to the future rather than to the past, were jostling one another for place and power in the forum, but none stood out head and shoulders above the others as the inevitable successor to Monroe.

Puzzled by this state of affairs, the congressional caucus nominated for the presidency W. H. Crawford of Georgia, a man of ability but not a commanding personality. Its decree was in regular form but it could not be enforced because, forsooth, three other candidates insisted on entering the lists. John Quincy Adams, son of the second President, regarded himself as heir apparent in virtue of his services as Secretary of State; while the frontier brought its hard fist down on the political table with emphasis, announcing the rights of Henry Clay of Kentucky and Andrew Jackson of Tennessee. "The wild men of the Mississippi region" could not be ignored but fortune postponed their mastery.

So divided were the returns from the polls that no one of the four had a majority of the presidential electors as required by the Constitution; Jackson stood at the top, Clay at the bottom. From this it followed that the election was thrown into the House of Representatives, where each state could cast only one vote—the vote of its delega-

tion—and men elected in calmer days held the floor under the leadership of Clay as Speaker. Upon the trained ears of the old political dynasty, the cries of Jackson's hordes swarming into the lobbies sounded like the voices of willful fanatics. Bent on defeating them at all costs, Clay, whose small number of votes left him outside the pale, threw his strength heavily to the right and by skillful management won the presidency for Adams with the office of Secretary of State for himself, perhaps, as alleged, quite accidentally.

Though the roaring flood of the new democracy was now foaming perilously near the crest, the great dike of proscriptive rights still held, for Adams could no doubt give to the government the tone of the old régime. He called himself a Republican in politics, having turned against the Federalists and affiliated with the Jeffersonians in the days when the latter were regarded by the New England aristocracy as "a Jacobinical rabble." Nevertheless, he was no horny-handed farmer, aproned mechanic, or bold Indian fighter, dear to the rising electorate of the age. Educated at Harvard and in the politest circles of Europe, Adams viewed public service as a kind of *noblesse oblige* to be kept untainted by the vulgar odors of loot and spoils—a service capable of protecting democracy by efficient administration against the inroads of the plutocracy.

Besides being out of lockstep in matter of political patronage, he was opposed to flinging western land out to impecunious members of Congress, avid speculators, and gambling farmers. Looking to the long future, he believed in preserving the public domain as a great national treasury of resources to be wisely and honestly managed with a view to revenues for roads, canals, and education in letters, arts, and sciences. Besides anticipating by nearly a hundred years some of the most enlightened measures of conservation, Adams foresaw in a livid flash the doom of slavery in a social war.

By no possible effort could he become a Jacksonian "mixer"; like his illustrious descendant, Henry Adams, he was destined to wander in space without finding rest or peace. From the beginning to the end of his administration, misfortune dogged his steps. When he appointed Clay head of the State Department, the resentment of Jackson's party broke all bounds, worshipers of "Old Hickory," seeing in the appointment conclusive proof that a "corrupt bargain" had defeated their Hero. With a feeling of righteous indignation, they began to prepare for the next election, filling Adams' four years with torment by abuse and with chagrin by gathering in his friends as they fled from the sinking ship. In a tidal wave the country repudiated Adams at the next election.

The campaign of 1828 was marked by extreme rancor—a bitterness akin to that of 1800 when the Jeffersonian hordes drove the elder Adams from power. Metropolitan newspapers, the clergy, federal office-holders, manufacturers, and bankers were in general hotly in favor of re-electing Adams; the richest planters of the Old South preferred him to Jackson, even if they had little love for a New England Puritan himself. Against this combination were aligned the farmers, particularly those burdened with poverty and debts, and the mechanics of the towns who shouted their "Hurrah for Jackson!" with a gusto.

Passions of rank and place, rather than definite issues, divided the two factions and in the mad scramble for power both resorted to billingsgate of the most finished quality. Though garbed in the mantle of respectability, the Adams faction pictured Jackson, to use the terse summary of a recent historian, Claude Bowers, "as a usurper, an adulterer, a gambler, a cockfighter, a brawler, a drunkard, and a murderer." It also turned on his wife, its national campaign committee even sinking so low as to send out bales of pamphlets attacking the moral character of his "dear Rachel" who, although she did smoke a pipe, was a woman of exemplary life. In this unsavory game, Jackson's faction, determined not to be outdone, portrayed Adams as a stingy Puritan, an aristocrat who hated the people, a corruptionist who had bought his own election, and a waster of the people's money on White House decorations; and accused Clay of managing Adams' campaign "like a shyster, pettifogging in a bastard suit before a country squire."

When the smoke of the fray had lifted, it was found that Adams had won nothing but the electoral votes of New England and not even all those; whereas Jackson had carried the rest of the Union, making an absolutely clean sweep in the South and West. The collapse of the Adams party was terrible to behold. Gentlemen and grand dames of the old order, like the immigrant nobles and ladies of France fleeing from the sansculottes of Paris, could discover no consolation in their grief. . . .

Into the lists Jackson entered as gladiator-at-large for the masses against the moneyed classes, declaring that the agricultural interest was "superior in importance" to all others and placing himself, as he said, at the head of "the humbler members of society— the farmers, mechanics, and laborers who have neither the time nor the means" of securing special favors for themselves. They heard him gladly and thought him their Sir Galahad. . . .

WESTWARD TO THE PACIFIC

Before the western outposts of Jacksonian Democracy, Louisiana and Missouri, had settled down comfortably in the Union a movement was in full swing to carry the Stars and Stripes through the neighboring territory of Mexico to the Pacific. Nothing could check its momentum; neither the protests of New England abolitionists nor the resistance of the Mexicans; neither the torrid heat of the desert nor the ice-bound passes of the mountains. Within a generation it came to a climax in the annexation of Texas, a war with Mexico, the conquest of California, and the adjustment of the Oregon boundary. In the eyes of abolitionists, the drive on Mexico was a slave-owners' plot, a conspiracy against a friendly country, the seizure of "more pens to cram slaves in."

Many incidents lent color to this thesis but the tough web of facts could not be stretched to cover it. There were other economic forces equally potent: the passion of farmers for more land, the lure of continental trade, and the profits of New England traffic in the Pacific Ocean. Besides all that there was an active body of unknown citizens who held several million dollars worth of the debt and land scrip of Texas and looked to the United States for security —a sum which exceeded in value all the slaves in the Lone Star State in 1845.

Neither slavery nor profit explains, however, the whole westward movement. There was Manifest Destiny which covered a multitude of things and was tinged with mystery by the imagination of the esoteric. According to the version of the seers a virile people turned their resolute faces toward the setting sun. Some of them acquired by fair negotiation lawful possessions in Texas; others pierced the desert and crossed the mountains to gather peltries and engage in honest trade. Their rights were scorned and their flag was insulted by incompetent and dishonest Mexican officials. Innocent persons were imprisoned and some were murdered by barbarians. In such circumstances silence was dishonorable, peace a folly, annexation a virtue. Such was the case submitted in the name of Manifest Destiny.

But this shining shield had a reverse side. The nationalist historians of Mexico present a different version of Manifest Destiny. A ruthless and overbearing race of men, greedy for land and trade, respecting no rights or laws which barred their way, deliberately set themselves to the work of despoiling their neighbor. They violated contracts; they intruded themselves into Mexican territory without passports or permits. Their official representatives at the Mexican capital fomented domestic intrigues, attempted to buy for a song what they intended to take by violence, and shrank not from corruption in gaining their ends. American citizens took part in revolutionary movements to overthrow a friendly government; American naval officers seized Mexican ports in time of peace, pulled down the Mexican flag, and hoisted the Stars and Stripes. Finally, Americans raised a revolution in Texas, tore that province away from a peaceful republic, and then made war to get more territory. Such was the Mexican view of the drama.

Although in this bitter controversy a judgment satisfactory to both parties can hardly be rendered, a number of pertinent facts force themselves upon the moralist who feels compelled to hold a court of justice and mercy. Above all it is necessary to take account of the state of Mexico during the first half of the nineteenth century. It is the fashion to speak of the "Mexican government," the "Mexican people," and "Mexican policies." Nothing could be more misleading. Such terms, with some show of propriety, may be used in referring to a settled country with a stable government capable of representing the masses; but even in such nations there are wild oscillations—like that which occurred when the United States, repudiating Wilson and the League of Nations, swung abruptly to Harding and isolation. What seems to be perfidy is sometimes a perfectly legitimate change of opinion.

II. DOCUMENTS

1. Nationalism

Throughout his career, Thomas Jefferson feared the centralization of political power and the effects of aggressive nationalism. He favored the maximum degree of local, representative democracy. Once in power, however, Jefferson proved a wily and expert manipulator of precisely the tendencies he claimed to despise. As Chief Executive, he increased greatly the power of presidential decision-making through diplomatic and executive actions. Nor was Jefferson an advocate of complete popular democracy. Believing in a "natural aristocracy" (by which he meant the rule of the best people), he despised "the ill-tempered and rude men of society who have taken up a passion for politics." He advised his politically-ambitious grandson to "consider yourself when with them, as among the patients of bedlam, needing medical more than moral counsel. . . . Get by them therefore, as you would an angry bull; it is not for a man of sense to dispute the road with such animals." Jefferson referred to precisely those groups in American society that would one day elect Andrew Jackson and that lent so much support to the expansionist movement of the 1840's. Here also, Jefferson's public career contradicted his avowed principles. Although fearful of unrestricted westward movement, his purchase of the Louisiana Territory provided the impetus for America's first powerful thrust outward.

John Quincy Adams, on the other hand, embodied much of the nationalist spirit of the later Jacksonian age. Adams wrote to a friend following his humiliating defeat by Jackson in 1828 that he had tried to improve the quality of national government and to expand its power. He lamented his failure and mourned that improvements, if made at all, would now come only "with the limping gait of state legislature and private adventure." Although a strong nationalist, Adams proved no fonder of Jacksonian politics than Jefferson might have been, and the electorate that brought Jackson to power repudiated Adams' strong centralizing tendencies. Nor did the Jacksonians share Adams' obvious contempt for private entrepreneurship or states' rights, as they were to demonstrate in waging political war on the "monopolistic" Second Bank of the United States.

THOMAS JEFFERSON

TO JOHN ADAMS

Monticello, October 28, 1813
I agree with you that there is a natural aristocracy among men. The grounds of this are virtue and talents. Formerly, bodily powers gave place among the aristoi. But since the invention of gunpowder has armed the weak as well as the strong with missile death, bodily strength, like beauty, good humor, politeness and other accomplishments, has become but an auxiliary ground of distinction. There is also an artificial aristocracy, founded on wealth and birth, without either virtue or talents; for with these it would belong to the first class. The natural aristocracy I consider as the most precious gift of nature, for the instruction, the trusts, and government of society. And indeed, it would have been inconsistent in creation to have formed man for the social state, and not to have provided virtue and wisdom, enough to manage the concerns of the society. May we not even say, that that form of government is the best, which provides the most effectually for a pure selection of these natural aristoi into the offices of government? The artificial aristocracy is a mischievous ingredient in government, and provision should be made to prevent its ascendency. . . . .

Reprinted from Koch and Pedens, eds., THE LIFE AND SELECTED WRITINGS OF THOMAS JEFFERSON *(New York: The Modern Library, 1944), pp. 632–34, 673–76.*

With respect to aristocracy, we should further consider, that before the establishment of the American States, nothing was known to history but the man of the old world, crowded within limits either small or overcharged, and steeped in the vices which that situation generates. A government adapted to such men would be one thing; but a very different one, that for the man of these States. Here every one may have land to labor for himself, if he chooses; or, preferring the exercise of any other industry, may exact for it such compensation as not only to afford a comfortable subsistence, but wherewith to provide for a cessation from labor in old age. Every one, by his property, or by his satisfactory situation, is interested in the support of law and order. And such men may safely and advantageously reserve to themselves a wholesome control over their public affairs, and a degree of freedom, which, in the hands of the *canaille* of the cities of Europe, would be instantly perverted to the demolition and destruction of everything public and private. The history of the last twenty-five years of France, and of the last forty years in America, nay of its last two hundred years, proves the truth of both parts of this observation.

But even in Europe a change has sensibly taken place in the mind of man. Science had liberated the ideas of those who read and reflect, and the American example had kindled feelings of right in the people. An insurrection has consequently begun, of science, talents, and courage, against rank and birth, which have fallen into contempt. It has failed in its first effort, because the mobs of the cities, the instrument used for its accomplishment, debased by ignorance, poverty, and vice, could not be restrained to rational action. But the world will recover from the panic of this first catastrophe. Science is progressive, and talents and enterprise on the alert. Resort may be had to the people of the country, a more governable power from their principles and subordination; and rank, and birth, and tinsel-aristocracy will finally shrink into insignificance, even there. This, however, we have no right to meddle with. It suffices for us, if the moral and physical condition of our own citizens qualifies them to select the able and good for the direction of their government, with a recurrence of elections at such short periods as will enable them to displace an unfaithful servant, before the mischief he meditates may be irremediable. . . .

TO SAMUEL KERCHEVAL

Monticello, July 12, 1816

I am not among those who fear the people. They, and not the rich, are our dependence for continued freedom. And to preserve their independence, we must not let our rulers load us with perpetual debt. We must make our election between *economy and liberty,* or *profusion and servitude.* If we run into such debts, as that we must be taxed in our meat and in our drink, in our necessaries and our comforts, in our labors and our amusements, for our callings and our creeds, as the people of England are, our people, like them, must come to labor sixteen hours in the twenty-four, give the earnings of fifteen of these to the government for

their debts and daily expenses; and the sixteenth being insufficient to afford us bread, we must live, as they now do, on oatmeal and potatoes; have no time to think, no means of calling the mismanagers to account; but be glad to obtain subsistence by hiring ourselves to rivet their chains on the necks of our fellow suffers. Our land-holders, too, like theirs, retaining indeed the title and stewardship of estates called theirs, but held really in trust for the treasury, must wander, like theirs, in foreign countries, and be contented with penury, obscurity, exile, and the glory of the nation. This example reads to us the salutary lesson, that private fortunes are destroyed by public as well as by private extravagance. And this is the tendency of all human governments. A departure from principle in one instance becomes a precedent for a second; that second for a third; and so on, till the bulk of the society is reduced to be mere automatons of misery, to have no sensibilities left but for sinning and suffering. Then begins, indeed, the *bellum omnium in omnia,* which some philosophers observing to be so general in this world, have mistaken it for the natural, instead of the abusive state of man. And the fore horse of this frightful team is public debt. Taxation follows that, and in its train wretchedness and oppression.

Some men look at constitutions with sanctimonious reverence, and deem them like the ark of the covenant, too sacred to be touched. They ascribe to the men of the preceding age a wisdom more than human, and suppose what they did to be beyond amendment. I knew that age well; I belonged to it, and labored with it. It deserved well of its country. It was very like the present, but without the experience of the present; and forty years of experience in government is worth a century of book-reading; and this they would say themselves, were they to rise from the dead. I am certainly not an advocate for frequent and untried changes in laws and constitutions. I think moderate imperfections had better be borne with; because, when once known, we accommodate ourselves to them, and find practical means of correcting their ill effects. But I know also, that laws and institutions must go hand in hand with the progress of the human mind. As that becomes more developed, more enlightened, as new discoveries are made, new truths disclosed, and manners and opinions change with the change of circumstances, institutions must advance also, and keep pace with the times. We might as well require a man to wear still the coat which fitted him when a boy, as civilized society to remain ever under the regimen of their barbarous ancestors. It is this preposterous idea which has lately deluged Europe in blood. Their monarchs, instead of wisely yielding to the gradual change of circumstances, of favoring progressive accommodation to progressive improvement, have clung to old abuses, entrenched themselves behind steady habits, and obliged their subjects to seek through blood and violence rash and ruinous innovations, which, had they been referred to the peaceful deliberations and collected wisdom of the nation, would have been put into acceptable and salutary forms. Let us follow no such examples, nor weakly believe that one generation is not as capable as another of taking care of itself, and of ordering its own affairs. Let us, as our sister States have done, avail ourselves of our reason and experience, to correct the crude essays of our first and unexperienced, although wise, virtuous, and well-meaning councils. And lastly, let us provide in our Constitution for its revision at stated periods. What these periods should be, nature herself indicates. By the European tables of mortality, of the adults living at any one moment of time, a majority will be dead in about nineteen years. At the end of that period then, a new majority is come into place; or, in other words, a new generation. Each generation is as independent of the one preceding, as that was of all which had gone before. It has then, like them, a right to choose for itself the form of government it believes most promotive of its own happiness; consequently, to accommodate to the circumstances in which it finds itself, that received from its predecessors; and it is for the peace and good of mankind, that a solemn opportunity of doing this every nineteen or twenty years, should be provided by the Constitution; so that it may be handed on, with periodical repairs, from generation to generation, to the end of time, if anything human can so long endure. It is now forty years since the constitution of Virginia was formed. The same tables inform us, that, within that period, two-thirds of the adults then living are now dead. Have then the remaining third, even if they had the wish, the right to hold in obedience to their will and to laws heretofore made by them, the other two-thirds, who, with themselves, compose the present mass of adults? If they have not, who has? The dead? But the dead have no rights. They are nothing; and nothing cannot own something. Where there is no substance, there can be no accident. This corporeal globe, and everything upon it, belong to its present corporeal inhabitants, during their generation. They alone have a right to direct what is the concern of themselves alone, and to declare the law of that direction; and this declaration can only be made by their majority. That majority, then, has a right to depute representatives to a convention, and to make the Constitution what they think will be the best for themselves. But how collect their voice? This is the real difficulty. If invited by private authority, or county or district meetings, these divisions are so large that few will attend; and their voice will be imperfectly, or falsely, pronounced. Here, then, would be one of the advantages of the ward divisions I have proposed. The mayor of every ward, on a question like the present, would call his ward together, take the simple yea or nay of its members, convey these to the county court, who would hand on those of all its wards to be the proper general authority; and the voice of the whole people would be thus fairly, fully, and peaceably expressed, discussed, and decided by the common reason of the society. If this avenue be shut to the call of sufferance, it will make itself heard through that of force, and we shall go on, as other nations are doing, in the endless circle of oppression, rebellion, reformation; and oppression, rebellion, reformation, again; and so on forever. . . .

JOHN QUINCY ADAMS

Upon this first occasion of addressing the Legislature of the Union, with which I have been honored, in presenting to their view the execution so far as it has been effected of the measures sanctioned by them for promoting the internal improvement of our country, I can not close the communication

Reprinted from John Quincy Adams, First Annual Message to Congress, Dec. 6, 1825, in J. D. Richardson, ed., COMPILATION OF THE MESSAGES AND PAPERS OF THE PRESIDENTS, 1789–1897 (Washington, 1907), II, 311–13.

without recommending to their calm and persevering consideration the general principle in a more enlarged extent. The great object of the institution of civil government is the improvement of the condition of those who are parties to the social compact, and no government, in whatever form constituted, can accomplish the lawful ends of its institution but in proportion as it improves the condition of those over whom it is established. Roads and canals, by multiplying and facilitating the communications and intercourse between distant regions and multitudes of men, are among the most important means of improvement. But moral, political, intellectual improvement are duties assigned by the Author of Our Existence to social no less than to individual man. For the fulfillment of those duties governments are invested with power, and to the attainment of the end—the progressive improvement of the condition of the governed—the exercise of delegated powers is a duty as sacred and indispensable as the usurpation of powers not granted is criminal and odious. Among the first, perhaps the very first, instrument for the improvement of the condition of men is knowledge, and to the acquisition of much of the knowledge adapted to the wants, the comforts, and enjoyments of human life public institutions and seminaries of learning are essential. So convinced of this was the first of my predecessors in this office, now first in the memory, as, living, he was first in the hearts, of our countrymen, that once and again in his addresses to the Congresses with whom he coöperated in the public service he earnestly recommended the establishment of seminaries of learning, to prepare for all the emergencies of peace and war—a national university and a military academy. With respect to the latter, had he lived to the present day, in turning his eyes to the institution at West Point he would have enjoyed the gratification of his most earnest wishes; but in surveying the city which has been honored with his name he would have seen the spot of earth which he had destined and bequeathed to the use and benefit of his country as the site for an university still bare and barren.

In assuming her station among the civilized nations of the earth it would seem that our country had contracted the engagement to contribute her share of mind, of labor, and of expense to the improvement of those parts of knowledge which lie beyond the reach of individual acquisition, and particularly to geographical and astronomical science. Looking back to the history only of the half century since the declaration of our independence, and observing the generous emulation with which the Governments of France, Great Britain, and Russia have devoted the genius, the intelligence, the treasures of their respective nations to the common improvement of the species in these branches of science, is it not incumbent upon us to inquire whether we are not bound by obligations of a high and honorable character to contribute our portion of energy and exertion to the common stock? The voyages of discovery prosecuted in the course of that time at the expense of those nations have not only redounded to their glory, but to the improvement of human knowledge. We have been partakers of that improvement and owe for it a sacred debt, not only of gratitude, but of equal or proportional exertion in the same common cause. Of the cost of these undertakings, if the mere expenditures of outfit, equipment, and completion of the expeditions were to be considered the only

charges, it would be unworthy of a great and generous nation to take a second thought. One hundred expeditions of circumnavigation like those of Cook and La Pérouse would not burden the exchequer of the nation fitting them out so much as the ways and means of defraying a single campaign in war. But if we take into the account the lives of those benefactors of mankind of which their services in the cause of their species were the purchase, how shall the cost of those heroic enterprises be estimated, and what compensation can be made to them or to their countries for them? Is it not by bearing them in affectionate remembrance? Is it not still more by imitating their example—by enabling countrymen of our own to pursue the same career and to hazard their lives in the same cause?

In inviting the attention of Congress to the subject of internal improvements upon a view thus enlarged it is not my design to recommend the equipment of an expedition for circumnavigating the globe for purposes of scientific research and inquiry. We have objects of useful investigation nearer home, and to which our cares may be more beneficially applied. The interior of our own territories has yet been very imperfectly explored. Our coasts along many degrees of latitude upon the shores of the Pacific Ocean, though much frequented by our spirited commercial navigators, have been barely visited by our public ships. The River of the West, first fully discovered and navigated by a countryman of our own, still bears the name of the ship in which he ascended its waters, and claims the protection of our armed national flag at its mouth. With the establishment of a military post there or at some other point of that coast, recommended by my predecessor and already matured in the deliberations of the last Congress, I would suggest the expediency of connecting the equipment of a public ship for the exploration of the whole northwest coast of this continent.

The establishment of an uniform standard of weights and measures was one of the specific objects contemplated in the formation of our Constitution, and to fix that standard was one of the powers delegated by express terms in that instrument to Congress. The Governments of Great Britain and France have scarcely ceased to be occupied with inquiries and speculations on the same subject since the existence of our Constitution, and with them it has expanded into profound, laborious, and expensive researches into the figure of the earth and the comparative length of the pendulum vibrating seconds in various latitudes from the equator to the pole. These researches have resulted in the composition and publication of several works highly interesting to the cause of science. The experiments are yet in the process of performance. Some of them have recently been made on our own shores, within the walls of one of our own colleges, and partly by one of our own fellow-citizens. It would be honorable to our country if the sequel of the same experiments should be countenanced by the patronage of our Government, as they have hitherto been by those of France and Britain.

Connected with the establishment of an university, or separate from it, might be undertaken the erection of an astronomical observatory, with provision for the support of an astronomer, to be in constant attendance of observation upon the phenomena of the heavens, and for the periodical publication of his observations. It is with no feeling of pride as an American that the remark may be made that on the comparatively small territorial surface of Europe there are existing upward of 130 of these light-houses of the skies, while throughout the whole American hemisphere there is not one. If we reflect a moment upon the discoveries which in the last four centuries have been made in the physical constitution of the universe by the means of these buildings and of observers stationed in them, shall we doubt of their usefulness to every nation? And while scarcely a year passes over our heads without bringing some new astronomical discovery to light, which we must fain receive at second hand from Europe, are we not cutting ourselves off from the means of returning light for light while we have neither observatory nor observer upon our half of the globe and the earth revolves in perpetual darkness to our unsearching eyes?

2. The American Democrat

Who was that "ill-tempered and rude" man who provoked Jefferson's contempt and John Quincy Adams' dismay? One popular Jacksonian fictional portrait of such a rugged individual, Simon Suggs, is the satirical hero of the following selection. Suggs, in both his strengths and weaknesses, represented a painfully true caricature in microcosm of homo democraticus *during the Age of Jackson, a man whose style placed him at the center of American political experience during the 1830's and 1840's.*

If the biography of Simon Suggs suggests certain basic economic and social characteristics of Jacksonianism, the careers of professional partisans offer us vivid glimpses of Jacksonian political attitudes. The major practical difference between Jefferson's so-called "Revolution of 1800" and Jackson's analogous "Revolution of 1828" lay in the technique of organization. While Jefferson had built his party around a political elite, the politicians who attached their fortunes to Jackson often came from the most modest personal backgrounds and built their careers around partisan activity at the local level. In the following selections, David Crockett, a professed "coonskin democrat" although a Whig Party regular, explains how to win an election, while Martin Van Buren's Autobiography provides some keen insights into the ambitions, values, and mentality of the era's successful professional party managers.

SIMON SUGGS, JR., ESQ.

This distinguished lawyer, unlike the majority of those favored subjects of the biographical muse, whom a patriotic ambition to add to the moral treasures of the country, has prevailed on, over the instincts of a native and professional modesty, to supply subjects for the pens and pencils of their friends, was not quite, either in a literal or metaphorical sense, a self-made man. He had ancestors. They were moreover, men of distinction; and, on the father's side in the first and second degrees of ascent known to fame. The father of this distinguished barrister was, and, happily, is Capt. Simon Suggs, of the Tallapoosa volunteers, and celebrated not less for his financial skill and abilities, than for his martial exploits. His grandfather, the Rev. Jedediah Suggs, was a noted divine of the Anti-Missionary or Hardshell Baptist persuasion in Georgia. For further information respecting these celebrities, the ignorant reader—the well-informed already know them—is referred to the work of Johnson Hooper, Esq.,

Reprinted from Joseph G. Baldwin, THE FLUSH TIMES OF ALABAMA AND MISSISSIPPI (New York: Hill & Wang, 1957), pp. 88–103.

one of the most authentic of modern biographers.

. . .

In the month of July, Anno Domini, 1810, on the ever memorable fourth day of the month, in the county of Carroll, and State of Georgia, Simon Suggs, Jr., first saw the light, mingling the first noise he made in the world with the patriotic explosions and rejoicings going on in honor of the day. We have endeavored in vain to ascertain, whether the auspicious period of the birth of young Simon was a matter of accident, or of human calculation, and sharp foresight, for which his immediate ancestor on the paternal side was so eminently distinguished; but, beyond a knowing wink, and a characteristic laudation of his ability to accomplish wonderful things, and to keep the run of the cards, on the part of the veteran captain, we have obtained no reliable information on this interesting subject. It is something, however, to be remarked upon, that the natal day of his country and of Simon were the same.

. . .

Simon's course at school was marked by many of the traits which distinguished him in after life; so true is the aphorism which the great Englishman enounced, that the boy is father to the man. His genius was eminently commercial, and he was by no means deficient in practical arithmetic. This peculiar turn of mind displayed itself in his barterings for the small wares of schoolboy merchandise—tops, apples, and marbles, sometimes rising to the dignity of a pen-knife. In these exercises of infantile enterprise, it was observable that Simon always got the advantage in the trade; and in that sense of charity which conceals defects, he may be said to have always displayed that virtue to a considerable degree. The same love of enterprise early led him into games of hazard, such as push-pin, marbles, chuck-a-luck, heads and tails, and other like boyish pastimes, in which his ingenuity was rewarded by marked success. The vivacious and eager spirit of this gifted urchin sometimes evolved and put in practice, even in the presence of the master, expedients of such sort as served to enliven the proverbial monotony of scholastic confinement and study: such, for example, were the traps set for the unwary and heedless scholar, made by thrusting a string through the eye of a needle and passing it through holes in the school bench—one end of the string being attached to the machinist's leg, and so fixed, that by pulling the string, the needle would protrude through the further hole and into the person of the urchin sitting over it, to the great divertisement of the spectators of this innocent pastime. The holes being filled with soft putty, the needle was easily replaced, and the point concealed, so that when the outcry of the victim was heard, Simon was diligently perusing his book, and the only consequence was a dismissal of the complaint, and the amercement of the complainant by the master, *pro*

falso clamore. Beginning to be a little more boldly enterprising, the usual fortune of those who "conquer or excel mankind" befell our hero, and he was made the scapegoat of the school; all vagrant offences that could not be proved against any one else being visited upon him; a summary procedure, which, as Simon remarked, brought down genius to the level of blundering mediocrity, and made of no avail the most ingenious arts of deception and concealment. The master of the old field school was one of the regular faculty, who had great faith in the old medicine for the eradication of moral diseases—the cutaneous tonic, as he called it—and repelled, with great scorn, the modern quackeries of kind encouragement and moral suasion. Accordingly, the flagellations and cuffings which Simon received, were such and so many as to give him a high opinion of the powers of endurance, the recuperative energies, and the immense vitality of the human system. Simon tried, on one occasion, the experiment of fits; but Dominie Dobbs was inexorable; and as the fainting posture only exposed to the Dominie new and fresher points of attack, Simon was fain to unroll his eyes, draw up again his lower jaw, and come to. Simon, remarking in his moralizing way upon the virtue of perseverance, has been heard to declare that he "lost that game" by being unable to keep from scratching during a space of three minutes and a half; which he would have accomplished, but for the Dominie's touching him on the raw, caused by riding a race barebacked the Sunday before. "Upon what slender threads hang the greatest events!" Doubtless these experiences of young Suggs were not without effect upon so observing and sagacious an intellect. To them we may trace that strong republican bias and those fervid expressions in favor of Democratic principles, which, all through life, and in the ranks of whatever party he might be found, he ever exhibited and made; and probably to the unfeeling, and sometimes unjust inflictions of Dominie Dobbs, was he indebted for his devotion to that principle of criminal justice he so pertinaciously upheld, which requires full proof of guilt before it awards punishment.

We must pass over a few years in the life of Simon, who continued at school, growing in size and wisdom; and not more instructed by what he learned there, than by the valuable information which his reverend father gave him in the shape of his sage counsels and sharp experiences of the world and its ways and wiles. An event occurred in Simon's fifteenth year, which dissolved the tie that bound him to his rustic *Alma Mater,* the only institution of letters which can boast of his connection with it. Dominie Dobbs, one Friday evening, shortly after the close of the labors of the scholastic week, was quietly taking from a handkerchief in which he had placed it, a flask of powder; as he pressed the knot of the handkerchief, *it* pressed upon the slide of the flask, which as it revolved, bore upon a lucifer match that ignited the powder; the explosion tore the handkerchief to pieces, and also one ear and three fingers of the Dominie's right hand—those fingers that had wielded the birch upon young Simon with such effect. Suspicion fell on Simon, notwithstanding he was the first boy to leave the school that evening. This suspicion derived some corroboration from other facts; but the evidence was wholly circumstantial. No positive proof whatever connected Simon with this remarkable accident; but the characteristic prudence of the elder Suggs suggested the expediency of Simon's leaving for a time a part of the country where character was held in so little esteem. Accordingly the influence of his father procured for Simon a situation in the neighboring county of Randolph, in the State of Alabama, near the gold mines, as clerk or assistant in a store for retailing spirituous liquors, which the owner, one Dixon Tripes, had set up for refreshment of the public, without troubling the County Court for a license. Here Simon was early initiated into a knowledge of men, in such situations as to present their characters nearly naked to the eye. The neighbors were in the habit of assembling at the grocery, almost every day, in considerable numbers, urged thereto by the attractions of the society, and the beverage there abounding; and games of various sorts added to the charms of conversation and social intercourse. It was the general rendezvous of the fast young gentlemen for ten miles around; and horse-racing, shooting-matches, quoit-pitching, cock-fighting, and card-playing filled up the vacant hours between drinks.

In such choice society it may well be supposed that so sprightly a temper and so inquisitive a mind as Simon's found congenial and delightful employment; and it was not long before his acquirements ranked him among the foremost in that select and spirited community. Although good at all the games mentioned, card-playing constituted his favorite amusement, not less for the excitement it afforded him, than for the rare opportunity it gave him of studying the human character.

• • •

. . . In his twenty-first year, Simon, starting out with a single mare to trade in horses in the adjoining State of Alabama, returned, such was his success, with a drove of six horses and a mule, and among them the very mare he started with. These, with the exception of the mare, he converted into money; he had found her invincible in all trials of speed, and determined to keep her. Trying his fortune once more in Alabama, where he had been so eminently successful, Simon went to the city of Wetumpka, where he found the races about coming off. As his mare had too much reputation to get bets upon her, an ingenious idea struck Simon—it was to take bets, through an agent, *against* her, in favor of a long-legged horse, entered for the races. It was very plain to see that Simon's mare was bound to win if he let her. He backed his own mare openly, and got some trifling bets on her; and his agent was fortunate enough to pick up a green-looking Georgia sucker, who bet with him the full amount left of Simon's "pile." The stakes were deposited in due form to the amount of some two thousand dollars. Simon was to ride his own mare—wild Kate, as he called her—and he had determined to hold her back, so that the other horse should win. But the Georgian, having by accident overheard the conversation between Simon and his agent, before the race, cut the reins of Simon's bridle nearly through, but in so ingenious a manner, that the incision did not appear. The race came off as it had been arranged; and as Simon was carefully holding back his emulous filly, at the same time giving her whip and spur, as though he would have her do her best, the bridle broke under the strain; and the mare, released from check, flew to and past the goal like the wind, some three hundred yards ahead of the horse, upon the success of which Simon had "piled" up so largely.

A shout of laughter like that which pursued Mazeppa, arose from the crowd (to whom the Georgian had communicated the facts), as Simon swept by, the involuntary winner of the race; and in that laugh, Simon heard the announcement of the discovery of his ingenious contrivance. He did not return.

. . .

The losses Simon had met with, and the unpromising prospects of gentlemen who lived on their wits, now that the hard times had set in, produced an awakening influence upon his conscience. He determined to abandon the nomadic life he had led, and to settle himself down to some regular business. He had long felt a call to the law, and he now resolved to "locate," and apply himself to the duties of that learned profession. Simon was not long in deciding upon a location. The spirited manner in which the State of Arkansas had repudiated a public debt of some five hundred thousand dollars gave him a favorable opinion of that people as a community of litigants, while the accounts which came teeming from that bright land, of murders and felonies innumerable, suggested the value of the criminal practice. He wended his way into that State, nor did he tarry until he reached the neighborhood of Fort Smith, a promising border town in the very *Ultima Thule* of civilization, such as it was, just on the confines of the Choctaw nation. It was in this region, in the village of Rackensack, that he put up his sign, and offered himself for practice. I shall not attempt to describe the population. It is indescribable. I shall only say that the Indians and half-breeds across the border complained of it mightily.

The motive for Simon's seeking so

remote a location was that he might get in advance of his reputation—being laudably ambitious to acquire forensic distinction, he wished his fame as a lawyer to be independent of all extraneous and adventitious assistance. . . .

It was not long before Simon's genius began to find occasions and opportunities of exhibition. When he first came to the bar, there were but seven suits on the docket, two of those being appeals from a justice's court. In the course of six months, so indefatigable was he in instructing clients, as to their rights, the number of suits grew to forty. Simon—or as he is now called —*Colonel Suggs,* determined on winning reputation in a most effective branch of practice—one that he shrewdly perceived was too much neglected by the profession—the branch of preparing cases *out of court* for trial. While other lawyers were busy in getting up the law of their cases, the Colonel was no less busy in getting up the facts of his.

One of the most successful of Col. Suggs' efforts, was in behalf of his landlady, in whom he felt a warm and decided interest. She had been living for many years in ignorant contentedness, with an indolent, easy natured man, her husband, who was not managing her separate estate, consisting of a plantation and about twenty negroes, and some town property, with much thrift. The lady was buxom and gay and the union of the couple was unblessed with children. By the most insinuating manners, Col. Suggs at length succeeded in opening the lady's eyes to a true sense of her hapless condition, and the danger in which her property was placed, from the improvident habits of her spouse; and, having ingeniously deceived the unsuspecting

husband into some suspicious appearances, which were duly observed by a witness or two provided for the purpose, he soon prevailed upon his fair hostess to file a bill of divorce; which she readily procured under the Colonel's auspices. Under the pretence of protecting her property from the claims of her husband's creditors, the Colonel was kind enough to take a conveyance of it to himself; and, shortly afterwards, the fair libellant; by which means he secured himself from those distracting cares which beset the young legal practitioner, who stands in immediate need of the wherewithal.

Col. Suggs' prospects now greatly improved, and he saw before him an extended field of usefulness. The whole community felt the effects of his activity. Long dormant claims came to light; and rights, of the very existence of which, suitors were not before aware, were brought into practical assertion. From restlessness and inactivity, the population became excited, inquisitive and intelligent, as to the laws of their country; and the ruinous effects of servile acquiescence in wrong and oppression, were averted.

• • •

One of the most harassing annoyances that were inflicted upon the emigrant community around him, was the revival of old claims contracted in the State from which they came, and which the Shylocks holding them, although they well knew that the pretended debtors had, expressly in consideration of getting rid of them, put themselves to the pains of exile and to the losses and discomforts of leaving their old homes and settling in a new country, in fraudulent violation of this object, were ruinously seeking to enforce, even to the deprivation of the property of the citizen. In one instance, a cashier of a Bank in Alabama brought on claims against some of the best citizens of the country, to a large amount, and instituted suits on them. Col. Suggs was retained to defend them. The cashier, a venerable-looking old gentleman, who had extorted promises of payment, or at least had heard from the debtors promises of payment, which their necessitous circumstances had extorted, but to which he well knew they did not attach much importance, was waiting to become a witness against them. Col. Suggs so concerted operations, as to have some half-dozen of the most worthless of the population follow the old gentleman about whenever he went out of doors, and to be seen with him on various occasions; and busying himself in circulating through the community, divers reports disparaging the reputation of the witness, got the cases ready for trial. It was agreed that *one* verdict should settle all the cases. The defendant pleaded the statute of limitations; and to do away with the effect of it, the plaintiff offered the cashier as a witness. Not a single question was asked on cross-examination; but a smile of derision, which was accompanied by a foreordained titter behind the bar, was visible on the faces of Simon and his client, as he testified. The defendant then offered a dozen or more witnesses, who, much to the surprise of the venerable cashier, discredited him; and the jury, without leaving the box, found a verdict for the defendant. The cashier was about moving for a new trial, when, it being intimated to him that a warrant was about to be issued for his apprehension on a charge of perjury, he concluded not to see the result of such a process, and indignantly left the country.

. . .

The most difficult case Col. Suggs ever had to manage, was to extricate a client from jail, after sentence of death had been passed upon him. But difficulties, so far from discouraging him, only had the effect of stimulating his energies. He procured the aid of a young physician in the premises—the prisoner was suddenly taken ill—the physician pronounced the disease smallpox. The wife of the prisoner, with true womanly devotion, attended on him. The prisoner, after a few days, was reported dead, and the doctor gave out that it would be dangerous to approach the corpse. A coffin was brought into the jail, and the wife was put into it by the physician—she being enveloped in her husband's clothes. The coffin was put in a cart and driven off—the husband, habited in the woman's apparel, following after, mourning piteously, until, getting out of the village, he disappeared in the thicket, where he found a horse prepared for him. The wife obstinately refused to be buried in the husband's place when she got to the grave; but the mistake was discovered too late for the recapture of the prisoner.

The tact and address of Col. Suggs opposed such obstacles to the enforcement of the criminal law in that part of the country, that, following the example of the English government, when Irish patriotism begins to create annoyances, the State naturally felt anxious to engage his services in its behalf. Accordingly, at the meeting of the Arkansas legislature, at its session of 184-, so soon as the matter of the killing a member on the floor of the house, by the speaker, with a Bowie knife, was disposed of by a resolution of mild censure, for imprudent precipitancy, Simon Suggs, Jr., Esquire, was elected solicitor for the Rackensack district. Col Suggs brought to the discharge of the duties of his office energies as unimpaired and vigorous as in the days of his first practice; and entered upon it with a mind free from the vexations of domestic cares, having procured a divorce from his wife on the ground of infidelity, but magnanimously giving her one of the negroes, and a horse, saddle and bridle.

The business of the State now flourished beyond all precedent. Indictments multiplied: and though many of them were not tried—the solicitor discovering, after the finding of them, as he honestly confessed to the court, that the evidence would not support them: yet, the Colonel could well say, with an eminent English barrister, that if he tried fewer cases in court, he settled more cases out of court than any other counsel.

The marriage of Col. Suggs, some three years after his appointment of solicitor, with the lovely and accomplished Che-wee-na-tubbe, daughter of a distinguished prophet and warrior, and head-man of the neighboring territory of the Choctaw Indians, induced his removal into that beautiful and improving country. His talents and connections at once raised him to the councils of that interesting people; and he received the appointment of agent for the settlement of claims on the part of that tribe, and particular individuals of it, upon the treasury of the United States. This responsible and lucrative office now engages the time and talents of Col. Suggs, who may be seen every winter at Washington, faithfully and laboriously engaged with members of Congress and in the departments, urging the matters of his mission upon the dull sense of the Janitors of the Federal Treasury.

May his shadow never grow less; and may the Indians live to get their dividends of the arrears paid to their agent.

DAVID CROCKETT

"Attend all public meetings," says I, "and get some friends to move that you take the chair; if you fail in this attempt, make a push to be appointed secretary; the proceedings of course will be published, and your name is introduced to the public. But should you fail in both undertakings, get two or three acquaintances, over a bottle of whiskey, to pass some resolutions, no matter on what subject; publish them even if you pay the printer—it will answer the purpose of breaking the ice, which is the main point in these matters. Intrigue until you are elected an officer of the militia; this is the second step towards promotion, and can be accomplished with ease, as I know an instance of an election being advertised, and no one attending, the innkeeper at whose house it was to be held, having a military turn, elected himself colonel of his regiment." Says I, "You may not accomplish your ends with as little difficulty, but do not be discouraged—Rome wasn't built in a day.

"If your ambition or circumstances compel you to serve your country, and earn three dollars a day, by becoming a member of the legislature, you must first publicly avow that the constitution of the state is a shackle upon free and liberal legislation; and is, therefore, of as little use in the present enlightened age, as an old almanac of the year in which the instrument was framed. There is policy in this measure, for by making the constitution a mere dead letter, your headlong proceedings will be attributed to a bold and unshackled mind; whereas, it might otherwise be thought they arose from sheer mulish

Reprinted from THE LIFE OF DAVID CROCKETT, THE ORIGINAL HUMORIST AND IRREPRESSIBLE BACKWOODSMAN *(Philadelphia, 1865), pp. 274–77.*

ignorance. 'The Government' has set the example in his attack upon the constitution of the United States, and who should fear to follow where 'the Government' leads?

"When the day of election approaches, visit your constituents far and wide. Treat liberally, and drink freely, in order to rise in their estimation, though you fall in your own. True, you may be called a drunken dog by some of the clean shirt and silk stocking gentry, but the real rough necks will style you a jovial fellow, their votes are certain, and frequently count double. Do all you can to appear to advantage in the eyes of the women. That's easily done—you have but to kiss and slabber their children, wipe their noses, and pat them on the head; this cannot fail to please their mothers, and you may rely on your business being done in that quarter.

"Promise all that is asked," said I, "and more if you can think of anything. Offer to build a bridge or a church, to divide a county, create a batch of new offices, make a turnpike, or anything they like. Promises cost nothing, therefore deny nobody who has a vote or sufficient influence to obtain one.

"Get up on all occasions, and sometimes on no occasion at all, and make long-winded speeches, though composed of nothing else than wind—talk of your devotion to your country, your modesty and disinterestedness, or on any such fanciful subject. Rail against taxes of all kinds, office-holders, and bad harvest weather; and wind up with a flourish about the heroes who fought and bled for our liberties in the times that tried men's souls. To be sure you run the risk of being considered a bladder of wind, or an empty barrel, but never mind that, you will find enough of the same fraternity to keep you in countenance.

"If any charity be going forward, be at the top of it, provided it is to be advertised publicly; if not, it isn't worth your while. None but a fool would place his candle under a bushel on such an occasion.

"These few directions," said I, "if properly attended to, will do your business; and when once elected, why a fig for the dirty children, the promises, the bridges, the churches, the taxes, the offices, and the subscriptions, for it is absolutely necessary to forget all these before you can become a thoroughgoing politician, and a patriot of the first water."

MARTIN VAN BUREN

Earnestly engaged in a successful and lucrative practice, I had no desire to be a candidate for an elective office, nor did I become one until the Spring of 1812, when I was forced into that position by circumstances with which I could not deal differently. But from my boyhood I had been a zealous partisan, supporting with all my power the administrations of Jefferson and Madison—including the Embargo and other restrictive measures. . . .

. . .

The Party which had raised Jefferson and Madison to the Presidency elected Mr. Monroe under the expectation that his Administration would be similar in its political aspects to those of his predecessors. The People of the United States had, during both of those Administrations, been divided into two and only two great political

Reprinted from Martin Van Buren, AUTOBIOGRAPHY (Washington, 1918), pp. 28, 122–25, 398–402, 445–47.

parties. It is not necessary and would only serve to render complex the views intended to be expressed to make any reference here to the particular character and tendency of their conflicting principles. For the present it needs only to be stated that in the ranks of one or the other of these parties were arrayed almost all the People who took an interest in the management of public affairs. These differences were first developed in Congress and in Society during the last term of of Gen. Washington's administration, had a partial and comparatively silent influence in the election of his successor, but were openly proclaimed and maintained with such earnestness during that successor's entire administration. The result of this conflict of opinions was the expulsion of John Adams from the office of President and the election of Thomas Jefferson in his place. Not intolerant by nature Mr. Jefferson made an ineffectual effort to allay the warmth of these party differences and to prevent them from invading and poisoning the personal relations of individuals. But, true to his trust, he not only administered the government upon the principles for which a majority of the People had shown their preference, but he carried the spirit of that preference into his appointments to office to an extent sufficient to establish the predominance of those principles in every branch of the public service. This he did, not by way of punishing obnoxious opinions, or to gratify personal antipathies, but to give full effect to the will of the majority, submission to which he regarded as the vital principle of our Government. Mr. Madison, elected by the same Party, tho' proverbial for his amiable temper and for the absence of any thing like a proscriptive disposition, pursued the same course, and upon the same principle—the performance of a public trust in regard to the terms of which there was no room for doubt.

The Administrations of Jefferson and Madison, embracing a period of sixteen years, were, from first to last, opposed by the federal party with a degree of violence unsurpassed in modern times. From this statement one of two conclusions must result. Either the conduct of these two parties which had been kept on foot so long, been sustained with such determined zeal and under such patriotic professions and had created distinctions that became the badges of families—transmitted from father to son—was a series of shameless impostures, covering mere struggles for power and patronage; or there were differences of opinion and principle between them of the greatest character, to which their respective devotion and active service could not be relaxed with safety or abandoned without dishonor. We should, I think, be doing great injustice to our predecessors if we doubted for a moment the sincerity of those differences, or the honesty with which they were entertained at least by the masses on both sides. The majority of the People, the sovereign power in our Government, had again and again, on every occasion since those differences of opinion had been distinctly disclosed, decided them in favor of the Republican creed. That creed required only that unity among its friends should be preserved to make it the ark of their political safety. The Country had been prosperous and happy under its sway, and has been so through our whole history excepting only the period when it was convulsed and confounded by the criminal intrigues and commercial disturbances of the Bank of the United States. To maintain that unity became the obligation of him whom its supporters had elevated to the highest place among its guardians. Jefferson and Madison so interpreted their duty. On the other hand, Mr. Monroe, at the commencement of his second term, took the ground openly, and maintained it against all remonstrances, that no difference should be made by the Government in the distribution of its patronage and confidence on account of the political opinions and course of applicants. The question was distinctly brought before him for decision by the Republican representatives from the states of Pennsylvania and New York, in cases that had deeply excited the feelings of their constituents and in which those constituents had very formally and decidedly expressed their opinions.

If the movement grew out of a belief that an actual dissolution of the federal party was likely to take place or could be produced by the course that was adopted, it showed little acquaintance with the nature of Parties to suppose that a political association that had existed so long, that had so many traditions to appeal to its pride, and so many grievances, real and fancied, to cry out for redress, could be disbanded by means of personal favors from the Executive or by the connivance of any of its leaders. Such has not been the fate of long established political parties in any country. Their course may be qualified and their pretentions abated for a season by ill success, but the cohesive influences and innate qualities which originally united them remain with the mass and spring up in their former vigour with the return of propitious skies. Of this truth we need no more striking illustrations than are furnished by our own experience. Without going into the details of events familiar to all, I need only say that during the very "Era of good feelings," the federal party, under the names of federal republicans and whigs, elected their President over those old republicans William H. Crawford, Andrew Jackson and John C. Calhoun—have, since his time, twice elected old school federalists—have possessed the most effective portions of the power of the Federal Government during their respective terms, with the exception, (if it was one) of the politically episodical administration of Vice President Tyler—and are at this time in power in the government of almost every free state. We shall find as a general rule that among the native inhabitants of each State, the politics of families who were federalists during the War of 1812, are the same now—holding, for the most part, under the name of Whigs, to the political opinions and governed by the feelings of their ancestors.

I have been led to take a more extended notice of this subject by my repugnance to a species of cant against Parties in which too many are apt to indulge when their own side is out of power and to forget when they come in. I have not, I think, been considered even by opponents as particularly rancorous in my party prejudices, and might not perhaps have anything to apprehend from a comparison, in this respect, with my contemporaries. But knowing, as all men of sense know, that political parties are inseparable from free governments, and that in many and material respects they are highly useful to the country, I never could bring myself for party purposes to deprecate their existence. Doubtless excesses frequently attend them and produce many evils, but not so many as are prevented by the maintenance of their organization and vigilance.

The disposition to abuse power, so deeply planted in the human heart, can by no other means be more effectually checked; and it has always therefore struck me as more honorable and manly and more in harmony with the character of our People and of our Institutions to deal with the subject of Political Parties in a sincerer and wiser spirit—to recognize their necessity, to give them the credit they deserve, and to devote ourselves to improve and to elevate the principles and objects of our own and to support it ingenuously and faithfully.

. . .

. . . Through the transactions of which I have spoken and the strong emotions excited by them in the breast of Gen. Jackson my position had become, in the phrase of the day, that of heir apparent to the succession. I needed no more than my experience for the past two years, confirmed by that of Messrs. Adams and Clay, to satisfy me of the great evils to which an Administration was exposed whose chief Cabinet officer occupied that position. They were of a nature impossible to escape the eyes of any but the foolhardy and blindly ambitious. It was not safe to found hopes of exemption from them on the examples of success in such situations furnished by the earlier periods of the Government. In those days the selection of candidates was confined to compartively few individuals and the republican party was not the theatre for Presidential intrigues upon any thing like the same scale as that since in vogue. No degree of abstinence or discretion on the part of the Minister plausibly suspected of aiming at the succession could protect an Administration thus encumbered from the assaults to which he would inevitably expose it. Whether he availed himself of his position to intrigue for

his advancement or not he would be charged with doing so by thousands who would believe him guilty of it and by other thousands in the ranks of the supporters of the Administration who would think themselves interested in spreading such a belief. Thus the design of working for my own elevation at the expiration of Gen. Jackson's first term was freely imputed to me whilst I solemnly affirm that I had been a steady advocate of his re-election and was exerting myself at the time to put down movements that were attempted in my behalf.

Near the close of the first year of the Administration, in reply to some givings out in my favor by Major Noah, of the *New York Courier and Enquirer* —an editor proverbially imprudent and who in the sequel became worse—the *Telegraph* stated as follows: "We KNOW that no one is more opposed to the agitation of that question [that of the succession] than Mr. Van Buren, and that he permits no fit opportunity of discountenancing and discouraging it to pass by unimproved." Without enquiry into the motives of this apparently friendly statement, the course of events makes it proper to say that it was made before the establishment of the *"Globe"* and before matters were ripe for an attack on me—perhaps before such a step was contemplated. It was at all events, at a time when the editor of the *Telegraph* hazarded nothing in saying about me what he honestly believed to be true, but no sooner had war been declared in form by Mr. Calhoun than my desire to precipitate the question in regard to the succession and my intrigues to secure my own elevation at the end of Gen. Jackson's first term were his daily themes. When I come to speak of my first nomination for the Presidency I will have occasion to refer to circumstances which will place my entire course upon this subject beyond the reach of cavil. Altho' it was not in his power to lay his hand upon a shred or semblance of evidence to show that my conduct upon the point in question had varied in the slightest degree, yet his views of his own interests having changed and the period having arrived for the development of projects which had been for some time in preparation, the absence and indeed non-existence of proof made no difference and I knew that it would make no difference in future either with him or with the affiliated presses of which he spoke to Mr. Duncanson, or with the opposition press in general. That was the vantage ground from which the attacks of all were to be made to the end of the war, which if the general should be re-elected and should live so long, was to last for a period of six years; a ground the strength and efficacy of which were likely to be constantly increased during that interval by the addition of new aspirants to the Presidency from our own ranks and to be brought to bear upon Congress, the press, the people and wherever else such aspirants might hope to discover recruits. In my cordial aversion to being made the cause of such a warfare upon the Administration of that honest old man who had devoted the remnant of his life and strength to the public service and upon the interests of the Country committed to his charge, the idea originated of resigning the high office to which I had been appointed. My inquietude was doubtless increased sensibly by the reflection that I had been the object of similar assaults before I came to Washington, and that I had hoped by the change in my field of action to throw off the hounds by whom personal character is hunted down. I was for many years, while in

the service of my state persistently charged with influencing the action of the appointing power for my own advancement when I was thoroughly conscious that there was not one among my contemporaries who estimated as lightly as I did the advantages of such appliances, or who was more disinclined by taste and by judgment than myself to meddle in them. Such incessant defamation added to the thousand vexations to which official station is otherwise exposed wore upon my health and spirits to an extent which would now be deemed incredible by such of my associates as judged only from what they saw of me in public, but which nevertheless made me at times heartily sick of public life; so much so that I often determined, during successive winters, to throw up the offices I held, in the spring and to confine my future exertions to my profession. These resolutions as they were from time to time formed were the subject of discussions in my family and occasionally communicated to my friends; the latter however did not believe in them, and I had perhaps no right to expect them to do so as, thro' causes more easily appreciated than described, I myself had so often contradicted my professions by my action when the time arrived for carrying them into effect. They were notwithstanding always sincere. Of the frequent occasions on which I was thus 'seriously inclined' one occurs to my recollection as I write to which I will refer. Whilst holding the offices of State Senator and Attorney General, I was one afternoon about to return to Albany from Schenectady whither I had been called by business. I found Colonel Aaron Burr at the hotel enquiring for a conveyance to Albany and as I travelled in my own carriage I offered him a seat. The period was after his return from

Europe and when his fortunes were at their lowest ebb. Our drive occupied us till a late hour of the evening during which I was entertained much by his free, caustic and characteristic observations. Whilst sounding me in regard to my political expectations, of which he was pleased to say complimentary things, I surprised him by the remark that I thought of giving up politics and of devoting myself to my profession and that with that view I meant to resign my place in the Senate in the ensuing spring. He was curious to know my reasons and I gave them in the spirit I have here indicated. After a brief reflection he answered, "Sir! you have gone too far to retreat. The only alternative left to you is to kick or to be kicked, and as you are not fool enough to prefer the latter you will not resign!"

My career in State politics had been in general successful and in the end signally such. After competing for a quarter of a century, the greater part of the time as the undisputed leader of my party in my County and State, with such men as De Witt Clinton, Ambrose Spencer, Abraham Van Vechten, William W. and William P. Van Ness, Elisha Williams, Thomas J. Grosvenor, Thomas J. Oakley, John Duer, Chancellor Jones, David B. Ogden, Harry Croswell, Solomon Southwick and William Colden, *mutatis mutandis,* I left the service of the State for that of the Federal Government with my friends in full and almost unquestioned possession of the State Government in all its branches, at peace with each other and overflowing with kindly feelings towards myself, and not without hope that I might in the sequel by good conduct be able to realize similar results in the enlarged sphere of action to which I was called. I soon found, however, that in respect to the practicability of carrying into effect the best intentions there was a peculiar difference between the two systems, which young Statesmen will do well to bear in mind. Whilst the public functionary connected with the State Government acts almost under the eyes of and in constant intercourse with those who are the judges of his actions and consequently has full opportunity to enable them to appreciate his motives, under the General Government the actions of the official are, with very few exceptions, to be passed upon by men a vast majority of whom can have no personal knowledge on the subject and who must weigh his conduct at a distance and decide from report. Having learned to estimate at its true value this important distinction and convinced by experience and observation of the aggravated effects which it promised to long continued harping upon the old theme, even false as it was, I felt that my success was at least doubtful. It should be borne in mind that in the days when this conclusion was arrived at respect was yet maintained for the obligation of Government to preserve the purity of the elective franchise, or as declared by President Jackson in his Inaugural address, to eschew "bringing the patronage of the Government into conflict with the freedom of elections." My apprehensions might well be derided at the present time when the contrary practices are indulged in by all parties with a license that contemns both right and decency and which threatens, if not seasonably arrested, to subvert our institutions.

Having accepted a high and responsible official trust, I was duly conscious that I was not at liberty to permit personal considerations to control my course in resigning it, and I certainly did not design to do so. The success of Gen. Jackson's Administration and his own tranquillity and comfort were to be promoted, in my judgment, by that step, nevertheless views and considerations of self obtruded themselves in all my deliberations in regard to it; it was not possible to exclude them altogether and to say how far I was influenced by them would require a greater proficiency in self-knowledge than I pretend to. They at all events mitigated the sacrifice involved in the course of which I decided when stimulated afresh by the plots, intrigues and calumnies by which I had been for two years surrounded, I recurred to my often formed and often abandoned resolution to retire from the political field.

• • •

I sailed from New York on the execution of my English mission on the 16th August, 1831, in the packet ship President, accompanied by Mr. Aaron Vail, the Secretary of Legation, and by my son Mr. John Van Buren. There were only three other passengers, among them an apparently amiable and certainly modest and retiring young gentleman who was a son of the celebrated Duke of Otranto.

Suddenly and I may say unexpectedly transferred from the turmoil and contentions of Washington—never perhaps more rampant than at that moment—to the quietude of a midsummer Ocean, I experienced sensations which tho' well remembered I would not find it an easy matter to describe. For more than a quarter of a century preceding the day on which I stepped on the deck of the "President" there had scarcely been one during which I had been wholly exempted from the disturbing effects of partisan agitation, too often of the most bitter description. Whether as a subordinate and doubtless, at times, over-zealous member of the political party in which I had almost

literally been reared from childhood, or as its leader for many years in my State, or as a Senator in Congress, active and ardent in Federal politics, or in the Cabinet of Gen. Jackson, first in point of rank and second to none in the confidence of its Chief, the responsibility and anxiety growing out of my successive positions, tho' varying in form had always absorbed my time and my faculties. During the two years immediately preceding my departure there had been few working days which had failed to bring their load of care to my door; the laborious occupation required by the details of the President's Message, the political and official demands upon my attention regularly and plentifully emptied upon my table from the mail-bags with the spoken alarms of timid croakings of complaining and rarer congratulations of satisfied friends by which every public man, resident at the seat of Government, is doomed to be beset—these were but new representations upon an enlarged scale of the same general features which had characterized my whole previous life. These constantly recurring sources of excitement had now, one and all, been suddenly closed. The first morning at sea came unaccompanied by any fresh supplies of the stimulating ailment to which my mind had been accustomed, and one tranquil day followed another only to carry me further from the sight and the sound of the political strife and labour in which I had been so ceaselessly and prominently participant.

When the first mixed feelings produced by this sudden and great change had sufficiently subsided my attention was naturally directed to a careful review of the more recent stirring scenes thro' which I had passed and of the steps which I had thought it proper to take to meet them. The result of this retrospect was an unhesitating conviction that the course I had pursued had been the wisest within my power—that which was best adapted to do the greatest attainable justice to every interest which it was my duty to respect. The momentary inconvenience to which I had exposed one of the truest friends man ever had by my resignation, my sense of which had been quickened by the scenes thro' which I had passed with him in its progress, was a source of sincere regret. That act had also led to other consequences, more particularly applicable to myself and to some extent injurious; but both seemed to me to have been unavoidable results of a step which was imposed upon me by considerations I was not at liberty to disregard, and I was confident that they would be more than made good by the advantages of my action to other and higher interests. Strengthened by this conviction and satisfied with the past, the time and the situation seemed favorable to a definite settlement of my future course. I have already said that by accepting the mission to England I regarded myself as having virtually abandoned whatever chance I might have acquired of reaching the Presidency, and that I had so informed Gen. Jackson. Reason and experience forbade the expectation that any political party would voluntarily encounter the risk of selecting as its candidate an individual peculiarly obnoxious to its adversaries and of whom strong jealousies were cherished by rival leaders within its own camp, after he had himself released it from even the appearance of obligation imposed by previous mutual relations and had left those rivals in undisputed possession of the field of competition. In the

calmer moments I now enjoyed I could think of no aspect in which that opinion could be considered that would cast a doubt upon its correctness. To have maintained the advance towards the Presidency at which I had arrived when I threw up the office of Secretary of State, the effectual course would have been to have retired absolutely from all public employment and to have entered upon the practice of my profession and the life of a private citizen. The disinterestedness of my motives would thus have been placed above the reach of cavil, and a majority of the people, eagerly attached to the President and indignantly resenting the injustice he was made to suffer, would, at the proper time, have demanded my elevation as the suitable reward for the sacrifices I had made to relieve him and to promote his success.

The dispassionate reconsideration of the subject, in my then favourable position for making it, only confirmed these first impressions; and to discard, totally and forever, the idea of becoming President became therefore the fixed and settled purpose of my mind.

That I was able to come to that conclusion with perfect equanimity was attributable in some degree to impressions in regard to the advantages and disadvantages, the pleasures and annoyances of public life derived from a full experience, of which I have often spoken. This was in truth the state of my mind at the time, however hard of belief it may seem to those among my contemporaries who are still on the stage of life and who regarded me as the "magician" I was called—never so much in my element or so happy as when employed in concocting and advancing political intrigues.

3. Popular Government

The mystique of American democracy during the Jacksonian years was similar in many respects to the German romantic ideal of "volksgeist," the spirit of the people. Both the life and writings of the historian, George Bancroft, exemplify this connection. From Harvard, Bancroft went on to complete his study at the University of Göttingen in Germany. There he was deeply influenced by such German idealists as Fichte and Herder, whose romantic nationalism found a strong response in the young and egalitarian American student. Surprisingly, Bancroft was a Brahmin from Boston whose passionate service in the cause of Jacksonian democracy shocked and scandalized his class while it rewarded him well. He was made Collector of Boston port and, through controlling the lucrative custom-house patronage, became a powerful leader in the Massachusetts Democratic party and eventually Secretary of the Navy under President Polk.

Bancroft's democratic mystique was identified directly with the process of westward expansion by William Gilpin, a soldier, explorer, speculator, and personal friend of Andrew Jackson. In the selection included here, Gilpin explains the function of democratic politics in providing boundless opportunities for achieving wealth and success on a continental scale.

Although unpopular, it was still possible to disapprove publicly of the direction of Jacksonian democracy. James Fenimore Cooper, author of the Leatherstocking novels, wrote one of the most powerful and thoughtful criticisms of popular government in the United States, addressing himself to the dangers of egalitarian government. Cooper viewed with alarm the tendencies exemplified in a campaign instruction sheet issued by Whig political leaders during William Henry Harrison's presidential race: "Let him say not one single word about his principles, or his creed—let him say nothing, promise nothing. Let no committee, no convention, no town meeting ever extract from him a single word about what he thinks now, or what he will do hereafter. Let the use of pen and ink be wholly forbidden as if he were a mad poet in bedlam." A selection from The American Democrat *presents Cooper's assessment of the disadvantages of democracy.*

GEORGE BANCROFT

I

The material world does not change in its masses or in its powers. The stars

Reprinted from George Bancroft, LITERARY AND HISTORICAL MISCELLANIES *(New York, 1855), pp. 408–11, 413–16, 421–28.*

shine with no more lustre than when they first sang together in the glory of their birth. The flowers that gemmed the fields and the forests, before America was discovered, now bloom around us in their season. The sun that shone on Homer shines on us in unchanging lustre. The bow that beamed on the patriarch still glitters in the clouds. Nature is the same. For her no new forces are generated, no new capacities are discovered. The earth turns on its axis and perfects its revolutions and renews its seasons without increase or advancement.

But a like passive destiny does not attach to the inhabitants of the earth. For them the expectations of social improvement are no delusion; the hopes of philanthropy are more than a dream. The five senses do not constitute the whole inventory of our sources of knowledge. They are the organs by which thought connects itself with the external universe; but the power of thought is not merged in the exercise of its instruments. We have functions which connect us with heaven, as well as organs which set us in relation with earth. We have not merely the senses opening to us the external world, but an internal sense, which places us in connection with the world of intelligence and the decrees of God.

There is a *spirit in man*—not in the privileged few; not in those of us only who by the favor of Providence have been nursed in public schools. *It is in man;* it is the attribute of the race. The spirit, which is the guide to truth, is the gracious gift to each member of the human family.

Reason exists within every breast. I mean not that faculty which deduces inferences from the experience of the senses, but that higher faculty which from the infinite treasures of its own consciousness originates truth and assents to it by the force of intuitive evidence; that faculty which raises us beyond the control of time and space, and gives us faith in things eternal and invisible. There is not the difference between one mind and another which the pride of philosophers might conceive. To them no faculty is conceded which does not belong to the meanest

of their countrymen. In them there can not spring up a truth which does not equally have its germ in every mind. They have not the power of creation; they can but reveal what God has implanted in every breast.

The intellectual functions, by which relations are perceived, are the common endowments of the race. The differences are apparent, not real. The eye in one person may be dull, in another quick, in one distorted, and in another tranquil and clear; yet the relation of the eye to light is in all men the same. Just so judgment may be liable in individual minds to the bias of passion, and yet its relation to truth is immutable and is universal.

In questions of practical duty, conscience is God's umpire, whose light illumines every heart. There is nothing in books which had not first and has not still its life within us. Religion itself is a dead letter wherever its truths are not renewed in the soul. Individual conscience may be corrupted by interest or debauched by pride, yet the rule of morality is distinctly marked. Its harmonies are to the mind like music to the ear; and the moral judgment, when carefully analyzed and referred to its principles, is always founded in right. The Eastern superstition which bids its victims prostrate themselves before the advancing car of their idols springs from a noble root and is but a melancholy perversion of that self-devotion which enables the Christian to bear the cross and subject his personal passions to the will of God. Immorality of itself never won to its support the inward voice; conscience, if questioned, never forgets to curse the guilty with the memory of sin, to cheer the upright with the meek tranquillity of approval. And this admirable power, which is the instinct of Deity, is the attribute of every man; it knocks

386

at the palace gate; it dwells in the meanest hovel. Duty, like death, enters every abode and delivers its message. Conscience, like reason and judgment, is universal.

II

I speak for the universal diffusion of human powers, not of human attainments; for the capacity for progress, not for the perfection of undisciplined instincts. The fellowship which we should cherish with the race receives the Comanche warrior and the Kaffir within the pale of equality. Their functions may not have been exercised, but they exist. Immure a person in a dungeon; as he comes to the light of day, his vision seems incapable of performing its office. Does that destroy your conviction in the relation between the eye and light? The rioter over his cups resolves to eat and drink and be merry; he forgets his spiritual nature in his obedience to the senses. But does that destroy the relation between conscience and eternity? "What ransom shall we give?" exclaimed the senators of Rome to the savage Attila. "Give," said the barbarian, "all your gold and jewels, your costly furniture and treasures, and set free every slave." "Ah," replied the degenerate Romans, "what then will be left to us?" "I leave you your souls," replied the unlettered invader from the steppes of Asia, who had learnt in the wilderness to value the immortal mind, and to despise the servile herd that esteemed only their fortunes and had no true respect for themselves. You cannot discover a tribe of men, but you also find the charities of life and the proofs of spiritual existence. Behold the ignorant Algonquin deposit a bow and quiver by the side of the departed warrior, and recognize his faith in immortality. See the Co-

manche chieftain, in the heart of our continent, inflict on himself severest penance; and reverence his confession of the needed atonement for sin. The Barbarian who roams our Western prairies has like passions and like endowments with ourselves. He bears within him the instinct of Deity, the consciousness of a spiritual nature, the love of beauty, the rule of morality.

And shall we reverence the dark-skinned Kaffir? Shall we respect the brutal Hottentot? You may read the right answer written on every heart. It bids me not despise the sable hunter that gathers a livelihood in the forests of Southern Africa. All are men. When we know the Hottentot better, we shall despise him less.

III

If it be true that the gifts of mind and heart are universally diffused, if the sentiment of truth, justice, love, and beauty exists in every one then it follows, as a necessary consequence, that the common judgment in taste, politics, and religion is the highest authority on earth and the nearest possible approach to an infallible decision. From the consideration of individual powers I turn to the action of the human mind in masses.

If reason is a universal faculty, the universal decision is the nearest criterion of truth. The common mind winnows opinions; it is the sieve which separates error from certainty. The exercise by many of the same faculty on the same subject would naturally lead to the same conclusions. But if not, the very differences of opinion that arise prove the supreme judgment of the general mind. Truth is one. It never contradicts itself. One truth cannot contradict another truth. Hence truth is a bond of union. But error not only contradicts truth, but may contradict itself; so that there may be many errors, and each at variance with the rest. Truth is therefore of necessity an element of harmony; error as necessarily an element of discord. Thus there can be no continuing universal judgment but a right one. Men cannot agree in an absurdity; neither can they agree in a falsehood.

If wrong opinions have often been cherished by the masses, the cause always lies in the complexity of the ideas presented. Error finds its way into the soul of a nation only through the channel of truth. It is to a truth that men listen; and if they accept error also, it is only because the error is for the time so closely interwoven with the truth that the one cannot readily be separated from the other.

Unmixed error can have no existence in the public mind. Wherever you see men clustering together to form a party, you may be sure that however much error may be there truth is there also. Apply this principle boldly, for it contains a lesson of candor and a voice of encouragement. There never was a school of philosophy nor a clan in the realm of opinion but carried along with it some important truth. And therefore every sect that has ever flourished has benefited Humanity, for the errors of a sect pass away and are forgotten; its truths are received into the common inheritance. To know the seminal thought of every prophet and leader of a sect is to gather all the wisdom of mankind.

IV

In like manner the best government rests on the people and not on the few, on persons and not on property, on the free development of public opinion and not on authority; because the mu-

nificent Author of our being has conferred the gifts of mind upon every member of the human race without distinction of outward circumstances. Whatever of other possessions may be engrossed, mind asserts its own independence. Lands, estates, the produce of mines, the prolific abundance of the seas may be usurped by a privileged class. Avarice, assuming the form of ambitious power, may grasp realm after realm, subdue continents, compass the earth in its schemes of aggrandizement, and sigh after other worlds; but mind eludes the power of appropriation. It exists only in its own individuality; it is a property which cannot be confiscated and cannot be torn away; it laughs at chains; it bursts from imprisonment; it defies monopoly. A government of equal rights must, therefore, rest upon mind; not wealth, not brute force, the sum of the moral intelligence of the community should rule the State. Prescription can no more assume to be a valid plea for political injustice. Society studies to eradicate established abuses and to bring social institutions and laws into harmony with moral right, not dismayed by the natural and necessary imperfections of all human effort, and not giving way to despair, because every hope does not at once ripen into fruit.

The public happiness is the true object of legislation, and can be secured only by the masses of mankind themselves awakening to the knowledge and the care of their own interests. Our free institutions have reversed the false and ignoble distinctions between men; and refusing to gratify the pride of caste, have acknowledged the common mind to be the true material for a commonwealth. Everything has hitherto been done for the happy few. It is not possible to endow an aristocracy with greater benefits than they have already enjoyed; there is not room to hope that individuals will be more highly gifted or more fully developed than the greatest sages of past times. The world can advance only through the culture of the moral and intellectual powers of the people. To accomplish this end by means of the people themselves is the highest purpose of government. If it be the duty of the individual to strive after a perfection like the perfection of God, how much more ought a nation to be the image of Deity. The common mind is the true Parian marble, fit to be wrought into likeness to a God. The duty of America is to secure the culture and the happiness of the masses by their reliance on themselves.

The absence of the prejudices of the Old World leaves us here the opportunity of consulting independent truth, and man is left to apply the instinct of freedom to every social relation and public interest. We have approached so near to nature that we can hear her gentlest whispers; we have made Humanity our lawgiver and our oracle; and, therefore, the nation receives, vivifies, and applies principles which in Europe the wisest accept with distrust. Freedom of mind and of conscience, freedom of the seas, freedom of industry, equality of franchises—each great truth is firmly grasped, comprehended, and enforced; for the multitude is neither rash nor fickle. In truth, it is less fickle than those who profess to be its guides. Its natural dialectics surpass the logic of the schools. Political action has never been so consistent and so unwavering as when it results from a feeling or a principle diffused through society. The people is firm and tranquil in its movements, and necessarily acts with moderation, because it becomes but slowly impregnated with new ideas; and effects no

changes except in harmony with the knowledge which it has acquired. Besides, where it is permanently possessed of power, there exists neither the occasion nor the desire for frequent change. It is not the parent of tumult; sedition is bred in the lap of luxury, and its chosen emissaries are the beggared spendthrift and the impoverished libertine. The government by the people is in very truth the strongest government in the world. Discarding the implements of terror, it dares to rule by moral force and has its citadel in the heart.

Such is the political system which rests on reason, reflection, and the free expression of deliberate choice. There may be those who scoff at the suggestion that the decision of the whole is to be preferred to the judgment of the enlightened few. They say in their hearts that the masses are ignorant; that farmers know nothing of legislation; that mechanics should not quit their workshops to join in forming public opinion. But true political science does indeed venerate the masses. It maintains, not as has been perversely asserted, that "the people can make right," but that the people can *discern* right. Individuals are but shadows, too often engrossed by the pursuit of shadows; the race is immortal. Individuals are of limited sagacity; the common mind is infinite in its experience. Individuals are languid and blind; the many are ever wakeful. Individuals are corrupt; the race has been redeemed. Individuals are time-serving; the masses are fearless. Individuals may be false; the masses are ingenuous and sincere. Individuals claim the divine sanction of truth for the deceitful conceptions of their own fancies; the Spirit of God breathes through the combined intelligence of the people. Truth is not to be ascertained by the impulses of an individual; it emerges from the contradictions of personal opinions; it raises itself in majestic serenity above the strifes of parties and the conflict of sects; it acknowledges neither the solitary mind nor the separate faction as its oracle, but owns as its own faithful interpreter the dictates of pure reason itself, proclaimed by the general voice of mankind. The decrees of the universal conscience are the nearest approach to the presence of God in the soul of man.

Thus the opinion which we respect is, indeed, not the opinion of one or of a few, but the sagacity of the many. It is hard for the pride of cultivated philosophy to put its ear to the ground and listen reverently to the voice of lowly humanity; yet the people collectively are wiser than the most gifted individual, for all his wisdom constitutes but a part of theirs. When the great sculptor of Greece was endeavoring to fashion the perfect model of beauty, he did not passively imitate the form of the loveliest woman of his age; but he gleaned the several lineaments of his faultless work from the many. And so it is that a perfect judgment is the result of comparison, when error eliminates error, and truth is established by concurring witnesses. The organ of truth is the invisible decision of the unbiased world; she pleads before no tribunal but public opinion; she owns no safe interpreter but the common mind; she knows no court of appeals but the soul of humanity. It is when the multitude give counsel that right purposes find safety; theirs is the fixedness that cannot be shaken; theirs is the understanding which exceeds in wisdom; theirs is the heart of which the largeness is as the sand on the seashore.

It is not by vast armies, by immense natural resources, by accumulations of treasure, that the greatest results in modern civilization have been accomplished. The traces of the career of conquest pass away, hardly leaving a scar on the national intelligence. The famous battle grounds of victory are, most of them, comparatively indifferent to the human race; barren fields of blood, the scourges of their times but affecting the social condition as little as the raging of a pestilence. Not one benevolent institution, not one ameliorating principle in the Roman state was a voluntary concession of the aristocracy; each useful element was borrowed from the democracies of Greece or was a reluctant concession to the demands of the people. The same is true in the modern political life. It is the confession of an enemy to Democracy, that *"all the great and noble institutions of the world have come from popular efforts."*

It is the uniform tendency of the popular element to elevate and bless humanity. The exact measure of the progress of civilization is the degree in which the intelligence of the common mind has prevailed over wealth and brute force; in other words, the measure of the progress of civilization is the progress of the people. Every great object connected with the benevolent exertions of the day has reference to the culture of those powers which are alone the common inheritance. For this the envoys of religion cross seas and visit remotest isles; for this the press in its freedom teems with the productions of maturest thought; for this the philanthropist plans new schemes of education; for this halls in every city and village are open to the public instructor. Not that we view with indifference the glorious efforts of material industry; the increase in the facility of internal intercourse; the accumulations of thrifty labor, the varied results of concentrated action. But even there it is mind that achieves the triumph. It is the genius of the architect that gives beauty to the work of human hands, and makes the temple, the dwelling, or the public edifice, an outward representation of the spirit of propriety and order. It is science that guides the blind zeal of cupidity to the construction of the vast channels of communication which are fast binding the world into one family. And it is as a method of moral improvement that these swifter means of intercourse derive their greatest value. Mind becomes universal property; the poem that is published on the soil of England finds its response on the shores of Lake Erie and the banks of the Missouri, and is admired near the sources of the Ganges. The defense of public liberty in our own halls of legislation penetrates the plains of Poland, is echoed along the mountains of Greece, and pierces the darkest night of Eastern despotism.

WILLIAM GILPIN

In *North America* a homogeneous unity of language, population, and manners is unavoidable. This is benignantly amplified by an undulating variety of contour, pervading equally the mountain system and the plains. This happy combination provokes the highest development and discipline of energy, and the most exalted civilization.

Here the vast arena of the Pacific basin fits itself to the basin of the Atlantic, edge to edge. The goal is reached where the zodiac of nations closes its circle. The gap between the

Reprinted from William Gilpin, MISSION OF THE NORTH AMERICAN PEOPLE (Philadelphia, 1874), pp. 127–30.

hemispheres is bridged over forever.

We are upon the *isothermal axis,* which is the trunk line (*the thalweg*) of intense and intelligent energy; where civilization has its largest field, its highest development, its inspired form.

There is an intoxicating grandeur in the panorama which unveils itself to the spectator looking out from the crest of the neighboring Cordillera. In front, in rear, and on either flank, Nature ascends to her highest standard of excellence.

Behold to the right the Mississippi Basin: to the left the Plateau of the Table Lands: beneath, the family of Parcs: around, the radiating backs of the primeval mountains: the primary rivers starting to the seas: a uniform altitude of 8000 feet: a translucent atmosphere, a thousand miles removed from the ocean and its influences: a checkered landscape, from which no element of sublimity is left out—fertility and food upon the surface; metals beneath; uninterrupted facility of transit.

Behold here the *panorama* which crowns the middle region of our Union; fans the immortal fire of patriotism; and beckons on the energetic host of our people!

Here, through the heart of our territory, our population, our States, our cities, our mines, our farms and habitations, will traverse the condensed commerce of mankind—where passengers and cargoes may, *at any time or place,* embark upon or leave the vehicles of transportation.

Down with the parricidal policy which will banish it from the *land*— from among the broadcast dwellings of the people—to force it on to the sterile ocean: outside of society, through foreign nations—into the torrid heats: along solitary, circuitous routes: imprisoned for months and dwarfed in great ships!

RAILWAYS, multiplied and spanning the continent, are essential domestic institutions; more powerful and more permanent than law, or popular consent, or political constitutions, to thoroughly complete the grand system of fluvial arteries which fraternize us into one people—to bind the *two seaboards* to this one *continental union,* like ears to the human head—to radicate the *rural* foundations of the Union so broad and deep, and establish its structures so solid, that no possible force or stratagem can shake its permanence—to secure such scope and space to progress, that equality and prosperity shall never be impaired or chafe for want of room!

. . . The North American people number *fifty millions* in strength. *Two millions* annually shift their homes. This force is, *par excellence,* the pioneer army of the North American people. This movement causes an uninterrupted pressure of the people from *east* to *west,* resembling the drift of the ocean which accompanies the great *tidal* wave.

Diurnally is the surface of the sea lifted up in silence and poured upon the coasts of the continents. Exactly similar to this is the movement, annually gathering force, and seen to impel our people through and through from the *eastern* to the *western* limit of the land.

The inscrutable force of *gravity,* which with minute accuracy holds the planets in their orbits, or causes each drop of rain to fall, sways the instinct of society. This gravitation presses from all directions upon the axis, and to the focus of intensity. This regular instinct of movement has been transiently interfered with by the artificial passions and demoralization of civil strife. It rapidly assumes again its temper and its regularity.

. . .

The *Mexican* column reaches us from the *south.* On the *north* the activity is great, and in close contact. These several columns simultaneously converge upon us. They increase *every moment* in numbers, weight, and celerity of motion.

We no longer march into the blind wilderness, dependent upon and chained *exclusively* to Europe in the rear. We open up in front the gorgeous arena of the ASIATIC OCEAN.

At present, the huge city of London monopolizes the imports from the *Oriental* world. These are stored there, and retailed to the people residing in the basin of the Atlantic.

Upon the labor of the American people, so far as they participate in the consumption of *Oriental wares,* is harnessed the frightful burden to support the British people and the British Empire, and to be devoured by their voracious despotism of trade.

The work of emancipation is accomplished by the intrepid energies and conquests of the pioneer army of North America. It only remains to be appreciated and accepted by the people.

We are about to supply by direct export the food and precious and base metals to 850,000,000 of neighboring Asiatics! To Japan: to China: to India. To the gorgeous islands of Borneo: Sumatra: Java. To the Philippines: the Celebes. To the Archipelagoes of the Sooloo Sea and Polynesia! These are *larger* in aggregate area, and more populous, than Europe; *and are nearer to us.*

Included within the *equatorial* zone, but approached by us through the *temperate* zone, they overflow with merchandises desirable to our people, in multitudinous affluence. To us will belong the prodigious carrying trade upon the seas for these infinite multitudes. The equatorial *heats* are outflanked and avoided. The conflict for dominion over the multiplied commerce of the world is fought, and the conclusive victory is won for our country.

A large majority of the American people now reside within the Mississippi Basin, and in this Asiatic front of our continent, which is born from us.

Nascent powers, herculean from the hour of their birth, unveil their forms and demand their rights. States for the pioneers; self-government for the pioneers; untrammelled way for the imperial energies of the forces of the Rocky Mountains and the Pacific Sea, may not long be withheld by covetous, arbitrary, and arrogant jealousy and injustice!

In the conflict for freedom, it is not numbers or cunning that conquers; but rather daring, discipline, and judgment, combined and tempered by the condensed fire of faith and intrepid valor.

As it is my hope, in these notes, to contribute what may be valuable, I adhere strictly to severe facts, and reject absolutely all theory and speculation. These facts are as indestructibly established as is the alphabet, and are as worthy of unquestioning faith and credence.

That we may look into the gathering achievements of the *near* future, without obscurity, and with an accurate prophetic vision, I may without censure submit what is within my own personal experience.

It fell to my lot, during the years from 1840 to 1845, alone and in extreme youth, to seek and chalk out, in the immense solitudes filling the space from Missouri to China, the lines of this dazzling empire of which we now hold the oracular crown—to have stood by its cradle—to be the witness of its miraculous growth.

It is not for me, in this season of gathering splendor, to speak *tamely* upon a subject of such intense and engrossing novelty and interest. I may properly here quote the concluding sentences of a report which I was required to make on the 2d of March, 1846, *to the United States Senate,* at that time brimful of illustrious statesmen. What I said then and there, in the first dawning twilight of our glory, I will now repeat:

"The calm, wise man sets himself to study aright and understand clearly the deep designs of Providence—to scan the great volume of nature—to fathom, if possible, the will of the Creator, and to receive with respect what may be revealed to him.

"Two centuries have rolled over our race upon this continent. From nothing we have become 20,000,000. From nothing we are grown to be in agriculture, in commerce, in civilization, and in natural strength, the first among nations existing or in history. So much is our *destiny*—so far, up to this time—*transacted,* accomplished, certain, and not to be disputed. From this threshold we read the future.

"The *untransacted* destiny of the American people is to subdue the continent—to rush over this vast field to the Pacific Ocean—to animate the many hundred millions of its people, and to cheer them upward—to set the principle of self-government at work—to agitate these herculean masses—to establish a new order in human affairs—to set free the enslaved—to regenerate superannuated nations—to change darkness into light—to stir up the sleep of a hundred centuries—to teach old nations a new civilization—to confirm the destiny of the human race—to carry the career of mankind to its culminating point—to cause stagnant people to be re-born—to perfect science—to emblazon history with the conquest of peace—to shed a new and resplendent glory upon mankind—to unite the world in one social family—to dissolve the spell of tyranny and exalt charity—to absolve the curse that weighs down humanity, and to shed blessings round the world!

"Divine task! immortal mission! Let us tread fast and joyfully the open trail before us! Let every American heart open wide for patriotism to glow undimmed, and confide with religious faith in the sublime and prodigious destiny of his well-loved country."

JAMES FENIMORE COOPER

ON DEMAGOGUES

A demagogue, in the strict signification of the word, is "a leader of the rabble." It is a Greek compound, that conveys this meaning. In these later times, however, the signification has been extended to suit the circumstances of the age. Thus, before the art of printing became known, or cheap publications were placed within the reach of the majority, the mass of all nations might properly enough be termed a rabble, when assembled in bodies. In nations in which attention is paid to education, this reproach is gradually becoming unjust, though a body of Americans, even, collected under what is popularly termed an "excitement," losing sight of that reason and respect

Reprinted from James Fenimore Cooper, THE AMERICAN DEMOCRAT *(New York, 1956), pp. 96–102.*

for their own deliberately framed ordinances, which alone distinguish them from the masses of other people, is neither more nor less than a rabble. Men properly derive their designations from their acts, and not from their professions.

The peculiar office of a demagogue is to advance his own interests, by affecting a deep devotion to the interests of the people. Sometimes the object is to indulge malignancy, unprincipled and selfish men submitting but to two governing motives, that of doing good to themselves, and that of doing harm to others. The true theatre of a demagogue is a democracy, for the body of the community possessing the power, the master he pretends to serve is best able to reward his efforts. As it is all important to distinguish between those who labor in behalf of the people on the general account, and those who labor in behalf of the people on their own account, some of the rules by which each may be known shall be pointed out.

The motive of the demagogue may usually be detected in his conduct. The man who is constantly telling the people that they are unerring in judgment, and that they have all power, is a demagogue. Bodies of men being composed of individuals, can no more be raised above the commission of error, than individuals themselves, and, in many situations, they are more likely to err, from self-excitement and the division of responsibility. The power of the people is limited by the fundamental laws, or the constitution, the rights and opinions of the minority, in all but those cases in which a decision becomes indispensable, being just as sacred as the rights and opinions of the majority; else would a democracy be, indeed, what its enemies term it, the worst species of tyranny. In this instance, the people are flattered, in order to be led; as in kingdoms, the prince is blinded to his own defects, in order to extract favor from him.

The demagogue always puts the people before the constitution and the laws, in face of the obvious truth that the people have placed the constitution and the laws before themselves.

The local demagogue does not distinguish between the whole people and a part of the people, and is apt to betray his want of principles by contending for fancied, or assumed rights, in favor of a county, or a town, though the act is obviously opposed to the will of the nation. This is a test that the most often betrays the demagogue, for while loudest in proclaiming his devotion to the majority, he is, in truth, opposing the will of the entire people, in order to effect his purposes with a part.

The demagogue is usually sly, a detractor of others, a professor of humility and disinterestedness, a great stickler for equality as respects all above him, a man who acts in corners, and avoids open and manly expositions of his course, calls blackguards gentlemen, and gentlemen folks, appeals to passions and prejudices rather than to reason, and is in all respects, a man of intrigue and deception, of sly cunning and management, instead of manifesting the frank, fearless qualities of the democracy he so prodigally professes.

The man who maintains the rights of the people on pure grounds, may be distinguished from the demagogue by the reverse of all these qualities. He does not flatter the people, even while he defends them, for he knows that flattery is a corrupting and dangerous poison. Having nothing to conceal, he is frank and fearless, as are all men with the consciousness of right motives. He oftener chides than commends, for

power needs reproof and can dispense with praise.

He who would be a courtier under a king, is almost certain to be a demagogue in a democracy. The elements are the same, though, brought into action under different circumstances, ordinary observers are apt to fancy them the extremes of opposite moral castes. Travellers have often remarked, that, Americans, who have made themselves conspicuous abroad for their adulation of rank and power, have become zealous advocates of popular supremacy, on returning home. Several men of this stamp are, at this moment, in conspicuous political stations in the country, having succeeded by the commonest arts of courtiers.

There is a large class of political men in this country, who, while they scarcely merit the opprobrium of being termed demagogues, are not properly exempt from the imputation of falling into some of their most dangerous vices. These are they, whose habits, and tastes, and better opinions, indeed, are all at variance with vulgar errors and vulgar practices, but, who imagine it a necessary evil in a democracy to defer to prejudices, and ignorance, and even to popular jealousies and popular injustice, that a safe direction may be given to the publick mind. Such men deceive themselves, in the first place, as to their own motives, which are rather their private advancement than the publick good, and, admitting the motives to be pure, they err greatly both in their mode of construing the system under which they live, and in the general principles of correcting evil and of producing good. As the greatest enemy of truth is falsehood, so is the most potent master of falsehood, truth. These qualities are correlatives; that which is not true, being false; and that which is not false, being true. It follows, as a pervading rule of morals, that the advancement of one is the surest means of defeating the other. All good men desire the truth, and, on all publick occasions on which it is necessary to act at all, the truth would be the most certain, efficient, and durable agency in defeating falsehoods, whether of prejudices, reports, or principles. The perception of truth is an attribute of reason, and the ground-work of all institutions that claim to be founded in justice, is this high quality. Temporary convenience, and selfish considerations, beyond a doubt, are both favored by sometimes closing the eyes to the severity of truth, but in nothing is the sublime admonition of God in his commandments, where he tells us that he "will visit the sins of the fathers unto the third and fourth generations of their children," more impressively verified, than in the inevitable punishments that await every sacrifice of truth.

Most of the political men of the day belong to this class of doubtful moralists, who, mistaking a healthful rule, which admonishes us that even truth ought not to be too offensively urged, in their desire to be moderate, lend themselves to the side of error. The ingenuity of sophisms, and the audacity of falsehoods receive great support from this mistaken alliance, since a firm union of all the intelligent of a country, in the cause of plain and obvious truths, would exterminate their correlative errors, the publick opinion which is now enlisted in the support of the latter, following to the right side, as as matter of course, in the train of combined knowledge. This is the mode in which opinions rooted in the wrong have been gradually eradicated, by the process of time, but which would yield faster, were it not for the latitude and delusion that self-ishness imposes on men of this class, who flatter themselves with soothing a sore that they are actually irritating. The consequence of this mistaken forbearance, is to substitute a new set of errors, for those which it has already taken ages to get rid of.

On the subject of government and society, it is a misfortune that this country is filled with those who take the opposite extremes, the one side clinging to prejudices that were founded in the abuses of the feudal times, and the other to the exaggerations of impracticable theories. That the struggle is not fiercer, is probably owing to the overwhelming numbers of the latter class, but as things are, truth is a sufferer.

The American *doctrinaire* is the converse of the American demagogue, and, in his way, is scarcely less injurious to the publick. He is as much a visionary on one side, as the extreme theoretical democrat is a visionary on the other. The first deals in poetry, the last in cant. The first affirms a disinterestedness and purity in education and manners, when exposed to the corruption of power, that all experience refutes; and the last an infallibility in majorities that God himself has denied. These opposing classes produce the effect of all counter-acting forces, resistance, and they provoke each others' excesses.

In the *doctrinaire*, or theorist of the old school, we see men clinging to opinions that are purely the issue of arbitrary facts, ages after the facts themselves have ceased to exist, confounding cause with effect; and, in the demagogue, or his tool, the impracticable democrat, one who permits envy, jealousy, opposition, selfishness, and the unconsciousness of his own inferiority and demerits, so far to blind his faculties, as to obscure the sense of justice, to exclude the sight of positive things, and to cause him to deny the legitimate consequences of the very laws of which he professes to be proud. This is the dupe who affirms that, "one man is as good as another."

These extremes lead to the usual inconsistencies and follies. Thus do we see men, who sign for titles and factitious and false distinctions, so little conscious of truth, as to shrink from asserting the real distinctions of their social station, or those they actually and undeniably possess; as if nature ever intended a man for an aristocrat, who has not the manhood to maintain his just rights; and those, again, who cant of equality and general privileges, while they stubbornly refuse to permit others to enjoy in peace a single fancied indulgence or taste, unless taken in their company, although nature, education and habits have all unfitted them to participate, and their presence would be sure to defeat what they could not, in the nature of things, enjoy.

The considerate, and modest, and just-minded man, of whatever social class, will view all this differently. In asserting his own rights, he respects those of others; in indulging his own tastes, he is willing to admit there may be superior; in pursuing his own course, in his own manner, he knows his neighbor has an equal right to do the same; and, most of all, is he impressed with the great moral truths that flatterers are inherently miscreants, that fallacies never fail to bring their punishments, and that the empire of God is reason.

III. RECENT INTERPRETATIONS

The political and ideological world of Jacksonian America has elicited new interest among American historians, especially those skilled in the application of behavioral techniques to political analysis. In one major recent study, *The Second American Party System*, Richard McCormick traced on a state-by-state basis the evolution of Jacksonian political parties from a sprawl of factional remnants during the 1820's to the disciplined national organizations of the 1840's.

McCormick's emphasis on the increased parallel growth of political professionalism and democratic values in mid-nineteenth-century America reinforces the central argument of Marvin Meyers' study of partisan ideology, *The Jacksonian Persuasion*. In the selection from this work which is included here, Meyers isolates a ruling paradox and moral dilemma felt by many Jacksonians, who found themselves trapped between the desire to restore a vision of republican virtue associated with the founding generation's agrarian world while at the same time they wished to exploit fully the opportunities of their own liberal capitalist society.

McCormick's description of the mass parties in Jacksonian America portrays the emergence of a new class of professional political managers who found it possible to combine economic interest and political ambition in their public lives, as when they dispensed banking privileges, awarded canal subsidies, or handled Western land sales. Thus, when seen as a problem in personal morality, the dilemma of McCormick's professionals resembles closely the paradox of Meyers' ideologists, and the two articles that follow suggest the close relationship between the political and moral *style* of Jacksonian America.

RICHARD P. McCORMICK

It would seem to be quite clear that the stimulus for the formation of the second party system was supplied by the revival of the contest for the presidency in 1824. With the expiration of Monroe's second term there was no notable Virginian to take his place; the weak and discredited Republican congressional caucus was unable to produce a disciplined solution to the problem of succession; and soon there were four candidates—all self-styled Republicans—contending for the presidency. Except in New England, where John Quincy Adams had virtually no opposition, the contest was extremely confused and did not at once produce new party alignments. Because it was so chaotic, and also because in many states one or another of the candidates enjoyed overwhelming support from local political leaders, voter participation was remarkably low.

The most important consequence of 1824, in terms of party formation, was that it projected Andrew Jackson to the fore as the rival to Adams. Looking ahead to 1828, rival political leaders from state to state began to calculate their courses of action with respect to what was termed the "presidential question." Obviously, many considerations entered into their appraisals, but the fact that loomed largest, no doubt,

was the highly sectional nature of the appeal of the two candidates.

This sectional bias was clearly revealed in the election of 1828. Adams swept New England, securing majorities of three-to-one or better in four of the six states. Jackson was equally impressive in the South, and won commanding majorities in most of the newer states of the West. Having no sectional candidate of their own in the race, the Middle States provided the major battleground of the election, and—except in Pennsylvania—the vote was extremely close. The party alignments that formed in the Middle States by 1828 tended to be durable, as Table 1 shows,[1] although in both New York and Pennsylvania the anti-Jackson forces lacked cohesion and were distracted by Antimasonry. With these important exceptions, we could say that a new two-party system had emerged in the Middle States by 1828 and that it had been given definition by the presidential contest. In New England, because of the overwhelming loyalty to the sectional favorite, the opposition Jacksonian parties were able to make little headway until after Adams had been defeated. But by 1829 the political balance had altered considerably, and the Jacksonians rapidly moved into a competitive position in most states. In the South and West—except for the very special case of Kentucky—the election of 1828 stimulated the temporary

Reprinted from Richard P. McCormick, "Political Development and the Second Party System," in William N. Chambers and Walter D. Burnham, eds., THE AMERICAN PARTY SYSTEMS *(New York: Oxford University Press, 1967), pp. 97–109, 111–12, by permission of the publisher.*

[1] It will be observed that the average differential between the total vote obtained by the presidential candidates in 1828 was 36 points, which would mean an average percentage of 68 for the victor and 32 for the defeated candidate.

TABLE 1. *Differential Between Percentages of Total Vote Obtained by Major Presidential Candidates, 1824–44*

STATE	1828	1832	1836	1840	1844
Maine	20	10	20	1	13
New Hampshire	7	13	50	11	19
Vermont	50	10	20	29	18
Massachusetts	66	30	9	16	12
Rhode Island	50	14	6	23	20
Connecticut	50	20	1	11	5
New York	2	4	9	4	1
New Jersey	4	1	1	4	1
Pennsylvania	33	16	4	1	2
Delaware	—	2	6	10	3
Maryland	2	1	7	8	5
Virginia	38	50	13	1	6
North Carolina	47	70	6	15	5
Georgia	94	100	4	12	4
Kentucky	1	9	6	29	8
Tennessee	90	90	16	11	1
Louisiana	6	38	3	19	3
Alabama	80	100	11	9	18
Mississippi	60	77	2	7	13
Ohio	3	3	4	9	2
Indiana	13	34	12	12	2
Illinois	34	37	10	2	12
Missouri	41	32	21	14	17
Arkansas	—	—	28	13	26
Michigan	—	—	9	4	6
Average Differential	36	36	11	11	9

formation of parties. Once the election was over, however, the alignments did not persist and politics continued to be conducted in what was essentially an unstructured fashion.

Despite the large issues that presumably were involved, the election of 1832 had remarkably little effect on party formation. In the South and West there were feeble efforts to organize support for Henry Clay, but in most states he fared even less well than had Adams in 1828. In the Middle States, the close balance that had become evident in 1828 persisted. The most striking shift occurred in New England, where in every state the Jacksonians made tremendous gains and captured Maine and New Hampshire. Perhaps

this remarkable upheaval can be attributed to the popularity of Jackson's policies regarding the bank, tariff, and internal improvements. Yet I am inclined to believe that the explanation is to be found quite simply in the fact that Clay lacked the strong sectional appeal that Adams had possessed.

How well developed, then, was the new party system by the end of 1832? In broad terms, it was well established in New England and the Middle States, despite the complications of Antimasonry. In every state the Jacksonians had acquired recognized leaders, constructed an elaborate party appartus, and enlisted in their ranks multitudes of voters who identified with the Jackson party. The opposition, plagued by the lack of a persistent standard bearer, nevertheless managed to maintain a competitive position, whether under the Adams, National Republican, or Antimasonic label. The South, except for Kentucky, could best be described as politically monolithic. Where nearly all political leaders and candidates were nominally, at least, of the Jacksonian persuasion, there could scarcely be a functioning two-party system. In certain of the newer states of the West what can only be described as a dual party system existed. There were temporary party formations in 1828 and 1832 for the purpose of contesting the presidential election, but in state and congressional elections the contests were either conducted on a non-party basis or, in some instances, on the basis of alignments quite different from those that obtained in the presidential elections. It is common, in describing American politics in this era, to assert that by 1828 or by 1832 a functioning party system existed; but it would be my contention that in many states the crucial stage of party formation had not yet been reached.

Slight as was the effect of the election of 1832 on party formation, it did reveal an undercurrent that was soon to assume the proportions of a tidal wave. Although Jackson retained, and even increased, his huge majorities throughout the South, there were strong manifestations of dissatisfaction with his running mate and heir-apparent, Martin Van Buren of New York. In Virginia, North Carolina, Georgia, and Alabama, factions that professed loyalty to Jackson also launched organized efforts to oppose Van Buren's candidacy for the vice-presidency, and there were similar signs of restiveness in other Southern states as well. Some of these early anti-Van Burenites were admirers of John C. Calhoun, and others were appalled at the prospect of having to support a Northerner for the presidency. Still others, no doubt, were calculating how they might exploit anti-Van Buren sentiment to advance their political fortunes within their particular states.

What can best be characterized as a political explosion rocked the South from Virginia to Mississippi in 1834 and 1835. With Jackson nearing the end of his tenure, the political consensus that seemingly had prevailed was abruptly replaced by a sharp cleavage in almost every state. Those who remained loyal to the Jackson party found themselves confronted with a virulent opposition that shared a common antagonism to Martin Van Buren. While some of those "antis" continued to profess their undying loyalty to Old Hickory and his policies, others declaimed against executive usurpation, the removal of bank deposits, and the tariff, or sounded the changes on states' rights. The new sides were drawn in the state and congressional elections of 1834 and 1835, and by 1836 the Southern opposition parties—often bearing the name Whig—had found their standard bearer in Hugh Lawson White of Tennessee.

In the Western states, too, the approach of the election of 1836 spurred the slow process of party formation. More-or-less well-organized Van Buren-Democratic parties faced bitter struggles with opposition parties pledged variously to a local hero—William Henry Harrison of Indiana—or to mixed White-Harrison tickets. In part because of the unprecedented personal campaign waged by Harrison, the election aroused considerable interest. The alignments that emerged in this election persisted, even though state elections in Illinois, Indiana, and Missouri continued for a few years to bear only a vague resemblance to party contests.

The least studied of all our presidential elections, the election of 1836, was of crucial importance in determining the ultimate outlines of the second party system. In marked contrast to the situation that had existed in 1832, there were now two parties contesting elections in every state, and—no less significantly—in the large majority of the states the parties were competitive. Although Van Buren eked out a victory in the 1836 election, the party that he headed had very different dimensions from the one that had twice swept Jackson into office. In the South, where Jackson had encountered little more than token opposition, Van Buren polled slightly less than 50 per cent of the popular vote. Jackson had won 100 per cent of the votes in Georgia and 95 per cent of the votes in Tennessee in 1832; Van Buren lost both of these states in 1836. In the West, too, Van Buren's strength was far less than that of Jackson. Only in New England did Van Buren enhance the strength of the Democratic party. In the evenly balanced Middle States there was no large shift.

In brief, the effect of Van Buren's candidacy was to end the monolithic character of Southern politics and delineate and strengthen alignments in the West, thereby giving a truly national dimension to the second party system. While in 1832 the victorious candidate had secured a two-to-one margin in eleven states, only one state remained in that category in 1836: New Hampshire, which Van Buren carried by a three-to-one margin. Fittingly enough, the state in which Van Buren found his weakest support was Vermont. Here, indeed, is a conundrum for political analysts.

The anti-Van Buren or Whig parties that had formed in the several states between 1834 and 1836, together with those in New England and the Middle States that had originated earlier, had yet to develop national cohesion and leadership. Such an achievement would be essential if they were to contest successfully for the presidency. Meeting at Harrisburg in December 1839, in one of the most astutely contrived conventions ever held, they performed the difficult feat by agreeing to unite on the best available hero, Old Tippecanoe Harrison, and by sedulously avoiding any semblance of a party platform. Thus effectively mobilized, the Whigs proceeded to put on a spectacular campaign that was to fix a new style in American political drama.[2] The exciting contest, waged furiously now in every state, stimulated an unprecedented outpouring of voters and sent Van Buren down to a crushing defeat in the electoral college, although the popular vote was far less lopsided.

The campaign of 1840 brought the second American party system at last to fruition. In every region of the country, and indeed in every state, politics was conducted within the framework of a two-party system, and in all but a handful of states the parties were so closely balanced as to be competitive.[3] In broad terms, it was the contest for the presidency that shaped this party system and defined its essential purpose. The same party system, however, was to be utilized as the framework within which competition for office at all other levels of government would be conducted. The two parties were similar in structure, employed similar campaign techniques, and performed similar functions. Although in specific features the parties remained somewhat differentiated from state to state, there had in fact occurred a nationalization of institutional forms and political styles. There was also a nationalization of political identities. Voters everywhere would respond to candidates and issues as Whigs or Democrats.

With this brief and even partial synopsis of party development in mind, it becomes possible to attempt some analyses of what it all signifies. We can approach this question by attempting some broad comparisons between the first and second party systems. But before engaging in this exercise, we might well pause to consider how politics was conducted in the absence of parties, for only with some understanding of this phase of our political history can we measure and evaluate the effects of parties.

Even after the appearance of the first party system, many states continued to

[2] The story of this memorable campaign is ably detailed in Robert G. Gunderson, *The Log Cabin Campaign* (Lexington, Ky., 1957).

[3] See Table 1. In twenty of the states in 1840 the margin between the two parties was 15 points or less and the average differential was only 11 points. Note the contrast between 1832 and 1840.

conduct politics on a non-party basis. An example is Tennessee, which did so for roughly forty years.[4] With no vestige of political parties, the Tennessee brand of politics featured hard-fought contests for seats in the legislature and in Congress that not uncommonly brought over 70 per cent of the electorate to the polls. In the process, the state produced a host of outstanding political figures, including not only Andrew Jackson but James K. Polk, Hugh Lawson White, John Bell, and Felix Grundy as well. Reference could readily be made to a dozen other states where as late as the 1820's, or even 1830's, political parties were nonexistent. Leaving aside the intriguing question of why parties were not formed, at least for the purpose of conducting state politics, it would no doubt be illuminating if we could answer the question of what functions usually ascribed to political parties were not being performed in some manner in Tennessee and other non-party states. Probably none of us would insist that representative government was inconceivable without political parties, but we may readily err in attributing to parties a larger and more comprehensive role in the American political process than they in fact deserve. Unfortunately, we know even less about pre-party politics in the United States than we do about party politics, with the result that as yet we are not well prepared to make reliable comparisons between the two systems.

We are on slightly firmer ground when we endeavor to compare the first

and the second party systems, although admittedly our knowledge of both is inadequate and the conceptual framework within which we structure our comparisons is incomplete. For the purposes of this essay, the comparative analysis must necessarily be kept within brief limits and deal only with large and readily visible attributes.

The first and second American party systems did not have precisely the same origins. It would seem that cleavages within Congress preceded and even forecast the formation of parties in the 1790's. In theoretical terms, it would be extremely important to be able to affirm that the first party system represented an "internally created" or "interior" type of party formation. Unfortunately, we cannot be sure how far this interior process of party formation might have proceeded, for superimposed on the impulse supplied by the congressional parties was the mobilization for the presidential contests in 1796 and 1800. It is my view that these contests for the presidency supplied a greater stimulus to party formation than did the congressional groupings. Nevertheless, the early existence of congressional alignments in the 1790's has no counterpart in the 1820's. Moreover, the parties of the 1790's possessed at the outset an issue-orientation that can hardly be discerned in 1824 or 1828. Finally, the first party system had a relatively rapid emergence, whereas the second was formed in stages over a period of roughly sixteen years.

Both party systems, the second more clearly than the first, were oriented toward contesting presidential elections. This orientation presents a striking contrast to the situation in other Western political systems, where parties have been oriented toward securing as large a representation as possible in the national legislature (although it

---

[4] Tennessee might be called a "one-party" state in the sense that nearly all public figures, as well as voters, identified themselves as Jeffersonian Republicans, or—after 1824— as Jacksonians. But there was no formal party structure, and vigorously contested elections were conducted without relevance to parties.

must be noted that in most cases it has been the legislature that names the functioning executive in such systems). It is this peculiarity, among others, that makes it so difficult to conceptualize American party systems in terms that would be relevant to other nations. In organizational terms, the congressional district has presented awkward problems for our parties, quite unlike the parliamentary constituencies in Europe. Why should the executive rather than the legislative branch have been the focal point for the party system, especially in the first half of the nineteenth century? No doubt an extended answer to this question could tell us much about the special character of American parties.

There were pronounced differences in the organizational structures of parties in the first and second party systems. The caucus reflected in part the prominent role taken by legislators —national and state—in guiding early party development, and it was extensively employed as a management device under the first party system.[5] In most states, as well as at the national level, party members within the legislature, often joined by non-legislators, performed extensive nominating functions and—usually through such agencies as central committees—directed party affairs generally. In many states, conspicuously in New England and Virginia, the caucus and its agencies operated a highly centralized party apparatus, although in time local party units increasingly employed delegate

conventions to nominate candidates for lesser offices. Two states, New Jersey and Delaware, were exceptional in that they instituted the state convention. Because of the great variations in constitutional structures from state to state, the precise forms of party organization and even the functions performed by the caucus differed widely; but in its most highly developed form— notably in Massachusetts—the caucus structure was highly integrated and extremely efficient. At the national level, party management was relatively weak. The Republican congressional caucus was a promising institution, which under slightly altered circumstances might have exerted a lasting influence on the structure of American parties, but for reasons that must be passed over it failed to develop and maintain its authority and grew increasingly ineffective, especially after 1816. The Federalists, with their small and geographically unrepresentative delegation in Congress, could scarcely use the caucus as an authoritative national agency, and they had little success in developing the convention as an alternative.

Under the second party system, the caucus was almost completely replaced by the convention as the characteristic device for party management. The changeover, which has not yet been studied thoroughly, had great theoretical significance. In addition to reflecting demands for popular participation in party affairs the convention also represented a highly practical solution to problems facing party leaders at a time when party identities in legislative bodies were extremely confused, or when incipient parties had too few legislative representatives to organize a respectable caucus. Much might be made of the fact that the Antimasonic party, the first clear example of what

---

[5] For interesting material on the caucus-style party organization under the first party system, see Cunningham, *Jeffersonian Republicans*, 162–6; Cunningham, *The Jeffersonian Republicans in Power: Party Operations 1801–1809* (Chapel Hill, 1963), 111–12, 127, 133, 137, 142, 145–6; and Fischer, *Revolution of American Conservatism*, 60–90 *passim*.

Maurice Duverger calls an "externally created" or "exterior" type of party in the United States, was especially zealous in developing the convention technique and, as we know, held the first national party convention. Whether the extralegislative origins of the Jackson and Adams parties in most—but not all—states would justify our describing them as "exterior" parties could lead to considerable debate. What would seem to be indisputable is that the shift from caucus to convention implied a loss in the political authority of legislative bodies. While they were suffering this loss, they were also experiencing general curtailment of their elective functions, as evidenced by the trend toward the popular choice of electors, governors, and other state officials. Again, one would like to be able to understand fully why this downgrading of the legislative branch occurred and what implications it had for our system of politics.

The widespread adoption of the convention system in the 1830's, with its hierarchy of delegate conventions and party committees extending from the smallest electoral unit up to the national conventions, made for an exceedingly elaborate and complex organizational structure. Because candidates had to be nominated at so very many different levels of government, elections were held so frequently, and the party system embraced the entire range of offices, the organizations that had evolved in most states by the 1840's were marvels of ingenuity and intricacy and required enormous manpower to staff them. In contrast to the diversity of organizational forms under the first party system, there was now a high degree of uniformity throughout the nation and in both major parties.

It is possible that the shift from the caucus to the convention may have tended greatly to emphasize the purely electoral functions of the party apparatus. The members of a caucus, in their dual capacity as legislators and party managers, may have been more concerned with matters of program and policy than were the members of conventions. It would also appear that in its most centralized form, the caucus structure imposed a much higher degree of discipline than was to prevail under the convention system. Despite their elaborate organization, the new parties of the second party system were actually decentralized structures. The party apparatus at each level of government, or within each type of constituency, possessed considerable autonomy. Party mechanisms were better designed for achieving agreement on nominations than for formulating policies. Perhaps the very complexity and magnitude of the formal organizational structure contributed to the rise of the professional party manager and the informal leader, or boss.

In discussing any formal party structures, whether of the caucus or convention type, the problem inevitably arises as to whether the formal structure reflected the actual locus of power or influence. Superficially, the delegate convention system of the 1830's and 1840's resulted in the "democratization" of parties, but we have yet to determine the degree to which conventions were genuine decision-making bodies. Perhaps they were, but they must also be viewed as having what might be termed a cosmetic function; that is, they gave a democratic appearance to what might in fact have been decisions determined by a party oligarchy. Indeed, Ostrogorski used the term "democratic formalism" to describe the convention structure.

The two party systems could also be compared with respect to participation.

The installation of the convention party structure unquestionably multiplied opportunities for party followers to assume roles as activists. This development was especially prominent in those states where previously there had been little or no formal party organization, but its effects could be noted everywhere. Moreover, intense interparty competition stimulated unprecedented levels of voter participation, not uncommonly rising to 80 per cent of the electorate, whereas prior to 1824 in a very large number of states it was exceptional for half of the eligible voters to participate regularly in elections.[6] Both in the comprehensiveness of their structures and in the universality of their appeal, then, the new parties could truly be characterized as mass parties.

One may properly speculate as to whether the measurable increase in voter participation had a direct influence on party programs and governmental actions. To put the question differently, when vast numbers of men who had formerly lacked the franchise or who had been apathetic entered the electoral arena, were there discernable

shifts in party attitudes or public policy? Did the parties and the governments become more "democratic"? This would be an extremely difficult question to answer, but I have the impression that the "new" voters tended to divide between the two parties in much the same proportion as the "old" voters.[7] We might conclude that both parties accommodated the new voters by modifying their appeals and their programs. An alternative conclusion could be that because the new voters did not enter predominantly into one party and make it the instrument for achieving their political goals, they had no great effect on the parties. Any sure evaluation of the effects of enlarged participation must depend on further studies, but at least we might agree that the mass participation that we associate with the second party system did affect the style of politics.

The extended form of participation in politics in the era of the second party system can scarcely be comprehended in purely political terms—that is, only in terms of rivalry between opposing power elites or interest groups for dominance in the state and for control over public policy. It would be difficult to account for all the phenomena of the system within these limited concepts, and the varieties of experiences that parties in this era afforded to the electorate went beyond the political sphere.[8] Those tens of thousands of men and women who attended the mammoth Whig festival at Nashville in 1840; those untold mil-

[6] See my "New Perspectives on Jacksonian Politics," *American Historical Review*, LXV (1960), 288–301, for illustrative data on the increase in voter participation. In those states where the parties were competitive after 1800, it was not uncommon for 70 per cent or more of the adult white males to vote, and on occasion higher levels were reached. But in states where the parties were unbalanced, or where elections were not contested on a party basis, participation would usually be under 50 per cent. There are, however, curious exceptions to these generalizations. Alabama recorded the suspiciously high figure of 97 per cent in a gubernatorial election in 1819, and Tennessee reached 80 per cent in the gubernatorial election of 1817. These, and other data that could be cited, suggest that high participation could be achieved in the absence of parties, and even in the absence of the stimulus of a presidential contest.

[7] See my "Suffrage Classes and Party Alignments: A Study in Voter Behavior," *Mississippi Valley Historical Review*, XLVI (1959), 397–410.

[8] M. Ostrogorski, among other foreign observers, has some extremely perceptive comments on the "ritual character" of American parties in *Democracy and the Party System in the United States* (New York, 1910), 408–12.

lions who carried torches, donned uniforms, chanted slogans, or cheered themselves hoarse at innumerable parades and rallies; those puffed-up canvassers of wards, servers of rum, and distributors of largesse; and all those simple folk who whipped themselves into a fury of excitement and anxiety as each election day approached, were thrilling to a grand dramatic experience, even a cathartic experience. There was no spectacle, no contest, in America that could match an election campaign, and all could identify with and participate in it.

Innumerable foreign observers saw clearly this amazing dimension of American politics. As Michael Chevalier perceived it, the political campaign and all its attendant pageantry and exaltation meant to Americans what religious festivals had meant to the peoples of Catholic Europe. Witnessing a post-election celebration of New York City Democrats, he was struck by the resemblance.

The procession was nearly a mile long; the democrats marched in good order to the glare of torches; the banners were more numerous than I had ever seen them in any religious festival; all were in transparency, on account of the darkness. On some were inscribed the names of the democratic societies or sections, . . . others bore imprecations against the Bank of the United States; *Nick Biddle* and *Old Nick* here figured largely and formed the pendant of our *libera nos a malo*. Then came portraits of General Jackson afoot and on horseback. . . . Those of Washington and Jefferson, surrounded with democratic mottoes, were mingled in all tastes and of all colors. Among these figured an eagle, not a painting, but a real live eagle, tied by the legs, surrounded by a wreath of leaves, and hoisted upon a pole, after the manner of the Roman standards. The imperial bird was carried by a stout sailor, more pleased than ever was a sergeant permitted to hold

one of the strings of the canopy, in a Catholic ceremony. From further than the eye could reach, came marching on the democrats. I was struck with the resemblance of their air to the train that escorts the *viaticum* in Mexico or Puebla. . . . The democratic procession, also, like the Catholic procession, had its halting places; it stopped before the house of the Jackson men to fill the air with cheers, and halted at the doors of the leaders of the Opposition, to give three, six, or nine groans.

. . . If these scenes were to find a painter, they would be admired at a distance, not less than the triumphs and sacrificial pomps, which the ancients have left us delineated in marble and brass; for they are not mere grotesques after the manner of Rembrandt, they belong to history, they partake of the grand; they are the episodes of a wondrous epic which will bequeath a lasting memory to posterity, that of the coming of democracy.[9]

Finally, the first and second party systems exhibited pronounced differences in their extent and their alignment. The parties of the 1790's had never really been extended to more than fifteen states, and in several of those they scarcely became rooted. The second party system comprehended every state, although there might well be some reservations about South Carolina. The first party system was, from one point of view, very badly aligned. Early in its history the New England states were heavily inclined toward the Federalist party, while in the South the Republicans possessed a lopsided supremacy. Although New England in time achieved a brief balance of parties, the South became virtually a one-party region. The second party system was extraordinary in that the two parties were fairly evenly

9 Michael Chevalier, *Society, Manners and Politics in the United States* (Boston, 1839), 318–19.

balanced in every region.[10] Between 1836 and 1852, as in no other period in our history, each of the parties was truly national in its extent.

. . .

. . . As the second party system reached maturity in the 1840's, it scarcely reflected the fact that the basic cleavage within the nation, transcending all others, was that which may be vaguely defined as North-South sectionalism. The first party system had mirrored this tension to the degree that after 1800 the Federalists were very largely a Northern party. The third party system as it finally became aligned in the 1870's also contained a decided sectional bias, with its solidly Democratic South and its Northern-oriented Republican party. In attempting to explain how the second party system produced not sectional parties but parties that were remarkably well balanced throughout the nation, we are confronted with a paradox. In the successive contests for the presidency between 1824 and 1836 strong sectional loyalties shaped the responses of political leaders and voters in each region to the opposing candidates. But by 1836 the end result of the series of realignments was a sectionally balanced party system. In brief, the explanation for the paradoxical character of the second party system is to be found in the peculiar circumstances associated with the contests for the presidency.

To recapitulate, the second party system did not emerge suddenly; it developed in a series of stages, and at each stage it was shaped by the sectional identifications of the candidates. With Andrew Jackson and John Quincy Adams as the candidates in 1828, a highly sectionalized vote resulted; New England went almost as overwhelm-

ingly for Adams as the South did for Jackson; only the Middle States were evenly divided. When Henry Clay was substituted for Adams, New England was no longer held together by its loyalty to a sectional favorite, and parties throughout the North came into balance. When Martin Van Buren was substituted for Jackson—and opposed by White and Harrison—the South and much of the new West ceased to be politically monolithic, as anti-Van Buren parties quickly mobilized. These sectional responses to the presidential candidates were crucial at the time of party formation. Once the parties had been formed and identities had been acquired by the voters, alignments tended to remain relatively firm. Thus highly sectional responses in a series of presidential elections resulted in the formation of non-sectional parties.

MARVIN MEYERS

James Parton, that excellent popular biographer of his eminent countrymen, consulted a map in 1859 to discover which notables had given their names most frequently to American places. I doubt that one can find a better brief guide to relative popularity, and to relative political significance for the people, than Parton's simple finding:

Washington	198 times
Jackson	191
Franklin	136
Jefferson	110
Clay	42

Washington the founder; Jackson the defender; Franklin the practical preceptor; Jefferson the republican sage;

Reprinted from Marvin Meyers, THE JACKSONIAN PERSUASION: POLITICS AND BELIEF (Stanford, Calif.: Stanford University Press, 1957), pp. 1–10, by permission of the publisher.

and far below, Clay the adjuster and promoter.[1]

To have routed British veterans at New Orleans and cleared a region for settlement in the Indian campaigns gave Andrew Jackson a strong initial claim to national attention; and the military style which made him Old Hickory, Old Hero, put the claim in its strongest terms. Yet there had to be more to account for the passionate involvement of men's loyalties with Jacksonian politics: there had been other generals, other battles, other colorful personalities. At first, the battlefield reputation was enough: the unfailingly acute Governor Ford of Illinois, an uneasy late Jacksonian, observed how eager politicians had flocked to the banner of "a popular and fortunate leader" in the early days. But Ford saw too, in the perspective of 1850, that Jackson had been the master figure of American political life during his two administrations and the eight years of his retirement, and that he "has since continued to govern, even after his death."[2]

Jackson entered the presidency a national hero out of the West; he became the great partisan protagonist of his generation. No man of his time was at once so widely loved and so deeply hated. His blunt words and acts assumed the character of moral gestures which forced men to declare themselves, for or against. The movement we have come to call Jacksonian Democracy borrowed more than a powerful name;

it projected into politics a fighting image of the man who would save the republic from its enemies. Exactly where and how Andrew Jackson and his party met is a question for biographers; but once joined, they excited and focused the concerns of a political generation. George Bancroft's memorial panegyric, for all its Transcendental claptrap, comes to a truth about Jackson's political significance:

Before the nation, before the world, before coming ages, he stands forth the representative, for his generation, of the American mind. And the secret of his greatness is this: by intuitive conception, he shared and possessed all the creative ideas of his country and his time; he expressed them with dauntless intrepidity; he enforced them with an immovable will; he executed them with an electric power that attracted and swayed the American people.[3]

From contemporary commentators to recent scholars there has been agreement upon initial facts: that politics substantially engaged the interest and feelings of American society; that Jacksonian Democracy was a large, divisive cause which shaped the themes of political controversy; that the second quarter of the nineteenth century is properly remembered as the age of Jackson. Here agreement ends. The limits of the subject are in dispute: Is Jacksonian Democracy to be considered primarily as an affair of party politics, or as a broad political, social, and intellectual movement? What message did Jacksonian Democracy carry to society, whom did it reach, what did it signify in the setting of the times? These are yet unsettled questions, for all the wealth of industry and talent spent upon them.

In one view of the subject, urban

[1] James Parton, *Life of Andrew Jackson*, I, 236. Publication data on editions cited in this footnote and all following footnotes may be found in the Bibliography [omitted here].

[2] Thomas Ford, *A History of Illinois*, pp. 103–4, 271. For an interesting sketch of the petty local maneuvering which led to Jackson's original candidacy, see Charles Grier Sellers, Jr., "Jackson Men with Feet of Clay," *American Historical Review*, LXII (April 1957), 537–51.

[3] George Bancroft, *Literary and Historical Miscellanies*, p. 479.

masses rise against a business aristocracy; in another, simple farming folk strike out at capitalist trickery; in still another, fresh forest democracy seeks liberation from an effete East. Some recent works discover at the heart of the movement hungry men on the make invading the positions of chartered monopoly. Some stress the strengthening of the presidency, or the heightening of nationalist sentiment. An older emphasis upon King Andrew, master demagogue, exploiting the gullibility of the masses for the sake of his own power, reappears in altered form—the shrewd politicos behind a popular hero learning to manage a new mass electorate by perfecting the organization and tactics of machine politics. Woven into many accounts are elements of the official Jacksonian version: the friends of limited and frugal government, equal rights and equal laws, strict construction and dispersed power, taking up from Jefferson the defense of the republic.[4]

These are not all the theses; and each is, of course, far more formidable in its author's custody than I have made it out in quick review. My object is simply to suggest the variety of plausible interpretations, and to suggest further the gaps and conflicts that invite a new effort to order our knowledge of Jacksonian Democracy. Much remains to be learned from precise and limited studies of the movement and the period; but now, I think, the need is to keep the focus wide: to ask the small questions with constant reference to the large.

Accepting the conclusions of Jacksonian scholarship as so many diverse hints to be considered when occasion gives them relevance, I have undertaken a new reading of some familiar sources. Somehow Jacksonian Democracy communicated a message which touched off powerful political emotions. What was this message, and what conditions gave it force? The questions are not easily answered.

---

[4] The historical interpretations of Jacksonian democracy are not, of course, so flat and monolithic as I make them out here. I have abstracted what seem to me central lines of argument and deployed them for my own purposes. The variety of interpretations may be represented by such works as Arthur M. Schlesinger, Jr., *The Age of Jackson;* Joseph Dorfman, *The Economic Mind in American Civilization,* Vol. II; Alexis de Tocqueville, *Democracy in America;* Frederick Jackson Turner, *The United States, 1830–1850;* M. Ostrogorski, *Democracy and the Party System in the United States;* Thomas P. Abernethy, *From Frontier to Plantation in Tennessee;* Louis Hartz, *Economic Policy and Democratic Thought;* and the excellent chapter iii in Richard Hofstadter, *The American Political Tradition,* together with the bibliographical essay, *ibid.,* pp. 353–57.

Vernon Louis Parrington's brief discussion of Jackson as an "Agrarian Liberal" is perhaps closer to the truth than many later studies; see his *Main Currents in American Thought,* II, 145–52. Harold C. Syrett has made a useful selection of Jackson's writings and assessed his

When the Jacksonian movement formed in the late 1820's America was far out upon a democratic course: [political democracy was the medium more than the achievement of the Jacksonian party.] The Jacksonians proclaimed popular principles with but little more insistence than the Whig supporters of Harry of the West or Old Tip. For

---

role in *Andrew Jackson.* Bray Hammond's revealing observations on Jacksonian economic aims, with special reference to banking, are discussed in Chapter 4, *infra.* A recent work by William N. Chambers, *Old Bullion Benton: Senator from the New West,* uses the opposing terms "enterprise" and "arcadia" as the key to Jacksonian party divisions; the similarity to my own conception will be apparent in the following pages. A penetrating critical essay by R. W. B. Lewis—*The American Adam*—suggests in its treatment of cultural spokesmen many parallels to my analysis of political spokesmen.

most of the country the Federalist conservatism of Hamilton or John Adams was stone dead: its ghost walked only in the speeches of Jacksonians trying to frighten honest citizens out of their opposition. Government by the people was largely a matter of consensus and of wont. Basic principles and institutions were firmly settled; only their legal elaboration—for example, in suffrage extension and the increase of elective offices—was recent and still in progress. There was some party conflict over details, none over the general democratic direction. The completion of a popular regime seemed to follow an unquestionable logic.

Indeed the most consequential political changes entered silently, without formal consideration or enactment: changes in the organization and conduct of parties. The winning of elections became to an unprecedented degree the business of professionals who managed powerful machines. On the surface such developments might suggest a bureaucratization of political life; in main effect, however, they brought a novel intimacy to the relation between the people and politics. The political machine reached into every neighborhood, inducted ordinary citizens of all sorts into active service. Parties tended to become lively two-way channels of influence. Public opinion was heard with a new sensitivity and addressed with anxious respect. The bureaucratic science of machine operation was effective only in association with the popular art of pleasing the many. As never before, the parties spoke directly, knowingly, to the interests and feelings of the public. The Jacksonians initiated much of the change in the instruments and methods of popular democracy; they adopted new party ways with a natural ease and competence which earned

them some electoral advantage; the Whigs understandably resented their success, and quickly followed their example. Thus the new party democracy, like democracy in the abstract, was a common element of politics and raised no substantial public issues between Jacksonians and their rivals. At most, the less successful partisans carped at the more successful.

Under the new political conditions parties were alert to interests everywhere in society. One is tempted to think that Jacksonian Democracy found a major class constituency, identified its concrete needs, catered to them in its program, won the interested vote, and so became a great political force; and that the Wigs did much the same thing with opposite interests and policies. Unfortunately, the scheme breaks down at critical points. The chief Jacksonian policies—opposition to special corporate charters, hostility toward paper money, suspicion of public enterprise and public debt—do not patently contribute to the needs of a distinctive class following. The parties show some interesting marginal variations in their sources of support; nonetheless—given the relatively loose class structure, the heavy concentration in the middle social ranks as then identified (farmers, mechanics, shopkeepers), the flexibility of careers and the mixture of interests—it seems clear that both parties must have reached broadly similar class constituencies to gain, as they did, only a little more or less than half the popular vote. In sum: social differences were subtly shaded and unstable; party policies were ambiguous in their probable effects upon group interests; and so no general and simple class difference appears in party preferences.

The flaws in this class-interest approach have provoked a reaction toward the view that the Jacksonian movement had no great insurgent mission. In this view, the parties were fraternal twins, devoted to the advancement of slightly varying business interests in a free economy, their essential similarity disguised by a series of practical quarrels which windy party leaders dressed up in a conventional grand rhetoric; the essential meaning of Jacksonian politics is found in the objective import of legal and institutional changes. But why did political language go so far beyond practical objects? Why did men respond out of all proportion to their manifest interests? How were they convinced that party differences were profound, persistent—mattered greatly? Why did some kinds of rhetoric touch the quick, others not? Here, as elsewhere, the revisionist temper seems too impatient with the impalpable motives, feelings, perceptions, which lie between external act and external consequences.

I have spoken of the sensitive relationship which developed between parties and people: not only interests but attitudes and feelings reached the receptive eye of politicians. And politics took on what might be called an expressive role, along with its traditional task of conducting the business of the state. Here one enters a region of elusive psychological fact buried in a fragmentary record of words and acts. But here I think the vital transaction between Jacksonians and their generation must be found.

The appeals of the Democracy were carried by ideas and rhetoric, by policies and public gestures. Taken singly, these elements point this way and that, and no one of them conveys a full notion of the party message that worked such large effects. Taken together, I think, they converge to form an urgent political message with a central theme. It will be my purpose to identify that theme and the nature of its appeal. "Ideology" is a conventional term for one aspect of my subject, "ethos" for another, but I have chosen the less formal "persuasion" to fit my emphasis upon a matched set of attitudes, beliefs, projected actions: a half-formulated moral perspective involving emotional commitment. The community shares many values; at a given social moment some of these acquire a compelling importance. The political expression given to such values forms a persuasion.

In Jacksonian political appeals I have found—as might be expected—distinct traces of every theme used by historians to explain the nature and import of Jacksonian Democracy. Jacksonian spokesmen drew upon an exhaustive repertory of the moral plots which might engage the political attention of nineteenth-century Americans: equality against privilege, liberty against domination; honest work against idle exploit; natural dignity against factitious superiority; patriotic conservatism against alien innovation; progress against dead precedent. A first ungraded inventory shows only a troubled mind groping for names to fit its discontent.

The great specific mission of Jacksonian Democracy was the war against the Monster Bank. Here the party formed, or found, its character. Here was the issue which stood for all issues. Broad popular fear and hatred of the Second Bank, evoked by Jacksonian appeals, cannot be understood simply as a matter-of-fact reaction to material injuries. The economic operations of the institution conferred some manifest general benefits, directly crossed the interests of only a limited group: its hand was not found upon men's throats or in their pockets. The Bank was called a Monster by Jacksonians. A monster is an unnatural thing, its acts are out of reason, and its threat cannot be estimated in ordinary practical terms. The effort to destroy the Monster Bank and its vicious brood— privileged corporations, paper money— enlisted moral passions in a drama of social justice and self-justification.

Broadly speaking, the Jacksonians blamed the Bank for the transgressions committed by the people of their era against the political, social, and economic values of the Old Republic. The Bank carried the bad seed of Hamilton's first Monster, matured all the old evils, and created some new ones. To the Bank's influence Jacksonians traced constitutional impiety, consolidated national power, aristocratic privilege, and plutocratic corruption. Social inequality, impersonal and intangible business relations, economic instability, perpetual debt and taxes, all issued from the same source.

Jefferson had brought into temporary equilibrium the formal ideal of a dynamic liberal society and the concrete image of a stable, virtuous yeoman republic. "It is," he wrote, "the manners and spirit of a people which preserve a republic in vigor." And God had made the independent citizen farmer "His peculiar deposit for substantial and genuine virtue." Nothing is more revealing than Jefferson's later concession of the need for domestic manufacturing, under the pressures of war: "Our enemy has indeed the consolation of Satan on removing our first parents from Paradise: from a peaceful agricultural nation he makes us a military and manufacturing one." [5] Now

[5] "Notes on Virginia," in *The Works of Thomas Jefferson*, ed. Paul Leicester Ford, IV, 85–86; "Letter to William Short, Nov. 28, 1814," in *The Writings of Thomas Jefferson*, ed. H. A. Washington, VI, 400.

Jacksonian society was caught between the elements—the liberal principle and the yeoman image—and tried again to harmonize them. Americans were boldly liberal in economic affairs, out of conviction and appetite combined, and moved their world in the direction of modern capitalism. But they were not inwardly prepared for the grinding uncertainties, the shocking changes, the complexity and indirection of the new economic ways. Their image of the good life had not altered: somehow, as men and as a society, they hoped to have their brave adventures, their provocative rewards, their open-ended progress, and remain essentially the same. The practical outcomes of the free pursuit of economic interest had never been legitimated, or even fully associated with the abstract liberal principle. Yet the ideological and material attachment to the liberal code was too deep to be severed, even in considerable distress.

Thus many found in the anti-Bank crusade, and in the Jacksonian appeal generally, a way to damn the unfamiliar, threatening, sometimes punishing elements in the changing order by fixing guilt upon a single protean agent. A laissez-faire society with this source of corruptions cut out would re-establish continuity with that golden age in which liberty and progress were joined inseparably with simple yeoman virtues. Under the Jacksonian persuasion men could follow their desires, protest their injuries, affirm their innocence. In this direction one can begin to meet the Jacksonian paradox: the fact that the movement which helped to clear the path for laissez-faire capitalism and its culture in America, and the public which in its daily life eagerly entered on that path, held nevertheless in their political conscience an ideal of a chaste republican

412

order, resisting the seductions of risk and novelty, greed and extravagance, rapid motion and complex dealings.[6]

The Jacksonian movement was forged in the Bank War. Its new machine carried its influence throughout American society; its Old Hero, at once the voice and the exemplar of Jacksonian values, linked the machine to the essential cause. However far Jacksonians went in adapting policies to the practical requirements of local conditions, special interests, and effective party operation, the movement continually returned to its core appeal: death to the Monster; life and health to the old republican virtues. How-

[6] There is a fascinating English parallel, suggested to me first by reading William Cobbett's *Life of Andrew Jackson*. The history is poor stuff, cribbed from an American biography; but the remarks of the old Federalist "Porcupine" of the Philadelphia press wars, turned angry social reformer back at home, reveal a profound admiration for the American "Irishman": "The bravest and greatest man now living in this world, or that ever has lived in this world, as far as my knowledge extends" *(ibid.,* pp. iii–iv). Cobbett praised Jackson for mastering the British (his book is dedicated to the Irish working people), the savages, and the Bank—"a monster perfectly insatiable; hypocritical as the crocodile, delusive as the syren, and deadly as the rattlesnake itself." Cobbett sees a perfect parallel between the Bank of the United States and the Bank of England in nature and social effects *(ibid.,* pp. vi–vii, 162, 185–86). All this is the more interesting because Cobbett is not in the "liberal" reform camp, and has no patience with "corn-bill nonsense, or HEDDEKASHUN" as social panaceas *(ibid.,* p. 196). G. D. H. Cole calls him an "agrarian tribune" who "wanted his old world back again, his memory—idealised like most men's early memories—of the England which he had known and loved before the great wars and the great factories came." G. D. H. Cole, *Persons and Periods,* p. 157. Cf. J. L. and Barbara Hammond, *The Bleak Age,* p. 32. For further evidence of Cobbett's social views and of his impression of nineteenth-century America, see, for example, *Rural Rides, A Year's Residence in the United States of America,* and *The Emigrant's Guide.*

ever carefully the knowledgeable voter looked to his immediate interests—when they could be linked plausibly to party policies—he would always see the moral choice proposed by Jacksonian Democracy. If the Jacksonian persuasion gained relevance and force from common social experience, common tradition, how then did the Whigs develop a distinct voice and a substantial following? Reducing a complex matter to the utmost simplicity: the Whig party spoke to the explicit hopes of Americans as Jacksonians addressed their diffuse fears and resentments. To say this is to reverse a common historical appraisal. The Federalists had been, at the end, a party of fear and resentment. There is some loose justice in deriving Whiggery from Federalism; but only if one recognizes that the language of mob terror and elite guidance had gone out of general use before Jacksonians and Whigs assumed political leadership. Some unregenerate Federalists who worried openly about the dangers of extreme democracy still survived; Whig party leaders tapped them for campaign funds and otherwise wished them out of sight.

What the Whigs deliberately maintained in the inheritance was the ambitious scheme for economic progress through banks, tariffs, and public promotion of internal improvements. Clay's American System, the nearest approach to a coherent Whig policy, was a popularization of Hamiltonian economic designs and John Marshall's flexibile interpretation of national authority. Whigs, too, fully associated themselves with the Old Republican idyll—Webster wept in memory of his father's forest hut; zealous clerks helped to clutter city streets with Harrison log cabins—but they felt no serious tension between past and present. Their cabin was a nostalgic prop, a publicity gimmick without focused moral content. The fulfillment of liberal premises in capitalist progress was for them entirely natural and unproblematic.[7]

The Whigs distinctively affirmed the material promise of American life as it was going; and they promised to make it go faster. They were inclined to see the corporation not as nameless monster but as an engine of progress; public debt not as a curse on honest labor but as a sound gamble on a richer future. Ironically, depression gave them their greatest popular success; yet they did not take depression as an omen of profound social maladjustment. They could see only that an imperious demagogue with primitive economic notions had thrown society into crisis by his spiteful war against the Bank. Indeed the Whigs were so markedly an anti-Jackson coalition

that often their positive message was obscured in mere personal invective. To some degree, perhaps, the Whigs did succeed in spreading the conviction that Jacksonian dictatorship menaced the integrity of the republic. Principally, however, the party appealed to interested hopes, offering concrete advantages to groups and sections, and a quickening of economic progress for society as a whole.

Succeeding chapters will present a series of related commentaries on the appeal Jacksonian Democrats made to their generation, and on the changing social situation which lent relevance and force to that appeal. Perhaps they can convey the effort of Jacksonian Democracy to recall agrarian republican innocence to a society drawn fatally to the main chance and the long chance, to the revolutionizing ways of acquisition, emulative consumption, promotion, and speculation —the Jacksonian struggle to reconcile again the simple yeoman values with the free pursuit of economic interest, just as the two were splitting hopelessly apart.

---

[7] See in this connection two recent discussions of Whig leaders: Clement Eaton, *Henry Clay and the Art of American Politics;* Richard N. Current, *Daniel Webster and the Rise of National Conservatism.*

HISTORIOGRAPHICAL NOTE

For most American historians, the parallel development of political egalitarianism and continental expansion during the Jacksonian era has appeared clear and intelligible. Differences in interpretation have been based on sharply divergent moral evaluations of the so-called "middle period." In recent years, however, scholars have addressed themselves increasingly to the shadings and contradictions in national development during these decades, most particularly to the paradoxes that marked the simultaneous evolution of political individualism and of a national political structure in American life. (See the previous discussion of Richard McCormick's study for elaboration of this point.)

Earlier historians had either praised Jacksonian democracy in unambiguous terms as a justified revolt against privileged "monopolies" such as the Second Bank of the United States or, in contrary fashion, had damned it for the vulgar and senseless destruction of such stabilizing institutions as the Bank. Many historians, in fact, consider the Bank War the crucial episode in Jacksonian politics and the key to the· period's basic political divisions. For even pro-Jacksonian scholars continue to disagree over the movement's vital center. Frederick Jackson Turner (*The United States, 1830–1850*) and Claude Bowers (*Making Democracy a Reality*) stress the personal support enjoyed by Jackson and the endorsement of democratic reforms by Southern and Western frontier settlers. Arthur Schlesinger Jr. (*The Age of Jackson*), on the other hand, has reworked the Beards' earlier economic class analysis of the epoch and emphasizes the ideological and political importance of eastern workingmen and their leaders to the Democratic party coalition, especially in its attack on monopolistic banking and business practices.

Other less favorable accounts of the Jacksonian years, although not disputing these sympathetic portraits of "King Andrew's" followers, have aimed hostile shafts at Jackson himself, indicting him as a sharp, mean-spirited, and decidedly *un*democratic opportunist. Thomas P. Abernathy (*From Frontier to Plantation in Tennessee*) has reassessed Jackson's place in Tennessee politics and sees him not as a convinced popular leader but, rather, as an avaricious frontier entrepreneur opposed to democratic reforms in his own state and allied with its oligarchy. Charles M. Wiltse, in his superb multi-volume life of John C. Calhoun, also criticized Jackson as a particularly unprincipled and vindictive politician driven in his actions as President, whether during the Bank War or the Nullification Crisis, primarily by bitter personal vendettas.

This disagreement over the moral nature of Andrew Jackson and his democracy has extended to the problem of continental expansion. Some historians have defended the acquisition of our western boundaries through war with Mexico as a legitimate fulfillment of America's "manifest destiny," while others have seen this territorial conquest, unlike more peaceful western settlement, as a clear betrayal of older national values. In the late nineteenth century, for example, Herman Von Holst (*The Constitutional and Political History of the United States*) wrote approvingly of American triumph in the Mexican War, because it extended to the Pacific the boundaries of Anglo-Saxon civilization, and this xenophobic attitude also marked Justin S. Smith's classic two-volume study of the Mexican War itself. James Ford Rhodes, on the other hand, echoed contemporary critics of the conflict in his *History of the United States Since the Compromise of 1850* by blaming the land-hunger and conspiratorial political ambitions of Southern slaveholders for provoking a needless and immoral conflict. In the present century, less heated nationalists like the diplomatic historian Samuel Flagg Bemis, realists if not fatalists, have sought to strike a balance between exuberance and dismay over continental expansion, condemning the war but approving the conquest. Norman Graebner (*Empire on the Pacific)* singled out for attention the previously neglected factor of northern commercial involvement on the Pacific Coast as a major catalyst of continental imperialism during the Jacksonian era. But Graebner, along with other recent diplomatic historians of the epoch, adopts a more impersonal tone in assessing the causes of nineteenth-century expansion and is more concerned with explaining rather than judging the process.

Similarly, "middle period" historians of political trends and territorial development have generally abandoned explicit value judgments of the era in an effort to characterize its underlying beliefs and assumptions. Joel Silbey, Richard McCormick, and Lee Benson have all published important re-evaluations of national political behavior. Benson's provocative work, *The Concept of Jacksonian Democracy: New York as a Test Case,* proposed that scholars pay closer attention to ethnic and religious determinants of voting behavior rather than dwelling obsessively on economic class antagonisms in explaining partisan divisions during the 1830's and 1840's. Silbey's elaborate analysis of congressional roll-call voting from 1841 to 1852, *The Shrine of Party,* has argued for the centrality of partisan rather than sectional influences on legislative voting during this decade.

Some revisionists have offered new explanations for the emergence of Jacksonian democracy itself. Thus, Richard Hofstadter, in *The American Political Tradition,* stressed the "jack" in Jacksonian ambitions, pointing to the entrepreneurial motives of many democratic politicians and their supporters, small-holding capitalists or "men on the make." Marvin Meyers has gone even further and described the entire "Jacksonian persuasion" as an effort by personally ambitious yet morally cautious Americans to preserve older Jeffersonian values without sacrificing available economic opportunities in their own time, while Louis Hartz *(The Liberal Tradition in America)* sees Jacksonian philosophy reflecting a basic American association of democracy and capitalism in a mobile society that lacked Europe's feudal traditions.

Few recent historians have disputed the fact that expansion appeared inevitable to most Americans during the 1840's as an extension of frontier democracy into the presumably "uncivilized" trans-Mississippi West. Albert K. Weinberg's pioneering study, *Manifest Destiny,* Frederick Merk's *Manifest Destiny and Mission in American Life,* and John William Ward's *Andrew Jackson: Symbol for an Age* all develop this particular insight. All three historians stress the crucial connection made by contemporaries between land hunger and an underlying emotional sense of "mission" toward the un-Americanized, a Jacksonian "errand into the wilderness" defined broadly enough to include Texas, California, Oregon, and the territory between. Western expansion gave the crude, aggressive, and harshly egalitarian political world of the 1830's and 1840's a continental realm of thought and action, one which Americans accepted with both greed and pride. The "men on the make" who fought politically under Whig and

Democratic banners shared a liberal capitalist ethos appropriate to their dominant political ideal, that of the independent producer—whether farmer, mechanic, or merchant—eager to exploit a land-rich, market-rich continent. As most recent historians have shown, their ideal is one still familiar to Americans. Simply stated, it envisioned economic success but without loss of moral integrity.

8. The Civil War

INTRODUCTION

When Abraham Lincoln took office on March 4, 1861, he confronted a unique situation, one that has not been faced by any other President. South Carolina, Georgia, Florida, Alabama, Mississippi, and Louisiana had passed "ordinances" of secession; Texas was soon to follow. Eight states in the upper South, from Virginia west to Missouri, were on the verge of secession. The federal government had been rendered inoperative in the deep South, except for mail deliveries. All federal installations in the seceded states had been seized, except for a few forts along the Florida coast and Ft. Sumter at the mouth of Charleston harbor. Lincoln immediately adopted a complex policy of attempting to keep as many of the "border" states in the Union as possible, of avoiding direct confrontations in the deep South, and of keeping up at least a symbolic federal presence in the seceded states. For this last purpose, the coastal forts were crucial. On his first full day in office, Lincoln learned that Ft. Sumter was running low on provisions. He tried to reinforce one of the Florida forts, in case Sumter had to be abandoned, but this attempt failed. Lincoln decided that to give up Sumter without a struggle would put a seal of approval on secession, so he informed South Carolina authorities that the garrison would be resupplied. The Confederate government, in turn, decided to "reduce" the fort, and opened fire on it on April 12, 1861.

Four years later, on April 9, 1865, Lee surrendered his army at Appomattox Court House. Six hundred thousand men had died in the war. Five days later, on the anniversary of the surrender of Sumter, Lincoln himself was assassinated. The Civil War which filled the four years between the fall of Ft. Sumter and the assassination of Lincoln was the most traumatic event of United States history. It grew out of decades of sectional controversy between the North and the South, and it determined the course of political, economic, and social history for decades to come. It was, in sum, the pivotal event of the nineteenth century.

In this chapter, we present a number of different analyses of the war. The first section contains selections from the work of men writing as historians who were also participants in the event, one as propagandist and the other as President of the Confederacy. The section of documents is a collection of various explanations of the sectional crisis and the war by politicians and newspaper editorials. Finally, there are recent interpretations by three modern historians. The "objective" conditions which presumably underlay the conflict—economic differences, the realities of political power, concrete social conflicts—are, of course, important to an understanding of the war. But it is at least as important to understand men's *perceptions* of these conditions as to know the conditions themselves. This chapter, then, is a sample of such perceptions, all of which are concerned with three basic and related questions: What *caused* the war? Could it have been avoided? and Who was to blame?

I. EARLY INTERPRETATIONS

The first histories of the Civil War were written by the men who lived through the traumatic years between the election of Lincoln in 1860 and the agreement at Appomattox in 1865. In the selections in this section, two men give diametrically opposed explanations of the causes of the conflict and, of course, place moral blame for the war on different shoulders. The first selection is a classic statement of the "slave-power conspiracy" theory of the war written by J. E. Cairnes, a professor at the University of Dublin. His book was published first in England and then, in 1864, in the United States under the title *The Slave Power*. The second selection is from a history of the Confederacy by its first and only President, Jefferson Davis, first published shortly after the end of the war. Cairnes and Davis attribute the war to different causes. Cairnes insists that the war had only one basic cause, the attempt of the slave South to extend its "peculiar institution" throughout the Union. Davis, naturally, did not agree. He argues that the war had nothing to do with slavery, but was the result of northern attempts to reduce the South to helplessness. For all their differences, Cairnes and Davis did agree on one point: the war was the result of a conspiratorial attempt by one section to subvert the Constitution and reduce the other to something like colonial status.

J. E. CAIRNES

The first announcement by South Carolina of its intention to secede from the Union was received in this country [England] with simple incredulity. There were no reasons, it was said, for secession. . . . But when the contest had passed beyond its first

Reprinted from J. E. Cairnes, THE SLAVE POWER (New York, 1864), pp. 2, 18–33.

stages . . . belief in the reality of the movement could no longer be withheld, and speculation was directed to the causes of the catastrophe. The theory at first propounded was nearly to this effect: Commercial and fiscal differences were said to be at the bottom of the movement.

The North fancied she had an interest in protection; the South had an obvious interest in free trade. . . . The civil war was thus described as having sprung from narrow and selfish views of sectional interests . . . and sustained by passions which itself had kindled; and the combatants were advised to compose their differences, and either return to their political partnership, or agree to separate and learn to live in harmony as independent allies.

. . .

One is tempted to ask, whether those who thus expound American politics suppose the present crisis to be an isolated phenomenon in American history, disconnected from all the past; or, to look at the question from another point of view, whether they imagine that the coincidence of the political division of parties with the geographical division of slave and free States is an accident—that, to borrow the expression of Jefferson, "a geographical line coinciding with a marked principle" has no significance. It seems almost trifling with the reader to remind him that the present outbreak is but the crowning result, the inevitable climax of the whole past history of American politics—the catastrophe foreseen with more or less distinctness by all the leading statesmen of America from Washington to Webster and Clay, which was the constant theme of their forebodings, and to escape or defer which was the great problem of their political lives. And equally superfluous does it seem to mention what was the grand central question in that history— the question to which all others were subordinate, and around which all political divisions ranged themselves.

Never surely was the unity of a national drama better preserved. From the year 1819 down to the present time the history of the United States has been one record of aggressions by the Slave Power, feebly, and almost always unsuccessfully, resisted by the Northern States, and culminating in the present war. At the time of the revolution, as is well known, slavery was regarded by all the great founders of the Republic, whether Northern or Southern men, as essentially an immoral system: it was, indeed, recognized by the Constitution, but only as an exceptional practice, a local and temporary fact. In the unsettled territory then belonging to the Union it was by a special ordinance prohibited. Even in 1819, although in the interval the Slave Power had pushed its dominion and pretensions far beyond their original limits, the claim was scarcely advanced for slavery to rank as an equal with free institutions in any district where it was not already definitively established, and certainly no such claim was acknowledged. Of this the Missouri Compromise affords the clearest proof, since, regarded as a triumph by the slave-owners, it only secured the admission of slavery to Missouri on the express condition that it should be confined for the future to the territory south of a certain parallel of latitude. But what has been the career of the Slave Power since that time? It is to be traced through every questionable transaction in foreign and domestic politics in which the United States has since taken part—through the Seminole war, through the annexation of Texas, through the Mexican war, through filibustering expeditions under Walker, through attempts upon Cuba, through the Fugitive Slave Law of 1850, through Mr. Clay's compromises, through the repudiation of the Missouri Compromise so soon as the full results of that bargain had been reaped, through the passing of the Nebraska Bill and the legislative establishment of the principle of "Squatter Sovereignty," through the invasion of Kansas, through the repudiation of "Squatter Sovereignty" when that principle had been found unequal to its purposes, and lastly, through the Dred-Scott decision and the demand for protection of slavery in the Territories —pretensions which, if admitted, would have converted the whole Union, the Free States no less than the Territories, into one great domain for slavery. This has been the point at which the Slave Power, after a series of successful aggressions, carried on during forty years, has at length arrived. It was on this last demand that the Democrats of the North broke off from their Southern allies—a defection which gave their victory to the Republicans, and directly produced the civil war. And now we are asked to believe that slavery has no vital connexion with this quarrel, but that the catastrophe is due to quite other causes—to incompatibility of commercial interests, to uncongeniality of social tastes, to a desire for independence, to anything but slavery.

. . .

But the difficulties of this theory do not end here. If the secession movement be a revolt against protective tariffs, why is it confined to the Southern States? The interest of the Cotton States in free exchange with foreign countries is not more obvious than that of Ohio, Indiana, Illinois, and Wisconsin. No class in these States has anything to gain by protective measures: nothing is produced in them which is endangered by the freest competition with the rest of the world: an artificial enhancement of European manufactures is to them as pure an injury as it is to South Carolina and Alabama: yet all these States are ranged on the side of the North in this contest, and resolute for the suppression of the revolt.

It is, however, by the watchword of "independence," still more than by

that of free trade, that the partisans of the South in this country have sought to enlist our sympathies in favour of that cause. We are told of the naturalness, the universality, the strength of the desire for self-government. We are reminded of the peculiar power of this passion among the Anglo-Saxon race. The act of the original thirteen States in severing their connexion with the mother country is dwelt upon; and we are asked why the South should not also be permitted to determine for itself the mode of its political existence? "It threatens none, demands nothing, attacks no one, but wishes to rule itself, and desires to be 'let alone:'" why should this favour be denied it? Now let it at once be conceded that the right to an independent political existence is the most sacred right of nations: still even this right must justify itself by reference to the ends for which it is employed. The demand of a robber or murderer for "independence" is not a claim which we are accustomed to respect; and it does not appear how our obligations are altered if the demand proceed from a robber or murderer nation—if national independence be sought solely and exclusively as a means of carrying out designs which are nothing less than robbery and murder on a gigantic scale.

. . .

The causes and character of the American contest are not for Englishmen questions of merely speculative interest. On the view which we take of this great political crisis will depend, not alone our present attitude towards the contending parties, but in no small degree our future relations with a people of our own race, religion, and tongue, to whom has been committed the task, under whatever permanent form of polity, to carry forward in the other hemisphere the torch of knowledge and of civilization. We may, according as we act from sound knowledge of the real issues which are at stake or in ignorance of them, do much to promote or to defeat important human interests bound up with the present contest, and to increase or to diminish the future influence for good of this country. It would indeed be a grievous misfortune if, in one of the great turning points of human history, Great Britain were found to act a part unworthy of the position which she occupies and of the glorious traditions which she inherits.

The present essay is intended as a contribution towards the diffusion of sound ideas upon this subject. The real and sufficient cause of the present position of affairs in North America appears to the writer to lie in the character of the Slave Power—that system of interests, industrial, social, and political, which has for the greater part of half a century directed the career of the American Union, and which now, embodied in the Southern Confederation, seeks admission as an equal member into the community of civilized nations. In the following pages an attempt will be made to resolve this system into its component elements, to trace the connexion of the several parts with each other, and of the whole with the foundation on which it rests, and to estimate generally the prospects which it holds out to the people who compose it, as well as the influence it is likely to exercise on the interests of other nations; and, if I do not greatly mistake the purport of the considerations which shall be adduced, their effect will be to show that this Slave Power constitutes the most formidable antagonist to civilized progress which has appeared for many centuries, representing a system of society at once retrograde and aggressive, a system

which, containing within it no germs from which improvement can spring, gravitates inevitably towards barbarism, while it is impelled by exigencies, inherent in its position and circumstances, to a constant extension of its territorial domain. The vastness of the interests at stake in the American contest, regarded under this aspect, appears to me to be very inadequately conceived in this country; and the purpose of the present work is to bring forward this view of the case more prominently than has yet been done.

But it is necessary here to guard against a misapprehension. The view that the true cause of the American contest is to be found in the character and aims of the Slave Power, though it connects the war ultimately with slavery as its radical cause, by no means involves the supposition that the motive of the North in taking up arms has been the abolition of slavery. Such certainly has not been its motive, and, if we keep in view its position as identified with legal government and constitutional rights in the United States, we shall see that this motive, even had it existed, could scarcely, at least in the outset, have been allowed to operate. Let us recall for a moment the mode in which the crisis developed itself. It must be remembered—what seems now almost to be forgotten—that the war was commenced by the South—commenced for no other reason, on no other pretext, than because a republican president was elected in the ordinary constitutional course. If we ask why this was made the ground for revolt, I believe the true answer, as I have just intimated, is to be found in the aims of the Slave Power,—aims which were inconsistent with its remaining in the Union while the Government was carried on upon the principle of restricting the extension of its domain. So long as it was itself the dominant party, so long as it could employ the powers of the Government in propagating its peculiar institution and consolidating its strength, so long it was content to remain in the Union; but from the moment when, by the constitutional triumph of the Republicans, the government passed into the hands of a party whose distinctive principle was to impose a limit on the further extension of slavery, from that moment its continuance in the Union was incompatible with its essential objects, and from that moment the Slave Power resolved to break loose from Federal ties. The war had thus its origin in slavery: nevertheless the proximate issue with which the North had to deal was not slavery, but the right of secession. For the constitution having recognized slavery within the particular states, so long as the South confined its proceedings within its own limits, the Government which represented the constitution could take no cognizance of its acts. The first departure from constitutional usage by the South was the act of secession, and it was on the question, therefore, of the right to adopt this course that the North was compelled to join issue.

The contest thus springing from slavery, and involving, as will be shown, consequences of the most momentous kind in connexion with the future well-being of the human race in North America, wore the appearance, to persons regarding it from the outside, of a struggle upon a point of technical construction—a question of law which it was sought to decide by an appeal to arms. It was not unnatural, then, that the people of this country, who had but slight acquaintance with the antecedents of the contest or with the facts of the case, should wholly misconceive the true nature of the issues at stake, and, disconnected as the quarrel seemed to have become from the question of slavery, should allow their sympathies, which had originally gone with the North, to be carried, under the skilful management of Southern agency acting through the Press of this country, round to the Southern side. Nevertheless, had the case of the North, regarded even from this point of view, been fairly put before the English people, it is difficult to believe that it would not have been recognized as founded, at least in its first phase, in reason and justice. When the South forced on a contest by attacking the Federal forts, what was Mr. Lincoln to do? Before acquiescing in its demand for separation, was he not at least bound to ascertain that that demand represented the real wish of the Southern people? But, after war had been proclaimed, or rather commenced, by the South, how was this to be done otherwise than by accepting the challenge? Was the Government at once to lower the standard of law before that of revolution, without even inquiring by whom the revolution was supported? But in truth the President's case was much stronger than this. The Government was in possession of evidence which at least rendered it very probable that at this time the separatists were in a minority in the South, even in those places where they were believed to be strongest. At the presidential election which had just been held, the votes for the unionist candidates in the extreme south exceeded those for the candidate who represented the secession; in the intermediate states, the unionist votes formed two-thirds of the constituency; in Missouri, three-fourths. Will it be said that, with such facts before him, which were surely a safer criterion of Southern feeling than the votes of conventions obtained under mob-terrorism, Mr. Lincoln should at once have acquiesced in the demand for secession, and quietly permitted the consummation of a conspiracy, which for deliberate treachery, betrayal of sacred trusts, and shameless and gigantic fraud, has seldom been matched? To have done so, would have been to have written himself down before the world as incompetent—nay, as a traitor to the cause which he had just sworn to defend.

The right of secession became thus by force of circumstances the ostensible ground of the war; and with the bulk of the Northern people it must be admitted it was not only ostensible but the real ground; for it is idle to claim for the North a higher or more generous principle of conduct than that which itself put forward. The one prevailing and overpowering sentiment in the North, so soon as the designs of the South were definitively disclosed, was undoubtedly the determination to uphold the Union, and to crush the traitors who had conspired to dissolve it. In this country we had looked for something higher; we had expected, whether reasonably or not, an anti-slavery crusade. We were disappointed; and the result was, as has been stated, a re-action of sentiment which has prevented us from doing justice to that which was really worthy of admiration in the Northern cause. . . .

The prevailing idea that inspired the Northern rising was, I have said, the determination to uphold the Union. Still it would be a great mistake to suppose that this idea represented the whole significance of the movement, even so far as this was to be gathered from the views of the North. While loyalty to the Union pervaded and held together all classes, another sentiment —the sentiment of hostility to slavery— though less widely diffused, was strong-

ly entertained by a considerable party, and came more directly into collision than the unionist feeling with the real aims of the seceders. "The abolitionists," conventionally so known, formed indeed a small band. They had hitherto advocated separation as a means of escape from connexion with slavery, but they now threw themselves with ardour into the war; not that they swerved from their original aim, but that they believed they saw in the war the most effectual means of advancing that aim by breaking with slavery for ever; because with true instinct they felt that, secession having been undertaken for the purpose of extending slavery, the most effectual means to defeat that purpose was to defeat secession. The anti-slavery feeling, however, prevails far beyond the bounds of the party known as "abolitionists." Outside this sect are a large number of able . . . men who, while refusing to pronounce the shibboleth of the abolitionists, share in a large degree their views. The effect of the war has been, as might have been supposed, to bring this class of politicians into closer union than before with the extreme sect. The two have now begun to act habitually together, and for practical purposes may be regarded as constituting a single party. Now it is these men, and not the mere unionists, whose opinions form the natural antithesis to the aims of the seceders. Between these and the South there can be no compromise; and, conformably to the law which invariably governs revolutions, they are the party who are rapidly becoming predominant in the North. The anti-slavery feeling is already rapidly gaining on the mere unionist feeling, and bids fair ultimately to supersede it. In the anti-slavery ranks are now to be found men who but a year ago were staunch supporters of slavery. Anti-slavery orators are now cheered to the echo by multitudes who but a year ago hooted and pelted them: they have forced their way into the stronghold of their enemies, and William Lloyd Garrison lectures in New York itself with enthusiastic applause. The anti-slavery principle thus tends constantly, under the influences which are in operation, to become more powerful in the North; and it is this fact which justifies the view of those who have predicted that it is only necessary the war should continue long enough in order that it be converted into a purely abolition struggle.

These considerations will enable the reader to perceive how, while the North has arisen to uphold the Union in its integrity, slavery is yet the true cause of the war, and that the real significance of the war is its relation to slavery. I think, too, they must be held to afford a complete justification of the North in its original determination to maintain the Union; but this is scarcely now the practical question. There was, at the first, reason to believe that a very considerable element of population favourable to the Union existed in the South. While this was the case, it was no less than the duty of the Federal government to rescue these citizens from the tyranny of a rebel oligarchy. But do grounds for that supposition still exist? Before the war broke out, it is well known that something like a reign of terror prevailed in the South for all who fell short of the most extreme standard of pro-slavery opinion. The rigour of that reign will hardly have been relaxed since the war commenced, and must no doubt have produced a very considerable emigration of loyal citizens. The infectious enthusiasm of the war will probably have operated to make many converts; and, under the influ-

ences of both these causes, the South, or at least that portion of the South which has led the way in this movement, has probably by this time been brought to a substantial unanimity of opinion, a conclusion which is strongly confirmed by the absence of any sign of disaffection to the Confederation among its population. Under these circumstances what is the policy to which Europe, in the interests of civilization, should give its moral support? This country has long made up its mind as to the impossibility of forcibly reconstructing the Union; perhaps it has also satisfied itself of the undesirableness of this result. Of neither of these opinions is the writer prepared to contest the soundness. But this being conceded, an all-important question remains for decision. On what conditions is the independence of the South to be established? For the solution of this question in the interests of civilization, a knowledge of the character and designs of the power which represents the South is requisite, and it is this which it is the aim of the present work to furnish. Meanwhile, however, it may be said that the definitive severance of the Union is perfectly compatible with either the accomplishment of the original design of the seceders—the extension of slavery, or the utter defeat of that design, according to the terms on which the separation takes place; and that therefore the severance of the Union by no means implies the defeat of the North or the triumph of the South. The Southern leaders may be assumed to know their own objects, and to be the best judges of the means which are necessary to their accomplishment; and we may be certain that no arrangement which involves the frustration of these objects will be acquiesced in until after a complete prostration of their strength. If this be so, it is important to ascertain what the objects of the South are. For if these objects be inconsistent with the interests of civilization and the happiness of the human race (and I shall endeavour to show that this is the case), then no settlement of the American dispute which is not preceded by a thorough humbling of the slave party should be satisfactory to those who have human interests at heart. This is the cardinal point of the whole question. The designs of the seceders are either legitimate and consistent with human interests, or the contrary. If they are legitimate, let this be shown, and let us in this case wish them God speed: if they are not, and if the Southern leaders may be taken to know what is essential to their own ends, then we may be sure that nothing short of the effectual defeat of the South in the present war will secure a settlement which shall be consistent with what the best interests of mankind require.

JEFFERSON DAVIS

At the period to which this review of events has advanced, one state had already withdrawn from the Union. Seven or eight others were preparing to follow her example, and others yet were anxiously and doubtfully contemplating the probably impending necessity of taking the same action. The efforts of Southern men in Congress, aided by the cooperation of the Northern friends of the Constitution, had failed, by the stubborn refusal of a haughty majority, controlled by radical purposes, to yield anything to

Reprinted from Jefferson Davis, THE RISE AND FALL OF THE CONFEDERATE GOVERNMENT *(Richmond, Va., 1938), I, 65–72.*

the spirit of peace and conciliation. This period, coinciding, as it happens, with the close of a calendar year, affords a convenient point to pause for a brief recapitulation of the causes which had led the Southern states into the attitude they then held, and for a more full exposition of the constitutional questions involved.

The reader of many of the treatises on these events, which have been put forth as historical, if dependent upon such alone for information, might naturally enough be led to the conclusion that the controversies which arose between the states, and the war in which they culminated, were caused by efforts on the one side to extend and perpetuate human slavery, and on the other to resist it and establish human liberty. The Southern states and Southern people have been sedulously represented as "propagandists" of slavery, and the Northern as the defenders and champions of universal freedom, and this view has been so arrogantly assumed, so dogmatically asserted, and so persistently reiterated, that its authors have, in many cases, perhaps, succeeded in bringing themselves to believe it, as well as in impressing it widely upon the world.

The attentive reader of the preceding chapters—especially if he has compared their statements with contemporaneous records and other original sources of information—will already have found evidence enough to enable him to discern the falsehood of these representations, and to perceive that, to whatever extent the question of slavery may have served as an *occasion,* it was far from being the *cause* of the conflict.

I have not attempted, and shall not permit myself to be drawn into any discussion of the merits or demerits of slavery as an ethical or even as a political question. It would be foreign to my purpose, irrelevant to my subject, and would only serve—as it has invariably served in the hands of its agitators —to "darken counsel" and divert attention from the genuine issues involved.

As a mere historical fact, we have seen that African servitude among us —confessedly the mildest and most humane of all institutions to which the name "slavery" has ever been applied —existed in all the original states, and that it was recognized and protected in the fourth article of the Constitution. Subsequently, for climatic, industrial, and economical—not moral or sentimental—reasons, it was abolished in the Northern, while it continued to exist in the Southern states. Men differed in their views as to the abstract question of its right or wrong, but for two generations after the Revolution there was no geographical line of demarkation for such differences. The African slave trade was carried on almost exclusively by New England merchants and Northern ships. Jefferson—a Southern man, the founder of the Democratic party, and the vindicator of state rights—was in theory a consistent enemy to every form of slavery. The Southern states took the lead in prohibiting the slave trade, and, as we have seen, one of them (Georgia) was the first state to incorporate such a prohibition in her organic Constitution. Eleven years after the agitation on the Missouri question, when the subject first took a sectional shape, the abolition of slavery was proposed and earnestly debated in the Virginia legislature, and its advocates were so near the accomplishment of their purpose, that a declaration in its favor was defeated by only a small majority, and that on the ground of expediency. At a still later period, abolitionist lec-

turers and teachers were mobbed, assaulted, and threatened with tar and feathers in New York, Pennsylvania, Massachusetts, New Hampshire, Connecticut, and other states. One of them (Lovejoy) was actually killed by a mob in Illinois as late as 1837.

These facts prove incontestably that the sectional hostility which exhibited itself in 1820, on the application of Missouri for admission into the Union, which again broke out on the proposition for the annexation of Texas in 1844, and which reappeared after the Mexican war, never again to be suppressed until its fell results had been fully accomplished, was not the consequence of any difference on the abstract question of slavery. It was the offspring of sectional rivalry and political ambition. It would have manifested itself just as certainly if slavery had existed in all the states, or if there had not been a negro in America. No such pretension was made in 1803 or 1811, when the Louisiana purchase, and afterward the admission into the Union of the state of that name, elicited threats of disunion from the representatives of New England. The complaint was not of slavery, but of "the acquisition of more weight at the other extremity" of the Union. It was not slavery that threatened a rupture in 1832, but the unjust and unequal operation of a protective tariff.

. . . The truth remains intact and incontrovertible, that the existence of African servitude was in no wise the cause of the conflict, but only an incident. In the later controversies that arose, however, its effect in operating as a lever upon the passions, prejudices, or sympathies of mankind was so potent that it has been spread like a thick cloud over the whole horizon of historic truth.

As for the institution of negro servitude, it was a matter entirely subject to the control of the states. No power was ever given to the general government to interfere with it, but an obligation was imposed to protect it. Its existence and validity were distinctly recognized by the Constitution in at least three places:

First, in that part of the second section of the first article which prescribes that "representatives and direct taxes shall be apportioned among the several States which may be included within this Union, according to their respective members, which shall be determined by adding to the whole number of free persons, including those bound to service for a term of years, and, excluding Indians not taxed, three fifths of all other persons." "Other persons" than "free persons" and those "bound to service for a term of years" must, of course, have meant those permanently bound to service.

Secondly, it was recognized by the ninth section of the same article, which provided that "the migration or importation of such persons as any of the States now existing shall think proper to admit shall not be prohibited by Congress prior to the year one thousand eight hundred and eight." This was a provision inserted for the protection of the interests of the slave-trading New England states, forbidding any prohibition of the trade by Congress for twenty years, and thus virtually giving sanction to the legitimacy of the demand which that trade was prosecuted to supply, and which was its only object.

Again, and in the third place, it was specially recognized, and an obligation imposed upon every state, not only to refrain from interfering with it in any other state, but in certain cases to aid in its enforcement, by that clause, or paragraph, of the second section of the fourth article which provides as follows:

No person held to service or labor in one State, under the laws thereof, escaping into another, shall, in consequence of any law or regulation therein, be discharged from such service or labor, but shall be delivered up on claim of the party to whom such service or labor may be due.

.   .   .

The preamble to the Constitution declared the object of its founders to be "to form a more perfect union, establish justice, insure domestic tranquillity, provide for the common defense, promote the general welfare, and secure the blessings of liberty to ourselves and our posterity." Now, however (in 1860), the people of a portion of the states had assumed an attitude of avowed hostility, not only to the provisions of the Constitution itself, but to the "domestic tranquillity" of the people of other states. Long before the formation of the Constitution, one of the charges preferred in the *Declaration of Independence* against the government of Great Britain, as justifying the separation of the colonies from that country, was that of having "excited domestic insurrections among us." Now, the mails were burdened with incendiary publications, secret emissaries had been sent, and in one case an armed invasion of one of the states had taken place for the very purpose of exciting "domestic insurrection."

It was not the passage of the "personal liberty laws," it was not the circulation of incendiary documents, it was not the raid of John Brown, it was not the operation of unjust and unequal tariff laws, nor all combined, that constituted the intolerable grievance, but it was the systematic and persistent struggle to deprive the Southern states of equality in the Union—generally to discriminate in legislation against the interests of their people; culminating in their exclusion from the territories, the common property of the states, as well as by the infraction of their compact to promote domestic tranquillity.

The question with regard to the territories has been discussed in the foregoing chapters, and the argument need not be repeated. There was, however, one feature of it which has not been specially noticed, although it occupied a large share of public attention at the time, and constituted an important element in the case. This was the action of the federal judiciary thereon, and the manner in which it was received.

In 1854 a case (the well-known Dred Scott case) came before the Supreme Court of the United States, involving the whole question of the status of the African race and the rights of citizens of the Southern states to migrate to the territories, temporarily or permanently, with their slave property, on a footing of equality with the citizens of other states with their property of any sort. This question, as we have seen, had already been the subject of long and energetic discussion, without any satisfactory conclusion. All parties, however, had united in declaring that a decision by the Supreme Court of the United States—the highest judicial tribunal in the land—would be accepted as final. After long and patient consideration of the case, in 1857, the decision of the Court was pronounced in an elaborate and exhaustive opinion, delivered by Chief Justice Taney—a man eminent as a lawyer, great as a statesman, and stainless in his moral reputation—seven of the nine judges who composed the Court concurring in it. The salient points established by this decision were:

1. That persons of the African race were not, and could not be, acknowledged as "part of the people," or citizens, under the Constitution of the United States;

2. That Congress had no right to exclude citizens of the South from taking their negro servants, as any other property, into any part of the common territory, and that they were entitled to claim its protection therein;

3. Finally, as a consequence of the principle just above stated, that the Missouri Compromise of 1820 insofar as it prohibited the existence of African servitude north of a designated line, was unconstitutional and void. . . .

Instead of accepting the decision of this then august tribunal—the ultimate authority in the interpretation of constitutional questions—as conclusive of a controversy that had so long disturbed the peace and was threatening the perpetuity of the Union, it was flouted, denounced, and utterly disregarded by the Northern agitators, and served only to stimulate the intensity of their sectional hostility.

What resource for justice—what assurance of tranquillity—what guarantee of safety—now remained for the South? Still forbearing, still hoping, still striving for peace and union, we waited until a sectional President, nominated by a sectional convention, elected by a sectional vote—and that the vote of a minority of the people—was about to be inducted into office, under the warning of his own distinct announcement that the Union could not permanently endure "half slave and half free," meaning thereby that it could not continue to exist in the condition in which it was formed and its Constitution adopted. The leader of his party, who was to be the chief of his cabinet, was the man [William Seward] who had first proclaimed an "irrepressible conflict" between the North and the South, and who had declared that abolitionism, having triumphed in the territories, would proceed to the invasion of the states. Even then the Southern people did not finally despair until the temper of the triumphant party had been tested in Congress and found adverse to any terms of reconciliation consistent with the honor and safety of all parties.

No alternative remained except to seek the security out of the Union which they had vainly tried to obtain within it. The hope of our people may be stated in a sentence. It was to escape from injury and strife in the Union, to find prosperity and peace out of it.

II. DOCUMENTS

1. Southern Anxieties

For a few southerners the desire for secession was as old as the Constitution itself, but the movement for secession did not gain a very substantial following until the 1850's. By then, two decades of abolitionist agitation, of rapid growth in the northern economy and population, of deepening gloom in the South had created an atmosphere that was more and more favorable to secession. One of the first intellectuals in the South to commit himself firmly to the radical cause was the South Carolina novelist William Gilmore Simms. The first document in this section is a letter in which Simms plotted secession. If Simms' attitudes are typical of the early "fire-eaters," then Cairnes was wrong about the slave-power "conspiracy"; Simms, in his letter, was conspiring to break the Union, not to dominate it.

The most brilliant proponent of the southern cause in the period between the Missouri Compromise of 1820 and the Compromise of 1850 was John C. Calhoun. In the second document in this section, a speech to the Senate on March 4, 1850, Calhoun looked to the future with typical forebodings. He revered the Union, but he argued that it could not be saved unless the northern states voluntarily redressed the balance of political power between the sections and guaranteed slavery against abolitionist attacks. Calhoun was "right," at least historically, but it is legitimate to ask whether any group of politicians, northern or southern, might reasonably have been expected to make the kind of voluntary concessions which he insisted on. As some twentieth-century historians have pointed out, Calhoun might just as well have argued that the Union could be preserved only if the South voluntarily surrendered its claims to the peculiar brand of "property" represented by the slaves.

In the months before Lincoln's election, there were many anxious meetings in the North and the South, some of which attempted to harden the lines of division and others which sought a way out of the impasse. The final stakes were enormous: control of the border states such as Virginia, which hung in the balance between secession and reluctant submission to a new, sectional administration. The third document in this section is the reaction of a Richmond newspaper to a political meeting in New York in January, 1860. The editorial's conclusion was the outcome of decades of mistrust and agitation: the people of the South could look only "to their own power and authority."

WILLIAM GILMORE SIMMS

TO NATHANIEL BEVERLEY TUCKER

Woodlands, Nov. 27 [1850]

You have seen by this time that Georgia has for the nonce surrendered to the Submissionists. This I feared would be the case. Indeed, I have no hope of the South *until after* the next Presidential election [1852]. The two great national parties must make one more dying effort under their old organizations. The result will crowd the field with discontents, and all the success will enure to the abolitionists. They will push their success. They lack the wisdom which knows when to stop, and in their insolence they will push the South to extremities. In all probability the fugitive Slave Bill will be repealed this coming session. The abolition of slavery will follow, soon or late in the District of Columbia and in all places directly under the control of the Fed. Gov. Four years will certainly bring about all these things & probably interdict the slave trade between the States. Five years at the utmost—unless there be a great revolution in public sentiment at the north,—which is scarcely possible—will see the dissolution of the Union, since every pretext will then be set aside utterly, by which our trading politicians

Reprinted from Oliphant, Odell, and Eaves, eds., THE LETTERS OF WILLIAM GILMORE SIMMS (Columbia, S.C.: University of South Carolina Press, 1952–1956), III, 75–77.

have succeeded in abusing the understanding of the people. That they should succeed—we need not wonder for the masses are very slow in general, particularly where the questions do not press directly & practically upon them, in detecting the treachery of old & long honored leaders. Were I to trust my feelings, I should say to S. C. secede at once. Let our State move *per se.* But here's the danger. None of the South. States stood to the rack in 1833 when S. C. threw herself into the breach—and owing to the same cause—the faithlessness & selfishness of trading politicians. Were S. C. to secede her ports would be blocked up—her trade would pass to Geo. and the appeal to Georgia cupidity—filled as that State is, with Yankee traders, would be fatal to her patriotism. It would be irresistible in keeping her in her position. The next consequence would be that S. C. would lose a large portion of her planting population. It would give a new impulse to emigration. They would abandon their lands & pass to Georgia & the west. Those who remained, goaded by privation, distress, loss of trade, profit, & perhaps property,—would rise up & rend their leaders to pieces. We must, at all hazards goad Geo. to extremities & give her no encouragement in her submission. With S. C. & Geo. moving for secession the effect would be conclusive upon all the South. British assistance could not be expected, unless they were shut out from *all* the cotton ports. Leave the majority of these open & they will encounter no contest with the U. S. for the trade of one or more of our Southern cities. Patience & shuffle the cards! Our emissaries must be at work. If we are to incur the imputation of rebellion, we must use all the arts of conspiracy. We must enter the field with the U. S. and hold out the proper lines to buyable politicians. We must show them that a confederacy of 13 South. States, must have the same foreign & domestic establishment now maintained by the 31 states; show them that we shall have the same offices to distribute among 13 now distributed among 31. and thus be able to *bid* more highly for their support. We must select our men, and give them their price. Meanwhile, events *must* favor us. The abolitionists *will* go on. . . . The South has but a single interest, and when it is no longer possible for her people to doubt in respect to its danger, there will be no longer difficulty in uniting them in its defence. They may well continue to doubt, while Va. the Mother of States, and as deeply interested as any, shows herself so perfectly quiescent. *Our* Legislature is in session,—a very feeble body, but full of spirit. They will probably call a convention of the people.

JOHN C. CALHOUN

I have, Senators, believed from the first that the agitation of the subject of slavery would, if not prevented by some timely and effective measure, end in disunion. Entertaining this opinion, I have, on all proper occasions, endeavored to call the attention of both the two great parties which divide the country to adopt some measure to prevent so great a disaster, but without

Reprinted from THE WORKS OF JOHN CALHOUN *(New York, 1851–1856), IV, 542–47, 551–59, 571–73.*

success. The agitation has been permitted to proceed, with almost no attempt to resist it, until it has reached a point when it can no longer be disguised or denied that the Union is in danger. You have thus had forced upon you the greatest and the gravest question that can ever come under your consideration—How can the Union be preserved?

To give a satisfactory answer to this mighty question, it is indispensable to have an accurate and thorough knowledge of the nature and the character of the cause by which the Union is endangered. Without such knowledge it is impossible to pronounce, with any certainty, by what measure it can be saved; just as it would be impossible for a physician to pronounce, in the case of some dangerous disease, with any certainty, by what remedy the patient could be saved, without similar knowledge of the nature and character of the cause which produced it. The first question, then, presented for consideration, in the investigation I propose to make, in order to obtain such knowledge, is—What is it that has endangered the Union?

To this question there can be but one answer,—that the immediate cause is the almost universal discontent which pervades all the States composing the Southern section of the Union. This widely-extended discontent is not of recent origin. It commenced with the agitation of the slavery question, and has been increasing ever since. The next question, going one step further back, is—What has caused this widely diffused and almost universal discontent?

It is a great mistake to suppose, as is by some, that it originated with demagogues, who excited the discontent with the intention of aiding their personal advancement, or with the disappointed ambition of certain politicians, who resorted to it as the means of retrieving their fortunes. . . . No; some cause, far deeper and more powerful than the one supposed, must exist, to account for discontent so wide and deep. The question then recurs—What is the cause of this discontent? It will be found in the belief of the people of the Southern States, as prevalent as the discontent itself, that they cannot remain, as things now are, consistently with honor and safety, in the Union. The next question to be considered is —What has caused this belief?

One of the causes is, undoubtedly, to be traced to the long-continued agitation of the slave question on the part of the North, and the many aggressions which they have made on the rights of the South during the time. I will not enumerate them at present, as it will be done hereafter in its proper place.

There is another lying back of it— with which this is intimately connected —that may be regarded as the great and primary cause. This is to be found in the fact that the equilibrium between the two sections, in the Government as it stood when the constitution was ratified and the Government put in action, has been destroyed. At that time there was nearly a perfect equilibrium between the two, which afforded ample means to each to protect itself against the aggression of the other; but, as it now stands, one section has the exclusive power of controlling the Government, which leaves the other without any adequate means of protecting itself against its encroachment and oppression. . . .

. . .

The result of the whole is to give the Northern section a predominance in every department of the Government, and thereby concentrate in it the two elements which constitute the Federal Government,—majority of States, and a majority of their population, estimated in federal numbers. Whatever section concentrates the two in itself possesses the control of the entire Government.

But we are just at the close of the sixth decade, and the commencement of the seventh. The census is to be taken this year, which must add greatly to the decided preponderance of the North in the House of Representatives and in the electoral college. The prospect is, also, that a great increase will be added to its present preponderance in the Senate, during the period of the decade, by the addition of new States. . . . This great increase of Senators, added to the great increase of members of the House of Representatives and the electoral college on the part of the North, which must take place under the next decade, will effectually and irretrievably destroy the equilibrium which existed when the Government commenced.

Had this destruction been the operation of time, without the interference of Government, the South would have had no reason to complain; but such was not the fact. It was caused by the legislation of this Government, which was appointed, as the common agent of all, and charged with the protection of the interests and security of all. The legislation by which it has been effected, may be classed under three heads. The first is, that series of acts by which the South has been excluded from the common territory belonging to all the States as members of the Federal Union—which have had the effect of extending vastly the portion allotted to the Northern section, and restricting within narrow limits the portion left the South. The next consists in adopting a system of revenue and disbursements, by which an undue proportion of the burden of taxation has been imposed upon the South, and an undue proportion of its proceeds appropriated to the North; and the last is a system of political measures, by which the original character of the Government has been radically changed. . . .

. . .

The result of the whole of these causes combined is—that the North has acquired a decided ascendency over every department of this Government, and through it a control over all the powers of the system. A single section governed by the will of the numerical majority, has now, in fact, the control of the Government and the entire powers of the system. What was once a constitutional federal republic, is now converted, in reality, into one as absolute as that of the Autocrat of Russia, and as despotic in its tendency as any absolute government that ever existed.

As, then, the North has the absolute control over the Government, it is manifest, that on all questions between it and the South, where there is a diversity of interests, the interest of the latter will be sacrificed to the former, however oppressive the effects may be; as the South possesses no means by which it can resist, through the action of the Government. But if there was no question of vital importance to the South, in reference to which there was a diversity of views between the two sections, this state of things might be endured, without the hazard of destruction to the South. But such is not the fact. There is a question of vital importance to the Southern section, in reference to which the views and feelings of the two sections are as opposite and hostile as they can possibly be.

I refer to the relation between the two races in the Southern section, which constitutes a vital portion of her social organization. Every portion of the North entertains views and feelings more or less hostile to it. Those most opposed and hostile, regard it as a sin, and consider themselves under the most sacred obligation to use every effort to destroy it. Indeed, to the extent that they conceive they have power, they regard themselves as implicated in the sin, and responsible for not suppressing it by the use of all and every means. Those less opposed and hostile, regard it as a crime—an offence against humanity, as they call it; and, although not so fanatical, feel themselves bound to use all efforts to effect the same object; while those who are least opposed and hostile, regard it as a blot and a stain on the character of what they call the Nation, and feel themselves accordingly bound to give it no countenance or support. On the contrary, the Southern section regards the relation as one which cannot be destroyed without subjecting the two races to the greatest calamity, and the section to poverty, desolation, and wretchedness; and accordingly they feel bound, by every consideration of interest and safety, to defend it.

This hostile feeling on the part of the North towards the social organization of the South long lay dormant, but it only required some cause to act on those who felt most intensely that they were responsible for its continuance, to call it into action. The increasing power of this Government, and of the control of the Northern section over all its departments, furnished the cause. It was this which made an impression on the minds of many, that there was little or no restraint to prevent the Government from doing whatever it might choose to do. This was sufficient of itself to put the most fanatical portion of the North in action, for the purpose of destroying the existing relation between the two races in the South.

The first organized movement towards it commenced in 1835. Then, for the first time, societies were organized, presses established, lecturers sent forth to excite the people of the North, and incendiary publications scattered over the whole South, through the mail. The South was thoroughly aroused. Meetings were held every where, and resolutions adopted, calling upon the North to apply a remedy to arrest the threatened evil, and pledging themselves to adopt measures for their own protection, if it was not arrested. At the meeting of Congress, petitions poured in from the North, calling upon Congress to abolish slavery in the District of Columbia, and to prohibit, what they called, the internal slave trade between the States—announcing at the same time, that their ultimate object was to abolish slavery, not only in the District, but in the States and throughout the Union. At this period, the number engaged in the agitation was small, and possessed little or no personal influence.

. . .

As for myself, I believed at that early period, if the party who got up the petitions should succeed in getting Congress to take jurisdiction, that agitation would follow, and that it would in the end, if not arrested, destroy the Union. I then so expressed myself in debate, and called upon both parties to take grounds against assuming jurisdiction; but in vain. . . . *That* was the time for the North to have shown her devotion to the Union; but, unfortunately, both of the great parties of that section were so intent on obtaining or retaining party ascendency, that all other considerations were overlooked or forgotten.

What has since followed are but natural consequences. With the success of their first movement, this small fanatical party began to acquire strength; and with that, to become an object of courtship to both the great parties. The necessary consequence was, a further increase of power, and a gradual tainting of the opinions of both of the other parties with their doctrines, until the infection has extended over both; and the great mass of the population of the North, who, whatever may be their opinion of the original abolition party, which still preserves its distinctive organization, hardly ever fail, when it comes to acting, to co-operate in carrying out their measures. . . .

Such is a brief history of the agitation, as far as it has yet advanced. Now I ask, Senators, what is there to prevent its further progress, until it fulfils the ultimate end proposed, unless some decisive measure should be adopted to prevent it? Has any one of the causes, which has added to its increase from its original small and contemptible beginning until it has attained its present magnitude, diminished in force? Is the original cause of the movement—that slavery is a sin, and ought to be suppressed—weaker now than at the commencement? Or is the abolition party less numerous or influential, or have they less influence with, or control over the two great parties of the North in elections? Or has the South greater means of influencing or controlling the movements of this Government now, than it had when the agitation commenced? To all these questions but one answer can be given: No—no—no. The very reverse is true. Instead of being weaker, all the elements in favor of agitation are stronger now than they were in 1835, when it first commenced, while all the elements of influence on the part of the South are weaker. Unless something decisive is done, I again ask, what is to stop this agitation, before the great and final object at which it aims—the abolition of slavery in the States—is consummated? Is it, then, not certain, that if something is not done to arrest it, the South will be forced to choose between abolition and secession? Indeed, as events are now moving, it will not require the South to secede, in order to dissolve the Union. . . .

. . .

The cords that bind the States together are not only many, but various in character. Some are spiritual or ecclesiastical; some political; others social. Some appertain to the benefit conferred by the Union, and others to the feeling of duty and obligation.

. . .

If the agitation goes on, the same force, acting with increased intensity, as has been shown, will finally snap every cord, when nothing will be left to hold the States together except force. But, surely, that can, with no propriety of language, be called a Union, when the only means by which the weaker is held connected with the stronger portion is *force*. It may, indeed, keep them connected; but the connection will partake much more of the character of subjugation, on the part of the weaker to the stronger, than the union of free, independent, and sovereign States, in one confederation, as they stood in the early stages of the Government, and which only is worthy of the sacred name of Union.

Having now, Senators, explained what it is that endangers the Union, and traced it to its cause, and explained its nature and character, the question again recurs—How can the Union be saved? To this I answer, there is but one way by which it can be—and that is—by adopting such measures as will satisfy the States belonging to the Southern section, that they can remain in the Union consistently with their honor and their safety. There is, again, only one way by which this can be effected, and that is—by removing the causes by which this belief has been produced. Do *this,* and discontent will cease—harmony and kind feelings between the sections be restored—and every apprehension of danger to the Union removed. The question, then, is—How can this be done? . . .

. . .

There is but one way by which it can with any certainty; and that is, by a full and final settlement, on the principle of justice, of all the questions at issue between the two sections. The South asks for justice, simple justice, and less she ought not to take. She has no compromise to offer, but the constitution; and no concession or surrender to make. She has already surrendered so much that she has little left to surrender. Such a settlement would go to the root of the evil, and remove all cause of discontent, by satisfying the South, she could remain honorably and safely in the Union, and thereby restore the harmony and fraternal feelings between the sections, which existed anterior to the Missouri agitation. Nothing else can, with any certainty, finally and for ever settle the questions at issue, terminate agitation, and save the Union.

But can this be done? Yes, easily; not by the weaker party, for it can of itself do nothing—not even protect itself —but by the stronger. The North has only to will it to accomplish it—to do justice by conceding to the South an equal right in the acquired territory, and to do her duty by causing the stipulations relative to fugitive slaves to be faithfully fulfilled—to cease the agitation of the slave question, and to provide for the insertion of a provision in the constitution, by an amendment, which will restore to the South, in substance, the power she possessed of protecting herself, before the equilibrium between the sections was destroyed by the action of this Government. There will be no difficulty in devising such a provision—one that will protect the South, and which, at the same time, will improve and strengthen the Government, instead of impairing and weakening it.

. . .

It is time, Senators, that there should be an open and manly avowal on all sides, as to what is intended to be done. If the question is not now settled, it is uncertain whether it ever can hereafter be; and we, as the representatives of the States of this Union, regarded as governments, should come to a distinct understanding as to our respective views, in order to ascertain whether the great questions at issue can be settled or not. If you, who represent the stronger portion, cannot agree to settle them on the broad principle of justice and duty, say so; and let the States we both represent agree to separate and part in peace. If you are unwilling we should part in peace, tell us so, and we shall know what to do, when you reduce the question to submission or resistance. If you remain silent, you will compel us to infer by your acts what you intend. In that case, California will become the test question. If you admit her, under all the difficulties that oppose her admission, you compel us to infer that you intend to exclude us from the whole of the acquired territories, with the intention of destroying, irretrievably, the equilibrium between the two sections. We would be blind not to perceive in that case, that your real objects are power and aggrandizement, and infatuated not to act accordingly.

I have now, Senators, done my duty in expressing my opinions fully, freely, and candidly, on this solemn occasion. In doing so, I have been governed by the motives which have governed me in all the stages of the agitation of the slavery question since its commencement. I have exerted myself, during the whole period, to arrest it, with the intention of saving the Union, if it could be done; and if it could not, to save the section where it has pleased Providence to cast my lot, and which I sincerely believe has justice and the constitution on its side. Having faithfully done my duty to the best of my ability, both to the Union and my section, throughout this agitation, I shall have the consolation, let what will come, that I am free from all responsibility.

RICHMOND SEMI-WEEKLY EXAMINER

Those who anticipated any beneficial results from the Union meetings in the free States, have little reason to rejoice at the evidences of popular sentiment and feeling recently given in the most conservative city of the North, and in the interior of the most wealthy, populous, and powerful State in the Confederacy. Not a fortnight has passed since every paper in the South teemed with the details of a grand Union meeting held in the city of New York. People were told that the dormant but potent conservatism of the Empire State was aroused, and in spite of the repeated failures of the spasmodic and intermittent efforts of

Reprinted from RICHMOND SEMI-WEEKLY EXAMINER, Editorial, January 6, 1860, in Dwight L. Dumond, ed., SOUTHERN EDITORIALS ON SECESSION (New York, 1931), pp. 5–11.

that enfeebled element in Northern society, the timid and credulous Union idolaters of the South begun to receive this and similar demonstrations in the seaboard cities of that section as omens of a popular reaction which was to end our political "thirty years' war," and to furnish a cure for all the ills to which the body politic is subject. But the ruling genius of free society was not alarmed by these magnificent delusions, nor did it sleep over them. The high priest of Black Republicanism was wandering back from his European tour, and the unexpected and unwelcome appearance of RICHARD THE LION-HEARTED amid the sports at Ashby de la Zouche did not appal the minions of his indolent and hollow-hearted brother, or encourage the English loyalists more, than the sudden arrival of SEWARD disconcerted the Conservative reactionists, and animated the Black Republican cohorts. The thunders of an hundred cannon, the vociferous greeting of an immense multitude, welcomed him to the commercial emporium of the Union; the authorities of the city voted him its freedom. At Albany, at Syracuse, at Auburn, he was received with every demonstration of public rejoicing, and with all the assurances of popular confidence and support. From the villages and rural districts of the interior came forth the sounds of a people's welcome, as if to a great public benefactor and a trusted representative of popular will and sentiment. And why was this seen, amid a people not apt to pay for what it has not received, nor particularly demonstrative of grateful or sudden impulses of any kind? Why was this ovation rendered to the living politician by those who had suffered the greatest genius their section had produced for half a century to sink almost unnoticed and unhonored to his grave, and have apparently forgotten him in less than a decade? Why does VAN BUREN vegetate at Lindenwold, and why do PIERCE and FILLMORE still live unnoticed, "all weak and withered of their force," and indebted for casual mention and kindly memory to Southern friends alone? . . . Why is DOUGLAS fast sinking in public esteem, even in the Northwest, and forced to cast his eye Southward "with the lingering last look of despairing?" These men had position, genius, ability, energy and great skill in public affairs, and all, save one, are in the vigor of life. Why should they fall, in despite of supports which generally sustain men greatly their inferiors? The answer is simple: They were at war with the popular sentiment, which is the law of the society in which they lived. Why does SEWARD head the political movements and lead the people, their agents and representatives in the Northern section of the Union? . . . . In the Northern States the popular power has no check but the popular reason and will. A law such as this acting upon a society singularly energetic and adventurous, greedy after wealth and lusting for power, has no limit but the measure of its own power, and that measure is the extent of the physical force of the numerical majority of the people. That force is stimulated to action by one unvarying and universal incentive: the desire for the acquisition and use of power and property. The temper to acquire, the spirit to appropriate, thus unrestrained, operates under a universal law of human nature with a continuous and unremitting energy, against which plighted faith and constitutional checks will ever prove feeble and worthless defenses. . . . We trust that the people of the South will close their ears to the delusive promises of the merchant princes in Fifth Avenue, and hearken to no more tattle about popular reactions which, like sorrow, "endure for a night," but unlike it, are not precursors of "joy that cometh in the morning." Let them look at this matter as it is, as a conflict that must be settled, as a danger that is upon them, as an issue which delays and subterfuges cannot avert, as a trouble inseparable from the political and social condition of the Confederacy. Let them look neither to the Federal Government nor to popular movements in the free States for comfort or succor in time of need. But to their own power and authority. They should insist that every public man, either in office or a candidate for one, should stand at once upon defined and common ground with the people of the South. Let them assume a position at once, which will ensure them equality in, or security and independence out of the Union. If they are to stay in the Union, they should know on what terms; but let them be prepared to achieve independence, and maintain their honor and equality in whatever political position they may have to assume.

2. Northern Fears and Divisions

Radicals in the North and the South were in agreement on one basic issue, that same issue on which Cairnes and Davis were later to agree: an evil conspiracy was afoot to undermine the Constitution and the "security" of the people. The violent language of some of the southern secessionists was matched by a passionate northern hatred of the "slave-power." In the 1850's, the men who had been able to control sectional antagonisms and bring about compromises—men like Webster, Calhoun, and Clay—were being replaced in government by those who were unwilling to play at the old game of sectional co-existence. The first document in this section is part of a speech on "the crime against Kansas," by an abolitionist leader, Senator Charles Sumner of Massachusetts. In this famous speech, Sumner hammered away at the image of the slave power as conspiratorial, consummately evil, and ruthless. As many abolitionists were fond of doing, he also openly charged the federal government with active participation in the "crime."

Some modern historians have built an interpretation of the war around such appeals to fear and hatred by both southern fire-eaters and northern abolitionists. The war, these historians have argued, was unnecessary and was brought on by the irrational emotions and prejudices created by the extremists on both sides. Such an interpretation depends, in part, on the assumption that there was a widespread but ineffectual "moderate" public opinion in both sections.

The second document in this section is an editorial from the Sioux City Register, *December 1, 1860. The paper had supported Douglas against Lincoln, and was still insisting after the election on compromise and concession. Before secession, it is probably true that the opinions expressed in this editorial were held by something approaching a majority in the North.*

CHARLES SUMNER

At last, in the latter days of November, 1855, a storm, long gathering, burst upon the heads of the devoted people. The ballot-boxes had been violated and a legislature installed which proceeded to carry out the conspiracy of the invaders; but the good people of the Territory, born to freedom and educated as American citizens, showed no signs of submission. Slavery, though recognized by pretended law, was in many places practically an outlaw. To the lawless borderers this was hard to bear; and, like the heathen of old, they raged particularly against the town of Lawrence, already known by the firmness of its principles and the character of its citizens as citadel of the good cause. On this account they threatened, in their peculiar language, to "wipe it out." Soon the hostile power was gathered for this purpose. The wickedness of this invasion was enhanced by the way in which it began. A citizen of Kansas by the name of Dow was murdered by a partisan of slavery in the name of "law and order." Such an outrage naturally aroused indignation and provoked threats. The professors of "law and order" allowed the murderer to escape, and, still further to illustrate the irony of the name they assumed, seized the friend of the murdered man, whose few neighbors soon rallied for his rescue. This transaction, though totally disregarded in its chief front of wickedness, became the excuse for unprecedented excitement. The weak Governor, with no faculty higher than servility to slavery, —whom the President, in official delinquency, had appointed to a trust worthy only of a well-balanced character,—was frightened from his propriety. By proclamation he invoked the Territory. By telegraph he invoked the President. The Territory would not respond to his senseless appeal. The President was false. But the proclamation was circulated throughout the border countries of Missouri; and Platte, Clay, Carroll, Saline, Howard, and Jackson, each of them contributed a volunteer company, recruited from the roadsides, and armed with weapons which chance afforded, known as "the shot-gun militia,"—with a Missouri officer as commissary general, dispensing rations, and another Missouri officer as general in chief; with two wagon-loads of rifles belonging to Missouri, drawn by six mules, from its arsenal at Jefferson City; with seven pieces of cannon belonging to the United States from its arsenal at Liberty; and this formidable force amounting to at least 1,800 men, terrible with threats, oaths, and whiskey, crossed the borders, and encamped in larger part on the Wakarusa over against the doomed town of Lawrence, now threatened with destruction. . . . For more than a week it continued, while deadly conflict was imminent. I do not dwell on the heroism by which it was encountered or the mean retreat to which it was compelled; for that is not necessary in exhibiting the crime which you are to judge. . . .

. . .

Five several times and more have these invaders entered Kansas in armed array, and thus five several times and more have they trampled upon the organic law of the Territory. These extraordinary expeditions are simply the extraordinary witnesses to successive, uninterrupted violence. They stand out conspicuous, but not alone. The spirit of evil, in which they had their origin, is wakeful and incessant.

Reprinted from OLD SOUTH LEAFLETS *(Boston, 1896–1907), IV, No. 83, 11–15, 21–24.*

From the beginning it hung upon the skirts of this interesting Territory, harrowing its peace, disturbing its prosperity, and keeping its inhabitants under the painful alarms of war. . . .

. . .

Murder stalks, Assassination skulks in the tall grass of the prairie, and the vindictiveness of man assumes unwonted forms. A preacher of the gospel has been ridden on a rail, then thrown into the Missouri, fastened to a log, and left to drift down its muddy, tortuous current. And lately we have the tidings of that enormity without precedent, a deed without a name, where a candidate for the legislature was most brutally gashed with knives and hatchets, and then, after weltering in blood on the snow-clad earth, trundled along with gaping wounds to fall dead before the face of his wife. . . .

In these invasions, with the entire subversion of all security in this Territory, the plunder of the ballot-box, and the pollution of the electoral franchise, I show simply the process in unprecedented crime. If that be the best government where injury to a single citizen is resented as injury to the whole State, what must be the character of a government which leaves a whole community of citizens thus exposed? In the outrage upon the ballot-box, even without the illicit fruits which I shall soon exhibit, there is a peculiar crime of the deepest dye, though subordinate to the final crime, which should be promptly avenged. In other lands, where royalty is upheld, it is a special offence to rob the crown jewels, which are emblems of that sovereignty before which the loyal subject bows, and it is treason to be found in adultery with the queen, for in this way may a false heir to be imposed upon the State; but in our Republic the ballot-box is the single priceless jewel of that sovereignty which we respect, and the electoral franchise, where are born the rulers of a free people, is the royal bed we are to guard against pollution. In this plain presentment, whether as regards security or as regards elections, there is enough, without proceeding further, to justify the intervention of Congress, promptly and completely, to throw over this oppressed people the impenetrable shield of the Constitution and laws. But the half is not yet told.

. . .

The work of Usurpation was not perfected even yet. It had already cost too much to be left at any hazard.

> "To be thus is nothing,
> But to be safely thus."

Such was the object. And this could not be, except by the entire prostration of all the safeguards of Human Rights. Liberty of speech, which is the very breath of a Republic,—the press, which is the terror of wrong-doers,—the bar, through which the oppressed beards the arrogance of law,—the jury, by which right is vindicated,—all these must be struck down, while officers are provided in all places, ready to be the tools of this Tyranny; and then, to obtain final assurance that their crime is secure, the whole Usurpation, stretching over the Territory, must be fastened and riveted by legislative bolt, spike, and screw, *so as to defy all effort at change through ordinary forms of law.* To this work, in its various parts, were bent the subtlest energies; and never, from Tubal Cain to this hour, was any fabric forged with more desperate skill and completeness.

Mark, sir, three different legislative enactments constituting part of this work. *First,* according to one act, all who deny, by spoken or written word, "the right of persons to hold slaves in this Territory," are denounced as felons, to be punished by imprisonment at hard labor for a term not less than two years,—it may be for life. . . . *Secondly,* by another act, entitled "An Act concerning Attorneys-at-law," no person can practise as attorney unless he *shall obtain a license* from the Territorial courts, which, of course, a tyrannical discretion will be free to deny; and, after obtaining such license, he is constrained to take an oath not only "to support" the Constitution of the United States, but also "to support and sustain"—mark here the reduplication—the Territorial Act and the Fugitive Slave Bill, thus erecting a test for admission to the bar calculated to exclude citizens who honestly regard the latter legislative enormity as unfit to be obeyed. And, *thirdly,* by another act, entitled "An Act concerning Jurors," all persons "conscientiously opposed to the holding slaves" or "who do not admit the right to hold slaves in this Territory" are excluded from the jury on every question, civil or criminal, arising out of asserted slave property, while, in all cases, the summoning of the jury is left without one word of restraint to "the marshal, sheriff, or other officer," who is thus free to pack it according to his tyrannical discretion.

For the ready enforcement of all statutes against Human Freedom the President furnished a powerful quota of officers, in the governor, chief justice, judges, secretary, attorney, and marshal. The legislature completed this part of the work by constituting in each county a Board of Commissioners, composed of two persons, associated with the probate judge, whose duty it is to "appoint a county treasurer, coroner, justices of the peace, consta-

bles, and *all* other officers provided for by law," and then proceeding to the choice of this very Board, thus delegating and diffusing their usurped power, and tyrannically imposing upon the Territory a crowd of officers in whose appointment the people had no voice, directly or indirectly.

And still the final, inexorable work remained to be done. A legislature renovated in both branches could not assemble until 1858, so that, during this long intermediate period, this whole system must continue in the likeness of law, unless overturned by the National Government, or, in default of such interposition, by the generous uprising of an oppressed people. But it was necessary to guard against possibility of change, even tardily, at a future election; and this was done by two different acts, under the *first* of which all who do not take the oath to support the Fugitive Slave Bill are excluded from the elective franchise, and under the *second* of which all others are entitled to vote who tender a tax of one dollar to the sheriff on the day of election; thus, by provision of Territorial law, disfranchising all opposed to Slavery, and at the same time opening the door to the votes of the invaders; by an unconstitutional shibboleth excluding from the polls the body of actual settlers, and by making the franchise depend upon a petty tax only admitting to the polls the mass of borderers from Missouri. By tyrannical forethought the Usurpation not only fortified all that it did, but assumed a *self-perpetuating* energy.

Thus was the Crime consummated. Slavery stands erect, clanking its chains on the Territory of Kansas, surrounded by a code of death, and trampling upon all cherished liberties, whether of speech, the press, the bar, the trial by jury, or the electoral franchise. And, sir, all this is done, not merely to introduce a wrong which in itself is a denial of all rights, and in dread of which mothers have taken the lives of their offspring,—not merely, as is sometimes said, to protect Slavery in Missouri, since it is futile for this State to complain of Freedom on the side of Kansas when Freedom exists without complaint on the side of Iowa and also on the side of Illinois,—but it is done for the sake of political power, in order to bring two new slaveholding Senators upon this floor, and thus to fortify in the National Government the desperate chances of a warning Oligarchy. As the gallant ship voyaging on pleasant summer seas is assailed by a pirate crew and plundered on its doubloons and dollars, so is this beautiful Territory now assailed in peace and prosperity and robbed of its political power for the sake of Slavery. Even now the black flag of the land pirates from Missouri waves at the mast-head; in their laws you hear the pirate yell and see the flash of the pirate knife; while, incredible to relate, the President, gathering the Slave Power at his back, testifies a pirate sympathy.

Sir, all this was done in the name of Popular Sovereignty. And this is the close of the tragedy. Popular Sovereignty, which, when truly understood, is a fountain of just power, has ended in Popular Slavery,—not in the subjection of the unhappy African race merely, but of this proud Caucasian blood which you boast. The profession with which you began of *All by the People* is lost in the wretched reality of *Nothing for the People*. Popular Sovereignty, in whose deceitful name plighted faith was broken and an ancient Landmark of Freedom overturned, now lifts itself before us like Sin in the terrible picture of Milton, which

"seemed woman to the waist, and fair,
But ended foul in many a scaly fold
Voluminous and vast, a serpent armed
With mortal sting: about her middle round
A cry of hell-hounds never ceasing barked
With wide Cerberean mouths full loud, and
    rung
A hideous peal; yet, when they list, would
    creep,
If aught disturbed their noise, into her
    womb,
And kennel there, yet there still barked
    and howled
Within, unseen."

The image is complete at all points; and with this exposure I take my leave of the Crime against Kansas.

SIOUX CITY REGISTER

That man must be blind to passing events who does not, in the widely extended and tumultuous excitement of the Southern people see fearful indications of imminent peril to our institutions. There is in the South a class of radical "fire eaters" whose sole aim for years, has been to inflame and exasperate the masses.—But all their efforts have hitherto been fruitless. The value of the Union has always largely preponderated over all real as well as immaginary [sic] wrongs to which public attention has been directed. The really distinguished statesmen of the South have always avowed their determination to sustain the Union, and their patriotic councils [sic] have been heeded.—It cannot be denied, however, that disaffection and open hostility has [sic] now reached an extent and intensity far beyond any precedent. In many of the States, if there be any re-

Reprinted from SIOUX CITY REGISTER, *Editorial, December 1, 1860, in Harold C. Perkins, ed.,* NORTHERN EDITORIALS ON SECESSION *(New York, 1942), pp. 109–11.*

liance in the usual sources of information, the secession party is very largely in the majority, embracing a large share of the talent and influence of these States; and while the border States will for the time being be found sustaining the Union and the Constitution; yet, it is exceedingly questionable whether in the event of a rupture, a common interest would not speedily unite all the Southern States in what would be regarded as an issue upon the question of slavery.

Of the results of such a contest it is hardly possible to form an adequate conception. Under the most favorable circumstances we can calculate upon nothing less than a literal destruction of all our industrial interests; a financial panic such as was never before known; a loss of confidence in all classes of securities; repudiation of indebtedness and universal bankruptcy. We shall have made a happy escape if in addition to all this we are not plunged in a civil war, which must in the nature of things be characterized by scenes of misery and ruin, horrible to contemplate. With such a condition of things it well becomes us calmly to survey the field—to see and acknowledge our errors, and strive by conciliation, and acts of justice, to calm the troubled waters, and avert the impending blow.

We must not expect to find the wrong all on one side, but direct attention to the mote in our own eye, as well as to the beam in that of our neighbors. There are certain land marks that have been lost sight of, and as a consequence our noble vessel has drifted far out of the established channel. Prominent among these is the constitutional requirement for the rendition of fugitives. Stubborn facts, oft repeated, should force from the North the admission that they have come far short

of their duty in this regard. Not only has every subterfuge been made use of to evade the plain provisions of law, but in numerous instances its ends have been defeated by the most lawless and revolutionary proceedings. And besides this, States in their sovereign capacity have declared the law null and void, and have made its enforcement a penal offence. For such proceedings we have no excuse, nor have we any reason to expect other than retaliatory measures of like character from those whose rights are thus wantonly disregarded. If we value the Union as we claim to, and deprecate the evils of disunion, we should manifest our feelings by a careful observance of the terms of the compact, by "rendering unto Cæsar the things that are Cæsar's." Were we to exhibit good faith in the discharge of this unquestionable duty, by a repeal of the offensive and unjust State Statutes, and by rendering that prompt and efficient aid in the enforcement of Congressional enactments, which is due from every law abiding citizen, it is probable that there would be no trouble in effecting an amicable adjustment of all other sources of alienation and discord.

It is conceded by all that the question of territorial jurisdiction, so far as slavery is concerned, is a mere abstraction; one which will never effect [sic] the status of a single slave in existance [sic],—and surely such a question is susceptible of settlement were other more important ones satisfactorily disposed of. It is manifest that all these distracting questions in and of themselves are less important than the impression that has grown out of them throughout the South, that there is a wide spread Northern hostility to their people and institutions, such an one too as will admit of no abatement until slavery shall have been overthrown, or the Union dissolved,—and if we would maintain the confederacy we must dispel that illusion. We must satisfy them that we do not seek any interferance [sic] with their domestic or local institutions; that we are willing that they alone should assume the responsibility of slavery within their respective borders, and continue it or not as to them may seem best. This is no less than the South have a right to demand, and no less than justice requires at our hands.

Under the impulse of an intense excitement it is by no means improbable that a step may be taken that will lead to results the most disastrous. The exercise of prudence, wisdom and patriotism, brought to bear at the right time, and in the right direction, may arrest the first step, which if once taken, may never be restored.

Never were the responsibilities of those holding commanding positions greater than in the present crisis. Will the venerable President of the United States acquit himself as becomes a contemporary and successor of JACKSON? Will he emulate the example of that great man whose administration he so nobly sustained[?] If so, his last official acts will be the most glorious ones of his protracted career as a statesman. DOUGLAS, though smarting under the pangs of a Waterloo defeat has spoken, and has acquitted himself nobly. He invokes his friends to rally as one man around the standard of the Union. There is yet another distinguished statesman, a representative of one of Kentucky's noblest families, who will prove untrue to the name of BRECKINRIDGE if he does not, in this critical hour raise his clarion voice for his country. There are hundreds of others whose council [sic] and influence would tend largely to allay the storm that menaces us. May they all prove themselves worthy the position they hold in the country's esteem.

3. Secession, Sumter, and War

Much of the long and inconclusive debate over the "causes" of the Civil War, and over the question of its inevitability, has resulted from the failure of politicians and historians to make clear distinctions between three separate elements: sectional conflict, secession, and war. Sectional conflict *was at least as old as the Constitution, and it involved a great many basic issues: control of the western territories and new states; tariff controversies; slavery; the general irritation that grew up between a commercial, industrial North and an agricultural South; and the conflict of ideologies and cultural styles.* Secession, *on the other hand, was born in the winter and spring of 1860–61. Like any political crisis, it was composed of a variety of specific events: the election of Lincoln, the secession of the states one by one, and the taking of federal installations, money, and weapons in the South. Finally* war *came to life in the Charleston harbor. Logically, at least, sectional conflict could have existed without leading to secession, and secession could have taken place without leading to war. The problem of explaining and placing "blame" for each of these three elements is therefore quite different and must be undertaken separately.*

On July 4, 1861, Abraham Lincoln spoke to the Congress in special session on the origins of the war. He made a careful distinction between the secession crisis and the war and placed the causal and moral responsibility for each squarely on the South. Characteristically, however, Lincoln did not stop with this sort of analysis, but insisted that a third and still larger issue was involved: Could a government built on republican and democratic principles survive? This issue, like the issues of secession and war, had been forced by the South, Lincoln argued, and the outcome was far more than a political or sectional question. Lincoln insisted, as he was to do throughout the war, that the fate of all the peoples of the world hung on the American contest.

ABRAHAM LINCOLN

Abraham Lincoln on the Coming of the Civil War, July 4, 1861

At the beginning of the present Presidential term, four months ago, the functions of the Federal Government were found to be generally suspended within the several States of South Carolina, Georgia, Alabama, Mississippi, Louisiana, and Florida, excepting only those of the Post Office Department.

Within these States, all the Forts, Arsenals, Dock-yards, Customhouses, and the like, including the movable and stationary property in, and about them, had been seized, and were held in open hostility to this Government, excepting only Forts Pickens, Taylor, and Jefferson, on, and near the Florida coast, and Fort Sumter, in Charleston harbor, South Carolina. The Forts thus seized had been put in improved condition; new ones has been built; and armed forces had been organized, and were organizing, all avowedly with the same hostile purpose.

The Forts remaining in the posses-

Reprinted from Abraham Lincoln, Message to Congress, July 4, 1861, in Roy P. Basler, ed., THE COLLECTED WORKS OF ABRAHAM LINCOLN *(New Brunswick, N.J.: Rutgers University Press, 1953–1955), IV, 421–26.*

sion of the Federal government, in, and near, these States, were either besieged or menaced by warlike preparations; and especially Fort Sumter was nearly surrounded by well-protected hostile batteries, with guns equal in quality to the best of its own, and outnumbering the latter as perhaps ten to one. A disproportionate share, of the Federal muskets and rifles, had somehow found their way into these States, and had been seized, to be used against the government. Accumulations of the public revenue, lying within them had been seized for the same object. The Navy was scattered in distant seas; leaving but a very small part of it within the immediate reach of the government. Officers of the Federal Army and Navy, had resigned in great numbers; and, of those resigning, a large proportion had taken up arms against the government. Simultaneously, and in connection, with all this, the purpose to sever the Federal Union, was openly avowed. In accordance with this purpose, an ordinance had been adopted in each of these States, declaring the States, respectively, to be separated from the National Union. A formula for instituting a combined government of these states had been promulgated; and this illegal organization, in the character of confederate

States was already invoking recognition, aid, and intervention, from Foreign Powers.

Finding this condition of things, and believing it to be an imperative duty upon the incoming Executive, to prevent, if possible, the consummation of such attempt to destroy the Federal Union, a choice of means to that end became indispensable. This choice was made; and was declared in the Inaugural address. The policy chosen looked to the exhaustion of all peaceful measures, before a resort to any stronger ones. It sought only to hold the public places and property, not already wrested from the Government, and to collect the revenue; relying for the rest, on time, discussion, and the ballot-box. It promised a continuance of the mails, at government expense, to the very people who were resisting the government; and it gave repeated pledges against any disturbance to any of the people, or any of their rights. Of all that which a president might constitutionally, and justifiably, do in such a case, everything was foreborne, without which, it was believed possible to keep the government on foot.

On the 5th of March, (the present incumbent's first full day in office) a letter of Major Anderson, commanding at Fort Sumter, written on the 28th of February, and received at the War Department on the 4th of March, was, by that Department, placed in his hands. This letter expressed the professional opinion of the writer, that re-inforcements could not be thrown into that Fort within the time for his relief, rendered necessary by the limited supply of provisions, and with a view of holding possession of the same, with a force of less than twenty thousand good, and well-disciplined men. This opinion was concurred in by all the officers of his command; and their

memoranda on the subject, were made enclosures of Major Anderson's letter. The whole was immediately laid before Lieutenant General Scott, who at once concurred with Major Anderson in opinion. On reflection, however, he took full time, consulting with other officers, both of the Army and the Navy; and, at the end of four days, came reluctantly, but decidedly, to the same conclusion as before. He also stated at the same time that no such sufficient force was then at the control of the Government, or could be raised, and brought to the ground, within the time when the provisions in the Fort would be exhausted. In a purely military point of view, this reduced the duty of the administration, in the case, to the mere matter of getting the garrison safely out of the Fort.

It was believed, however, that to so abandon that position, under the circumstances, would be utterly ruinous; that the *necessity* under which it was to be done, would not be fully understood—that, by many, it would be construed as a part of a *voluntary* policy—that, at home, it would discourage the friends of the Union, embolden its adversaries, and go far to insure to the latter, a recognition abroad—that, in fact, it would be our national destruction consummated. This could not be allowed. Starvation was not yet upon the garrison; and ere it would be reached, *Fort Pickens* might be reinforced. This last, would be a clear indication of *policy,* and would better enable the country to accept the evacuation of Fort Sumter, as a military *necessity.* An order was at once directed to be sent for the landing of the troops from the Steamship Brooklyn, into Fort Pickens. This order could not go by land, but must take the longer, and slower route by sea. The first return news from the order was received just one week before the fall of Fort Sumter. The news itself was, that the officer commanding the Sabine, to which vessel the troops had been transferred from the Brooklyn, acting upon some *quasi* armistice of the late administration, (and of the existence of which the present administration, up to the time the order was despatched, had only too vague and uncertain rumors to fix attention) had refused to land the troops. To now re-inforce Fort Pickens, before a crisis would be reached at Fort Sumter was impossible—rendered so by the near exhaustion of provisions in the latter-named Fort. In precaution against such a conjuncture, the government had, a few days before, commenced preparing an expedition, as well adapted as might be, to relieve Fort Sumter, which expedition was intended to be ultimately used, or not, according to circumstances. The strongest anticipated case, for using it, was now presented; and it was resolved to send it forward. As had been intended, in this contingency, it was also resolved to notify the Governor of South Carolina, that he might expect an attempt would be made to provision the Fort; and that, if the attempt should not be resisted, there would be no effort to throw in men, arms, or ammunition, without further notice, or in case of an attack upon the Fort. This notice was accordingly given; whereupon the Fort was attacked, and bombarded to its fall, without even awaiting the arrival of the provisioning expedition.

It is thus seen that the assault upon, and reduction of, Fort Sumter, was, in no sense, a matter of self defence on the part of the assailants. They well knew that the garrison in the Fort could, by no possibility, commit aggression upon them. They knew—they were expressly notified—that the giving of bread to the few brave and hungry men of the garrison, was all which would on that occasion be attempted, unless themselves, by resisting so much, should provoke more. They knew that this Government desired to keep the garrison in the Fort, not to assail them, but merely to maintain visible possession, and thus to preserve the Union from actual, and immediate dissolution—trusting, as herein-before stated, to time, discussion, and the ballot-box, for final adjustment; and they assailed, and reduced the Fort, for precisely the reverse object—to drive out the visible authority of the Federal Union, and thus force it to immediate dissolution.

That this was their object, the Executive well understood; and having said to them in the inaugural address, "You can have no conflict without being yourselves the aggressors," he took pains, not only to keep this declaration good, but also to keep the case so free from the power of ingenious sophistry, as that the world should not be able to misunderstand it. By the affair at Fort Sumter, with its surrounding circumstances, that point was reached. Then, and thereby, the assailants of the Government began the conflict of arms, without a gun in sight, or in expectancy, to return their fire, save only the few in the Fort, sent to that habor, years before, for their own protection, and still ready to give that protection, in whatever was lawful. In this act, discarding all else, they have forced upon the country, the distinct issue: "Immediate dissolution, or blood."

And this issue embraces more than the fate of these United States. It presents to the whole family of man, the question, whether a constitutional republic, or a democracy—a government of the people, by the same people—can, or cannot, maintain its territorial integrity, against its own domestic foes. It presents the question, whether discontented individuals, too few in numbers to control administration, according to organic law, in any case, can always, upon the pretences made in this case, or on any other pretences, or arbitrarily, without any pretence, break up their Government, and thus practically put an end to free government upon the earth. It forces us to ask: "Is there, in all republics, this inherent, and fatal weakness?" "Must a government, of necessity, be too *strong* for the liberties of its own people, or too *weak* to maintain its own existence?"

So viewing the issue, no choice was left but to call out the war power of the Government; and so to resist force, employed for its destruction, by force, for its preservation.

III. RECENT INTERPRETATIONS

In his address to the Congress, Lincoln took the moral high ground. Faced with secession, he had been prepared to be patient, to do almost nothing, and to let "time, discussion, and the ballot-box" bring the South to its senses and restore the Union; but the South had made a willful decision to go ahead on its ruinous course. In taking his position—which had obvious political and propaganda value—Lincoln set the stage for the debate that has dominated historians' discussions of the war in recent decades. Since about 1940, the primary question of interpretation among historians has been, "Could the Civil War have been avoided by careful and rational action on both sides, or was the contest 'irrepressible'?"

The most famous statement of the view that the war was not necessary and was thus a tragic waste was by J. G. Randall, an Indianan by birth, who taught in Virginia for eight years before and during World War I. On the eve of another war, in 1940, Randall published an essay on "The Blundering Generation," in which he argued that the Civil War had been a costly, brutal mistake, wrought by men who simply stumbled irrationally into a conflict that they could and should have avoided. "It is difficult," Randall concluded, "to achieve a full realization of how Lincoln's generation stumbled into a ghastly war, how it blundered during four years of indecisive slaughter, and how the triumph of the Union was spoiled by the manner in which the victory was used."

Randall's argument, which quickly became very influential, was angrily challenged in 1949 by Arthur Schlesinger, Jr., a young Harvard historian with the experience of World War II fresh in his mind. The problem with Randall's "revisionist" view, according to Schlesinger, was simply that it had either to ignore or to apologize for the real cause—in the moral sense of "cause"—of the war, slavery. Like Hitler's Germany, the South, with its system of chattel slavery, created a moral crisis which *had* to be resolved by force of arms.

Historians may be less influenced by the wars they write about than by those they live through or participate in. Randall wrote in memory of what many intellectuals by the 1930's had decided was the unnecessary and wasteful participation of the United States in World War I. Schlesinger's essay of 1949 was overwhelmed by the memory of the recent crusade against Nazism. In the midst of the Cold War, another historian, David Potter, attacked the problem of inevitability with a moral perspective influenced by years of "co-existence" with Soviet Russia, an almost annual decision by both the Americans and the Russians to stave off the ultimate conflict for at least a little longer. In a 1962 preface to a new edition of his *Lincoln and His Party in the Secession Crisis,* Potter took a position somewhere between Randall's and Schlesinger's. The issues dividing North and South were real and compelling, he agreed with Schlesinger. But a temporary peace in 1861 might have had the same "merit" then as a temporary peace in 1961. So, Potter decided, a compromise along the lines of the Crittenden proposals *was* possible and *was* probably the most reasonable course of action that either side could have taken.

J. G. RANDALL

When one visits a moving picture, or reads [Joseph] Hergesheimer's *Swords and Roses,* which is much the same thing, he may gather the impression that the Civil War, fought in the days before mechanized divisions, aerial bombs, and tanks, was a kind of *chanson de geste* in real life. "The Civil War in America," writes Hergesheimer, "was the last of all wars fought in the grand manner. It was the last romantic war, when army corps fought as individuals and lines of assault . . . charged the visible enemy." "The war created a heroism . . . that clad fact in the splendor of battle flags." Hergesheimer feeds his readers chunks of sombre beauty, winterless climate, air stirred with faint cool music, fine houses, Spanish moss and cypress, trumpet vine and bay blossom, live oaks and linden,

Reprinted from J. G. Randall, "The Blundering Generation," MISSISSIPPI VALLEY HISTORICAL REVIEW, *XXVII (1940), 3–8, 10–16, 18–19, 21–24, 27–28, by permission of the publisher.*

bridal wreath, japonica, moonflower, and honeysuckle. . . .

The picture is filled in with red-lined cape, French sabre, yellow sash and tassels, The Bugles Sang Truce, The Dew is on the Blossom, orders given when asleep, animal vitality dancing in brilliant eyes.

Escapists may put what they will between the covers of a book; unfortunately the historian must be a realist. Whatever may be the thrill, or the emotional spree, of treating the Civil War romantically, it may be assumed that this has not been neglected. This paper, therefore, will attempt a very different task, that of weighing some Civil War realities, examining some of the irrational ideas of war "causation," and pondering some aspects of the Civil War mind. . . .

One seldom reads of the Civil War in terms of sick and wounded. . . . A Union surgeon at Bull Run reported extreme difficulty in inducing field officers to listen to complaints of disease resulting from foul tents into which fresh air was "seldom if ever" admitted.

Because ambulances were on the wrong side of the road, this also at Bull Run, twelve thousand troops had to pass before some of the wounded could be taken to the emergency hospital. Wounded men arriving from the field were thrust into freight cars where they lay on the bare floor without food for a day; numbers died on the road. One of the officers refused hospital admittance to wounded soldiers not of his regiment. Medical supplies were thrown away for want of transportation, injured men were exposed to heavy rain, gangrene resulted from minor wounds.

Romance and glory suggest at least the memory of a name. This implies an identified grave, but after making calculations based upon the official medical history issued by the surgeon general, the student would have to inform dear Blanche, or perhaps Mr. Ripley, that if the surgeon general's figures are right the unknown dead for the Civil War exceeded the number killed in battle! In round numbers there were about 110,000 Union deaths from battle, but the surgeon general reported that in November, 1870, there were 315,555 soldier graves, of which only 172,109 had been identified by name, leaving over 143,000 unidentified graves. . . . It is no more satisfactory to realize that about half the Union army became human waste in one form or another, as dead, disabled, deserted, or imprisoned.

"Jeb" Stuart may have worn gold spurs, but the common soldier was more familiar with fleas. . . . Without exposing all the euphemisms that obscure the truth of this subject, it may be noted that the great majority of Union deaths were from causes medically regarded as preventable, leaving aside the cynical assumption that war itself is not preventable. Pneumonia,

typhus, cholera, miasmic fever, and the like hardly find their way into the pages of war romance, but they wrought more havoc than bayonets and guns. Where there was danger of infection the rule-of-thumb principle of the Civil War surgeon was to amputate, and from operating tables, such as they were, at Gettysburg, arms and legs were carried away in wagon loads. . . .

One does not often speak or read of the war in reality, of its blood and filth, of mutilated flesh, and other revolting things. This restraint is necessary, but it ought to be recognized that the war is not presented when one writes of debates in Congress, of flanking movements, of retreats and advances, of cavalry and infantry, of divisions doing this and brigades doing that. In the sense of full realism war cannot be discussed. The human mind will not stand for it. For the very word "war" the realist would have to substitute some such term as "organized murder" or "human slaughterhouse." In drama as distinguished from melodrama murder often occurs offstage. In most historical accounts, especially military narratives, the war is offstage in that its stench and hideousness do not appear.

With all the recent revisionist studies it is difficult to achieve a full realization of how Lincoln's generation stumbled into a ghastly war, how it blundered during four years of indecisive slaughter, and how the triumph of the Union was spoiled by the manner in which the victory was used. In the hateful results of the war over long decades one finds partisanship at its worst. To see the period as it was is to witness uninspired spectacles of prejudice, error, intolerance, and selfish grasping. The Union army was inefficiently raised, poorly administered, and often badly commanded. In government there was deadlock, cross purpose, and extravagance. One can say that Lincoln was honest, but not that the country was free from corruption during the Lincoln administration. There was cotton plundering, army-contract graft, and speculative greed. Where Lincoln was at his best, where he was moderate, temperate, and far-seeing, he did not carry his party with him. Even those matters dissociated from the war, such as homesteading and railroad extension, came to be marred by exploitation and crooked finance. The period of the Civil War and the era of Jim Fisk and Jay Gould were one and the same generation.

If it was a "needless war," a "repressible conflict," as scholars now believe, then indeed was the generation misled in its unctuous fury. To suppose that the Union could not have been continued or slavery outmoded without the war and without the corrupt concomitants of the war, is hardly an enlightened assumption. If one questions the term "blundering generation," let him inquire how many measures of the time he would wish copied or repeated if the period were to be approached with a clean slate and to be lived again. Most of the measures are held up as things to be avoided. Of course it is not suggested that the generation of the sixties had any copyright on blundering. It is not that democracy was at fault. After all, civil war has not become chronic on these shores, as it has in some nations where politics of force is the rule. One can at least say that the Civil War was exceptional; that may be the best thing that can be said about it. A fuller measure of democracy would probably have prevented the war or at least have mitigated its abuses. To overlook many decades of American democracy and take the Civil War period as its test,

would be to give an unfair appraisal. Nor does this probing of blunders involve lack of respect for the human beings of that generation. As individuals we love and admire them, these men and women who look at us from the tin-types and Brady photographs of the sixties, though we may have "malice toward some." The distortions and errors of the time were rather a matter of mass thinking, of social solidification, and of politics.

. . .

War causation tends to be "explained" in terms of great forces. Something elemental is supposed to be at work, be it nationalism, race conflict, or quest for economic advantage. With these forces predicated, the move toward war is alleged to be understandable, to be explained, and therefore to be in some sense reasonable. . . .

War-making is too much dignified if it is told in terms of broad national urges, of great German motives, or of compelling Russian ambitions. When nations stumble into war, or when peoples rub their eyes and find they have been dragged into war, there is at some point a psychopathic case. Omit the element of abnormality, or of bogus leadership, or inordinate ambition for conquest, and diagnosis fails. In the modern scene it fails also if one omits manipulation, dummies, bogeys, false fronts, provocative agents, made-up incidents, frustration of elemental impulses, negation of culture, propaganda that is false in intent, criminal usurpation, and terrorist violence. These are reflections on the present bedeviled age, but their pertinence to the subject at hand is seen in the fact that scholarly discussions in explanation of war on the economic or cultural basis frequently include the Civil War as a supposedly convincing example. The writer doubts seriously whether a consensus of scholars who have competently studied the Civil War would accept either the cultural motive or the economic basis as the effective cause.

If one were to explain how this or that group or individual got into the Civil War, he could rely on no one formula. He would have to make up a series of elements or situations of which the following are only a few that might be mentioned: the despairing plunge, the unmotivated drift, the intruding dilemma, the blasted hope, the self-fulfilling prediction, the push-over, the twisted argument, the frustrated leader, the advocate of rule or ruin, and the reform-your-neighbor prophet. Robert Toombs said he would resist Stephen A. Douglas though he could see "nothing but . . . defeat in the future"; there is your despairing plunge. Young Henry Watterson, a Tennessee antislavery Unionist who fought for the Confederacy, is an example of the unmotivated drift. To many an individual the problem was not to fight with the side whose policies he approved of, but to be associated with the right set. Such an individual motive could not by a process of multiplication become in any reasonable sense a large-group motive. Yet it would be understandable for the individual. Usually in war time individuals have no choice of side, though in the American Civil War they sometimes did, especially on the border. Even where such choice was possible, the going to war by the individual in the sixties was due less to any broad "cause" or motive than to the fact that war existed, so that fighting was the thing to do. The obtaining of soldiers is not a matter of genuine persuasion as to issues. War participation is not a proof of war attitude.

The intruding dilemma was found in the great border and the great upper South where one of two ugly courses had to be chosen, though neither choice made sense in terms of objectives and interests in those broad regions. The self-fulfilling prediction is recognized in the case of those who, having said that war must come, worked powerfully to make it come. The blasted hope, i.e. the wish for adjustment instead of butchery, was the experience of most of the people, especially in the border and upper South. The frustrated leader is seen in the Unionist who came to support secession, or in such northerners as Thurlow Weed and William H. Seward who sought compromise and then supported war. The plea that "better terms" could be had out of the Union, which implied a short secession gesture though uttered by determined secessionists, was the crafty argument for secession to be used in addressing Unionists. This might be dubbed the twisted argument. The push-over is seen in the whole strategy of secession leaders by which anti-secession states and Union-loving men were to be dragged in by the accelerated march of events.

These are things which belong as much to the "explanation" of the Civil War as any broad economic or cultural or elemental factor. It should be remembered how few of the active promoters of secession became leaders of the Confederacy; their place in the drama was in the first act, in the starting of trouble. Nor should sectional preference cause one to forget how large a contribution to Union disaster, and how little to success, was given by northern radicals during the war. Clear thinking would require a distinction between causing the war and getting into the war. Discussion which overlooks this becomes foggy indeed. It was small minorities that caused the war;

then the regions and sections got into it. No one seems to have thought of letting the minorities fight it out. Yet writers who descant upon the causation of the war write grandly of vast sections, as if the fact of a section being dragged into the slaughter was the same as the interests of that section being consciously operative in its causation. Here lies one of the chief fallacies of them all. . . .

. . . None of the "explanations" of the war make sense, if fully analyzed. The war has been "explained" by the choice of a Republican president, by grievances, by sectional economics, by the cultural wish for southern independence, by slavery, or by events at Sumter. But these explanations crack when carefully examined. The election of Lincoln fell so far short of swinging southern sentiment against the Union that secessionists were still unwilling to trust their case to an all-southern convention or to cooperation among southern states. In every election from 1840 to 1852 Lincoln voted for the same candidate for whom many thousands of southerners voted. Lincoln deplored the demise of the Whig party and would have been only too glad to have voted in 1856 for another Harrison, another Taylor, or another Fillmore. Alexander Stephens stated that secessionists did not desire redress of grievances and would obstruct such redress. Prophets of sectional economics left many a southerner unconvinced; it is doubtful how far their arguments extended beyond the sizzling pages of *DeBow's Review* and the agenda of southern commercial congresses. The tariff was a potential future annoyance rather than an acute grievance in 1860. What existed then was largely a southern tariff law. Practically all tariffs are one-sided. Sectional tariffs in other periods have existed without producing war. Southern independence on broad cultural lines is probably more of a modern thesis than a contemporary motive of sufficient force to have carried the South out of the Union on any cooperative, all-southern basis.

It was no part of the Republican program to smash slavery in the South, nor did the territorial aspect of slavery mean much politically beyond agitation. Southerners cared little about actually taking slaves into existing territories; Republicans cared so little in the opposite sense that they avoided the prohibition of slavery in those territorial laws that were passed with Republican votes in February and March, 1861. Things said of "the South" often failed to apply to southerners, or of "the North" to northerners. Thwarted "Southern rights" were more often a sublimation than a definite entity. "The North" in the militant pre-war sense was largely an abstraction. The Sumter affair was not a cause, but an incident resulting from pre-existing governmental deadlock; Sumter requires explanation, and that explanation carries one back into all the other alleged factors. In contemporary southern comments on Lincoln's course at Sumter one finds not harmony but a jangling of discordant voices. Virginia resented Lincoln's action at Sumter for a reason opposite to that of South Carolina; Virginia's resentment was in the anti-secessionist sense. By no means did all the North agree with Lincoln's course as to Sumter. Had Lincoln evacuated Sumter without an expedition, he would have been supported by five and a half of seven cabinet members, Chase taking a halfway stand and Blair alone taking a positive stand for an expedition. What Lincoln refused as to Sumter was what the United States government had permitted in general as to forts and arsenals in the South. Stronger action than at Sumter was taken by Lincoln at Pickens without southern fireworks. There is no North-versus-South pattern that covers the subject of the forts. Nor is the war itself to be glibly explained in rational North-versus-South terms.

Let one take all the factors—the Sumter maneuver, the election of Lincoln, abolitionism, slavery in Kansas, cultural and economic differences—and it will be seen that only by a kind of false display could any of these issues, or all of them together, be said to have caused the war if one omits the elements of emotional unreason and overbold leadership. If one word or phrase were selected to account for the war, that word would not be slavery, or state-rights, or diverse civilizations. It would have to be such a word as fanaticism (on both sides), or misunderstanding, or perhaps politics. . . .

The fundamental or the elemental is often no better than a philosophical will o' the wisp. Why do adventitious things, or glaringly abnormal things, have to be elementally or cosmically accounted for? If, without proving his point, the historian makes war a thing of "inevitable" economic conflict, or cultural expression, or *Lebensraum,* his generalizations are caught up by others, for it would seem that those historians who do the most generalizing, if they combine effective writing with it, are the ones who are most often quoted. The historian's pronouncements are taken as the statement of laws whether he means them so or not; he is quoted by sociologists, psychologists, behaviorists, misbehaviorists, propagandists, and what not; he becomes a contributor to those "dynamic" masses of ideas, or ideologies, which are among the sorriest plagues of the present age. As to wars, the ones that have not happened are perhaps best to study. Much could be said about such wars. As much could be said in favor of them as of actual wars. Cultural and economic difficulties in wars that have not occurred are highly significant. The notion that you must have war when you have cultural variation, or economic competition, or sectional difference is an unhistorical misconception which it is stupid in historians to promote. Yet some of the misinterpretations of the Civil War War have tended to promote it.

What was the mind of America in Lincoln's day? It was human, which means it was partly simian! It was occidental. It was New World. It was American, though one would have to be a Stephen Benét to state what that means. It had somewhat of a sense of humor, though not enough. It was southern, or Yankee, or midwestern, or otherwise sectional. It was the mind of the McGuffey reader, by which a world of ready-made ideas is suggested. It was Victorian; it had inhibitions which today appear as droll as its unrepressed whiskers. It was less mechanized than today, being of the horse-and-buggy age. It was soul-searching. It was Christian and it was chiefly Protestant; yet the one most numerous faith was Catholic. Religiously it was fundamentalist. It was not profoundly philosophical and took with resentment the impact of Darwinism. Though polyglot it was far from cosmopolitan. The soapbox flavor or the backwoods tang was characteristic of its humorists. It was partly conditioned by racial backgrounds, such as the Dutch, German, Irish, Anglo-Saxon, or Scandinavian. It differed in the degrees of its Americanization; there was a staggering at variant distances from immigrant ancestors. Often the recent immigration, such as the German or Scandinavian, took American democracy with more simple faith than the seasoned American. When disillusion came to such, it came hard.

. . .

In spite of much nobility of sentiment, the Civil War mind seems a sorry *melange* of party bile, crisis melodrama, inflated eloquence, unreason, religious fury, self-righteousness, unctuous self-deception, and hate. Bad party feeling was evident when Seward appeared in the Senate on January 9, 1860, "& not a man from the democracy save Douglas . . . came to greet him." "D—n their impudence," was the comment of William P. Fessenden. Yet this was more than a year before the war opened. It was a time of crisis psychosis. Men felt they were living in great days. The generation had its self-consciousness of mission and destiny. Even the private soldier filled his letters with exalted talk. At the beginning of the war a Massachusetts soldier, telling of a rail journey from Boston to New York, wrote: "Refreshments were lavished upon us . . . cannon sent their boom over hill and dale and bells peeled [*sic*] their tocsin of warning . . . that our train was approaching bearing a Regiment of brave hearts to the defence of our country's capitol [*sic*]." Passing the "Constitution" he wrote: "May they [the colors] ever float over that notable ship . . . as she rides proudly upon the waters of the Union." This proudly riding epistle was but a soldier's letter to his brother. Similar attitudes were characteristic of the South; Mrs. Chesnut referred to "the high-flown style which of late seems to have gotten into the very air."

. . .

When war came and as the struggle dragged on, demands for peace were regarded as a kind of defeatism, of surrender to forces which northern idealists considered destructive and evil.

Peace became a matter of politics, of anti-Lincoln agitation, of what was called Copperhead disloyalty. . . .

Denunciation of war easily became denunciation of rebellion; this readily passed over into a demand to put down rebellion. The cause of peace as a crusade found a new orientation when war actually existed, for non-resistance could not stop the torrent. It was the dilemma of the pacifist. When peace men face an existing war begun by what they consider an aggressor, their attachment to peace becomes outraged indignation against those who, in their opinion, have broken the peace. . . .

. . .

It is not of record that Lincoln's Cabinet contained a "minister of national enlightenment and propaganda"; yet propaganda itself was not lacking. In the public "enlightenment" of that time there was boasting, there was rumor, there were atrocity tales, and there was falsehood. Atrocity stories were found not only in newspapers but in congressional reports. There were circumstantial accounts of Confederates bayoneting wounded captives, kicking heads about like footballs, insulting women, and engaging in gruesome tortures. William B. Hesseltine has shown that anti-southern horror tales were not without governmental inspiration in the North and that the secretary of war, the surgeon general, and the committee on the conduct of the war took· pains to spread tales of the sufferings of northern prisoners in the South. Motives were various: tales might be spread to carry forward the abolitionist's denunciation of southern cruelty, to satisfy the moral sense by besmirching the foe, or to discourage surrender into southern hands. When the backfire came and these atrocity stories led to questions as to why prisoners were not exchanged, it became necessary to invent the tale that exchange had been stopped by a vicious South intent upon destroying the lives of prisoners. . . .

. . .

President Lincoln, who once owned a newspaper, by no means neglected publicity. Naturally he addressed the people in occasional speeches, in his two inaugurals, his proclamations, and his messages to Congress. Beyond this there was the use of patronage for newspapers, an obscure subject yet to be explored, and there was the case of J. W. Forney whose Philadelphia *Chronicle* and Washington *Chronicle* were known as Lincoln organs. In March, 1862, the President asked Henry J. Raymond for an article in the *Times*. So much of the writing on Lincoln has been of the sentimentally stereotyped variety that people have overlooked Lincoln's trenchant comments on his own times, on wartime profits, on corruption, and on the manner in which every "foul bird" and "every dirty reptile" came forth in war time. It is safe to say that Lincoln saw the war more clearly and faced it more squarely than Emerson. He faced it with an amazing lack of hatred and rancor.

The Civil War generation, not alone military and political events, but life and *mores*, social conditions and thought-patterns that accompanied the war as well as non-war aspects of the age, will receive further attention by inquisitive historians. . . . History has its vogues and its movements. Just as Americans beginning about 1935 executed something like an about-face in their interpretation of the World War, including American participation in it and attitudes preceding it, so the re-telling of the Civil War is a matter of changed and changing viewpoints. In the present troubled age it may be of more than academic interest to re-

examine the human beings of that war generation with less thought of the "splendor of battle flags" and with more of the sophisticated and unsentimental searchlight of reality.

ARTHUR SCHLESINGER, JR.

The Civil War was our great national trauma. A savage fraternal conflict, it released deep sentiments of guilt and remorse—sentiments which have reverberated through our history and our literature ever since. Literature in the end came to terms with these sentiments by yielding to the South in fantasy the victory it had been denied in fact; this tendency culminated on the popular level in *Gone with the Wind* and on the highbrow level in the Nashville cult of agrarianism. But history, a less malleable medium, was constricted by the intractable fact that the war had taken place, and by the related assumption that it was, in William H. Seward's phrase, an "irrepressible conflict," and hence a justified one.

As short a time ago as 1937, for example, even Professor James G. Randall could describe himself as "unprepared to go to the point of denying that the great American tragedy could have been avoided." Yet in a few years the writing of history would succumb to the psychological imperatives which had produced *I'll Take my Stand* and *Gone with the Wind;* and Professor Randall would emerge as the leader of a triumphant new school of self-styled "revisionists." The publication of two vigorous books by Professor Avery Craven—*The Repressible Conflict* (1939) and *The Coming of the Civil War*

Reprinted from Arthur Schlesinger, Jr., "The Causes of the Civil War: A Note on Historical Sentimentalism," PARTISAN REVIEW, XVI (1949), 969–81, by permission of the author.

(1942)—and the appearance of Professor Randall's own notable volumes on Lincoln—*Lincoln the President: Springfield to Gettysburg* (1945), *Lincoln and the South* (1946), and *Lincoln the Liberal Statesman* (1947)—brought about a profound reversal of the professional historian's attitude toward the Civil War. Scholars now denied the traditional assumption of the inevitability of the war and boldly advanced the thesis that a "blundering generation" had transformed a "repressible conflict" into a "needless war."

The swift triumph of revisionism came about with very little resistance or even expressed reservations on the part of the profession. Indeed, the only adequate evaluation of the revisionist thesis that I know was made, not by an academic historian at all, but by that illustrious semi-pro, Mr. Bernard De Voto; and Mr. De Voto's two brilliant articles in *Harper's* in 1945 unfortunately had little influence within the guild. By 1947 Professor Allan Nevins, summing up the most recent scholarship in *Ordeal of the Union,* his able general history of the eighteen-fifties, could define the basic problem of the period in terms which indicated a measured but entire acceptance of revisionism. "The primary task of statesmanship in this era," Nevins wrote, "was to furnish a workable adjustment between the two sections, while offering strong inducements to the southern people to regard their labor system not as static but evolutionary, and equal persuasions to the northern people to assume a helpful rather than scolding attitude."

This new interpretation surely deserves at least as meticulous an examination as Professor Randall is prepared to give, for example, to such a question as whether or not Lincoln was playing fives when he received the news of his nomination in 1860. The following notes are presented in the interests of stimulating such an examination.

The revisionist case, as expounded by Professors Randall and Craven, has three main premises. First:

1) that the Civil War was caused by the irresponsible emotionalization of politics far out of proportion to the real problems involved. The war, as Randall put it, was certainly not caused by cultural variations nor by economic rivalries nor by sectional differences; these all existed, but it was "stupid," as he declared, to think that they required war as a solution. "One of the most colossal of misconceptions" was the "theory" that "fundamental motives produce war. The glaring and obvious fact is the artificiality of war-making agitation." After all, Randall pointed out, agrarian and industrial interests had been in conflict under Coolidge and Hoover; yet no war resulted. "In Illinois," he added, "major controversies (not mere transient differences) between downstate and metropolis have stopped short of war."

Nor was the slavery the cause. The issues arising over slavery were in Randall's judgment "highly artificial, almost fabricated. . . . They produced quarrels out of things that would have settled themselves were it not for political agitation." Slavery, Craven observed, was in any case a much overrated problem. It is "perfectly clear," he wrote, "that slavery played a rather minor part in the life of the South and of the Negro."

What then was the cause of war? "If one word or phrase were selected to account for the war," wrote Randall, ". . . it would have to be such a word as fanaticism (on both sides), misunderstanding, misrepresentation, or perhaps politics." Phrases like "whipped-up crisis" and "psychopathic case" adorned

Randall's explanation. Craven similarly described the growing sense of sectional differences as "an artificial creation of inflamed minds." The "molders of public opinion steadily created the fiction of two distinct peoples." As a result "distortion led a people into bloody war."

If uncontrolled emotionalism and fanaticism caused the war, how did they get out of hand? Who whipped up the "whipped-up crisis"? Thus the second revisionist thesis:

2) that sectional friction was permitted to develop into needless war by the inexcusable failure of political leadership in the fifties. "It is difficult to achieve a full realization of how Lincoln's generation stumbled into a ghastly war," wrote Randall. ". . . If one questions the term 'blundering generation,' let him inquire how many measures of the time he would wish copied or repeated if the period were to be approached with a clean slate and to be lived again."

It was the politicians, charged Craven, who systematically sacrificed peace to their pursuit of power. Calhoun and Adams, "seeking political advantage," mixed up slavery and expansion; Wilmot introduced his "trouble-making Proviso as part of the political game;" the repeal clause in the Kansas-Nebraska Act was "the afterthought of a mere handful of politicians;" Chase's Appeal to the Independent Democrats was "false in its assertions and unfair in its purposes, but it was politically effective"; the "damaging" section in the Dred Scott decision was forced "by the political ambitions of dissenting judges." "These uncalled-for moves and this irresponsible leadership," concluded Craven, blew up a "crack-pot" crusade into a national conflict.

It is hard to tell which was under attack here—the performance of a particular generation or democratic politics in general. But, if the indictment "blundering generation" meant no more than a general complaint that democratic politics placed a premium on emotionalism, then the Civil War would have been no more nor less "needless" than any event in our blundering history. The phrase "blundering generation" must consequently imply that the generation in power in the fifties was *below* the human or historical or democratic average in its blundering. Hence the third revisionist thesis:

3) that the slavery problem could have been solved without war. For, even if slavery were as unimportant as the revisionists have insisted, they would presumably admit that it constituted the real sticking-point in the relations between the sections. They must show therefore that there were policies with which a non-blundering generation could have resolved the slavery crisis and averted war; and that these policies were so obvious that the failure to adopt them indicated blundering and stupidity of a peculiarly irresponsible nature. If no such policies could be produced even by hindsight, then it would seem excessive to condemn the politicians of the fifties for failing to discover them at the time.

The revisionists have shown only a most vague and sporadic awareness of this problem. "Any kind of sane policy in Washington in 1860 might have saved the day for nationalism," remarked Craven; but he did not vouchsafe the details of these sane policies; we would be satisfied to know about one. Similarly Randall declared that there were few policies of the fifties he would wish repeated if the period were to be lived over again; but he was not communicative about the policies he would wish pursued. Nevins likewise blamed the war on the "collapse of American statesmanship," but restrained himself from suggesting how a non-collapsible statesmanship would have solved the hard problems of the fifties.

In view of this reticence on a point so crucial to the revisionist argument, it is necessary to reconstruct the possibilities that might lie in the back of revisionism. Clearly there could be only two "solutions" to the slavery problem: the preservation of slavery, or its abolition.

Presumably the revisionists would not regard the preservation of slavery as a possible solution. Craven, it is true, has argued that "most of the incentives to honest and sustained effort, to a contented, well-rounded life, might be found under slavery. . . . What owning and being owned added to the normal relationship of employer and employee is very hard to say." In describing incidents in which slaves beat up masters, he has even noted that "happenings and reactions like these were the rule [sic], not the exception." But Craven would doubtless admit that, however jolly this system might have been, its perpetuation would have been, to say the least, impracticable.

If, then, revisionism has rested on the assumption that the non-violent abolition of slavery was possible, such abolition could conceivably have come about through internal reform in the South; through economic exhaustion of the slavery system in the South; or through some government project for gradual and compensated emancipation. Let us examine these possibilities.

(1) *The internal reform argument.* The South, the revisionists have suggested, might have ended the slavery system if left to its own devices; only the abolitionists spoiled everything by letting loose a hysteria which caused the southern ranks to close in self-defense.

This revisionist argument would have been more convincing if the decades of alleged anti-slavery feeling in the South had produced any concrete results. As one judicious southern historian, Professor Charles S. Sydnor, recently put it, "Although the abolition movement was followed by a decline of antislavery sentiment in the South, it must be remembered that in all the long years before that movement began no part of the South had made substantial progress toward ending slavery. . . . Southern liberalism had not ended slavery in any state."

In any case, it is difficult for historians seriously to suppose that northerners could have denied themselves feelings of disapproval over slavery. To say that there "should" have been no abolitionists in America before the Civil War is about as sensible as to say that there "should" have been no anti-Nazis in the nineteen-thirties or that there "should" be no anti-Communists today. People who indulge in criticism of remote evils may not be so pure of heart as they imagine; but that fact does not affect their inevitability as part of the historic situation.

Any theory, in short, which expects people to repress such spontaneous aversions is profoundly unhistorical. If revisionism has based itself on the conviction that things would have been different if only there had been no abolitionists, it has forgotten that abolitionism was as definite and irrevocable a factor in the historic situation as was slavery itself. And, just as abolitionism was inevitable, so too was the southern reaction against it—a reaction which, as Professor Clement Eaton has ably shown, steadily drove the free discussion of slavery out of the South. The extinction of free discussion meant, of course, the absolute extinction of any hope of abolition through internal reform.

(2) *The economic exhaustion argument.* Slavery, it has been pointed out, was on the skids economically. It was overcapitalized and inefficient; it immobilized both capital and labor; its one-crop system was draining the soil of fertility; it stood in the way of industrialization. As the South came to realize these facts, a revisionist might argue, it would have moved to abolish slavery for its own economic good. As Craven put it, slavery "may have been almost ready to break down of its own weight."

This argument assumed, of course, that southerners would have recognized the causes of their economic predicament and taken the appropriate measures. Yet such an assumption would be plainly contrary to history and to experience. From the beginning the South has always blamed its economic shortcomings, not on its own economic ruling class and its own inefficient use of resources, but on northern exploitation. Hard times in the eighteen-fifties produced in the South, not a reconsideration of the slavery system, but blasts against the North for the high prices of manufactured goods. The overcapitalization of slavery led, not to criticisms of the system, but to increasingly insistent demands for the reopening of the slave trade. Advanced southern writers like George Fitzhugh and James D. B. DeBow were even arguing that slavery was adapted to industrialism. When Hinton R. Helper did advance before the Civil War an early version of Craven's argument, asserting that emancipation was necessary to save the southern economy, the South burned his book. Nothing in the historical record suggests that the southern ruling class was preparing to deviate from its traditional pattern of self-exculpation long enough to take such a drastic step as the abolition of slavery.

(3) *Compensated emancipation.* Abraham Lincoln made repeated proposals of compensated emancipation. In his annual message to Congress of December 1, 1862, he set forth a detailed plan by which States, on an agreement to abolish slavery by 1900, would receive government bonds in proportion to the number of slaves emancipated. Yet, even though Lincoln's proposals represented a solution of the problem conceivably gratifying to the slaveholder's purse as well as to his pride, they got nowhere. Two-thirds of the border representatives rejected the scheme, even when personally presented to them by Lincoln himself. And, of course, only the pressure of war brought compensated emancipation its limited hearing of 1862.

Still, granted these difficulties, does it not remain true that other countries abolished slavery without internal convulsion? If emotionalism had not aggravated the situation beyond hope, Craven has written, then slavery "might have been faced as a national question and dealt with as successfully as the South American countries dealt with the same problem." If Brazil could free its slaves and Russia its serfs in the middle of the nineteenth century without civil war, why could not the United States have done as well?

The analogies are appealing but not, I think, really persuasive. There are essential differences between the slavery question in the United States and the problems in Brazil or in Russia. In the first place, Brazil and Russia were able to face servitude "as a national question" because it was, in fact, a national question. Neither country had the

American problem of the identification of compact sectional interests with the survival of the slavery system. In the second place, there was no race problem at all in Russia; and, though there was a race problem in Brazil, the more civilized folkways of that country relieved racial differences of the extreme tension which they breed in the South of the United States. In the third place, neither in Russia nor in Brazil did the abolition of servitude involve constitutional issues; and the existence of these issues played a great part in determining the form of the American struggle.

It is hard to draw much comfort, therefore, from the fact that other nations abolished servitude peaceably. The problem in America was peculiarly recalcitrant. The schemes for gradual emancipation got nowhere. Neither internal reform nor economic exhaustion contained much promise for a peaceful solution. The hard fact, indeed, is that the revisionists have not tried seriously to describe the policies by which the slavery problem could have been peacefully resolved. They have resorted instead to broad affirmations of faith: if only the conflict could have been staved off long enough, then somehow, somewhere, we could have worked something out. It is legitimate, I think, to ask how? where? what?—at least, if these affirmations of faith are to be used as the premise for castigating the unhappy men who had the practical responsibility for finding solutions and failed.

Where have the revisionists gone astray? In part, the popularity of revisionism obviously parallels that of *Gone with the Wind*—the victors paying for victory by pretending literary defeat. But the essential problem is why history should be so vulnerable to this literary fashion; and this prob-

lem, I believe, raises basic questions about the whole modern view of history. It is perhaps stating the issue in too portentous terms. Yet I cannot escape the feeling that the vogue of revisionism is connected with the modern tendency to seek in optimistic sentimentalism an escape from the severe demands of moral decision; that it is the offspring of our modern sentimentality which at once evades the essential moral problems in the name of a superficial objectivity and asserts their unimportance in the name of an invincible progress.

The revisionists first glided over the implications of the fact that the slavery system was producing a closed society in the South. Yet that society increasingly had justified itself by a political and philosophical repudiation of free society; southern thinkers swiftly developed the anti-libertarian potentialities in a social system whose cornerstone, in Alexander H. Stephen's proud phrase, was human bondage. In theory and in practice, the South organized itself with mounting rigor against ideas of human dignity and freedom, because such ideas inevitably threatened the basis of their own system. Professor Frank L. Owsley, the southern agrarian, has described inadvertently but accurately the direction in which the slave South was moving. "The abolitionists and their political allies were threatening the existence of the South as seriously as the Nazis threaten the existence of England," wrote Owsley in 1940; ". . . Under such circumstances the surprising thing is that so little was done by the South to defend its existence."

There can be no question that many southerners in the fifties had similar sentiments; that they regarded their system of control as ridiculously inadequate; and that, with the book-burning, the censorship of the mails, the gradual illegalization of dissent, the South was in process of creating a real machinery of repression in order more effectively "to defend its existence." No society, I suppose, encourages criticism of its basic institutions. Yet, when a democratic society acts in self-defense, it does so at least in the name of human dignity and freedom. When a society based on bond slavery acts to eliminate criticism of its peculiar institution, it outlaws what a believer in democracy can only regard as the abiding values of man. When the basic institutions are evil, in other words, the effect of attempts to defend their existence can only be the moral and intellectual stultification of the society.

A society closed in the defense of evil institutions thus creates moral differences far too profound to be solved by compromise. Such a society forces upon every one, both those living at the time and those writing about it later, the necessity for a moral judgment; and the moral judgment in such cases becomes an indispensable factor in the historical understanding.

The revisionists were commendably anxious to avoid the vulgar errors of the post-Civil War historians who pronounced smug individual judgments on the persons involuntarily involved in the tragedy of the slave system. Consequently they tried hard to pronounce no moral judgments at all on slavery. Slavery became important, in Craven's phrase, "only as a very ancient labor system, probably at this time rather near the end of its existence"; the attempt to charge this labor system with moral meanings was "a creation of inflamed imaginations." Randall, talking of the Kansas-Nebraska Act, could describe it as "a law intended to subordinate the slavery question and hold it in *proper* proportion" (my italics).

I have quoted Randall's even more astonishing argument that, because major controversies between downstate and metropolis in Illinois stopped short of war, there was reason to believe that the Civil War could have been avoided. Are we to take it that the revisionists seriously believe that the downstate-metropolis fight in Illinois—or the agrarian-industrial fight in the Coolidge and Hoover administrations—were in any useful sense comparable to the difference between the North and South in 1861?

Because the revisionists felt no moral urgency themselves, they deplored as fanatics those who did feel it, or brushed aside their feelings as the artificial product of emotion and propaganda. The revisionist hero was Stephen A. Douglas, who always thought that the great moral problems could be solved by sleight-of-hand. The phrase "northern man of southern sentiments," Randall remarked, was "said opprobriously . . . as if it were a base thing for a northern man to work with his southern fellows."

By denying themselves insight into the moral dimension of the slavery crisis, in other words, the revisionists denied themselves a historical understanding of the intensities that caused the crisis. It was the moral issue of slavery, for example, that gave the struggles over slavery in the territories or over the enforcement of the fugitive slave laws their significance. These issues, as the revisionists have shown with cogency, were not in themselves basic. But they were the available issues; they were almost the only points within the existing constitutional framework where the moral conflict could be faced; as a consequence, they became charged with the moral and political dynamism of the central issue. To say that the Civil War was fought over the "unreal" issue of slavery in the territories is like saying that the Second World War was fought over the "unreal" issue of the invasion of Poland. The democracies could not challenge fascism inside Germany any more than opponents of slavery could challenge slavery inside the South; but the extension of slavery, like the extension of fascism, was an act of aggression which made a moral choice inescapable.

Let us be clear what the relationship of moral judgment to history is. Every historian, as we all know in an argument that surely does not have to be repeated in 1949, imports his own set of moral judgments into the writing of history by the very process of interpretation; and the phrase "every historian" includes the category "revisionist." Mr. De Voto in his paraphrases of the revisionist position has put admirably the contradictions on this point: as for "moral questions, God forbid. History will not put itself in the position of saying that any thesis may have been wrong, any cause evil. . . . History will not deal with moral values, though of course the Republican radicals were, well, culpable." The whole revisionist attitude toward abolitionists and radicals, repeatedly characterized by Randall as "unctuous" and "intolerant," overflows with the moral feeling which is so virtuously excluded from discussions of slavery.

An acceptance of the fact of moral responsibility does not license the historian to roam through the past ladling out individual praise and blame: such an attitude would ignore the fact that all individuals, including historians, are trapped in a web of circumstance which curtails their moral possibilities. But it does mean that there are certain essential issues on which it is necessary for the historian to have a position if he is to understand the great conflicts of history. These great conflicts are relatively few because there are few enough historical phenomena which we can confidently identify as evil. The essential issues appear, moreover, not in pure and absolute form, but incomplete and imperfect, compromised by the deep complexity of history. Their proponents may often be neurotics and fanatics, like the abolitionists. They may attain a social importance only when a configuration of non-moral factors—economic, political, social, military—permit them to do so.

Yet neither the nature of the context nor the pretensions of the proponents alter the character of the issue. And human slavery is certainly one of the few issues of whose evil we can be sure. It is not just "a very ancient labor system"; it is also a betrayal of the basic values of our Christian and democratic tradition. No historian can understand the circumstances which led to its abolition until he writes about it in its fundamental moral context. "History is supposed to understand the difference between a decaying economy and an expanding one," as Mr. De Voto well said, "between solvency and bankruptcy, between a dying social idea and one coming to world acceptance. . . . It is even supposed to understand implications of the difference between a man who is legally a slave and one who is legally free."

"Revisionism in general has no position," De Voto continues, "but only a vague sentiment." Professor Randall well suggested the uncritical optimism of that sentiment when he remarked, "To suppose that the Union could not have been continued or slavery outmoded without the war and without the corrupt concomitants of war is hardly an enlightened assumption."

We have here a touching afterglow of the admirable nineteenth-century faith in the full rationality and perfectibility of man; the faith that the errors of the world would all in time be "outmoded" (Professor Randall's use of this word is suggestive) by progress. Yet the experience of the twentieth century has made it clear that we gravely overrated man's capacity to solve the problems of existence within the terms of history.

This conclusion about man may disturb our complacencies about human nature. Yet it is certainly more in accord with history than Professor Randall's "enlightened" assumption that man can solve peaceably all the problems which overwhelm him. The unhappy fact is that man occasionally works himself into a log-jam; and that the log-jam must be burst by violence. We know that well enough from the experience of the last decade. Are we to suppose that some future historian will echo Professor Nevins' version of the "failure" of the eighteen-fifties and write: "The primary task of statesmanship in the nineteen-thirties was to furnish a workable adjustment between the United States and Germany, while offering strong inducements to the German people to abandon the police state and equal persuasions to the Americans to help the Nazis rather than scold them"? Will some future historian adapt Professor Randall's formula and write that the word "appeaser" was used "opprobriously" as if it were a "base" thing for an American to work with his Nazi fellow? Obviously this revisionism of the future (already foreshadowed in the work of Charles A. Beard) would represent, as we now see it, a fantastic evasion of the hard and unpleasant problems of the thirties. I doubt whether our present revisionism would make much more sense to the men of the eighteen-fifties.

The problem of the inevitability of the Civil War, of course, is in its essence a problem devoid of meaning. The revisionist attempt to argue that the war could have been avoided by "any kind of sane policy" is of interest less in its own right than as an expression of a characteristically sentimental conception of man and of history. And the great vogue of revisionism in the historical profession suggests, in my judgment, ominous weaknesses in the contemporary attitude toward history.

We delude ourselves when we think that history teaches us that evil will be "outmoded" by progress and that politics consequently does not impose on us the necessity for decision and for struggle. If historians are to understand the fullness of the social dilemma they seek to reconstruct, they must understand that sometimes there is no escape from the implacabilities of moral decision. When social conflicts embody great moral issues, these conflicts cannot be assigned for solution to the invincible march of progress; nor can they be bypassed with "objective" neutrality. Not many problems perhaps force this decision upon the historian. But, if any problem does in our history, it is the Civil War.

To reject the moral actuality of the Civil War is to foreclose the possibility of an adequate account of its causes. More than that, it is to misconceive and grotesquely to sentimentalize the nature of history. For history is not a redeemer, promising to solve all human problems in time; nor is man capable of transcending the limitations of his being. Man generally is entangled in insoluble problems; history is consequently a tragedy in which we are all involved, whose keynote is anxiety and frustration, not progress and fulfillment. Nothing exists in history to assure us that the great moral dilemmas can be resolved without pain; we cannot therefore be relieved from the duty of moral judgment on issues so appalling and inescapable as those involved in human slavery; nor can we be consoled by sentimental theories about the needlessness of the Civil War into regarding our own struggles against evil as equally needless.

One must emphasize, however, that this duty of judgment applies to issues. Because we are all implicated in the same tragedy, we must judge the men of the past with the same forbearance and charity which we hope the future will apply toward us.

DAVID POTTER

. . . It would be dated indeed to reissue this book without giving some attention to the bearing of the scholarship of the last two decades upon it. For inasmuch as my study dealt with the coming of the Civil War, it was almost by definition controversial, and it touched upon two questions which have been the focus of sharp and extensive dispute. One of these is the question whether the Civil War could have been and should have been avoided. This, of course, is a vast problem, and in its full extent reaches back to the earliest divergence between Northern and Southern societies. In its philosophical aspects, it involves all the great questions of causation, of historical inevitability, and of determinism. Obviously my book, with its sharp focus on the events of a five-

Reprinted from David Potter, LINCOLN AND HIS PARTY IN THE SECESSION *(New Haven, Conn.: Yale University Press, 1962), pp. xvii–xxiii, by permission of the publisher.*

month interval, did not attempt to deal either with the broad background of sectional antagonism or with the nature of historical forces. I was working on the immediate circumstances which led to the outbreak of war at a particular time—April 1861—and not on the underlying forces of antagonism which were back of these circumstances. If my narrative helps to explain anything, it helps to explain why war came when it did; it certainly does not explain at all why North and South were antagonistic to one another at this time; nor does it measure the depth of their antagonism. In a sense, therefore, there is hardly occasion for me to discuss whether a result was unavoidable from the operation of forces which I have not examined.

But I did suggest very strongly . . . that the Crittenden Resolutions represented a possible basis for compromise, and I presented evidence throughout that the Crittenden Plan commanded a great deal of support both in the North and in the South—so much, in fact, that if Lincoln had supported it, it might have been adopted. I still think the evidence is impressive, and I still believe that if Lincoln had supported the Compromise it might have been adopted.

This, of course, means that I believed there was a possible alternative to war in 1861. It does not mean that I regarded the crisis as an artificial one, or the sources of sectional antagonism as being in any sense superficial. It does not mean that I subscribed to the doctrine that conflict was "needless" or "repressible," for, as I asserted . . . "the slavery issue was certain to arouse emotions which no compromise could pacify—therefore it was beyond compromise." Yet to say that the fundamental source of friction was bound to cause deep antagonism is not, I think, the same as to say that this antagonism had inevitably to take the form of armed combat, and it is certainly not the same as to say that it had to take the form of armed combat at an exact time—April 1861—no sooner, no later.

The Crittenden Compromise had many of the same qualities and the same limitations as the Compromise of 1850. The chief limitation was that it did not and could not settle the slavery question. But within this limitation, it was perhaps less heavily freighted with bones of potential controversy than the Compromise of 1850. At least, it contained no Fugitive Slave Law, and it did not hold any such built-in ambiguities as later made the formula of popular sovereignty a source of chronic conflict. Perhaps it had almost as much popular backing at the beginning of 1860 as the Compromise of 1850 commanded at the beginning of the earlier year. Perhaps, also, it would have been a stopgap, or, as some would say, a "mere stopgap." The Compromise of 1850 is now widely regarded as such a stopgap; yet there is some question whether it failed in its own provisions or whether it was undone by the repeal of the Missouri Compromise in 1854.

I am very reluctant to dismiss Crittenden's plan as a stopgap so long as we maintain a double standard on the subject of stopgaps. For our evaluation of them depends very much upon whose gaps are being stopped. Thus no *modus vivendi* with the Soviet Union can be much more than a stopgap today, given our basic disagreements with that country. But we would be prone to regard it as most praiseworthy to defer a showdown, even for as much as five years. Our attitude is not unrelated to the fact that this would assure us of five years of immunity from being killed by the Russians. It is quite true, no doubt, that if war had been averted in 1861, it would not have meant a settlement of the issues. It would only have meant an indeterminate interval of immunity from being killed by the Rebs or the Yanks, as the case may be—immunity specifically for those who were killed between 1861 and 1865. Since all of these individuals would be dead by now even if the Rebs or the Yanks had not killed them, we can afford to be very bland about how right it was that the issue was met in 1861, and was not put off. All I suggest is that historians who believe so zealously in the virtue of facing up to issues in the past ought not to believe in the expedients of peace in the present. If an interval of peace, without any fundamental solution of issues, is worth something today, it was worth something in 1861. In 1861, as today, it would be worth a great deal less than a real peace—a real settlement of the basic issues.

Those who despite the advantages of a stopgap peace will point out, of course, that the Civil War did settle the basic issues. It saved the Union, and it freed 4,000,000 slaves. Certainly this is true, and it is important. But it can hardly be said that these immense values were gained at a bargain. For every six slaves who were freed, approximately one soldier was killed; for every ten white Southerners who were held in the Union, one Yank or one Reb died. A person is entitled to wonder whether the Southerners could not have been held and the slaves could not have been freed at a smaller per-capita cost. Certainly few would have purchased these gains at the time if they had known the price, and the mere fact that it has already been paid is not a reason for historians to let it go without questioning now.

The so-called revisionists, who have been most explicit in questioning the necessity for the war, have stressed certain themes: namely that the Republicans were quite prepared to guarantee the continued existence of slavery in all the slave states, and that the difference between what the Republicans proposed to do about slavery and what the Democrats proposed to do was not worth a war (this is, of course, very different from saying that slavery was not worth a war); that North and South had formed unreal, emotional stereotypes of one another, and that the opposing groups fought against these illusory stereotypes, rather than against one another; and that the war resulted from a breakdown of reason and would not have happened if reason had prevailed. In connection with these themes, they have been severely criticized for their moral indifference concerning slavery; for their failure to perceive that overwrought emotions and exaggerated stereotypes are the reflex rather than the cause of deep antagonisms; and for the fallacy that irrational forces are unreal forces. On all of these counts, it seems to me that revisionism is vulnerable, though it by no means follows that everyone associated with revisionism is open to these criticisms. For myself, to repeat, my study makes no attempt to analyze the long-range history of sectional antagonism, and I do not think that a compromise averting war in 1861 would have solved the basic issues or cleared up the basic problem any more than the Compromise of 1850 did. I certainly do not think the issues or the antagonisms were in any sense unreal, nor of anything less than major importance. If I believe there was an alternative course available in 1861, it is not because I am abstractly converted to the power of rationality but because the concrete evidence seems to me to show that a majority in the South did not want disunion and that a majority in the North did not want to press the question of slavery in the territories. I have discussed this evidence at length in my book, but here let me merely point out that in the election of 1860 the combined vote for Douglas and Bell in the slave states exceeded the vote for Breckinridge, and that the combined vote for Douglas, Bell, and Breckinridge in the states which stayed with the Union exceeded the vote for Lincoln. Over all, Lincoln received almost precisely the same proportion of the popular vote in 1860 that Herbert Hoover received in 1932 (39.9% and 39.6%). The evidence further seems to me to show that the Crittenden proposals commanded so much support in 1861 that if the President-elect had thrown his weight in the balance for them rather than against them, they would have been voted in Congress. If this had occurred, the fire-eating secessionists would still have resisted them bitterly, but again the evidence indicates that fire-eaters almost failed to carry their program anyway, and if the Crittenden proposals had been thrown into the balance against them, they could hardly have gained the minimum support which they needed and which they only barely gained as it was. The Southern Unionists had beaten them in 1850 and might have done so again.

This, of course, would not have solved the ultimate problem. It would have resulted only in temporary peace. But what peace is more than temporary? Peace is essentially finite and temporal, and can be gained only by installments—not in perpetuity. Our peace with the Soviet Union for some seventeen years now has never appeared more than temporary, and indeed future historians may say that it was not worth our while to preserve such a tenuous peace. If it has any merit, it is only the merit of being better than war, and that is the merit which peace in 1861 might have had.

HISTORIOGRAPHICAL NOTE

More has been written about the Civil War than about any event in American history. There are still new sources that historians can use, and there will be new interpretations, but we have come closer to a full account of the causes, course, and consequences of the Civil War than of any episode in the national past. The only way to make any sense whatever of the many proposed interpretations of the war is to categorize and group them, with the understanding that such grouping inevitably leads to oversimplification.

The most simple grouping has been proposed by a philosopher, William Dray. There have been, according to Dray, only three fundamentally different ways of looking at the war: a "conspiracy" interpretation, a "conflict" interpretation, and a "revisionist" interpretation. According to the first approach, the war was a defensive action by one side against an active and willful conspiracy by the other. According to the second, the war resulted from underlying and powerful conflicts between the sections, conflicts that rendered political leaders on both sides helpless to alter the course of events. The third, or "revisionist" interpretation, argues that leaders could have restrained events, but "blundered" into war by failing to do so. These three groupings, incidentally, exhaust the general possibilities of "blaming" individuals or groups for the war. Within a conspiracy interpretation, one side or the other acted freely and was to blame; the other was *not* free to determine the outcome and was thus free of blame. Within a conflict interpretation, neither side was to blame, since neither side was free of fundamental historical forces which led to war. Within a revisionist interpretation, both sides—in some mixture or other—were to blame, since both sides were free to have done otherwise.

The conspiracy interpretation is the oldest. It was put forward even before the war by men like Sumner and Simms, and during and after the war by others like Cairnes and Davis. But the dominance of the conspiracy theory was broken in the 1880's and 1890's by the new atmosphere of reconciliation that flooded the country, and by the work of one historian in particular, James Ford Rhodes. In a massive *History of the United States from the Compromise of 1850* (Seven vols., New York, 1893–1906), Rhodes insisted that the war was an inevitable result of the conflict over one issue, slavery. The South, he said, was not "guilty" of the institution of slavery; slavery was simply a fact of history that the war generation had inherited and could not escape. But the North was not guilty, either, of its abolitionism; abolitionism, like slavery, was an uncontrollable outcome of history.

From about World War I, the conflict interpretation shifted away from Rhodes' preoccupation with slavery and toward an economic analysis approach. Influenced primarily by Charles Beard, a new generation of historians insisted that the basic conflict was economic, and that the Civil War should be seen as a "Second American Revolution," the triumph of industrial capitalism. At the same time, however, other conflict historians were interpreting the war as the outcome of the complex development of two separate "civilizations," North and South, with different folkways, institutions, economic structures, and beliefs. But whether the underlying cause was slavery, economic interests, or divergent civilizations, the conflict interpretation still sought to get around any question of blame by insisting always that the individual actors of the drama were governed by a script that they had not written and had no power to edit.

It was this sort of moral "flabbiness"—as he thought of it—that Randall reacted against in his essay on "The Blundering Generation." He was joined in his "revisionism" by Avery O. Craven, whose most important revisionist book was frankly titled, *The Repressible Conflict, 1830–1861* (University, La., 1939). The revisionist point of view was also accepted, though incompletely, by Allan Nevins, a journalist turned influential historian. Nevins' *Ordeal of the Union* (Four vols., New York, 1947–1950) was history in the grand manner, a vast study of a type seldom attempted by American historians since the turn of the century. The book summed up the wisdom of Nevins' generation of scholars, and was heavily influenced by Randall's and Craven's attitudes.

Since World War II, there has been a considerable shift back toward Rhodes' version of the conflict interpretation. Arthur Schlesinger's "Note on Historical Sentimentalism" was the harbinger of similar interpretations of the war to be produced by his contemporaries, interpretations best summed up in Kenneth Stampp's *And the War Came* (Baton Rouge, 1950). More recently, there have been a number of requests for moderation, such as David Potter's 1962 preface, and cries for a more "scientific" approach to the subject, such as Lee Benson's essay on "Causation and the American Civil War," *History and Theory,* 1 (1961).

There are, fortunately, two lengthy surveys of the many different ways that Americans have tried to understand the Civil War, surveys that not only summarize changing interpretations but attempt to explain why the changes have come about: Howard K. Beale's classic essay, "What Historians Have Said about the Causes of the Civil War," in *Theory and Practice in Historical Study* (Social Science Research Council, Bulletin No. 46, 1946); and T. J. Pressley's less sophisticated but more recent and exhaustive *Americans Interpret Their Civil War* (Princeton, 1954).